PATTERN RECOGNITION: HUMAN AND MECHANICAL

PATTERN RECOGNITION: HUMAN AND MECHANICAL

SATOSI WATANABE
University of Hawaii

A Wiley-Interscience Publication
JOHN WILEY & SONS
New York • Cichester • Brisbane • Toronto • Singapore

Library of Congress Cataloging in Publication Data:

Watanabe, Satoshi, 1910–
Pattern recognition.

"A Wiley-Interscience publication."
Bibliography: p.
Includes index.
1. Pattern perception. I. Title.

Q327.W365 1985 001.53′4 84-7354
ISBN 0-471-80815-6

Printed in the United States of America

10 9 8 7 6 5 4 3 2 1

To

Dorothea

for her patience and cheerful encouragement

Preface

This book is an elementary introduction to a new domain of science commonly called pattern recognition, excluding, however, its subfield called picture processing. It addresses two kinds of readers: those of the non-scientific audience who do not like mathematical formulas and those specialized students of science who have been exposed to mathematical theories on pattern recognition but do not understand what they are really doing with those sharp quantitative tools.

Although the current interest in pattern recognition stems obviously from the possibility of its partial simulation and replacement by the computer, the subject of the present study is primarily the human cognitive capabilities, ranging from concrete object perception to abstract theory building. The title originally considered for this book was: "Form, Figure, Feature," implying that our task here lay in explication of the general concept (Form) in terms of class-characteristics (Feature) derived from the intuitive image (Feature) of a class as suggested by class-samples (paradigms). The study of this mental activity is, however, at present forced to be reformulated under the impact of the recent developments of psychology and neurophysiology. The present book, includes, beside the mathematical modeling, both non-mathematical, historical descriptions (Chapters 1-4) and a currently developing new vista over the entire field of cognition (Epilogue).

Before finalizing the manuscript, I also considered a subtitle: "An Epistemometrical Foundation of Pattern Recognition." The term epistemometry, which was used in the preface of my earlier book, *Knowing and Guessing* [W-10], designates an attitude developed during our series of research on the problem of knowledge and concept formation. It may be characterized as follows:

1. Represents a new natural extension of a branch of philosophy, epistemology.
2. Represents an empirical science--a quantitative theory based on empirical facts about the process of knowing. It is not a branch of the traditional philosophy, nor of mathematics, nor, least of all, of statistics. It is an independent discipline by itself.
3. Does not side with the so-called empiricist camp in the classical empiricist-rationalist battle. It recognizes the fact that innate ideas are necessary in making "knowing" possible, but, at the same time, maintains that these innate ideas are the results of the philogenetic outgrowth, through evolution, of the interaction between life and its environments.
4. Corrects the overemphasis of the "digital-linguistic-logical-deductionist" approach prevalent among researchers in cognitive sciences, simply because the basic cognitive capabilities are present already in the prelingual animals and human infants (Section 10.5 and E-3).
5. Maintains that the formation of concepts is possible only with the help of a value-oriented ponderation (Chapter 4). As such it has affinity with the epistemological relativism held by such philosophers as Feyerabend, Putnam, Kuhn, the ontological relativity maintained by Quine, and the inductive relatively pointed out by Goodman [F-5, G-3, K-8, P-11, Q-1]. We think, however, that a more cautious attitude is required than in the popular epistemological relativism with regard to the arbitrariness of historical developments of natural science [W-17, W-32].
6. Considers mental description as well as physical description as experimental facts.

The identify theory of mind-body relation à la Feigl is assumed, but only in an approximate sense [F-3, W-34] (see also Section E-3).

7. Makes a clear distinction between deductive and inductive processes, without losing sight of the fact that a real process of thinking is an interplay of deduction and induction. At variance with R. Carnap and his followers, we should abide by the old definition of deduction as a derivation of particular proposition from a general proposition and the definition of induction as the reverse process [C-5, W-10]. Pattern recognition is an inductive process [W-24].
8. Locates the vital essence of science in its inductive theory-building. The axiomatization and programmation of a theory is a cadaver of a science. Despite the final deductive expositions of their results, the true creative logicians and mathematicians are strong inductionists.
9. Takes the view that induction is never free of inductive ambiguity. In the presence of inductive ambiguity, what propels a science is a heuristic principle which is neither unique nor necessary. It does not guarantee success.
10. Believes that the study of human pattern recognition as a science is beneficial to and benefited from the development of mechanical applications of pattern recognition as a technique. The totality of scientific-technological efforts to unravel and simulate the process of pattern recognition, in the broadest sense of the word, is tantamount to the entire epistemometry. See Epilogue for a discussion of the unbridgeable gap between the present-day computer and the human brain.

An epistemometrical point of view, as characterized above, can be said to have started in 1959 when Professor Brand Blanshard, then chairman of the philosophy department of Yale University, asked me, an IBM physicist, to take over course on "inductive logic," which Professor Arthur Papp had been scheduled to give. I am certain that the philosophical level of my course was nothing comparable to the one that the famous young-deceased philosophical genius would have attained. But, one thing notable of mention was that in my course the inductive ambiguity was traced back to the asymmetrical application of symmetrical conditional probabilities, and the idea of the theorem of the Ugly Duckling was introduced as another expression of inductive ambiguity. This theorem was announced in a session organized by Professor Russell Hanson but was not published [W-18, W-19].

About the same time (1960) my research at IBM Research Laboratory became more and more concentrated on pattern recognition. In the past twenty years, the materials included in this book have been topics of my courses at the University of Hawaii, Yale University, Columbia University, Rutgers University, Fordham University and Sophia University (Tokyo) and subjects of lectures at various institutions and conferences in Europe, the United States, and Japan. As a consequence, it contains some earlier results in pattern recognition, but is entirely rewritten in the spirit of the new ideas about heuristics which have been reformulated quite recently [W-46, W-47]. There is a certain amount of duplication of my earlier book, *Knowing and Guessing* [W-10], but an independent reading is entirely possible, although some cross-references are made for possible usefulness.

I witnessed and modestly participated in the genesis and development of pattern recognition in the United States, and the contents of this book owe greatly to the works of my colleagues and contemporary experts in this field. But, at the same time, this book may be more truthfully described as a record of my reactions as a non-American-trained researcher, non-engineer, and non-mathematician, to these important achievements of technology, which have been brought about mostly by American-trained researchers, engineers, and mathematicians. I hope the reader will tolerate an autobiographic overtone in order to make this self-styled textbook more readable and more vivid.

I am indebted to many friends and colleagues who made this book possible, and to two young collaborators who have worked closely with me from my

Yale years on, Dr. Tsuguchika Kamimura and Dr. Casimir Kulikowski. I am indebted greatly to Dr. Francis W. Dauer for exciting discussions and for his tutorial efforts in philosophical problems although I was not always a docile student. Others who have inspired and assisted me in scholarly research are mentioned in the appropriate places in the text.

Being interspersed at different junctures with innovative yet unorthodox ideas, this book has to expect at best a controversial acceptance. The courageous decision on the part of Miss Beatrice Shube of John Wiley and Sons, Wiley-Interscience Division, to publish this book is highly appreciated by the author. The first manuscript was typed up by Mrs. Alberta Smith. The second much revised typescript was prepared by Mrs. Ethel Shintaku and assistants. The final accurate camera-ready copy was typed by Ms. Susan Yamane and Ms. Glenna Sumiye. This book owes its birth in the present elegant form greatly to Mrs. Barbara Whitehouse-Jones, who edited the manuscript and coordinated efforts for the production of camera-ready copy.

Satosi Watanabe

Honolulu
September, 1984

Contents

PATTERN RECOGNITION: HUMAN AND MECHANICAL

CHAPTER 1
Pattern Recognition as Seeing-One-In-Many

1.1 PATTERN AND RECOGNITION

The intellectual enterprises usually grouped under the name of pattern recognition are so diversified and comprehensive that many people are tempted to introduce a neologism, more general or more dignified than pattern recognition. But, I myself have no objection to the rubrique: pattern recognition. Although this name emphasizes only one aspect of this group of intellectual activities, it is neither too abstract nor too concrete, neither pompous nor overly modest. This term is particularly convenient because it serves well the purpose of extricating the essential common nature underlying the various activities in this general area. In addition to this advantage, the terminology is neutral as to the question whether we are talking about the human activities such as sensation, perception, cognitive judgement, or about their mechanical simulation by the computer. As was the case with cybernetics, the technique of mechanization is advanced by a study of human prototypes, and the biomedical and psychological understanding profits from our efforts in developing methods of mechanical simulation. It is, therefore, often convenient to use a common terminology to cover these two areas, although it is on the other hand also important not to overlook a deep-lying crevasse between them.

Now, what is a pattern? When do we speak of a pattern? For instance, when iron filings are scattered on a sheet of paper they spread out more or less uniformly and there is no pattern to speak of. But, by some accident, perhaps due to an irregular deviation of the paper from a perfect horizontal plane, the density of filings may become relatively high at certain places, and, a pattern appears. It may look like a river, or a dog's head. In another case, because of a magnet positioned under the paper, the filings may show something like what we learn in physics as magnetic lines of force (see Fig. 1.1.1). In such cases, we say that a pattern has appeared. Be it a blob or lines of force or something without name, a pattern is the opposite of chaos; it is an entity, vaguely defined, that could be given a name--i.e. a something. It is important to notice, when we see a river, a dog's head or lines of force, that we are somehow associating the present particular case before the eyes to other cases of

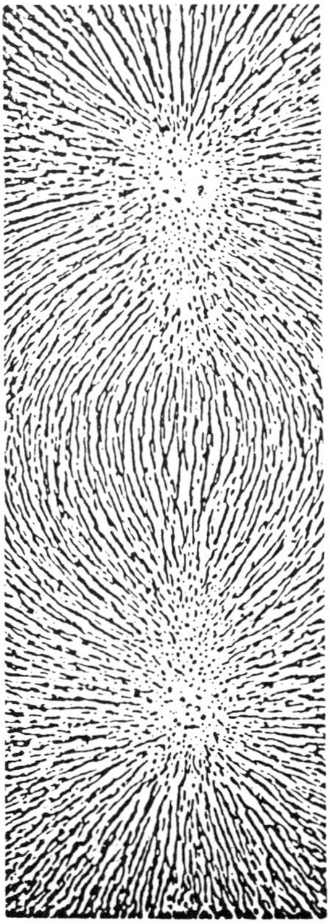

Figure 1.1.1 A collection of pieces of broken line segments seen as a set of lines of force of a magnetic field.

Figure 1.1.2 An example of double meaning: Wittgenstein's duck-rabbit. Either a duck or a rabbit <u>is seen but not both</u> simultaneously.

rivers, dogs' heads and lines of force, recognizing similarity.

The situation may be regarded as a special case of what Wittgenstein said about "seeing something_1 as something_2" [W-14]. The verb "see" has two usages, according to him, such as "I see this rose" and "I see this picture as a rabbit" (see Fig. 1.1.2). What we call "pattern" corresponds to something_2 in this formulation. Something_2 as such does not exist in the same level of language as something_1 in the picture. It can be seen by our mind's eye. It is an ideal construction. Sometimes, something_2 has a name; sometimes, it has no name. In some cases, we have to describe the structure cf the nameless thing by mentioning the known constituent building blocks and how they are put together in some familiar, definable way.

In cases exemplified by Wittgenstein's duck-rabbit, there can be two, or even more, somethings recognizable, and the most conspicuous fact is that when one pattern is recognized the other one disappears at that time and vice versa (see Fig. 1.1.2). It is the same in many examples of figure-ground switching of Gestalt psychologists, and a similar thing can be said about Rorschach inkblots. There is no mixture, no co-existence (see Fig. 1.1.3, Fig. 1.1.4). Yet it is not true if we say that only one of them is the true reality. This is somewhat like Bohr's complementarity. In any event, what is important here is that something_2 is a result of cooperation of external stimuli and a certain kind of

Figure 1.1.3 A favorite example of double meaning used by Gestalt psychologists--a flip-flop alternation of figure and ground.

mental activity of associating one case with other similar, or at least related, cases.

Now if we substitute "recognize" for "see" and "pattern" for "$something_2$" in the phrase "to see $something_1$ as $something_2$," we can talk more specifically about pattern recognition. Let us consider a few examples out of ordinary conversation: "I recognize this flower as plumeria"; "I recognize this tartan as Gordon." These sentences contain perfectly normal usages of the word "recognize" in the sense of recognizing a pattern. They share one important common feature, i.e., the idea of different individual objects belonging to the same class. The plumeria flower I have in my hand is not the same plumeria flower I have previously seen, but I recognize this one as a member of the same family as the earlier samples of plumeria. The necktie I have in my hand at this moment is an entirely different object from the kilt I saw yesterday, and the dimension of weave pattern on the tie is smaller, yet I consider these two to belong to the same class as far as the arrangement of colors is concerned.

Thus, we may say that recognition usually means identification of an object as a member of a family which we already know, or we are familiar with, thereby reducing many to one. Before going into the examination of the meaning of the word "family" or "class," we may ask ourselves if it is necessary for us to know already, or to be familiar with, the class when we use the word recognize. The answer is no.

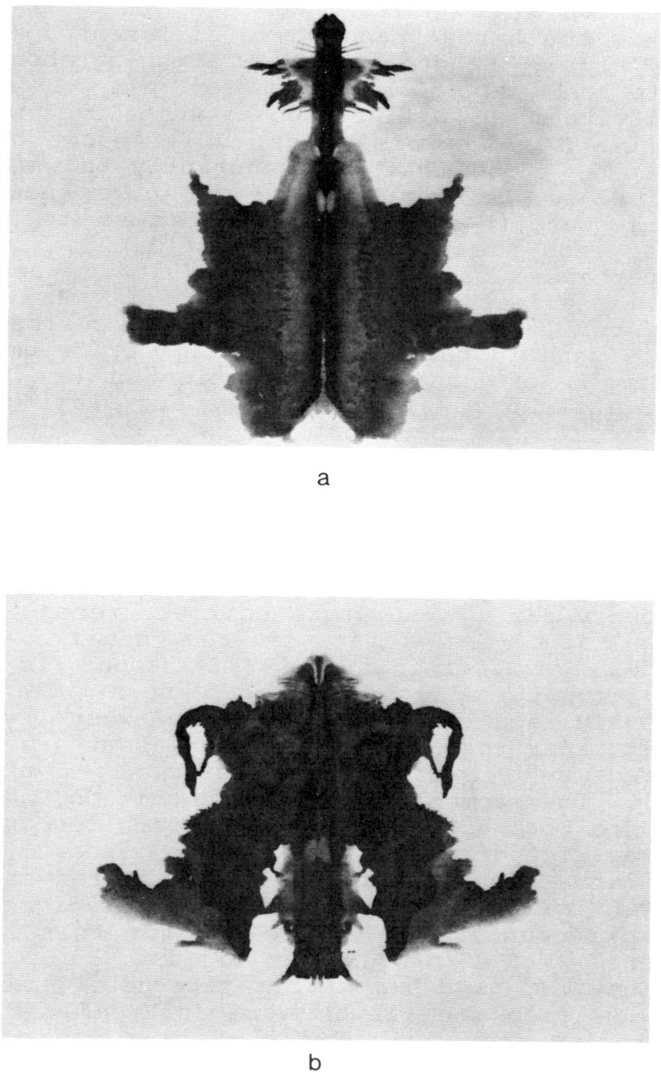

a

b

Figure 1.1.4ab An example of multiple meaning: Rorschach's inkblots. Reprinted with permission. Copyright 1921 (renewed 1948) Verlag Hans Huber, Bern, Switzerland.

Suppose we have a visitor coming from an island where there are no birds. We take him to the zoo and show him the birds' cage where different species are freely flying. He does not know anything about birds, but it will not take long for him to start to classify them. He will recognize white ones with long legs, green-red colored ones, small brown ones with red beaks, those that sit constantly in water, etc. In this case, he does not have any prior knowledge of classes. But, it is his natural instinct to recognize groups and make a classification of his own--perhaps one of the simplifying tendencies of human intellect. We can think of many similar incidents. This act of classification corresponds to what is usually called "clustering" or "clumping" in the jargon of pattern recognition. It consists of making a group of similar things and placing them in a "box." We may say that it is a cognition rather than re-cognition. It is the taking cognizance of the existence of a group of similar objects.

This example shows that word recognition has actually two meanings: assigning an object to a so far unknown class of objects, and identifying an object as a member of the already known class. Webster's dictionary has two separate entries: recognition and re-cognition. The first is the usual one which includes both meanings and the second is the one which specifically involves known classes. I previously used the word "cognition" when I wanted to make it clear that we were talking about a case which involved formation of new classes, i.e. clustering [W-10]. The term "pattern recognition" generally refers to both activities, but pattern recognition in the restricted sense, i.e., the general pattern recognition minus clustering, will be referred to as "pattern recognition proper" or "paradigm-oriented pattern recognition." The reason for this last term reference will be presently clarified.

The word pattern has an interesting etymology. It comes from the French word "patron" (which also means model, template) whose original meaning was a master, protector as well as anything that was supposed to be followed or imitated.* Obviously, the

---

*A quiz for recreation: Why does a "patron of restaurant" mean the owner in French, and a customer in English?

modern meaning of pattern is more "democratic," and it now includes not only the one imitated but also those which imitate, making up together a family of similar beings. In this sense, pattern means any object qua a sample of a class. The idea behind this etymology is that a group of objects is defined by a typical case, examplar, or archetype. The German word for pattern, "Muster," which comes from Italian "mostra," has also a similar association of ideas. A Mustersohn is an exemplary son, and Blumenmuster means a flower pattern. The modern meaning of the word "pattern" does not presuppose the existence of a central object, which is the master of other imitations. We shall refer to these two views: one with the "patron" and the other without "patron," as "epicentric concept" and "aggregative concept" of pattern. This distinction shows up in different context throughout the work of pattern recognition.

When the French and Germans speak of pattern recognition, they usually prefer to use their words corresponding to English "form" to their patron or Muster (reconnaissance de forme, Formenerkennen). This usage is quite natural in their modern languages, but in the deep bottom layer of semantic riches of the word form, we can detect an association to the idea of form conceived by Greek philosophers. For Aristotle the "Form" was as real as the existence of individual objects. In the somewhat caricatured version of Plato's philosophy, the "Form" or "Idea" is an ideal, real object that exists in an eternal world different from the actual world of daily experience, and individual concrete objects of this world are nothing but defective copies of the "Form." Such a concept of form is a typical example of what we called epicentric concept of pattern. We said at the beginning of this section that the pattern exists in the mind's eye of the beholder. Neither Plato nor Aristotle would have accepted such a view that does not give reality to the form. If we have to investigate the concept of pattern, we have therefore to start our study with a review of the philosophical history of the concept of form (see Chapter 3). We shall have to show how the philosophical concept of general ideas is related to the common sense view that a class is a collection of similar objects.

The reader might have noticed that pattern recognition can be characterized as discerning one thing or one form in a field of perception consisting of many parts or many examples. More precisely, we can recognize two meanings in "seeing-one-in-many":

1. In a single case of scenery, recognition of one object in the collection of parts, as seeing a face in the collection of points of different greyness,
2. In a case of collection of many sceneries, different items are called by a single name such as plumeria which can be of different sizes, colors, and of different individualities.

But, in all processes of pattern recognition, the mental activity of unification, or integration, as modern psychologists call it, is at work. For a further discussion, see Section E-2.

1.2 PARADIGM AND SIMILARITY

We said that the pattern is an object as a member of a class. For this reason, the pattern often plays a double role of an individual object and of a class. We can easily discover this fact by reflecting on the way the word pattern is usually used in ordinary language. The reason for this curious double role can be explained also by analyzing the mechanism by which we form a concept in mind.

Logicians would define a concept, or the class corresponding to it, by its intension or its extension. The intension is the collection of predicates which just defines the concept. The extension is the collection of individual objects which correspond to the concept and make up the class. In other words, the extension is the collection of all objects that satisfy all the predicates included in the intension. But, in the real life situation, we need neither intension nor extension. We usually "define" a class by class samples (paradigms). According to the usually accepted version of Platonic philosophy all tables are imperfect imitations (material realizations) of the ideal table or the "form" of table which is somewhere in the world of Idea. But we cannot describe such a table, and we actually need no ideal table; all we need is a few actual tables to know what table is. If a mother shows a few dogs to her child, he will become capable of deciding whether any other animal is a dog or not. Theoretically speaking this is not a definition of a class, but it generates in the human mind a working capability of distinguishing a member from a nonmember of a class.

What we call pattern recognition (in the narrow sense, i.e., excluding clustering) is precisely this process: having been shown a few paradigms (and perhaps a few negative paradigms) of a class, one becomes capable of telling whether or not a new object (whose properties are made known but whose classification is unknown) belongs in this class. Together with clustering, this pattern recognition, in this sense, lays the basic pattern of human formation of classified knowledge. We have spoken of objects as if they were limited to birds or flowers, but the same action can be applied to abstract objects, and the product would become scientific knowledge. Therefore, we cannot condemn some of the enthusiastic experts of pattern recognition claiming that all intellectual acts are pattern recognition. Indeed, inductive inference and pattern recognition are basically identical in their essential function--inferring a generality from a few concrete cases.

The use of the term paradigm in this sense (i.e. as an individual object standing for a class) has been practiced by the author since more than twenty years ago. It is a very appropriate one, because the term not only means a typical example but was also used traditionally by some Greek philosophers to mean the "Form." In the modern half-philosophical jargon, the term is often used in the sense of an ideological type of theories under the influence of Thomas Kuhn's famous book, *Scientific Revolution* [K-8], but this epidemic use is, as Kuhn himself regrets, a rather unfortunate fad.

If the paradigms are given, and if the required value of similarity is assumed, we can have the following picture of the process of paradigm-oriented pattern recognition. Around each paradigm we can define a domain of similarity, and any datum of individual item will be decided to belong, or not to belong, to the same class as the paradigm, whereby the paradigm plays the major role of an epicenter. In the simple case, all the given paradigms are found located in the domain of similarity of one another. In the other extreme, each paradigm is in the domain of one and only one other paradigm. In this case we have an example of chain effect. In the most general case, each paradigm is in the domain of similarity of at least one other paradigm. In this case, we shall speak of "disjunctive subclasses of similarity," because the total domain for the class is the disjunction of the domains of similarity of separate paradigms. The class characteristic is then an invariant property which remains unchanged for the displacement within this entire domain.

The extension of the set suggested by paradigms has a definite meaning when the definition of similarity is uniquely defined. But in reality, the concept of similarity depends on the weight we attach to each variable, on the threshold placed on the degree of nearness of the values of variables, and on the global situation about the distribution of paradigms. This is exactly the counterpart of the "inductive ambiguity" that is inevitable in any kind of inductive process.

In a practical case of paradigm-oriented pattern recognition, we have to recognize the existence of two stages:

1. the "tutorial stage" or "learning stage" during which the machine (or human) is shown paradigms and has to determine the class domain, and
2. the "application stage" or "decision stage" in which the machine is shown a newcomer whose class belonging is not known and has to make the decision as to the class affiliation.

In the "adaptive" mode of the learning stage, the paradigms (of known class-affiliation, of course) are shown to the machine, not all at one time, but one by one. The machine decides step by step and modifies its disjunctive domain of similarity, and the next paradigm is used as a test of this tentative domain. The correction will be made if the test proves to be negative, and the disjunctive domain of similarity is adaptively improved.

The task of producing the disjunctive domain of similarity (for simplicity, it will be called decision domain) on the basis of the paradigms requires a certain process of computation. The result of computation is essentially the condition on the properties of the members of the class. Therefore, in a way, it is a derivation of "intension" from the paradigm. But, we should remember that the result will depend on the adopted algorithm used in this computation. Once the class is defined by the intension, the application would become, in essence, a process of "sorting," which is one of two basic functions of the computer, the other one being logical operations which includes calculation.

Along with the two kinds of pattern recognition, i.e., the clustering and the paradigm-oriented pattern recognition, we should perhaps mention the existence of a third kind: "structure-oriented pattern recognition." In the paradigm-oriented pattern recognition, at least the number of classes is explicitly given, and each class is suggestively exemplified by paradigms. But in the "structure-oriented pattern recognition" the number of class is not explicitly given and can become infinite. Neither is given the paradigms. But, it is known that a member of each class is constructed by a certain number of elementary building blocks of known properties according to a certain combination of known rules of composition. This third class of pattern recognition, in spite of the apparent difference from the first two, will be shown in Chapter 10 to be essentially the same as the second class of pattern recognition.

1.3 PAVLOVIAN GENERALIZATION AND INDUCTION

The scientific method of inductive inference must have had its philogenic prototype in the everyday life strategy of survival through the use of past experience to foresee a future event, whereby the guiding principle is that similar causes will result in similar effects--an idea that was fostered in the environment in which the aphorism: "natura non facit saltus" was mostly correct. The utilization of this type of vague causality in life is not uniquely invented by conscious animals. The conditioned reflex is eminently the precursor of the practical usage of causality for the purpose of survival. Thus, it is not surprising that from the beginning Pavlov emphasized this effect of "generalization" in conditioned reflex [P-8, P-9]. If an animal is trained to stimulus S resulting in response R, it will react to stimulus S', which is not identical to S but close to S giving the same response R. This generalization is obviously the first sign of that mental activity that will develop into pattern recognition because it urges the organism to bundle together similar situations.

Whether the subject is capable of distinguishing S' from S is a separate problem, although for the extension of conditioned reflexes to conception of causality, the generalization plays a more important role when the subject is capable of discriminating S' from S. But at the stage of experiments with conditioned reflexes, the stimuli are simple excitations of sensory organs, and the difference between S' and S is, for instance, a difference in pitch or in mixing ratios of overtones in auditory experiments or a difference in skin positions of two points of contact. Thus, the generalization was confused with the absence of discriminating capability. Even as late as 1964 in a symposium on "generalization," the distinction between two kinds of problems could become a significant topic of discussion [M-6].

The objective data about generalization are limited practically only to the "gradient curve of generalization," i.e. a plot of the intensity of response against the distance between S and S', using the same appropriate units, e.g., the number of trained responses plotted against the frequency of the sound used as stimulus. The shape of the curve, particularly its symmetry, the position of the peak, which sometimes does not exactly coincide with the original stimulus S, the change with times after the training, etc., could become topics of discussion. An extension of the curve to a surface using a multi-dimensional distance measure between S and S' is an interesting subject, because of its analogy to inductive ambiguity, but it has not been investigated to a desirable degree.

Of course, Pavlov himself made an assumption with regard to the neurophysiological mechanism, but a more methodical scientific study was started by Jerzy Konorski of Poland who published the classical book entitled *Conditioned Reflex and Neuron Organization*, in England as early as 1948 [K-12]. In this book, he rejected Pavlov's "irradiation theory" of generalization, according to which the excitation caused by training stimulus takes place at a point in the cortex and it is, in generalization, irradiated to a neighboring point which corresponds to a generalized stimulus. He rejects the point-representation of a stimulus and believes that the connection between neurons has a hierarchial structure, and one stimulus, when it reaches the cortex, spreads to a complex function (a pattern) of cortical points. The generalization is caused by a partial overlap of two patterns. In its generality, this theory seems to be closer to the idea of researchers of today (see Section E-3 for more modern interpretation).

The research in the neurophysiological area is, of course, strongly handicapped by the scarcity of experimental methods. The only available data of that time were taken mainly from the cases of accidental and intentional lesions in brains.

An experiment done by Werner K. Honig of Dalhousie University was designed so that any asymmetry between S and S' was eliminated, and the data showed only the effect in the context of discrimination versus generalization. Figure 1.3.1 is an example of the generalization gradient, in which the ordinate is the percentage of the "identity key" being pecked at, whereas the abscissa is the difference in frequency (in millimicron) of the lights corresponding to S and S'. Four different pigeons were trained to peck at the "identity key" when two lights simultaneously shown were of identical wavelength, and to peck at the "difference key" when the two lights were of wavelengths with a difference of 40 millimicrons. The wavelengths themselves of the lights were chosen between 500 mμ and 570 mμ and presented to the subject randomly. When the response had become 80% correct in the training period, the subject passed to the test period. Again a pair of two lights were shown, between 500 and 570 mμ, with a difference varying between 0 and 70 mμ. The rate of total responses, both identity and difference keys, was constantly

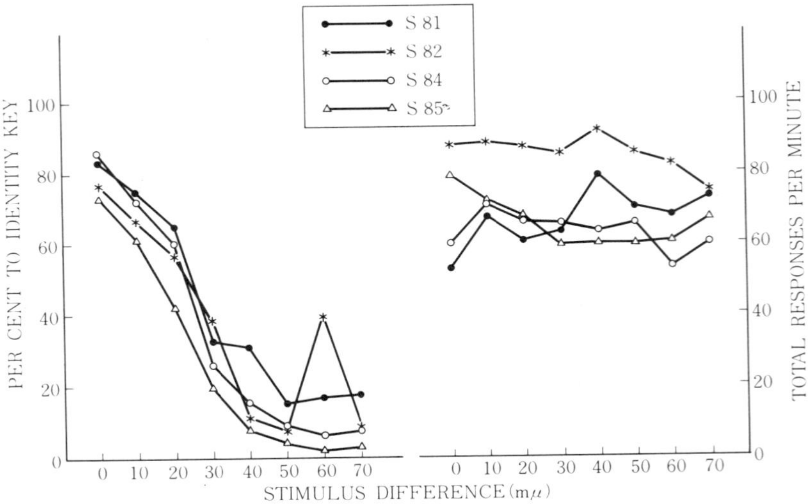

Figure 1.3.1 An example of the generalization gradient. The ordinate is the strength of "identification" and the abscissa is the "distance." (After figure by Werner K. Honig of Dalhousie University.)

about 80%. The percentage of identity key is given in Fig. 1.3.1.

This experiment does not reproduce the natural situation in which the phenomenon of generalization manifests itself. In particular, the simultaneous training for discrimination and identification (by arbitrarily fixing the distance of "different" examples) will tend to alter the "range of generalization" (the range of stimuli in which the positive response is appreciable). But the general shape of the gradient curve is more or less the same in different cases of the similar experiment. In the case of human reaction patterns, the variables of stimuli are multi-dimensional and the range of generalization can be intentionally changed. Even for animals, it is important to note that the range of generalization is determined, not only by the physical nature of the incoming stimuli, but also by the factors pertinent to the organism. For an individual organism, the range of generalization is innately fixed, because it is probably mainly determined by the overlap of neuronic patterns on the cortex. If we consider, however, the phylogenic development of the nervous system, the structure of neurons must be a result of the gradual adaptation to the environment in which life had to live and survive. Indeed, without the non-zero and non-infinite ranges of generalization, the organism could not have survived. Another example of epistemometrical principle that the innate framework of thinking in individual organisms is a result of is phylogenic adaption to experience.

For actual purposes of survival, some ranges of generalization may be too broad and some may be too narrow. The conscious animal can have the capability of deciding which variables to choose and how far to generalize them, although it cannot be sure, in advance, of the adequacy of their generalization in each individual case of application of their causal laws, which is essentially an extension of past experience. This is because a new situation is never exactly the same as before, and the range of generalization can be far beyond the capability of discrimination.

This uncertainty is to be found at the root of inductive ambiguity, which pervades all branches of science and their applications, including pattern recognition. There is no infallible rule guiding human intelligence in choosing the best strategy in face of this ambiguity. In a problem of deductive nature, there is a set of rules of logic, but in a problem of inductive nature, there are at best only a few vaguely conceived heuristic rules which sometimes are useful but can be unsuccessful. They are not "necessary" rules, but are often found to be worthwhile. Their reliability is somehow like that of the esthetic rule of golden section or the principle of simplicity or the principle of parsimony.

1.4 "PRÄGNANZ" AND CONCEPTUAL ADAPTATION

By now the reader can see why this chapter is called "pattern recognition as seeing-in-one-in-many." But, as explained in Section 1.1, we can discriminate two kinds of seeing-one-in-many involved in pattern recognition:

1. when seeing an animal face in a cloud or seeing an array of lines-of-force in a layer of iron filings, one sees a form in an individual case of picture or scenery consisting of many parts,
2. when calling many flowers by a single name of plumeria or many weaving patterns by a single name of family plaid, one puts many examples in one class.

What we have noted in the last section was an example of (b) because many incidents of similar cases were perceived or conceived as one in the sense of Pavlovian generalization.

What we are discussing in this section is primarily the case (a) but we have to note that (a) is a necessary prerequisite for (b). For if a picture, or a scene, or a pattern is not seen as one thing, we cannot put it as a member of a class. When a cloud with a fox face is put into a class of fox faces, it is not as a collection of many white points which constitute the cloud, but as a single item called fox face. But, the interesting part of the two-stage process is that these two stages have a lot in common. The secret is that both consist of discerning a form in a collection of many. A division into two stages may be regarded as an artificial explanation. In reality, the same process of seeing-one-in-many or form-discerning goes on in a ladder of stages. Indeed, a number of classes usually constitute one higher order class. That is why this section applies also for higher order form-seeing, although admittedly each stage of the hierarchy of form-discerning has its peculiar characteristic and requires a different precaution.

The form of a picture or scenery is a global character, not a local character, of a perceived picture. The first school that pointed out the importance of a form was Gestalt psychology. The precursor was von Ehrenfels and his Graz school who about 1890 remarked that in the description of a perception by local sensations, many ordinary visual characteristics such as round, angular, slender are completely missing. For the occurrence of these characteristics, single stimuli or mere addition of such stimuli will not suffice [V-5]. These characteristics remain invariant for a change in size

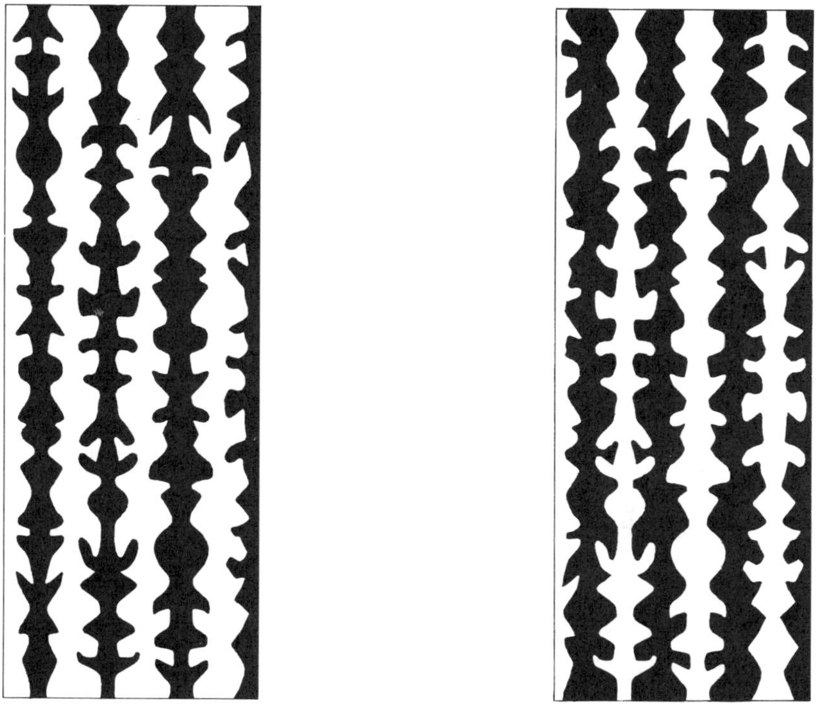

Figure 1.4.1 Picture (left) is seen in black; picture (right) is seen in white. The symmetric arrangement has more "Prägnanz." Adapted from *Principles of Gestalt Psychology* by Kurt Koffka, copyright 1935 by Harcourt Brace Jovanovich, Inc.; renewed 1963 by Elisabeth Koffka; United Kingdom copyright 1935 by Routledge and Kegan Paul. Reproduced by permission of the publishers and Mrs. Elisabeth Koffka.

or in color. Similar invariant features exist in the dimension of time, for instance, the same melody can be recognized, even played, by different instruments or in different keys. The name "Gestalt" was introduced by von Ehrenfels.

Wertheimer who is considered by many as the founder of the Gestalt psychology is often said to have been the first to "deny the existence of sensory elements as parts of perceptual experience" [W-49, W-50]. But von Ehrenfels and his followers had considered the global characteristic already as a "produced idea" or the "idea of extrasensory origin" [K-13]. In any event, according to Köhler [K-14], we have to note two meanings of the German word, Gestalt, one meaning one independent thing, i.e., an articulate figure we perceive in the visual field, and the other meaning the shape of such a figure. The first aspect of Gestalt is what we shall study in Chapter 2 from a slightly different view. The term "form" has a connotation of the <u>shape</u> of a <u>separate object</u> that we perceive in a mosaic of visual stimuli. In fact, one of these two aspects of Gestalt is not possible without the other aspect of Gestalt. The principle by which the Gestalt is formed in the mind is what is called by Wertheimer the principle of "Prägnanz." This is a vaguely conceived principle which lies at the bottom of form-discerning. According to Koffka [K-13], it embraces such properties as regularity, symmetry, and simplicity.

Fig. 1.4.1 is a good example of the law of "Prägnanz" devised by Bahnsen. In the left figure or the right figure the observer can see either the black stripes or the white stripes as "figures" as is the case in many known figure-ground experiments. But, the actual experiments showed that the majority of observers saw as "figure" the black stripes in the left figure, and white stripes in the right figure. The preferred figure is of course the "simple" one. To use the modern jargon, the information content of the preferred figure is smaller than the nonpreferred figure (the one seen as ground). This is a simple example of "the principle of minimum entropy" which states that we adjust our conceptual framework so that the entropy of the object becomes minimum. This principle was discovered by research entirely different from the Gestalt psychologists, but the coincidence of the tenets of the two principles is is amazing (see Chapter 6).

The principle of Prägnanz is often simplified as principle of organization, but this name gives an erroneous impression because in order to talk about an organization forming the whole, the parts must exist before the whole. Wertheimer's idea of the organization of parts is different. For him, the whole (Gestalt) preexists the parts, and the whole is divided into parts whose existence is guaranteed only through their mutual relation and their relation to the whole. The same kind of remark is necessary in order to interpret the famous explanation in terms of physical Gestalten (such as electromagnetic fields). We should note that the structure of a field (such as a solution of the Laplace equation) is nothing but a human mental construct. To say that the field exists in the external world is a short hand for "in the man-made theory, there is such a thing as field obeying such and such mathematical equation," which shows a strong structuredness. We should always come back to the fact that there is no such real thing in the external world as figure and ground. These ideas are nothing but a result of the mental adaptation to the exterior world. The habit of seeing something which has a higher degree of Prägnanz (i.e. a low entropy) is also developed thorugh phylogenic experience. This, of course, does not imply that everything comes from the environment, but that everything is a result of an accumulation of experience through generations and generations of interaction between the observing subject and the observed object.

We shall devote Chapter 5 to a detailed discussion of the relationship between inductive inference and pattern recognition. It is rather easy to see that a paradigm-oriented pattern recognition is a case of induction. We have at hand finite examples (paradigms) of class, say, A, and we have to "induce" therefrom a general hypothesis, applicable to an infinite number of cases, that a member of class A has such and such properties. The actual finite set of paradigms has a great number of common properties, and we can use any combinations or functions of observed variables as generalized variables, as far as paradigms are concerned. But not all of them are relevant and useful for generalization. Some combinations or functions of original variables will prove successful (when the general rule is used for a certain purpose) and some will not. This is the origin of inductive ambiguity. Here is the field where a heuristic principle has to play a role, be it a principle of Prägnanz or a principle of minimum entropy or some other principle, none of which can give foolproof advice. It should be noted, that the success can be, in the last analysis, judged by the usefulness of the resulting classification for a given purpose. In the case of an inductive inference of a natural law, the purpose may be the formulation of a simple, elegant, mathematical law. The empirical "validity" alone does not determine the unique formulation of a natural law.

In pattern recognition, the heuristic of minimum entropy is used mainly in the following manner. Each case of paradigm is represented as a point in the space of available variables or functions or both, which can have some relevance to the desired classification. A group of paradigms thus form a "cloud" of points in this space. We adjust and select our choice of variables so that the cloud shows a sign of simplicity, symmetry, elegance, articulation, etc. We shall see in Chapter 6 and in chapters that follow how such a program works--a program of conceptual adaptation so as to see a form in the given data.

Referring to Fig. 1.1.4, Rorschach inkblots, we should note that left and right symmetry is built into the picture to give the figure a certain degree of Prägnanz, so that the subject is induced to look for something meaningful. But it is so contrived that there is not a single obvious answer to the question: "What do you see in this picture?" The association in the mind of the subject will be at work to give an answer to this question.

Two of the major factors that make pattern recognition possible, namely, inductive generalization and the esthetic heuristic, were discovered more than half a century ago by two scholars (Pavlov, Wertheimer), who are renowned for the discoveries apparently remote from the problems of pattern recognition. The author thanks the psychologist, Prof. O. Miyagi, for the enlightening conversation between them regarding the benefit inherited from the early psychologists.

CHAPTER 2
Pattern Recognition as Perception

2.1 OBJECT AND FEATURES

Whether we like it or not, under all the works of pattern recognition lies tacitly the Aristotelian view that the world consists of a discrete number of self-identical objects provided with, other than fleeting accidental properties, a number of fixed or very slowly changing attributes. Some of these attributes represent the peculiarity of a particular object; the rest of these attributes, which may be called "features," determine the class to which the object belongs. The assignment of a class to an object is essentially the task of pattern recognition. The features, therefore, are invariant properties when we pass from one particular object to another object within a class, and also when we change the mode of presentation of the same object to our observation.

The traditional approach to pattern recognition is to start with various methods of taking "neutral" data and then later consider classification. For those readers who are not familiar with the practice of pattern recognition we prepared Appendix A-1, Data Taking. Appendix A-2 explains Fourier transformation and Fourier optics as an example of extracting "invariant" features from the data.

It would be a commonsensible view to consider the "raw" data about the properties as provided by our sensory organs or instruments of observation or both and by the class-assignment as made by our cognitive judgment on the basis of the raw data. This picture of two-stage process of cognition is often deliberately reproduced in the mechanical design of pattern recognition, but we should ask ourselves whether such a picture is applicable to the natural perception in animals and man. This is the first question posed in this chapter.

The second question pertains to the idea of a discrete number of self-identical objects. What we see with our eyes are patches of colors that blend continuously into one another, or more precisely, one two-dimensional extension with continuously changing hues and shades. What falls on our ears is equally a continuously extending one-dimensional flow. The segmentation of nature into discrete objects probably has its ontogenetic and phylogenetic psychological origin closely related to the primitive animistic picture of the world; however, we can explain to some extent this object-segmenting tendency by the physiological effect of the Mach band. We shall further see this problem in connection with the convergence of sensory informations in the association area of the cortex.

The third question we should keep in mind while reading this chapter is whether the traditional separation between dispassionate cognition and affective evaluation, between knowledge and value, and between epistemology and axiology, is so clear-cut as is usually assumed. The same theme will reappear also in Chapter 4 and in Epilogue E-3.

The fourth question, which is related to the first question but bridges us over to Chapter 3 on the controversy about the universal, is whether the concept we use in classification is imposed by experience of the external world or more or less pre-determined by the innate nature of our minds, or perhaps by something that transcends our actual world of experience.

Keeping these questions in mind, let us study a few interesting facts in the realm of sensory science and animal perception, which is the primordial type of pattern recognition. The mechanical methods of pattern recognition will profit from the study of the natural perception, and the sensory science and epistemology will profit from the effort to make a mechanical facsimile of the natural perception. Of course, we have to expect that one approach which is successful in natural pattern recognition may not always be the best approach in the mechanical counterpart.

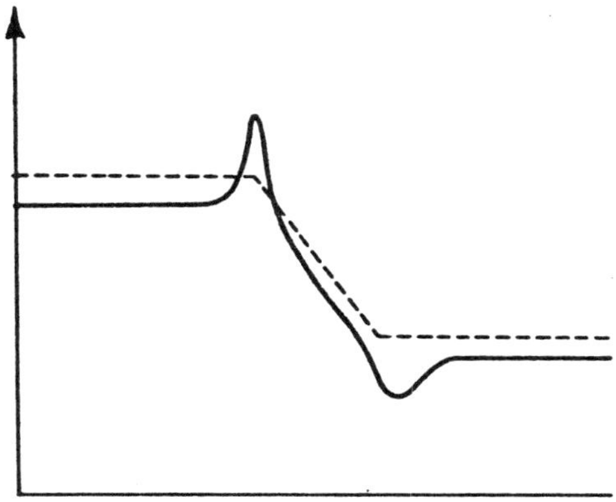

Figure 2.2.1. Mach's curve. The subjective intensity of Mach's curve shown here is the physical intensity plus a term proportional to the upward convexity of the physical intensity.

2.2 CONTOUR AND FIGURE

This section relates to the fact that when we ask someone, adult or child, sophisticated or naive, to draw a picture of something, he is likely to draw the contour lines of the object, whereas there are no such lines in physical signals from the object. This phenomenon has been a long-standing enigma, and there have been many would-be answers. But, the fact is that, apart from any explanations belonging to the conceptual level, a physiological effect underlying this phenomena has now become clarified, thanks to a series of investigations of which the very first dates back more than one century to Ernst Mach's 1865 paper [M-2, M-3]. The source of the following description is Mach's papers, Ratliff's book [R-2] and a personal conversation with Georg von Békésy (see also [V-3, V-4, K-5]).

What is known as the Mach band is the following phenomenon. Suppose the light intensity is distributed like the solid line of Figure 2.2.1. The left portion has a constant high light intensity, the central part represents a gradual decrease in intensity, and the right portion shows again a constant but lower intensity. In other words, the inclination is zero in the left portion and in the right portion, but it has a negative constant value in the central portion. If a human eye sees such a distribution of light, it sees an additional change of intensity as shown by a dotted curve on top of the solid curve. Where the inclination suddenly decreases, we see an additional increase of intensity, and where the inclination suddenly increases, we see an additional dip in intensity. Note that this statement need not be changed if we invert the positive x-direction of Figure 2.2.1.

If we want to see this effect by an experiment, the simplest way is to paint concentric zones on a round disk following Mach, so that the physical light intensity distribution along the radial direction becomes like the solid line of Figure 2.2.1 when we rotate the disk by an electric motor. We shall see, in addition to the three concentric zones, one bright band and one dark band between the zones. Mach expressed this effect by the formula

$$K = I - c \frac{\partial^2 I}{\partial x^2} , \tag{2.2.1}$$

where I is the physical intensity of light, K is the intensity that the human eye sees, x is the x-axis of Figure 2.2.1 or the radial direction on Mach's disk. The second derivative becomes positive where the curve is concave upward, and negative where the curve is convex upward, hence the formula (2.2.1) represents the phenomenon explained above.

Mach's papers in physics and philosophy were well remembered by many readers, but his papers in physiology had quickly fallen into oblivion. But, the young physicist von Békésy remembered them, when a photographic record of a spectral line of a star started a controversy. The line in the photographic plate looked to the naked eye like two lines, suggesting that the two lines were caused by a double star due to the Doppler effect, whereas the photometric observation showed only one line. von Békésy gave immediately a solution to the controversy, by explaining the two lines as the Mach bands on both sides of a single line.

Our explanation used one dimension, but a similar psychological effect can naturally happen in a two-dimensional light distribution, and Mach already wrote a formula which is essentially

$$K = I - c\left(\frac{\partial^2 I}{\partial x^2} + \frac{\partial^2 I}{\partial y^2}\right), \tag{2.2.2}$$

where the operation in the parentheses is what is called the Laplacian. It is very interesting that the early pattern recognition engineers who struggled with picture processing introduced a digital equivalent of the Laplacian without knowing the works of Mach or von Békésy, in order to obtain the contour of an object.

An interesting anecdote is that Mach, who was known to be a pure positivist, was afraid that he would be criticized for introducing the "subjective" intensity (K) into his theory and tried to forestall such objections by declaring "even illusion is a fact that requires explanation." As a matter of fact, he even wrote that this effect must be caused by an interaction of neighboring cells on the retina. This theory at that time was only a conjecture, because neurophysiology in the modern sense then was still to be born.

This conjecture was proven to be true 90 years after Mach's theory by the discovery of "lateral inhibition" by Hartline and Ratliff [H-4, H-11] in 1950. When light falls on a spot on the retina, a positive signal is emitted through the optical nerve fiber originating from that spot on the retina. The lateral inhibition consists of suppressing the signals originating from the neighboring optical cells around the first irradiated point. This action can be expressed mathematically by the response function which is positive on the point and negative on the neighboring points (the von Békésy function). Hearing the news of this discovery, von Békésy immediately knew that this must be the mechanism of the Mach band.

Relegating a mathematical treatment to Appendix 2, we can qualitatively understand why it is so. The first derivative is essentially the difference of the values of a curve between two neighboring points. Repeating this process of difference taking twice, we can see that the second derivative (with a sign change) amounts to taking twice the value of the curve at a point and subtracting the value of the left-neighbor point and the value of the right-neighbor point. Therefore, it is easy to

Figure 2.2.2 *(a)* is the original picture.

understand that the lateral inhibition corresponds to the negative of the second derivative.

If we idealize the sensory response by mathematical formulae like (2.2.1) and (2.2.2), and make the transient zone (what we called middle portion in Figure 2.2.1) tend to zero, the additional increase and additional decrease would formally cancel each other. But insofar as there exists a finite transient zone, narrow as it may be, the contrast between the bright zone and the dark zone

Figure 2.2.2 (b) is the contour of *(a)* obtained by the Fourier optics method simulating the Laplacian operator.

will make the contour very real. Even if the width of the transient zone becomes zero, the distance between the neighboring points previously mentioned is finite, and this finite distance will determine the distance between the bright zone and the dark zone. This distance is therefore physiologically determined. In any event, the contour vision is a real phenomenon from the point of view of sensory science, and not a simple subjective construction.

Figure 2.2.2 (c) is the same as *(b)* but the horizontal distance between the maximum and the minimum of Mach's curve is assumed to be finite; *(b)* is the limiting case where the distance tends to zero.

In computer simulation, we can do three things to see the contour: use the extended version of Laplacian keeping the distance between neighboring points finite; use the absolute value of the Laplacian (or even of the gradient, i.e., the first derivative along the steepest descent); or use

Fourier optics and apply the Laplacian to the amplitude instead of the intensity of the picture. Figure 2.2.2b is the contour obtained by the third method from the original Figure 2.2.2a in our laboratory in Hawaii. Figure 2.2.2c corresponds to the case where the maximum and minimum in the sense of Figure 2.2.1 are separated by a finite distance. In these pictures the intensity instead of the amplitude is photographed, therefore we see two bright lines (see Appendix 2).

von Békésy assumed a similar effect in the auditory sensation even before the actual discovery of lateral inhibition in optical sensation. Before von Békésy's work, people used to believe in Helmholtz's theory which claimed that a stationary acoustic wave was produced in the cochlea and that the sensitive hairlike cells, whose own frequency corresponded to the impinging wave, sensed that pitch. von Békésy showed that the acoustic wave produced in the cochlea is not a stationary wave, but a damped traveling wave. The envelope of this traveling wave has a maximum whose position depends on the frequency. The hair cell which is located near the maximum point senses the frequency. The trouble with this theory was that the maximum was not sharp enough to explain the extreme sensitivity of aural sensation on pitches. To explain this sharpness, von Békésy imagined something like the Mach band which would enhance the maximum. Unfortunately, this conjecture was proven recently not to be exactly tenable because the auditory nerve fibers are so connected that only neighbor cells on one side exert inhibition [D-2, R-3, S-6, Z-1]. As a result, the first derivative instead of the second derivative is added to the straight sensation. Yet von Békésy's idea that the sharpening of auditory sensation is affected by the inhibitive action of the neighboring cells seems to be still true.

In later years, von Békésy tried and succeeded in extending his theory of sharpening of sensation by lateral inhibition to all kinds of sensation other than the eye and the ear. When the author visited von Békésy's hospital bed immediately after his death in 1971 in Honolulu, there was on the bedside table an experimental setup consisting of a rotating disk very much like Mach's disks.

We have seen in Figure 1.1.3 that the picture represents a goblet or two faces according as our "attention" is shifted from one aspect to another. The object we "see" at one instant is called the "figure," and the suppressed aspect is called "ground." Now, from the point of view of the usage in ordinary language of the term contour, we have to say that the contour is to be considered to belong to the figure, not to the ground. Therefore, the contour from one instant to another changes its affiliation. But, all the same, the contour vision makes the figure more conspicuous. It is interesting to note that the term figure often means the contour of the conspicuous object, i.e., of the figure in the Gestalttheoretic vocabulary. For instance, when we say that she has a good figure, it is implied that we make abstraction of the hue of the skin, or of the ugliness of the face, or of the physiognomy.

If a picture is given like Figure 1.1.3, there is no reason to decide which one of the two alternatives is the "correct" interpretation, although there may be a difference in the degree of Prägnanz. But, if the same picture is a part of a larger picture which represents a group of bottles and glasses, the interpretation of the picture as a goblet may be judged to be the right one. Therefore, the decision of figure-ground may be said to be context dependent. Again, if the observer is unfamiliar with this type of goblet, he will not see the goblet aspect of the picture at all. Thus the notion of context should be extended not only to all the coexisting objects but also to the background of the observer.

Coming back to the context-free case, i.e., assuming that both aspects are equally valid, we have to note an important fact, already mentioned, that when one aspect is seen, the other aspect completely disappears. In other words, two alternative figures are not simultaneously tenable. Yet, it is not justifiable to say that one aspect is correct and the other is incorrect. Both have an equal right to reality although they are conflicting with each other. Such a situation fits perfectly well with Niels Bohr's epistemological principle of complementarity, which he introduced to explain the wave-particle duality of an elementary particle. The reality can have two conflicting aspects, either of which is correct and consistent, yet both not simultaneously tenable.

The lesson we draw from this section is that already at the stage of peripheral organs, our sensation already modifies the incoming physical signals in such a way to facilitate pattern recognition in terms of discernible objects.

2.3 PSEUDOCONCEPT

We saw that the sensory organs of animals detect not only the simple variables of physical stimuli but also the first and second spatial derivatives of them when these are useful for the purposes of life. But, the derivatives are still relatively simple variables closely related to the physical variables. In nature, some of the peripheral organs send signals to the nervous center which are quite complicated functions of incoming physical stimuli. In higher animals, complicated functions of physical signals are mostly formed on the cortex of the cerebrum to represent "concepts," but in the lower animals whose brains are not developed, quite complicated functions seem to be formed at the peripheral levels which in higher animals would correspond to concepts. If we agree that the pattern is recognized by the "mind's eye," the "mind" must be said to be extended to the peripheral sensory organs. Let us describe briefly the famous research made by Lettvin et al. [L-3, L-4] on the frog's eye. It is a classical example showing that the goal-matching information selection and something similar to the formation of "concepts" start already right after the retina, i.e., before the signals reach the brain. Even a simple geometrical or physical variable corresponds to a concept, but what we call concepts in this section are those which correspond to very complicated functions of physical stimuli.

In the frog's eye, light falls on about one million receptors (rods and cones), and the signals go out of the eye in a bundle of optic nerve fibers which are actually the axons* of the so-called "ganglia" cells, of which there are about one half million. In the back layer of the eye, the receptors and the ganglia cells are connected by bipolar cells. There are also a total of 2 1/2 to 3 1/2 million horizontal connecting cells. As a result, one rod or cone is connected to a large number of ganglia cells, and conversely one ganglion cell is connected to many thousands of receptors. The two bundles of optic nerve fibers coming from the left and right eyes are crossed and connected to the optic tectum which lies on the dorsal side of the brain.

Lettvin and collaborators detected electric signals in individual axons in the optic nerves and in cells in the optic tectum. In the frog's eye, there is no fovea. Some ganglion cells have a receptive field (area that they "see") of only a few degrees in diameter (1° - 4°), and some react to a very wide field. In the optic nerve fibers, the geometric relations of receptive fields of ganglion cells are all mixed up, but they seem to be restored when they arrive in the optic tectum. The cells in the optic tectum, however, are no longer connected to definite receptive fields but react to the more global feature of the entire field.

Lettvin et al. discovered five major groups of optical fibers: Group 1, boundary detectors--the receptive fields of these fibers are 2° to 4° in diameter, and they respond to any sharp boundary between two areas with different greyness. The sharpness of the boundary is important, not the degree of contrast between the two greynesses. Motion of the boundary enhances the electric discharge, but is not necessary to cause the discharge. Group 2,

---

*A nerve cell consists of a cell body, dendrites (signal input) and an axon (signal transmission and output). Both dendrites and axon-ends divide into small branches establishing contact with other nerve cells. A potential peak (spike) travels along an axon with various velocities peculiar to each cell. The intensity of response is inversely related to the interval between consecutive spikes. The propagation of signals by electric spikes, unlike the electric current in metals, is determined by the motion of ion concentration and is, therefore, much slower than the light velocity.

convexity detectors--these fibers have receptive fields of 3° to 5°. They respond only to sharp boundaries between two areas of different degrees of greyness, provided the boundary is curved and the "inside" area is darker than the "outside" area (i.e., the darker area is convex), and provided the boundary has moved or is moving. In other words, these nerve fibers respond strongly to a small dark object that has moved or is moving. When such an object moves into the receptive field and stops, it causes a long-lasting discharge which stops if the light is turned off, and does not restart if the light is turned on again, unless the object moves again. Groups 1 and 2 belong to what is called unmyelinated fibers (i.e., fibers that are not covered with soft, white, fatty sheaths), and make up about 97% of the optic nerves. The signals travel at velocities between 20 and 50 cm/sec. Groups 3 and 4, which occupy the remaining 3% of fibers are myelinated, and the signals travel much faster at various velocities between 1 to 10 m/sec. Group 3, moving boundary detectors--in contrast to Group 1, these fibers respond only when the boundary is moving or changing. In contrast to Group 2, the discharge stops when the object stops. The discharge response becomes more frequent when the boundary is sharp, and the speed of the motion is high. Group 4, dimming detectors--respond by a prolonged discharge to any dimming of illumination in the entire receptive field, which is as large as 15°. They are insensitive to the existence of boundaries or motions of objects.

The fibers belonging to Group 5 are very few and their function is not studied in detail, except that their firing rate seems to be an indicator of the average illumination. The darker the illumination, the higher the firing rate. It is significant that the authors observed nerve fibers with very high speed (20 m/sec), which they assumed carried messages from the brain to the retina, in contrast to the great majority of nerve cells that carry messages in the opposite direction. It is also interesting that they anatomically recognized four different types of dendritic connections of ganglion cells at the back of the retina. Some cells have connections at one particular depth, some others have connections at more than one particular depth. Some have horizontal widespread connection and some others have more concentrated connection. They could establish with sufficient plausibility a correspondence between the functional types and the anatomic types. For instance, the dimming detector respondent to the general darkening of the wide field is identified with the one-level widespread type.

At the brain end of the optic fibers, the four major types of axons end at four different depths in the outer layer of the optic tectum. Below the outer layer there are nerve cells which receive signals from the optic fibers. Among these cells, Lettvin and collaborators recognized two major types of neurons. The first type is named "newness" neurons. If an object moves across the neurons' receptive fields, which are as wide as 30°, the neurons respond with frequencies dependent upon the jerkiness, velocity, direction of the motions, and the size of the object. The peculiarity of these cells is that they do not respond for at least 5 to 10 sec when we repeat the same motion of the same size object in the same direction. Even after 20 sec the response remains weak. If the first movement and the second movement are at right angles, there is no interference; the second movement is new.

The second type of neurons is called "sameness" neurons by those authors. If a small object, 1° or 2° in diameter, is brought into the field (which is almost as wide as the entire visual field), the nerve cell starts to "notice" after a short time. After the starting time, the response continues as long as the object is in the field and becomes intense every time the object makes any kind of jerky move. The authors report a particularly interesting phenomenon in the case where they showed two objects at once. At least with a subclass of sameness neurons, it was observed that they respond only to one or the other of the two objects at one time and not to both of them simultaneously, although their attention may shift from one to the other when one of them stops.

The frog's survival depends upon factors as the sky, pond, small insects, snakes, etc. It is obvious that the four types of ganglion cells are developed to send signals selectively pertinent to these vital factors. (Group 2 is often called "bug detector.") It is amazing that such a selection of variables takes place already right behind the retina instead of in the brain. In the optic tectum, there is already a prototype of memory and also a special faculty of concentrating attention to one object of concern.

The bug detectors send signals corresponding to the concept "bug-ness," although we cannot say that the peripheral organ literally forms a concept. Similarly, the frog can see the snake-like objects and pond-like objects. With this type of concept-like sensation on one extreme and the sophisticated genuine concepts in human intelligence on the other extreme, we can further recognize a third kind of class, which may be called behavioral categories of stimuli. For instance, in the T-maze experiment, an untrained rat will go up the entrance branch and turn to the left and to the right with an approximately equal probability (relative frequency). But, if a food pellet is placed consistently on the left branch, it starts to turn to the left with an increasingly higher probability, until finally it ends up turning consistently to the left. We cannot say that there is a particular inborn behavioral distinction between left and right, nor can we say that the rat has created a concept of left and right. But, its response pattern looks as if it learned the "concept" of left and right, and causally associated left with food.

The fact that the rat has extracted the "pseudoconcept" of left and right among other possibilities can be shown by simultaneously illuminating one or the other of the two exit branches randomly. It will soon discover that there is no relation between light and food, and will learn to turn to the left to get the food. But, on the other hand, if we do not fix the location of the food pellet and place it on the illuminated side, the rat will probably learn to turn to the illuminated branch.

What is important to remember at this point is that the selective formation of a pseudoconcept or a response category is intimately related to what is valuable for survival--in this case, the food pellet. In the T-maze experiment, and in many other similar experiments of learning and conditioned reflexes*, the animals learn to notice selectively such a feature or pattern in the situation in which they are placed and their responses based on that feature would lead to acquisition of a desirable "reward." Pattern recognition in humans is not basically different, but somewhat in the same way as science can become independent of technology, we are capable of carrying out a pattern recognition task which is not directly related to an immediate profit. For a further discussion of the subtle interrelation between the value-system and the concept formation, see Chapter 4, and Epilogue 3.

We have learned two important things in this section pertinent to the work of pattern recognition: (1) The choice of observational variables in animals is directly related to their value situation, (2) The concept formation is not exclusive to human intelligence, but its prototype exists already in lower animals and is often carried out not necessarily at the cortex. At this level, we cannot distinguish between observed variables and concepts.

Thus, for a computerized pattern recognition, the most vital thing is to choose good observational variables which may be quite different from the simple variables that physicists would use to describe the physical aspects of the incoming stimuli. The physicists' variables are chosen so as to make the physical laws not only possible but also simple. The value for them here is the scientific truth described by the physical laws.

2.4 SYNTHESIS OF SENSORY STIMULI

Since the pioneering investigation of Lettvin et al. opened a new era of neurophysiological study of perception, more than 20 years have passed. During this time a fantastic number of experimental results in this field have been accumulated. It is therefore

---

*A Russian scholar, Bongard [B-9], recently emphasized that animals can learn many things that do not exist as unconditioned reflexes, showing that Pavlovian theory is too narrow to explain the whole gamut of learning processes. Compare this idea, however, with the findings described in the next section, where some concepts are shown to be innate.

impossible for a layman like the present author even to try to make a brief survey of the new progress. It may be of some interest, however, to pick up randomly a few topics from the newer findings that have relevance to pattern recognition. The animals used now for experiments are usually monkeys and cats which certainly have more similarity to humans than the frog.

One of the most valuable projects that requires a great deal of tedious and careful labor is the mapping of the interconnections of neurons. The cortex can be divided into three areas: (1) the receptor area where sensory stimuli arrive, (2) the motor area where a new decision of action is emitted to the effectors, and (3) the association area where presumably complex information processing takes place. The neurons in this area are eventually connected to the receptor area and the motor area, but the flow of information within this area is highly complicated. In general, three types of connection are observed in the association cortex: divergent type--starting from one neuron or a few neurons, the signals diverge to many different regions; parallel type--signals from a small region are converged to a small region; convergent type--signals from different regions are conveyed to a single neuron or to a small region (see Chavis and Pandya [C-6]). The convergence type of connection is interesting, because, as we have seen, pattern recognition aims at finding one image in a field consisting of many "parts." In the converging type of connection, a neuron can receive signals not necessarily of the same kind.

The perception of depth (i.e., the 3-D view) is made possible primarily due to the disparity of the left and right visual signals, and, in fact, Bishop and others have discovered neurons which are sensitive to the left and right disparity (see for instance [B-10]). But a perfect 3-D image requires more than the disparity of binocular view. Sakata reports that a visual fixation neuron, which fires when a certain point is gazed at, shows a positive response at a certain direction and a negative response at a different direction. A similar discrimination is shown with regard to the distance of the object gazed at, which demonstrates that on such a neuron, not only the visual signal but also the information about the muscular tensions (which are governed by a motor decision) converge and help the depth sensation [S-13]. It is, at least, now clear that the perfect 3-D effect is produced by a synthesis of many different stimuli.

Apart from the visual fixation neurons, there are visual tracking neurons which fire when following a moving point. Sakata discovered that the same tracking neuron fires either by a moving point or by a background moving in the opposite direction and fires more strongly by both motions together [S-14]. This provides, as Sakata rightly points out, a neurophysiological backing to the idea of "induced motion" discovered by Gestalt psychologist K. Dunker (see p. 282 of [K-13]).

Helmholtz, in spite of his fame as an early proponent of neurophysiological explanation, is known to have insisted on the necessity of innate mental (instead of physical) activity to make the 3-D vision possible. The newer researches seem to show that what was called "mental" was just a result of confluence of many sensory (and perhaps even motor) signals. But, note that this visual faculty is not acquired nor learned but innate. Also note that this neurophysiological explanation does not deny the coexistence of mental activities simultaneous with physical activities.

More close to pattern recognition is the discovery by Perrett et al. [P-10] of visual neurons in the monkey that respond exclusively to human and simian faces. The responses were found to be relatively constant for such transformations as inversion, change in color, and change in size, but the response diminishes drastically when the front view is changed to the profile. The fact that different neurons of this group respond to different parts (eye, mouth or hair) of the face shows that these cells did not represent the last stage of synthesis, but are very close to the formation of the idea of "face-ness." The facial recognition is known to be present in newborn animals showing that this recognition is definitively an innate capability necessary for survival.

On a more abstract level, Sato and collaborators [S-15] discovered a small number of neurons which respond exclusively to one or another of four geometrical figures (cross, circle, triangle, square). The response was found not to depend on size, color, illumination and, above all, on training but depends strictly on the mentioned kinds of figures. This is a striking capability of form-discrimination. If this new discovery stands all possible criticisms, it will show that there is an innate idea of cross, circle, triangle, and square. Could there be, however, as many kinds of neurons as there are possible geometrical forms? Is this capability limited to a small number of nice, simple forms with a high degree of Prägnanz? Could this give support to the philosophy of Cubism in painting?

It is meaningful to ask if there is anything in the neurophysiological findings that is necessarily bound up with the Aristotelian view of nature that the world consists of a discrete number of self-identical objects with fixed attributes (see Chapter 3). The fact of contour vision and the existence of visual fixation neurons and visual tracking neurons certainly encourage the use of the idea of self-identical objects. But, these neurophysiological findings by no means confirm or necessitate the Aristotelian view; they only invite us to assume the short-term sameness of a discerned "object." On the other hand, some neurons may be said to have inborn capacities of perceiving certain "forms," certain "---nesses," such as "face-ness, triangle-ness, etc.," whereas some other alien properties such as size, color, illumination are abstracted away. We should remember that Plato did not believe in particular objects because they are mixtures of fleeting properties and insisted on the permanence of innate "ideas." It is, of course, a far-fetched comparison, but note that the content of the neuronic responses is unique, innate, abstract, and seems to pre-exist and supercedes the concrete particular objects with multifarious, ever-changing, often deceiving properties. We thank Dr. Sakata for imparting some of the recent discoveries in neurophysiology. He let us know by a recent private communication that he had discovered a visual neuron of the monkey that is exclusively sensitive to the clockwise motion of an object and a neuron that is sensitive to the counterclockwise motion of an object. He said that so far he could not find neurons exclusively sensitive to vertical and horizontal motion. See Epilogue 3 for more about the recent findings in neurophysiology and our comments.

2.5 PERCEPTION AS MENTAL CONSTRUCT

In the last two sections we relied on the commonsensible view that the neurophysiological phenomena and the mental process have intimate correspondence. This assumption is very difficult to prove and forms the center of the long-standing philosophical controversy over the mind-body problem. The author has his own theory about this problem [W-33, W-34] but does not want to go into the philosophical arguments here. Rather in this book he will proceed with the assumption (which is allowed according to our theory) that there is a rough (but not exact) parallelism between the neurophysiological-behavioral description and the mental description. See Epilogue 2. Furthermore, we take the view that consciousness or awareness is not limited to man and that the ratio of consciousness to unconsciousness gradually diminishes when we go down the scale of complexity of organic beings.

From this point of view, human beings provide a very useful case because we can get verbal reports of inner experience, which should not be so different from the animal experience. In this respect, we differ from those philosophers who are too strongly influenced by the linguistic theories and the ordinary language philosophy. They tend to believe that our intelligence and thought are based on, and conditioned by, our language. Their theory will be shattered by the recent experimental discoveries that show that human children can recognize patterns and classify objects before they start to talk or understand others talking. This is not surprising from our continuous viewpoint of the animal-man transition. In this section, we shall include more of the human introspective reports in addition to purely non-mental findings.

One of the important facts we emphasized in the last three sections was that sensation and perception are not a passive and unbiased transmission of physical stimuli, but they are an <u>active</u> selective formation of <u>valuable</u> information. It is interesting to note that such a statement would have aroused less sensation in the 19th century than in the first half of this century. Remember that Goethe's Farbenlehre was based on the theory that the eye is an active agent rather than a passive recipient. Kant could advance his theory, which for the sake of simplification we might call a theory of innate ideas, without arousing a resistance it would have caused in this century. This century with its deluge of technological successes which were essentially based on the 19th-century classical physics brought about a new Zeitgeist, championed by the Wiener circle which preached unification of sciences under the banner of logical empiricism, but, the trend had to change quickly. The middle of this century may be epitomized as a reaction to empiricism, calling for a return, in a guise or another, to what may be roughly called the Kantian tendency. The author still remembers having participated in a conversation one evening at the AAAS (American Association for Advancement of Science) meeting at Denver in 1961, in which Lettvin tried to explain his discoveries to Herbert Feigl (the last remaining great member of the Wiener circle, and who had an open mind) saying that his discoveries about the frog's eye can be understood only in terms of the "Kantian" view, but not in terms of the passive philosophy of logical empiricism. In the field of philosophy of science, the trend toward the "Kantianism" gained more and more momentum, and in the field of perception psychologists have become more and more convinced that a simple "passive" view had to be abandoned.

The weakest form of the "active" theory of perception may be an emphasis on "attention." Among many others who expressed similar ideas in the 19th century, Franz Brentano held the view that the distinctive feature of the mind was its "Dirigiertsein," i.e. attention being directed on one object. Applied to visual perception, this may mean that the eye can actually see only one thing out of many things in the visual field, or one part out of the whole, or an aspect out of more than one. According to Brentano, the phenomenon of "directedness" can be seen in presentation (Vorstellang), judgment, and emotion. His often quoted idea of "intentional inexistence" (we can think of something that does not exist) gave the starting point to Edmund Husserl's phenomenology. In the mid-20th century, many psychologists rediscovered the importance of attention in various aspects of human mental activity.

One of the most interesting phenomena showing the surprising faculty of attention of human perception is what is called the "cocktail party effect." The human ear can hear discriminately one particular person's voice in a noisy room where many people simultaneously talk. Psychologists in experiments in visual perception discovered what they call "fragmentation." If a subject is forced to see the same view for a long time, some part of the view disappears completely from perception leaving only the part on which attention is concentrated. Again, when many characters are shown simultaneously, the human recognizer immediately reads characters one after another, whereas the mechanical recognizer programmed for reading characters would be unable to concentrate attention on one character at a time, and then shift the attention.

The concentration of attention on one part of the visual field is the simplest case, where the mechanical recognizer can be expected to be programmable to cope with the task. But, the overlapping in the same dimensionality, such as double exposure photography or the case of a cocktail party effect may be more difficult, if not impossible, for the mechanical recognizer.

The case of Gestalt-theoretical flip-flop of figure and ground may be included as an example of attention concentration and shifting. As we remarked before, it is important to note that it is possible to shift from one object or one aspect to another object or another aspect and that at one instant we cannot share attention to two objects or to two aspects.

It may be a little questionable to include the following problem as a case of attention concentration and shifting, but it is interesting to view the discovery of invariance in pattern recognition as a shift of attention to the invariant properties of the object and a rejection from attention of the non-invariant properties of the object. It is significant that a young child has no hesitation in classifying the same letter rotated in different angles as one thing, whereas little older children have more difficulty in classifying them as the same letter.

It should be remembered that a prototype of "attention" and its "switching" were observed in the frog's eye in connection with "sameness" and "newness" neurons, and it may be justifiable to think that attention and its switching constitute the very fundamental nature of the nervous system.

The attention implies a nonpassive selection but is not really an active modification of incoming signals. The case of the Mach band is a definitive modification, however, it is physiologically determined and not an alteration of signals due to the mental activity of the observing subject. Some of the psychological illusions are definitively subject-dependent. Hallucinations are mental phenomena of seeing nonexisting objects and their contents are independent from outside optical stimuli. Even without going to the extreme of hallucinations, we can mention cases of our active modification. For instance, we shall read Q as O, without noticing that we modified our perception if the letter is placed in a position in a word where usually O stands instead of Q. A similar thing can be said about ш and щ, or わ and ね. Here "familiarity" plays an important role, and we can characterize such phenomena as "context-dependent," or Gestalt-dependent, or global sensing perception.

An important subclass of Gestalt-dependence is what some psychologists call "physiognomical perception." A secretary can often tell whether her boss has a bad mood today, without being able to say why she judges so. A dog will jump into a car, when it perceives that the master is going to make a long trip, out of fear that it may be left behind alone. This response happens even if the master takes a very careful deceiving technique. The fortune teller usually has a well developed sense of physiognomical perception.

Another example of "global perception," where things are seen that exist in no way in the details of the view, is used in the Rorschach test. In Figure 1.1.4, we saw an example of the Rorschach picture. The doctor asks, "What do you see in this ink-blot?" The answer is supposed tc reveal the emotional, intellectual, and characterological trend of the subject. The objects of value, fear, desire, suspicion, suppression, familiarity, etc., will emerge in this test. We can see the emotion-laden complex through this test. This "what" in this question corresponds to $something_2$ in Wittgenstein's "I see $something_1$ for $something_2$." In the language of pattern recognition, it is the class into which an object is placed. (That is why it is subject to inductive ambiguity.) It is important to know that the answer is not dictated by the object [$something_1$] and is very much dependent on the emotional and evaluative situation of the subject.

We have repeated again in this section that perception is not a simple "passive" act. If this active aspect is explained only in terms of our innate categories, it is a Kantian view. We want to draw the attention of the reader to the fact that the active aspect is, in a deeper analysis, an emotion-dependent and value-dependent mental construct, not a colorless Kantian category (see Epilogue 2 for more about the modern cognitive psychology).

CHAPTER 3
Pattern Recognition as Categorization

3.1 CONTROVERSY OVER UNIVERSALS AND REALISM

We stated in Chapter 1 that the task of pattern recognition is to place a particular object into a class corresponding to a concept. In Chapter 2, we learned that the idea of particular objects and the idea of concepts begin to be formed in the prelingual stage of sensation and perception. In this section we shall talk about the full-fledged cognition found in a lingual animal, man. The main concern here is the relationship between the particular objects and the general concepts.

To discuss this problem intelligently, we have to survey briefly that aspect of the history of philosophy that centered around the so-called controversy over the universals. The universal means a concept or general notion. If our cognitive judgment states "this is a desk," then "this" is a particular object, and "desk" is a universal.

Usually, three points of view regarding the status of the universal are recognized in the ancient and medieval history of philosophy. One view maintains that the universal has a real existence. This view is traditionally called "realism." The opposite view is that the universal is just a name devoid of any real existence. It is called "nominalism." The third view, which may be located in between, is "conceptualism." It maintains that the universal does not exist in the external world, but it has a real existence in our mind. If we define the three views this way, the distinction among them is clear-cut, but if we want to classify any real philosopher into one of the three, we sometimes encounter considerable difficulty.

Another difficulty with this definition is in regard to what we should understand by reality. We have to leave this crucial question unanswered, however, because the discussion about reality, particularly in this connection, will tend to deviate too much from our major interest. The reader should interpret the term reality in his own way.

Usually, Plato and Aristotle are considered the chief proponents of the oldest view, "realism." Although these two philosophers differ considerably with regard to the understanding of the term "Form," both agree that the Form in the sense of universal is a reality. Some modern students of Plato say that the position of the problem of the universal itself is strongly Aristotelian, and Plato should not be considered as a founder of what is usually called "realistic" view of the universal. We shall come back briefly to this question in a short while, and let us proceed to the traditional description of Plato's realism.

For Plato, the particular object called "desk" does not have a real existence, only a deceptive, temporary, illusory existence, and what really is is the Form or Idea (of the desk). This sensible world of experience has no reality, but the eternal world of Form has reality. The particular object is only an imperfect copy of the ideal Form. We should remember the distinction made in the Introduction between the epicentric view and aggregative view of class. The Platonian theory of Form may be considered as a kind of epicentric view of pattern.

The capacity we have of judging a particular object as a desk (or something else) according to Plato is inborn in us. We have an "innate idea" of desk, which we have inherited from our former life in the eternal world of Form. The particular object has the function of reminding us of, or evoking, the innate idea of the desk. We have alluded to the Kantian theory of innate idea in Chapter 2, and we have described it as opposed to the empiric point of view. Platonic theory of former life (as put in Socrates' mouth in Plato's Meno) as the source of innate idea gives us a theoretical possibility of bridging the opposition between empiricism and apriorism. Whether or not Plato and Kant would agree with us, if we replace the experience in the former life by the long chain of generations in the process of evolution, we can say that our innate ideas are after all products of experience through evolution.

Of course, products of an interaction between the active subject and the object acted upon is not a one-way determination by the external world.

To the modern mind, the assertion that this world of experience is unreal and the world of Ideas is real may be difficult to absorb. Think of a geometrical figure like "triangle." A triangle drawn on paper is not a real triangle as defined by geometry. Because we can speak of deviation from, or approximation to, a real triangle, we cannot deny the reality (in a certain sense) of a geometrically defined triangle, which is the Form of triangle. An actual triangle drawn by a human hand is a poor imitation and not a true triangle.

In fact, the main domains for which Plato introduced the idea of Form were a field of abstract concepts (such as goodness, friendship, and kindness, etc.) and a field of mathematical concepts (such as numbers, figures, etc.). Application to the concrete objects (such as desk or book, etc.) was, so to speak, an overextension. In the field of abstract idea, we can speak of a wrong definition, which shows that there is a correct, ideal mode of existence. This is made possible by the existence of Forms. Therefore interpretation of Form as a universal is not quite appropriate. The Form is not a perfect object in the best of the worlds, but it means rather the essential nature or functional meaning of the objects covered by the same name. To understand Form as an ideal object is to force Plato's philosophy into Aristotle's framework.

Since the mid 1950's, modern analytic philosophers have started to apply their method to the study of classical philosophy, and a new vista has been opened up also over Plato's philosophy. According to Fujisawa [F-4], we can divide Plato's activities into three chronological periods: From Charmides to Cratylus; from Symposium (or Phaedo) to Phaedrus; from Parmenides to the end (Epist. VII). Fujisawa also classifies various terms Plato used in connection with the Form-particular relation into three groups: ἔχειν (have) and related words, μετέχειν (participate) and related words, and παράδειγμα (paradigm), and εἰκών (image). Fujisawa traces how these classes were introduced, abandoned, and modified in meaning during the three periods. The first group (i.e. "have"-group) is used primarily where the particular object is described as having such and such observable property--x has F, where both x and F belong to the empirical world. The second group ("participate"-group) was used in the first period already but was not attached to a specific philosophical meaning but in the second period acquired a specific assignment to designate that a particular object participated in the general Form: x participates in Φ, where x belongs to this world, but Φ belongs to the world of Ideas. This group of words became the target of controversy in Parmenides (first work of the third period) and was abandoned completely thereafter. The third group ("paradigm"-group) was used also in the first period, but was not assigned to a specific philosophical meaning. In the second period it was used in the same meaning as the participate-group, in describing the relation between x and Φ. A curious thing is that after the participate-group was abandoned, the paradigm group survived until the end of Plato's life. It may be that the paradigm group was judged less likely to arouse the misunderstanding described in Parmenides, or perhaps Plato thought of giving a new nuance to the paradigm group. Fujisawa thinks that unless the relation between F and Φ is not clarified, the description in terms of participation is not sufficient, and that the description in terms of paradigm is more appropriate to express the relation between F and Φ.

It is therefore important to understand the meaning of the controversy in Parmenides, which is often called the Third Man Argument (TMA). The gist of TMA, if translated into modern language, would become something like this: Probably the trouble was started by the disciples of Plato who could not see the difference between "x has such and such property F" and "x participates in the Form Φ of that property." According to the Aristotelian world view, Form is also an object, albeit in the different eternal world. If there are n particular objects belonging to a Form, the total number of objects belonging to the class would become (n+1). Those (n+1) objects would require (n+2)-nd object which would be the Form of the first (n+1) object. This concept would call for an infinite number of objects, a typical case of infinite regression.

Fujisawa made a comprehensive index for the Japanese version of the collected works of Plato; of interest is the entry for the term Paradeigma. He noticed two major classes I and II of meanings in which the term is used, one as a general concept and the other as a particular example of concept. The first class was divided into two subclasses: Ia, paradigm as a Form, and Ib, paradigm as a perfect model to be imitated. The second class II included meanings such as typical example, and concrete instances. Admittedly, toward the end of his career, the emphasis was placed more and more on the meaning of class Ia. The term covered both the universal and the particular. In Timaeus, of the third period, the particular object is reduced, somewhat like in modern physics, to the field (χώρα , τόπος), which is an empty space where the Form is reflected. The true actors are not elementary particles, but physical laws that make the actors dance. Nevertheless, what is most important in the Platonic Form is that it is "one" standing for many, not one in addition to the many, but one covering all of them simultaneously. The author owes sincere thanks to Professor N. Fujisawa of Kyoto University who was kind enough to read the draft version of this manuscript and to point out many minor mistakes.

All theoretical works on pattern recognition as practiced today are essentially based on the Aristotelian philosophy. Hence it is well nigh impossible to revise single-handedly the entire theoretical structure on a new philosophy. But the reader will notice that my theory about the object-predicate exchange (Sections 4.4 and 7.3) and the exposition in the Epilogue (in particular, E-3) are strongly influenced by the Platonic philosophy and that some innovative views on pattern recognition emerge. The main role played in the Epilogue will be called paradigmatic symbol.

Passing now to Aristotle, this "scientific" philosopher recognized the reality of particular objects. The particular object, according to Aristotle, consists of two "real" elements: Matter and Form. Matter is a material out of which an object is made and endows real existence as a material object. The wood is the Matter of a wooden desk. What makes a desk be a desk is not only the material, but how the material is cut into pieces of different shapes, and how these pieces are put together to form a desk. This is the Form. Because we can make different things out of wood, the Matter represents "potentiality." The desk becomes an actual desk on account of the Form, therefore the Form represents "actuality." The doublet, potentiality-actuality, is one of the leading motifs in Aristotelian philosophy.

It is well-known that Aristotle always speaks of the four causes: material cause, formal cause, efficient cause, and final cause. The first two causes are as we have seen in the example of a desk. For a cabinetmaker to make a desk, he has to intervene with tools such as a saw, nails and a plane. This physical intervention is the efficient cause. The final cause is the purpose for which we make a desk. Aristotle recognizes that the final cause and the formal cause tend to coincide. Among these four causes, those that remain attached to the desk are the Matter and Form, whereas the physical operation passes away and the final cause is incorporated in the Form. Therefore, Aristotle speaks of two real elements in the actual desk.

The basic reason why Aristotle could not agree with Plato was Aristotle's obsession with the idea of "substance." Like Plato he was always concerned with the question, "What is being?" In trying to answer that question Plato was concerned with "function"; Aristotle was concerned with "thing." For Aristotle, there were two kinds of substances. The primary substance (not to be confused with prime matter) is a concrete object, provided with attributes. The secondary substance is the universal or species to which concrete objects belong, labeled also with the same attributes. These two substances are not of the same degree of importance. In his mind, the concrete objects are the basic reality. For him, the object-attribute relation is closely related to the grammatical constituents of subject-predicates. Rightly or wrongly, modern pattern recognition is deeply rooted in this Aristotelian dualistic view, which we shall call the "object-predicate" duality in this book. This view contributed, in some sense to the progress of this science, but we have to recognize its limitations too. We shall point them out from time to time in this book. See the Section on Object-Predicate Inversion, which aims at a liberation from the obsession about the particular object - a partial return to Platonism. See [A-5, A-6] for anti-Aristotelian logic.

After Plato and Aristotle, there were many philosophers who discussed the problem of Forms and universals, but we shall limit ourselves only to mentioning two representative scholars: Augustine who was a Platonian, and Thomas Aquinas who was an Aristotelian. Augustine was different from Plato in identifying the world of Form as God's mind (concept), thus establishing a kind of bridge to conceptualism. Thomas Aquinas belongs to a later time, and we see a little more affinity with science, perhaps because the idea of prime matter (matter without attribute) was much discussed during the medieval age. Aquinas seems not to have been committed so much to the Aristotelian primary substance. His remarkable point was that he emphasized the existence of similarity (resemblance) among the members of a universal. There is no doubt that the ancient philosophers recognized also similarity within a universal, but we can probably name Thomas Aquinas as the first one who pushed similarity to the forefront. Being an Aristotelian, however, he did not say that similarity is the only ground for which a collection of objects were put together as a group. See also [R-4, R-5].

3.2 NOMINALISM AND CONCEPTUALISM

To locate the general attitude of the modern engineers toward pattern recognition in the context of philosophical controversy over universals, we have to continue our quick survey of the historical developments. In the medieval age, a reaction to the Platonic and Aristotelian realism was bound to come, but slowly. The first man to whom the germ of this new anti-realism is attributed is Boethius. Roscelin and Garland went far beyond Boethius, but St. Anselm was quick to denounce them as "extreme nominalists." Abeland and William of Ockham, although counted as nominalists, may be said to have tried to restore some objectivity in the universal. On the other hand, Thomas Aquinas, labeled usually as a realist, was strongly influenced by anti-realism. Spinoza and Hobbes were considered as nominalists in a broad sense.

There was a whole gamut of anti-realism, but one of its common denominators was that the human mind could apprehend the particular, whereas the realists maintained it can apprehend particulars only in virtue of apprehending universals. If they had pushed nominalism to the extreme, they would have arrived at the idea that there is nothing common among the particulars covered by the same general name, but there was no such drastic proposal even among the nominalists of the medieval age.

In the seventeenth and eighteenth centuries, we see a renewed discussion of the universal by British empiricists, such as John Locke, Bishop Berkeley, and David Hume. They are sometimes classified as nominalists, sometimes conceptualists, but this distinction is not as important as what they actually said. The following statement by Locke (*Essay Concerning Human Understanding*) [L-2] sets the general pattern of the British conceptualism.

"General and universal belong not to the real existence of things, but are the inventions and creatures of the understanding, made by it for its own use, and concern only signs, whether words or ideas." (Note that if we choose "words," it would become nominalism; if we emphasize "idea," it would become conceptualism. But, we shall presently see that the name conceptualism is more appropriate for Locke.) He continues,

> Words are general when used for signs of general ideas, and so are applicable indifferently to many particular things; and ideas are general, when they are set up as the representatives of many particular things; but universality belongs not to things themselves, which are all of them particular in their existence, even those words and ideas which in their signification are general. When therefore we quit particulars, the generals that rest are only creatures of our own making, their general nature being nothing but the capacity they are put into the understanding, of signifying or representing many particulars. For the signification they have is nothing but a relation that by the mind of man is added

> to them.... The sorting of things under names is the workmanship of the understanding, taking occasion from <u>the similitude it observes among them</u> to make abstract general ideas, and set them up in the mind, with names annexed to them, as patterns or formal (for in that sense the word form has a very proper signification), to which as particular things are found to agree, so they come to be of that species, have that denomination, or are put into that classes.

In Book III, Chapter 3, Sections 12-13 of [L-2], Locke speaks of observed similitudes, but he does not say whether similitudes exist among particulars or are in the beholder's eyes. Note further that the word "pattern" is used; the underlines are added by the author.

What is important for today's engineers of pattern recognition to remember about Locke is that he rightly pointed out the role of "abstraction" in the formation of a universal. For Locke, the "idea" can be either simple or general. The simple idea is an image of a particular object. (He did not suspect that this too can be a mental construct.) But the general or abstract idea is a mental fabrication made from a juxtaposition of simple ideas. Being an empiricist, he did not believe in innate ideas. The process by which the general idea is extracted from simple ideas is an abstraction. The abstraction consists of leaving out of the particular ideas of various individual objects of a class all features that are not common to them all, and retaining only what is common to them all (see Book II, Chapter 11, Section 9 and Book III, Chapter 3 of [L-2]). The reader should notice that what we said at the beginning of this Chapter about the extraction of invariant features is precisely the same procedure as Locke's abstraction.

Locke's theory of general idea became a target of George Berkeley's violent attack. If we interpret "general idea" as a mental image, then Berkeley's criticism of Locke's theory is understandable, particularly when the method of abstraction is applied not to a pure abstract concept such as white or large but to a class of concrete objects such as man or triangle. Berkeley would say that we cannot have an image of a man who is neither tall nor short, or an image of a man who is simultaneously tall and short. Even if we think of a man in general, we have to imagine a man with a certain tallness. A man without height is indeed impossible. The point is therefore well taken, if we want to make a psychological theory of mental image of a general idea. Here emerges again a problem we mentioned in connection with Plato's problem of many versus one, which we shall return to in the Epilogue.

If we did not interpret the "idea" as a mental image, but as a logical condition (of man or of whiteness), we would find nothing wrong with Locke's abstraction. It would be an abstract symbol, not a "mental image".

To Berkeley, "to be is to be perceived," therefore, the interpretation of general idea as mental image is quite natural and can become a target of criticism. Besides, it should be mentioned that Locke is known for his emphasis on the distinction between primary qualities (properties that an individual object has independently of the observer) and secondary qualities (the property dependent on the observer). This distinction lies obviously not quite parallel to, but behind, the distinction between concrete idea and abstract idea, because the concrete idea (or the single components of it) is given by experience of an individual whereas the abstract idea is "craftmanship" of the mind. When Berkeley abolished the distinction between the primary and secondary qualities in favor of the latter, the distinction between the concrete and universal idea was destined to disappear.

David Hume begins the section entitled, "Of Abstract Ideas" which treats the problem of universals in *A Treatise of Human Nature,* Part I, Section VII [H-6] as follows:

> A great philosopher [meaning Berkeley] has ... asserted, that all general ideas are nothing but particular ones, annexed to a certain term, which gives them a more extensive signification, and makes them recall upon occasion other individuals, which are similar to them. As I look upon this to be one of the greatest and most

> valuable discoveries that has been made of late years in the republic of letters, I shall here endeavour to confirm it by some arguments which I hope will put it beyond all doubt and controversy.

Hume states that the general term "man" either represents at once men of all sizes and all qualities, or represents no particular man at all. It is commonly argued, according to Hume, that since the human mind has a finite capacity, the first alternative is impossible and that the abstract ideas have been supposed to represent no degree either of quantity or quality. Hume, however, favors the first alternative with a special interpretation of terms.

He argues first that it is impossible to conceive any quantity or quality, without forming a precise notion of its degree, but second that in spite of the finiteness of the mental capacity, "we can at once form a notion of all possible degrees of quantity and quality, in such a manner, at least, as, however imperfect, may serve all the purpose of reflection and convention." Everything that exists, is, for Hume, particulars. "Abstract ideas are therefore in themselves individual, however they may become general in their representation. The image in the mind is only that of a particular object, tho' the application of it in our reasoning be the same, as if it were universal."

"When we have found a resemblance among several objects, that often occur to us, we apply the same name to all of them, whatever difference we may observe in the degrees of quantity and quality, and whatever other differences may appear among them. After we have acquired a <u>custom</u> of this kind, the hearing of that name revives the idea of one of these objects, and makes the <u>imagination</u> conceive it with all its particular circumstances and proportions," (Chapter VII).

Here, we see the kernel of his theory of general ideas which parallels his theory of induction (although he never uses the term induction [H-6, H-7]). This parallelism is, to the present author, one of the greatest discoveries in the philosophy of science. We refer to earlier chapters, in particular to Chapter IV, entitled "Of the Connection or Association of Ideas" where Hume made a similar distinction between the simple idea and complex ideas as Locke did, but originality lies in his explanation as to how certain complex ideas are formed from simple ideas by connection or association of the latter.

All simple ideas may be separated and reunited differently by the imagination. There is no fixed rule for recombination by the imagination, but there exist certain guiding principles. These principles are to be regarded "as a gentle force, which commonly prevails. ... nature in a manner pointing out to everyone these simple ideas, which are most proper to be united in a complex one. The qualities from which this association arises, and by which the mind is after this manner convey'd from one idea to another, are three, viz. Resemblance, Contiguity in time or place, and Cause and Effect." The complex idea of a class is thus formed by association due to resemblance. The induction associates two events as cause and effect. The reader will find an echo of "a gentle force which commonly prevails" in our characterization of the heuristic "as a non-necessary, non-compelling advice," which is useful in discussing a class (see Chapter 5).

He depicts the nature of association as a "kind of attraction, which in the mental world will be found to have as extraordinary effects as in the natural, and to show itself in as many and as various forms. Its effects [of association] are everywhere conspicuous; but as to its causes [of association], they are mostly unknown, and must be resolv'd into original qualities of human nature, which I pretend not to explain." He thus attributes this capacity of association to human nature, but he rejects innate ideas because they mean fixed association. As we know, Kant made his a priori category of causality out of Hume's empirical "human nature" of association by the qualities of cause and effect.

Before passing to the next section, we should mention a few remarks by Hume of minor importance on similarity. Hume notices that sometimes two objects are associated not by their direct similarity, but by each one's similarity to a third object. (Note a related observation we made with regard to Fig. A.1.3 of this book.) Another interesting remark (added in the Appendix to the third volume of Hume's original edition) is his interest in the fact that resemblance does not necessarily imply formation of a general idea. For instance, he says, "Blue and green are different simple ideas, but are more resembling than blue and scarlet." He notes also when (1) one globe of white marble, (2) one cube of white marble, and (3) one globe of black marble are presented, (1) and (2) resemble each other with regard to the "aspect" of color and (1) and (3) resemble each other with regard to the "aspect" of figure.

3.3 SIMILARITY THEORY

The commonsensical view of classes is that of a collection of similar objects. One might say that after many centuries of scholastic detour, the philosophers with and after Hume have come back to this simple-minded yet robust commonsensical view. The theory of general concepts based on similarity has regained some respectability, but we should note that the most important contribution by Hume, namely, that similarity is a product of association formed by mental habit, is left out of consideration by most of the proponents of the similarity theory.

Those who hold the similarity theory, though diverse in details of their arguments, agree more or less on the following two points:

1. What really exist are particulars, not universals.
2. It is not the case that members of a class covered by a general concept have an identical common element which non-members do not have. (If they had a common element it would justify a realism.) The particulars in a class are bound together only by similarity.

The practitioners of mechanical pattern recognition usually share this view too; however, these two points raise several serious questions. Relegating the most serious objection to this view to the next chapter, we shall limit ourselves here to the criticism already raised by different philosophers, and to some simple counter-examples we can find in our daily life.

Recently, Strawson [S-8] presented cogent arguments against the first point. To quote, "Grant that the existence of universals is no more than the fact, or the possibility, that particular things do, or might, exemplify them. But acknowledge that the fact or possibility of their being exemplified is no less than the fact of their existence." He says that we can apprehend or perceive a particular thing only by referring to its general characters. We can indeed not recognize a particular dog without using a concept of dog, a concept of color, a concept of size, etc. Therefore, the existence of particulars and that of universals are mutually dependent.

Further, Strawson applies Quine's criteria for existence to universals: (a) To be is to be the value of a variable, and (b) To be requires having an identity. In plain language, (a) means that an object that exists has to be a subject of a predicate or predicates. (Remember what we have called the Aristotelian view of the world at the beginning of Chapter 2.) Usually, Quine's criteria are thought to apply only to particular things, but Strawson argues that they apply just as well to universals. According to Strawson, particular things exist only in the space-time, whereas the universals exist only in our thought. This standpoint may be characterized as a special variation of conceptualism with realistic leaning.

There are two ways to interpret the second theme of the theory of similarity. One way is to say that similarity is not an attribute of an object, but a relationship between two objects. If we consider a pair of objects as one particular thing, then similarity (or its absence) can be considered as a property of a pair of things. Those who oppose this view would say that it is a realism in disguise, and that if we want to be consistent, we should apply the similarity view also to the general concept of similarity. But, this similarity view of similarity immediately encounters a serious difficulty, namely, that of defining the similarity between two particular similarities, where we have to resort to similarity of similarity, etc. And we can never end the chain of infinite regression. Of course, there is an argument that we do not need to flee forever, and we can cut the chain somewhere in a finite domain. But this argument is as obscure as the argument of infinite regression itself.

Another question is: Assuming that similarity is not a realistic attribute, do we have, or can we achieve, an objective judgment or at least an intersubjective consensus as to similarity of two things? Many negative answers are at hand.

For instance, suppose we have a whale, an elephant, and a tuna fish. The whale and elephant are similar because they are mammals, but the whale and tuna fish are similar because they live in water. This shows that similarity depends on the aspect we are using in the judgment of similarity.

Persons of a race remote from one's self all look similar, whereas persons of one's own race all look different. Discrimination seems to depend on remoteness. Is this an effect akin to Weber-Fechner's law? In any event similarity depends on perspective and remoteness.

Suppose we have three square wood panels whose sides are (a) 1 cm, (b) 2 cm, and (c) 2.8 cm. Since the difference between (a) and (b) is 1 cm, while the difference between (b) and (c) is 0.8 cm, we may say that (b) and (c) are more similar than (a) and (b). If we take areas, however, instead of the length of the side, we have (a) 1 cm^2, (b) 4 cm^2, and (c) 7.84 cm^2. Therefore, (a) and (b) are more similar than (b) and (c). One may say that this again is a case of dependence of similarity on the aspect. If we want to build a shelf in a narrow space, the aspect of the side may be more useful. If we sell building materials, the aspect of area may be more pertinent.

For Japanese-speaking people green and blue are so similar that they often form a single category, because the Japanese word blue (ao) often covers both green and blue. The distinction between French *saucisse* and *saucisson* does not exist in the minds of English-speaking people. The distinction between the English desk and table is also absent in the German mind. The desk for them is only a subclass of the table, not another class. Rat and mouse have almost opposite emotional connotations in European languages, whereas it is almost impossible to make a difference between them for the Japanese-speaking people. All these aspects show the language dependence of similarity. To admit a language dependence is, of course, different from adherence to nominalism, but there is no such thing as an intersubjective or intercommunal consensus.

In Chapter 2, we learned that there is strong evidence that the origin of general ideas is to be found in the prelingual stage of evolution. In general, the philosophers of linguistic leaning exaggerate the dependence of thought on languages; however, this does not mean that we can ignore the influence of language on the general concepts.

In relation to linguistic influence on human thought, we should not neglect what Wittgenstein said with regard to general concepts (see Sections 66 and 67 of [W-14], Anscomb's version, p. 31). He takes as an example what is called "games." He declares that there is nothing common in various activities called under the same name. He says, like many other similarity-theoreticians, that similarities and relations, etc., bind them together under the same name. What is new is that he points out that some games are bound together by some kind of similarity such as "winning and losing" and some other games are bound together by some other kind of similarity such as "amusement." And these different similarities are overlapping, so that all kinds of activities form a family called games. He writes: "We see a complicated network of similarities overlapping and crisscrossing: sometimes overall similarities, sometimes similarities of detail." He chooses the word *"Familienähnlichkeit"* ("family resemblance") to express his idea.

Therefore Wittgenstein's theory sometimes is taken as a special case of the similarity theory, allowing disjunction of subgroups. Barnbrough wanted to claim that Wittgenstein initiated a new third position between nominalism and realism, but his claim is not well-founded [B-4] p. 207. Although Wittgenstein acknowledges that the family is not bound merely by a common name, he knows that the concept of games, for instance, depends on what people consider as games. And this depends obviously on the linguistic-behavioral community and its habit of classification. For instance, there could very well be a community which does not consider gambling and marathon running as the same kind of activities. And this dependence on the kind of community is probably an undeniable fact of life. Recognition of the societal and linguistic influence on the small details of concepts is different from the recognition of language as the major determinant of human concepts. See also [H-10] as one of the first books on pattern recognition that referred to Wittgenstein.

Apart from the explication of similarity as an association of ideas, Hume's emphasis on the degree of similarity has a great importance for the problem of general ideas. We can't say that to recognize coincidence of a property between two objects amounts to a concession to realism, because we can always quantize continuous variables and reduce the description to yes-or-no statements of categorical predicates. Conversely, most of the categorical predicates can be considered as approximations to reality. There are two ways of introducing a degree of similarities. When we use categorical predicates, we can use the number of predicates shared (i.e., simultaneously affirmatively satisfied) by two objects is a usual measure of similarity. Two men are said to resemble each other, when both are taller than 5 feet 8 inches, both wear eyeglasses, their eye colors are both non-black, etc.

When we use n continuous variables, we can consider an n-dimensional space and define a formula of distance between two points in the space. The concept of distance which is often more convenient than similarity is such that the larger the distance, the smaller the similarity. Simple examples of the relation between distance D and similarity S are a linearity:

$$S + D = \text{constant} \qquad (3.3.1)$$

or inverse proportionality,

$$S \cdot D = \text{constant} \qquad (3.3.2)$$

but these are not the only possible ones.

When we define a concept of distance, it is customary to require the so-called triangular relation: If D(A,B) represents the distance between object A and object B, then the distances between A and B, B and C, and C and A should satisfy

$$D(A,B) + D(B,C) \geq D(A,C). \qquad (3.3.3)$$

Of course, this rule is still so lenient that all sorts of concepts of distance are allowed. The so-called Euclidean distance is only just one possible case, although it is very commonly used:

$$D(x,y) = \sqrt{\sum_{i=1}^{n} (x_i - y_i)^2}, \qquad (3.3.4)$$

where x_i, $i = 1, 2, \ldots, n$ is the i-th coordinate of point x in the n-dimensional space subtended by the n variables; similarly, for point y.

3.4 ABSTRACTION, SIMILARITY, AND CATEGORIZATION

The foregoing discussions are based on the assumption that the world consists of a discrete number of objects subject to a discrete number of attributes, affirmatively or negatively. The logical notation for a proposition P(a) which expresses that object a satisfies property P, reflects this "Aristotelian" view. To give a mathematical expression to this picture of the world, it is convenient to use a matrix representation, which we call Aristotelian table or object-predicate table [W-7].

Let $X = \{x_i\}$, $i = 1, 2, \ldots, m$ be the collection of objects under examination and $Y = \{y_j\}$, $j = 1, 2, \ldots, n$ be the collection of predicates that are used to describe the objects. The Y is assumed to be such that proposition $y_j(x_i)$ is either true or false for each i and each j. To make this assumption be always true, it is sometimes useful to agree that $y_j(x_i)$ is true when the predicate originally meant by y_j is applicable to x_i and found to be true, and $y_j(x_i)$ is false when the predicate originally meant by y_j either is applicable to x_i and found to be false or is not applicable. The object-predicate table A (for Aristotle) is an n x m matrix with m rows and n columns whose element $A(x_i,y_j)$ or A_{ij} is equal to 1 or 0 according to whether the proposition $y_j(x_i)$ is confirmed to be true or false, i.e., according as the predicate y_j is affirmed (satisfied) by x_i or is negated (not satisfied) by x_i. Because of the aforesaid convention we can increase X and Y indefinitely and still define the values of A_{ij}.

We have mentioned before, and we shall discuss again later, the questionable nature of the assumption that we can always identify a self-identical object. But we shall not take time in this section to analyze this assumption, which is necessary to introduce set X. As far as set Y is concerned, it is mandatory to assume the "compatibility" of the predicates in Y, or, more generally, they should be "adequate" predicates. It is a common occurrence in atomic physics and psychology that two predicates, say, y_j and y_k, are incompatible, i.e., they change the values, when we change the order of observation, i.e., when we observe first y_j and second y_k or first y_k and second y_j. This is a case of what was called "pseudo-predicates" [W-22], [W-15], [W-34], [W-35]. Pseudo-predicates or inadequate predicates are those which cannot be assumed to have definite sets of objects that clearly affirm or negate them. Sallantin claims that non-compatibility exists even among some ordinary predicates (such as determination of medical signs) which are usually assumed to be purely "primary qualities" [S-7]. Y is assumed to be a collection of predicates that are genuine predicates and mutually compatible, i.e., those whose values are definite and do not depend on the order of their observation. See A-5,A-6 for anti-Aristotelian logic.

Second, we have to adhere primarily to an empirical viewpoint. The assignment of value to the object-predicate table must be based on the information obtained by observation. Human sensory organs do complicated manipulation of physical stimuli. Also, logical operations of the observational data are inevitable. For instance, a predicate y_j and its negation $\neg y_j$ are equivalent as information content and are interchangeable--0 becomes 1 and 1 becomes 0. Instead of two variables y_j and y_k we can use $y_j \cap y_k$, and $y_j \cup y_k$ if we are ready to lose part of the information. The loss of information is obvious because we cannot reconstruct the values of y_j and y_k separately from the values of $y_j \cap y_k$ and $y_j \cup y_k$. But, sometimes we want purposely to lose part of the information, to limit our knowledge to only useful information.

It is obvious that if we introduce a new predicate from the old predicate by the use of the logical connectives $(\neg, \cup, \cap)$, the entries for these new predicates will be obtained by the use of truth-value tables for these connectives. But, if there are some constant (i.e., valid for all members of X) relations between observationally independent predicates, these relations bring some new information. If one observation y_j determines whether an animal has a gill, and another y_k determines whether the animal lives in water most of the time, we shall have $y_j \rightarrow y_k$ (if y_j then y_k), although $y_j \neq y_k$ (because a porpoise lives in water). This means that if $A_{ij} = 1$ then $A_{ik} = 1$, but, if $A_{ij} = 0$, A_{ik} can be either 0 or 1. A row of matrix which has $A_{ij} = 1$ and $A_{ik} = 0$ does not appear in the observational object-predicate table.

This constraint is due to an empirical law. More generally, the constraints may be due to an accidental situation created by the finite size of X. On the other extreme, if we increase X as much as possible, the number of constraints will become smaller and smaller. The remaining constraint may be considered purely "analytical." If we include in X all the objects in all possible conceivable worlds, the remaining constraint will be due to logical reasons. From this point of view, we might understand the idea of Quine [Q-2] and White, that the distinction between synthetic truth and analytic truth is not as clear-cut as traditional philosophy usually assumes, because no constraint holds in <u>all</u> possible worlds. If we include all possible worlds, what remains will be considered as (Boolean) logical constraint. If we further include the non-Boolean worlds into our consideration, we shall be left with only very few fundamental constraints. If we go backward, we shall gradually see more and more of logic-dependence, language-dependence, theory-dependence, nature-dependence, and finally pure contingence (see pp. 363-366 of [W-10] for more discussion). At the same place, we can see the difference between our object-predicate table and Carnap's "state description" [C-5].

Now, let us go back to the ordinary cases where X consists of a finite number of accessible objects and Y consists of usually used observations. First, let us consider Locke's idea of abstraction. Suppose G is a subset of X, $G \subset X$, consisting of all available particular objects covered by a complex idea (general concepts) C. Then, the abstraction, according to Locke's idea, must be a collection of those predicates (features) common to all members of G.

$$F = \{y_j \mid A_{ij} = 1, \quad \text{for all } x_i \in G\}. \qquad (3.4.1)$$

The members of G are characterized by the condition that $A_{ij} = 1$ for all $y_j \in F$. We can take the conjunction of all such predicates

$$f = \bigcap_{y_j \in F} y_j \qquad (3.4.2)$$

and call f the conjunctive feature of G.

According to the above derivation, it is clear that if $x_i \in G$, then $f(x_i)$, i.e., x_i satisfies f, but it is not clear that if $x_i \in (X - G)$, $\neg f(x_i)$, i.e., x_i does not satisfy f. However, we shall show in the next section that for any arbitrary collection of objects, we can define f such that $f(x_i)$ if, and only if, x_i belongs to the collection. The same general concept C can therefore be seen from either the aspect of collection of objects or from the aspect of collection of predicates. The former, i.e., G, is the extension of C and in the latter, i.e., F or f is the intension of C. The extension expresses the richness in membership, and the intension expresses the richness in characterization. We shall discuss the notions of extension and intension more rigorously in the next section, but here we would like to give a general idea of the quantitative aspects of intension and extension.

We should note that we have to expect that if we increase the number of samples that constitute G, some of the predicates y_j of F will drop out. Therefore, when we have a limited G and guess what F would be in the limiting case of large G, the mental process is a generalization and a case of inductive inference. Some of the predicates will be expected to survive in this process, and these may be considered to be more essential to characterize the general idea C. But, such a characterization is possible only on the assumption that there exists a unique limiting F for a given general idea.

If we call the number of members of G extension of concept C, and the number of members of F intension of concept C, we have obviously

$$\frac{d\,\mathrm{Ext}(C)}{d\,\mathrm{Int}(C)} \leq 0, \qquad (3.4.3)$$

where

$$\text{Ext}(C) = \text{Card. } G \tag{3.4.4}$$

$$\text{Int}(C) = \text{Card. } F \tag{3.4.5}$$

Indeed, if we increase the number of characterization of G, it will tend to drive out some members of G. The equality sign in (3.4.3) can happen because an addition of predicate sometimes does not change the set G. For instance, if F includes in addition to the adjective "--is a biped mammal," the phrase "--is a speaking animal," then this addition would not change the set; disregarding the existence of mums. The set is still the set of human beings.

To count the extension of G, it is more convenient to assume that there are no two rows in the object-predicate table which are exactly the same, because as far as our description is concerned, they are "identical." If we add a new independent member to Y, it may happen that one single row will split in two.

If we denote by F' the feature of another group G' which could be the complementary group X - G or of any other competitive group; i.e., if

$$F' = \{y_j | A_{ij} = 1, \quad x_i \in G'\} \tag{3.4.6}$$

then the discriminating feature F_d of G from G' would be

$$F_d = F - F \wedge F'. \tag{3.4.7}$$

Each term in this expression will become smaller as X increases.

If X consists of several classes and the remainder, i.e., if

$$X = G_1 \vee G_2 \vee \ldots \vee G_\mu \vee R$$

$$G_\rho \wedge G_\sigma = \Phi \qquad \rho, \sigma = 1, 2, \ldots, \mu$$

$$G_\rho \wedge R = \Phi \qquad \rho = 1, 2, \ldots, \mu$$

we can say that the given objects are categorized into μ categories and the remainder.

What has been said so far applies to any kind of collection of objects. It is true that if members of the class do not resemble each other a great deal, the number of common features F will become small, but, we can still formally define F as well as f. In order to give some meaning to a collection of objects, we have to introduce the idea of similarity.

Thus, we have now to interpret the similarity theory in terms of the object-predicate table. Each row A_{ij}, i = fixed, j = 1, 2,..., n, represents the properties of an object. The similarity between two objects x_i and x_k is to be defined in terms of A_{ij} and A_{kj}, with i = fixed, k = fixed, j = 1, 2,..., n. As indicated earlier, it is often convenient to use a distance instead of a similarity, such that similarity S and distance D stand in the relation:

$$dS/dD < 0. \tag{3.4.8}$$

The simplest way is to use the so-called Hamming distance

$$D_{ik} = \sum_{j=1}^{n} |A_{ij} - A_{kj}| \tag{3.4.9}$$

which measures the number of y_j's for which object i and object k have different entries. The so-called Tanimoto distance defined by

$$D_{ik} = \frac{W(i,k)}{W(i) + W(k) - W(i,k)} \tag{3.4.10}$$

with

$$W(i) = \sum_{j=1}^{n} A(x_i,y_j), \quad W(i,k) = \sum_{j=1}^{n} A(x_i,y_j)A(x_k,y_j) \tag{3.4.11}$$

amounts to giving more emphasis to affirmative entries (1) than to negative entries (0). This may, in some cases, be useful, but logically y_j and $\neg y_j$ are perfectly equivalent. Therefore, the ground for adoption of this definition is rather weak. Of course, the choice of definition of distance is not limited to these two. It is usually assumed that $D_{ik} = D_{ki}$.

Now, two objects x_i and x_k may be considered as similar, when the distance between them is less than a threshold θ:

$$D_{ik} \leq \theta. \tag{3.4.12}$$

If a family is to be defined by similarity, we shall have

$$x_i \varepsilon G \text{ and } x_k \varepsilon G \text{ iff } D_{ik} \leq \theta \tag{3.4.13}$$

If we want to allow a disjunctive definition of families of similar objects, in accordance with Wittgenstein, we can write

$$G = \vee G_\rho, \tag{3.4.14}$$

where each G_ρ is defined by similarity (3.4.13) and the disjunction is defined by the condition that ($x_i \varepsilon G$ and $x_k \varepsilon G$) means that there exists a series of G's: G_α, G_β, ..., G_ω such that

$$x_i \in G_\alpha, \; x_k \in G_\omega$$

and (3.4.15)

$$G_\alpha \wedge G_\beta \neq \phi, \; G_\beta \wedge G_\gamma \neq \phi, \ldots, G_\psi \wedge G_\omega \neq \phi.$$

If we decrease the threshold θ, the similarity increases, as a result of which the condition for membership in G will be more restrictive. This will cause Int(C) to become larger and Ext(C) to become smaller.

3.5 INTENSION AND EXTENSION

In Section 3.4, we have dealt with intension and extension mainly from the point of view of the greater-smaller relation and did not concern ourselves about their actual values. For this limited purpose, it was sufficient to define Y vaguely as the set of predicates used in the description of objects observed, and X as the set of available objects.

But, in defining Y we could include or exclude $\neg y_j$ when y_j is already included in Y without altering the content of the description. This approach will change the value of Int(C) as defined by (3.4.5). Again, in addition to two predicates y_j and y_k, we may include or exclude $y_j \cap y_k$ and/or $y_j \cup y_k$ in Y, without changing the information content, but this will also alter the value of the Int(C). To have a really fixed value of Int(C), we should probably include all the logical combinations of the starting predicates.

As a matter of fact, the so-called raw data are outputs of sensory organs and observation instruments. They are, as we have seen in Chapter 2, results of complicated functions of physical inputs, including logical operations. What is important is the information content, and not the question as to which are the original predicates. For instance, when there are two original predicates y_j and y_k, we can just as well take y_j and $y_j \Cup y_k$ [$= (y_j \cup y_k) \cap (\neg y_j \cup y_k)$] instead of y_j and y_k as original predicates without changing the information contents. Indeed if we write $z_j = y_j$ and $z_k = y_j \Cup y_k$, then we can write $y_j = z_k$, $y_k = z_j \Cup z_k$. There is no logical ground why y_j and y_k should be considered "atoms", whereas z_j and z_k should be considered "molecules". For if we take z_j and z_k as "atoms", then y_j and y_k become "molecules." (The names "atoms" and "molecules" are used here according to the usage of some philosophers, and they are different from what should be called atoms and molecules according to the lattice theory.) In any event, we can state that there is no logical or empirical reason for the so-called logical atomism as philosophical doctrine.

If we have two object-predicate tables, one with y_j and y_k, the other with z_j and z_k, whereas all the rest is the same, the intention of C calculated from them can be different. Indeed, if the intension of a general concept includes y_k but not y_j, the contribution to Int(C) from these two columns in the table is 1, but if we use z_j and z_k instead of y_k and y_j, the contribution will become 2. To avoid all these anomalies, we should include all the logically non-equivalent combinations of starting predicates.

Another argument for including all logical combinations in Y is that the conjunctive feature f (3.4.2) which is the most important predicate may or may not be found in the original Y. But if we include all possible predicates in Y, the class predicate f will certainly be found among the members of the extended Y.

As the table is originally defined, subset G may contain many objects which have the same description; this will introduce an inconvenient superfluity of objects in definition of Ext(X). In order to fix this ambiguity, we can introduce a convention that we write only one row for all these objects which have the same description by Y. The extension Ext(C) will become the number of different "object-types" included in G in the table. Even if we extend the Y by logical combinations, clearly such an extension will not change Ext(C). Of course, if we introduce a new independent predicate other than logical combinations of the original predicates, one object-type may split into two, changing the extension. But as far as we do not increase the scope (i.e., the content of information), the extension of C will not change.

Let us now call $\hat{Y}$ the full enlargement of Y by including all possible logical combinations. A member of Y, say y, is a member of $\hat{Y}$, but a member of $\hat{Y}$, say $\hat{y}_i$, may or may not be a member of Y. To obtain the entries for the enlarged object-predicate table, we should use the following rule:

$$A(x_i, \neg\hat{y}_j) = 1 - A(x_i \hat{y}_j) \text{ for all } i \tag{3.5.1}$$

$$A(x_i, \hat{y}_j \cap \hat{y}_k) = A(x_i, \hat{y}_j) A(x_i, \hat{y}_k) \text{ for all } i \tag{3.5.2}$$

$$A(x_i, \hat{y}_j \cup \hat{y}_k) = A(x_i, \hat{y}_j) + A(x_i, \hat{y}_k) - A(x_i \hat{y}_j) A(x_i, \hat{y}_k) \tag{3.5.3}$$

If we take $\hat{y}_k = \neg\hat{y}_j$, we get from $A(x_i, \hat{y}_j \cap \neg\hat{y}_j) = A(x_i, \emptyset) = 0$ for all i, and from $A(x_i, \hat{y}_j \cup \neg\hat{y}_j) = A(x_i, \square) = 1$ for all i. Thus, $\emptyset$ and $\square$ will be members of $\hat{Y}$.

To express in words what is meant by (3.5.1) through (3.5.3), we can say (1) $\neg\hat{y}_j$ is obtained from $\hat{y}_j$ by exchanging 1 with 0, (2) $\hat{y}_j \cap \hat{y}_k$ is obtained by putting 1 where both $\hat{y}_j$ and $\hat{y}_k$ have 1 and putting 0 otherwise, and (3) $\hat{y}_j \cup \hat{y}_k$ is obtained by putting 1 where either $\hat{y}_j$ or $\hat{y}_k$ or both have 1 and putting 0 otherwise.

From the n original predicates y_j ($\in$ Y), we can formally construct $m = 2^n$ different object types. But, in an actual table some object types may be missing. The reason for the absence of certain types may be classified into four general cases: (1) A sheer accident due to the finiteness of the collection X, (2) A logical reason --for instance, if Y contains a predicate y_j and its negation $\neg y_j$ all the rows with entries 1 in both columns y_j and y_k will be missing, (3) A semantic reason. For instance, if y_j means "is red," and y_k means "is colored" then all the object types with 1 for y_j and 0 for y_k will be missing, (4) An empiric reason--for instance, if y_j means "... has gills" and y_k means "... lives (most of the time) in water," then the type with 1 for y_j and 0 for y_k will be missing for an empiric reason.

Cases that violate (2) above do not really appear, therefore we can ignore them. The absence of certain types due to (1), (3), or (4) above does not show any difference in appearance. They can be written in the form of a logical relation (not logical connective), i.e., either equivalence (=) or implication ($\rightarrow$). Note that one equivalence amounts to two implications. Each time there exists one implication ($\rightarrow$), entries for y's become pairwise equal. For instance, if $y_j \rightarrow y_k$, then pairs: (y_j and $y_j \cap y_k$), ($\neg y_j \cap y_k$, and $y_j \Cup y_k$), ($\neg y_k$ and $\neg y_j \cap \neg y_k$)(y_k and $y_j \cup y_k$), ($y_j \cup y_k$ and $\neg(y_j \Cup y_k)$), ($\neg y_j$ and $\neg y_j \cup \neg y_k$), ($y_j \cap \neg y_k$ and $\emptyset$), and ($\neg y_j \cup y_k$ and $\square$) become identical (see Table 3.5.1).

As for the possible predicate types in Y, we note that for one y_j, we can have 0 or 1 for each x_i. Therefore, the number of predicate types, i.e., the number of different columns in the table with m objects is 2^m. If all the formally possible object-types for the original Y are available, the number will be 2^{2^n}. Each time there is an "implication" relation among $\hat{y}_j \in \hat{Y}$, this number becomes one half of what would be in the absence of the implication. The collection of all the predicate types constitutes the complete Boolean lattice. The types of predicates in $\hat{Y}$ can be classified into those which have r ones and m-r zeros, with r = 0, 1,..., m. The integer r is called the rank of a predicate; r = 0 corresponds to $\emptyset$ and r = m to $\square$. There are m $\hat{y}$'s with r = 1; these are atoms in the sense of lattice theory. If we consider a fixed r, there are $\binom{m}{r}$ different ways of placing one in r places out of m possible places. Therefore the total number of possible ways of distributing ones and zeros is $\sum_{r=0}^{m} \binom{m}{r} = (1 + 1)^m = 2^m$, coming back to the same number of predicate-types. There is a one-to-one correspondence between an atomic predicate and an object type, because for a given atomic predicate $\hat{y}_j$, there is only i such that $A_{ij} = 1$ and for a given i, there is only one $\hat{y}_j$ that has only one 1 along the column and precisely on the i-th row.

It is obvious that the extension of a predicate with rank r, say $\hat{y}_j$, can be considered as a disjunction of r atoms. This is a predicate that applies to these r different object-types of the last section. Therefore r is the extension of the predicate in question. If we apply this description to a collection of r objects G of last section, then the predicate $\hat{y}_j$ of rank r under consideration corresponds to f of last section.

On the other hand, all predicates that are implied by the predicate $\hat{y}_j$ in question correspond to properties shared by all the objects covered by $\hat{y}_j$. Consider a predicate with rank r+1 that is implied by $\hat{y}_j$. Such a predicate has one more one in the column than $\hat{y}_j$. There are (m-r) places to place the one, hence there are (m-r) different predicates of rank r+1 which are implied by $\hat{y}_j$. Similarly, there are $\binom{m-r}{2}$ different predicates of rank r+2 that are implied by $\hat{y}_j$, etc. There are $\binom{m-r}{m-r-1} = \binom{m-r}{1} = (m-r)$ predicates of rank (m-r-1) + r = m-1 that are implied by $\hat{y}_j$, and of rank m we have one predicate $\square$. In total $1 + \binom{m-r}{1} + \binom{m-r}{2} + \ldots \binom{m-r}{1} + 1 = 2^{m-r}$ that are implied by $\hat{y}_j$, including $\hat{y}_j$ itself. The collection of these predicates is the F of the last section. Any of these numbers (except the one with m = r) decrease with increasing r.

We can take any of these numbers that are decreasing the function of r as the intension of $\hat{y}_j$, as far as (3.4.3) is concerned. But for symmetry's sake, we can adopt the number of predicates of rank m-r that are implied by y_j. Thus

$$\text{Int}(C) = m-r$$

$$\text{Ext}(C) = r,$$

where C is the general concept corresponding to the collection of objects G.

We note that this way of defining G and F have nothing to do with the internal relation such as similarity among object-types. Any arbitrary collection of object-types can be dealt with in the same way. The idea of similarity will be discussed in the next chapter.

The reader can test the knowledge he has learned with the help of Table 3.5.1.

		Y		$\hat{Y}$					
	rank in x	1	2	0	1	1	2	2	3
	y	y_1	y_2	$\emptyset$	$\neg y_2$	$\neg y_1 \cap y_2$	y_1	$y_1 \cup \neg y_2$	$\square$
	x	$y_1 \cap y_2$	$y_1 \cup y_2$	$y_1 \cap \neg y_2$	$\neg y_1 \cap \neg y_2$	$y_1 \Cup y_2$	$\neg y_1 \cup \neg y_2$	$\neg(y_1 \Cup y_2)$	$\neg y_1 \cup y_2$
$\hat{X}$ / X	x_1	0	0	0	1	0	1	1	1
$\hat{X}$ / X	x_2	0	1	0	0	1	1	0	1
$\hat{X}$ / X	x_3	1	1	0	0	0	0	1	1
$\hat{X}$	x_4	1 0	0 1	0 1	1 0	0 1	0 1	1 0	1 0
	rank in $\hat{X}$	2 1	2 3	0 1	2 1	1 2	2 3	3 2	4 3

Table 3.5.1 Consider first only X which consists of three object-types with $(A_{i1}, A_{i2}) = (0,0)$, $(0,1)$, $(1,1)$, respectively. Since there are two original predicates ($n = 2$), there could be in principle four ($2^n = 4$) object-types. But, one of them is missing ($m = 3$), causing a constraint $y_1 \to y_2$ As a result, a pair of predicates that can be formed in terms of y_1 and y_2 coincides with another, reducing the total number of elements of the completed Boolean lattice $\hat{Y}$ from its maximum value sixteen ($2^{2^n} = 16$) to eight

$(2^m = 8)$. The atoms corresponding to x_1, x_2, x_3 are respectively $\neg y_2$, $\neg y_1 \cap y_2$ and y_1. Now add x_4 which is characterized by $A_{41} = 1$ and $A_{42} = 0$. The m of this extended $\hat{X}$ is 4. The constraints disappear and the predicate-types become 16. The rank with respect to X and that with respect to $\hat{X}$ are not the same. For instance, y_1 and $y_1 \cap y_2$ have the same rank 1 with respect to X, but they become respectively 2 and 1 with respect to $\hat{X}$. Starting with two predicates y_1 and y_2, which constitute Y, we can build a total of 16 predicates that form $\hat{Y}$. But as far as the description of X (but not $\hat{X}$) is concerned, two predicates $y_1 \cap y_2$ and $y_1 \cup y_2$ become identical with y_1 and y_2 respectively, thus appearing under the same rubric of Y.

CHAPTER 4
Pattern Recognition as Value-Oriented Ponderation

4.1 THEOREM OF THE UGLY DUCKLING†

To persuade that two objects are similar, it is natural to enumerate the properties that are commonly owned by the objects. The more properties are shared, the more similar they are. For such an argument it is only fair for the arguers to be allowed to use all possible predicates that are applicable to the objects. For instance, let A mean "... his left eye is damaged," and B means "... his right eye is damaged," then $A \Cup B$ will mean "... his one eye, but not two, is damaged." Two persons can be called similar, if they are blind in one eye but not totally blind. We see therefore that the complex predicate $A \Cup B$ is not an unnatural predicate at all. We should therefore discuss similarity from the point of view of **fully** enlarged predicate lattice $\hat{Y}$, instead of a limited starting set of predicates. In lieu of using the object-predicate table, we shall discuss the problem in this section using the Euler diagram (or the Venn diagram) and the lattice diagram to give the reader a chance to familiarize himself with other methods of mental representation.

Let us start with the case of two starting predicates, A and B, without any constraint. Figure 4.1.1 is the Euler diagram where we see two contours named A and B. The area contained in A corresponds to

---

*To avoid the rather uneuphonic gerundive form "weighting" we borrow the French word "ponderation."

†The author mentioned this theorem in a lecture in 1961 [W-18], and stated and proved it rigorously in a lecture at Brussels in 1962 [W-19]. Quine quoted this paper in his paper, [Q-1], which treats a somewhat related subject.

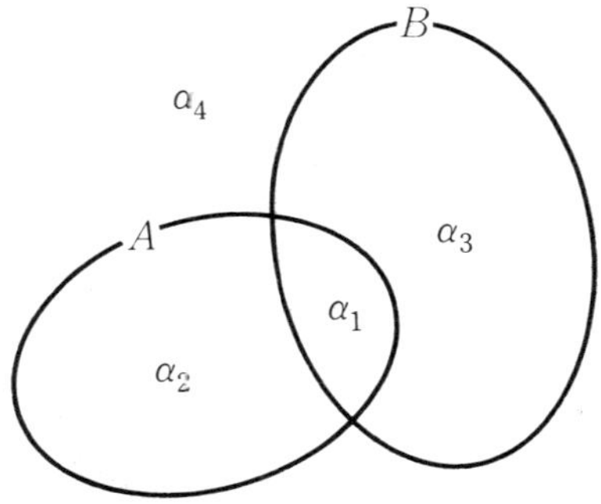

Figure 4.1.1 Euler's diagram with 4 atoms.

predicate A; similarly with B. The area contained in both A and B, denoted by α_1, corresponds to predicate conjunction A ∩ B. The area contained in either A or B or both, corresponds to disjunction A ∪ B. That is the total area of α_1, α_2, and α_3. ¬A corresponds to the area outside the contour A. In other words, the conjunction A ∩ B is the common area ("meet," "intersection") of area A and area B. The disjunction is the joint area ("join," "union") of A and B. The negation of A is the area outside of A. These last definitions by words of logical connectives are valid whether or not there is a constraint.

We see that there are four "atomic" areas, i.e., areas which are not divided any further, denoted α_1, α_2, α_3, α_4 in the figure. Each atom is inside of some predicates and outside of some predicates. For instance, α_2 is the "meet" of the area of A and area of ¬B, therefore α_2 = A ∩ ¬B, that is α_2 is inside of A and outside of B (see Table 4.1.1). There are four atoms in this case of absence of constraints:

Table 4.1.1

α_1	A ∩ B
α_2	A ∩ ¬B
α_3	¬A ∩ B
α_4	¬A ∩ ¬B

Atomic predicates that can be formed from two starting predicates A and B when there is no constraint.

Since there is no smaller subdivision than atoms, any area (i.e. any predicate) can be considered as a join of some atomic areas, for instance, A $\Cup$ B being defined inside A or inside B but not inside both, hence, A B = $\alpha_2 \Cup \alpha_3$. The number of atoms that constitute a predicate is called its rank r. There are $\binom{4}{2} = 6$ ways to pick up 2 out of 4 atoms. Therefore there are 6 predicates of rank 2. Similarly there are $\binom{4}{3} = 4$ predicates of rank 3. Finally, we can think of a predicate that does not contain any atom, i.e., the predicate of rank 0. This is called constantly false predicate ∅. On the other end, the predicate that contains all atoms is called constantly true predicate □; ∅ can be said to correspond to vanishing area and □ to the total area. There are, in total, $\sum_{r=0}^{4} \binom{4}{r} = (1 + 1)^4 = 16$ possible predicates in this case of absence of constraints (see Tables 4.1.2 and 4.1.3).

Table 4.1.2

$\alpha_1 \cup \alpha_2$	A
$\alpha_1 \cup \alpha_3$	B
$\alpha_2 \cup \alpha_3$	A $\Cup$ B
$\alpha_1 \cup \alpha_4$	¬(A $\Cup$ B)
$\alpha_3 \cup \alpha_4$	¬A
$\alpha_2 \cup \alpha_4$	¬B

Predicates of rank 2 that can be formed from two starting predicates A and B in the absence of constraints.

Table 4.1.3

$\alpha_1 \cup \alpha_2 \cup \alpha_3$	A ∪ B
$\alpha_2 \cup \alpha_3 \cup \alpha_4$	¬A ∪ ¬B
$\alpha_1 \cup \alpha_2 \cup \alpha_4$	A ∪ ¬B
$\alpha_1 \cup \alpha_3 \cup \alpha_4$	¬A ∪ B

Predicates of rank 3 that can be formed from two starting predicates A and B in the absence of constraints.

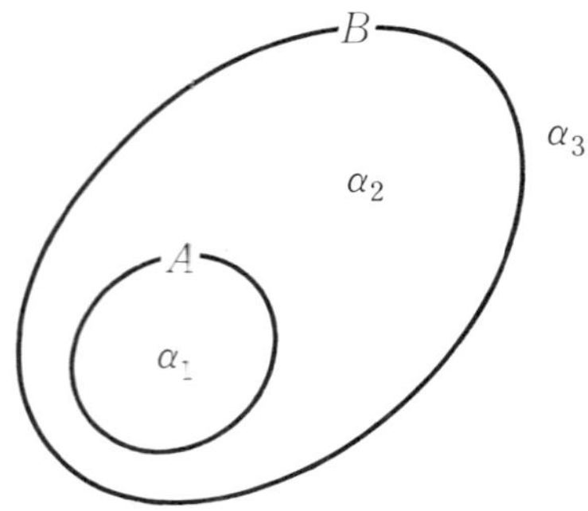

Figure 4.1.2 Euler's diagram with 3 atoms.

A case of two predicates A and B with constraints $A \to B$ is depicted in Figure 4.1.2. The difference in this case from Figure 4.1.1 is that the atom α_2 of Figure 4.1.1 has now collapsed to become equivalent to $\emptyset$. That is $A \cap \neg B = \emptyset$. We know that $A \cap \neg B = \emptyset$ or $\neg A \cup B = \square$ is equivalent to $A \to B$. The number of atoms is now three. Therefore, the number of predicates of rank r is $\binom{3}{r}$ instead of $\binom{4}{r}$ and the total number of predicates is $\sum_{r=0}^{3} \binom{3}{r} = (1 + 1)^3 = 8$ (see Figure 4.1.2).

The lattice diagram can be obtained by placing predicates of the same rank on the same level, and ordering the levels according to the ranks. Two predicates of successive ranks are connected by a straight line if the predicate of lower rank implies the predicate of higher rank, i.e., the area of the lower rank predicate is included in the area of the higher rank predicate. Thus the lattice diagrams corresponding to the Euler diagram of Figures 4.1.1 and 4.1.2 are given in Figures 4.1.3 and 4.1.4.

So far we explained the case of two starting predicates, n=2. But, let us repeat the same thing in the case of an arbitrary number of predicates. Each object has to affirm or negate each of the n predicates. Therefore 2^n possible object types are thinkable. Each object type corresponds therefore to one atomic predicate. However, if there is a constraint, the number of the atoms will decrease, hence in general the number m of atoms is $\leq 2^n$. The

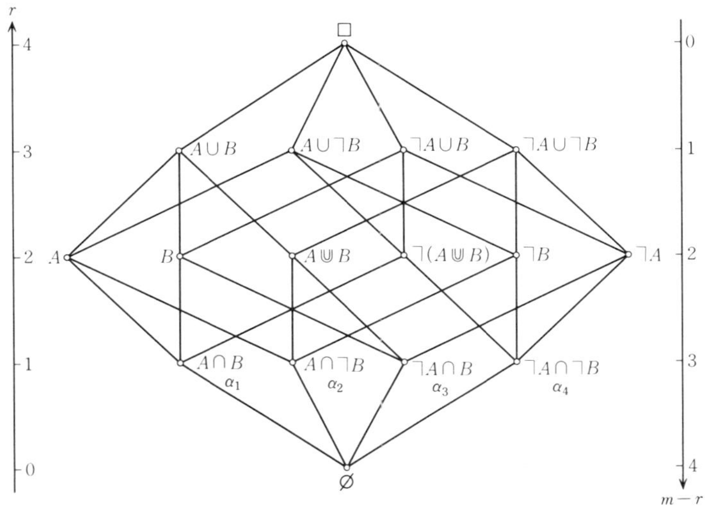

Figure 4.1.3 Lattice produced by 2 starting predicates without constraints. There are 4 atoms and 16 predicates.

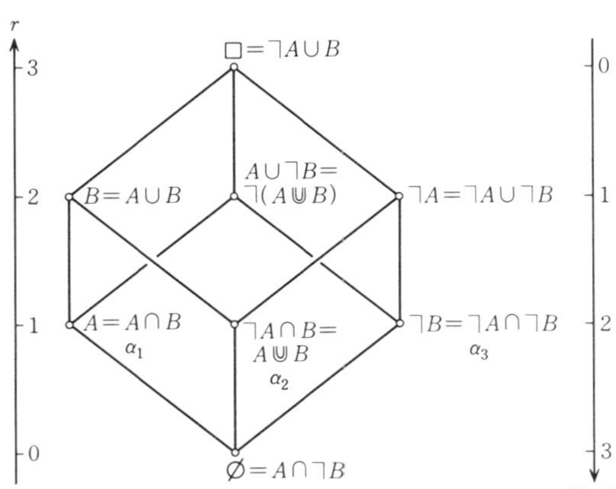

Figure 4.1.4 Lattice produced by 2 starting predicates with one implicational constraint.

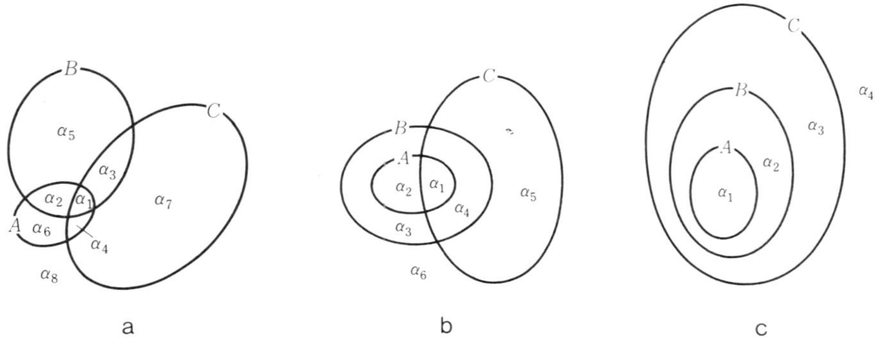

Figure 4.1.5 Euler's diagram for lattices produced by 3 starting predicates. *(a)* Without constraints (8 atoms). *(b)* With 1 constraint (6 atoms). *(c)* With 2 constraints (4 atoms).

number of predicates of rank r is $\binom{m}{r}$ and the total number of predicates is $\sum_{r=0}^{m} \binom{m}{r} = 2^m$. Figure 4.1.5 is for the case n=3: (a) is for the case of no constraints; (b) is for the case of one implicational constraint; (c) is for the case of two implications.

A class of objects can be defined either by its extension, which is a collection G of object-types, or by the intension F, which is the collection of all predicates that are implied by at least all atoms that correspond to the object-types included in G. The conjunctive intension f is the conjunction of all these predicates. The numerical extension of f is its rank, r, i.e., the level height in the lattice diagram, and the numerical intension of f is the depth of the level calculated downward from the maximum height, i.e., m-r. We should note that this number m-r is exactly the number of predicates of rank (m-1) that include the given r atoms, i.e., (m-r-1), other atoms. There are in total m atoms but r are already used, leaving (m-r) atoms still available. Therefore, there should be $\binom{m-r}{m-r-1} = m-r$ possible ways of forming such a predicate. The conjunction of these (m-r) predicates will turn out to be f, because atoms not included in the original r atoms defining G will be missing at least in one of the (m-r) predicates of rank (m-1).

Let us finally notice two invariances involved in the lattice structure. One is called the reciprocity theorem in logic. A simultaneous exchange of affirmation and negation, i.e., 1. A with ¬A, and, conjunction with disjunction, i.e., 2. ∩ with ∪, the constant falsehood with constant truth, i.e., 3. ∅ with □, and the right-directed implication with left-directed implication, i.e., and 4. → with ← will transform a valid logical theorem into another valid theorem. This, in terms of the lattice diagram, amounts to a 180° rotation of the diagram. The exension and intension will be exchanged. At the same time a predicate of rank m-1 and an atom will be exchanged. If, for instance, a theorem says that if A → B, then A ∩ ¬B = ∅, then another theorem will say that if ¬A ← ¬B then ¬A ∪ B = □ is valid.

Another invariance theorem says that any theorem that is valid according to lattice theory will remain valid for any permutation of atoms. Then we can see that the lattice diagram is completely symmetrical for any permutation of two atoms.

We stated that we can equally set up the same completed Boolean lattice either starting A and B or starting A and A ⋓ B. From the present notation (see Figure 4.1.1) A and B are $(\alpha_1 \cup \alpha_2)$ and $(\alpha_1 \cup \alpha_3)$, whereas A and A ⋓ B are $(\alpha_1 \cup \alpha_2)$ and $(\alpha_2 \cup \alpha_3)$. Therefore, these alternative ways of representation correspond simply to an exchange of two atoms α_1 and α_2.

Let us discuss the problem of similarity. When two objects are selected, it is customary to use the number of predicates shared by them as the degree of similarity. As we have seen, two objects, which are distinguishable by the predicates used, correspond to two atoms, say, α_i and α_j. Atoms are predicates of rank 1. There is, of course, no predicate of rank 1 shared (affirmed simultaneously) by these two atoms, but there is one predicate of rank 2 that is shared by these two objects--$\alpha_i \cup \alpha_j$. Now a predicate of rank 3 shared by the two objects must consist of three atoms of which two are α_i and α_j. Because there are m atoms and two of them are already used, the choice is to pick up one out of m-2. Hence, there are $\binom{m-2}{1} = m-2$ predicates of rank 3 that are shared by the two objects.

Similarly, a predicate of rank r shared by the two objects contains the two atoms, α_i and α_j, plus (r-2) atoms that can be chosen out of (m-2). Hence there are $\binom{m-2}{r-2}$ predicates of rank r shared by the two objects. Here r can be any integer between 2 and m, inclusive. The total number of predicates shared by the two objects is $\sum_{r=2}^{m}\binom{m-2}{r-2} = (1+1)^{m-2} = 2^{m-2}$. These numbers, $\binom{m-2}{r-2}$ and 2^{m-2}, are completely independent of the choice of α_i and α_j, hence they are applicable to any two objects.

We can thus state the Theorem of the Ugly Duckling: "Insofar as we use a finite set of predicates that are capable of distinguishing any two objects considered, the number of predicates shared by any two such objects is constant, independent of the choice of the two objects." This theorem is true also if we limit the number of predicates of any given rank.

If we decide to measure similarity of two objects by the number of predicates of a given rank, or by the total number of all possible predicates that are shared by the two objects, then we can say

"Any arbitrary two objects are equally similar" Thus, a swan and a duck, and two swans (insofar as distinguishable) are equally similar. This theorem is mathematically a very simple theorem, but it has a very profound meaning for the study of pattern recognition. If we use the concept of distance D instead of similarity, the situation is the same; the distance between a pair of objects is the same for any choice of the pair.

Relegating to the next section the discussion of a method to salvage ourselves out of the awkward situation we are now placed in due to the Theorem of the Ugly Duckling, let us adduce here a typical case of misunderstanding of logical and linguistic nature that people are likely to become victims of. A certain researcher recently claimed that the "conjunctive classes" are the only permissible classes that can be used in the generalization in pattern recognition. What he means is the following. Suppose that the language provides us with two pairs of predicates (A) big, small; (B) red, non-red. Four conjunctive classes: 1. big and red, 2. small and red, 3. big and non-red, and 4. small and non-red are the only allowable groupings. But, we can show that there is no such thing as allowable groupings from the logical point of view or from the linguistic point of view. The language we use could be so well-developed and so rich that there is another pair of predicates: (C) meissen, delft where meissen = big $\Cup$ red, and delft = $\neg$(big $\Cup$ red). Then, we shall have to admit four more classes: 5. big and meissen, 6. small and meissen, 7. big and delft, and 8. small and delft. These four groupings are exactly those which are forbidden from the first point of view. We can't say that red and non-red are atomic whereas meissen and delft are artificially contrived molecules, because we can write red = big $\Cup$ meissen, non-red = $\neg$(big $\Cup$ meissen). In other words, seen from the point of view of the predicates (meissen, delft), the pair (red, non-red) is molecular. From the logical point of view as well as from the linguistic point of view, there is no reason to prefer one point of view to another, or even to distinguish one from the other. The only difference is a pragmatic one. Perhaps from the point of view of pigment to be used, (red, non-red), is a meaningful classification, but from the point of view of business the classification (meissen, delft) may be more meaningful. This again is a manifestation of the inductive ambiguity we encounter when we want to make a class out of an object.

4.2 AXIOLOGICAL OVERCOMING OF RADICAL NOMINALISM

When we review the history of theories about the relation between particular objects and general concepts, we understand that philosophers, after making centuries of detour around realism, conceptualism, and nominalism, have come to one version or another of the similarity theory, which is in a way a return to the common sense view of classes: (1) things that really exist are particular objects and (2) a class corresponding to a general concept consists of particular objects which resemble one another. The resemblance or similarity between two objects, again in the common sense view, is measured by the maximum number of predicates that are shared by them. The theorem of the Ugly Duckling shows that, according to this definition of similarity, the degree of similarity between any arbitrary pair of objects is the same. In other words, there is no such thing as similarity or dissimilarity in the world, as far as empirical data and their logical treatment are concerned. This destroys the similarity theory completely and we are left with the conclusion that a general concept is applicable to any arbitrary set of objects. There is no better name for such a view than "radical nominalism." This term was used to describe a somewhat similar view in the Medieval Age, but our view is supported by a more rigorous logical consideration.

The radical nominalism in this sense is impossible to defeat. Yet, can we live without the concept of similarity and that of class in the actual world? Obviously not! Since our argument for the radical nominalism was based on the logical treatment of empirical data, we shall have to introduce an extra-experiential or extra-logical element or both into our argument, if we are to reinstate similarity and the universal in some sense.

More specifically, in the foregoing we treated all predicates (of the same rank) equally. This must be the cause of the disturbing consequence. Some predicates must be more "important" in some sense than some others. To be similar may be to share more of the important predicates. But, how can we evaluate the scale of importance? To answer this question, we have to reflect on the reason why we use similarity and classification in life. The answer is because it is useful. In other words, our scale of importance must be such that the resulting classifications carry utility or value. We can overcome the radical nominalism only by axiological considerations. I do not hereby mean any ultimate value, but various instrumental values toward more fundamental ends.

To reach a classification useful in formulating zoology, it serves the purpose better to put the whale with the elephant rather than with the tuna. In this case, predicates that characterize the mammals are important, and, in view of such predicates, the elephant and the whale are similar. To reach a classification useful in administration of industries, it serves the purpose better to put the whale with the tuna rather than with the elephant. The predicate: "can be caught in the sea," is more important here, and the whale and the tuna are similar in this respect.

It is instructive to observe how the sensory organs have developed themselves in such a way that the more important predicates are directly observed, whereby importance is mainly dictated by the value of survival. To individual animals, these particular predicates are so-to-speak innate ideas, but they are without any doubt results of the long experience through evolution (see p. 126 in Quine's essay on ontological relativity, [Q-1]).

In this section, we discussed the problem in terms of discrete predicates which require a yes or no response, but, a similar argument can be advanced in terms of continuous variables. First, a continuous variable can always be quantized so that it can be considered as a group of yes-or-no variables, with any given desired accuracy. In this sense, the continuous case is also subject to the Theorem of the Ugly Duckling. But we can consider any continuous functions of the given variables as new continuous variables too. Given n variables, we can introduce their arbitrary functions so as to make any two objects nearer to each other than any other two objects, using the Euclidean distance. Conversely, by introducing an arbitrary definition of distance, we can alter the relation of distance between objects any way we want. The situation is actually worse than in the case of the Theorem of the Ugly Duckling. If we decide to use the Euclidian distance, we have to choose the variables in such a way that a useful classification will ensue. Unimportant variables can also be eliminated from consideration.

In the case of discrete predicates, let us consider how we can introduce mathematically the idea that predicates should not be treated as equally important, i.e., each predicate has to be assigned a different weight, a preferential ponderation. We have to keep in mind that this weight is not a constant attribute of the predicate, but varies depending **essentially** upon the use we are going to make of the resulting classification.

Let us denote by w_j the weight which we attach to predicate y_j. [From now on we consider only the Boolean completion of a predicate lattice, therefore, we do not write the cap on the y's.] We agree that

$$w_j \geq 0, \qquad \sum_{j=1}^{n} w_j = 1 \tag{4.2.1}$$

and that the larger the value of w_j, the more "important" the predicate y_j. The upper end of summation n is the number of nonequivalent predicates, that is 2^m, where m is the given object-types. We introduced the Hamming distance between two objects x_i and x_k by

$$\sum_{j=1}^{n} |A_{ij} - A_{kj}| , \tag{4.2.2}$$

where each term is 0 or 1. Correspondingly, we can define a natural similarity by

$$S_{ik} = \frac{1}{n} \sum_{j=1}^{n} \{1 - |A_{ij} - A_{kj}|\} . \tag{4.2.3}$$

This quantity has a prima facie minimum zero and prima facie maximum 1. But due to the Theorem of the Ugly Duckling, there are $2^{m-2} = n/4$ predicates for which $A_{ij} = A_{kj} = 1$. There must be just as many predicates (which are negatives of the first group of predicates) for which $A_{ij} = A_{kj} = 0$. The remaining predicates have $|A_{ij} - A_{kj}| = 1$. Therefore

$$S_{ik} = \frac{1}{2} \tag{4.2.4}$$

for any pair (x_i,x_k). This is another expression of the Theorem of the Ugly Duckling.

Now, introducing the preferential ponderation w_j, we should redefine the similarity as

$$S_{ik} = \sum_{j=1}^{n} w_j \{1 - |A_{ij} - A_{kj}|\} . \qquad (4.2.5)$$

This quantity becomes 1 if $w_j = 0$ for those summanden which are 0, and it becomes 0 if $w_j = 0$ for those summanden which are 1. S_{ik} is then a non-negative quantity that varies between 0 and 1

$$0 \leq S_{ik} \leq 1 , \qquad (4.2.6)$$

which is a nice characteristic as a measure of similarity.

If we want to define a class (universal) as a collection of similar objects, we should introduce a set as follows: Two objects, x_i, $x_k \in X$, belong to the set G: $x_i \in G$ and $x_k \in G$ if and only if

$$S_{ik} \geq \theta \qquad (S_{ik} = S_{ki}) \qquad (4.2.7)$$

with a suitable threshold θ, which should be fixed at a value larger than 1/2. If we want to allow for a disjunctive set of similar objects, H, we can require that $x_i \in H$ and $x_k \in H$ if and only if there is at least a series of sets of the type (4.2.7) G_1, G_2, ..., G_μ, such that $x_i \in G_1$, $x_k \in G_\mu$ and

$$G_\rho \wedge G_{\rho+1} \neq \emptyset \text{ with } \rho = 1, 2, \ldots, \mu-1$$

and

$$H = G_1 \vee G_2 \vee \ldots \quad \vee G_\mu . \qquad (4.2.8)$$

The threshold θ could be different for each subset.

We thus conclude that we can see similarity, hence grouping of objects, only because of an "uneven" emphasis on the empirical data about the objects. If we give a mathematical formulation to this unevenness, it is convenient to use the entropy function.

$$S = -\sum_{i=1}^{n} w_i \log w_i \qquad (4.2.9)$$

which takes its minimum 0 when one of the w's is 1 and the others 0, and its maximum log n when all w's are equal and $\frac{1}{n}$.

The situation created by the uneven distribution of w's can be interpreted as follows. If we take, without any bias, the raw data provided by the results of observation and logical treatments we cannot see any "clumping" among the objects. We can see a "form" in this amorphous chaos only by modifying our conceptual framework. The degree of this modification can be measured by log n -S.

The lesson learned in this section is that epistemology can subsist only through its interaction with axiology. It will be deprived of its major function, concept formation, if it relies only on observational experience and logical manipulation. What makes cognition possible is the evaluative ponderation, whose origin is aesthetic and emotional in the broadest sense of the terms.

4.3 NONSIMILARITY GROUPING

This section and the next have little to do with the title of the chapter, value-oriented ponderation, but they have one thing in common with Sections 4.1 and 4.2 in that they point out the weakness of the simple-minded similarity theory as a epistemological foundation of the general concept, hence, also as a foundation of pattern recognition. In this section we want to show that similarity is not the only kind of bond or source of cohesion among the elements tied together under a concept. Take, for instance, the concept of family. Husband, wife, and children are called a family not because of their mutual similarity. What is the nature of the bond that binds together Father, Son and Holy Ghost? Certainly it is not similarity. The Trinity is a concept not simply because it represents one and the same God, but because it manifests itself under three different aspects. What, again, is the nature of the bond that binds "stone," "scissors," and "paper" in the game of

Janken, which is widely practiced among children of Southeast Asia and the Far East? The bond is a trilateral circular relation: stone defeats scissors, scissors defeats paper, and paper defeats stone. These examples are groupings by multi-lateral relations, rather than by a binary relation, which similarity is. Even if we limit ourselves to bilateral relations, a strong bond between elements can be found also in "opposition" or "contrast" rather than similarity, such as "black and white" and "right and wrong."

To clarify our point let us introduce an example that can easily be given a mathematical expression. We call the example "a voting pattern in U.N.," but the U.N. here is a fictitious league of nations. To make visualization easy we call four groups of nations S (Soviet Union and satellites), A (United States and allies), T (the Third World), and N (genuine neutrals). The voting pattern of the first three groups, S, A, and T, is motivated by the following basic principle. [1] If two of three groups vote "No," the third group will not vote "Yes," because this "Yes" is wasted. If one of the three wants to vote "Yes," it lures one of the remaining two to vote also "Yes." [2] If two of the three groups vote "Yes," the third group will not vote "Yes," because the third group does not like the friendship of the other two and would like to show its independence. The fourth group is completely indifferent and independent of what the others may be doing. The patterns of voting would, therefore, look like Table 4.3.1.

In this table, the predicate y_j means "vote yes" for the j-th proposed resolution; there are eight voting patterns. We observe first that each row of the four groups has four ones and four zeros. There is no tendency for yesmanship, nor for nomanship. Now let us take two groups out of four groups; there are of course $\binom{4}{2} = 6$ pairs. Each pair has two (1,1), two (0,0), two (0,1) and two (1,0). That is, there is no tendency for similarity, no tendency for opposition, and each of six pairs has exactly the same pattern. Now we take a supragroup of three voting groups, such as (S,A,T), (A,T,N), etc. There are $\binom{4}{3} = 4$ supragroups. But here we see a distinction between

Table 4.3.1

	y_1	y_2	y_3	y_4	y_5	y_6	y_7	y_8
S	1	1	1	1	0	0	0	0
A	1	1	0	0	1	1	0	0
T	0	0	1	1	1	1	0	0
N	0	1	0	1	0	1	0	1

S, A, T, N are fictitious Soviet group nations, fictitous American group nations, fictitious Third World group nations, and fictitious neutral group nations, respectively. The y's are the proposed resolutions. The entry "1" means "yes" vote and "0" means "no" vote.

(S,A,T) and the remaining three (A,T,N), (T,N,S), (N,S,A). (S,A,T) exhibits four voting patterns (1,1,0), (1,0,1), (0,1,1), and (0,0,0) whereas each of the remaining three exhibits eight patterns, which consists in addition to the four already mentioned ones, four new ones: (1,0,0), (0,1,0), (0,0,1), and (1,1,1). The supragroup (S,A,T) avoids (1,0,0), (0,1,0), and (0,0,1) because of the voting policy [1] and avoids (1,1,1) because of the voting policy [2].

This example was originally introduced under the name of "four girls in a dormitory" [W-10], but we explained the same mathematical structure here as a problem of voting patterns. The main point is that there exists mathematically demonstrable grouping due to m-partite relations, with $m > 2$. The traditional theory of grouping due to similarity is nothing but the most elementary case. We can make a much more complicated example, but this one is the simplest we can think of for $m > 2$.

The reader may be curious to know what will happen if we enlarge the Y (which consists of eight $\underset{\sim}{y}$'s in the above example) to its Boolean completion $\hat{Y}$. It is easy to see that the special characteristic supragroup (S,A,T) disappears, just as all similarity disappears in the extended object-predicate table.

Not to waste too much space in this book, the reader is referred to the Generalized Theorem of the Ugly Duckling for the mathematical proof (see p. 378 [W-10]). The proof is based, as is the simple Theorem of the Ugly Duckling, on the invariance of the Boolean lattice for any permutation of lattice atoms. Therefore, the grouping due to multilateral relations is detectable also only if we have a preferential ponderation on the available predicates.

We said that clustering consists in discovering groupings in the given data (admitting of course that there is a preferential ponderation). Now, all the existing mathematical algorithms, except ones later explained in this book, are totally incapable of discovering grouping due to m-partite relation with $m > 2$. Most engineers, just as traditional philosophers, do not realize that there exist all kinds of grouping of elements due to more-than-two-partite relations. A mathematical method that enables us to extricate such multipartite relations will be explained in Section 6.5.

4.4 OBJECT-PREDICATE INVERSION

The thinking described in this section started as a kind of computational trick. When we introduced in 1961 the idea of object-predicate table, we noted [W-7]* "Mathematically, there exists a complete symmetry between the x_i and the y_j, and what will be stated in terms of the x_i can also be stated, mutatis mutandis, in terms of the y_j, and vice versa." (The notations x_i and y_j here are the same as in the preceding sections.) The technical advantage of this "object-predicate inversion" was developed mainly in connection with the method of diagonalization of covariance matrix [W-8] and will be explained in Chapter 7. In this chapter on the analysis of the similarity theory, we shall discuss some of the more

*The idea of "more-than-two-object relation," with the same example as in Table 4.3.1, was also introduced in this 1961 paper [W-7]. It is surprising that practically nothing has been done to exploit this potentially important subject in the last twenty years.

philosophical problems lurking behind this technical possibility.

We have stated that the similarity theory which is inevitably involved in all works of mechanical pattern recognition is based on two pillars: (1) the real existence of particular objects, (2) similarity among particular objects. As far as the second point is concerned, we have shown that from the point of view of empirical data and of logical manipulation, there is no such thing as similarity. But we can salvage the idea of similarity by introducing preferential ponderation of predicates, the origin of which can be traced to human values in practical life. In this section we will analyze the first assumption, namely, the concept of particular object.

Ordinary language is, without exception, based on the pattern of thinking: subject + predicate. We have submitted in the earlier chapter that the very origin of this pattern of thinking may be attributed to the animistic view of the world and unwarranted extension of the idea of the self-identical "I" as an active subject. The subject-predicate pattern was also adopted as the basic assumption in Aristotelian philosophy. The view however that the world consists of discrete number of objects is by no means a self-evident assumption. We want to introduce in this section further doubt of a different sort on the assumption of particular objects.

In the first place, how do we identify an object? It is identified by observation, just as a predicate is confirmed or denied by an observation. A raven is identified by first observing all kinds of predicates that ravens are supposed to satisfy and then by observing some special marks of this-ness, such as the one that lives in a certain tree, or the one that has a defective right wing or some other characteristic. Sometimes, the identity is supposed to be confirmed by continuous same-ness. (Remember, the frog's eyes have the same-ness perception.) This confirmation is nothing but a continuous observation of some predicates. We mentioned a recent work of Strawson [S-8], which maintains that a particular object can be identified only through testing applicability of some general concepts, which, in our context, amount to observations of some predicates. If we agree that an object can be identifiable only by a group of observations, the object-predicate relation is no more than a relation between two groups of observations.

We can look at the problem from a slightly different angle. We have already stated that the idea of particular objects in Aristotle is intimately related to his obsession about "substance." The object-predicate relation is, in this sense, a relation between a "substance" concept and a "function" concept. If the substance refers to "what," then the function refers to "how." The predicate is a description of how a thing is, such as black or large, or heavy. The first systematic assault on the substance concept, as is known to the author, is the Buddhistic principle of anatta.

The Brahmanism from which Buddhism is born as a kind of reformation was espoused firmly to the idea of substance. The basic tenet of Brahmanism is the unity of the world soul (the Brahman) and the individual soul (atman, etymologically identical with German Atmen). Called either brahman or atman, it is as indestructible, unchanging, self-perpetuating, everlasting as any genuine substance. One of the basic tenets of Buddhism is the negation of substance atman [hence, anatman (Sanscrit) = annatta (Pali)]. What looks like a constant unchanging substance is nothing more than a causal chain of temporary occurrences. The metaphor of life as a flame, therefore, acquires a deep metaphysical significance in Buddhism. But, we are not interested in ancient philosophy. We wanted only to note that the doubt about the substance concept is nothing new.

If we see a shift of priority from substance to function in the transition from Brahmanism to Buddhism, the Platonist philosopher, Professor Fujisawa, sees a reverse shift from Plato to Aristotle. According to him, most of the criticism against Plato's Idea (Form) is based on the Aristotelian bias that forced the Idea into the role of substance, which Plato did not intend. For Plato the Idea is not a thing, but it is a state, a function, a meaning.

Two milleniums later, we see that the modern developments in physical science manifest also a shift from substance to function. Toward the end of the nineteenth century, the concept of ether played the role of the ultimate substance that permeated the entire universe. At that time, Einstein declared that the ether has no material properties and had best be considered as a pure void, capable of carrying electromagnetic waves. (Compare the Platonic concept of field, see Section 3.1.) Similarly, the modern atomism has gradually deprived the constituent building blocks of material attributes and comes close to the view that all properties of elementary particles are no longer fixed attributes but variable quantities whose actual values require explanation. This means that the modern "atoms" are the prima materia devoid of any fixed attributes, only a symbolic carrier of variable functions.

The fact that the modern elementary particle has lost the status of substance is most conspicuously demonstrated by the empirical discovery that if we assume self-identity for an elementary particle we come to a theoretical conclusion that contradicts experiments. The Aristotelian way of describing the physical state of an elementary particle would be that "a particle P is in a quantum state Q." If P had self-identity, then particle P_1 in a quantum state Q and particle P_2 in Q would be different situations. But, if an electron E_1 and electron E_2 are indistinguishable, then there is no sense in saying that E_1 instead of E_2 is in quantum state Q. In fact, the theoretical statistical conclusion on the basis of the complete identity of all electrons and the conclusion on the basis of the individual self-identity of each electron are different, and the experiment favors definitively the former alternative. The empirical fact is that an elementary particle does not possess individual self-identity.

On the other hand, quantum states are distinguishable. Therefore, the correct way of describing the physical state is not "particle P is in quantum state Q," but "quantum state Q is occupied by a certain number N of the particle of a certain kind." That is, the roles of object and predicate are, so-to-speak, interchanged.

We do not mean that we should deny the self-identity of a macroscopic object, but, we do mean that it would be worthwhile to try to interchange the roles of object and predicate. That might show as a hidden aspect of reality. At least, we should keep in mind that the Aristotelian view of object-predicate is not the only valid way to look at the world.

It has to be admitted that if we do exactly the same thing with respect to X as with respect to Y, for instance, introduce a "Boolean completion" $\hat{X}$ of X in the same way as we introduced a Boolean completion $\hat{Y}$ of Y, we immediately get into apparent trouble. We shall have to introduce an object that simultaneously affirms and denies a predicate. We may have to give such an object a special status of "fictitious object." It may be also of some interest to consider the reciprocity of intension and extension (Section 4.1) as an expression of the principle of basic interchangeability of predicate and object, and to exploit to the extreme the implication of the invariance of the lattice graph for a 180° rotation. See Chapter 7 for further discussion of object-predicate inversion. See also Appendix [A-4] for another aspect of the idea of elimination of object.

CHAPTER 5
Pattern Recognition as Induction

5.1 INDUCTION AND INDUCTIVE AMBIGUITY

We have noted that the paradigm-oriented pattern recognition is an inductive process. The reason is that in the paradigm-oriented pattern recognition a class is produced by generalization based on a finite number of paradigms, whereas in an induction a universal rule is produced by generalization based on a finite number of paradigmatic evidences. In both cases, generalization is an extension to "similar" situations. To see this parallelism more clearly, we shall start with surveying the theoretical views about induction (see [W-24]).

Traditionally, induction is considered as the opposite process of deduction: deduction is the derivation of particular facts from a general rule, and induction is the derivation of a general rule from a finite number of particular facts. Because the first derivation is usually a logical inference, and the second derivation is usually non-logical inference, the distinction between induction and deduction is defined by some authors (such as Rudolf Carnap and Max Black) as one between logical or demonstrable inference and probabilistic and non-demonstrable inference [B-5, C-5]; however, this alternative definition leads not only to confusion but also to an erroneous conclusion. Indeed, there does exist a probabilistic deduction and a logical refutation in induction. Another more dangerous mistake is committed by the second definition of the distinction, because this view, as was the case with Carnap, leads to the ignorance of the fundamental asymmetry of conditional probabilities. See later discussion in Chapter 8.

A simple example of deductive inference is: (H) Men are mortal, (A) Socrates is a man, (D) Socrates is mortal. The corresponding inductive inference is: (D) Socrates died, Plato died, Wittgenstein died etc. (A) They are all men, (H) Men are mortal. A probabilistic example of deductive inference is: (H) A man is, with 95% probability, right-handed, (A) Nothing else except the fact that Mr. X is a man is known, (D) Mr. X is, with 95% probability, right-handed. The corresponding induction is: (D) 95% of men examined were found to be right-handed. (A) They are nonbiased random samples of men, (H) Men are, with 95% probability, right-handed.

H stands for a hypothesis assumed (general rule), A for an auxiliary fact, D for an experimental datum. We have to assign a probability to each proposition of three categories. The probability of A is usually assumed to be unity, because it is assumed to be a fact. The statement of hypothesis H is such that the probability of occurrence of the empirical event D on the assumption of H and A is determined: $p(D|H \cap A)$. This is the deductive probability. In the case of a logical deduction, this probability is unity or zero. The inductive probability (or credibility) is the degree of confidence we place on H on the basis of D and A: $p(H|D \cap A)$. This probability is, according to Bayes' theorem, proportional to $p(D|H \cap A) \times p(H)$ where $p(H)$ is the degree of confidence we would place on the hypothesis H without taking into consideration the evidential fact D and the auxiliary fact A. The a posteriori inductive probability $p(H|D \cap A)$ and its a priori inductive probability $p(H)$ can be given a natural interpretation only from the standpoint of personalistic foundation of probability [W-10]. Those authors, such as Hans Reichenbach, who believe in the frequency view of probability have to make recourse to a round-about argument for induction, which Herbert Feigl called "vindication" [F-3, R-6].

We are customarily told that David Hume was the first to point out that induction is not a logical inference, but he never used the word induction, nor did he directly discuss the process of inductive inference. What he was interested in was the connection between cause and effect. To establish causality on a really firm basis, he thought he would have to show *necessary connection* between cause and effect other than spatial contiguity, temporal succession, and joint occurrence. Of course, if we interpret necessary connection as a logical necessity, it is hopeless to establish such a connection. Even if we interpret necessary connection in the sense of an empirical law, what can be shown is only a finite number of cases of factual conjoint occurrence. Hume thought that the connection of cause and effect is, like in the case of "universal," an association in the mind created by "habit" generated by a repeated observation of conjoint occurrence of cause and effect.

If the connection between cause and effect is not a necessary one, it follows that the generation of a general causal law from a finite number of empirical examples cannot be a necessary process, and pervasive skepticism about induction is inevitable. Usually, the Humean psychologism is attacked by philosophers, because they look for a "justification" for induction. But, the greatness of Hume resides precisely in the fact that he pointed at the same origin both in the formation of universal ideas and in the formation of general rules by induction. We shall touch upon this matter again in the Epilogue.

In spite of this early discovery by Hume that induction has no logical foundation, there exists a persistent tendency among philosophers to reduce induction to logical inference. One of such futile efforts is represented in recent years by Karl Popper's theory of infirmation [P-6]. If the hypothesis states such and such phenomenon will not occur, and if this phenomenon actually happens, then this hypothesis is rejected. This process, called infirmation, is a perfectly legitimate logical process. But, the error of this infirmation theory is that it claims that the process of evaluation of hypothesis consists exclusively of this infirmation. The positive process of induction lies in the fact that if the hypothesis predicts such and such phenomenon with a large probability and if such a phenomenon occurs with high frequency, then the evaluation of the hypothesis becomes higher. The process of infirmation is a logical conclusion, but the most substantial body of the process of induction lies in this latter process of confirmation by positive evidence.

That the probabilistic model of induction includes both infirmation and confirmation can be easily seen from what we said about the degree of confidence we place in hypothesis H on the ground of the empirical fact D, which is, $p(H|D\cap A) \propto p(D|H\cap A)\,p(H)$. The case of infirmation is: $p(H|D\cap A) = 0$ because $p(D|H\cap A) = 0$. The case of confirmation can be seen that the larger the deductive probability, $p(D|H\cap A)$, the larger the inductive probability, $p(H|D\cap A)$, provided that p(H) remains the same [W-10, W-13, W-23, W-51].

An important fact is that the confirmation is not the only factor that determines the evaluation of a hypothesis. Consider, for instance, the case of the well-known example, invented by Nelson Goodman, of grue emeralds [G-3]. Suppose we have two hypotheses: (H_1) All emeralds are green, (H_2) All emeralds are grue (where grue means green up to today and blue from tomorrow). Then all the evidence so far confirms H_1 and H_2 to an equal degree. But, most people would place more confidence in H_1. This factor of evaluation is neither evidential nor logical. As far as the evidences, i.e., the empirical facts predicted by the hypothesis, are concerned, the evaluation should be the same for both hypotheses. The difference must originate from some a priori consideration (a priori in the sense of prior to the evidential fact).

The reason why the hypothesis H_1 is preferred may evoke different explanations, such as the "entrenchment" in the language (green is more "entrenched" in the language than grue). One possible explanation may be that the green-meter (the machine which distinguishes green from non-green) is simpler in construction than the grue-meter (see [W-10] for a more detailed discussion of Goodman's paradox).

If we use the probabilistic version of induction, we have the inductive probability which is proportional to $p(D|H\cap A)p(H)$, where $p(D|H\cap A)$ is the deductive probability of the evidential fact D on the basis of H and A. The factor p(H) is to be evaluated apart from the evidential fact D, therefore it is the place where the extra-evidential, extra-logical consideration is to be reflected [W-10, W-13, W-23]. That there is a place in the mathematical model to insert the a priori factor of evaluation shows that the probability theory sides with the theory that confirmation (represented by the factor $p(D|H \cap A)$) is not the exclusively decisive factor.

In both categorical and probabilistic cases, we have to admit that the quantitative strength of the extra-evidential, extra-logical consideration cannot be uniquely determined, and to this extent, the induction always leaves "inductive ambiguity." We can notice, however, that if we repeat experiments, the effect of confirmation will eventually overwhelm that of the a priori factor. On the other hand, insofar as the size of the body of evidence is finite, we can always change the value of the a priori factor to counteract the evidential factor (see [W-10]).

If we look at the historical process of theory evolution in natural sciences, the actual workers in science are never bothered by an overabundance of possible hypotheses. The truth is, on the contrary, that it is difficult to think of even one new potential hypothesis - i.e., to use the jargon introduced by Peirce [P-4] - to do abduction.* The inductive ambiguity does not even raise its ugly head. The Kuhnian theory of scientific revolutions leaves the reader with the impression that the scholars have, in principle, a choice of many theories at their disposal and that they choose the one that harmonizes with their Zeitgeist and social ideology. This is not the case. A scholar would grab any one possible hypothesis, if any one fortunately occurs to his mind [W-17]. Or does Kuhn's theory mean that a scholar is always so narrow minded that he can think of only one type of theory that his time and social condition impose on him?

The reason for this actual scarcity of hypotheses is that the scientific mind has a strong feeling about the harmonious coherence of his entire theoretical structure [D-4]. This principle of "coherence" includes not only the logical consistency of different parts of one's theoretical structure, but also esthetic harmony among them. Among these extra-evidential factors, one important element can be formulated as the principle of simplicity, although this is not the sole principle of the

*Introduce a new hypothesis implies also that we attach a non-zero prior probability to that hypothesis, which is necessary for its survival.

extra-evidential, extra-logical consideration (see Section 5.4).

If a hypothesis is invalidated by an empirical fact, we can, by the use of the Duhem-Quine [D-3] method, amend the hypothesis so that the hypothesis becomes again compatible with the empirical facts. But, attachment of many such Duhemian amendments will give an ugly appearance to the hypothesis, violating the principle of simplicity, thus leading to a very low plausibility for the amended hypothesis.

An extra-logical, extra-evidential guiding principle like the use of simplicity, while providing no guarantee for a "correct" conclusion of induction, often leads to a successful progress of inferential process. Such a tactical guide is called "heuristic."

Some comments on Carnap's theory of induction and its background should be given here. The most harmful bias which is widespread among philosophers and mathematicians and hinders a correct appreciation of the depth and breadth of inductive ambiguity stems from the so-called "necessary view" of probability, which is usually associated with such eminent names as Keynes [K-6] and Carnap [C-5]. According to this view, there holds one and only one relation of a certain kind called probability relation between any two propositions, taken as the analogues of the logical notions of premise and consequence in analogies to logical implications. This relation corresponds to a numerical value, which depends only on the relation between the two propositions and not on human opinions or any other element outside these two propositions. Thus, Carnap* introduces the probability c(h,e) of a hypothesis h which is a function only of the relation between the hypothesis h and the relevant evidence e. That this view is entirely untenable in the case of induction was demonstrated previously by the present author [W-13, W-23, W-51].

We have to know the basic asymmetry that cannot be avoided when we use the concept of conditional probability [W-10]. Carnap's c-function, c(h,e), by definition is the conditional probability of h on the

*It is understood that Carnap shifted his view in his last years, but the name Carnap is used here as the author of his famous book mentioned as [C-5] in the bibliography.

ground of e, $P(h|e)$. The asymmetry is between $P(h|e)$ and $P(e|h)$. In general when we have two propositions which are dependent on each other, say, A, and B, we can think of five different probabilities, which are related to one another by the relation

$$p(A|B)P(B) = p(A \cap B) = p(B|A)P(A).$$

It is pointed out in [W-10], that the first and most important task before making use of these probabilities is to determine which of the five probabilities are determined by the nature of the problem. If $p(A \cap B)$ is determined, all the remaining four can be derived from it, but, in most of the problems, $p(A \cap B)$ is not determined, and only one of the two conditional probabilities $p(A|B)$ or $p(B|A)$ is determined by the nature of the problems. If $p(A|B)$ is determined by the problem, we cannot determine arbitrarily in addition $p(B|A)$ because this determination can immediately contradict the given value of $p(A|B)$. All that can be further determined in addition to the given value of $p(A|B)$ is $p(B)$.

In the case of the deduction-induction complex, deductive probability, $p(e|h)$, is determined by the nature of the problem, because the hypothesis or law has to give the prediction about the data to be obtained by the experiment. This is determined by the relation between h and e. If it is so, then the inverse conditional probability, i.e., inductive probability $p(h|e)$ is not determined by the relation between h and e, because $p(h|e)$ is given by $p(e|h)p(h)/p(e)$. This relationship depends on $p(h)$ which represents the prior probability of h which is not determined by the relation of h and e. The probability $p(e)$ on the denominator has nothing to do with the hypothesis h, of which the credibility is in question. This argument of the inevitable asymmetric use of symmetrical conditional probabilities shows clearly that Carnap's assumption that $c(h,e)$ is determined by the necessary relation between h and e is completely invalid; $c(h,e)$ should include its extra-evidential evaluation that determines $p(h)$.

Only the principle of simplicity has been mentioned as the factor determining the prior probability of a hypothesis. To be more truthful to the situation, we should mention a broader list of the extra-evidential factors, such as:

1. Effect of other competing hypotheses. If a more credible hypothesis is competing with a given hypothesis, the credibility of the latter will become less than in the absence of the former,
2. In a scientific theory, hypotheses of different areas and different levels have to be structured into a harmonious and consistent system. Two hypotheses which are equally well confirmed by the evidence may have different credibilities depending on how well they harmonize with other hypotheses in a theory,
3. Scientists often believe in one hypothesis more than in another because it is simpler or more elegant, or simply more to his taste. Such an esthetic evaluation is not only inevitable but also quite helpful in efficient induction,
4. A hypothesis H is often a (probabilistically) deductive consequence of another hypothesis of higher level which can become more credible through a direct confirmation via other hypotheses of lower levels, then the hypothesis H becomes more credible in spite of the fact that its deductive consequences are not tested by any evidence.

In the cases where the agreement of a hypothesis with evidence is not a matter of degree, but a matter of dichotomic yes or no, the same inductive arbitrariness that has been described above takes a slightly different aspect. Often, more than one hypothesis, indeed possibly infinitely many hypotheses, agree perfectly with the available body of evidence. The difference in hypotheses often can be reduced to the difference in predicate used in generalizing the available cases of evidence. Then, the choice among the hypotheses with perfect evidential agreement becomes a matter of choice among the predicates. This is very much the same situation we encountered with respect to the choice of predicate in pattern recognition we discussed in the last chapter. Human intelligence shows an inherited (yet empirically developed through evolution) wisdom in choice of predicate in generalizing the evidential confirmation. This wisdom is obviously extra-logical and extra-evidential and gives a guide in the face of inductive arbitrariness.

The factors mentioned above, which are extraneous to the "necessary relation" between the hypothesis and the evidence, are certainly the most common source of inductive ambiguities, but there is another kind of inductive ambiguity which may be considered separately. The above introduced factors affect the evaluation of the hypotheses, but in order to evaluate them, we shall first have to produce them, because evidently the hypotheses are inscribed nowhere in nature so that we can read them. The act of generating hypotheses, which may be called abduction to borrow Charles Peirce's terminology, is usually excluded from the theorization of inductive process. Some people believe that it is an unpredictable act of genius outside the realm of rational formulation. Some other people claim that it is a mechanical process, which grinds out all possible hypotheses one by one. Neither of these two extreme views seems to correspond to the actual process of hypotheses generation or abduction. Poincaré's view about the invention in mathematics suggests the existence of an esthetic referee guarding the threshold between the conscious and the unconscious admitting into the conscious only those hypotheses presented by the unconscious which have esthetic appeal. Undeniably, there is a certain element of truth in this conjecture in the sense that abduction is not a purely logical or necessary process. The abduction is another aspect of inductive arbitrariness, because we cannot generate or handle all possible hypotheses, and the choice of those which are actually placed for evaluation is made in a highly contingent fashion. We shall discuss more about this later.

We would like to comment on the fact that the existence of inductive ambiguity becomes a very simple matter if we consider the problem in reference to the lattice structure of predicates we used in connection with the theorem of the Ugly Duckling. In a given set of N data points, each falling on one of its lattice-theoretic atoms, let P be the disjunction of these N atoms. The inductive generalization is any predicate Q which is implied by P. There are obviously 2^{n-N} such possible generalizations, where n is the number of independent atoms in the lattice. The inductive ambiguity corresponds to the arbitrariness of choice of one among these 2^{n-N} alternatives. The difficulty lies of course also in determining the set of n atoms.

5.2 PATTERN RECOGNITION AS AN INDUCTIVE PROCESS

It is often pointed out that pattern recognition is a special kind of induction, but no serious efforts have been made to examine how the various aspects of pattern recognition fit in the general framework of inductive inference. The purpose of this section is to try to do just that, based upon the mathematical model of induction previously proposed by the author [W-10, W-13, W-23, W-51] and explained in the last section. It is hoped that such an attempt will benefit both the abstract study of inductive inference in general and the practical exploration of methods of pattern recognition. Since the time of David Hume [H-6] inductive inference has been known to be a non-necessary inference, hence pattern recognition cannot be free from arbitrary elements inherent in any inductive inference. It is then very important in a methodological study to clarify how the inductive arbitrariness creeps into the method, and what kind of guiding principle of non-logical nature is actually practiced to make the method work as a technique.

We shall refer to the mathematical model of induction of the last section and try to interpret the process of pattern recognition according to this model, exposing the junctures where the inductive ambiguities occur.

Inductive inference is, in a certain sense, the inverse process of deductive inference. We will start our discussion with a brief sketch of deductive inference which involves three components: 1. Hypothesis or Law H_j, $j=1, 2, \ldots, N$; 2. Auxiliary Condition A_k, $k=1, 2, \ldots, M$; and 3. Experimental Data D_i, $i=1, 2, \ldots, n$. For example, H_j could be a dynamical law of some kind, and A_k could be the initial and boundary conditions, and D_i may be the final condition to be predicted on the ground of H_j and A_k. In another example, hypothesis H_j may predict that an animal of a certain given species has probability 1/2 of having red eyes (D_1) and the probability 1/2 of having blue eyes (D_2). A_k may state that a particular object O at hand is a (randomly taken sample of) animal of this particular species. The deductive consequence is that object O has an equal probability of being red eyed and blue eyed. In a still simpler example, H_j may state that all men are mortal, A_k may state that Socrates is a man, and these two premises give probability one to the particular D_i which says that Socrates is mortal. The basic task of deduction is, then, the calculation of probability $p(D_i|H_j \cap A_k)$, or, in the categorical case, the determination of the D_i which makes the probability one.

Generally, this conditional probability must be averaged with the help of the probability $p(H_j \cap A_k)$ to obtain the most probable D_i. But in many practical cases, this last probability can be replaced by $p(H_j) \cdot P(A_k)$ where $p(H_j)$ is assumed to be unity for a particular H_j because it is taken for a law, and $p(A_k)$ is assumed to be unity because it is an observed fact. In any event, we see that the general theory must be based on the probability measure $p(H_j \cap A_k \cap D_i)$ defined on the product space $\{H_j\} \times \{A_k\} \times \{D_i\}$, where $\{H_j\}$ is the set of hypotheses at hand, $\{A_k\}$ is the set of possible auxiliary conditions, and $\{D_i\}$ is the set of possible outcomes.

In the usual inductive inference, we are first given D_i and A_k, and we are interested in guessing the right H_j, i.e., we are interested in evaluating the inverse conditional probability $p(H_j|D_i \cap A_k)$. In a second type of inductive inference, we are given D_i and H_j, and we are interested in deriving $p(A_k|D_i \cap H_j)$. In the third type of inductive inference we are given only D_i, and we are interested in deriving $p(A_k \cap H_j|D_i)$.

In the first type of induction, we can assume one particular A_k to be the case, hence we can write $p_k(H_j|D_i) = p(H_j|D_i \cap A_k)$, which assigns an a posteriori probability (in the sense of "after the experience of D_i") to hypothesis H_j. This is an act of hypothesis evaluation. This inductive conditional probability, or credibility, is connected with the corresponding deductive probability $p_k(D_i|H_j) = p(D_i|H_j \cap A_k)$ by the well-known Bayes formula.

$$p_k(H_j|D_i) = \frac{p_k(D_i|H_j)p_k(H_j)}{\sum\limits_{\ell} p_k(D_i|H_\ell)p_k(H_\ell)} = \frac{p_k(D_i|H_j)p_k(H_j)}{p_k(D_i)} \tag{5.2.1}$$

The most important fact concerning this Bayes formula is that the deductive conditional probability $p_k(D_i|H_j)$ satisfies the Keynesian postulate, because it is determined solely by the definition of H_j and D_i, whereas the inductive conditional probability $p_k(H_j|D_i)$ does not satisfy the postulate because it depends on the prior probability $p_k(H_j)$ and the denominator $p_k(D_i)$. It is rather surprising that this mathematical formula agrees with our general remarks about the extra-evidential factors, because it provides a place, namely, the prior probability, where we can include these factors in the evaluation of a given hypothesis. Moreover, the effect of other competing hypotheses can reflect itself through the denominator (see [W-10] for more details and (1) of Section 5.1).

Except for these extra-evidential factors, the two conditional probabilities are proportional to each other giving a certain justification to the so-called likelihood approach, which consists of ignoring the difference in the prior probabilities (see Section 8.4). A special case of this last remark is the fact that the formula incorporates the condition of logical refutation (infirmation). If the hypothesis H_j gives probability zero to D_i and if this D_i nevertheless happens, the credibility of H_j becomes zero. Other than the case of infirmation, the likelihood method has only a poor excuse that "we don't know how to do it better." It can be easily shown that we can use (5.2.1) successively in a sequential experimentation by substituting the a posteriori probability of a stage for the a priori probability of the next stage, thus "improving" the evaluation of the hypothesis. As the number of stages increases, the influence of the prior probability of H_j on the a posteriori probability of H_j decreases, yet insofar as the experience is finite, the prior probability can always offset the evidential factor [W-23] (see also the next section).

The task of pattern recognition is obviously closely related to the inductive inference, but it has its own peculiarity. Suppose that H_j states that each member of class I has probability $f^j{}_I(D_i)$ of giving experimental result (a representation vector) D_i, and each member of class II has probability $f^j{}_{II}(D_i)$ of giving experimental result D_i. The content of H_j expressed by $f^j{}_k(D_i)$ may be called a statistical definition of class k. Let A_I state that an object O at hand belongs to class I and A_{II} state that O belongs to class II. The deductive probability of object O having the experimental value D_i is then given by $p(D_i) = \sum_j \sum_k p(D_i|A_k \cap H_j)p(A_k \cap H_j) = \sum_j [f^j{}_I(D_i)p(A_I) + f^j{}_{II}(D_i)p(A_{II})]p(H_j)$. When A_k is given, we may write $p_k(D_i) = \sum_j p_k(D_i|H_j)p(H_j)$ where $p_k(D_i|H_j)$ is either $f^j{}_I(D_i)$ or $f^j{}_{II}(D_i)$ depending on K = I or k = II.

During the so-called training period, the classifier, human or machine, is shown a D_i with its class affiliation, i.e., A_k. The effect of the training lies in the evaluation of hypothesis H_j by the Bayesian rule (5.2.1) in which the probabilities have now to be interpreted respectively as the probabilities of hypothesis $p(H_j)$, and the deductive distribution functions, $f^j{}_k(D_i)$. The formula expresses the "improvement" of the quality of the credibility through the experimental facts, $(D_i \cap A_k)$. In the training period, this process of improvement goes on sequentially.

When we come to the application period of the pattern recognition process, the classifier is given D_i and is asked the probability of its class-affiliation A_k, i.e., it is required to evaluate $p(A_k|D_i)$ which would be given by

$$p(A_k|D_i) = \frac{\sum_j p(D_i|A_k \cap H_j)p(H_j)p(A_k)}{\sum_j \sum_k p(D_i|A_k \cap H_j)p(H_j)p(A_k)}. \qquad (5.2.2)$$

This is a case of the second type of inductive inference mentioned above. In a usual pattern recognition algorithm only one H_j is taken as true at one time; as a result, we do not question the probability $p(H_j)$ and use $p(A_k|D_i) = p_j(D_i|A_k)p(A_k)/\sum_k p_j(D_i|A_k)p(A_k)$ instead of (5.2.2).

We may rationalize this procedure by saying that the hypothesis that receives the highest a posteriori credibility during the training period by (5.2.1) is assumed to be the law in the application period. But, this is not justifiable from a more fundamental point of view, and the $p(H_j)$ of (5.2.2) should be equated to the last stage a posteriori probability $p_k(H_j|D_i)$ of the training period. The evaluation of credibility of H_j, even after accumulation of experimental facts, ultimately depends on the original extra-evidential evaluation of H_j, hence it is not determined by the experimental data only. Usually the prior probability of class $p(A_k)$ is taken from the actual relative frequency of members of class I and members of class II in the training period. But, this also is not always justifiable. In fact, the known class-samples and the unknown class-samples may be taken from two different populations. In general, being a prior probability, $p(A_k)$ can reflect also all other considerations that the classifier may have and has not necessarily determined value.

This analysis shows that pattern recognition actually involves two stages of inductive inference of different kinds, and inevitably extra-evidential, non-necessary factors are involved in each stage. The usual method of pattern recognition is so formulated that these inductive ambiguities are entirely invisible.

As we shall state more clearly later, the assumptions that there exists such a thing as a distribution (density) function for the samples of a class and that we can evaluate such a function with reliability from a small number of samples are quite dubious; these doubts can also be thrown against the inductive model of pattern recognition described above. But, what I intended in this Section was to expose, in addition to these doubts, what the usual statistical methods tend to hide, i.e., inductive ambiguities in pattern recognition.

We shall now study the problem of clustering. By clustering we mean the task of grouping a given set of objects into a certain number of subsets, whereby nothing more than the properties of each object is known. The subsets here are required to be created in such a way that members of the same subset are tied together more intensely by some kind of bond than members of different subsets. In the case of pattern recognition, on the other hand, the number of classes and a certain number of paradigms, i.e., class-samples, are first given (in the training stage), and other objects are later given (in the application stage) without class-assignments. The classifier is then required to place these late-comers into the classes which have been exemplified by the paradigms. In reference to the mathematical model, pattern recognition assumes that the classifier knows at least the number of classes with certainty, and also, more or less distinctly, the set $\{H_j\}$ of competitive hypotheses, i.e., possible statistical definitions of classes. In the clustering problem, we have to create both of these, hence its task is abductive, according to Peirce's terminology. For this reason, clustering involves further inductive ambiguities over and above those involved in pattern recognition. Since the nature of "hypotheses" in the classification problem is different from the hypotheses as candidate natural laws in science, the ambiguity which arises in clustering has its own peculiarities.

The bond by which members of a class are supposed to cohere may be of a different nature: similarity, contrast, triangular relation, etc. But, since the majority of problems of clustering is based on the bilateral relation of similarity, we shall limit the following discussion here to the case of similarity, although we can extend a similar discussion easily to more complicated kinds of multilateral relations. If the definition of similarity can be made now on a purely logical basis, then we shall have to acknowledge that there is a certain logical, hence necessary, ground for the abductive phase of clustering. But, as we have seen, there is no logical basis in the idea of similarity.

Similarity depends on the purpose for which we use the classification, and the classification depends on the concept of similarity. Clearly, this looks like a vicious circle, but the solution is that we can in principle evaluate the quality of a classification by its utility, and the concept of similarity is indirectly evaluated through it. But, this process is doubly laden with ambiguity. First, utility depends on the purpose which varies according to the circumstances, and second, even if the purpose is fixed, there is no unique way of measuring utility quantitatively. Above and beyond this theoretical ambiguity, we have to mention the ambiguity in the practical circumstances. We usually measure the dissimilarity by the Euclidian distance in a space subtended by accidentally available measurements. The choice of variables is entirely arbitrary. Thus, the abduction involved in clustering is not only laden with the difficulties inherent in any abduction, but is further troubled by difficulties peculiar only to clustering.

In the above discussion, we have slightly over-simplified the problem, giving probably the impression that clustering is purely an abduction and pattern recognition is purely a double induction. In actual problems, these two aspects are usually intermingled. For instance, the training period of the parametric approach to pattern recognition may be described as evaluation of the members of a well-defined set $\{H_j\}$ of hypotheses, but the non-parametric approach does not always assume a well-defined set $\{H_j\}$, and includes often an abductive aspect in itself.

Since we have studied the general nature of pattern recognition and clustering, let us go a little farther into the techniques of pattern recognition and discuss where ambiguities occur. As we have seen in the foregoing, the training period can be described as a stage where the inductive probability of the first kind $p(H_j|D_i \cap A_k)$ is determined. If each object is represented by an n-component vector x, then D_i is a point in the corresponding n-dimensional space. A_k designates the class to which this point belongs. In some cases, A_k can be considered as the (n + 1)st component of the vector. In many practical problems, we do not need to know the exact value of the probability $p(H_j|D_i \cap A_k)$, but only to obtain the particular H_j that would maximize this probability. The estimation of the values of parameters in the parametric approach can be considered as doing just that. In this case, the set $\{H_j\}$ is well-defined in such a way that for each k, $p(D_i|H_j \cap A_k) = p(x|H_j \cap A_k)dx$ is a function of a given type containing yet-to-be-determined parameters which depend on H_j. The most plausible values of parameters may be interpreted as those which maximize

$p(H_j|x \cap A_k)$. This process involves a basic indeterminacy, because the value of the prior credibility $p(H_j)$ cannot be determined on a necessary basis. We usually camouflage this indeterminacy by giving an equal (or almost equal) value to all $p(H_j)$.

In the application stage, we are concerned with the inductive probability of the second kind $\sum_j p(A_k|H_j \cap D_i)p(H_j)$ or simply $p_j(A_k|D_i) = p(A_k|H_j \cap D_i)$ with the H_j which has the highest credibility at the moment. In this expression, the D_i is the vector of the new object whose class-belonging is yet to be determined. If there are only two classes I and II, the probability of the object belonging to class I is larger than the probability of its belonging to class II if and only if

$$f(x) = \frac{p(I|H_j \cap x)}{p(II|H_j \cap x)} > 1. \tag{5.2.3}$$

If the loss due to "misclassifying" an object of class I into class II is larger than the loss due to "misclassifying" an object of class II into class I, then one would classify the object to class I if and only if

$$f(x) > \theta \tag{5.2.4}$$

with θ less than unity. In the opposite case, θ must be larger than unity. If the loss function is known, then θ can be determined. The border surface, or "decision function"

$$f(x) - \theta = 0 \tag{5.2.5}$$

depends on the loss. The loss means the negative of utility and is dependent on the usage for which the classification is made. Here is another juncture where the logical indeterminacy resides.

After we have decided on a value of θ, we can replace $f(x) - \theta$ by the simplest possible function $g(x)$ such that the three conditions $g(x) \gtreqless 0$ coincide with the three conditions $f(x) - \theta \gtreqless 0$. For instance, if $p(I|H_j \cap x)$ and $p(II|H_j \cap x)$ are linear in x (within a certain domain of x), then f(x) is not linear, but we can readily find a linear function g(x). If we assume that g(x) is linear, quadratic, etc., in x, it results in restricting the class of possible H_j's. The limitation of H_j to a certain class represents an extra-evidential arbitrary choice which is another aspect of inductive indeterminacy.

We will now summarize the inductive aspect of pattern recognition and show more intuitively the inductive ambiguity and its usual rescue practiced in pattern recognition. We will limit the summary to the case of paradigm-oriented pattern recognition of two classes: Class I and Class II.

We are given two groups of paradigm points, each point being labeled either class I or class II. Starting from the finite number of given examples, we are asked to divide the entire space, which is a set of infinite number of points. This involves a task of infinite ambiguity because it is an inductive process. It is like figuring out an entire image, basing oneself on a few strokes painted by an artist. We have to figure out an n-dimensional "form" or "order" from zero-dimensional token points.

If it were possible, we might introduce a transformation of n variables, such that in the new variables the paradigm points of each group become located close together, and the distance between these two small regions becomes very large. However, theoretically there are an infinite number of possible transformations, and practically it is very difficult to find a simple transformation which does this. Instead of introducing an n-dimensional transformation, the practitioners of pattern recognition often project the n-dimensionally scattered paradigm groups on a less-than-n dimensional subspace such that in this subspace, the points are more "orderly" distributed, in the sense that points of each class are aggregated together whereas points of different classes are segregated far apart. Such a transformation is a first step in seeing an "order" in the given data. We shall analyze the idea of "order" in the next section. This is an extra-logical, extra-evidential guiding principle used in overcoming the enormous ambiguity in the inductive process called pattern recognition.

In the case of the actual historical development of scientific theories, we noticed that the inductive ambiguity does not trouble the scientists, because it is difficult to produce even a single hypothesis satisfying evidence and the requirement of coherence, which the latter, in the main, is an extra-evidential, extra-logical guideline. In the case of pattern recognition, the inductive ambiguity usually leaves a tremendous field of freedom of choice.

The next step in the pattern recognition, after the variables are so chosen that some degree of order is established, is to divide the territory in two, when the number of classes is two. Here, the principle of simplicity is often applied, sometimes successfully. But, there is no guarantee of success. The simplest method would be to divide the n-dimensional by an (n-1)-dimensional hyperplane. In the case of two dimensions this method defines a straight line. If a hyperplane does not work, they might try a second-order (n-1)-dimensional hypersurface, etc. It is easily expected that, if we insist on a low-order hypersurface, the separation might violate some of the class-designation of paradigms. It is often left to the good sense of the researcher to make a compromise between the dictate of paradigms and the principle of simplicity, another judgment outside the realm of evidence and logic.

See [W-52] for a method of reducing clustering problems to a method of paradigm-oriented pattern recognition. See [W-53] for a method of reducing pattern recognition problems to a clustering problem.

5.3 LEARNING AS PATTERN FORMATION

Learning is a process in which the response behavior converges to one of the alternative possibilities when a subject is placed in a repetitive environment. Before the learning process sets in, the response behavior usually shows randomness or disorderliness, but in the measure as learning progresses, the behavior starts to show some set pattern leading to a unique response category.

It is often said that learning is a convergence of response pattern toward the "right" response alternative. But, this statement contains two judgments, one descriptive, the other evaluative. The purely behavioral description should limit itself to the convergence to one of the many categories.

Whether the observer calls this alternative a right one or a wrong one is a subjective, often anthropomorphic after-thought having nothing to do with the essence of learning process. Learning a "wrong" response is also a learning. The observer should, rather, learn that the response pattern to which the living organism converges usually reveals the hidden "value" dictated by the purpose of survival.

It is easy to expect that learning as convergence of behavior to one of the alternative behavioral categories can be characterized as a decrease of entropy, if this quantity is defined in terms of relative frequencies of different alternatives taken by the subject. The basic idea of learning as an entropy-decreasing process was introduced by the present author in a 1962 paper [W-36].

What is important is the fact that if we take a different set of response categories even in an obvious process of learning, we lose sight of a process of behavioral convergence. Imagine that we categorize a rat's behavior in a T-maze experiment by the evenness and oddness of the number of steps it makes in the passage, instead of the left turns and right turns, we would see no convergence of response pattern. Therefore a learning process cannot be characterized as an entropy-decreasing phenomenon with respect to an arbitrary set of behavioral categories. Rather, a learning process is to be characterized by the existence of a particular set of behavioral categories, by the use of which we can observe a convergence of response, or an entropy decrease. In other words, we have to formulate our conceptual framework so as to see a certain pattern, or regularity, or order in the behavior. Learning theory must be therefore concerned primarily with the conceptual adaptation which enables the observer to see the convergence of response.

The same is true with pattern recognition in general. We have to formulate our conceptual framework in order to see a form, order, regularity or pattern in a collection of data.

Now we can recognize two kinds of learning: behavioral and cognitive. The former includes all learning processes of animals and skill learning of humans. Learning at school where the progress of learning is tested by a multiple-choice type examination is a typical case of cognitive learning. If we characterize the learning process by the behavioral categories of marking a check on one of the different alternatives on the answer sheet, we can classify the cognitive learning as a special case of behavioral convergence. However, we do not need necessarily to reduce the cognitive learning to a behavioral learning, and we can set up a mathematical model of cognitive learning interpreting the latter as a convergence of selection of hypothesis in the inductive process.

The mathematical proof of an entropy decrease in inductive learning through the application of the Bayesian formulae to a repetitive environment was given in 1960 [W-13]. The same principle of entropy-decrease was then experimentally verified in the non-cognitive learning [W-36].

We shall now reproduce the outline of the mathematical theory of entropy convergence in the case of Bayesian learning. Assume that we have a set of hypotheses, $\mathcal{H} = \{H_1, H_2, \ldots, H_N\}$, a set of auxiliary facts, $A = \{A_1, A_2, \ldots, A_M\}$ and a set of possible experimental data $\mathcal{D} = \{D_1, D_2, \ldots, D_n\}$. The hypothesis usually determines the method of calculating the deductive probabilities $p(D_i|H_j \cap A_k)$. Induction is an inverse process, i.e., calculating the posteriori probability, $p(H_j|D_i \cap A_k)$, on the basis of obtained experimental results. In simple cases, the element A_k is fixed and the deductive probability given by the hypothesis H_j can be written $p(D_i|H_j)$, and the goal of induction is to derive the inverse conditional probability:

$$p(H_j|D_i) = \frac{p(D_i|H_j)p(H_j)}{\sum_{k=1}^{n} p(D_i|H_k)p(H_k)} \quad . \qquad (5.3.1)$$

Here $p(H_j)$ is the a priori probability, or the prior probability, which measures the degree of confidence attached to the hypothesis H_k on the ground of different considerations outside the experimental data D_i. It is this prior probability that reflects our extra-logical, extra-evidential consideration. The principle of simplicity, for instance, tends to give a large prior probability to a "simple" hypothesis.

Suppose we are placed in a repetitive environment such that the experimental D_i appears with empirical probability γ_i.

Suppose we repeat the same experiments ν times and we obtain the results, $D^{(1)}, D^{(2)}, \ldots D^{(\nu)}$, each of which is a member of the set $\mathcal{D}$. We write ν_i the number of the results D_i in the sequence, $D^{(1)}, D^{(2)}, \ldots D^{(\nu)}$, so that $\sum_{i=1}^{n} \nu_i = \nu$. If we write $\alpha_i = \nu_i/\nu$, we obtain by the repeated use of formula (5.3.1)

$$p^{(\nu)}(H_j|\alpha_1,\alpha_2,\ldots,\alpha_n) = \frac{\prod_{i=1}^{n} [p(D_i|H_j)]^{\alpha_i \nu} p(H_j)}{\sum_{k=1}^{N} \prod_{i=1}^{n} [p(D_i|H_k)]^{\alpha_i \nu} p(H_k)} . \tag{5.3.2}$$

Due to the law of large number, we shall have

$$\lim_{\nu \to \infty} \alpha_i = \gamma_i , \tag{5.3.3}$$

where γ_i is the probability with which the result D_i is produced in our experiment. γ_i is the limiting relative frequency.

If we replace α_i for a finite ν by its limiting value γ_i, we can demonstrate the average inverse H-theorem which says

$$\frac{d\bar{S}^{(\nu)}}{d\nu} \leq 0 \quad \text{for } \nu > \nu_0 , \tag{5.3.4}$$

where ν_0 is a certain number and $\bar{S}$ is the "average" $(\alpha_i = \gamma_i)$ of

$$S^{(\nu)} = - \sum_{j=1}^{N} p^{(\nu)}(H_j|\alpha) \log p^{(\nu)}(H_j|\alpha) . \tag{5.3.5}$$

The denominator in (5.3.2) is independent of H_j and serves only the purpose of normalization. We have therefore

$$\log p^{(\nu)}(H_j|\alpha) = \nu \sum_{i=1}^{n} \alpha_i \log p(D_i|H_j) + \log p(H_j) + \text{const.} \tag{5.3.6}$$

We can draw two important conclusions from this formula: (1) The effect of the prior probability becomes weaker and weaker as we increase ν, but on the other hand, (2) Insofar as ν is finite, we can undo the empiric effect expressed by the first term by changing the values of the prior probabilities.

It is interesting to note that by adding a constant term $-\nu \sum_{i=1}^{n} \alpha_i \log \alpha_i$, which does not depend on H_j, we can write the first term of (5.3.6) in the form

$$-\nu \sum_{i=1}^{n} \alpha_i \log[\alpha_i/p(D_i|H_j)] = \nu V[\alpha, p(D|H_j)], \tag{5.3.7}$$

where

$$V(p,w) = -\sum_i p_i \log(p_i|w_i). \tag{5.3.8}$$

The convenience of the V-function will be explained in the next chapter. If there is only one hypothesis H_k such that

$$\underset{j}{\text{Min}}\, V[\gamma, p(D|H_j)] = V[\gamma, p(D|H_k)] \tag{5.3.9}$$

the entropy defined in (5.3.5) will obey the law

$$\lim_{\nu \to \infty} \bar{S}^{(\nu)} \to 0. \tag{5.3.10}$$

We can conclude that if there is one, and only one, hypothesis H_k that predicts the probability $p(D_i|H_k)$ equal to the given relative frequency γ_i for all empirical results, i.e., for all i, then the confidence we place on this hypothesis H_k becomes in the long run unity. This fact can be interpreted as a derivation or justification of the "frequency view" of probability from the "subjective view" of probability. The reverse derivation, i.e., an acceptable justification of the subjective view from the frequency view of probability is unknown to the author. From the purely subjective point of view, the quantity $p(D_i|H_k)$ is also the degree of confidence of obtaining the experimental result D_i, but by the convergence theorem, it becomes justifiable to interpret $p(D_i|H_k)$ as relative frequency γ_i. Another approach to make the subjective probability empirically measurable has been developed by Toda and Finetti (see [W-10] for the literature on this matter).

We have learned three important lessons in this section. First, in the learning process, we can observe a gradual formation of pattern or organization in the response-behavior, which before the onset of learning shows chaos or disorganization. Second, this possibility of observing the formation of behavioral pattern depends critically on the categories that we use in describing the behaviors. Therefore, the detection of pattern depends on a conceptual adaptation to the process we observe. Third, the existence of pattern can be expressed by a small value of entropy and the formation of pattern by the decrease of entropy.

5.4 PRINCIPLE OF SIMPLICITY

In Section 5.1 we saw that in pattern recognition and induction, a special kind of ambiguity is inevitable and that in order to obtain a solution we have to use a heuristic guideline, such as the principle of simplicity, which can claim neither a unique nor universal validity. We want to examine in this section a simple case of application of the principle of simplicity and show that the principle can be formulated at least in this case as a principle of entropy minimization.

From the time life was created on earth, living organisms have been exposed to an excessive amount of complex information about the environment. Modern life is still the continuation of the same fight against complexity and abundance of information. The concept-formation or pattern recognition and the establishment of general laws have been a weapon serving to simplify the complexity and abundance in the sense that it bundles together many cases as a single item. The principle of simplicity can be considered as a habit developed through this mental process of simplification [W-38].

We consider the case where the experimental data are numerical values of a variable, say y, as a function of variable x. The "extraction" of formula $y = f(x)$ as a continuous function of x, when the number of data points is finite, is obviously an inductive process. The same process can be considered also as pattern recognition, where the given points are the paradigms and the formula $y = f(x)$ is a definition of the class for which this finite number of points serves as class samples. Usually, it is tacitly understood that the number of points is growing with time. Learning of the law, or definition of the class, is usually supposed to be tested by the future sample points. Thus, this problem often bears the significance of a forecast, as do all the inductive processes.

The question is to decide a function $y = f(x)$ such that

$$y_i = f(x_i) \qquad i=1,2,\ldots,N \qquad (5.4.1)$$

where the pair (x_i, y_i) is the i-th of the N given data points. In some cases, we can allow some "inaccuracy" Δx, Δy for the given data (5.4.1); however, we shall use the expression (5.4.1). If one chooses, one may understand the equality = in the approximate sense. The "evidence" for the induction is the data points (5.4.1).

Of course, there is a continuously infinite number of possible answers. But, we usually connect the points by a smooth curve provided the number of points is large enough. This last condition may be interpreted as meaning, for instance, that the distance between x_i and the next point x_{i+1} is sufficiently small so that a drastic change of the value of y between y_i and y_{i+1} is not likely to happen, whereby "drastic change" means, for instance, that the change is comparable with or larger than $(y_{i+1}-y_i)$. This condition is a guess of extra-evidential nature, and there is no guarantee that this condition will be satisfied for the future arrivals.

What is meant by "smooth"? A smooth curve may be paraphrased also as a simple curve. If we allow a rapidly changing curve, it is not a simple solution, in the sense that there are a great number of rapidly changing curves. We may note that a smooth curve has fewer concrete cases than a rugged curve. The principle of simplicity is at work in the sense that the class of a smooth curve has a smaller extension. Indeed, the smooth, simple curve has larger intension because the restricting conditions for such a curve are greater.

To make the problem simpler, let us assume not only that f(x) is a single-valued function, but also that it is a polynomial, i.e., it is a solution of the equation

$$\frac{d^s y}{dx^s} = 0 \cdot \tag{5.4.2}$$

The hypotheses from among which we are supposed to choose one is of the type: f(x) is a solution of (5.4.2) with a fixed s, and satisfies the given conditions (5.4.1). That is, all the hypotheses in competition have the same degree of confirmation by the evidence; the only deciding factor is the extra-logical, extra-evidential consideration. Let us assume as the guiding principle in this selection the principle of simplicity, which, on the level of ordinary language, would advise us to choose the smallest value of s which is compatible with the N given restrictions. We will now give a mathematical interpretation to this guiding principle.

The extension of a hypothesis can be characterized by the entropy function

$$S = -\sum_{i=1}^{n} p_i \log p_i \ , \tag{5.4.3}$$

where p_i is the weight the hypothesis places on the i-th particular case included in the hypotheses, with i=1,2,...,n, where n is the number of particular cases allowed by the hypotheses. If all the particular cases have the same weight, S becomes the Hartley type entropy

$$S = \log n \ , \tag{5.4.4}$$

which corresponds to the (logarithmic) extension introduced in the last chapter.

Now, the solution of (5.4.2) with a fixed s has the form

$$y = \sum_{i=0}^{s-1} a_i x^i \tag{5.4.5}$$

allowing for s constants a_i. If we allow a_i to have a continuous value we cannot handle it in the framework of the usual information theory. Therefore, let us assume there is an inevitable inaccuracy for a_i and an upper and lower limit for its values, so that the total number of possible values of each a_i is a fixed integer p. As a result, the number of possible curves for a fixed value of s, is p^s.

A more rigorous way to treat the entire matter is to replace the differential equation (5.4.1) by a difference equation and quantize the x-y-space into $p \times p$ meshes. The result is the same: the number of possible curves in the quantized space obeying the difference equation of the s-th order is p^s (see [W-10]).

The logarithmic extension of the hypothesis is therefore

$$S = s \log p \ . \tag{5.4.6}$$

The proportionality of this entropy to s is understandable, because we shall have to specify s initial values to choose one out of p^s curves (5.4.5) which are allowed.

If there are N experimental data points, the curve has to pass these N points. This represents N constraints on the curve (5.4.1). If $s > N$, there is always a solution or solutions for a_i, $i = 0,1,\ldots,s-1$. If the N equations of (5.4.1) for the a_i's are linearly independent, the number of the curves obeying the hypothesis and the constraints becomes p^{s-N}. The corresponding entropy will then be

$$S = (s-N) \log p \ . \tag{5.4.7}$$

In case there is dependence among N equations, we need only to count the number of linearly independent equations as N in this equation.

The principle of minimum entropy will advise us to choose the hypothesis for which this entropy is the smallest, i.e., the one with the smallest s, because p and N are given. The degree of polynomials corresponding to the hypothesis is (s-1) at most. Therefore, the principle of minimum entropy can be translated as the principle of simplicity, because the smaller the degree (s-1) of polynomial, the simpler and the "smoother" the curve will be. The conclusion is the same whether we take (5.4.7) or (5.4.6) as the expression of the entropy.

It is interesting to consider the probability of error brought about by assuming the hypothesis. (1) If the hypothesis is correct, (2) if there are N experimental data points, (3) if there is only one "correct" polynomials curve, (4) if we can assume that all of the p^{s-N} curves are equally probable, then the probability that the chosen curve among the p^{s-N} possible ones is the correct one is $1/p^{s-N}$. This means that the smaller the value (s-1), the larger the probability of obtaining the correct answer. In other words, the principle of minimum entropy leads to the minimum error probability. But, this is not an interesting fact because we are interested in the probability of correctness of <u>the hypothesis</u>, and not in the probability of correctness of <u>a single possible curve</u>, allowed by the hypothesis.

But if we are interested in the probability of a curve allowed by the hypothesis, and if we are perfectly sure that the hypothesis is correct, then it is in general true that a concrete case obeying a hypothesis with small extension, i.e., with small entropy is more desirable, in the sense that the probability of error of the concrete case is small. But this does not seem to be a correct argument for the principle of simplicity. The idea of justifying the principle of simplicity on the ground of probability of error was advanced by J. Pearl [P-7].

So far we have assumed the case $s > N$. But the case $N > s$ is equally important. In the former case, when N is given we can reduce s until $s = N$ following the advice of the minimum entropy principle. But if $N > s$, we encounter a new situation. It is obvious that when N is larger than s, it is easier to match the empirical data by a higher degree polynomial. If $N > s$, we cannot satisfy all N equations (5.4.1) with only s parameters a_i; we have to resort to a compromise, for instance, by minimizing the "total square error,"

$$\sum_{i=1}^{N} [y_i - f(x_i)]^2 \qquad (5.4.8)$$

where y_i is the experimental value and f(x) is the theoretical value obtained by (5.4.5). Obviously the "total mean square error" can be made smaller when we have more parameters to vary.

Of course, the minimum entropy principle will still advise us to take as small as possible a value of s, insofar as the total square error does not become too large. The factor that sways us from one side [error estimate (5.4.8)] to the other [small entropy (5.4.6)] is definitively the reliability of the experimental data y_i. The reasonable way to determine the value of y_i is to take the average of $\nu(>1)$ observed data of the variable at x_i. If ν is larger, the value of y_i becomes more reliable, and it would be wiser to decrease the total square error even at the expense of a larger value of s. But if ν is small, the decision by the least mean square error becomes unreliable, due to inevitable fluctuation. And in that case, we had better listen to the wisdom of the minimum entropy principle.

It should also be noted that as ν increases, the spurious fluctuations of y will decrease at a rate proportional to $1/\sqrt{\nu}$, and the requirement on f(x) due to (5.4.8) will become smoother and smoother, so that a fewer number of s will be required, in agreement with the principle of simplicity. This conclusion is very much analogous to the philosophy behind AIC which will be explained in Section 8.4.

In inductive inference and pattern recognition there cannot be any one "necessary" or "logical" choice that is left open by the confirmation or by the paradigms among many alternatives of generalization. The principle of simplicity adopted often in induction and pattern recognition is one of the possible guiding principles, but it is not backed by any guarantee of "correctness" although in many cases it proves to be successful, and it is "intuitively" suggested by extra-logical, extra-evidential consideration. Such a principle is typically a "heuristic" principle. The principle of simplicity was shown in this section to be formulatable as a principle of minimum entropy.

5.5 HEURISTIC PRINCIPLES IN ARTIFICIAL INTELLIGENCE

So far in this chapter we have emphasized the distinction between deduction and induction. After having made clear the basic difference in nature of the two processes, we have now to turn to the fact that in human thinking these two processes are complementary to each other and are necessarily needed almost simultaneously in solving problems.

In basically inductive processes, deductive elements intervene in two junctures. First, in any inductive creation and evaluation of hypotheses, we have always to keep in mind that only those hypotheses are acceptable that deductively imply, or deductively give non-zero probabilities to evidential facts. Secondly, as has been explained in connection with what is called infirmation, any hypothesis which implies non-occurrence of a certain fact has to be abandoned if this fact actually takes place. This second juncture is a purely logical reasoning, but need not be added ad hoc from outside to the inductive reasoning. Indeed, we have seen that the process of infirmation is automatically incorporated in the probabilistic model of induction.

In the basically deductive processes, inductive elements intervene for the following reasons [W-10]. In a typically deductive problem we are given a set of premises or axioms, a set of logical laws, and a theorem to be demonstrated. The task is to connect the axioms to the theorems starting from the axioms by a string of theorems that are deductively derivable with the help of logical laws from theorems that have already appeared in the string. If we construct all possible such strings that can sprout from the axioms, one must eventually end up with finding the theorem to be demonstrated on one of the strings. But, as the stage in the string increases, the strings fan out rapidly - roughly speaking, exponentially with the number of stages - into an enormous number of strings. As a result, it is, even with a very fast computer, impossible to check all possible strings. This "exponential" fanning out of deductive strings or deductive trees is a common phenomenon of all deductive tasks [W-58]. For instance, checker playing is strictly a deductive task. If we can check all possible developments of a game, we could, in principle, determine logically the best stratagem at the initial stage. But, according to Arthur Samuel's estimate in the 1960's, it would take 10^{40} centuries to check all possible developments with the best computer of that date [S-9].

One possible way to shorten the computing time is to produce "inductively" an intermediate goal from the final goal. In a theorem proving problem, we can inductively produce an intermediate theorem which would entail the final theorem. If this theorem can be connected to the axioms, then the problem is solved. This method of producing an intermediate goal was first introduced by Gelernter [G-1], in his geometry problem-solving program, and the inductive status of this production of the intermediate goal was clarified by the author [W-10]. The method was adopted later by Newell, Shaw, and Simon [N-3] and other authors of the so-called artificial intelligence programs. The production of an intermediate theorem from the final theorem is inductive in nature, therefore it cannot be free from inductive ambiguity and does not guarantee success of the stratagem. Accordingly, it is called a "heuristic" principle in the program. Most researchers are not aware that this "non-necessary" nature of the heuristic principle stems from the inductive ambiguity.

Artificial Intelligence (AI) is said to be an effort to emulate on the computer the human intellectual process in solving problems, and, through this effort, to study the nature and function of human intelligence. But workers in this field, in spite of some brilliant results on particular problems, usually exhibit the following characteristic shortcomings:

1. Do not clearly realize the basic distinction between induction and deduction, therefore, do not know what part of their programs

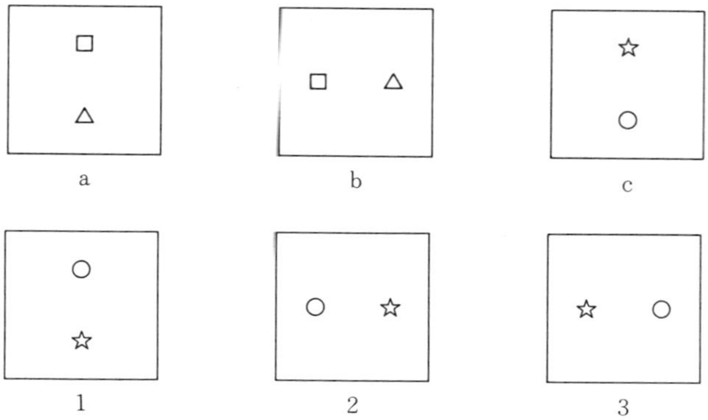

Figure 5.5.1 Which one (x) of six figures stands in the same relationship to (c) as figure (b) stands in relation to figure (a)? The obvious answer (3) is not a logical conclusion.

represents inductive and deductive processes.

2. Are usually trained strongly in logic and very poorly in natural sciences. Therefore, they emphasize the logical aspect, and suppress the inductive aspect of human reasoning.
3. Usually smuggle man-made heuristic rules or principles into the program, without saying so, then pretend that everything man can do can be done by a computer.
4. Are little concerned about a general theory and, with a few exceptions, their papers or books describe individual particular problem-solving algorithms.

Let us examine how AI is intimately related to pattern recognition and inductive ambiguity. One of the simplest examples is the problem of discovering similar relations. We are asked to find "x such that the relation of a to b is the same as the relation of c to x" in six pictures labeled a, b, c, 1, 2, 3, as shown in Figure 5.5.1. The "natural" answer is obviously "3."

To give a logical expression to this judgment, we could introduce the following 16 predicates p_{ij},

$i = 1, 2, 3, 4$; $j = 1, 2, 3, 4$, where p_{ij} is the conjunction of p_i and q_j defined by

p_1 = is a square
p_2 = is a triangle
p_3 = is a star
p_4 = is a circle
q_1 = occupies the upper position
q_2 = occupies the lower position
q_3 = occupies the left position
q_4 = occupies the right position

and

$$p_{ij} = p_i \cap q_j, \quad i = 1, 2, 3, 4, \quad j = 1, 2, 3, 4. \tag{5.5.2}$$

Let us introduce the propositions P and Q by

$$P = \text{One of the two objects is } p_{11} \cup p_{31}$$
$$Q = \text{One of the two objects is } p_{13} \cup p_{33} \tag{5.5.3}$$

Of course there is redundancy in the P_{ij}'s, due to the limited number of cases mentioned in Figure 5.5.1. For instance, P is equivalent to

$$P^* = \text{One of the two objects is } p_{22} \cup p_{42} \tag{5.5.4}$$

Since $P = P^* = P \cap^{\dagger} P^*$, we write only P.

Then, the relation of a to b as well as the relation of c to 3 is characterized as

$$P \rightarrow Q \tag{5.5.5}$$

But if we introduce

$$Q' = \text{One of the two objects is } p_{13} \cup p_{34} \tag{5.5.6}$$

† Here, $\cap$ is an exclusive disjunction.

then the relation of a to b is the same as the relation of c to 2: P → Q'. Therefore there is no logical ground why

a to b = c to 3   in compliance with (5.5.5)

should be preferred to

a to b = c to 2   in compliance with (5.5.6).

Yet, the choice (5.5.5) is "more natural" than (5.5.6). The reason why it looks more natural is that one tends to think of the transition a to b as a motion of the object "square" from the upper position to the left position (and a motion of the triangle from the lower position to the right position), and to require the object star to perform the same motion. This conforms with the habit generated with the usual solid physical objects which keep supposedly the squareness and starness throughout transition. This is an accidental habit contingent upon the usual concept of object and has nothing to do with logic or evidence. In short, this arbitrariness is a case of inductive arbitrariness, on the face of which, if a choice is made, it has an extra-evidential, extra-logical origin. The reader may have already noticed that the production of concept P from the paradigms a and c and the production of concept Q or Q' are typical cases of pattern recognition, as well as of inductive inference. The usual writings on AI not only ignore the inductive nature of the problem but also are unaware of logical ambiguity inherent in inductive reasoning. Worst of all, they do not confess their contraband of illogical biases.

Another typical case of AI is the game-playing programs such as for checkers and chess. The secret, introduced by Samuel [S-9], is the conversion of a deductive proposition that this situation is bound to win, to lose, or to be indecisive to an inductive proposition that we can attach such and such probability (degree of expectation) to the hypothesis that this board situation is leading to a win. The key to a success of such a program is, therefore, the evaluation function which is supposed to be proportional to the probability of wins. The reason why this probability is not a deductive probability but an inductive probability is that it is a variable which changes with accumulation of experience and it is not determined by the hypothesis itself.

The board-situation-evaluating function is usually assumed to be a linear function

$$v = \sum_{i=1}^{n} c_i y_i \qquad (5.5.7)$$

of a feature vector y_i with coefficients c_i. The choice of features y_i is made essentially by a study of human experience with the game. The values of c's are to be inductively determined by the experience, and a learning program was written by Samuel to change the values according to the experience. The machine can help calculate this suggested change, but the principle by which this change takes place is again man made.

If v of (5.5.7) is an instantaneous evaluation, there is also an accumulative evaluation. The method here can be said to be a partial return to the deductive nature of the problem. The computer surveys all the possible developments for a finite number of future steps. (If this number becomes infinite, the program would be deductive.) At each step, the opponent (human player) is assumed to play the best move (i.e. the most "unfavorable" for the computer program), and the computer is assumed to play the most "favorable" move for it. The "favorableness" of the last stage is evaluated by an instantaneous evaluation function. The assumption that the (human) opponent chooses the best move for him is a philosophy inherited from von Neumann's game theory and is not guaranteed to be fulfilled in reality.

There are records of past games in history, and some board situations are known to lead definitively to a win. These specially good board situations are used for two purposes. One, they are put in a read-only memory with the prescription as to how to proceed from there. Then the computer is supposed to look up the records, and switch to the prescriptions if the board situations are found to coincide with one of these specially good board situations. Two, the evaluation function (5.5.7) must be so adjusted that it gives its maximum or near-maximum values when the board situation is any one of these specially good ones.

Once the evaluation function is decided, the computer precedes mechanically (i.e., deductively) according to what the evaluation function dictates, but we should not forget that the evaluation function is the result of an inductive process and is not an infallible adviser.

There are several programs that aim at decreasing the distance or difference between the present intermediate stage and the final goal. But, the authors keep silence over the non-computer origin of the definition of the concept of distance or difference. One of the examples is the program called SAINT, written by Stagle [S-16], which allows the computer to perform indefinite integration.

The computer is given "standard forms" and "translation rules" in memory. When a problem in the form of an indefinite integral is given as an input, the computer applies to the integrand different transformations to bring it to a form that matches one or some of the standard formulae of indefinite integration. If the problem is solvable and if the allowed time is infinite, the computer could try all possible combinations of transformation rules to reach a form that coincides with one of the standard formulae, and the problem is solvable deductively. Since the allowable time is limited, the program has to resort to a heuristic method that is of extra-computer origin. In this program, it takes the form of a "degree of difficulty" (a kind of distance from the final goal) which is the integrated form. In Stagle's program, the degree of difficulty of an integrand is, 0, 1, 2, 3, etc., according as it is x, x^2, e^{x^2}, xe^{x^2}, etc. The number is of course arbitrary, but the choice of these categories (such as x^2, xe^{x^2}, etc.) is definitively a reflexian of inductive ambiguity. The degree of difficulty is defined as the largest of the degrees of difficulty of different terms that compose a complex integrand. The computer transforms the given original integrand into different forms, and then selects the least difficult one and pursues further transformation to make the difficulty still smaller. If this branch faces too high a difficulty, it goes back to another branch which was judged more difficult at the earlier stage. This is done in a fashion similar to the "mountain-climbing method" in the extremum problem, which never guarantees a success.

Another example is the well-publicized Newell-Shaw-Simon's GPS (general problem solver) [N-3]. This program uses what the authors call "mean-ends analysis," which compares the present step and the final goal and decides what to do in order to decrease the "difference." Here again, the categories by which the difference is observed and the degree of difference are defined by the programmer and not by the computer. It is well-known that this grandiloquent program is a very slow processor of problems.

An interesting program which is different in nature from these essentially deductive problem-solving ones is Buchanan et al. DENDRAL [B-11]. This program attempts to arrive at obtaining a chemical structure formula from the experimental data from mass spectrograms of chemical compounds. The chemical formula is supposed to be known but the structure is to be determined.

Even for relatively simple organic compounds, the valence-theoretically possible structures may be some thousands of structural formulae. Each of these thousands is a "hypothesis." The desired result is the most plausible hypothesis, in the presence of evidential data. Therefore the task is preeminently inductive. What the program does is to imitate a human chemist. The only shortcoming, from the methodological point of view, is that the authors do not specify what is confirmation, infirmation, and extra-evidential judgment, and what is machine feasible, what is man made.

The operation of the program attempts to reduce the number of acceptable hypotheses on the basis of the spectral data. For instance, some structures assume the existence of a certain subgroup of atoms that precludes certain spectral lines. If the precluded spectral peaks do exist, the assumed structure is infirmed. This is essentially the logical **refutation** of a hypothesis. On the affirmative side, the existence of certain spectral peaks is consistent with the existence of a certain type of substructure. This is a case of empirical confirmation of hypothesis with the use of a wide range of anterior knowledge. The program excludes also the structure which is unstable. This knowledge about stability and instability originates from a broad experience in chemistry and not the "evidence" which is the spectrum of the substance here. Therefore, this exclusion of a large number of hypotheses is extra-evidential, belonging to the domain of inductive ambiguity that is reflected in the prior probability of a hypothesis in the Bayesian model of inductions.

At the end of the program, only a few hypotheses will have survived the scrutiny. But, we have to know that a whole amount of human inductive knowledge outside the strict domain of evidential confirmation is put into the computer. The present author himself is also to be blamed, for in his paper on mechanical experiment on induction he kept silent on his smuggling into the computer of a human bias, in this case in the form of equal a priori probability on all the hypotheses [W-13].

Undoubtedly a great deal of valuable results in the area of AI has been obtained in the U.S. during about the last 20 years, but this success was marred by the over publicity and ungrounded claims made by the big centers at the earlier stage of development to attract research funds.

In order to secure, however, further growth of this field the researchers will have to become aware of the handicaps that are placed on the U.S. researcher due to his intellectual environment and heritage. For one thing, the empirical positivism, in spite of its undeniable contribution to the science of knowledge, preached three theses which have turned out to be harmful to the development of scientific epistemology: (1) R. Carnap confused probability with induction [C-5]; (2) R. Carnap held the necessary view of probability [C-5]; (3) K. Popper held that the scientific theories are selected only by the excluding process of infirmation [P-6]. If you combine (1) and (2), you are led to conclude that induction is a "necessary" process, therefore can be performed by the computer. The author remembers that he objected to Carnap precisely on these points as early as 1952 when Carnap gave a lecture on probability at the American Physical Society meeting in Chicago. As far as point three is concerned, infirmation is only a small portion of inductive process and that is the only one that can be done solely by logical machine. If this is taken as the whole story, the entire human science would become a very poor structure indeed.

Another heritage harmful to AI is the Deweyan pragmatism which otherwise did a great deal of good for the progress of technology. In an effort to emphasize the importance of "problem solving", the followers of Dewey's philosophy ignore the necessity to clarify the fundamentally important distinction between induction and deduction. The philosophical infantilism found in the works in the field of AI has a great deal to blame on the pragmatistic theory of knowledge.

CHAPTER 6
Pattern Recognition as Entropy Minimization

6.1 STRUCTURE AND ENTROPY

The aim of pattern recognition is to discover a form or more specifically, a structure, in a system consisting of partial subsystems. The antonym of form or structure is amorphism or chaos. The characteristic of something chaotic or amorphous is that the knowledge of the state of a partial subsystem does not give any clues regarding the state of other parts of the same whole system. The existence of a form or structure or pattern, therefore, presupposes the interdependence or correlation or cooperation of subsystems. Of course, the mere existence of such a structure does not guarantee a successful discovery of the structure. Hence, pattern recognition requires, as was emphasized earlier, a mental adaptation to make such a structure emerge in our perception or in a mechanical simulation thereof.

In recent years, a great deal of attention has been directed toward structured systems, physical or biological. We can conveniently trace the origin of this interest back to two, more or less disparate, roots: the structure-generating nature of living organisms which seems "to climb uphill the slope that the innert matter descends" [B-6, W-42] and the "cooperative" properties manifested by physical objects that are the opposite of chaos, whereby the chaos is ideally typified by the ideal gas. The first root goes back at least to 1907 when Henri Bergson published his famous *Évolution Créatrice*. One of the most conspicuous events along the second root may be Heisenberg's theory of ferromagnetism of 1929, according to which magnetization is due to parallel alignment of tiny magnetic zones in which the electron spins are parallel [H-8]. Other than ferromagnetism, the cooperative phenomena included crystalline structure, phase transition, superconductivity, and others.

In the postwar years, these two areas seem to approach each other, or at least, to have an overlapping subdomain, and they became subjects of study of what is nowadays called thermodynamics of dispersive systems [G-4], or synergetics [H-9]. The researchers in this field noticed that an open system, under certain circumstances, reaches a stationary state far from equilibrium, where the physical entropy takes a much smaller value than would be otherwise expected. The favorite topics of these theories have come to include Bénard's votices, lasers, temporal and spatial striations in colloids, chemical evolution that precedes biological evolution, some life phenomena, and so on. This is a definitive progress, and the whole approach seems to be on the right track. But there is danger of overlooking a fine point that is important.

The thermodynamics of dispersive phenomena or synergetics do not include in their domain the formation of structure in the crystal, or systems at very low temperature. It is a very old idea to compare the orderly structure of living organisms to crystals. Even the famous *Physical Aspect of the Living Cell* [S-18] of Schrödinger compares living cells to a system at zero temperature. But the orderliness of living matter and the orderliness of crystals are of an entirely different nature from the point of view of thermodynamics. The former is to be explained as a non-equilibrium, steady state of an open system, necessarily at a finite temperature, whereas the latter is the characteristic of the equilibrium state of a closed system at a very low temperature, ideally at the absolute zero temperature.

This discrepancy suggests that a thermodynamical investigation in terms of temperature and physical entropy is not an adequate approach to what we understand under the headings of structure, organization, order, or cooperation, as such. Of course, a small value of physical entropy is often associated with what we call structure, but this fact is, so to speak, a by-product of the definition of physical entropy. It is desirable to introduce a quantity directly from the point of view of orderliness or structuredness, in such a way that it may have applicability to all areas of orderliness, including, of course, these two areas of orderliness.

Originally, the concept of entropy was introduced by Clausius [C-10] in 1865 to formulate a thermodynamical law, now called Second Principle, whose essential content had been discovered by Sadi Carnot [C-11] at the beginning of the 19th century in his research about the efficiency of a heat engine. The definition of entropy was therefore given purely in terms of thermodynamical quantities. The increment dS of entropy was defined as $\Delta Q/T$ where ΔQ is the amount of heat energy given to the system at absolute temperature T. Towards the end of the century, efforts were made by such physicists as Boltzmann [B-7], Gibbs [G-5], and Maxwell [M-5] to reinterpret the entropy from the standpoint of the atomistic view of the physical world. As a result, expressions such as $S = \log(\text{probability})$ or $S = -\Sigma p_i \log p_i$ or $S = -\Sigma p_i \log p_i/w_i$ had been introduced. But, it was still a thermodynamical quantity. The first step toward the independence of entropy from thermodynamics may be said to have been taken in 1932 by von Neumann [V-1] in his book on the foundation of quantum mechanics in which he introduced what he called "microscopic entropy":

$$S = -\text{Trace } \sigma \log \sigma \qquad (6.1.1)$$

where σ is a non-negative hermitian matrix whose trace (diagonal sum) is unity. In terms of the diagonal elements, p_1, p_2, ..., p_n of σ, (6.1.1) takes the familiar form

$$S = -\Sigma p_i \log p_i \quad . \qquad (6.1.2)$$

But (6.1.1) is a more general concept than (6.1.2), because the expression by a matrix σ of our probabilistic knowledge about the object system is more general than the expression in terms of a mere probability distribution, p_i. Von Neumann used his microscopic entropy to demonstrate the irreversibility of the process of physical observation and did not make any reference to structuredness or cooperative phenomena.

The first paper which used this quantity as a measure of structuredness was written in 1939 by the present author under the direction of W. Heisenberg to discuss the properties of the nuclear matter [W-40]. In 1936 Niels Bohr emphasized the strong "cooperation" among nuclear particles or nucleons (protons and neutrons), which alone could explain the peculiar behavior of atomic nuclear matter in excited states, i.e., at a high "temperature" [B-8]. It was Heisenberg who thought that this cooperative nature of nucleons under nuclear force must be the key in explaining the properties of nuclei also in the ground state, i.e., in equilibrium at zero temperature. It was the present author who thought of using the "microscopic entropy" (6.1.1) of each nuclear particle as the indicator of the degree of their cooperation in the nuclear matter at any temperature. We called this entropy "Bausteinentropie" (building block entropy) to make it clear that this is not the thermodynamical entropy. We explained why this Bausteinentropie plays the double role of a measure of inexactitude of our knowledge of each Baustein (building block) and of a measure of strength of mutual dependence of constituent parts.

The aspect of the entropy function (6.1.1) as the measure of cooperation was explained in great detail in a series of papers published in 1944 in Japanese [W-39]. Figures 6.1.1 and 6.1.2 were taken from the 1944 paper to explain the idea of cooperation. It is assumed that one nucleon is located at the origin of the x-axis. The full line represents the probability density of presence of a second nucleon. Figure 6.1.1a is the case where no nuclear force is acting between nucleons. Figure 6.1.2a is for two nucleons of different kinds, i.e., one is a proton and the other is a neutron, or they are both protons or both neutrons but of different spin. In other words, the two are such that they can belong to the same alpha particle. Figure 6.1.1b is for two particles of the same charge (i.e., both protons or both neutrons) and having the same spin. The dip in Figure 6.1.1b shows that they cannot occupy the same place because of the Pauli principle. The difference between Figure 6.1.2 and Figure 6.1.1 is that in Figure 6.1.2 the nuclear force is "switched on." We see that the particles that can

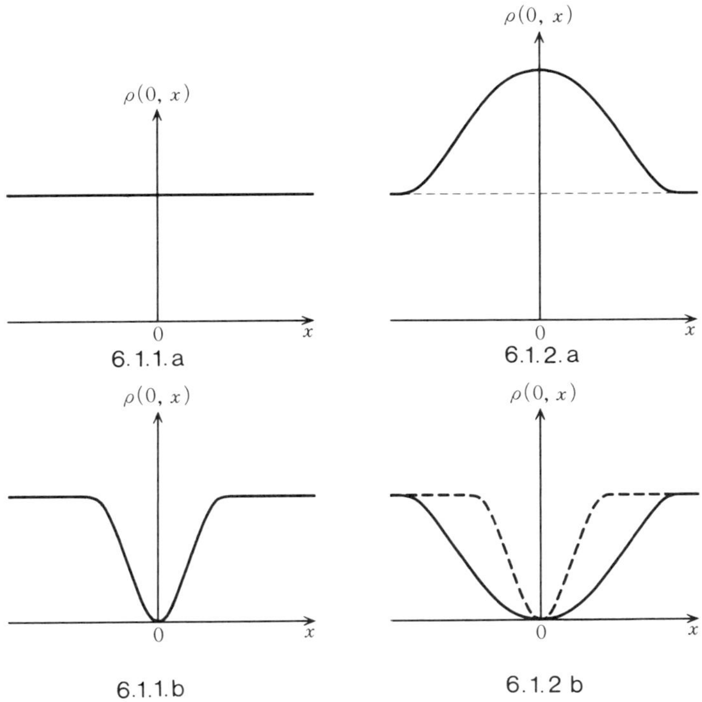

Figures 6.1.1 and 6.1.2 In the case where one nuclear particle is known to be located at x = 0, the probability density of the second nuclear particle being located at x is given by the curves of these four graphs. Fig. 6.1.1*a* is for two particles of different kinds in the absence of nuclear force. Fig. 6.1.1*b* is for two particles of the same kind in the absence of nuclear force. The particles tend to repel each other because of the Pauli principle. Fig. 6.1.2*a* is the same as Fig. 6.1.1*a* but with the nuclear force switched on. The particles tend to attract each other because of the tendency toward the formation of an alpha particle. Fig. 6.1.2*b* is the same as Fig. 6.1.1*a* but now the nuclear force is switched on. The repulsive tendency is further enhanced.

enter the same alpha particle have the tendency to attract each other, whereas the particles that cannot enter the same alpha particle repel each other. This is a typical case of cooperative phenomena. Note that if we measure the density of each nucleon separately, it is not changed at all due to the nuclear force. The only difference caused by the nuclear force is the bilateral property or relation between two constituent particles. It is proven that the Bausteinentropie is increased when the nuclear force is switched on. In the jargon of the latter part of this section, the nuclear force causes the structure function to increase. The curves were originally obtained by Euler and Volz quoted by von Weizsäcker [E-3, V-2]. These authors, however, did not discuss the change in terms of entropy, which was done in [W-39].

The cooperative phenomenon we see in the nuclear matter in a stable state is a property of a closed system at zero temperature, entirely different from the non-equilibrium structure of an open system that we discussed recently in thermodynamics of dispersive systems or in synergetics. But the formulation of structuredness, in terms of the information theoretic entropy, can be applied also to the case of non-equilibrium structure. Thus, the structure theory in the modern spirit of informatics was founded in 1939 just before the outbreak of the war. The idea of using the entropy function (6.1.2) as a measure of uncertainty was taken up by the founders of Information Theory, Wiener, and Shannon and Weaver, [W-41, S-10] about 10 years after the idea was formulated by physicists on a more general basis in the form of (6.1.1). (The density matrix is a more general concept than the probability distribution.) The idea of cooperation was rediscovered in 1951 under the name of redundancy [S-11]. Of course the idea of channel capacity is to be credited to the information theoreticians.

With the explanation given in this section, the reader must have been left with a conflicting impression that, on one hand, the entropy of a constituent part contributes to the degree of organization, whereas on the other hand, it is generally known that the smaller the value of entropy the more marked the degree of structure. In order to solve this apparent puzzle we shall have to go back to what we said at the beginning of this section. The existence of structure means that the knowledge of a part allows us to guess easily the rest of the whole. In other words, the possible variety of the state of the whole is restricted in spite of the variety of states of individual parts separately taken. If there is no correlation of interdependence among parts, the entropy of the whole is the sum of the entropies of parts. Therefore, the comparison must be made between the entropy of the whole and the sum of the entropies of the parts. The stronger the structure, the more markedly the sum of partial entropies will overwhelm the entropy of the whole. Therefore the strength of structure will be very naturally expressed by a formula:

$$\begin{aligned} J &= \text{strength of structure} \\ &= (\text{sum of partial entropies}) \\ &- (\text{entropy of whole}) \end{aligned} \tag{6.1.3}$$

For instance, if the entire system is seen as consisting of two parts, and the variables $x^{(1)}$ and $x^{(2)}$ represent the two parts, the strength will be

$$\begin{aligned} J = &- \sum p(x^{(1)}) \log p(x^{(1)}) - \sum p(x^{(2)}) \log p(x^{(2)}) \\ &+ \sum p(x^{(1)}, x^{(2)}) \log p(x^{(1)}, x^{(2)}) \end{aligned} \tag{6.1.4}$$

If a closed physical system is in an equilibrium state, the entire system will be in a pure state expressible as a psi-function. Therefore, the entropy of the whole will be zero as a result, and J will simply become the sum of Bausteinentropies. But in an open system, the state of the whole system is expressible only in terms of a density matrix. Therefore, the entropy of the whole is not necessarily zero. However, in a discussion of a physical system in equilibrium, the structure appears to be an increasing function of the (constituent) entropy.

In non-physical application, it often happens that the partial entropies do not appreciably change from one case to another. Therefore, the structure appears to be a decreasing function of the (total) entropy. This is the reason why it is not erroneous to say, in these applications, that the smaller the entropy the stronger the structure [W-5, W-6, W-10, W-48].

Returning to pattern recognition, we can take as our heuristic principle the adjustment of our conceptual framework so as to maximize the structure function, or--as it comes to the same thing in many cases--to minimize the entropy. It cannot, however, be anything more than a heuristic guiding principle, for there cannot be a necessary, unique solution in a pattern recognition problem [W-46, W-47, W-56].

To answer the question as to what could be meant by conceptual framework, we should remember that pattern recognition starts with observation of selected, say n, variables and ends with a single binary variable which decides whether or not a particular object belongs to a certain class. Therefore, the conceptual framework is here a set of variables, and our adjustment then should follow our guiding principle for the selection and reduction of variables. The reduction of dimensionality is usually done not in one single stroke, but in several steps.

A step in reduction of dimensionality involves usually a transformation of variables and a rejection of unimportant ones. One necessary condition we have to emphasize is that the transformation should be such that amorphism or uniformity is transformed into amorphism or uniformity, otherwise we might create a form that does not exist objectively. One of the transformations often used is a projection of points in the n-dimensional space onto an m-dimensional subspace ($m < n$). The dimensions orthogonal to this subspace are rejected. When $m = 1$, it becomes a one-stroke dimension-reduction. An orthogonal rotation of axes and a subsequent rejection of "unimportant" axes can be considered also as a variety of the projection method.

As we use the entropy function, we have to know the statistical population and its instantiations. For usual applications, all possible objects belonging to a class form the population and an individual object is an instantiation (see Section 6.4). In some cases, all possible objects of all possible classes form the population and an object of any class is an instantiation (see Section 6.3). But, as in a particular application in Section 6.5, each object is considered as a stochastic variable, and each observation on each object as an instantiation. As a result, to each object can be assigned an observed value of its entropy (see Section 6.6, in which we use the Hartley type of entropy--a special case of (6.1.2) where the p's are equal).

6.2 ENTROPY FUNCTIONS

Most of the useful properties of the entropy function

$$S(p) = - \sum_{i=1}^{n} p_i \log p_i \geq 0 \tag{6.2.1}$$

with

$$p_i \geq 0, \quad \sum_{i=1}^{n} p_i = 1, \quad 0\log 0 \equiv 0 \tag{6.2.2}$$

stem from Gibbs' theorem (p. 135 of [G-11]) about the relative entropy function V or the Gibbs' function G:

$$G(p, w) = - V(p, w) = + \sum_{i=1}^{n} p_i \log \frac{p_i}{w_i} \geq 0 \tag{6.2.3}$$

with

$$w_i \geq 0, \quad \sum_{i=1}^{n} w_i = 1. \tag{6.2.4}$$

The theorem asserts that V(p, w) is non-positive and that V vanishes if and only if $p_i = w_i$ for all i = 1, 2, ..., n.

The proof is very easy with the help of the definition of a function f of two non-negative variables:

$$f(x, y) = x(\log x - \log y) - x + y, \tag{6.2.5}$$

from which follows

$$\frac{\partial f}{\partial x} = \log x - \log y; \quad \frac{\partial^2 f}{\partial x^2} = \frac{1}{x}, \tag{6.2.6}$$

which shows that as a function of x, f is positive everywhere except at x = y, where f = 0. Hence

$$f(p_i, w_i) = p_i(\log p_i - \log w_i) - p_i + w_i \geq 0 \tag{6.2.7}$$

where equality holds if and only if $p_i = w_i$. Because $-V(p, w) = \sum_{i=1}^{n} f(p_i, w_i)$, we have proven the theorem.

The crucial point in this proof is the convexity (toward the x-axis) of the f-function, which stems from the concavity of the addendum in the definition of the S-function: $-x\log x$. This function is zero at $x = 0$ and $x = 1$, but everywhere else it is non-negative, $0 < x < 1$. In a loose use of language the function: $-x\log x$ is a measure of the deviation of x from idempotency. The equation $x^2 = x$ has two solutions: $x = 0$ and $x = 1$. As is well-known, the maximum of the S-function is log n which is realized when $p_i = 1/n$ for all i, and the minimum is 0 which is realized when one of the p's is 1 and the rest are 0. The function, log n - S, is a measure of unevenness, i.e., the deviation from the uniform distribution: $p_i = 1/n$ for all i.

The Gibbs' function, G = -V, is a good measure of the deviation of the distribution $\{w_i\}$ from the distribution $\{p_i\}$. In particular, if the deviation is small:

$$w_i = p_i + \Delta p_i; \quad \sum_{i=1}^{n} \Delta p_i = 0 \qquad (6.2.8)$$

it is easy to see

$$G = \sum_{i=1}^{n} (\Delta p_i)^2. \qquad (6.2.9)$$

We assumed in the above that n is finite, but no serious difficulty arises when n becomes denumerably infinite. But, when n becomes a continuous infinity, we must be a little careful, at least as far as the S-function is concerned. The integral

$$S = -\int_a^b p(x) \log p(x)\, dx \qquad (6.2.10)$$

is not an invariant for a probability-preserving transformation: $x \rightarrow y$, with $p(x)\, dx = p(y)\, dy$. In contrast the continuous counterpart of the G-function

$$G = \int p(x) \log \frac{p(x)}{w(x)} dx \qquad (6.2.11)$$

is an invariant for a probability-preserving transformation, because $p(x)/w(x) = p(y)/w(y)$.

As far as a small difference between the p's and the w's is concerned, as we can see from (6.2.9), the G-function, or V-function is symmetric with respect to w and p, but if the difference becomes larger, the G- or V-function is no longer symmetric with respect to w and p. For certain theoretical considerations and also for some applications, we would like to have a symmetric function expressing the difference between w and p. For that purpose, we introduce a W-function

$$W(p, w) = W(w, p) = V(p, w) + V(w, p) \leq 0. \qquad (6.2.12)$$

If we write out W in terms of the probability distributions, we obtain

$$\begin{aligned} W = &- \Sigma p_i \log p_i - \Sigma w_i \log w_i \\ &+ \Sigma p_i \log w_i + \Sigma w_i \log p_i . \end{aligned} \qquad (6.2.13)$$

Because the maximum of V is zero, which is reached when the two distributions become identical, we can state the same theorem also for W. The minimum of V, as well as that of W, is $-\infty$. This will take place, in the case of V, when $w_i = 0$ for an i for which p_i is non-zero, and in the case of W, where there is at least one i for which either p_i or w_i is zero and the other is non-zero. If this last condition is not satisfied, W is finite and will become small if S(p) and S(w), which are the first two terms of (6.2.13), become separately small and if the overlap of the p and w, which is measured by the last two terms of (6.2.13), becomes small. Since a negative quantity is awkward to handle, it is better to use an H-function:

$$\begin{aligned} H(p, w) &= H(w, p) = - W(p, w) = - W(w, p) \\ &= G(p, w) + G(w, p) \geq 0 \end{aligned} \qquad (6.2.14)$$

If the W-function is called the overlap function, the H-function may be called the discrepancy function.

Let us assume that the index i, i = 1, 2, ..., n used in (6.2.3) is actually a double index i, j, i = 1, 2, ..., n_i, j = 1, 2, ..., n_2, $n_1 \times n_2 = n$, so that

$$p_i^{(1)} = \sum_{j=1}^{n_2} p_{ij}, \quad p_j^{(2)} = \sum_{i=1}^{n_1} p_{ij}. \tag{6.2.15}$$

If we take w

$$w_{ij} = p_i^{(1)} \cdot p_j^{(2)}, \tag{6.2.16}$$

Gibbs' theorem becomes

$$\begin{aligned} - V(p, w) &= J(p^{(1)}, p^{(2)}) = S^{(1)} + S^{(2)} - S \\ &= - \sum_{i=1}^{n_1} p_i^{(1)} \log p_i^{(1)} - \sum_{j=1}^{n_2} p_j^{(2)} \log p_j^{(2)} \\ &+ \sum_{i=1}^{n_1} \sum_{j=1}^{n_2} p_{ij} \log p_{ij} \geq 0. \end{aligned} \tag{6.2.17}$$

The equality in (6.2.17) holds if and only if

$$w_{ij} = p_{ij}$$

i.e.

$$p_i^{(1)} \cdot p_j^{(2)} = p_{ij} \text{ for all i and all j.} \tag{6.2.18}$$

This means that

$$S = S^{(1)} + S^{(2)} \tag{6.2.19}$$

if and only if $p_i^{(1)}$ and $p_j^{(2)}$ are probabilistically independent. This is the so-called additivity of the S-function. This allows us to interpret $J(p^{(1)}, p^{(2)})$ as a measure of interdependence, or in the context of the last section, as a measure of structuredness.

If we interchange p and w in (6.2.17) we obtain a theorem

$$S^{(1)} + S^{(2)} + \sum_{i=1}^{n_1} \sum_{j=1}^{n_2} p_i^{(1)} p_j^{(2)} \log p_{ij} \leq 0 \quad (6.2.20)$$

where equality holds if and only if $p^{(1)}$ and $p^{(2)}$ are statistically independent. In general cases, we can set the upper limit and lower limit

$$S \leq S^{(1)} + S^{(2)} \leq - \sum_{i=1}^{n_1} \sum_{j=1}^{n_2} p_i^{(1)} p_j^{(2)} \log p_{ij} \quad (6.2.21)$$

By the repeated use of Gibbs' theorem, we can similarly obtain a theorem for the case where the index i in (6.2.2) actually is a N-ple index $(i_1, i_2, \ldots, i_N)$, $i_k = 1, 2, \ldots, n_k$, $\prod_{k=1}^{N} n_k = n$.

$$J = \sum_{k=1}^{N} S^{(k)} - S \geq 0 \quad (6.2.22)$$

with

$$S^{(k)} = - \sum_{i_k=1}^{n_k} p_{i_k}^{(k)} \log p_{i_k}^{(k)} \quad (6.2.23)$$

and

$$p_{i_k}^{(k)} = \left[\sum_{i_1=1}^{n_1} \cdot \sum_{i_2=1}^{n_2} \cdots \sum_{i_N=1}^{n_N} / \sum_{i_k=1}^{n_k} \right] p(i_1, i_2, \ldots, i_N) \quad (6.2.24)$$

The division by $\sum_{i_k=1}^{n_k}$ indicates that in the multiple summation on the numerator, the summation sign $\sum_{i_k=1}^{n_k}$

is missing. The equality in (6.2.22) holds if and only if

$$p(i_1, i_2, \ldots, i_N) = p^{(1)}_{i_1} \cdot p^{(2)}_{i_2} \cdot \ldots p^{(N)}_{i_N} \qquad (6.2.25)$$

for all i_k, $k = 1, 2, \ldots, N$, $i_k = 1, 2, \ldots, n_k$. The quantity J measures the strength of organization or structure among N-partial systems which constitute the whole system.

As mentioned earlier, the Gibbs' theorem is based on the concavity of the function $-x\log x$. Therefore, the idea was immediate that a much simpler function with concavity such as $-x^2$ would do a similar job as the logarithmic entropy function, although we may have to abandon the additivity of the logarithmic entropy. The present author had this idea already when he wrote his 1939 paper [W-40], but did not use such an alternative entropy function in that paper. But, in his paper of 1944, he published this idea [W-39], and included it briefly in his 1969 book [W-10].

Basing ourselves in the concavity of $-x^2$, we can introduce, as a substitute of the S-function,

$$T(p) = 1 - \sum_{i=1}^{n} p_i^2 = \sum_{i \neq j}^{n} \sum^{n} p_i p_j \geq 0. \qquad (6.2.26)$$

The maximum of this function is $1 - (1/n) = (n-1)/n$, which is realized when all $p_i = \frac{1}{n}$; the minimum is 0, which is realized when one of the p_i is one and all the other p_i are zero. Therefore, the property is very much the same as the S-function. The T-function is another measure of evenness, and $-T$ or simply $\sum_{i=1}^{n} p_i^2$ may be considered as a good measure of unevenness. What corresponds to Gibbs' theorem here is the simple fact that

$$-U(p, w) = \sum_{i=1}^{n} (p_i - w_i)^2 \geq 0 \qquad (6.2.27)$$

is non-negative and becomes zero if and only if $w_i = p_i$ for all i.

Different from the V-function, the U-function is symmetrical with respect to the p_i and the w_i:

$$U(p, w) = U(w, p) \tag{6.2.28}$$

We do not need to introduce here a counterpart of the symmetrical W.

The U can be rewritten

$$U(p, w) = T(p) + T(w) - 2(1 - \sum_{i=1}^{n} p_i w_i). \tag{6.2.29}$$

The maximum of U is 0, which is reached when the two distributions p_i and w_i are identical and the minimum is -2, which is reached when T(p) and T(w) are individually zero; the p_i and the w_i are such that for every i, either or both of p_i and w_i are zero. This last condition is more convenient than the minimization condition of V or W, since, the minimum condition for U is such that the p_i and w_i are separately and sharply concentrated, and the two peaks are located at different values of i. For this reason, as an overlap function, U is much more convenient than V or W. To make a distinction between the two groups: (S, T) and (U, V, W), we shall call the former group form-finding entropies and the latter group discriminatory entropies.

For a multi-class overlap or discrepancy, we can take the sum of W's pairwise defined. For instance, 3-distribution p^1, p^2, p^3, we can take

$$W(p^1, p^2, p^3) = W(p^1, p^2) + W(p^2, p^3) + W(p^3, p^1)$$

$$V(p^1, p^2, p^3) = V(p^1, p^2) + V(p^2, p^3) + V(p^3, p^1). \tag{6.2.30}$$

As we mentioned, in the first work of 1939 on the information-theoretic entropy (in contrast to the thermodynamical entropy), our state of knowledge was assumed to be expressible in terms of density matrix which reduces to a probability distribution when all the observables are commutative, which is not always true in atomic physics. For this reason, to formulate a completely parallel theory to the ordinary information theory, we need a generalized version of Gibbs' theorem:

$$\mathrm{Trace}(\sigma_1 \log \sigma_1) - \mathrm{Trace}(\sigma_1 \log \sigma_2) \geq 0 \qquad (6.2.31)$$

where σ_1 and σ_2 are two density matrices which do not necessarily commute with each other. The proof of this generalized Gibbs' theorem is given in Appendix 9.8 of [W-10].

In Section 1.4 we learned that according to the principle of Prägnanz of Gestalt psychologists we form a mental image that shows a high degree of regularity, simplicity, symmetry, organization, and articulation. It is surprising that the minimum entropy principle we have arrived at from a different point of view implies to a great degree the identical tenet. In fact, the regularity means that due to the rules that govern the image there is redundancy (expressible as entropy-decrease) in the information carried by the parts of the scenery. The perfect left-and-right symmetry reduces the entropy of the picture to one half. We have seen in Section 5.4 that the principle of simplicity can be derived from the principle of minimum entropy. We have seen that when two probability distributions have a low value of the Gibbs' entropy, the two distributions are articulately distinct. We have to be somewhat careful, when we apply the entropy-consideration to the Bayesian formula of evaluation of a hypothesis about the probability distribution. There are two places where the entropy function plays a role. As far as the "confirmation" of the hypothesis is concerned, a higher value of the Gibbs' function (between the experimental and theoretical distributions) tends to give a high value of evaluation. But, as far as the evaluation of the "prior" probability is concerned, the principle of minimum entropy will have its role to play (see Section 8.4).

6.3 PRINCIPAL AXIS METHOD

We have seen that apart from the final decision-making process with regard to classification of objects, the major mathematical aspect of pattern recognition can be regarded as a reduction of dimensionality. One way of reducing the number of dimensions is to perform a transformation of variables so that some variables become more important than others. The more important variables may be considered "features" by which we should proceed to make the final classification. If we ignore the less important variables, we can say that we have reduced dimensionality. Because the class-generation (clustering) or class-assignment (pattern recognition) is the next step, this step of dimensionality reduction may be called one of the methods of preprocessing. If we take all the available observed points of all classes, this preprocessing will serve the purpose of preparation for clustering. If we take only sample points of one class, this method will serve the purpose of class-feature extraction.

With regard to the allowable transformations, we must mention the necessary precautions that should be taken to insure that the transformation of variables must maintain the invariance of spatial uniformity in the reduced dimensionality. The safest kind of transformation complying with this rule would be a rotation, or rectangular transformation, in the Euclidean space. A translation is, of course, another surely allowable transformation.

To conduct the program described above, we first have to introduce a measure of importance of each variable or axes. If this measure of importance is non-negative and so normalized that the values of the measure of importance of all axes add up to unity, then we can define an entropy with these values. The aim of the transformation is to make the values of importance as unevenly distributed as possible so that we can ignore the less important axes. In terms of entropy, this would be translated into a minimization of entropy.

Suppose we are given N objects, which are subjected to observation of n variables. The data then can be expressed as N vectors of n components: $\{x_i^{(\alpha)}\}$, i=1, 2,..., n; α=1, 2,..., N. Let us assume that each vector is normalized so that

$$\sum_{i=1}^{n} (x_i^{(\alpha)})^2 = 1. \qquad (6.3.1)$$

If we introduce a weight:

$$\rho_i = \frac{1}{N} \sum_{i=1}^{N} (x_i^{(\alpha)})^2 \tag{6.3.2}$$

we have, of course,

$$\rho_i \geq 0 \text{ and } \sum_{i=1}^{n} \rho_i \;. \tag{6.3.3}$$

We can interpret ρ_i as the importance of the i-th axis in representing the collection of the N given vectors. Then, the entropy mentioned above will be

$$S = - \sum_{i=1}^{n} \rho_i \log \rho_i . \tag{6.3.4}$$

Now we rotate the axes, or apply an orthogonal transformation

$$x_i \rightarrow x'_j = \sum_{k=1}^{n} T_{jk}\, x_k \tag{6.3.5}$$

with the condition of orthogonal transformation:

$$T_{ji} = (T^{-1})_{ij} \text{ or } T^t = T^{-1}. \tag{6.3.6}$$

The weight ρ'_i of the i-th axis of the new coordinate system is then given by

$$\rho'_i = G'_{ii} \tag{6.3.7}$$

where

$$G'_{ij} = \Sigma T_{ik}\, G_{k\ell} (T^{-1})_{\ell j} = \frac{1}{N} \sum_{\alpha=1}^{N} x'^{(\alpha)}_1 x'^{(\alpha)}_j \tag{6.3.8}$$

with

$$G_{k\ell} = \frac{1}{N} \sum_{\alpha=1}^{N} x_k^{(\alpha)} x_\ell^{(\alpha)} . \tag{6.3.9}$$

In other words, the ρ_i are the diagonal elements of the scatter matrix G in the x-coordinate system, and the ρ_i' are the diagonal elements of the scatter matrix in the x'-coordinate system. The entropy in the new coordinate system is

$$S' = - \sum_{i=1}^{n} \rho_i' \log \rho_i' . \tag{6.3.10}$$

The desired axes are such that they minimize S'. Suppose that the x'-axes are indeed those that minimize S', we have of course that

$$S' \leq S \tag{6.3.11}$$

for any starting x-axes. Fixing now conversely the optimal axes, we can obtain any x-axes by a reverse transformation T^{-1}. Hence, the optimal axes can be characterized by (6.3.11) with any arbitrary T.

The theorem published in 1964 [W-1, W-2] claims the following:

The optimal coordinate axes that minimize the entropy S' are the eigenvectors of the G-matrix and the ρ' in this optimal coordinate system are the eigenvalues of the G-matrix.

We are now going to prove the inverse of this theorem, i.e., that the S-value calculated in a coordinate system determined by the eigenvectors of the G-matrix is not larger than the S-value in any other coordinate system. If the S-value calculated in any one of the eigenvector systems is the same, and if the stated inverse theorem is true, then the original theorem must be true: the S-minimizing coordinate system is one of the eigenvector coordinate systems of G.

Since in the eigenvector coordinate systems the G-matrix must have a diagonal form

$$G_{ij}' = \lambda_i \, \delta_{ij} \tag{6.3.12}$$

If we pass to the non-primed coordinate system by the inverse transformation T^{-1}, we shall have

$$G_{k\ell} = \sum_i \sum_i (T^{-1})_{ki} \lambda_i \delta_{ij} (T)_{j\ell}. \qquad (6.3.13)$$

In this expression, we can consider $(T^{-1})_{ki}$ as the k-th component in the non-primed system of the i-th eigenvector of the matrix G. Indeed if we multiply $(T^{-1})_{\ell m}$ from the right, and sum over ℓ, we obtain the equation

$$\sum_\ell G_{k\ell}(T^{-1})_{\ell i} = \sum_i (T^{-1})_{ki} \lambda_i, \qquad (6.3.14)$$

which is the equation defining eigenvalues and eigenvectors.

The S-value in the primed coordinate system is

$$S'(\lambda) = - \sum_{i=1} \lambda_i \log \lambda_i, \qquad (6.3.15)$$

whereas the S-value in the non-primed coordinate system is

$$S(\rho) = - \sum_{k=1}^{n} \rho_k \log \rho_k, \qquad (6.3.16)$$

where the ρ and the λ are related according to (6.3.13) by

$$\rho_k = G_{kk} = \sum_{i=1}^{n} A_{ki} \lambda_i \qquad (6.3.17)$$

with

$$A_{ki} = (T^{-1})_{ki} T_{ik}. \qquad (6.3.18)$$

Due to the fact that T^{-1} is the inverse of T, we have

$$\sum_{k=1}^{n} A_{ki} = 1 \qquad (6.3.19)$$

and

$$\sum_{i=1}^{n} A_{ki} = 1. \qquad (6.3.20)$$

Because T (therefore also T^{-1}) is an orthogonal transformation, we have, with the help of (6.3.6),

$$A_{ki} = (T_{ik})^2 \geq 0. \qquad (6.3.21)$$

Hence A_{ki} is a probability distribution with respect to i as well as to k. In the jargon of the Markov chain, A_{ki} is a doubly-stochastic matrix.

If there is an r-ple degeneracy in the i-th eigenvalue, this eigenvalue does not determine an eigenvector, but rather an r-dimensional eigensubspace. But, no matter what r directions we take as the eigenvectors corresponding to this eigenvalue, the S-value is the same. Thus, the optimal coordinate system is not uniquely determined, but the S-value is the same.

The theorem will be proven, if we can prove

$$S(\rho) \geq S'(\lambda), \qquad (6.3.22)$$

where the ρ and the λ are connected by (6.3.17) by a doubly-stochastic matrix (6.3.18). This is the famous simple H-theorem [W-10] whose proof is as follows:

Since the f-function:

$$f = -x\log x \qquad (6.3.23)$$

is a convex (upward) function

$$\frac{d^2f}{dx^2} = -\frac{1}{x} \leq 0, \quad \text{for } x \geq 0 \qquad (6.3.24)$$

a tangent straight line to the f-curve has a larger value than the value of f for the same x:

$$f(x_o) + \frac{df(x_o)}{dx}(x-x_o) \geq f(x), \qquad (6.3.25)$$

where x_o is the point of osculation.

If we put

$$x_o = \Sigma A_{k\ell}\ \lambda_\ell \tag{6.3.26}$$

we get for $x = \lambda_i$

$$f(\Sigma A_{k\ell}\ \lambda_\ell) + \frac{df(x_o)}{dx}(\lambda_i - \Sigma A_{k\ell}\lambda_\ell) \geq f(\lambda_i). \tag{6.3.27}$$

Now multiply each term by A_{ki} and sum over i; then we get, due to (6.3.20)

$$f(\Sigma A_{k\ell}\ \lambda_\ell) \geq \sum_i A_{ki} f(\lambda_i). \tag{6.3.28}$$

Sum over k we then obtain due to (6.3.19)

$$\sum_k f(\sum_\ell A_{k\ell}\ \lambda_\ell) \geq \sum_i f(\lambda_i), \tag{6.3.29}$$

which is the desired result (6.3.22).

It is interesting that all we used was the convexity of the f-function, therefore we can use the polynomial entropy instead of the logarithmic entropy. As a result, we can characterize the optimal coordinate system by the T-function instead of the S-function. We come to the same result (see Section 7.7).

It is convenient to label the eigenvalues of the G-matrix according to their magnitudes:

$$\lambda_1 \geq \lambda_2 \geq \cdots \geq \lambda_n. \tag{6.3.30}$$

The fact that the λ's are more "uneven" than the ρ's--which is what is meant by the entropy minimization principle--can be translated so that the λ_i is the fastest descending function of i. Those axes corresponding to small λ's have very small importance in representing the collection of objects. Hence, the possibility presents itself that we can reasonably fix a threshold value for λ_i, so that the dimensions corresponding to the indices larger than this i can be eliminated. In actual application, the λ_i decreases often suddenly at a certain value of i. That is usually chosen as the threshold. When the

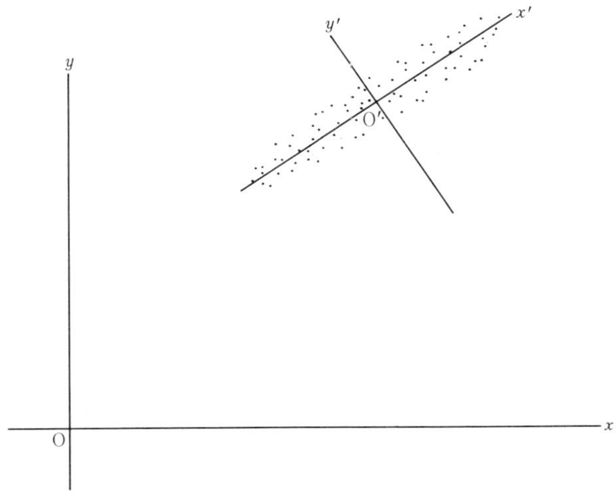

Figure 6.3.1 In this illustration neither the x-axis nor the y-axis serves effectively to discriminate the points from one another, but the x'-axis will serve the purpose more effectively, whereas the y'-axis will perform very poorly.

diagonalization of the covariance matrix is used to reduce the dimensionality, the method is sometimes called SELFIC (self featuring information compression) (see Section 7.2).

Figure 6.3.1 shows the geometrical meaning of this entropy minimization method. In this case, we shifted the origin first to the average of all vectors, and then applied the entropy minimization. In the x-y-representation, both x and y are almost equally important, but x'-y'-representation, the spread in y'-direction is very small and the y'-axis may be deemed as unimportant.

The G-matrix after the shift of the coordinate origin to the centroid is often called covariance, and the diagonalization of G-matrix is called rotation to the principal axis of the covariance. Therefore, the method we reached as a consequence of the principle of entropy minimization is often referred to as the method of the rotation to the principal axis of the covariance matrix. We shall discuss other aspects of the method of principal axis in the next chapter.

6.4 DYNAMIC COALESCENCE MODEL--CLUSTERING AS MERGER

The dynamical coalescence model is an algorithm introduced by the present author in 1974 and has proved to be quite successful in various practical clustering problems [W-54, W-55, W-56]. The motivation for this invention was twofold.

First, being mechanical simulations of human perception, the methods of pattern recognition may profit from imitating a certain special dynamical aspect of human perception, which we have not discussed in Chapter 2 on pattern recognition as perception. Namely, a human perceptor-observer tends to see motion in a statical picture by imagination, and the contents of this imagination participate in the generation of the "form" he sees in the picture. For instance, a futuristic picture of a horse with many legs suggests the running of the horse. Or, in a picture of a car suspended in the air off the edge of a cliff, we can see already an impending disaster.

In trying to see a "form" in a collection of points, the formation of pattern will be aided by some imaginary motion of the points. For instance, when we say we see a fox's face in a cloud, the cloud as it is may not have a distinct shape of a fox, but, we add different imaginary deformations onto the actual cloud to make it look like a form.

The second motivation comes from our interest in discovering entropy-decreasing phenomena in nature, whereas most of the usual happenings in the physical world are accompanied by an increase of entropy. An apparent entropy decrease in living organisms has already been mentioned in Section 6.1. Other examples that challenge our imagination are coalescence of vortices, flip-over of tippy top, and others [W-42]. In these phenomena, the physical entropy decrease of the system is made possible by an entropy increase in an adjacent system or by a conversion of mechanical energy into heat energy. That is why these phenomena are interesting.

The most conspicuous case of apparent entropy-decrease, for the present author, has been always the formation of stars and nebulae some time (perhaps 10 billion years) after the big bang, which itself (isolated from the rest) represents an entropy increasing phenomenon. The formation of stars and nebulae, seen only in terms of geometrical distribution, is indeed an entropy decreasing phenomena.

Combining these two motivations, we come to an idea that formation of clusters in perceptual grouping can be best modeled by a dynamical motion of points under mutual attraction. Such a motion will realize a decrease of spatial entropy accompanying the formation of a form, in agreement with our principle of minimization of entropy.

Usual clustering algorithms are bound up with the static concept of probability density function of which the given objects are stochastic samples. We here introduce a new image of clustering process which is quite different from such a statical model. A uniform distribution of stars in the space under mutual gravitational attraction is known to be unstable. The slightest deviation from the absolute and infinite uniform distribution will set the system into motion and will end up forming clusters of stars. A slight clustering tendency in the original configuration will be enhanced and made conspicuous. This process, of course, is complicated by the fact that the gravitational potential energy is converted into kinetic energy and this kinetic energy will cause orbital motions around each other. Suppose now that the entire system is immersed in a viscous fluid to dampen the inertial motion. Each star will, under these conditions, reach the so-called terminal velocity which is proportional to the gravitational force acting on it. Suppose further that the stars are made of deformable and sticky material and that they coalesce to form a new star when they touch one another. These coalesced stars will gravitate and coalesce again forming larger and larger stars until finally they become a unique star into which all astral masses have merged. Each coalesced star at different stages of this process can be considered as a cluster. Our proposed model of clustering is based on such an image, except for one difference: the force of attraction is assumed to have no singularity at zero distance and to have a finite range so that its magnitude becomes very small but not entirely zero at larger distances beyond the range.

A better image of the process may be obtained by supposing the points to be clustered are represented by oil drops of unit mass and of radius r_0, suspended in water or some other liquid. It is assumed that the density of oil and that of water are equal, so that there is no effect of the earth's gravitation. These oil drops attract each other by a force dependent on the distance, and if two drops come in contact with each other, they coalesce and form a bigger drop with the total mass of both. The force acting on an oil drop is the attractive force and the resistive force due to the viscosity of "water." This resistance is assumed to be proportional to the velocity of the oil drop and directed opposite to the velocity. Under such circumstances, the oil drop will immediately (provided the viscosity is high enough) reach the so-called terminal velocity. This terminal velocity is constant, i.e., has no acceleration. Therefore, it will be proportional to the attractive force acting on it. As the process of coalescence goes on, the oil drop will become heavier and heavier. Its mass m is equal to the number of original points which have been merged to form the drop because the mass of each original point is assumed to be unity. The force between two oil drops is in general a function of the masses of the two. The force is assumed to have a "range" σ, such that the force becomes very weak beyond this range. If the force decreases with distance, an oil drop would be most strongly drawn to its near neighbors and coalesce with them which will result in a chain effect.

Unless the force becomes literally zero beyond the range, the process of coalescence goes on until all of the oil drops form a final single drop. This corresponds to a hierarchical clustering. If we stop the process when the number of drops has become ν, we have accomplished a ν-ary clustering.

This dynamic coalescence method has the following advantages:

1. Because each point is under the influence of all other points, the model is capable of reflecting the global situation of the distribution of all points. This is definitely a great advantage over many other algorithms which consider only the influence of neighboring points.
2. Instead of searching the optimum or local optimum by methods such as hill-climbing, exchange-of-members, and trial-and-error, the suggested algorithm follows the solution

of a differential (or difference) equation. Therefore, once the parameters involved in the algorithm are selected, the entire process goes on smoothly and uniquely to the end. Usually, problems in information sciences are formulated as optimum problems for which we can find only a would-be solution which may be a true solution or a local or approximate solution.

3. Choosing the parameters suitably, we can adjust the degree to which the chain effect is taken into account. We can further enhance the chain effect by modifying the force formula.
4. The process does not follow a step-by-step division of the set of objects into smaller and smaller subsets as many algorithms do, but a step-by-step merger of members.
5. We can obtain any number of clusters, ranging from one to N_0 (the number of the initially given objects). The method provides a hierarchical tree which we can trim at any stage.
6. Choosing values of the parameters involved, we can obtain different clustering trees.

We will now specify in detail the dynamical aspects of the model. We start with N_0 objects of equal "mass," so that a cluster that is formed from m original objects will have mass m. The number of clusters at time t is designated by N(t). The clusters are labeled by superscript α, β, γ, ..., so that the position, radius and mass of the α-th cluster will be denoted by $x^{(\alpha)}$, $r^{(\alpha)}$ and $m^{(\alpha)}$. The radius is assumed to be given by

$$r^{(\alpha)} = (m^{(\alpha)})^{\frac{1}{n}} r_0, \tag{6.4.1}$$

where r_0 is a constant that is equal to the radius of each original object if it has a unity mass. For the reason that will become clear later, this constant r_0 will be called coalescence parameter. Equation (6.4.1) is suggested by the image of a sphere of constant density, but it could be replaced by a different law without changing the general features of the model very much.

The motion of the clusters is determined by the dynamical equation

$$\frac{dx^{(\alpha)}}{dt} = F^{(a)}, \tag{6.4.2}$$

where

$$F^{(\alpha)} = A\sum_{\beta} \frac{x^{(\beta)}-x^{(\alpha)}}{|x^{(\beta)}-x^{(\alpha)}|} f^{(1)}_{\alpha\beta} \tag{6.4.3}$$

with

$$f^{(1)}_{\alpha\beta} = (m^{(\alpha)}m^{(\beta)})^{\rho}\ g(|x^{(\beta)}-x^{(\alpha)}|), \tag{6.4.4}$$

where ρ is usually taken to be 1.

If we want to include the second order effect in the equation in order to enhance the chain effect, we can replace (6.4.3) by

$$F^{(\alpha)} = A\sum_{\beta} \frac{x^{(\beta)}-x^{(\alpha)}}{|x^{(\beta)}-x^{(\alpha)}|} [f^{(1)}_{\alpha\beta} + \varepsilon f^{(2)}_{\alpha\beta}], \tag{6.4.5}$$

where ε is a constant to be adjusted suitably. $f^{(2)}$ is in the "closed-end model"

$$f^{(2)}_{\alpha\beta} = \sum_{\gamma} f^{(1)}_{\alpha\gamma}\ f^{(1)}_{\gamma\beta} \tag{6.4.6}$$

and in the "open-end model"

$$f^{(2)}_{\alpha\beta} = \sum_{\gamma} f^{(1)}_{\alpha\beta}\ f^{(1)}_{\beta\gamma}. \tag{6.4.7}$$

By the same token, we can introduce still higher-order terms. In general, if we use a term of the r-th order $f^{(r)}$, the computer time will increase with N_O roughly proportionally to N_O^{r+1}, where N_O is the number of original sample points. However, this is considerably more amenable than the exponential growth exp N_O characteristic of the usual clustering algorithms. It was found by experience that the first order force sufficiently shows the chain effect.

The mass-dependent factor in (6.4.4) is inserted to represent the fact that the larger the lump the stronger the force that it exerts, hence $\rho \geq 0$. The "force" is attractive, therefore $A \geq 0$. We tried three types of "force":

Gaussian: $$g(\xi) = c \exp[-\xi^2/(2\sigma^2)] \tag{6.4.8}$$

Cauchy: $$g(\xi) = c \frac{\sigma}{\xi^2 + \sigma^2} \tag{6.4.9}$$

Square-Well: $$g(\xi) = c \quad \text{if } \xi \leq \sigma \tag{6.4.10}$$

$$= 0 \quad \text{if } \xi > \sigma$$

The Gaussian and Cauchy forces produce a hierarchical clustering and will eventually reach a unique one final clump, hence if we want to have two or more clumps, we have to stop the process at a specified time. The Square-Well force may, depending on the case, stop before the number of clumps becomes one.

The process of coalescence is determined by the following rule. Two clumps α and β coalesce when they touch each other, i.e., $|x^{(\alpha)} - x^{(\beta)}| = r^{(\alpha)} + r^{(\beta)}$, and a new clump of mass $(m^{(\alpha)} + m^{(\beta)})$ at position

$$(x^{(\alpha)}m^{(\alpha)} + x^{(\beta)}m^{(\beta)})/(m^{(\alpha)} + m^{(\beta)}) \tag{6.4.11}$$

will be created. To solve the equation (6.4.2) we take a finite difference Δt and calculate a small change of position

$$\Delta x^{(\alpha)} = F^{(\alpha)} \Delta t \tag{6.4.12}$$

at a time.

The dynamical coalescence model is originally meant to be a tool in clustering. We can modify it so as to be applicable to paradigm-oriented pattern recognition (see [W-54]).

We shall give two illustrations of the method. Figure 6.4.1 shows that the method is suitable to the case where the chain effect is marked. The starting configuration is a) and the final configuration d). We stopped when N became 2.

In Figure 6.4.2 the original configuration is produced by two normal distributions. The distance between the centers of the two distributions was 5 units, while the standard deviation of each normal distribution was 1.25 units. In Figure 6.4.1, each coalesced center is represented by a point. In Figure 6.4.2 a coalesced center is a circle whose area is proportional to the number of original points included in that cluster.

The entropy change during the process of coalescence can be measured in two ways: In one way we divide the space in n meshes into which the original points will be distributed. Let ρ_i be the fraction of the original points coalesced into clusters whose centers are located in the i-th mesh. Then

$$S = -\sum_{i=1}^{n} \rho_i \log \rho_i . \qquad (6.4.13)$$

In the other way, let μ_α be the fraction of the original points which are coalesced into the α-th coalesced cluster. Then

$$S = -\sum_{\alpha=1}^{N} \mu_\alpha \log \mu_\alpha , \qquad (6.4.14)$$

where N is the number of clusters at time t. In either way, insofar as the force does not vanish at a finite distance, we have $S \to 0$ with $t \to \infty$.

6.5 COHESION METHOD--CLUSTERING AS CLEAVAGE

In the last section we visualized the process of clustering as a gradual merger of constituent parts. In this section, on the contrary, the clustering process will be regarded as a splitting of a whole into parts. What is the natural way of making a cleavage in a loosely aggregated body of mass? The

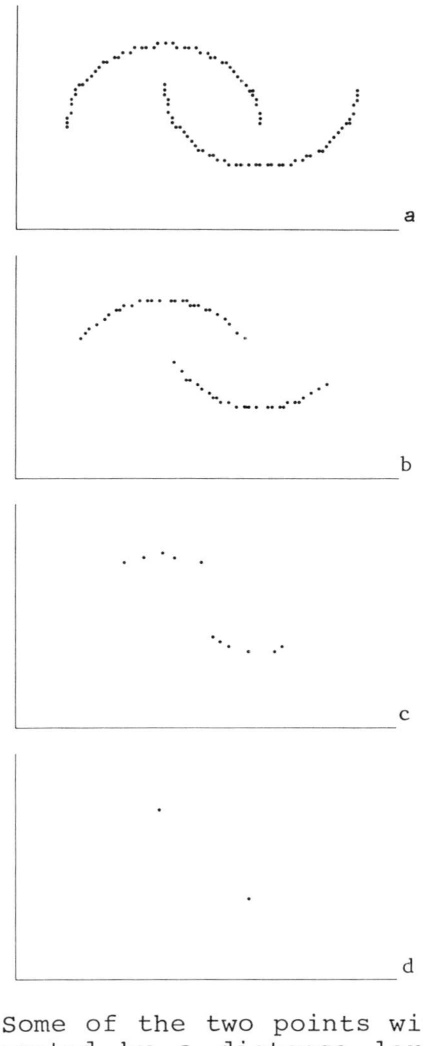

Figure 6.4.1 Some of the two points within the same group are separated by a distance larger than the distance between some of the two points belonging to two different groups. The dynamic coalescence model of clustering embodies such a "chain effect." The series *a, b, c, d* shows different stages of the process of coalescence ending with two clusters. This experiment was helped by E. Harada.

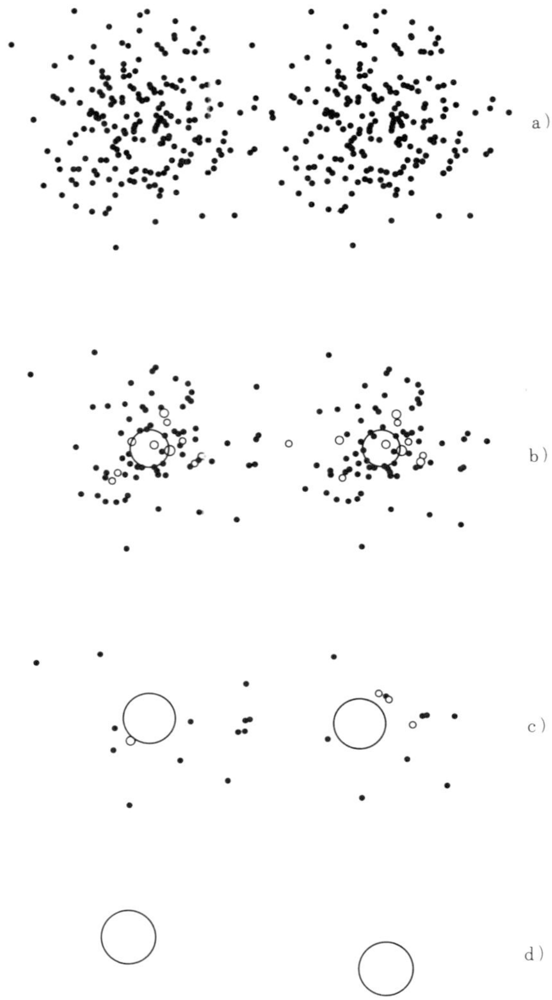

Figure 6.4.2 An illustration of another example of gradual coalescence, also ending with two clusters. This method is very sensitive to the global situation of the distribution of points. This experiment was done by Professor S. Tomita.

answer would be that the splitting surface would be such that the two partial bodies themselves are internally solidly cohered together whereas the two are mutually weakly cohered to each other. A splitting of a body into more than two parts would follow the same pattern. The mutual cohesion between parts would be weak, whereas internal cohesion of each part would be strong.

In the preceding chapters, the objects to be classified were supposed to have known properties. Therefore the cohesion to be considered was relation definable in terms of these properties. The most fundamental one was the similarity relation. Similar objects form a class--the basic idea of the classification. But, we have seen not only that dissimilarity (opposition) could be also a relation that binds objects, but also, as shown in the section on the example of the fictitious U.N., that irreducibly multilateral relations could cause cohesion of a group (see Section 4.3).

However, what we have said at the beginning of this section goes still further beyond the case of objects with known properties. For instance, suppose we have a group of people and some pairs among them know each other and some do not. Cohesion within a partial group will be the strongest if every pair in it knows each other. A natural split of a whole group of people into subgroups would be such that within each subgroup people know one another with very few exceptions. The cleavage surfaces in a group like this will be such that they cut as few bonds of acquaintance as possible.

Let $X = \{x_1, x_2, \ldots, x_m\}$ be the set of given objects. We split this set into ν disjoint subsets, $X_1, X_2, \ldots, X_\nu$,

$$X_\rho \subset X, \qquad \rho=1, 2, \ldots, \nu \tag{6.5.1}$$

such that

$$\bigcup_{\rho=1}^{\nu} X_\rho = X, \tag{6.5.2}$$

$$X_\rho \wedge X_\sigma = \phi, \ \rho\neq\sigma. \tag{6.5.3}$$

Suppose we can define a nonnegative set function

$$C(X_\rho) \geq 0 \qquad \rho=1, 2, \ldots, \nu, \qquad (6.5.4)$$

which we call cohesion. It is in many practical cases possible to assume the supra-additivity of the C-function:

$$C(X_\rho \vee X_\sigma) \geq C(X_\rho) + C(X_\sigma) \qquad (6.5.5)$$

or

$$J(X_\rho, X_\sigma) \equiv C(X_\rho \vee X_\sigma) - C(X_\rho) - C(X_\sigma) \geq 0 \qquad (6.5.6)$$

For instance, we can take as $C(X_\rho)$ the number of bonds of acquaintance in the group X_ρ of people. We see immediately that the supra-additivity is satisfied, because some members of group X_ρ may know some members of group X_σ.

Our stated policy about splitting is that we should divide $X_\tau = X_\rho \vee X_\sigma$ into two subsets X_ρ and X_σ such that J becomes minimum. This policy will maximize the intra-subset cohesion and minimize the inter-subset cohesion.

A repeated use of the formula (6.5.5) allows us to write for a multiple splitting the J-minimizing policy with

$$X_\tau = X_\rho \vee X_\sigma \vee \ldots \vee X_\omega \qquad (6.5.7)$$

$$X_\rho \wedge X_\sigma = \phi, \ \rho \neq \sigma, \text{ etc.}, \qquad (6.5.8)$$

$$C(X_\tau) \geq C(X_\rho) + C(X_\sigma) + \ldots + X_\omega \qquad (6.5.9)$$

$$\begin{aligned} J(X_\rho, X_\sigma, \ldots, X_\omega) &= C(X_\tau) \\ - C(X_\rho) - C(X_\sigma) - \ldots &- C(X_\omega) \geq 0 \end{aligned} \qquad (6.5.10)$$

As the reader might have already guessed, the entropic expression of interdependence, which we introduced in (6.2.17) and (6.2.22), can play the role of the J-function of this section, (6.5.6), (6.5.10). Correspondingly, the C-function would become, in the context of entropic analysis of organization,

$$C(X) = S(x_1) + S(x_2) + \ldots + S(x_m) - S(X) \geq 0, \qquad (6.5.11)$$

where X is the set consisting of m objects x_1, x_2, ..., x_m, each of which is considered as a stochastic variable having entropy $S(x_i)$. Applying this definition to each subset of objects we have

$$\begin{aligned} J(X_\rho, X_\sigma, \ldots, X_\omega) &= C(X_\tau) - C(X_\rho) \\ &- C(X_\sigma) - \ldots - C(X_\omega) = S(X_\rho) \qquad (6.5.12) \\ &+ S(X_\sigma) + \ldots + S(X_\omega) - S(X_\tau) \geq 0 \end{aligned}$$

The entropy function is infra-additive:

$$S(X_\rho \vee X_\sigma) \leq S(X_\rho) + S(X_\sigma) \qquad (6.5.13)$$

for $X_\rho \wedge X_\sigma = \phi$, therefore C-function becomes supra-additive, (6.5.5).

The clustering problems generally have no definite meaning unless we know how many classes we want to make. For a given ν, we can compare the J-values of different ways of making ν subsets. But, the above method does not mention how to compare two divisions with different ν's.

The following strategy is a practical way of proceeding in the case where we might want to make two or more classes.

1. Apply only dichotomy (division into two) to the entire set. If one of the J-values is very much lower than the others, we should end this stage with that dichotomy.
2. If there are two or more J-values which are more or less equal to each other and much lower than the others, we execute all the dichotomies corresponding to the near-minimum J-values. The desired classes are those subsets which are "meet" (conjunction) of the results of the dichotomies.

3. If we want more classes than those thus obtained, we should repeat (1) to (3) to each of the classes.

Now we want to show that the C-function defined with the entropies does indeed represent the relations such as similarity, dissimilarity, and higher-order correlation we have discussed earlier. Let us assume that we are given an object-predicate table with m objects $X = \{x_1, x_2, \ldots, x_m\}$, and n binary predicates $Y = \{y_1, y_2, \ldots, y_n\}$. If we limit ourselves to a subset of "more important" predicates taken from the completed lattice $\hat{Y}$, the number of predicates simultaneously affirmed by two objects can be regarded as a mark of similarity. If we agree that a predicate y_j and its negation $\neg y_j$ are both included in Y, a simultaneous affirmation of y_j and a simultaneous negation of y_j will equally contribute to the similarity.

Let us focus our attention on two rows x_i and x_k in Table 4.3.1. Let $n_1(x_i) = n - n_0(x_i)$ be the number of 1's (affirmations) in the row of x_i; $n_0(x_i)$ is the number of 0's (negations)--similarly for $n_1(x_k)$ and $n_0(x_k)$. Further, let $n_{11}(x_i, x_j)$ be the number of columns on which 1 appears on both the i-th row and the k-th row. Similarly, $n_{10}(x_i, x_k)$ is the number columns on which 1 appears on the i-th row and 0 appears on the k-th row--similarly, for $n_{00}(x_i, x_k)$, $n_{01}(x_i, x_k)$.

If the 1's on the i-th row and 1's on the k-th row are distributed at random, then we shall have

$$\frac{n_{11}(x_i, x_k)}{n} = \frac{n_1(x_i)}{n} \cdot \frac{n_1(x_k)}{n} . \qquad (6.5.14)$$

But if the 1's in the i-th row and 1's in the k-th row have a tendency to coincide more frequently than by accident we shall have

$$\frac{n_{11}(x_i, x_k)}{n} > \frac{n_1(x_i)}{n} \cdot \frac{n_1(x_k)}{n} , \qquad (6.5.15)$$

which may be regarded as a sign of similarity.

To simplify the notation, we introduce

$$\alpha = \frac{n_{11}(x_i, x_k)}{n}, \quad \beta = \frac{n_{10}(x_i, x_k)}{n} \tag{6.5.16}$$

$$\gamma = \frac{n_{01}(x_i, x_k)}{n}, \quad \delta = \frac{n_{00}(x_i, x_k)}{n}.$$

We have obviously

$$\alpha+\beta = \frac{n_1(x_i)}{n}, \quad \gamma+\delta = \frac{n_0(x_i)}{n} \tag{6.5.17}$$

$$\alpha+\gamma = \frac{n_1(x_k)}{n}, \quad \beta+\delta = \frac{n_0(x_k)}{n}.$$

The condition of similarity in affirmative becomes

$$\frac{\alpha}{(\alpha+\beta)(\alpha+\gamma)} > 1 ; \tag{6.5.18}$$

the condition of similarity in negation becomes

$$\frac{\delta}{(\beta+\delta)(\gamma+\delta)} > 1 . \tag{6.5.19}$$

Taking the logarithms of these two quantities and joining them with relative weight α and δ, we obtain a good measure of similarity,

$$C^+ = \alpha\log\frac{\alpha}{(\alpha+\beta)(\alpha+\gamma)} + \delta\log\frac{\delta}{(\delta+\beta)(\delta+\gamma)} . \tag{6.5.20}$$

A positive value of C^+ indicates similarity, and the magnitude can be regarded as its degree.

The dissimilarity is marked by

$$\frac{n_{10}(x_i, x_k)}{n} > \frac{n_1(x_i)}{n}\frac{n_0(x_k)}{n} \tag{6.5.21}$$

or

$$\frac{\beta}{(\alpha+\beta)(\beta+\delta)} > 0 ; \tag{6.5.22}$$

and similarly

$$\frac{\gamma}{(\gamma+\delta)(\alpha+\gamma)} > 1 \ . \tag{6.5.23}$$

The quantity corresponding to C^+ is

$$C^- = \beta\log\frac{\beta}{(\beta+\alpha)(\beta+\delta)} + \gamma\log\frac{\gamma}{(\gamma+\delta)(\gamma+\alpha)} \ , \tag{6.5.24}$$

which is a good measure of dissimilarity. The larger the C^- the stronger is the degree to which the two objects x_i and x_k are dissimilar.

If we multiply the numerator, α, of (6.5.18) by

$$\alpha + \beta + \gamma + \delta = 1 \tag{6.5.25}$$

we obtain from (6.5.18)

$$\theta > 0 \tag{6.5.26}$$

with

$$\theta \equiv \alpha\delta - \beta\gamma \tag{6.5.27}$$

Similarly, also from (6.5.19), we obtain (6.5.26), which shows that two conditions (6.5.18) and (6.5.19) are equivalent. Further, by a similar manipulation, we can show that (6.5.22) and (6.5.23) are equivalent to each other and to

$$\theta < 0 \tag{6.5.28}$$

If a y_j and its negation $\neg y_j$ are listed in Y, we have

$$\alpha = \delta \quad \text{and} \quad \beta = \gamma \tag{6.5.29}$$

and

$$\alpha + \beta = \tfrac{1}{2} \ . \tag{6.5.30}$$

In this special case, the conditions of similarity of (6.5.18) and (6.5.19) become simply $\alpha > \frac{1}{4}$ and its conditions of dissimilarity of (6.5.22) and (6.5.23) become $\alpha < \frac{1}{4}$.

Under this simplifying condition of (6.5.29) and (6.5.30), we can compare easily the different

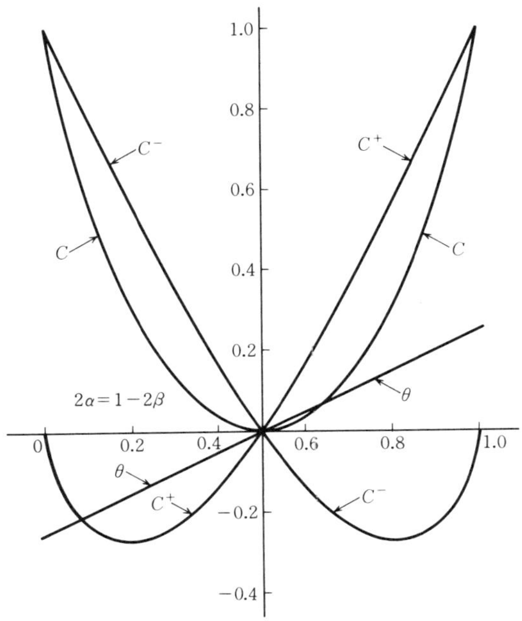

Figure 6.5.1 This figure shows the relationship among the indices of similarity: α, θ, and C^+, and the indices of dissimilarity: β and C^-. The sum of C^+ and C^-, which is C, is the degree of interdependence.

quantities characterizing similarity and dissimilarity (see Figure 6.5.1).

Now if we add C^+ and C^-, we obtain

$$\begin{aligned} C = C^+ + C^- &= -(\alpha+\beta)\log(\alpha+\beta) - (\alpha+\gamma)\log(\alpha+\gamma) \\ &\quad - (\beta+\delta)\log(\beta+\delta) - (\delta+\gamma)\log(\delta+\gamma) \\ &\quad + \alpha\log\alpha + \beta\log\beta + \gamma\log\gamma + \delta\log\delta \\ &= S(x_i) + S(x_k) - S(x_i, x_k) = J(x_i, x_k) . \end{aligned} \tag{6.5.31}$$

Then we see that the bilateral cohesion function represents the combined effect of similarity and dissimilarity. If two objects show neither similarity nor dissimilarity, the C-function becomes zero.

Next we want to show that our cohesion method is capable of unveiling irreducibly multilateral relations among objects that can contribute to formation of classes. As an example, we shall take the case of the voting pattern of the fictitious United Nations (see Table 4.3.1). We have four rows, x_1, x_2, x_3, x_4 and eight columns. The entire set is $X = \{x_1, x_2, x_3, x_4\}$. There are four subsets of three members, $X_{123} = \{x_1, x_2, x_3\}$, $X_{234} = \{x_2, x_3, x_4\}$, $X_{341} = \{x_3, x_4, x_1\}$, $X_{412} = \{x_4, x_1, x_2\}$. There are six subsets of two members $X_{12} = \{x_1, x_2\}$, etc.

Each object has four 1's and four 0's which means that each of two possible cases occur with probability 1/2. Therefore, the entropy of each object is $S = -\frac{1}{2}\log\frac{1}{2} - \frac{1}{2}\log\frac{1}{2} = \log 2$. Next, each group of two, for instance x_1 and x_2, has probability $\frac{1}{4}$ for each of four possible alternatives, (0, 0), (0, 1), (1, 0) and (1, 1). Hence, any group of two members has entropy $S = 4(-\frac{1}{4}\log\frac{1}{4}) = \log 4$. For groups of three, there are two kinds. For a group of three members, there could in principle be eight possible combinations of values, (0, 0, 0), (0, 0, 1), (0, 1, 0), (1, 0, 0), (0, 1, 1), (1, 0, 1), (1, 1, 0) and (1, 1, 1). As a matter of fact, for any one of the four subsets of three members, except $\{x_1, x_2, x_3\}$, these eight possibilities appear with probability 1/8. Hence, the entropy of the three subgroups of three members is log 8, but only for the subset $\{x_1, x_2, x_3\}$, the combinations of values (0, 0, 1), (0, 1, 0), (1, 0, 0) and (1, 1, 1) are missing. Each of the remaining four possibilities (0, 0, 0), (0, 1, 1), (1, 0, 1), and (1, 1, 0) appear with equal probability. $S(x_1, x_2, x_3) = \log 4$. $S(x_2, x_3, x_4) = S(x_3, x_4, x_1) = S(x_4, x_1, x_2) = \log 8$.

As for the entire set of four objects, there are sixteen possible combinations of values, but in Table 4.3.1 only eight possibilities are present with probability 1/8. Hence entropy of the entire set is log 8.

From these values of entropy, we can calculate the cohesion:

$$
\begin{aligned}
C^{(4)}(x_1, x_2, x_3, x_4) &= 4x\log 2 - \log 8 = \log 2\,, \\
C^{(3)}(x_1, x_2, x_3) &= 3x\log 2 = \log 4\,, \\
C^{(3)}(x_2, x_3, x_4) &= C^{(3)}(x_3, x_4, x_1) = C^{(3)}(x_4, x_1, x_2) \\
&= 3x\log 2 = \log 8\,, \\
C^{(2)}(x_1, x_2) &= C^{(2)}(x_2, x_3) = C^{(2)}(x_3, x_4) \\
&= C^{(2)}(x_1, x_3) = C^{(2)}(x_2, x_4) = C(x_3, x_1) \\
&= 2x\log 2 - \log 4 = 0\,, \\
C^{(1)}(x_1) &= C^{(1)}(x_2) = C^{(1)}(x_3) = C^{(1)}(x_4) = 0\,.
\end{aligned}
\tag{6.5.32}
$$

There are four ways of splitting a set of four members into a subset of three members and a subset of one member, and three ways of splitting the set of four into two subsets of two. If we calculate the J-value for all these seven ways of dichotomies, they are all log 2 except the split

$$\{x_1, x_2, x_3, x_4\} \rightarrow \{x_1, x_2, x_3\}\ \{x_4\}$$

for which $J = 0$. If we obey the principle of minimization of entropy, which coincides with the principle of the least resistant cleavage, we have to divide the total voting members into two groups: a subgroup consisting of pro-American, pro-Soviet, pro-Third World nations and a subgroup of perfectly neutral nations. This shows that our method of cohesion is capable of unravelling a hidden structure due to purely multilateral relations.

The idea of using the J-function for the purpose of classification and concept formation was already developed in 1957 [W-5, W-7]. The first applications of this method to a real problem were carried out by Francis W. Dauer in 1961, [D-1], and Casimir Kulikowski in 1965, unpublished (see also [W-10]). Kaminuma [K-17] developed an ingenious computer program to carry out the strategy efficiently and with co-workers obtained useful results.

6.6 DISCRIMINANT SURFACE

This section is concerned with an application of the principle of entropy minimization to the problems of paradigm-oriented pattern recognition [W-46, W-47, W-56]. When sample points known to belong to m classes are given in the n-dimensional space, assuming we can appropriately divide the space into m disparate domains in agreement with the paradigm points, then it would become possible for us to locate a newcomer into an appropriate class. The surfaces between these domains are the discriminant surfaces. In this section, we shall limit ourselves mainly to the two-class case, m=2, and the surface will be assumed to be a hyperplane of (n-1) dimensions. Generalization of the method to more than two-class cases is possible at least in principle. If we allowed the discriminant surface to be curved surfaces of any order, we would be able to satisfy the paradigm points perfectly, but an excessively gerrymandering surface is not realistic, and it becomes a delicate problem to find a reasonable compromise between the ideal of simplicity and the compliance with the paradigms.

To determine a hyperplane, it suffices to specify the direction of the normal to the plane and to decide where the plane should cut the normal. Let us first take up the direction of the normal. Suppose we project all paradigm points on this normal line and segment the normal into small intervals labeled by the index j. Let p^i_j, i = 1, 2; j = 1, 2, 3,... represent the relative frequency of paradigms of class i placed in the j-th interval. The entropy-minimization principle for two classes requires the minimization of the W-function, (6.2.13),

$$W(p^1,p^2) = -\sum_{j=1}^{\infty} p^1{}_j \log p^1{}_j - \sum_{j=1}^{\infty} p^2{}_j \log p^2{}_j + \sum_{j=1}^{\infty} p^1{}_j \log p^2{}_j + \sum_{j=1}^{\infty} p^2{}_j \log p^1{}_j \quad (6.6.1)$$

or its polynomial counterpart, (6.2.27)

$$U(p^1,p^2) = -\sum_{j=1}^{\infty} (p^1{}_j)^2 - \sum_{j=1}^{\infty} (p^2{}_j)^2 + 2\sum_{j=1}^{\infty} p^1{}_j p^2{}_j \ . \quad (6.6.2)$$

The mathematical minimization of W and U would be realized if the following two conditions would be satisfied: (1) For each i, one interval has $p^i{}_j = 1$ (concentrated in one interval); (2) $p^1{}_j = 1$ and $p^2{}_k = 1$ imply $j \neq k$ (no overlap). The direction of the normal should be such that U or W becomes minimum when the given paradigms are projected on this normal. The logarithmic entropy W is slightly inconvenient because $W = -\infty$ can be realized if $p^1{}_j$ is finite for a j for which $p^2{}_j = 0$, or if $p^2{}_j$ is finite for j for which $p^1{}_j = 0$. For this reason, the polynomial entropy is slightly more convenient.

But, depending on the given paradigms, the realization of the mathematically possible minimum cannot be reached by rotation of the normal. In such a general case, the minimization condition on W or U will require (1) minimization of intraclass "spread" represented by the first two terms of (6.6.1) or (6.6.2), and (2) maximization of interclass distance, i.e., minimization of the last two terms of (6.6.1) or the last term of (6.6.2). These two conditions, which are aimed at also in the Fisher's discriminant (see Chapter 9), are intuitively understandable, but it is significant that they ensue from the minimum-entropy principle.

When we have sufficiently many paradigms, we can obtain probability density function and may be able to use

$$W(p^1,p^2) = -\int p^1(x)\log \frac{p^1(x)}{p^2(x)}\,dx - \int p^2(x)\log \frac{p^2(x)}{p^1(x)}\,dx \tag{6.6.3}$$

or

$$V(p^1,p^2) = -\int [p^1(x) - p^2(x)]^2 dx . \tag{6.6.4}$$

The continuous expression W, (6.6.3), is invariant for a probability preserving transformation, but V is not.

The next question is where to draw the plane whose normal is decided by the above procedure. Suppose we are given paradigms of two classes, and let N^1 and N^2 be their respective numbers. Suppose the discriminant surface separates the n-dimensional space into two parts: part 1, supposedly representing class 1, and part 2 representing class 2. Let $N^i{}_j$, i=1,2; j=1,2 be the number of paradigms of class i placed in the part j of the space. Then

$$\sum_{j=1}^{2} N^i{}_j = N^i . \tag{6.6.5}$$

Let p^i, be defined by

$$p^i{}_j = N^i{}_j / N^i , \tag{6.6.6}$$

where

$$p^i{}_j \geq 0, \quad \sum_{j=1}^{2} p^i{}_j = 1 \quad \text{for each } i . \tag{6.6.7}$$

Keeping the normal as decided already, we can move the surface so that the following entropy becomes minimum:

$$W(p^1,p^2) = -\sum_{j=1}^{2} p^1{}_j \log \frac{p^1{}_j}{p^2{}_j} - \Sigma p^2{}_j \log \frac{p^2{}_j}{p^1{}_j} \quad (6.6.8)$$

or

$$U(p^1,p^2) = -\sum_{j=1}^{2} (p^1{}_j - p^2{}_j)^2 . \quad (6.6.9)$$

If all paradigms of class 1 are placed on one side of the discriminant, and all paradigms of class 2 are placed on the other side of the surface, both W and U become minimum. The inverse of this statement is true only for U.

If the surface can be allowed to be gerrymandered, we can always realize the minimization condition. But, if we are limited to a flat hyperplane, we cannot necessarily reach the minimum of U (which is -2). If this is possible, we speak of a separable case. If the case is not separable even if we allow ourselves to change the direction of the normal, the perceptron will not work. In our method, we can decide the normal as well as the position of the plane following the principle of minimum entropy.

We decided the normal by projecting paradigm points on a straight line. This procedure can be considered as a dimensionality reduction to one-dimensional space. Similarly, by projecting the paradigm points on a more than one-dimensional subspace, we can decide the subspace requiring the minimization of entropy. Thus, the same entropy-minimization principle can be used as a general tool of dimensionality reduction. This is possible because the expressions (6.6.1) - (6.6.4) can be used for a subspace of any dimensionality. The case of projection on the normal of a plane is just the simplest example. The strategy will be to choose the subspace such that the entropy calculated on the projected subspace becomes minimum.

Diday et al. [D-5] introduced a criterion in the process of projection of paradigm points onto a subspace of less dimensionality. We want to show that a principle of minimum entropy can engender, under certain conditions, a criterion similar to Diday-Lemoine's. For simplicity, we show the calculation for the case of one-dimensional subspace, but an extension to higher dimensional subspace will be obvious. Let us assume that the two paradigm density curves $p^1(x)$ and $p^2(x)$ can be approximated by two normal distributions

$$p^1(x) \propto \exp[-(x-x_{01})^2/(2\sigma_1^2)] \qquad (6.6.10)$$

$$p^2(x) \propto \exp[-(x-x_{02})^2/(2\sigma_2^2)] \;. \qquad (6.6.11)$$

Then the W-function will become

$$W(p^1,p^2) \propto$$

$$\frac{1}{\sigma_1^2} (x-x_{01})^2 \exp[-(x-x_{01})^2/(2\sigma_1^2)]\, dx$$

$$+ \frac{1}{\sigma_2^2} (x-x_{02})^2 \exp[-(x-x_{02})^2/(2\sigma_2^2)]\, dx$$

$$- \frac{1}{\sigma_2^2} (x-x_{02})^2 \exp[-(x-x_{01})^2/(2\sigma_1^2)]\, dx$$

$$- \frac{1}{\sigma_1^2} (x-x_{01})^2 \exp[-(x-x_{02})^2/(2\sigma_2^2)]\, dx \;. \qquad (6.6.12)$$

The first integral is the moment of inertia of the points of class 1 about their center of gravity. The second integral is the same for class 2. Provided that the two centers x_{01} and x_{02} are sufficiently distant, the third integral becomes the moment of inertia of the center of class 1 about the center of class 2. Similarly, the fourth integral represents the moment of inertia of class 2 about the center of class 1, because if the distance between x_{01} and x_{02} is larger than σ_1 and σ_2, the contribution in the third (fourth) integral comes mainly from the points around the center of class 1 (class 2).

The minimization of $W(p^1,p^2)$ therefore implies the minimization of the moment of inertia of points of class 1 (class 2) about the center of class 1 (class 2) and the maximization of the moment of inertia of the center of class 1 (class 2) about the center of class 2 (class 1). This is, in essence, the same as the Diday-Lemoine criterion in the multiclass clustering. The expression of equations (6.6.10) and (6.6.11) is written in the one-dimensional case, but it is obvious how to generalize in the multidimensional case. We assumed the normal distribution in equations (6.6.10) and (6.6.11), but we can consider this assumption as a rough approximation in order to clarify the relationship between the principle of minimum entropy and the Diday-Lemoine criterion. In general, we can use the entropy function to obtain a dimensionality reduction. For the multiclass case, we can take W or U of the type (6.2.30).

6.7 INFORMATION COMPRESSION

In the preceding sections of this Chapter, we have seen various applications of the principle of entropy minimization as a heuristic guide in our conceptual adaptation, whose ultimate aim lies in revealing a few articulately distinct classes in a vast sea of given data. The balance sheet of such a classificatory effort is essentially a comparison between the number of possible input data and the number of resulting classes. This comparison is therefore a comparison of the input "information" (that an object is one of the possible alternative input data) and the output "information" (that the object belongs to one of the possible classes).

We consider a set A of N possible objects and a set of its subsets

$$B_i \subset A, \qquad i=1,2,\ldots,M , \tag{6.7.1}$$

such that, at least ideally,

$$B_i \cap B_j = \emptyset, \qquad i \neq j \tag{6.7.2}$$

$$A = \bigcup_{i=1}^{M} B_i . \tag{6.7.3}$$

Each subset or class B_i is characterized by some conditions on its members, but it is inevitable that one of them is a meaningless catch-all subset. Indeed, practically in any application, some of the conceivable objects do not make any sense and have to be rejected at a certain stage out of consideration. Because we cannot usually assign a probability to each possible object, we had best use Hartley's definition of information which is the logarithm of possible alternatives to express the amount of information that an object is a member of a set or subset. Hartley's entropy is the usual expression of entropy in which all the probabilities are purposely put equal to one another. Then the input information is log N and the output information is log M. The amount of classificatory effect is the information compression,

$$r = \text{compression rate} = \log \frac{N}{M} = \log N - \log M. \quad (6.7.4)$$

This is a measure of the effectiveness of the classification in which the useful information of amount of log M is extracted from the given information in the amount of log N. In an extreme case, the result is a dichotomic answer as to whether an object belongs or does not belong to a class, the resulting information log M is just one bit.

The input information contains a tremendous amount of irrelevant or redundant information. Therefore, information compression means, above all, elimination of useless information. Establishment of a catch-all subclass is one way of eliminating useless information. The dimensionality reduction in the sense of the SELFIC method is certainly another (see Section 7.2). There could be many other ways. The desired total compression rate of log N/M is usually very large; as a consequence, the entire information compression in many cases is executed in several steps. In any event, the information compression in the above sense is another aspect of entropy minimization.

From observation of actual cases of pattern recognition, one may probably summarize the situation as follows:

1. The larger the information compression in one step the better it is, but the larger the compression rate the more difficult the task is. (We ignore the question of goodness or appropriateness of information compression.)
2. If the information compression is to be made in steps, it is desirable that the burden of information compression be distributed more or less evenly over different steps.
3. It is desirable to pass through a step in which it is easy to define a distinction between meaningful and meaningless subsets.

Because the information compression rate is defined by a logarithmic function, the rate is "additive" in the sense that if the transition from $N = N_0$ to $M = N_\nu$ is done through successive steps: $N_0 \to N_1 \to N_2 \to N_3 \to \dots \to N_\nu$, we have

$$r = \sum_{i=1}^{\nu} r_i$$

$$r_i = \log \frac{N_{i-1}}{N_i} . \qquad (6.7.5)$$

If we consider r_i as a kind of "labor," it is natural, if ν is given, to equalize the labor in each stage, which is the meaning of (2) above.

As an illustration, we adopt the representation of object as points in an n-dimensional Euclid space. Suppose that the set A of possible objects occupies the volume L^n in the n-dimensional space and that points within an elementary volume h^n are experimentally indistinguishable. The dimension n is the number of measured quantities of objects to be classified. Then, the number of possible alternatives $N = (L/h)^n$ is usually enormously large compared with the number M of classes. One stroke compression $\log[(L/h)^n/M]$ is usually very difficult not only because it is difficult to find a dividing surface satisfying the paradigms, but also because there appears to be too much arbitrariness. This necessitates preprocessing effecting a dimensionality reduction. If we first reduce the dimensionality from n to n'--we assume the same order of indistinguishableness per dimension in the new space--the information compression is done in two steps. The first step amounts to $\log[(L/h)^n/(L/h)^{n'}] = (n-n')\log(L/h)$ and the second step amounts to $\log[(L/h)^{n'}/M]$. Although the total is the same as before, this division in two steps usually makes the task considerably easier.

The method of SELFIC (self-featuring-information-compression, see Section 7.2), based on diagonalization of the covariance matrix, is a powerful tool in the first step information compression. As the second step information compression, a volume method (a volume in the reduced n'-dimensional subspace is assigned to a class) or a subspace method (an n"-dimensional subspace of the n'-dimensional subspace is assigned to a class, as in the CLAFIC-method, Section 7.6) can be used.

To illustrate point (3), let us take up a "Toshiba" ZIP-code reading machine and find out how the information compression takes place in steps in the machine. This machine is not only the first machine that was successfully used in a post office, but was also the only machine that could read handwritten ZIP code. To simplify the description, we shall ignore in the following some of the technical details of the functions of the machine. Those who are interested in the precise description should read the original report by the engineers who developed the machine [G-6] or an abbreviated explanation [W-27].

This machine locates the ZIP code numbers on the envelopes or postcards, contracts the size of the figures if they are too large, reduces the continuous greyness to two values, black and white, adjusts the thickness of each stroke, and finally produces a 32 X 32 binary (1 and 0) matrix corresponding to 32 X 32 black and white mesh points for each read character. Of these 32 rows and 32 columns, each intersection of 16 (every other) rows and 32 columns are used as "sampling points." At each sampling point, a small 3 X 3 submatrix is taken, covering adjacent rows and adjacent columns. There could be 2^9 different (3 X 3) matrices, but they are classified into seven different types: blank, vertical, increasing, decreasing, high horizontal, low horizontal, and miscellaneous. The miscellaneous class is a big "junk box" (see Figure 6.7.1). Figure 6.7.2 shows five black and white distributions that are classified as "increasing." Each of the seven types includes several configurations of black and white mesh points. For instance, all five configurations mentioned in Figure 6.7.2 belong to the type classified as "increasing." Each of the seven configuration types serves as an elementary component for a composite structure.

As far as a single 3 X 3 submatrix is concerned, $2^9 = 512$ possibilities are compressed into seven possibilities, i.e., nine bits are compressed into $\log_2 7 = 2.81$ bits. But a new redundancy is introduced by the overlapping of the 3 X 3 submatrices. The original representation can carry one bit at each of 32 X 32 points at maximum. (Of course the majority of the possibilities does not correspond to any character.) In the new representation the maximum information of $\log_2 7 = 2.81$ bits cannot be actually carried at each of the 32 X 16 points, because there are some inevitable mutual constraints between neighboring points in this description. The average must be of course less than two bits per point because the original information was one bit per one out of 32 X 32 points, which corresponds to two bits per one out of 32 X 16 points. But, as far as the memory device in the machine is concerned, the second representation would require even more space because we have to provide 32 X 16 X log 7 bits of capacity as compared with 32 X 32 X 1 bits. Therefore, the first stage of the operation by the machine does not result in any substantial information compression, but it prepares the ground for a large and meaningful compression at the next stage.

Each of the 16 rows, or rather 16 horizontal zones, is now characterized by a string consisting of seven components. There could be 7^{32} different configurations in a horizontal zone, but they are

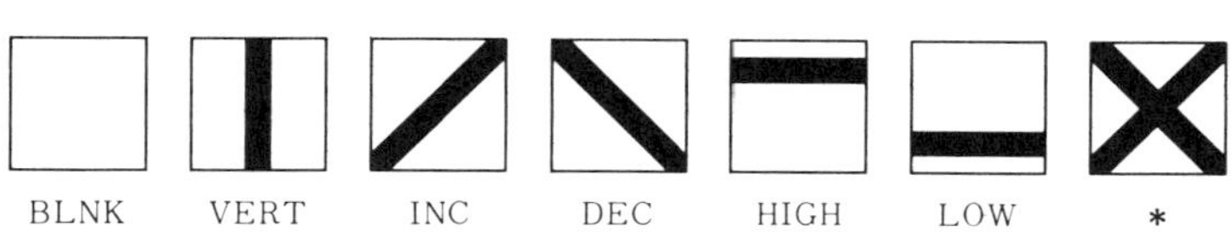

Figure 6.7.1 Seven lowest-level atoms characterizing 3 X 3 meshes.

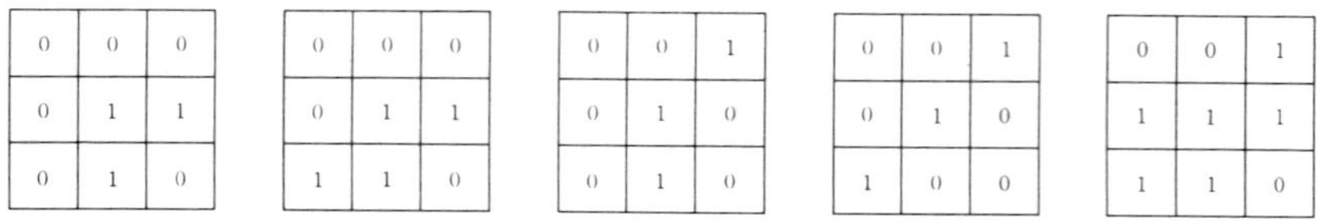

Figure 6.7.2 Five kinds of black-and-white distributions classified as "increasing."

classified again into 16 zone types: blank, vertical, increasing, decreasing, bar, cap, cup, parallel, etc. (see Figure 6.7.3). Each zone type serves as a secondary component subject to further structuring. Each horizontal zone type comprises, of course, many configurations of horizontal zones. For instance, a zone of the structure: blank-increase-high-decrease-blank is considered CAP, where blank stands for a run of arbitrary number of blanks, and high can stand for several highs in a row, etc. This rule, incidentally is an example of what we called in Appendix 1 "run contraction," which proves to be useful in many problems of pattern recognition. The run contraction makes it more economical to use a sequential logic, because what is important is a transition of states rather than the state of each position. Each 32-unit-long horizontal zone can, in the absence of constraints, be any one of the 7^{32} possible strings which are classified into 16 classes. Bit-wise, this is a compression from $\log_2(7^{32}) = 89.9$ bits down to $\log_2 16 = 4$ bits; the ratio is as much as 85.9 per zone.

To recover important information lost by the use of run contraction, the designers of the machine introduced an additional bit of information to each of the secondary components, splitting each zone type into "with asterisk" and "without asterisk." The zone called "with asterisk" means that the first black mesh point on the last row of the previous (i.e., one above) zone and the first black mesh point on the second row of the zone under consideration have the same column label, or have a difference of ± 1. The zone designated "without asterisk" means that it has column labels different by more than one unit. Thus, the asterisk indicates whether or not the blacks of the two zones start approximately at the same horizontal position (i.e., column label). Even including this additional bit, the information

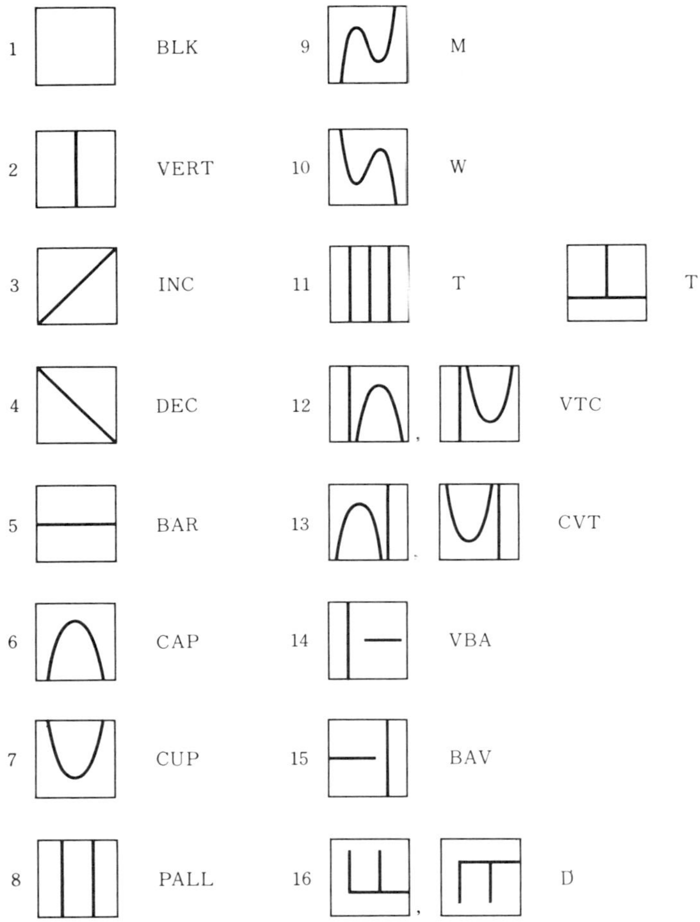

Figure 6.7.3 Sixteen intermediate atoms characterizing horizontal zones.

content of the new zone characterization is five bits. The compression ratio is 89.9 - 5 = 84.9.

There are 16 horizontal zones, and each zone can belon to any one of 16 X 2 zone types or secondary components, hence there are 32^{16} different global configurations. Depending on the structure of these components, the global configuration is classified into 10 different figures; 0, 1, 2, ..., 9. For instance, the global configuration obeying the sequence rule (called diagram), CAP - PALL - CUP - CAP - PALL - CUP, will be classified as 8 (see Figure 6.7.4). CAP means the convex-upward piece (finishing with two ends), which will be continued downward by two vertical lines that will be closed by the cup-shaped concave-upward piece, finishing the upper loop of the figure 8; the same applies for the lower loop. Of course, many of the similar sequences can be interpreted as 8. For instance, we can see that if we put one BAR between CUP and the second CAP, it will still look like 8. Similarly, if there are two PALL's instead of one PALL it will not change the 8-ness of the figure, another example of run-contraction. At this stage of information compression, a great deal of possibilities are rejected as meaningless, not belonging to any of the the 10 meaningful alternatives.

From the point of view of information compression, 32^{16} possibilities or 80 bits is reduced to 11 classes (including nonsense figures) or log 11 = 3.2... bits. The information reduction rate is 80-3.2... = 76.8. To repeat, the total input information $\log N_0 = \log_2 2^{32X32} = 1024$, the result of the first rewriting is $\log N_1 = \log 7^{16X32} = 1438.72$. After the second rewriting, $\log N_2 = 32^{16} = 80$. After the final compression $\log N_3 = \log_2 11 = 3.2...$. The

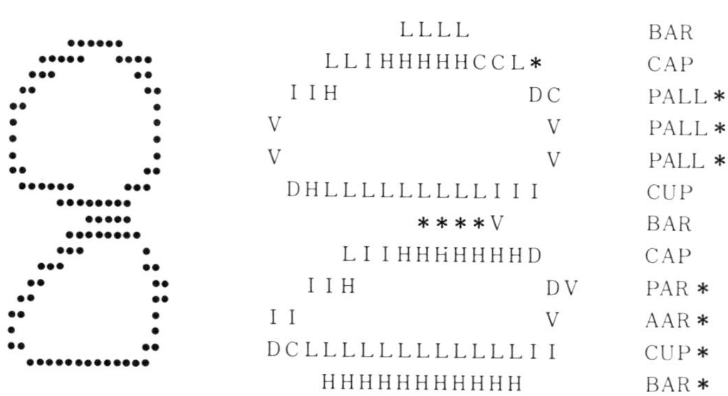

Figure 6.7.4 The vertical series, BAR, CAP, PAR, CUP, CAP, PAR, CUP, BAR, is deciphered as an 8.

compression ratio $r_i = \log N_{i-1} - \log N_i$ is far from the ideal equal partition $(1/3)(\log N_0 - \log N_3)$, but the success of the machine is admirable.

About 70 standard global diagrams are stored (and can be updated). The input diagram is compared with the standard diagrams. A perfect match is not sought, but the minimum discrepancy is sought. If the minimum discrepancy is larger than a certain threshold, or if some amount of minimum discrepancy is obtained for more than one numeral, the input is rejected. If the input is rejected, the horizontal zones are taken, with respect to those rows which were not used, as the center of the 3 X 3 matrix in the first pass and recognition is tried again.

The secret of success of this ZIP code reader is its methodology which consists of regarding a figure as composed, in a certain regular fashion, of constituent components. This methodology is to be compared to the atomistic view of the physical world. Instead of regarding the multifarious world as consisting of milliards of different objects, it considers, in agreement with Occham's dictum, the existing objects as consisting of a very limited number of atoms, whereby the multifariousness is attributed to how the atoms are put together. Somewhat like the modern atomism, which puts the elementary particles at the very bottom and then acknowledges the "secondary" constituent components of atoms and molecules, the ZIP code machine assumes three layers of atoms. At the very bottom there are two atoms of black and white meshes, followed by seven first-order constituents of mesh characterization, such as increasing, decreasing, vertical, etc. On the third layer, there are 16 zone characterizations, such as CAP, CUP, etc., and finally there are 10 figures which are numerals.

About the same time as this ZIP code machine was developed, theoreticians mostly in the United States started a new movement in pattern recognition differently called the grammatical approach, structural approach, and syntactical approach. Depending on the author, the nuance and emphasis are different, but the underlying tenet is the same: a figure is to be considered as consisting of a limited number of atomic components, which are put together obeying certain rules. From the point of view of information compression, the total rate of compression is divided up into more than one step. A clever way of choosing the atomic figures and grammatical rules makes it easy to distinguish meaningful compositions from meaningless compositions, thus effecting efficient information compression. In Chapter 10, we shall discuss the problem of figures consisting of atoms under structural laws and analyze the claimed difference of the grammatical approach from the other approaches. The content of this section was published in [W-26] and [W-27].

6.8 MINIMUM ENTROPY PRINCIPLE IN CONTROL THEORY

It is well known that Norbert Wiener started his famous book, *Cybernetics*, with the first chapter on the Newtonian and Bergsonian concepts of time, in which he stated to the effect that the new "theory of control" (cybernetics) requires a new concept of time in line with Bergson's idea of irreversible "durée," in particular, with the idea of time of life going in the opposite direction to the physical time of ever increasing entropy [W-41]. It is surprising that most of the followers of Wiener ignored this fundamental tenet of cybernetics [W-42].

The present author, in the meantime, tried two approaches in the general line of thought of entropy-decrease in cybernetical systems. One was that the theory of learning, which maintains that the essence of learning process, whether it refers to cognitive learning or to learning of behavioral skill, can be expressed as a process of decreasing entropy, provided the entropy is defined by the probabilities of alternative responses [W-36]. Another was the theory of minimum entropy as a heuristic principle, which is useful in discovering algorithms in pattern recognition [W-47].

In this section, we want to show that the principle of minimum entropy can lead to the same conclusion as the stability theory of Liapounoff in the problem of control theory (see Letov [L-6]).

The control action has to fulfill two conditions:

1. The "position" or "state" of the controlled system should coincide with the "goal."
2. The dynamics governing the controlled system and the controlling system must be such that the desired position of the controlled system should be stable.

The central point, however, is the second one of stability. The first condition becomes, then, one of setting the parameters in this stability condition so that the final state becomes the desired goal.

The stability can be formulated in the following way. Under the given state of the controlling system, there are, in general, a collection of states of the controlled system that are allowed. If the states in the collection that are not very far from the goal state converge with time to a single final state that agrees with the goal, then we have a "stable" goal. If indeed by some disturbance, the state of the controlled system fluctuates around the goal state, the actual controlled system will automatically come back to the goal state. To characterize the desired convergence of the various states in the collection, it would be best to introduce an entropy, suitably defined, that would measure the extension of variety, i.e., some function that is an increasing function of the number of the alternative states. The convergence of fluctuations will be described as a decrease with time of such an entropy. Thus the most important feature of control action can be expressed as minimum entropy principle.

If the entropy is defined as the entropy in theoretical physics, the decrease of entropy of the controlled system must be more than compensated by an increase of entropy in the environment (including the controlling system). Therefore, the controlled system is an entropy decreasing subsystem imbedded in the entropy-increasing environment. Such an interaction between the subsystem and the environment is usually realized by friction, which has the effect of decreasing the entropy of the subsystem by converting mechanical energy into heat (see [W-42]). One of the simplest examples of a controlled system is a simple harmonic oscillator which will be described by the differential equation:

$$\ddot{x} + w^2 x = 0 \qquad (6.8.1)$$

whose solution is

$$x = a \cos wt + b \sin wt \ . \qquad (6.8.2)$$

Since the kinetic energy is $(1/2)\,\dot{x}^2$ and the potential energy is $(1/2)\,w^2x^2$, the total energy E is

$$E = (1/2)(\dot{x}^2 + w^2x^2) = (a^2 + b^2)w^2/2 \ . \qquad (6.8.3)$$

The pair of canonical variables (q,p) is here $q = x$, $p = \dot{x}$. The trajectory in the phase-space, i.e., the (q,p)-space, corresponding to the energy E is

$$\frac{1}{\sqrt{2}\,E}\,(p^2 + w^2q^2) = 1 \ . \qquad (6.8.4)$$

The volume (area) A of this ellipse, which corresponds to the extension of all cases below the energy E, is π times (major axis) times (minor axis), i.e.

$$A = 2\pi\,\frac{E}{w} = \pi\,\left(\frac{1}{w}\,\dot{x}^2 + w\,x^2\right) \qquad (6.8.5)$$

or the entropy is

$$S = \log A = \log \frac{2\pi E}{w} \ . \qquad (6.8.6)$$

To make the dimension correct, we should divide A by a constant h whose dimension is that of action,

$$S = \log \frac{E}{h\nu} \ , \qquad (6.8.7)$$

where

$$w = 2\pi\nu \ . \qquad (6.8.8)$$

Now we introduce a frictional force and shift the origin, and assume, instead of (6.8.1)

$$\ddot{y} + r\,\dot{y} + w_o^2\,(y - y_o) = 0 \ . \qquad (6.8.9)$$

If we put $x = y - y_o$ and put (6.8.10)

$$w = (w_o^2 - r^2)^{1/2} \tag{6.8.11}$$

we can write the solution of (6.8.9) as

$$x = e^{-rt} (a \cos wt + b \sin wt) \ . \tag{6.8.12}$$

If we define the energy by $(\dot{x}^2 + w^2x^2)/2$, its value will decrease by the decay factor exp (-2rt). The phase volume A will decay also by the same factor. This factor comes from the decay factor in (6.8.12). The entropy will have an additive term (-2rt) which will cause S of (6.8.6) to become $-\infty$. If we quantize the phase space and assume that the final state has only one quantum, then the argument of (6.8.7) will stop at $E = h\nu$, and the minimum entropy will become 0. For our discussion in the next section, it will be more convenient to use the exponential of S, i.e., A. As far as the decrease and increase are concerned, whether we use A or S does not make any difference, because the exponential function and logarithmic function are monotonic functions of their arguments.

Of course the energy of the total system is conserved, and the loss of energy of the controlled system is compensated by the generation of heat by friction. Similarly, the loss of entropy by the controlled system is more than compensated by the increase of entropy due to absorption of heat by the surrounding system.

As we let the process continue, we have

$$\begin{aligned} &t \to \infty \\ &x \to 0, \text{ i.e., } y \to y_o \\ &A \to 0 \qquad S \to -\infty \ . \end{aligned} \tag{6.8.13}$$

The goal position is $y = y_o$ which is stable because we have only the one-way process: $A \to 0$, and we can never reverse the process, except through an external intervention. Thus the fluctuation is destined to be damped out and a stable control is realized.

A version of control theory takes Liapounoff's method as the main pillar of the theory. We want to show that the entropy function (or its exponential) can be considered as a Liapounoff function. We take n variables, $q_1, q_2, \ldots, q_n$, describing the controlled system. The origin of these variables is supposed to have been shifted to the steady position of the controlled system. Liapounoff considers a function $V(q_1, q_2, \ldots, q_n)$ of these coordinates which is positive

$$V(q_1, q_2, \ldots, q_n) > 0 \qquad (6.8.14)$$

except that at the origin it is assumed to vanish,

$$V(0, 0, \ldots, 0) = 0 \qquad (6.8.15)$$

or

$$\lim_{q_k \to 0} V(q_1, q_2, \ldots, q_n) = 0 \ . \qquad (6.8.16)$$

The dynamical law governing the variables is such that

$$\frac{dV}{dt} < 0 \qquad (6.8.17)$$

as far as

$$q_k \neq 0, \qquad r = 1, 2, \ldots, n \ . \qquad (6.8.18)$$

Then no matter where we start at $t = 0$, the controlled system will land the origin at a certain time, which could be either finite or infinite, and will remain at this position. This is the Liapounoff model of stability.

Liapounoff particularly considers the case where the dynamical law can be written in the form:

$$\frac{dq_k}{dt} = F_k(q_1, q_2, \ldots, q_n) \ , \qquad (6.8.19)$$

where F_k is a function of the coordinates. Then, we have

$$\frac{dV}{dt} = \sum_{k=1}^{n} \frac{\partial V}{\partial q_k} \frac{dq_k}{dt} = \sum_{k=1}^{n} \frac{\partial V}{\partial q_k} F_k$$

$$= \sum_{s=1}^{n} \left[\sum_{k=1}^{n} \left(\frac{\partial V}{\partial q_k}\right)^2 \right]^{1/2} \cdot F_s \cos(s \cdot n)$$

$$= \left[\sum_{k=1}^{n} \left(\frac{\partial V}{\partial q_k}\right)^2 \right]^{1/2} F_n , \tag{6.8.20}$$

where F_n is the normal component of the vector F_k ($k = 1, 2, \ldots, n$), "normal" meaning the upward normal to the surface: V = constant. If $F_n < 0$, we can realize (6.8.17) and we achieve the stability. In our case, we can put

$$q_1 = x, \quad q_2 = \dot{x} . \tag{6.8.21}$$

Then the dynamical laws:

$$\frac{dq_1}{dt} = F_1, \quad \frac{dq_2}{dt} = F_2 \tag{6.8.22}$$

with

$$F_1 = q_2, \quad F_2 = - w^2 q_1 - r q_2 \tag{6.8.23}$$

will be equivalent to

$$\ddot{x} + r\dot{x} + w^2 x = 0 . \tag{6.8.24}$$

The V can be equated to the exponential of the entropy A.

$$V \equiv \pi \left(w q_1^2 + \frac{1}{w} q_2^2\right) > 0 \text{ except at origin} \tag{6.8.25}$$

$$\frac{dV}{dt} = \frac{\partial V}{\partial q_1} \frac{dq_1}{dt} + \frac{\partial V}{\partial q_2} \frac{dq_2}{dt}$$

$$= - (2\pi\, r/w)\, q_2^2 < 0 \tag{6.8.26}$$

satisfying Liapounoff's condition of stability. Thus we see that the minimum entropy principle comes to the same conclusion as Liapounoff's theory of stability.

Those readers who are versed in the literature on the stability problems in the control theory might have the impression that the content of this section is another elementary example of the Liapounoff function. But, the intention of this section is rather the opposite: It is meant to suggest that the Liapounoff function, being a measure of the magnitude of fluctuations from the equilibrium point, can be considered as a kind of entropy function, not necessarily defined in physical variables and in the form of a logarithmic function, and that the stability theory can be considered as a special case of the minimum entropy principle.

CHAPTER 7

Pattern Recognition as Covariance Diagonalization

7.1 PRINCIPAL AXIS METHOD

The methods widely used under the names, such as Karhunen-Loeve expansion, diagonalization of covariance matrix, principal axis method, SELFIC, and factor analysis differ only in emphasis placed on particular aspects of one and the same mathematical tool and are based on the same theoretical structure. In the last chapter we have seen that the heuristic principle of entropy minimization led to this mathematical tool.

Some authors consider the data processing using this approach (1) as something entirely outside the problem complex of pattern recognition and exclude it from their textbooks. Some consider this approach (2) as a useful preprocessing tool to be applied prior to the essential part of pattern recognition. Some others consider it (3) as an integral part of pattern recognition.

We think that the point of view (1) is too narrow and fruitless. One way of looking at pattern recognition is to consider its major part as lying in discriminating one class from another in a space subtended by feature variables. In this viewpoint, the preparation of feature space from the observed data would be called a preprocessing of data, justifying (2). But, on the other hand, the entire process of pattern recognition can be considered as a gradual, or step-by-step, reduction of dimensionality of variables, starting from the raw observed quantities, and consumating in a single variable with two values, indicating membership and nonmembership of an object in a class, supporting the viewpoint (3). See, in addition, Section 7.6 on CLAFIC and Section 7.7 on DIRECLADIS, for application of the principal axis method to class discrimination.

The first work that introduced the method of principal axis into the field of pattern recognition was a paper in 1965, entitled "Karhunen-Loeve Expansion and Factor Analysis--Theoretical Remarks and Applications" [W-2]. This was the first paper to demonstrate the entropy-minimizing property of the eigenvectors of the covariance matrix already explained in Chapter 6. The idea of object-predicate inversion or reciprocation is even older than the idea of using the principal axis method for pattern recognition. It was introduced in connection with the use of the object-predicate table [W-7, W-48], but the idea was proved to be useful in connection with the practical application of the principal axis method [W-8]. In his dissertation of 1970 Kaminuma [K-9] traced the history of the principal axis method back to E. Schmidt's theory of 1907 [S-12] on integral equations and pointed out that the theory had already shown why the eigenvalues in the "object-picture" turn out to be the same. It is true that in 1901 Pearson [P-1] had the idea of diagonalizing the covariance matrix in connection with the line of thought that finally led to the method of factor analysis. But, because the computer was not available at that time, he could not carry out his dream. Schmidt's theory is far more advanced mathematically than Pearson's casual remarks and proves most of the important properties of the principal axis method including the mathematical counterpart of the reciprocity theorem but excepting the entropy-minimizing property.

In Japan, Iijima [I-1] seems to have independently thought of diagonalizating the covariance matrix for the purpose of pattern recognition. In 1970, Tomita [T-3] proved independently from Schmidt the identity of eigenvalues of covariance matrix in the object-picture and the predicate-picture. In the United States, a paper in 1966 by Fu et al. had probably the strongest influence on proliferation of the method of principal axis in the field of pattern recognition. Also see Kaminuma [K-9] for various applications of the principal axis method in physics and chemistry.

To explain specifically the properties of the principal axis method, we will describe mathematically the situation in which the method works, although there will be some duplication of what we described in Section 6.3. We are supposed to be given a collection of, say N, objects, with known properties, expressed by n variables, binary or continuous. We subject these n variables to an orthogonal transformation, (i.e., reflection or rotation), to find the coordinate axes such that some variables become conspicuously more important than others relative to the collection. The importance is to be a measure of participation of an axis in expressing statistically the collection of N objects. We have to know that a small difference, such as one between O and Q or between ш and щ, which is important for a certain discrimination, could be lost in a host of other information.

The data from which we start are N vectors with n components: $x_i^{(\alpha)}$, $i = 1,2,\ldots,n$; $\alpha = 1,2,\ldots,N$. To have more flexibility, we give a weight function $\omega^{(\alpha)}$ to each object, such that

$$\omega^{(\alpha)} \geq 0 \ , \quad \sum_{\alpha=1}^{N} \omega^{(\alpha)} = 1 \ . \tag{7.1.1}$$

The G-matrix is defined by

$$G_{ij} = \sum_{\alpha=1}^{N} \omega^{(\alpha)} x_i^{(\alpha)} x_j^{(\alpha)} \Big/ \tau \tag{7.1.2}$$

with

$$\tau = \sum_{\alpha=1}^{N} \sum_{i=1}^{n} \omega^{(\alpha)} \cdot (x_i^{(\alpha)})^2 \tag{7.1.3}$$

It is assumed that the Euclidean distance in the n-dimensional real space defined by the x_i's has the meaning of a suitable measure of difference or dissimilarity between objects for the purpose of clustering or pattern recognition. Instead of explicitly writing $\omega^{(\alpha)}$, we can multiply each $x_i^{(\alpha)}$ by $\sqrt{\omega^{(\alpha)}}$ and simplify the G-matrix

$$G_{ij} = \sum_{\alpha=1}^{N} x_i^{(\alpha)} \; x_j^{(\alpha)} \Big/ \tau \; , \qquad (7.1.4)$$

$$\tau = \sum_{\alpha=1}^{N} \sum_{i=1}^{n} (x_i^{(\alpha)})^2 \; . \qquad (7.1.5)$$

The G-matrix thus defined is normalized in the sense that its diagonal sum is unity, but each vector is not normalized. In many applications, however, it can be assumed that each vector is normalized, and τ becomes simply N. If we shift the origin of each variable so that

$$\sum_{\alpha=1}^{N} x_i^{(\alpha)} = 0 \; , \qquad (7.1.6)$$

the G-matrix becomes the covariance matrix. Under the same assumption, if we consider τ of (7.1.4) as dependent on i and j and replace τ by

$$\tau_{ij} = \left[\sum_{\alpha=1}^{N} (x_i^{(\alpha)})^2 \cdot \sum_{\alpha=1}^{N} (x_j^{(\alpha)})^2 \right]^{1/2} , \qquad (7.1.7)$$

the G-matrix can be considered as the autocorrelation function. In physicists' jargon, the original G-matrix corresponds to the density matrix in a real space.

Obviously, we have for all i and for all j

$$G_{ij} = G_{ji} \quad \text{(symmetric)} \; , \qquad (7.1.8)$$

$$G_{ii} \geq 0 \quad \text{(nonnegative diagonal)}, \qquad (7.1.9)$$

and

$$\sum_{i=1}^{N} G_{ii} = 1 \quad \text{(normalized)} \; . \qquad (7.1.10)$$

Without altering the Euclidean distance, we can change the coordinate system by an orthogonal transformation

$$G_{ij} \to G'_{ij} = \sum_{k,l} T_{ik} G_{k\ell} T_{j\ell} , \qquad (7.1.11)$$

with
$$T_{ji} = (T^{-1})_{ij} . \qquad (7.1.12)$$

The three basic properties (7.1.8), (7.1.9), and (7.1.10) of G-matrix remain unchanged by this transformation. So does the value of τ in the sense of (7.1.3), (7.1.5), or (7.1.7).

The invariant properties of (7.1.9) and (7.1.10) allow us to define an entropy

$$S' = - \sum_{i=1}^{N} \rho'_i \log \rho'_i , \qquad (7.1.13)$$

with
$$\rho' = G'_{ii} ,$$

where ρ'_i can be interpreted as the "importance" of the i-th coordinate, or the degree to which the i-th coordinate in the primed coordinate system participates in representing the ensemble of vectors. The value of S' depends naturally on the choice of the primed coordinate system.

The eigenvector $\psi_i^{(k)}$ and the corresponding eigenvalue $\lambda^{(k)}$ of the symmetric matrix G are defined by

$$\sum_{j=1}^{n} G_{ij} \psi_j^{(k)} = \lambda^{(k)} \psi_i^{(k)} , \qquad (7.1.14)$$

where the eigenvalues $\lambda^{(k)}$, $k = 1,2,\ldots,n$, are the n roots of the algebraic equation

$$\det|G_{ij} - \lambda\delta_{ij}| = 0 . \qquad (7.1.15)$$

We agree to label these n roots by the convention

$$\lambda^{(1)} \geq \lambda^{(2)} \geq \ldots \geq \lambda^{(n)} \geq 0 . \qquad (7.1.16)$$

Although an r-ple root determines only an eigenspace of r dimensions, we can agree to define the eigenvectors so that

$$\sum_{i=1}^{n} \psi_i^{(k)} \psi_i^{(\ell)} = \delta_{k\ell} \tag{7.1.17}$$

and

$$\sum_{k=1}^{n} \psi_i^{(k)} \psi_j^{(k)} = \delta_{ij} \tag{7.1.18}$$

for all n eigenvectors.

It is easy to see that we can write the G-matrix in the form

$$G'_{ij} = \sum_{k=1}^{n} \lambda^{(k)} \delta_{ik} \delta_{kj} \tag{7.1.19}$$

and

$$G_{ij} = \sum_{k=1}^{n} \lambda^{(k)} \psi_i^{(k)} \psi_i^{(k)}, \tag{7.1.20}$$

where the primed coordinate system is supposed to be subtended by the n eigenvectors of the G-matrix.

We have seen already that the entropy (7.1.13) becomes minimum where the primed coordinates coincide with the eigenvectors of the G-matrix. This means that the $G'_{ii} = \lambda^{(i)} = \rho'_i$ defined by this coordinate system are most sharply concentrated (i.e., most unevenly distributed). On the other hand, ρ'_i is the degree to which the coordinate x'_i is used to represent the given collection of vectors. If S' is small, some of the n primed coordinates are used to a very insignificant degree. In this sense, it is easy to expect that the mathematical expression representing the collection of vectors would suffer very little from an appreciable error if we ignore the coordinates with little ρ'_i in the primed coordinates. This idea leads to the minimum error property of the eigenvector coordinates, which will be briefly explained. In the following expressions, the eigenvalues of G-matrix will be denoted by λ_i, and the diagonal elements of G in any other coordinate system will be denoted by ρ_i,

$$\rho_i = G_{ii} = \sum_{j=1}^{n} A_{ij} \lambda_j \; , \tag{7.1.21}$$

$$A_{ij} = (T_{ij})^2 = T_{ij} T_{ji}^{-1} \tag{7.1.22}$$

due to the orthogonality of transformation, entailing

$$\sum_i A_{ij} = \sum_j A_{ij} = 1 \; , \tag{7.1.23}$$

which is the double stochasticity. See (7.1.12) and (7.1.20)).

The mathematical representation of the α-th vector is

$$\left\{ x_i^{(\alpha)} \right\} \; , \; i = 1,2,\ldots,n \; (\infty) \; .$$

If we take only the first m terms, the error committed is

$$\sum_{i=m+1}^{n} (x_i^{(\alpha)})^2 \; .$$

The average in the collection is

$$\sum_{i=m+1}^{n} \omega^{(\alpha)} (x_i^{(\alpha)})^2 = \sum_{i=m+1}^{n} G_{ii} = 1 - \sum_{i=1}^{m} G_{ii} = 1 - \sum_{i=1}^{m} \rho_i \; .$$

The same quantity in the eigenvector coordinates is

$$1 - \sum_{i=1}^{m} \lambda_{ii} \; .$$

The theorem to be proved is, for any m,

$$\sum_{i=1}^{m} \rho_i \leq \sum_{i=1}^{m} \lambda_i \; , \tag{7.1.24}$$

(i.e., the error is the smallest on the average in the eigenvector system). We have not specified the labeling of the ρ's, but (7.1.24) is meant to be true even if the labeling is such that $\sum_{i=1}^{m} \rho_i$ becomes maximum, that is,

$$\rho_i \geq \rho_2 \geq \cdots \geq \rho_n \ . \qquad (7.1.25)$$

The proof given below for this theorem is due to Professor S. Kakutani (oral communication). It uses the following lemma:

Lemma: For any given integer m and for a given doubly stochastic matrix A_{ij} $(i,j = 1,2,\ldots,\infty)$ there exists another doubly stochastic matrix B_{ij}, such that $B_{ij} = 0$ for $i > m$ or $j > m$ and $B_{ij} \geq A_{ij}$ for $1 \leq i \leq m$ and $1 \leq j < m$.

Proof of the lemma: Let D denote the class of $m \times m$ matrices with nonnegative elements C_{ij} $(i,j = 1,2,\ldots,m)$ that satisfy $p_j \equiv \sum_{i=1}^{m} C_{ij} \leq 1$ and $q_i \equiv \sum_{j=1}^{m} C_{ij} \leq 1$. A row (column) whose row sum q_i (column sum p_j) is less than unity is said to be deficient. The total number, δ, of deficient rows and columns is called the degree of deficiency of the matrix $||C_{ij}||$. The degree zero, $\delta = 0$, means that the $m \times m$ matrix is doubly stochastic. A simple fact to note about the deficient rows and columns is that if there are one or more deficient rows (columns) then there is at least one deficient column (row). This can be understood easily if one notes that the sum of all row sums is equal to the sum of all column sums:

$$\sum_{i=1}^{m} p_i = \sum_{j=1}^{m} q_j = \sum_{i=1}^{m} \sum_{j=1}^{m} C_{ij} \ . \qquad (7.1.26)$$

We now prove the following statement by induction with respect to δ. If $||C_{ij}||$ is a matrix belonging to D and has degree of deficiency $\delta\,(\neq 0)$, there exists another matrix $||C'_{ij}||$ belonging to D with degree $\delta-1$ or $\delta-2$ such that $C'_{ij} \geq C_{ij}$. Among δ deficient row sums and column sums of C_{ij}, let the row sum q_k be one of the largest. (The argument goes exactly the same way when a column sum is the largest.) Because of the fact mentioned above, there is at least one column, say, the ℓ-th, that is deficient, since there is a deficient row $q_k < 1$. Increase the element $C_{k\ell}$ until the k-th row becomes nondeficient, $q_k = 1$. This will not make the ℓ-th column larger than unity, since the k-th row has the largest among the deficient rows and columns. The matrix thus obtained will be denoted by $||C'_{ij}||$. This matrix $||C'_{ij}||$ differs from $||C_{ij}||$ only by one element at the intersection of the k-th row and the ℓ-th column, and $C'_{k\ell} \geq C_{k\ell}$; hence we can write in general $C'_{ij} \geq C_{ij}$ $(i,j = 1,2,\ldots,m)$. The degree of deficiency of $||C'_{ij}||$ will be either $\delta-1$ or $\delta-2$ according as whether $q_k > p_\ell$ or $q_k = p_\ell$. We can continue this process until the degree of deficiency is 2, then these two deficient rows will be eliminated by one stroke. The case $\delta = 1$ cannot happen, as explained earlier.

Thus, the rewritten matrix is no longer deficient. Coming back to the statement of the lemma, let the matrix $||A'_{ij}||$ be defined as an $m \times m$ matrix such that $A'_{ij} = A_{ij}$ for $1 \leq i \leq m$ and $1 \leq j \leq m$. Then this $||A'_{ij}||$ is a member of D, and the above proof shows that there exists a nondeficient (doubly stochastic) matrix $||B'_{ij}||$ belonging to D, such that $B'_{ij} \geq A'_{ij} = A_{ij}$ for $1 \leq i \leq m$ and $1 \leq j \leq m$. The B_{ij} of the lemma can be defined by $B_{ij} = B'_{ij}$ for $1 \leq i \leq m$ and $1 \leq j \leq m$ and $B_{ij} = 0$ otherwise. This completes the proof of the lemma.

The proof of the minimum error theorem (7.1.24) is now easy: Let ε_{ij} $(i,j = 1,2,\ldots,m)$ be defined by

$$B_{ij} = A_{ij} + \varepsilon_{ij} \; ; \; \varepsilon_{ij} \geq 0, \tag{7.1.27}$$

where A_{ij} and B_{ij} $(i = 1,2,\ldots,\infty)$ are related as in the foregoing lemma. Because the matrix A_{ij} and B_{ij} are doubly stochastic, we have

$$\sum_{j=1}^{m} \varepsilon_{ij} = \sum_{j=m+1}^{\infty} A_{ij} \; . \tag{7.1.28}$$

$$\sum_{j=1}^{m} \lambda_j = \sum_{i=1}^{m} \sum_{j=1}^{m} B_{ij}\lambda_j \qquad \left[\text{since } \sum_{j=1}^{m} B_{ij} = 1\right]$$

$$\geq \sum_{i=1}^{m} \sum_{j=1}^{m} A_{ij}\lambda_j + \sum_{i=1}^{m} \sum_{j=1}^{m} \varepsilon_{ij}\lambda_{m+1} \qquad [(7.1.16) \text{ and } (7.1.27)]$$

$$\geq \sum_{i=1}^{m} \sum_{j=1}^{m} A_{ij}\lambda_j + \sum_{i=1}^{m} \sum_{j=m+1}^{\infty} A_{ij}\lambda_j \qquad [(7.1.16) \text{ and } (7.1.28)]$$

$$= \sum_{i=1}^{m} \rho_i \ . \qquad [(7.1.21)]$$

This completes the required proof.

7.2 DIFFERENT ASPECTS OF THE PRINCIPAL AXIS METHOD

In this section, we would like to enumerate different aspects of the principal axis method that prove to be useful in applications. Some of the properties may have been mentioned before, and some of them will be explained in more detail in the later sections, but a brief overview of the entire method may be of some meaning.

1. Minimum Entropy. As we noted in Chapter 6 and repeated again in the foregoing paragraphs, the optimum coordinate system that minimizes the entropy defined in terms of the measure of participation of coordinates is nothing but the coordinate system defined by the eigenvectors of the G-matrix.
2. Uncorrelatedness. If we want to extract fewer and more important variables, it will be desirable that they be statistically independent, because a presence of

interdependence means redundancy and mutual duplication of information carried by these variables. This hypothetical ideal is not necessarily realized by the optimal coordinate system, but the next best property of uncorrelatedness is guaranteed. If we use τ of (7.1.7) in (7.1.4), the G_{ij} becomes the expression of correlation between the i-th component and j-th component in the ensemble. The optimal coordinate makes all the nondiagonal elements of the G vanish; that means there is no correlation between x_i' values and x_j' values in the ensemble. Besides, it may be well to remind ourselves that absence of correlation in the case of a family of normal distributions implies absence of statistical interdependence. Otherwise, statistical independence implies uncorrelatedness, but not vice versa.

3. Minimum Error. If we approximate each n-dimensional vector $\{x_i^{(\alpha)'}\}$, $i = 1,2,\ldots,n$ by a retrenched m-dimensional vector $\{x_i^{(\alpha)'}\}$, $i = 1,2,\ldots,m$, with $m < n$, the total error for all the vectors in the ensemble is represented by

$$E_{n,m} = \sum_{\alpha=1}^{N} \sum_{i=1}^{n} (x_i^{(\alpha)'})^2 - \sum_{\alpha=1}^{N} \sum_{i=1}^{m} (x_i^{(\alpha)'})^2 . \tag{7.2.1}$$

For any fixed value of m, the optimal coordinates minimize this over-all error. The proof was given in the last section.

4. Karhunen-Loève Expansion. In the discussion in the foregoing paragraphs, we have assumed that the given data are a set of n observations on each object (i.e., the α and i in $\{x_i^{(\alpha)}\}$ runs over discrete numbers). But, there are in reality many continuous data from observation of objects, such as seismographic records, meteorological records, medical records, and so on. In such

cases, the observed data on each object should be a continuous function: $f^{(\alpha)}(u)$, $\alpha = 1,2,\ldots,N$. Rigorously speaking, the data may not be "continuous" in the mathematical sense, but this does not matter; it is assumed to be "piecewise continuous" in an approximate sense, as idealization. In addition to this, it is often convenient to assume $f^{(\alpha)}(u)$ to be square integrable in a continuous domain, say [a,b]. The Karhunen-Loève expansion was well known in the mid-1900s among electrical engineers as the best expansion of a set of continuous functions by a certain set of fundamental continuous functions. This is the error-minimizing expansion with a finite number of terms corresponding to (7.2.1). The motivation for using the Karhunen-Loève expansion was for us the convenience in describing continuous medical records by a finite number of parameters. It was Eugene Wong who suggested the use of K-L expansion for this process. The idea of using the same mathematical tool for the purpose of dimension reduction in the sense of pattern recognition came later. The passage from the continuous case to the discrete case and vice versa required only a very easy trick well known to quantum physicists. The Schmidt theory, as published in 1907, assumed the case where both i and α in $\{x_i^{(\alpha)}\}$ are continuous and it was conceived as part of a theory of integral equation. We shall explain how we can go from one end to another in Section 7.3.

5. Factor Analysis. About the time our research work was going on with the K-L expansion, a psychologist in a nearby laboratory was doing some research using factor analysis. We noticed some resemblance between the K-L method and the mathematical tool called factor analysis. One of the purposes of the 1935 paper [W-2], was thus to study systematically this resemblance, hence the title of the paper: *Karhunen-Loève Expansion and Factor Analysis*. The factor analysis is a, so to speak, home-baked, mathematical

tool of psychologists, gradually developed from the early years of this century. In psychology or many other fields, there are often many measurable variables which are obviously correlated. For instance, the weight of a person and his height, his hip-circumference, and so on are closely related, but they are not simple functions of one another. Then, it is a natural desire for a scientist to discover an independent "common cause" behind these closely related variables, and to distinguish the particularity of each variable from the effect of the "common causes." Factor analysis is a method which enables us to find such common factors and particular factors. We shall discuss this method of factor analysis from the point of view of pattern recognition in Section 7.4.

6. SELFIC. The method of SELFIC (self-featuring information-compression) is a program to decrease the dimensionality of the representation space, without committing an appreciable overall error when the data are given as an ensemble of vectors. The qualification "self" is inserted in the name SELFIC to emphasize that the discrimination to which the method eventually leads depends on the ensemble itself and not on an external criterium. This error, in fraction, is E (n,m) of (7.2.1) divided by the first term of (7.2.1). The error depends on two factors, (1) the value of m, and (2) the choice of the primed framework, for a given m. Suppose we have already decided to use the optimal coordinate, then the "goodness" of the approximation is measured by "one minus fractional error", that is, "fidelity" σ defined as the ratio of the second term of (7.2.1) to the first term, which in the optimal coordinate system equals

$$\sigma = \sum_{i=1}^{m} \lambda_i \Big/ \sum_{i=1}^{n} \lambda_i = \sum_{i=1}^{m} \lambda_i , \qquad (7.2.2)$$

where the convention (7.1.16) is adopted.

The curve of the fidelity σ as a function of m is a steplike, convex (upward), monotonously increasing function. In most of the actual applications, it was found that σ becomes very large, say, 0.95 for m, considerably smaller than n. This is a good indication of the effectiveness of the SELFIC for the dimensionality reduction. The m-dimensional subspace thus defined is the retrenched subspace which can replace the original n-dimensional representation space with an overall error less than $1-\sigma$. The dimensionality of such a retrenched representation space is defined by the minimum value of m such that σ (fidelity) (7.2.2) is equal to or larger than a certain predetermined threshold. In many cases, as we increase the number m, the fidelity σ jumps up suddenly to a very large value, and we can use the increased value of σ as the threshold in such a case.

A few remarks regarding the actual application may be in order here. If we do not apply the shift of origin (7.1.6) for each measurement, the first eigenvector tends to represent the general feature common to all the objects in the collection, which does not serve the purpose of discriminating one object from another in the ensemble. If we apply (7.1.6) on the variable x_i, there will be positive values of x_i as well as negative values. Further, it should be noted that this formalism does not distinguish positive values from negative values, because the entire method depends on the square of the x_i's.

The SELFIC method admittedly allows for only linear (even only, orthogonal) transformations. If the linear transformation does not give any good result we could try either of the following two artifices to include some of the non linear transformation. One method is to augment the n-dimensional vector $\{x_i\}$ by additional components which are products and powers of the original components. For instance, if we take only the second degree terms, there will be n(n+1)/2 additional terms of the type: $x_i x_j$, $i,j = 1,2,\ldots,n$. These components are not independent from the original components, but treating them as if they were new independent variables, we can sometimes extract better features.

Another method is to introduce a set of orthonormal base functions defined in the n-dimensional space $\{\chi_i(x_1 x_2,\ldots x_n)\}$ $i = 1,2,\ldots,\infty$, and replace the vector $\left\{x_1^{(\alpha)}, x_2^{(\alpha)}, \ldots, x_n^{(\alpha)}\right\}$ by $\left\{\chi_i(x_1^{(\alpha)}, x_2^{(\alpha)}, \ldots, x_n^{(\alpha)})\right\}$, where now the index i specifies the components. We can limit ourselves to a finite number, say ν, of base functions, and we obtain a ν-dimensional representation. Between the orthogonal transformation and the nonlinear transformation, there is a big region of nonorthogonal linear transformations. We can take as the χ's not necessarily mutually orthogonal functions but some appropriate mutually linearly independent functions. The products of the x's are an example of such functions.

7. CLAFIC or AFFINE REPRESENTATION. The method of principal **axis** is primarily a preprocessing before we start classification, hence no consideration is given to paradigms or discriminating surfaces. But, the CLAFIC (class-featuring information compression), [W-3, W-21, K-19], is one device to introduce an idea of class within the framework of the method of principal **axis**. This method is not only useful in paradigm-oriented pattern recognition, but is also important by opening up a new vista of the subspace representation of classes in the feature space. As we have seen in connection with the discriminating surface, the usual way of representing a class in the n-dimensional feature space is to identify a class with an n-dimensional domain in this space. The subspace method or affine representation identifies a class as an m-dimensional subspace ($m<n$) (passing the

origin) in this n-dimensional representation space.

The idea of CLAFIC is as follows. In the usual application of the principal **axis** method, namely, the SELFIC, we take all the sample vectors to calculate G, whether we do not know their class affiliation or we wittingly ignore it. In CLAFIC, we take only the paradigms of a class, say C_1, and with a suitable fidelity, say $\sigma = 0.95$, we define a subspace of m ($<< n$) dimension. A simple application of this situation is to decide any vector, representing a newcomer, to belong to class C_1 if it is found in this subspace, and not to belong to class C_1, if it is not in this subspace. But this decision procedure is not realistic, because (1) there should always be in-between cases for any decision procedure, and (2) the subspace is defined only by an approximation: $\sigma = 0.95$.

Rather, we should project the vector of the newcomer onto the subspace and regard the ratio of the length (squared) of the projection to that of the original vector as the probability of the newcomer belonging to class C_1. If we do this, we have to define the probability of not belonging to class C_1 as the ratio of the projection onto the (n-m)-dimensional complementary subspace of the m-dimensional subspace of C_1. Then the probability of belonging to C_1 and the probability of belonging to $\neg C_1$ (i.e., not belonging to C_1) will add up to unity.

So far, so good. A little complication could occur when there is more than one class. If the subspace of C_i and the subspace of C_j $(j \neq i)$ are mutually orthogonal, there is no problem. And this can very well be the case, or at least approximately the case, if the dimensions of each subspace are all very small compared with n. But, if this is not the case, we need a special consideration, which we explain in Section 7.6. In Section 7.7 a new method called DIRECLADIS will be described which allows coping with many-class problems.

8. REPREX. When we apply the SELFIC method to a concrete problem using a computer, the major computation burden will be laid on the calculation of eigenvalues and eigenvectors of the $n \times n$ G-matrix. If the number N of vectors is sufficiently large, these eigenvalues and eigenvectors do not change by taking another collection of vectors taken from the same population. So, insofar as we are dealing with the same kind of problems, we do not need to repeat the calculation. All we need is to calculate the vector components in the coordinate systems defined by the eigenvectors. The calculation of eigenvectors requires an $n \times n$ matrix inversion. If n becomes larger than say 150, the matrix inversion becomes very complicated even with a very fast computer. Hence, we can consider $n < \ell$ as a practical limit to the method with $\ell \approx 150$, or so. While there is an upper limit to the number n, there is practically no limit to the allowable value of the number N. All that a large number of N does is a large number of terms to be added in calculation of G (7.1.2), and does not mean any serious computational burden.

If the data are such that n is larger than N, so that, say, $n > \ell > N$, can we not interchange the role of n and N, since the data are after all only numbers with double indices, $x_i^{(\alpha)}$, $i = 1,2,\ldots,n$ and $\alpha = 1,2,\ldots,N$ allowing us to interpret $x_i^{(\alpha)}$ either as the i-th component of the α-th vector or the α-th component of the i-th vector, leading us to the doorway to a problem of very far-reaching significance concerning interchangeability or reciprocity of predicate (variable) and object?

The papers in 1959 [W-5], 1960 [W-6] and 1961 [W-7] may be the first papers that explicitly dealt with this problem in information sciences. But, a germ of the idea can be already found in the old statement in the traditional exposition of logic to the effect that the extension (number of objects satisfying) and the intension (number of predicates satisfied) of a concept are inversely proportional. In fact, P(a) can be interpreted that object a satisfies predicate P, or predicate P is such that it is satisfied by object a. We can still go a step further and ask how we identify object a. The only pragmatic answer is to test its properties. Thus, P(a) is a relation of a predicate (P) to a group of predicates that identify object a. Similarly, in the continuous case $x_i^{(\alpha)}$ can be interpreted as the result of the i-th test on object α, or as the result of the α-th test on the i-th variable. A variable can be characterized by the values it takes on various objects, just in the same way as an object can be characterized by the values it takes on various variables. We have discussed more of the philosophical considerations about the object-predicate reciprocation in [W-8] and in this book in Chapter 4, Section 4.4.

Before studying the mathematical problem connected with the predicate-object reciprocity, we want to enlarge the vocabulary of the SELFIC method. By determining a suitable value of fidelity σ, we can define the m-dimensional subspace subtended by m new **important** predicates $\psi_i^{(k)}$ $k = 1,2,\ldots,m$, each of which is a linear combination of n original coordinate axes (unit vectors), $e_i^{(\ell)} = \delta_{i\ell}$, $\ell = 1,2,\ldots,n$. We can ask of each object vector $\{x_i^{(\alpha)}\}$ what percentage of its weight lies in this "important" subspace? Since the importance is determined by the average weight of vectors in the ensemble, we may say that the larger this percentage the more "representative" the object is. A vector which has most of its weight outside the subspace is a "loner." Thus, we may define the "representativeness" of an object vector $\{x_i^{(\alpha)}\}$ by

$$J^{(\alpha)} = \sum_{k=1}^{m} \left(\sum_{i=1}^{n} x_i^{(\alpha)} \psi_i^{(k)} \right)^2 \Big/ \sum_{i=1}^{n} x_i^{(\alpha)2}$$

$$= \sum_{k=1}^{m} x_k'^{(\alpha)2} \Big/ \sum_{k=1}^{n} x_k'^{(\alpha)2} \quad , \tag{7.2.3}$$

where the primed components are those along the optimal coordinate axes:

$$x_k^{(\alpha)'} = \sum_{i=1}^{n} T_{ki} \, x_i^{(\alpha)} = \sum_{i=1}^{n} \psi_i^{(k)} x_i^{(\alpha)} \tag{7.2.4}$$

(see Section 6.3). By requiring a suitable threshold θ

$$J^{(\alpha)} \geq \epsilon \tag{7.2.5}$$

we can limit the number of representative objects to $N^* < N$. This method of extracting "representative" objects was called REPREX [W-10]. The m is to be defined as the minimum value of m in (7.2.1) so that σ is equal to or larger than a certain predetermined threshold.

9. <u>Object-Predicate Reciprocation</u>. The method of object-predicate reciprocation has a rich philosophical background as well as many useful applications, but we shall here proceed to explain it from the point of view of representative objects and representative predicates.

   Now, we "reciprocate" object and predicate and define the matrix $(H^{(\alpha\beta)})$ corresponding to G_{ij} by

$$H^{(\alpha\beta)} = \sum_{i=1}^{n} \omega_i x_i^{(\alpha)} x_i^{(\beta)} \Big/ \sum_{i=1}^{n} \omega_i \sum_{\alpha=1}^{N} x_i^{(\alpha)2} \tag{7.2.6}$$

$$\omega_i \geq 0 \; , \; \sum_{i=1}^{n} \omega_i = 1 \; . \tag{7.2.7}$$

Instead of n × n matrix G_{ij}, we have here an N × N matrix $H^{(\alpha\beta)}$, and we can define a subspace in the N-dimensional representative space. The vectors in this space are n vectors of N components, $\{x_i^{(\alpha)}\}$, $\alpha = 1, 2,\ldots,N$. In the same way as we could define the N* representative objects from among N objects, we can define a set of n* representative predicate variables from among n predicate variables. Suppose, we have the situation $n > \ell > N$, then it is easier to obtain the eigenvectors and eigenvalues of $H^{(\alpha\beta)}$ than those of G_{ij}. Then we can obtain n* representative predicate variables, so that $n^* < \ell$.

At this point we have to refer to the basic theorem of reciprocation which we shall explain in the next section. According to the theorem, the nonzero eigenvalues of $H^{(\alpha\beta)}$ and those of G_{ij} are exactly the same, and the eigenvectors of $H^{(\alpha\beta)}$ corresponding to its nonzero eigenvalues can be derived from the corresponding eigenvectors of G_{ij} without solving the equation (7.1.15). This entails several important results.

Depending on whether $n > N$ or $N > n$, we should apply the diagonalization method to $H^{(\alpha\beta)}$ or G_{ij}. It is particularly important when the smaller of N and n is smaller than a certain number ℓ for which the matrix inversion is easy. Once we have obtained the eigenvalues and eigenvectors in the easier of the two, we can obtain therefrom the solutions for the more difficult one.

Since the nonzero eigenvalues of $H^{(\alpha\beta)}$ and G_{ij} are the same, the fidelity with respect to $H^{(\alpha\beta)}$ is the same as the fidelity with respect to G_{ij} for a given value of m. If, therefore, we reduce the dimensionality by specifying a certain value of fidelity, the dimensionality of the retrenched space will turn out to be the same in either representation. We can define the representative predicates and representative objects by requiring a certain minimum percentage of weight in either of the m-dimensional retrenched spaces. This, however, does not guarantee that the number n* of the representation predicates and the number N* of the representative objects should be the same.

7.3 EIGENVECTORS OF ASYMMETRIC MATRIX

Schmidt's theory of asymmetric kernel [S-12] will be adapted to our problem and explained, for this limited application, in this section. Our observational data $\{x_i^{(\alpha)}\}$, $\alpha = 1,2,\ldots,N$; $i = 1, 2,\ldots,n$ can be considered a $N \times n$ asymmetric matrix.

$$x_i^{(\alpha)} \equiv K(\alpha,i) \quad . \tag{7.3.1}$$

The original paper of Schmidt assumed both α and i to be continuous and their ranges of variation were assumed to be identical, but the present modification is a formal one and the restitution of the original format is trivial. Since in the continuous case the simultaneous eigenvalue equations, which will be shown presently, become a set of simultaneous integral equations, the asymmetric matrix $K(\alpha,i)$ is more properly called an asymmetric kernel. Although the theory is rather simple from the present-day standard, the date of publication of such an important paper (1907) is rather surprising, anticipating the actual application by more than half a century. We shall explain the theory following more or less the elegant line of presentation of Schmidt's paper.

Suppose there is a pair of functions $\phi(\alpha)$ and $\psi(i)$ such that

$$\phi(\alpha) = \frac{1}{\chi} \sum_{i=1}^{n} K(\alpha,i)\ \psi(i)\ ,\ \chi \neq 0 \tag{7.3.2}$$

and

$$\psi(i) = \frac{1}{\chi} \sum_{\alpha=1}^{N} \phi(\alpha)\ K(\alpha,i),\quad \chi \neq 0 \quad . \tag{7.3.3}$$

We call ϕ and ψ eigenfunctions of the asymmetric matrix $K(\alpha,i)$ for eigenvalue χ.

We now define

$$H(\alpha,\beta) = \sum_{i=1}^{n} K(\alpha,i)\ K(\beta,i) \tag{7.3.4}$$

$$G(i,j) = \sum_{\alpha=1}^{N} K(\alpha,i)\ K(\alpha,j)\ . \tag{7.3.5}$$

We see that this $G(i,j)$ corresponds to N times G_{ij} of (7.1.4) if each vector x_i^α is normalized in the sense

$$\sum_{i=1}^{n} (x_i^\alpha)^2 = 1\ . \tag{7.3.6}$$

We note that although $K(\alpha,i)$ is real, it is not symmetric, that is, it is not guaranteed that

$$K(\alpha,i) = K(i,\alpha)\ . \tag{7.3.7}$$

However, $H(\alpha,\beta)$ and $G(i,j)$ are real and symmetric

$$H(\alpha,\beta) = H(\beta,\alpha);\ G(i,j) = G(j,i)\ . \tag{7.3.8}$$

Now, if we insert (7.3.2) into (7.3.3) or vice versa, we obtain

$$\phi(\alpha) = \frac{1}{\chi^2} \sum_{\beta=1}^{N} H(\alpha,\beta)\phi(\beta) \tag{7.3.9}$$

and

$$\psi(i) = \frac{1}{\chi^2} \sum_{j=1}^{n} C(i,j)\psi(j)\ . \tag{7.3.10}$$

This means $\phi(\alpha)$ and $\psi(i)$, which are simultaneous solutions of (7.3.2) and (7.3.3), are respectively eigensolutions of (7.3.9) and eigensolutions of (7.3.10) corresponding both to the same eigenvalue χ^2.

Suppose we are given, at the outset, two equations (7.3.9) and (7.3.10), which look like two independent definitions of eigensolutions of two kernels, H and G. But, in reality, they are so intimately related that we do not need to solve them separately. The eigensolution of one equation for a given value of χ^2 can be derived from the eigensolution of the other equation for the same value of χ^2. The relations that allow us to pass from one set of eigensolutions to another set of eigensolution are precisely Eqs. (7.3.2) and (7.3.3). This simplification is of course made possible due to the relations, (7.3.4) and (7.3.5), that exist between two kernels, G and H.

To see this mechanism more closely, we start from (7.3.9) and assume that we obtained a solution $\phi(\alpha)$ of it with a certain value of χ^2. Then, with the help of (7.3.3), we define a $\psi(i)$ from this $\phi(\alpha)$. Then, substituting (7.3.9) for $\phi(\alpha)$ of the right-hand side of (7.3.3), we obtain

$$\psi(i) = \frac{1}{\chi} \sum_{\alpha=1}^{N} \phi(\alpha)\, K(\alpha,i)$$

$$= \frac{1}{\chi^3} \sum_{\alpha=1}^{N} \sum_{\beta=1}^{N} H(\alpha,\beta)\, K(\alpha,i)\phi(\beta).$$

With the aid of the definition of $H(\alpha,\beta)$, (7.3.4), this becomes

$$\psi(i) = \frac{1}{\chi^3} \sum_{\alpha=1}^{N} \sum_{\beta=1}^{N} \sum_{j=1}^{n} K(\alpha,j)\, K(\beta,j)\, K(\alpha,i)\phi(\beta) .$$

Performing first the summation over β, we obtain, using again (7.3.3) and definition (7.7.5)

$$\psi(i) = \frac{1}{\chi^2} \sum_{j=1}^{n} G(i,j)\psi(j) ,$$

which shows that $\psi(i)$ obtained from $\phi(\alpha)$ is nothing but the eigensolution of (7.3.10) corresponding to the same χ^2. Similarly, starting from (7.3.10) and (7.3.2) we obtain (7.3.9). Thus, when symmetric matrices G and H are defined with the help of an asymmetric matrix K, a pair of solutions, $\phi(\alpha)$ and $\psi(i)$ of the simultaneous equation defined by K with the eigenvalue χ, are respectively eigensolution of H and eigensolution of G, corresponding both to eigenvalue χ^2, provided that $\chi \neq 0$. If $\psi(i)$ here corresponds to $\psi_i^{(k)}$ of (7.1.14) with a particular k, and $\phi^{(k)}(\alpha)$ is related to $\psi_i^{(k)}$ by (7.3.2), i.e.,

$$\phi^{(k)}(\alpha) = \frac{1}{\chi^{(k)}} \sum_i K(\alpha,i)\ \psi_i^{(k)} , \qquad (7.3.11)$$

then we shall have

$$\lambda^{(k)} = \chi^{(k)2} . \qquad (7.3.12)$$

We have seen before that the eigenvalue of G (i.e., $\chi^2 = \lambda$) is positive, but in the present context we can prove this fact as follows. Using (7.3.2) and (7.3.3), we can write

$$\sum_\alpha (\phi(\alpha))^2 = \frac{1}{\chi} \sum_{\alpha=1}^{N} \sum_{i=1}^{n} \phi(\alpha)\ K(\alpha,i)\psi(i)$$

$$= \frac{1}{\chi^2} \sum_{i=1}^{n} \left[\sum_{\alpha=1}^{N} \phi(\alpha)\ K(\alpha,i)\right]^2 . \qquad (7.3.13)$$

Now, because (7.3.9) is linear in ϕ, and H is real, we can limit ourselves to real ϕ (or to purely imaginary ϕ), then (7.3.13) shows that χ^2 must be positive. Then χ could be either positive or negative. But, we can avoid a negative χ just by changing the sign of ϕ or ψ in (7.3.2) and (7.3.3).

Since $\psi^{(k)}(i)$ is an eigenvector of the symmetric matrix G(i,j) corresponding to eigenvalue $\chi^{(k)2}$

$$\psi^{(k)}(i) = \frac{1}{\chi^{(k)2}} \sum_{j=1}^{n} G(i,j)\ \psi^{(k)}(j), \qquad (7.3.14)$$

the series of functions $\psi^{(1)}(i)$, $\psi^{(2)}(i)$... will form a system of orthonormal fundamental function such that

$$\sum_{i=1}^{n} \psi^{(k)}(i)\ \psi^{(\ell)}(i) = \delta_{k\ell} , \qquad (7.3.15)$$

with the inverse orthonormal relations

$$\sum_{k=1}^{n} \psi^{(k)}(i)\ \psi^{(k)}(j) = \delta_{ij} \ . \tag{7.3.16}$$

If the eigenvalue $\chi^{(k)2}$ is r-ply degenerate, it does not determine a single eigenvector but an r-dimensional eigensubspace, but we can arbitrarily take r eigenvectors which satisfy the orthonormal relations. Starting from the $\psi^{(k)}(i)$, we can define $\phi^{(k)}(\alpha)$ by (7.3.2), and the orthonormal relations of the $\phi^{(k)}(\alpha)$'s can be derived for the orthonormal relation of $\psi^{(k)}$. For instance,

$$\begin{aligned}\sum_{\alpha=1} \phi^{(k)}(\alpha)\phi^{(\ell)}(\alpha) &= \frac{1}{\chi^{(k)}\chi^{(\ell)}} \sum_{\alpha=1}^{N} \sum_{i=1}^{n} \sum_{j=1}^{n} \\ &\quad K(\alpha,i)K(\alpha,j)\psi^{(k)}(i)\psi^{(\ell)}(j) \\ &= \frac{1}{\chi^{(k)}\chi^{(\ell)}} \sum_{i=1}^{n} \sum_{j=1}^{n} \\ &\quad G(i,j)\psi^{(k)}(i)\psi^{(\ell)}(j) \\ &= \frac{\chi^{(k)}}{\chi^{(\ell)}} \sum_{j=1}^{n} \psi^{(k)}(j)\psi^{(\ell)}(j) = \delta_{k\ell}.\end{aligned} \tag{7.3.17}$$

From this follows that the eigensubspace of r-dimensions in the (i,j) space is mapped onto an r-dimensional eigensubspace in its (α,β) space. Thus, the two matrices of N-dimensions and n-dimensions have, except for the eigenvalues 0, the same eigenvalues of the same degree of degeneracy. If $N < n$, the covariance matrix G will be singular, but H could be nonsingular and we can invert it and attain the eigenvalues and eigenvectors. After the eigenvector of H is obtained, we can calculate the eigenvector of G with the help of (7.3.3).

If $\psi^{(k)}(i)$ is the eigenvector of G corresponding to the eigenvalue $\lambda^{(k)}$, we can write as in (7.1.20)

$$G(i,j) = \sum_{k=1} \lambda^{(k)} \psi^{(k)}_{(i)} \psi^{(k)}_{(j)} . \qquad (7.3.18)$$

Similarly,

$$H(\alpha,\beta) = \sum_{k=1} \lambda^{(k)} \phi^{(k)}(\alpha) \phi^{(k)}(\beta) . \qquad (7.3.19)$$

Multiply by $\psi^{(k)}(j)$ the equation (7.3.2) for a particular $\chi^{(k)}$ and sum over k

$$\sum_{k=1}^{n} \chi^{(k)} \phi^{(k)}(\alpha) \psi^{(k)}(j) = \sum_{k=1}^{n} \sum_{i=1}^{n} K(\alpha,i)\, \psi^{(k)}(i) \psi^{(k)}(j)$$

$$= K(\alpha,j) . \qquad (7.3.20)$$

Hence,

$$K(\alpha,j) = \sum_{k=1}^{n} \chi^{(k)} \phi^{(k)}(\alpha) \psi^{(k)}(j) . \qquad (7.3.21)$$

Kaminuma suggests interpreting (7.3.2) and (7.3.3) intuitively as meaning that $\psi(i)$ and $\phi(\alpha)$ are filter coefficients for the given input $K(\alpha,i)$ resulting respectively in the outputs $\phi(\alpha)$ and $\psi(i)$ [K-11]. Computationally, the theorem of reciprocation provides us with a method to cope with the problem with a large n which leads to a difficulty for matrix inversion, due to a large size of matrix and to the singularity of the matrix. Tomita and Kaminuma applied the method to the problems of digitization of a two dimensional figure, particularly to character recognition [T-3, T-4, K-10]. The "object" is a character, the predicate is

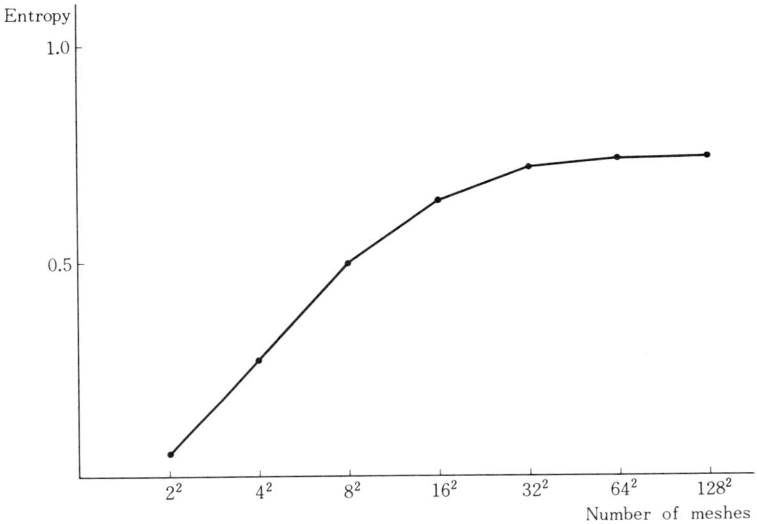

Figure 7.3.1 The entropy (information) increases at the beginning with the increasing number of meshes, but later reaches a plateau. From this stage on, any finer meshes will bring no further information. The entropy can be calculated either in the "object"-picture or in the "predicate"-picture, but of course we should choose the easier way.

---

the greyness of the printed or written characters, in each of the meshes. The number N is the number of characters, and the n is the number of meshes which could very easily be several hundreds or thousands. The greyness should be quantized, but the problem related to the fineness of quantization is irrelevant to us in the present context. We assume the number of quantization to be fixed at present.

The interesting question is how fine should the mesh-size be? In the (i,j) picture we cannot answer, but we can answer in the (α, β) picture. We should notice that the entropy S is the same in both pictures, for the same degree of fineness, which in this case is determined by the dimensionality n. The authors report that the S-value calculated in the (α, β) picture increases and converges to a certain value as we increase the number n of meshes. We can stop increasing n, where the entropy value starts to reach approximately a plateau. The S value in this example can be considered as the amount of information that the characters carry (as determined by the fixed number of quantization) (see Figure 7.3.1). Incidentally, it is interesting to notice that $H(\alpha, \beta)$, as can be seen from the definition (7.3.4), represents the degree of overlap of the characters α and β.

7.4 FACTOR ANALYSIS

After we had developed the method of SELFIC and had applied it effectively to problems in pattern recognition, in 1963 a psychologist friend of ours called our attention to the fact that the method of factor analysis practiced by some psychologists also used diagonalization of the correlation matrix. To our still bigger surprise, we subsequently learned that the idea of diagonalization of the correlation matrix had been proposed as early as 1901 by Karl Pearson [P-1]. The problem of factor analysis, however, was introduced by Charles Spearman in 1904 and originally had nothing to do with the method of diagonalization [S-1]. It was only in 1933 due mainly to Truman L. Kelley and Harold Hotelling, that a relation was established between the method of diagonalization and the problem of factor analysis [H-1, K-1]. It took another twenty years for the method of diagonalization to become practicable and useful thanks to the advent of electronic computers. In this section, we should like to describe the purpose of factor analysis and briefly explain how that purpose is realized by the diagonalization of correlation matrix. The reader will be interested to see that entirely different motivations lead to the same mathematical means.

Assume that an experiment consists of observation of n different variables, x_i, $i = 1, 2, \ldots, n$. We make N sets of observation and we identify each set of observed values by superscript α, so that $x_i^{(\alpha)}$ means the observed value of the i-th variable belonging to the α-th set ($\alpha = 1, 2, \ldots, N$). Each observation may belong to a different subject (object of psychological observation) or to the same subject at a different time. We assign probability or relative frequency $\omega^{(\alpha)}$ to the α-th set of observed values.

When the number n of variables is relatively large, they are likely to be correlated to one another. This should be clear if one considers for example a case like: height, weight, bust, waist, hip of a person, or a set of various kinds of tests pertaining to a child's intelligence. In cases like these it is quite natural to assume that there is a much smaller number of mutually uncorrelated variables (probably directly unobservable), of which these observed variables are functions. In a rough usage of words, we may regard these "hidden" variables as "causes" and the observed variables as "effects." If we succeed in uncovering a small number of such underlying causes, we may claim to have "explained" the complicated observational results in terms of simpler basic variables. It is customary to call such basic causative variables "common factors." Factor analysis aims to discover such common factors.

The first simplifying hypothesis to test would be to assume linear relations between the common factors and the observed variables, however, it would be too much to hope to realize $m<n$ for $x_i = \sum_{j=1}^{m} a_{ij} y_j$, $i = 1,2,\ldots,n$, where m variables y_j are the common factors. Although the x's are correlated, it is natural to assume that each variable has also its peculiar, individual cause of variation. Hence, we may assume

$$x_i = \sum_{j=1}^{m} a_{ij} y_j + b_i z_i \quad i = 1,2,\ldots,n \ , \qquad (7.4.1)$$

where the y's are "common" factors and the z_i are "specific" factors. In reference to each observation, we may write

$$x_i^{(\alpha)} = \sum_{j=1}^{m} a_{ij} \ y_j^{(\alpha)} + b_i z_i^{(\alpha)} \ . \qquad (7.4.2)$$

It is customary in factor analysis to adjust the range of variables so that each variable has mean value zero and standard deviation unity:

$$\langle x_i^{(\alpha)} \rangle_\alpha = \sum_{\alpha=1}^{N} \omega^{(\alpha)} x_i^{(\alpha)} = 0 \ ,$$

$$\langle x_i^{(\alpha)2} \rangle_\alpha = \sum_{\alpha=1}^{N} \omega^{(\alpha)} (x_i^{(\alpha)})^2 = 1 \quad i=1,2,\ldots,n \tag{7.4.3}$$

$$\langle y_j^{(\alpha)} \rangle = \sum_{\alpha=1}^{N} \omega^{(\alpha)} y_j^{(\alpha)} = 0 \ ,$$

$$\langle y_i^{(\alpha)2} \rangle_\alpha = \sum_{\alpha=1}^{N} \omega^{(\alpha)} (y_j^{(\alpha)})^2 = 1 \quad j=1,2,\ldots,m \tag{7.4.4}$$

$$\langle z_i^{(\alpha)} \rangle_\alpha = \sum_{\alpha=1}^{N} \omega^{(\alpha)} z_i^{(\alpha)} = 0 \ ,$$

$$\langle z_i^{(\alpha)2} \rangle_\alpha = \sum_{\alpha=1}^{N} \omega^{(\alpha)} (z_i^{(\alpha)})^2 = 1 \quad i=1,2,\ldots,n \ . \tag{7.4.5}$$

It may be noted that due to the assumption (7.4.3) the condition (7.1.6) of Section 7.1 is satisfied and the denominator τ of (7.1.5) (7.1.7) becomes unity. It is further assumed that all the new variables are mutually uncorrelated.

$$\langle y_j^{(\alpha)} y_k^{(\alpha)} \rangle_\alpha = \sum_{\alpha=1}^{N} \omega^{(\alpha)} y_j^{(\alpha)} y_k^{(\alpha)} = \delta_{jk}$$

$$j,k = 1,2,\ldots,m \tag{7.4.6}$$

$$\langle z_i^{(\alpha)} y_j^{(\alpha)} \rangle_\alpha = \sum_{\alpha=1}^{N} \omega^{(\alpha)} z_i^{(\alpha)} y_j^{(\alpha)} = 0$$

$$i=1,2,\ldots,n; \ j=1,2,\ldots,m \tag{7.4.7}$$

$$<z_i^{(\alpha)} z_k^{(\alpha)}>_\alpha = \sum_{\alpha=1}^{N} \omega^{(\alpha)} z_i^{(\alpha)} z_k^{(\alpha)} = \delta_{ik}$$

$$i,k=1,2,\ldots,n \; . \qquad (7.4.8)$$

Due to these normalization conditions G_{ij} of (7.1.2) becomes

$$G_{ij} = <x_i^{(\alpha)} x_j^{(\alpha)}>_\alpha = \sum_{k=1}^{m} a_{ik}a_{jk} + b_i^2 \, \delta_{ij}$$

$$i,j=1,2,\ldots,n \; , \qquad (7.4.9)$$

where diagonal elements are, in view of (7.4.3).

$$G_{ii} = \sum_{k=1}^{m} (a_{ik})^2 + b_i^2 = 1 \quad . \qquad (7.4.10)$$

The last formula can be interpreted as meaning that the average magnitude of the observed variable (which is unity) consists of two parts, "communality" and "specificity":

$$A_i + B_i = 1 \quad , \qquad (7.4.11)$$

with

$$A_i = \sum_{k=1}^{m} (a_{ik})^2, \; B_i = b_i^2 \qquad (7.4.12)$$

The communality A_i and specificity B_i of variable x_i measure the degree to which this variable depends respectively on common factors and on specific factors. The total communality

$$A = \sum_{i=1}^{n} A_i = \sum_{i=1}^{n} \sum_{k=1}^{m} (a_{ik})^2 \qquad (7.4.13)$$

then measures, in a certain sense, the extent to which the reduction of variables to common factors--the main purpose of factor analysis--is successful. On the other hand, it is also desirable to make the number m of common factors as small as possible, since after all the purpose is to explain "many" observable variables in terms of "few" elementary causes. But, understandably the smallness of m and the largeness of A are usually working against each other. This can be easily seen by considering a case with very small m and a case with very large A.

A successful factor analysis must rely on a suitable compromise of these two desirable features (large A and small m). In fact, there cannot be a unique solution in factor analysis anyway. The basic source of this ambiguity resides in the fact that for the given set of n variables x, we introduce n + m new variables y and z increasing the degree of freedom tremendously. Without some more or less arbitrary additional conditions, there could be no hope of obtaining the unique common factors. We shall presently show below one way of obtaining a set of solutions.

In (7.4.13), the total communality A is decomposed into communalities of individual observable variables. Another way of decomposing it is to put

$$A = \sum_{j=1}^{m} I_j \ , \quad I_j = \sum_{i=1}^{n} (a_{ij})^2 . \tag{7.4.14}$$

The quantity I_j is a measure of how strongly the common factor y_j influences observed variables. We may probably call it "influence" of y_j. We, of course, are looking for strongly influential factors. The constituent terms $(a_{ij})^2$ are so to speak the influence of factor y_j on variable x_i. If $(a_{ij})^2$ has appreciable values for many x's, the influence may be said to be widespread or general, and if it is limited to a few x's the influence has a narrow reach. We may then introduce an entropic function

$$S_j = -\sum_{i=1}^{n} q_{ij} \log q_{ij} \ , \tag{7.4.15}$$

with

$$q_{ij} = (a_{ij})^2 \Big/ \sum_{i=1}^{n} (a_{ij})^2 \tag{7.4.16}$$

and call it "generality" of influence of common factor y_j. The maximum of S_j is log n and the minimum is zero. Factor analysis introduces "common" factors and "specific" factors, but among the common factors some may be more "common" (i.e., less specific) than some others. The generality defined in (7.4.15) measures the degree of the commonness in this sense. A common factor with generality zero is no different from a specific factor. It influences only one observed variable. The measure S of generality was introduced in [W-2].

The problem is for us to make the "influence" of the common factors as strong as possible, whereby the constraints are the given experimental data G_{ij}. The variation can be made by changing the transformation coefficients a_{ij}. The way to formulate this problem as an extremum problem is as follows. Let y_1 be the most influential common factor, y_2 the next most influential common factor, and so on. Then we should require $\delta I_1 = 0$, $\delta I_1 + \delta I_2 = 0$, $\delta I_1 + \delta I_2 + \delta I_3 = 0$, and so forth under the constraint $\delta G_{ij} = 0$ or $\delta R_{ij} = 0$ where

$$R_{ij} = G_{ij} - b_i^2 \delta_{ij} = \sum_{k=1}^{m} a_{ik} a_{jk} . \qquad (7.4.17)$$

The coefficients b_i are kept constant during the variation of a_{ij}. Introducing $m \times n^2$ Lagrange multipliers $\mu_{ij}^{(\ell)}$, we can write the extremum problem in the form of m equations.

$$\delta \left(\sum_{k=1}^{\ell} I_k \right) + \delta \sum_{i=1}^{n} \sum_{j=1}^{n} \mu_{ij}^{(\ell)} R_{ij} = 0 \qquad (7.4.18)$$

$$\ell = 1,2,3,\dots,m.$$

The coefficients $\mu_{ij}^{(\ell)}$ are to be determined so as to satisfy (7.4.17). Since R_{ij} is a symmetric matrix the cofficients $\mu_{ij}^{(\ell)}$ can be assumed to be symmetric too. Every time we have a different ℓ in the summation of I_k, we may have a different set of coefficients $\mu_{ij}^{(\ell)}$, hence we put a superscript (ℓ) on $\mu_{ij}^{(\ell)}$. For $\ell = m$, the equation would mean extremization of the total communality, but this is actually already fixed by the given R_{ij} since $A = \sum_i R_{ii}$.

In terms of a_{ij}, equation (7.4.18) becomes, in virtue of (7.4.14) and (7.4.17),

$$\delta \sum_{k=1}^{\ell} \sum_{i=1}^{n} (a_{ik})^2 + \delta \sum_{i=1}^{n} \sum_{j=1}^{n} \mu_{ij}^{(\ell)} \sum_{k=1}^{m} a_{ik} a_{jk} = 0 \tag{7.4.19}$$

or

$$\sum_{k=1}^{\ell} \sum_{i=1}^{n} \left(a_{ik} + \sum_{j=1}^{n} \mu_{ij}^{(\ell)} a_{jk} \right) \delta a_{ik} + \sum_{k=\ell+1}^{m} \sum_{i=1}^{n} \sum_{j=1}^{n} \mu_{ij}^{(\ell)} a_{jk} \delta a_{ik} = 0 . \tag{7.4.20}$$

Since we have used Lagrange's multipliers we can regard each δa_{ik} as independent and obtain

$$a_{ik} + \sum_{j=1}^{n} \mu_{ij}^{(\ell)} a_{jk} = 0 \quad 1 \le k \le \ell, 1 \le i \le n \tag{7.4.21}$$

$$\sum_{j=1}^{n} \mu_{ij}^{(\ell)} a_{jk} = 0 \quad \ell+1 \le k \le m, 1 \le i \le n . \tag{7.4.22}$$

If we consider a_{jk} as the j-th component of the k-th vector in a set of ℓ vectors [each k corresponding to a factor in (7.4.1)], we can interpret these two equations as meaning the following: There exists a symmetric $n \times n$ matrix $\mu_{ij}^{(\ell)}$ such that $\{a_{jk}\}$ for a given value of k is one of its eigenvectors corresponding to eigenvalue -1 if $1 \le k \le \ell$ and eigenvalue 0 if $\ell < k \le m$, and that the a_{jk} thus obtained satisfy the condition (7.4.17) with the given R_{ij}. The eigenvalue -1 is ℓ-ply degenerate allowing for ℓ linearly independent eigenvectors. The eigenvalue 0 is $(m-\ell)$-ply degenerate allowing for $(m-\ell)$ linearly independent eigenvectors. We can, if we want, enlarge the set of vectors so that k runs from 1 to n, by introducing (n-m) eigenvectors of the matrix $\mu^{(\ell)}$, which being an $n \times n$ matrix can have n eigenvectors.

Thanks to our previous study of the correlation matrix, it is now easy for us to write down both μ_{ij} and a_{jk}, satisfying (7.4.21), (7.4.22) and (7.4.17). Let $\xi_i^{(k)}$ be the eigenvector of the $n \times n$ symmetric matrix R_{ij}, corresponding to eigenvalue $\lambda^{(k)}$

$$\sum_{j=1}^{n} R_{ij}\ \xi_j^{(k)} = \lambda^{(k)}\xi_i^{(k)} , \qquad (7.4.23)$$

where k runs from 1 to n. Some λ's may be zero, but we can define ξ's for them too. We can impose the orthonormal condition on the n eigenvectors, so that

$$\sum_{i=1}^{n} \xi_i^{(k)}\ \xi_i^{(\ell)} = \delta_{k\ell} , \quad \sum_{k=1}^{n} \xi_i^{(k)}\ \xi_j^{(k)} = \delta_{ij} . \qquad (7.4.24)$$

We can then write R_{ij} also in the form

$$R_{ij} = \sum_{k=1}^{n} \lambda^{(k)}\xi_i^{(k)}\xi_j^{(k)} . \qquad (7.4.25)$$

Comparing this with (7.4.17) we can immediately think of a possible solution

$$a_{ik} = \lambda^{(k)\frac{1}{2}}\xi_i^{(k)} , \qquad (7.4.26)$$

if we can assume that m is such that

$$\lambda^{(k)} = 0 \quad \text{for } k > m . \qquad (7.4.27)$$

It may be noted that (7.4.26) is sufficient but not necessary in order to satisfy (7.4.17). We should remember that a_{ik} must also satisfy an equation of the type (7.4.21), (7.4.23). But, in the present case, we can easily write down $\mu_{ij}^{(\ell)}$ such that (7.4.21), (7.4.22) are satisfied by (7.4.26). In fact, we can define $\mu_{ij}^{(\ell)}$ as a symmetric matrix given by

$$\mu_{ij}^{(\ell)} = -\sum_{k=1}^{\ell} \xi_i^{(k)} \xi_j^{(k)} \qquad (7.4.28)$$

which has an ℓ-ple eigenvalue -1 and $(n-\ell)$-ple eigenvalue 0. Different from (7.4.25), the summation with respect to k runs here only up to ℓ. The eigenvectors corresponding to eigenvalue -1 are $\{\xi_i^{(k)}\}$ with $k \leq \ell$ and the eigenvectors corresponding to eigenvalue 0 are $\{\xi_i^{(k)}\}$ with $\ell < k \leq n$. According to (7.4.26), the $\{a_{ik}\}$ is the same vector as $\{\xi_i^{(k)}\}$, except that the latter is normalized as in (7.4.24). We have kept the specific value of ℓ so far, but we now see that the different values result only in different numbers of terms in the summation in (7.4.28) and all the rest actually does not depend on ℓ.

With the help of (7.4.26), we can now write (7.4.1) in the form

$$x_i^* \equiv x_i - b_i z_i = \sum_{k=1}^{m} \left(\lambda^{(k)\frac{1}{2}} y_k\right) \xi_i^{(k)}, \qquad (7.4.29)$$

which shows that the common factor y_k is the component of the vector x_i^* in the direction of the vector $\xi^{(k)}$ divided by a constant $\lambda^{(k)\frac{1}{2}}$. It may further be noted that the influence of a common factor defined in (7.4.14) is now given, in view of (7.4.26) and (7.4.14) by

$$I_k = \sum_{i=1}^{n} (a_{ik})^2 = \lambda^{(k)} \qquad . \qquad (7.4.30)$$

The search for "influential" factors is now translated as a search for an eigenvector $\xi^{(k)}$ with large $\lambda^{(k)}$.

Now, in order to satisfy the conditions that I_1 is the largest and I_2 is the second largest, and so on, we should determine the label k of $\lambda^{(k)}$ so that

$$\lambda^{(1)} \geq \lambda^{(2)} \geq \dots \geq \lambda^{(m)} \qquad . \qquad (7.4.31)$$

Under this agreement, the a_{ik} of (7.4.26) becomes the desired solution.

The condition (7.4.27) may be interpreted as having the following meaning. The trace of G_{ij} is n by definition (7.4.10). The trace of R_{ij} is therefore n minus $\sum_{i=1}^{n} b_i^2$ due to (7.4.17). The total sum of n eigenvalues $\lambda^{(k)}$ must equal this difference, but the sum of the first m λ's can equal this since some of λ's could be zero. This means that we determine the number m of common factors by the condition

$$\sum_{k=1}^{m-1} \lambda^{(k)} < \sum_{k=1}^{m} \lambda^{(k)} = \sum_{k=1}^{n} \lambda^{(k)} = \text{trace } (R_{ij}) \ . \tag{7.4.32}$$

If the b's change, the number of dimensions m will change since R_{ij} changes.

In the psychological literature the specific factors are often separated again into two factors:

$$b_i z_i = b_i' u_i + b_i'' v_i \ , \tag{7.4.33}$$

where u_i should represent the purely characteristic variability of the i-th variable x_i, and v_i should represent the inevitable noise peculiar to the observation of the variable x_i. As we have seen in relation to generality (7.4.15), the distinction between common factor and specific factor is a matter of degree. It does not seem therefore to be very natural to separate the u's from the y's as is done by the traditional practitioners of factor analysis. I would rather advise to abolish the u's from the beginning and assume m=n. Those variables y_j with small generality values S_j should then be considered as specific factors. As far as the v's are concerned, it may be possible to evaluate their coefficients b"'s from the experiment, if the experiments refer to a repeatable observation as in physical sciences. But in biology, psychology, and sociology the experiments are not always reproducible and it is hard to evaluate the b"'s. In such a case we might do as well without v's too. If we do not introduce u's and v's from the beginning, the entire methodology of factor analysis becomes identical with our SELFIC. The "common factors" y's with small I_j are to be considered as "specific factors." But, we may say that the study of factor analysis increases our insight into the meaning of the SELFIC method. The "importance" of the optimal axes will play the role of the "influence" of this factor.

Another peculiar procedure widely adopted by the users of factor analysis is that they often apply a second linear transformation to the common factors obtained by factor analysis until the variables after the second transformation seem to acquire "intuitively clear" meanings. This does not make much sense (unless the λ's have almost the same value), since it would be much wiser to adapt our mental attitude so that the common factors with large generalities start to look familiar and intuitively clear to us. It may be added that it is customary in factor analysis to call the common factors obtained by the diagonalization of correlation matrix "principal components."

7.5 KARHUNEN-LOÈVE EXPANSION

The series of research that led us in the early 60s to the idea of the SELFIC method started actually as an attempt to develop a method for computer processing of continuous signals, such as seismic records, medical records, electroencephalograms, and so forth. To load a computer with such signals, we have of course to discretize them first. The simplest method is that of sampling the value of the function at constant intervals, but this may not be the most economical or the most efficient way. A more general way of discretizing a continuous signal is to expand it according to a set of orthogonal base functions and use the expansion coefficients as a representation of the function. (The sampling method is actually a very special case of such an expansion according to Someya-Shannon's theorem [S-2, W-4].) The maximum efficiency may then be translated as the fastest convergence of such an expansion, since the number of coefficients necessary to represent the function within a given error allowance will become the smallest. The speed of convergence of the expansion, of course, depends on the collection of functions one intends to represent by the coefficients. If one has only one function at hand, one can use a base function set which includes this particular function as one of the members. One has only one coefficient. If one has N linearly independent functions, one needs N coefficients to express each one of them without any error. But if N is very large yet not independent, we may need less than N coefficients, particularly, if we do not require the absolute absence of any error. More generally, we may formulate the problem as follows: Given a finite or infinite set of continuous functions possibly with different statistical weights, (i.e., given an ensemble of continuous functions), what is the base function set which allows on the average the fastest converging expansion? The answer had long been known under the name of Karhunen-Loève expansion.

In actual computer-oriented problems, the continuous functions are given anyway only by the sampled values. For this reason, the problem mentioned above becomes in reality that of passing from the enumerable (actually finite) sampled values of functions to the coefficients of the fastest converging expansion. Consequently, our work started with developing an enumerable (finite) version of the Karhunen-Loève expansion interpreting the fastest convergence as the optimality of coordinate system. We soon discovered the entropy minimizing property of the optimal coordinate system, and placed this fact as the central concept of the SELFIC. After having shown the practical usefulness of the methods, we proved true intimate mathematical relationship between Karhunen-Loève expansion and the method of factor analysis [W-2]. For the rest of this section, we shall show how Karhunen-Loève expansion leads to the same mathematical problem of diagonalization of the correlation matrix.

In Section 7.2, we introduced two sets of variables, α and i. The SELFIC method required both α and i to be discrete. Schmidt's original theory assumed both α and i to be continuous. In the Karhunen-Loève expansion, we have to assume α to be discrete and i to be continuous, but all three cases are essentially the same. But, because of the importance of the Karhunen-Loève expansion, we repeat the explanation for the half-continuous, half-discontinuous case in this section. The advanced reader may not need to read this section.

Suppose we are given an ensemble of N functions $f^{(\alpha)}(u)$, $\alpha = 1,2,\ldots,N$, square-integrable in the domain $u_1 \leq u \leq u_2$ of the continuous variable u, with weight $w^{(\alpha)}$ attached to the α-th function. We take a set of complete, orthonormal, real base functions $\{\psi_i(u)\}$, $i = 1,2,\ldots,\infty$, defined in the same domain

$$\int_{u_1}^{u_2} \psi_i(u)\ \psi_j(u)\ du = \delta_{ij}\ , \tag{7.5.1}$$

so that $f^{(\alpha)}(u)$ can be expanded as

$$f^{(\alpha)}(u) = \sum_{i=1}^{\infty} x_i^{(\alpha)} \psi_i(u)\ , \tag{7.5.2}$$

where the expansion coefficients $x_i^{(\alpha)}$ are given by

$$x_i^{(\alpha)} = \int_{u_1}^{u_2} \psi_i(u)\ f^{(\alpha)}(u)\ du\ . \tag{7.5.3}$$

The expansion (7.5.2) means the convergence

$$\lim_{m \to \infty} g_m^{(\alpha)}(u) = f^{(\alpha)}(u)\ , \tag{7.5.4}$$

where $g_m^{(\alpha)}(u)$ is the sum of the first m terms on the right hand side of (7.5.2)

$$g_m^{(\alpha)}(u) = \sum_{i=1}^{m} x_i^{(\alpha)} \psi_i(u)\ . \tag{7.5.5}$$

The difference between the finite sum $g_m^{(\alpha)}(u)$ and its limiting value $f^{(\alpha)}(u)$ is

$$\delta_m^{(\alpha)}(u) = f^{(\alpha)}(u) - g_m^{(\alpha)}(u) = \sum_{i=m+1}^{\infty} x_i^{(\alpha)} \psi_i(u)\ , \tag{7.5.6}$$

which depends on u, but for any u it tends to zero as $m \to \infty$. The average of the square of $\delta_m^{(\alpha)}(u)$ in the domain $[u_1, u_2]$ is $1/(u_2-u_1)$ times

$$\delta_m^{(\alpha)\,2} = \int_{u_1}^{u_2} \left[\delta_m^{(\alpha)}(u)\right]^2 du = \sum_{i=m+1}^{\infty} (x_i^{(\alpha)})^2 \ . \tag{7.5.7}$$

The last equality is obtained in virtue of (7.5.1). A fast convergence of (7.5.3) in the domain $[u_1,u_2]$ may be interpreted as meaning smallness of $\delta_m^{(\alpha)2}$ for each m.

The average of $\delta_m^{(\alpha)\,2}$ in the ensemble $\{f^{(\alpha)}(u), w^{(\alpha)}\}$ is

$$\delta_m^2 = \sum_{\alpha=1}^{N} \delta_m^{(\alpha)} w^{(\alpha)} = \sum_{\alpha=1}^{N} \sum_{i=m+1}^{\infty} w^{(\alpha)} (x_i^{(\alpha)})^2 \ , \tag{7.5.8}$$

or

$$\delta_m^2 = \sigma - \sum_{\alpha=1}^{N} \sum_{i=1}^{m} w^{(\alpha)} (x_i^{(\alpha)})^2 \ , \tag{7.5.9}$$

where $\sigma = \delta_o^2$ or more explicitly

$$\sigma = \sum_{\alpha=1}^{N} \sum_{i=1}^{\infty} w^{(\alpha)} (x_i^{(\alpha)})^2 = \sum_{\alpha=1}^{N} w^{(\alpha)} \int_{u_1}^{u_2} \left[f^{(\alpha)}(u)\right]^2 du \ . \tag{7.5.10}$$

The goal is now to minimize δ_m^2 for the given ensemble $\{f^{(\alpha)}(u), w^{(\alpha)}\}$ and for each m by varying the set of base functions $\{\psi_i(u)\}$. To carry out such a program we have to know how the coefficients $x_i^{(\alpha)}$ change as we vary the set of base functions, say, from $\{\psi_i(u)\}$ to $\{\psi'_i(u)\}$. The coefficients in the second representation by $x_i^{(\alpha)\prime}$ will be

$$x_i^{(\alpha)\prime} = \int_{u_1}^{u_2} \psi'_i(u)\ f^{(\alpha)}(u)\ du \ . \tag{7.5.11}$$

If we expand the function $\psi'_i(u)$ as

$$\psi'_i(u) = \sum_{j=1}^{\infty} T_{ij}\psi_j(u) \ , \tag{7.5.12}$$

the expressions (7.5.3) and (7.5.11) immediately yield

$$x_i^{(\alpha)\prime} = \sum_{j=1}^{\infty} T_{ij}\, x_j^{(\alpha)} . \qquad (7.5.13)$$

The condition that the set $\{\psi'_i(u)\}$ is also orthogonal and normalized

$$\delta_{ij} = \int_{u_1}^{u_2} \psi'_i(u)\ \psi'_j(u)\ du = \sum_k T_{ik}T_{jk} , \qquad (7.5.14)$$

which means the transformation T is an orthogonal transformation:

$$T^{-1} = T^t .$$

This transforms the problem of the fastest converging expansion into a problem exactly the same as one of the minimization of errors discussed in Section 7.1, except that the number n there should be replaced by an enumerable infinity. The reader will easily check for himself that none of the essential parts of the proof given there depends on the finiteness of n. Hence, the answer to our present problem can be easily given from what we learned there. Namely, the optimal set of base functions $\{\psi'(u)\}$ must be such that

$$G'_{ij} = \sum_{\alpha=1}^{N} w^{(\alpha)} x_i^{(\alpha)\prime} x_j^{(\alpha)\prime} \Big/ \tau \qquad (7.5.15)$$

becomes diagonal. Note that σ is independent of the base functions we use. With the help of (7.5.10), G'_{ij} can be written

$$G'_{ij} = \int_{u_1}^{u_2} \psi'_i(u)\,(u|G|u')\ \psi'_j(u')\ du\ du' , \qquad (7.5.16)$$

with

$$(u|G|u') = \sum_{\alpha=1}^{N} w^{(\alpha)} f^{(\alpha)}(u)\ f^{(\alpha)}(u') \Big/ \tau . \qquad (7.5.17)$$

It is now easy to see that if we take as $\psi'_i(u)$ the eigenvectors $\xi_i(u)$ of $(u|G|u')$, the matrix G'_{ij} will become diagonal. In fact the eigenvector $\xi_i(u)$ is defined by

$$\int_{u_1}^{u_2} (u|G|u') \; \varepsilon_i(u') \; du' = \lambda_i \xi_i(u) \tag{7.5.18}$$

and G'_{ij} becomes

$$G'_{ij} = \lambda_j \int_{u_1}^{u_2} \xi_i(u)\xi_j(u) \, du \; . \tag{7.5.19}$$

Since $(u|G|u')$ is symmetrical, that is,

$$(u|G|u') = (u'|G|u) \; , \tag{7.5.20}$$

we can write for $\xi_j(u)$

$$\int_{u_1}^{u_2} (u|G|u')\xi_j(u) \; du = \lambda_j \xi_j(u') \; . \tag{7.5.21}$$

Multiplying (7.5.18) by $\xi_j(u)$ and integrating with respect to u, we obtain

$$\int_{u_1}^{u_2}\int_{u_1}^{u_2} \xi_j(u)(u|G|u')\xi_i(u')du\,du' = \lambda_i \int_{u_1}^{u_2} \xi_j(u)\xi_i(u)du \; . \tag{7.5.22}$$

Similarly from (7.5.21)

$$\int_{u_1}^{u_2}\int_{u_1}^{u_2} \xi_i(u')(u|G|u')\xi_j(u)du\,du' = \lambda_j \int_{u_1}^{u_2} \xi_i(u')\xi_j(u')du' \; . \tag{7.5.23}$$

Subtracting (7.5.23) from (7.5.22), we obtain

$$(\lambda_i - \lambda_j)\int_{u_1}^{u_2} \xi_i(u)\xi_j(u)du = 0 \; , \tag{7.5.24}$$

or

$$\int_{u_1}^{u_2} \xi_i(u)\xi_j(u)du = 0 \quad \text{if } \lambda_i \neq \lambda_j \ . \tag{7.5.25}$$

If $\lambda_i = \lambda_j$, we do not have this, but we can choose $\xi_i(u)$ so that

$$\int_{u_1}^{u_2} \xi_i(u)\xi_j(u)du = \delta_{ij} \tag{7.5.26}$$

for all i and all j. With the help of (7.5.26), G'_{ij} of (7.5.19) becomes

$$G'_{ij} = \lambda_i \delta_{ij} \ . \tag{7.5.27}$$

To realize the minimization of δ_m^2, all we now need is to agree to label the base function $\{\xi_k(u)\}$ so that

$$\lambda_1 \geq \lambda_2 \geq \cdots \ . \tag{7.5.28}$$

As far as the entropy theorem (the Basic Theorem of SELFIC) is concerned, the only difference here from the previous case is that the entropy is now defined by the sum of infinite terms

$$S' = - \sum_{k=1}^{\infty} \rho'_k \log \rho'_k \ , \tag{7.5.29}$$

where $\rho'_k = G'_{kk}$ and, if the $\psi'_i(u)$ are the $\xi'_i(u)$, then $\rho'_k = \lambda_k$. Everything goes the same way as before because the prototype H-theorem remains valid for the case $N = \infty$.

7.6 CLAFIC-MOSS

In the foregoing sections of this chapter, we ignored the class affiliation of vectors and concentrated our attention on the aspect of dimension reduction. But in this section, we shall apply the same method to the cases where we are interested in distinguishing classes when the paradigms are given with their class-belonging and the newcomer is supposed to be, at least with some probability, located in each of the classes suggested by paradigms. First, we shall discuss the case of one class, to which an object either belongs or does not belong. CLAFIC (class-featuring-information-compression) is applicable in this case [W-3, W-10]. Next, we shall discuss the method of MOSS (multiclass-subspace) which can be used in the cases where more than one class are coexisting. Recently, we notice a sign of renewed interest in the subspace method. See for instance, Kohonen [K-23].

Both CLAFIC and MOSS use what we called the affine-space representation in contrast to the metric-space representation used by almost all the other methods of clustering and pattern recognition. See Appendix A-3 and A-5. The difference lies in the fact that a class occupies a subspace (passing the origin) in the affine-space representation while it occupies a zone or region in the metric-space representation. In the former, similarity of two vectors can be represented by the cosine between the two vectors while the dissimilarity in the latter can be represented by the distances between the two. Actually, the SELFIC already should be classified also as an affine-space representation, but we do not need to introduce explicitly the ideas of similarity. We could do without discussing this point.

In SELFIC, we represented an object as a vector in the n-dimensional space and we found out that if we allow small errors, all the vectors of appreciable importance can be located in an n-dimensional subspace, with m considerably smaller than n. We can, of course, apply the same method only to the vectors of one class, and we shall get a small subspace of very small m. This space is dependent on its fidelity σ we require as a measure of permissible error. Let us call the subspace the eigensubspace of the class.

If a newcomer happens to be totally in this eigensubspace of class C, we can decide that it belongs with probability one to class C. If the vector representing the new object has a nonzero projection on this eigensubspace, the cosine (the ratio of the length of this projection to the original vector length) squared can be taken to be the probability of the new object belonging to class C. Then, one minus this probability is its probability of not belonging to C or belonging to any class other than C and can be geometrically understood as the cosine squared between the original vector and its projection on the subspace formed by all vectors perpendicular to vectors of the C-subspace. This simple idea of CLAFIC, introduced in [W-3], does not apply when there is more than one class and was developed into MOSS in various papers [K-3, K-19, R-7, W-10, W-19, W-21, W-44].

The complications that can happen in the multiclass case are due to the following situations. (1) The eigensubspaces of two different classes can have a nonvanishing intersection. (2) The eigenspaces of all classes, pairwise, could be mutually nonorthogonal. (Two subspaces are said to be orthogonal if every vector in one subspace is orthogonal to all the vectors of the other subspace.)

The first difficulty can be at least formally eliminated if the intersection is declared to belong to the "reject-class." The second difficulty causes different troubles: (2a) the two eigenspaces have very small angles between them so that the discrimination becomes practically very difficult; (2b) the sum of the squares of cosines between a vector and different eigensubspace does not add up to unity; as a result, we cannot interpret them as probabilities of the object belonging to different classes; (2c) as explained later and also in the Appendix, this picture involves a logical anomaly. All these troubles will disappear if we apply to the vectors a nonorthogonal transformation so that the eigensubspaces of different classes all become mutually orthogonal. Of course, if n is large and the number M of classes is small, in reality both difficulties (1) and (2) actually do not cause practical troubles, but we must here present a general theory that can cope with both difficulties. In the following, we briefly explain such a general theory of MOSS which of course includes the simple case of CLAFIC.

As a mathematical tool convenient to describe the method MOSS, we shall start with explaining the mathematical tool called projection operator.

The projection operator P in the n-dimensional real space is an $n \times n$ real, symmetric, idempotent matrix, that is,

$$P^t = P \; ; \; P_{ji} = P_{ij} \tag{7.6.1}$$

and

$$P^2 = P \; ; \; \sum_{k=1}^{n} P_{ik} P_{kj} = P_{ij} \; . \tag{7.6.2}$$

The relations are obviously invariant for an orthogonal transformation, $P \to UPU^t$ with $U^t = U^{-1}$. Hence, (7.6.2) will be true even if we go to the coordinate in which P is diagonal. This means that the eigenvalues of P must be 0 or 1. The eigenvectors corresponding to eigenvalue 1 form a subspace (passing the origin) of m dimensions, where

$$m = \text{trace } P \; ; \; m = \sum_{i=1}^{n} P_{ii} \; . \tag{7.6.3}$$

Let's remember that the diagonal sum is invariant for an orthogonal transformation, hence m is the number of 1's standing on the diagonal in the diagonalized form of P. We can take arbitrarily a set of m mutually orthogonal (normalized) vectors in this m-dimensional subspace, which we denote $\xi^{(k)}$, $k = 1,2,...,m$.

$$\xi^{(k)t}\xi^{(\ell)} = \delta_{k\ell} \; ; \; \sum_{i=1}^{n} \xi_i^{(k)} \xi_i^{(\ell)} = \delta_{k\ell} \; . \tag{7.6.4}$$

The matrix P can be written as

$$P = \sum_{k=1}^{m} \xi^{(k)} \xi^{(k)t} \; ; \; P_{ij} = \sum_{k=1}^{m} \xi_i^{(k)} \xi_j^{(k)} \; . \tag{7.6.5}$$

The ξ's are eigenvectors of P corresponding to eigenvalue 1. The matrix P defines the subspace subtended by the $\xi^{(k)}$, $k = 1,2,...,m$, and conversely a subspace defines a projection operator P. Subspace and projection operator correspond one-to-one; consequently we may use synonymously the terms subspace and the **projection** operator corresponding to it.

The eigenvectors corresponding to eigenvalue 0 form a subspace of (n-m) dimensions. If we take arbitrarily $(n-m)$ mutually orthogonal, normalized vectors $\xi^{(k)}$, $k = m+1, m+2, \ldots, n$, in this subspace we can form a set of n base vectors $\xi^{(k)}$, $k = 1,2,\ldots,n$. If we express the matrix P using its own eigenvectors, $\xi^{(k)}$, $k = 1,2,\ldots,n$, as the base vectors, the matrix will have first m diagonal elements equal to 1 and all other elements equal to 0. If we apply an orthogonal transformation that leaves invariant the subspace subtended by the first m eigenvectors (and hence the subspace subtended by the last $(n-m)$ eigenvectors, too), this particular form of the matrix will remain unchanged. If we express the matrix P using a set of base vectors other than the eigenvectors, the matrix will not have this particular form.

If we multiply the matrix P from the left on an arbitrary vector x, the resultant x' will be the projection of x on the subspace defined by P. We can see this by observing

$$x' = Px = \sum_{k=1}^{m} (\xi^{(k)t}x)\,\xi^{(k)};$$

$$x_i' = \sum_{k=1}^{m} \left(\sum_{j=1}^{n} \xi_j^{(k)} x_j \right) \xi_i^{(k)}. \qquad (7.6.6)$$

The matrix 0 is obviously a projection operator satisfying (7.6.1) and (7.6.2) and corresponds to the subspace of 0 dimension, and the projection of any vector on this subspace is zero. The matrix 1 (identity matrix) is also a projection operator and corresponds to the entire n-dimensional space, and the projection of any vector on this subspace is the original vector itself. The matrix $(1-P)$ obeys also (7.6.1) and (7.6.2), meaning that it is a projection operator. It defines the subspace subtended by the eigenvectors of P corresponding to eigenvalue 0. The obvious relation

$$x = Px + (1-P)x \qquad (7.6.7)$$

means that x is the vectorial sum of the projection of x on the subspace of P and the projection of x on its complementary subspace.

Two subspaces are said to be orthogonal, if every vector of one subspace is orthogonal to all vectors of the other subspace. It is easy to see that this condition is equivalent to the condition that the projection operators P_1 and P_2 corresponding to them satisfy

$$P_1 P_2 = P_2 P_1 = 0 \ ;$$

$$\sum_{k=1}^{n} P_{1_{ik}} P_{2_{kj}} = \sum_{k=1}^{n} P_{2_{ik}} P_{1_{kj}} = 0, \qquad ((7.6.8)$$

which we write also

$$P_1 \perp P_2 \ . \qquad (7.6.9)$$

Note that $P_1 P_2 = 0$ implies that $P_2 P_1 = 0$, since $P_2 P_1 = P_2^t P_1^t = (P_1 P_2)^t = 0^t = 0$. The orthogonality relation is not transitive. A special case of orthogonality is $P \perp (1-P)$:

$$P(1-P) = P-P^2 = P-P = 0 \qquad (7.6.10)$$

$$\sum_{k=1}^{n} P_{ik} (1-P)_{kj} = P_{ij} - \sum_{k=1}^{n} P_{ik} P_{kj} = P_{ij} - P_{ij} = 0 .$$

Subspace P_1 is said to be "included in" subspace P_2 if every vector of P_1 is a vector of P_2. It is easy to see that this condition is equivalent to

$$P_1 P_2 = P_2 P_1 = P_1 \ ; \qquad (7.6.11)$$

$$\sum_{k=1}^{n} P_{1_{ik}} P_{2_{kj}} = \sum_{k=1}^{n} P_{2_{ik}} P_{1_{kj}} = P_{1_{ij}} \ ,$$

which we also write

$$P_1 \to P_2 \ . \qquad (7.6.12)$$

Indeed, (7.6.11) says that $P_1 x = x$ implies $P_2 x = x$. Note that $P_1 P_2 = P_1$ implies $P_2 P_1 = P_1$ and vice versa, since $P_2 P_1 = P_2^t P_1^t = (P_1 P_2)^t = P_1^t = P_1$. The inclusion relation is transitive. If P_1 is included in P_2, that is, if (7.6.11) is the case, the difference $P_2 - P_1$ is a projection operator satisfying (7.6.1) and (7.6.2). The fact that $(1-P)$ is a projection operator is a special case of this theorem. It should be noted that

$$O \rightarrow P \rightarrow 1 \text{ for any } P \ . \tag{7.6.13}$$

Subspaces P_1 and P_2 are said to be "compatible" if there exists a set of base vectors $\xi^{(k)}$, $k = 1,2,\ldots,n$ such that subspace P_1 as well as subspace P_2 is subtended by some of the ξ's. This condition can be expressed as commutativity of matrices P_1 and P_2

$$\begin{gathered} P_1 P_2 = P_2 P_1 \ ; \\ \sum_{k=1}^{n} P_{1_{ik}} P_{2_{kj}} = \sum_{k=1}^{n} P_{2_{ik}} P_{1_{kj}} \ , \end{gathered} \tag{7.6.14}$$

Which we also write

$$P_1 \sim P_2 \ . \tag{7.6.15}$$

The compatibility relation is not transitive. If (7.6.12) then (7.6.15). If P_1 and P_2 are compatible, the product

$$\begin{gathered} Q = P_1 P_2 = P_1 P_2 ; \\ Q_{ij} = \sum_{k=1}^{n} P_{1_{ik}} P_{2_{kj}} = \sum_{k=1}^{n} P_{2_{ik}} P_{kj} \end{gathered} \tag{7.6.16}$$

is easily seen to be a projection operator and

$$Q \rightarrow P_1 \text{ and } Q \rightarrow P_2 \ . \tag{7.6.17}$$

The three subspaces $P\,-Q$, $P\,-Q$, and Q are mutually orthogonal [provided (7.6.15)]

$$\left.\begin{aligned} (P_1 - Q) &\perp (P_2 - Q) \\ (P_2 - Q) &\perp Q \\ Q &\perp (P_1 - Q) \ . \end{aligned}\right\} \tag{7.6.18}$$

Hence, we can select a single set of orthogonal base vectors such that some of them belong to subspace P_1-Q, some others belong to subspace P_2-Q, and some others belong to subspace Q. Subspace P_1 is subtended by the base vectors of the first group and the base vectors of the third group. Subspace P_2 is subtended by the base vectors of the second group and the base vectors of the third group. The remaining base vectors subtend the complementary subspace $1 - (P_1-Q) - (P_2-Q) - Q = 1 + Q - P_1 - P_2$. It is easy to show that this expression is a projection operator. Q is the intersection of two compatible subspaces P_1 and P_2. Hereafter we decide not to write the indices that refer to the components with respect to a particular coordinate system.

The projection operators, being matrices, can be added, subtracted, and multiplied, but the result of such an arithmetic operation is not necessarily a projection operator. We have, however, the following rules: (1) if $P_1 \sim P_2$, then $P_1 P_2$ $(=P_2 P_1)$ is a projection operator; (2) if $P_1 \to P_2$ then $P_2 - P_1$ is a projection operator; (3) if $P_1 \perp P_2$, then $P_1 + P_2$ is a projection operator. The first two have already been mentioned. The third one is easy to prove.

Now we can introduce "conjunction" $P_1 \cap P_2$ of two projection operators P_1 and P_2 with the help of the concept of inclusion $(\to)$. A projection P_3 is said to be conjunction $P_1 \cap P_2$ if P_3 satisfies the conditions: (i) $P_3 \to P_1$ and $P_3 \to P_2$, and (ii) if $X \to P_1$ and $X \to P_2$, then $X \to P_3$. With some mathematical manipulation, we can prove that the infinite product of P_1 and P_2 can be considered to be P_3:

$$P_3 = P_1 \cap P_2 = \ldots P_1 P_2 P_1 P_2 P_1 P_2 \ldots \quad . \tag{7.6.19}$$

It is readily seen that P_3 corresponds to the subspace consisting of all vectors that belong to both P_1 and P_2. In other words, P_3 is the common subspace (i.e., the intersection of subspace P_1 and subspace P_2). It may be noted that if $P_1 \sim P_2$ then $P_1 \cap P_2 = P_1 P_2 = P_2 P_1$. We defined conjunction with the help of inclusion, but we can conversely define inclusion by conjunction. $P_1 \to P_2$ is equivalent to $P_1 = P_1 \cap P_2$. Special cases are $0 \cap P = 0$ and $1 \cap P = P$ for all P.

The derivation of $(1-P_1)$ from P_1 is called "complementation" and we write

$$\neg P = (1-P) . \tag{7.6.20}$$

From this definition follow the three basic laws of complementation:

i) $\neg\neg P = P$ (double negation)

ii) $P_1 \rightarrow P_2$ is equivalent to $\neg P_2 \rightarrow \neg P_1$ (contraposition) (7.6.21)

iii) if $P \rightarrow \neg P$ then $P = 0$. (self-contradiction)

From our definition, we have $0 = \neg 1$ and $1 = \neg 0$.

The "disjunction" $P_1 \cup P_2$ can now be defined by

$$P_1 \cup P_2 = \neg(\neg P_1 \cap \neg P_2) \tag{7.6.22}$$

$$= 1 - [\ldots(1-P_1)(1-P_2)(1-P_1)(1-P_2)\ldots] . \tag{7.6.23}$$

The disjunction $P_1 \cup P_2$ thus defined is a subspace formed by all the linear combinations of a vector in P_1 and a vector in P_2. Thus $P_1 \cup P_2$ includes also vectors which are not found in either P_1 or P_2. Actually, the disjunction can be defined first by conditions similar to the ones used in defining the conjunction; just invert the direction of arrows, and then prove with the help of (7.6.21) that the conjunction and disjunction are related by de Morgan's rule (7.6.28) Then, it is as well justified to define the disjunction directly by de Morgan's rule as (7.6.28). $P_1 \rightarrow P_2$ is equivalent to $P_2 = P_1 \cup P_2$. Special cases are $0 \cup P = P$ and $1 \cup P = 1$ for all P.

The conjunction and disjunction thus defined obey the following five basic laws:

i) Idempotent law:

$$P_1 \cap P_1 = P_1, \; P_1 \cup P_1 = P_1 \; ; \tag{7.6.24}$$

ii) Commutative law:

$$P_1 \cap P_2 = P_2 \cap P_1 ,$$
$$P_1 \cup P_2 = P_2 \cup P_1 ; \quad (7.6.25)$$

iii) Associative law:

$$(P_1 \cap P_2) \cap P_3 = P_1 \cap (P_2 \cap P_3) ,$$
$$(P_1 \cup P_2) \cup P_3 = P_1 \cup (P_2 \cup P_3) ; \quad (7.6.26)$$

iv) Absorptive law:

$$P_1 \cap (P_1 \cup P_2) = P_1 ,$$
$$P_1 \cup (P_1 \cap P_2) = P_1 ; \quad (7.6.27)$$

v) de Morgan's law:

$$\neg(P_1 \cap P_2) = \neg P_1 \cup \neg P_2 ,$$
$$\neg(P_1 \cup P_2) = \neg P_1 \cap \neg P_2 . \quad (7.6.28)$$

This shows that the projection operators, including 0 and 1, (7.6.13), form a complemented lattice.

It is very important to note that the distributive laws:

$$(P_i \cap P_2) \cup P_3 = (P_1 \cup P_3) \cap (P_2 \cup P_3) , \quad (7.6.29)$$

$$(P_i \cup P_2) \cap P_3 = (P_1 \cap P_3) \cup (P_2 \cap P_3) \quad (7.6.30)$$

do not in general hold. For instance, suppose that P_1 and P_2 are respectively x-direction and y-direction (each one is a one-dimensional subspace) and P_3 is another direction in the x-y-plane. Then $P_1 \cap P_2 = 0$, hence the left-hand side of (7.6.29) is $0 \cup P_3 = P_3$. But, on the right-hand side both $(P_1 \cup P_3)$ and $(P_2 \cup P_3)$ are the x-y-plane; as a result the right-hand side becomes also the x-y-plane. Hence, the distributive law breaks down. This lattice is nondistributive.

It should be noted if the three projection operators P_1, P_2, and P_3 are mutually compatible, that is, if

$$P_1 \sim P_2, \; P_2 \sim P_3, \; P_3 \sim P_1 . \quad (7.6.31)$$

the distributive laws (7.6.29) and (7.6.31) will apply. This is easy to understand. For instance, the left-hand side as well as the right-hand side (7.6.29) become the subspace subtended by coordinates that are included both in P_1 and P_2 and those defining P_3, whereby the coordinates are those that can be commonly used defining P_1, P_2, and P_3. Such a coordinate system exists because of (7.6.31). The logical implication of the breakdown of the distributive laws is separately discussed in the Appendix. Leaving the discussion of the preparation of mathematical tools, we return to the problem of CLAFIC and MOSS.

Let $x_\alpha^{(k)}$ be an n-dimensional vector representing the α-th paradigm (class-sample) of the k-th class, $\alpha = 1, 2, \ldots, \nu^{(k)}$; $k = 1,2,\ldots,M$. There are M classes, and there are $\nu^{(k)}$ paradigms (class-samples) in class k. The autocorrelation matrix $G^{(k)}$ for class k is defined by

$$G^{(k)} = \sum_{\alpha=1}^{\nu^{(k)}} x_\alpha^{(k)} x_\alpha^{(k)t} \Big/ \sum_{\alpha=1}^{\nu^{(k)}} x_\alpha^{(k)t} x_\alpha^{(k)} \qquad (7.6.32)$$

which is normalized so that

$$\text{trace } G^{(k)} = 1 \, . \qquad (7.6.33)$$

The orthonormal base vectors peculiar to the k-th class, $\{\psi_j^{(k)}\}$, $(j = 1,2,\ldots,n)$, are defined as the eigenvectors of $G^{(k)}$

$$G^{(k)}\psi_j^{(k)} = \lambda_j^{(k)}\psi_j^{(k)} \quad (j=1,2,\ldots,n) \, , \qquad (7.6.34)$$

where the λ's are nonnegative, and, due to (7.1.10), sums up to unity:

$$\sum_{j=1}^{n} \lambda_j^{(k)} = 1 \, . \qquad (7.6.35)$$

We choose the index j so that

$$\lambda_1^{(k)} \geq \lambda_2^{(k)} \geq \ldots \geq \lambda_n^{(k)} \, . \qquad (7.6.36)$$

In most of the examples we encounter in pattern recognition, the eigenvalues $\lambda_j^{(k)}$ decrease very fast with j, which means that the paradigm vectors of class k on the average have very little weight (square of components) along the directions $\psi_j^{(k)}$ for large j. This indicates that the vectors of class k are located in a subspace subtended by the $\psi_j^{(k)}$'s with small j's only. If we determine the dimensionality $m^{(k)}$ of the subspace by the condition

$$\sum_{j=1}^{m^{(k)}-1} \lambda_j^{(k)} < \sigma^{(k)} \leq \sum_{j=1}^{m^{(k)}} \lambda_j^{(k)}, \qquad (7.6.37)$$

the subspace so defined accounts on the average for about $100\,\sigma^{(k)}$ % of the weight of the paradigms of class k. We are usually surprised to see that for a relatively large value of $\sigma^{(k)}$ (say, 0.95) the dimension $m^{(k)}$ of the subspace becomes very small compared with m. This fact supports the subspace model of pattern recognition. In practice, we take the same value $\sigma^{(k)}$ for different classes in order to treat different classes on an equal footing. An appropriate value of σ in the case of SELFIC, in which we make only one subspace regardless of class affiliation, can be determined more or less by hunch and experience. It is obvious that a small σ will entail a smaller degree of overlap of subspaces of different classes. In our present case, however, we may determine σ so that the class discrimination becomes optimal.

The subspace for class k can now be represented by the projection operator

$$P^{(k)} = \sum_{j=1}^{m^{(k)}} \psi_j^{(k)} \psi_j^{(k)t} \; . \qquad (7.6.38)$$

Since the $\psi_j^{(k)}$'s are supposed to be normalized

$$\text{trace } P^{(k)} = m^{(k)} \; . \qquad (7.6.39)$$

If a new vector x of unknown class-affiliation arrives, we can take the projection in each subspace and assign to it the class which gives the largest projection, that is, the class k which maximizes $x^t \cdot P^{(k)} \cdot x$. This was the basic idea of CLAFIC. We shall now continue to describe the further developments of this idea.

The subspace $P^{(k)}$ consists of those feature variables that have high weights in the collection of paradigms of class k. But, this does not guarantee that the subspaces for two different classes do not contain the same variables. Such common variables have no discriminating power and should be taken out of consideration. We therefore define the "retrenched" subspace $P^{(k)'}$ by subtracting the overlapped subspaces from each subspace $P^{(k)}$.

$$P^{(k)'} = P^{(k)} - \bigcup_{\ell \neq k} (P^{(k)} \cap P^{(\ell)}) , \qquad (7.6.40)$$

where $P^{(k)} \cap P^{(\ell)}$ is the "overlap" of $P^{(k)}$ and $P^{(\ell)}$. Because each term $(P^{(k)} \cap P^{(\ell)})$ is a subspace of $P^{(k)}$, the merger of them under $\bigcup_{\ell \neq k}$ is also a subspace of $P^{(k)}$. Hence, the difference $P^{(k)'}$ is a projection operator, having the form of $P_1 - P_2$ with $P_2 \rightarrow P_1$. Since $P_2 \rightarrow P_1$ implies that P_1 and P_2 are compatible, we can also write $P_2 = P_2 \cap P_1 = P_1 P_2$. Hence, $P_1 - P_2 = P_1 - P_1 P_2 = P_1(1-P_2) = P_1 \cdot \neg P_2 = P_1 \cap \neg P_2$. Applying this transformation, we can also rewrite (7.6.40) as

$$\begin{aligned} P^{(k)'} &= P^{(k)} \cap \bigcap_{\ell \neq k} (\neg P^{(k)} \cup \neg P^{(\ell)}) \\ &= P^{(k)} \cdot \neg \bigcup_{\ell \neq k} (P^{(k)} \cap P^{(\ell)}) \\ &= P^{(k)} \cdot \bigcap_{\ell \neq k} (1 - P^{(k)} \cap P^{(\ell)}) . \qquad (7.6.41) \end{aligned}$$

The dimension $m^{(k)'}$ of the retrenched subspace is in general smaller than the original subspace.

$$m^{(k)'} = \text{trace } P^{(k)'} \leq m^{(k)} . \qquad (7.6.42)$$

These retrenched subspaces contain no common vectors with one another. We can see this point by noticing

$$P^{(k)'} \cap P^{(\ell)'} = P^{(k)} \cap P^{(\ell)} \cap \bigcap_{p \neq k} (\neg P^{(k)} \cup \neg P^{(p)})$$

$$\cap \bigcap_{q \neq \ell} (\neg P^{(\ell)} \cup \neg P^{(q)}) , \qquad (7.6.43)$$

where there must be a term $(\neg P^{(k)} \cup \neg P^{(\ell)})$ under the conjunctions $\bigcap_{p \neq k}$ and $\bigcap_{q \neq \ell}$ which will cancel the first term $P^{(k)} \cap P^{(\ell)}$, since the conjunction of a projection operator and its complement becomes 0. Hence,

$$P^{(k)'} \cap P^{(\ell)'} = \delta_{k\ell} P^{(k)'} , \qquad (7.6.44)$$

expressing that the $P^{(k)'}$ are projection operators and contain no common vectors if $k \neq \ell$.

The total class-subspace occupied by vectors of all the retrenched class-subspaces is given by $\bigcup_{k=1}^{M} P^{(k)'}$, and the dimension of this total class-subspace is at most n but in general less than n. The subspace orthogonal to the total class-subspace,

$$P^{(M+1)'} = \neg \bigcup_{k=1}^{M} P^{(k)'} = 1 - \bigcup_{k=1}^{M} P^{(k)'}, \qquad (7.6.45)$$

can be considered as consisting of vectors which are either not included in the original class-subspaces or included in more than one original subspace. Hence, we consider this as a "reject" subspace and name it the (M+1)-st class.

The next step is to introduce a linear transformation that will turn the class-subspaces until they belong orthogonal to one another. To do this, we take $m^{(k)'}$ orthogonal vectors in $P^{(k)'}$, i.e., we take $m^{(k)'}$ orthogonal degenerate eigenvectors of $P^{(k)'}$ corresponding to eigenvalue unity. If we take all such vectors for all k including the reject class $P^{(M+1)'}$, we shall get exactly n vectors, which we denote by $\eta^{(a)}$, $a = 1,2,...,n$, and the components of $\eta^{(a)}$ in the original coordinate systems by $\eta_\rho^{(a)}$, $\rho = 1, 2,...,n$. The vectors $\eta^{(a)}$ are not uniquely determined (due to the degeneracy of eigenvalue 1), but this ambiguity does not affect the result of the linear transformation we are going to introduce. The linear transformation L we are now considering is such that the transforms $\eta^{(a)*}$ of $\eta^{(a)}$ by L becomes all orthogonal, that is,

$$\eta^{(a)*t}\eta^{(b)*} = \sum_{\sigma=1}^{n} \eta_\sigma^{(a)*}\eta_\sigma^{(b)*}$$

$$= \delta_{ab}(a,b = 1,2,...,n) \tag{7.6.46}$$

where

$$\eta_\sigma^{(a)*} = \sum_{\rho=1}^{n} L_{\sigma\rho}\,\eta_\rho^{(a)} \; . \tag{7.6.47}$$

Such an L can be given by the condition

$$\sum_{\rho=1}^{n} L_{\sigma\rho}\eta_\rho^{(a)} = \delta_{\sigma a} \quad \sigma, a = 1,2,...,n \; . \tag{7.6.48}$$

By this transformation (7.6.48), the vectors $\eta^{(a)}$ belonging to the same subspace $P^{(k)'}$ will remain orthogonal and its magnitude will remain unchanged provided the $\eta^{(a)}$ are originally in a class. As a result, the subspace corresponding to a class remains internally unchanged. Two vectors $\eta^{(a)}$ belonging to two different subspaces $P^{(k)'}$ are made orthogonal to each other by the transformation (7.6.48).

In general, a nonorthogonal linear transformation L changes a projection operator P into LPL^t (not LPL^{-1}) which is no longer necessarily a projection operator. But, by the special linear transformation L, the $P^{(k)'}$ are transformed into

$P^{(k)*}$ which are projection operators and mutually orthogonal. The components of $P^{(k)*}$ are given by

$$P_{\rho\sigma}^{(k)*} = \left(L\, P^{(k)'} L^t\right)_{\rho\sigma} = \sum_{a\epsilon k} \eta_\rho^{(a)*} \eta_\sigma^{(a)*} , \tag{7.6.49}$$

with the summation with respect to a extending over those vectors included in the subspace $P^{(k)'}$. The product of two such operators becomes

$$\left(P^{(k)*} P^{(\ell)*}\right)_{\rho\sigma} = \sum_{\mu=1}^{n} \sum_{a\epsilon k} \sum_{b\epsilon \ell} \eta_\rho^{(a)*} \eta_\mu^{(a)*} \eta_\mu^{(b)*} \eta_\sigma^{b*}$$

$$= \sum_{a\epsilon k} \eta_\rho^{(a)*} \eta_\sigma^{(a)*} \delta_{k\ell} = P^{*(k)} \delta_{k\ell}, \tag{7.6.50}$$

where the condition (7.6.46) has been used. Equation (7.6.50) shows at once that the $P^{(k)*}$ are not only projection operators (idempotency) but are also mutually orthogonal.

From this point on every vector, paradigm, or new sample is transformed by the L-transformation, and then we proceed to the next stage of consideration, namely, the problem of discrimination. There remains a certain ambiguity whether the G-matrices should be transformed according to the same formal rule as (7.6.49) or redefined by the same formula as (7.6.32), except using the vectors with asterisks in both numerator and denominator. In the former case the condition (7.6.33) will no longer be rigorously true, but the difference should be very little anyway because the paradigm vectors lie more or less entirely in the $P^{(k)}$ space, and the L-transformation will not alter the internal structure of each subspace.

We have to discuss next the decision procedure using these class-subspaces. From now on the asterisk is omitted on quantities, but all of them, including the new samples, are supposed to have been subjected to the L-transformation.

The quantity in which we are first interested is the probability of an average paradigm vector of class k appearing in subspace $P^{(\ell)}$. This obviously will be given by

$$p(\ell|k) = \text{trace } (G^{(k)} \cdot P^{(\ell)}) / \text{trace } G^{(k)} , \tag{7.6.51}$$

which is normalized with respect to subspaces $P^{(\ell)}$, where ℓ runs from 1 to M+1:

$$\sum_{\ell=1}^{M+1} p(\ell|k) = 1 . \tag{7.6.52}$$

Obviously, $p(k|k)$ will be the largest among $p(\ell|k)$.

The inverse conditional probability that an arbitrary vector in the $P^{(\ell)}$ belongs to class k will be given, with the help of the prior probability $p(k)$ of class k, by

$$q(k|\ell) = p(\ell|k)\; p(k) \Big/ \sum_{k=1}^{M} p(\ell|k)\; p(k) , \tag{7.6.53}$$

which is normalized with respect to M classes:

$$\sum_{k=1}^{M} q(k|\ell) = 1 . \tag{7.6.54}$$

When a new object with vector y (after the L-transformation) arrives, we have to determine in which subspace it is located. The probability of vector y being in subspace $P^{(\ell)}$, or the fraction of its weight in subspace $P^{(\ell)}$ is given by

$$w(\ell|y) = y^t\, P^{(\ell)} y \big/ y^t y \tag{7.6.55}$$

with

$$\sum_{y=1}^{M+1} w(\ell|y) = 1 . \tag{7.6.56}$$

If y is located in subspace $P^{(\ell)}$, it will belong to class k with probability $q(k|\ell)$, hence we can conclude that the probability of y belonging to class k is

$$q(k|y) = \sum_{\ell=1}^{M+1} q(k|\ell)\, w(\ell|y) , \qquad (7.6.57)$$

with

$$\sum_{k=1}^{M} q(k|y) = 1 . \qquad (7.6.58)$$

The quantity $q(k|y)$ thus defined is proportional to $p(k)$, $p(\ell|k)$, and $w(\ell|y)$, which seems to be quite reasonable.

Our decision rule will be to assign class k_o which maximizes $q(k|y)$, that is,

$$q(k_o|y) = \operatorname*{Max}_{k}\, q(k|y) \qquad (7.6.59)$$

The reader may be disturbed by the fact that in this formalism there is no probability $q(M+1|y)$ of y belonging to the reject class, but this is because we have introduced the reject subspace but not the reject class. The way to utilize the reject subspace for a useful purpose is to compare the probability $w(M+1|y)$ of y being in the reject subspace with the probability $p(M+1|k_o)$ of an average vector of the assigned class being in the reject subspace. If the former is considerably larger than the latter, we have to conclude that the assignment is not well founded. We can make a criterion of the type

$$w(M+1|y) \le \theta = \gamma\, p(M+1|k_o), \qquad (7.6.60)$$

where θ is the threshold for admittance in class k_o, and the parameter γ is a real number larger than unity. If we decrease the threshold θ, the number of the paradigms of class k_o being rejected will increase and at the same time the number of the misclassification of paradigms will decrease. We can adjust θ so that the weighted sum of these two undesirable numbers will be a minimum.

An interesting possibility is that we can determine the yet undetermined parameter, fidelity, σ by requiring the maximum discrimination. The discrimination can be measured by the unevenness of $q(k|y)$, because if $q(k|y)$ is distributed more or less evenly over different k's, the decision made by (7.6.59) will be unreliable. A good measure for this would be the entropy function

$$S(y) = - \sum_{k=1}^{M} q(k|y) \log q(k|y) \ . \qquad (7.6.61)$$

In practice, the best way would be to determine the value of σ by the requirement that the average entropy $S(y)$ for the given paradigms will become minimum, that is, the most desirable value σ_o of σ can be given by

$$S(\sigma_o) = \underset{\sigma}{\text{Min}}\ S(\sigma) \ , \qquad (7.6.62)$$

where

$$S(\sigma) = \sum_{k=1}^{M} \frac{1}{\nu^{(k)}} \sum_{\alpha=1}^{\nu^{(k)}} S(x_\alpha(k)) \ . \qquad (7.6.63)$$

Although the expression (7.6.61) does not show the dependence of $S(y)$ on σ, it is obvious that the value of $S(y)$ depends on σ.

7.7 DIRECLADIS

The method explained in this section was invented just before the completion of the manuscript of this book, but because of the possible richness of its future development, we decided to fit it into the main body of the volume [W-68]. It has three interesting features:

1. it allows an automatic reduction of dimensionality serving the purpose of class-discrimination;
2. it shows the superiority of polynomial entropy functions to the logarithmic entropy functions for the purpose of pattern recognition; and

3. as a byproduct, it gives a much simpler justification of the principal axes method than the theory known up to now and explained in the earlier sections.

The principal **axis** method in the form of SELFIC is effective in reducing the dimensionality of the representation space when the data are a collection of vectors whose class-affiliation is unknown or to be ignored. Mathematically this purpose is realized by minimizing the simple entropy through an n-dimensional rotation, where the entropy is defined by

$$S = - \sum_{i=1}^{n} p_i \log p_i \ , \qquad (7.7.1)$$

with

$$p_i = G_{ii} \ , \qquad (7.7.2)$$

and

$$G_{ij} = \frac{1}{N} \sum_{\alpha=1}^{N} x_i^{(\alpha)} x_j^{(\alpha)} \ . \qquad (7.7.3)$$

In this expression, $x_i^{(\alpha)}$ is the i-th component of the normalized n-component vector representing the α-th of the N samples of unidentified class affiliation. The dimensionality reduction is effected by taking only those eigenvectors of the G-matrix corresponding to large eigenvalues to form the reduced representation space. As explained in Section 6.2, the minimization of the S-function roughly corresponds to the minimization of the polynomial entropy:

$$T = 1 - \sum_{i=1}^{n} p_i^2 \ . \qquad (7.7.4)$$

See Theorem 2 below.

We introduced in (6.2.12) the discriminatory entropy of two probability distributions $\{p_i\}$ and $\{q_i\}$:

$$W = - \sum_{i=1}^{n} p_i \log (p_i/q_i) - \sum_{i=1}^{n} q_i \log (q_i/p_i) \qquad (7.7.5)$$

and the polynomial counterpart in (6.2.27)

$$U = -\sum_{i=1}^{n} (p_i - q_i)^2 . \qquad (7.7.6)$$

We can, in our case, define p_i by Equations (7.7.2), (7.7.3) for the G-matrix of class 1 and q_i by the same equations for the G-matrix of class 2. We have explained in Section 6.2 that the smaller the value of W or of U, the sharper the distribution of each class and the smaller the overlap of the two distributions. The advantage of the polynomial entropy over the logarithmic entropy was also pointed out in Section 6.2.

In the DIRECLADIS, pronounced daiakleidis, standing for Dimension Reduction for Class Discrimination, method, we rotate the coordinate axes until we reach the minimum of W or of U, and in that optimal coordinate system we select those axes that appreciably contribute to the negative value of W or of U. Note that the maximum of U is zero and the minimum of U is minus two.

We shall first prove a mathematical theorem that will make our task in quest of the optimal coordinate system possible.

THEOREM 1. The coordinate axes that minimize the discriminatory entropy U of Equation (7.7.6) are the eigenvectors of the matrix:

$$D_{ij} = G_{ij}^{(1)} - G_{ij}^{(2)} . \qquad (7.7.7)$$

PROOF. Let the eigenvectors and corresponding eigenvalues of the symmetric matrix D be ξ_k and λ_k, $k = 1,2,\ldots,n$. Note that D is symmetric, but not nonnegative like G, and has a vanishing diagonal sum:

$$\text{trace } D = 0 . \qquad (7.7.8)$$

If T represents the transformation matrix from the ξ-coordinates to the x-coordinates, it should satisfy

$$T^{-1} = T^t \qquad (7.7.9)$$

because it is a rotation. The expression of U of Equation (7.7.6) in the ξ-coordinates system will be

$$U_o = - \sum_{k=1}^{n} \lambda_k^2 = - \sum_{k=1}^{n} (D_o^2)_{kk} \tag{7.7.10}$$

and in the x-coordinates system

$$U = - \sum_{i=1}^{n} (D_{ii})^2 \geq - \sum_{i=1}^{n} (D_{ii})^2$$

$$- 2 \sum\sum_{i>k} (D_{ik})^2 = - \sum_{i=1}^{n} (D^2)_{ii} , \tag{7.7.11}$$

as D_{ij} is symmetric. Further we have

$$- \sum_{i=1} (D^2)_{ii} = - \sum\sum_{kk} T_{ik} D_{okk}^2 T_{ki}^t = - \sum\sum_{ik} A_{ik} \lambda_k , \tag{7.7.12}$$

where A_{ik} is, due to Equation (7.7.9), doubly stochastic:

$$\sum_{i=1}^{n} A_{ik} = 1, \sum_{k=1}^{n} A_{ik} = 1, A_{ik} \geq 0 , \tag{7.7.13}$$

as

$$A_{ik} = T_{ik} T_{ki}^t = T_{ik} T_{ki}^{-1} = (T_{ik})^2 . \tag{7.7.14}$$

Combining (7.7.11) and (7.7.12), we obtain, on account of (7.7.13)

$$U \geq - \sum_{k=1}^{n} \lambda_k = U_o , \tag{7.7.15}$$

completing the proof.

This conclusion provides the answer to the problem posed earlier, namely, the optimal coordinate system is the one consisting of the eigenvectors of the D-matrix. The more important coordinates for the purpose of discrimination are the ones corresponding to larger values of λ_n. We can number the coordinates according to the magnitude of the square of the corresponding eigenvalues

$$\lambda_1^2 \geq \lambda^2 \geq \ldots \geq \lambda_n^2 \tag{7.7.16}$$

We can decide the threshold for adoption of coordinates ξ_k, with $k \geq \nu$ such that

$$\sum_{k=1}^{\nu-1} \lambda_k^2 < \sigma \leq \sum_{k=1}^{\nu} \lambda_k^2 \tag{7.7.17}$$

choosing the value of σ appropriately.

We can now see that the whole elaborate theory of the K-L expansion is not necessary because it is obvious that we can prove:

THEOREM 2. The coordinate axes that minimize the simple polynomial entropy T of Equation (7.7.4) are the eigenvectors of the G-matrix of Equation (7.7.3).

PROOF. All we need is to replace the D-matrix of the proof of Theorem 1 by the G-matrix.

When there are M (≥ 2) classes, we can take "important" discriminatory variables for each of $\binom{M}{2}$ pairs of classes, but there may be a great deal of redundancy, and the total number of variables could even become larger than n. We propose the following method: 1. to avoid linear dependency among variables and 2. to attach weight to each variable according to its contribution to the discriminatory power. Suppose $\xi^{(k)}$ is the k-th eigenvector of the D-matrix between Class 1 and Class 2 corresponding to the eigenvalue λ_k. We attached to this variable the weight:

$$\omega^{(k)} = \lambda_k^2 \Big/ \sum_{k=1}^{\nu} \lambda_k^2 \ . \tag{7.7.18}$$

Similarly, we attach to each eigenvector of the D-matrix of another pair a weight proportional to the square of the corresponding eigenvalue. We then make a new G-matrix:

$$G_{ij} = \left[1\Big/\binom{M}{2}\right] \sum_{\text{pairs}} \sum_{k} \omega^{(k)} \xi_i^{(k)} \xi_j^{(k)}. \quad (7.7.19)$$

The ω's are normalized within each pair of classes, and the first factor in (7.7.19) is inserted so that G-matrix as a whole is normalized.

Let $\eta^{(\gamma)}$, $\gamma = 1,2,...,n$ be the eigenvectors of the G-matrix of Equation (7.7.19) corresponding to the eigenvalue, χ_γ, where the numbering γ is determined by

$$\chi_1 \geq \chi_2 \geq \cdot\cdot \geq \chi_n \cdot \quad (7.7.20)$$

We take ν' eigenvectors $\eta^{(\gamma)}$, $\gamma = 1,2,...,\nu'$ such that

$$\sum_{\gamma=1}^{\nu'} \chi_\gamma \geq \sigma > \sum_{\gamma=1}^{\nu'-1} \chi_\gamma \quad (7.7.21)$$

defining the threshold σ in an appropriate manner. These variables are the desired set of discriminatory features.

There have been two earlier attempts known to the present author to generalize the K-L method to cope with a many-class discrimination problem. One is the CLAFIC-MOSS method (see Section 7.6) which presents an interesting mathematical problem but involves a large number of complications when there is overlap of classes. Another is the one proposed by Fukunaga and Koontz, [F-7]. This method is strictly a two-class algorithm and cannot be generalized to a more-than-two class case. The DIRECLADIS seems to be the most straightforward in philosophy and the simplest in manipulation. This method promises various interesting uses, but the shortness of time after the discovery does not allow for the development of further applications. (See [W-66,W-68] for a few simple examples worked out by I. Suzuki.)

CHAPTER 8
Pattern Recognition as Statistical Decision Making

8.1 BAYESIAN INDUCTION REVIEWED

We shall review in this chapter some of the important results obtained by application of the statistical method to pattern recognition, in particular, in those cases where the probability distribution of members of a class is involved. We have to keep in mind that the actually available class-samples are always finite in number, and any generalization starting from a finite size of samples and approaching an infinite population tends to conceal the basic ambiguity involved in any generalization in induction or pattern recognition. The deterministic ideology, which still prevails among some researchers, encourages the ignoring of the importance of the "prior probability" in the Bayesian formula (making the ill-founded likelihood theory popular), which is the only factor in the statistical theory that can reflect the inductive ambiguity.

In this chapter and the next, we are mainly concerned with paradigm-oriented pattern recognition--a two-stage process of training and classification. In the training period we are shown paradigms (class-samples), and in the classification period we are shown a new sample of unknown class and required to place it into one of the classes exemplified by the paradigms. In the following, we limit ourselves to the case where the objects, paradigms or nonparadigms, are all represented by vectors in an n-dimensional space. These vectors may be the result of a set of n observations, or the result of an appropriate method of dimensionality reduction. The training stage is to be used to infer the definition of classes, or in statistical language, to determine the probability distribution in the representation space of points of each class.

The second stage is to determine to which of its distributions the new vector should belong. In other words, the training period is supposed to determine the conditional probability $p(x|A_k)$, where x is a point in the space and A_k is the class. In other words, $p(x|A_k)$ is the probability density for points of class A_k having position x. The classification period is to be guided by the inverse conditional probability $p(A_k|x)$, which is the probability of the position x belonging to class A_k [K-7].

The real question that we have to answer is: to which class should we classify a point at x? The "decision function" d(x) is then to be defined as

$$d(x) = A_k , \tag{8.1.1}$$

where

$$p(A_k|x) = \underset{j}{\text{Max}}\ p(A_j|x) . \tag{8.1.2}$$

To discuss the probability distribution of points of a class $p(x|A_k)$ we must assume the existence of a "population" of an infinite number of points of the class A_k. But, this is a questionable assumption. In reality, an actual class consists of a finite number of real objects. Hence, there is no such thing as a population. Secondly, even if there exists a mechanism to produce our infinite number of members of a class, we are given in actuality only a finite number of paradigms to determine $p(x|A_k)$, making the estimation of $p(x|A_k)$ a risky task at best, and a fictitious idealization at worst. The real task of classification can be done only with the help of the inverse conditional probability $p(A_k|x)$, which on the basis of the theory of probability can be derived only from $p(x|A_k)$ with the help of the Bayesian inversion, which necessarily involves an undeterminable prior probability.

In Chapter 5, we showed that pattern recognition is an inductive process, and the only mathematically acceptable mode of induction is the Bayesian formula in which the inductive ambiguity is represented by the nonuniqueness of the prior probability. Let us review the derivation by which the basic asymmetry of the Bayesian formula is introduced.

Suppose we have a conditional probability $p(A|B)$ and its inverse, $p(B|A)$. We have evidently

$$p(A|B)\ p(B) = p(A \cap B) = p(B|A)\ p(A) \qquad (8.1.3)$$

from which we can derive two symmetrical Bayes' formulae:

$$p(B|A) = \frac{p(A|B)\ p(B)}{\sum_B p(A|B)\ p(B)} \qquad (8.1.4)$$

and

$$p(A|B) = \frac{p(B|A)\ p(A)}{\sum_A p(B|A)\ p(A)}, \qquad (8.1.5)$$

where both are valid. The asymmetry arises from the fact that in many actual cases one of the two conditional probabilities $p(A|B)$ and $p(B|A)$, say $p(A|B)$, is fixed by the nature of the problem and as a result the other, $p(B|A)$, has to be derived from it by the Bayesian formula by assigning the value of the prior probability, $p(B)$, which is not fixed by the nature of the problem.

For instance, in the problem of relation between the transmitted signal A and the received signal B, the probability of $p(B|A)$ is determined by the physical properties of the communication channel, whereas $p(A|B)$ depends on $p(A)$ which depends on the relative frequency of A used by the transmitter. A similar thing can be said about the scientific cause A and the causal effect B, because the conditional probability $p(B|A)$ is a natural law whereas $p(A)$ depends on the relative probability with which the initial state A is prepared in the experiment. These examples show that the asymmetry does not exist in the mathematics but does exist in the actual situation for which the formula is used. For more about this asymmetry, see [W-10].

In our problem of pattern recognition, we stated in Chapter 5 that two kinds of induction are involved: $p(H|A \cap D)$ and $p(A|H \cap D)$, where H is a hypothesis regarding the distribution of points D of objects of Class A. The hypothesis by its nature determines the conditional probability $p(D|H \cap A)$; as a result the two inductive probabilities, $p(H|A \cap D)$ and $p(A|H \cap D)$, involve two prior probabilities, $p(H)$ and $p(A)$. The indeterminacy of these prior probabilities reflects the inductive ambiguity. We have said that a heuristic principle is often useful as a guiding principle in narrowing the inductive ambiguity, although it is neither unique or infallible. This must, in the present case, be true in determining $p(H)$ and $p(A)$. The old-fashioned school of deterministic epistemology pretends to be able to dictate the prescription to determine unambiguously the prior probabilities, but it is doomed to fail because it ignores the basic nature of induction in human intelligence.

There are some people who believe in the so-called "principle of maximum entropy," which sometimes is used as a justification for determining the prior probability in the Bayesian formula in a certain way. We may have to briefly digress to explain where such an illusion comes from. The only area of experience where something like this mystical principle could have its origin is the determination of the initial state in macroscopic experiments in physics. The macroscopic specification of the initial state of an experiment determines a certain boundary condition which gives a set of restrictions on the microscopic state of the system. If we leave the system for a "long time" comparable to the relaxation time of the system, the microscopic state will, due to the ergodic theorem, run around all over the region of the phase space permitted by the macroscopic constraints. The probability of stay in a portion of the phase space will be, according to the ergodic theorem, proportional to the volume of the portion, or to the number of quantum states included in this portion. In a macroscopic experiment, the initial "instant" is a "long time" in the scale of relaxation time. That is what we once called "telescoped eternity" or telescoped Minkowsky space [W-67]. For that reason, the microscopic state has probability of being in a small portion of the region permitted by the constraints proportional to the volume of that portion. In other words, the probability distribution is uniform in that allowed region of the phase space, no matter what microscopic state we start with. In that sense the entropy is maximum. This situation becomes realized only because of the existence of a unit of state of equal a priori probability, the ergodic theorem, and the telescoped eternity. In the general area of application of the Bayesian formula, such a special situation does not exist.

To obtain the principle of maximum entropy in the usually acclaimed form we need only change each microscopic state in the above explanation to each hypothesis and limit the constraints only to the form linear in probabilities. The believers in this principle treat it as a divine edict and congratulate themselves on seeing some of the results, otherwise obtainable from the ergodic theorem, directly ensuing from the edict. This is a topsy-turvy argument and represents deductionism in bad taste. There is no such thing as a set of disjoint and exhaustive hypotheses with equal a priori probability, except by relying on the whims of linguistic contingencies [W-10]. This is the same mistake that Carnap committed in the past. All we can do at this juncture is to warn the readers against such a nonscientific myth. (See also Dias and Shimony [D-7] for another kind of criticism against Jaynes' principle of maximum entropy.) Another myth about the application of Bayes' theorem is the principle of maximum likelihood, which we shall criticize in Section 8.4. Now let us go back to the general discussion of the Bayesian induction.

In order to carry out the program according to the above explained Bayesian formula, we have to specify three sets: $\{H_j\}$, $j = 1,2,\ldots,N$; $\{A_k\}$, $k = 1,2,\ldots,M$; and $\{D_i\}$, $i = 1,2,\ldots,L$. H_j is a proposition of the type: an object belonging to Class A will have such and such probability of having position x_i. A_k has the type: an object belongs to Class A_k and D_i has the type: an object has position x_i. The content of $H_j \in \{H_j\}$ may be a certain function of two variables $p(x_i|A_k)$. If the class of functions is limited to a certain type of functions, differing from one another by the value of a set of parameters θ, we have a parametric case. If the difference among the H_j's is not only the values of parameters involved in H_j, we have a nonparametric case. In general, in the case of pattern recognition, the paradigms have a designated class affiliation. Therefore, we can evaluate $p(x_i|A_k)$ for each class separately. We have a finite number ν of empirical data $x^{(1)}$, $x^{(2)}, \ldots x^{(\nu)}$, of Class A_k which can be used for evaluation of H_j. Hence, the first inversion is the derivative: $p(H_j | x^{(1)}, x^{(2)}, \ldots x^{(\nu)}) \propto p(x^{(1)}, x^{(2)}, \ldots, x^{(\nu)} | H_j) \cdot p(H_j)$. The first factor represents the confirmation by the (finite) evidence $x^{(\alpha)}$, $\alpha = 1,2,\ldots,\nu$, for H_j, and the second factor is the a priori evaluation. This factor represents all the knowledge about it, other than the empirical data. As we shall soon see, if the size of evidence becomes infinite, the a priori factor becomes unnecessary. If the size of the evidence is finite, $p(H_j)$ represents all nonevidential factors including the very fact that the evidence used is finite.

The x_i in $\{D_i\}$ can be either continuous or discrete but for simplicity of description we assume here the x_i to be discrete. Since the occurrence of x_i can be considered statistically independent (random samples of "population" of x of Class A_k) we have

$$p(H_j | x^{(1)}, x^{(2)}, \ldots, x^{(\nu)}) \propto \prod_i [p(x_i | H_j)]^{\nu_i} p(H_j) \ , \tag{8.1.6}$$

where ν_i is the number of $x^{(\alpha)}$'s, $\alpha = 1,2,\ldots,\nu$, which are identical with x_i. Further putting

$$\frac{\nu_i}{\nu} = \alpha_i \ , \tag{8.1.7}$$

we can write

$$p(H_j | x^{(1)}, x^{(2)}, \ldots, x^{(\nu)}) \propto \prod_i [p(D_i | H_j)]^{\alpha_i \nu} p(H_j) \tag{8.1.8}$$

if we take the logarithm of this quantity

$$\log p(H_j|x^{(1)}, x^{(2)},\ldots,x^{(\nu)})$$
$$= \nu\sum_i \alpha_i \log p(x_i|H_j) + \log p(H_j) + \text{const} . \tag{8.1.9}$$

Or noticing that $\sum\alpha_i \log \alpha_i$ is independent of H_j, we can write with the help of the V-function (6.2.3)

$$\log p(H_j|x^{(1)}, x^{(2)},\ldots,x^{(\nu)})$$
$$= \nu\, V(\alpha,p(x|H_j)) + \log p(H_j) + \text{const} . \tag{8.1.10}$$

The first term for (8.1.9) or in (8.1.10) represents the degree of empirical confirmation of hypothesis H_j, whereas the second term represents the extra-evidential evaluation. The first term in (8.1.9) is sometimes called the (logarithmic) likelihood of hypothesis H_j. Here we can see the important theorem [W-10] concerning the conflict between the empirical (evidential) and the a priori (extra-evidential). Insofar as ν is finite, we can upset the empirical assessment of a hypothesis by changing the a priori evaluation. If $\nu \to \infty$, the extra-evidential evaluation is powerless in the presence of the empirical evaluation by an infinitely large evidence.

If $\nu \to \infty$, we can expect α_i to converge to a fixed limit γ_i which is the "objective" (in reality fictitious) relative frequency of the occurrence of paradigm type x_i in the population of A_k. In any human experience, however, ν is finite, and consequently the α_i fluctuates about the final value γ_i. As a result of the finiteness of ν, the likelihood function will, on the average, be different from the likelihood function for $\nu \to \infty$. As Akaike [A-3, A-4] has done and as we shall show in Section 8.4, this average discrepancy can be evaluated. Since this discrepancy is a result of the finiteness of ν, we can include this in the extra-evidential evaluation $p(H_j)$.

Returning to (8.1.10), we see that the larger the "entropy" $V(\alpha,p(x|H_j))$, the higher the evaluation of H_j. This has nothing contradictory to the heuristic principle of minimum entropy. Being a heuristic principle, the minimum entropy principle can affect the extra-evidential probability $p(H_j)$, but not the evidential evaluation, which is represented here by a V-function in (8.1.10).

8.2 PROBABILISTIC DECISION MAKING

In this section, we assume that we know already the probability densities $p(x|A_j)$ of various classes, A_j, $j=1,2,\ldots,M$, and we discuss the method to reach a decision function $d(x)$ for a new arrival at x. The task consists of first deriving the decision probabilities $p(A_j|x)$ and of then deriving the decision function on the basis of these probabilities.

The two kinds of probabilities, $p(x|A_j)$ and $p(A_j|x)$, are obviously mutually inverse conditional probabilities. Of these two, it seems more natural to consider the first $p(x|A_j)$ as determined by the nature of the problem, hence the second should be expressed by Bayes' formula in terms of the first.

$$p(A_j|x) = \frac{p(x|A_j)p(A_j)}{p(x)} = \frac{p(x|A_j)p(A_j)}{\sum_{k=1}^{M} p(x|A_k)p(A_k)} . \qquad (8.2.1)$$

It is important to remember that the denominator is independent of A_j and serves only the purpose of normalization so that

$$\sum_{j=1}^{M} p(A_j|x) = 1 . \qquad (8.2.2)$$

The prior probability $p(A_j)$ is "prior" in the sense that it is the probability of a newcomer belonging to class A_j without using the knowledge that it is located at x. If the paradigms and the newcomer are taken absolutely at random from the identical multiclass population, one may use the relative frequency of different classes in the paradigms as $p(A_j)$. If we have any other information, however, we have the freedom to change the $p(A_j)$. It also often happens that the paradigms of each class are given separately so that the number of paradigms in each class used in the training period has nothing to do with the prior probabilities $p(A_j)$ of the new arrival. In such a case we have to rely on some other indication about the class-belonging of the newcomer other than its location x to evaluate $p(A_j)$. In the worst case, we have to use the same value 1/M for all M classes, but this is indeed a very poor estimation. This is equivalent to using the "likelihood" instead of the Bayesian probability.

Since the denominator is independent of A_j, the decision function (8.1.1) can be characterized by

$$g_k(x) = \underset{j}{\text{Max}}\ g_j(x) \quad , \tag{8.2.3}$$

where the "discriminant function" g_j is given by

$$g_j(x) = p(x|A_j)p(A_j) \tag{8.2.4}$$

or any strictly monotonic function of $p(x|A_j)p(A_j)$. In the case of two classes, $g_1(x) - g_2(x)$ is also called discriminant function.

The procedure of choosing the class A_k which has the maximum decision probability $p(A_j|x)$ requires a certain caution when applied to certain types of problems. In fact, in some applications, an error of misplacing an object of class A_j into class A_k has a much more serious consequence than misplacing an object of class A_k into class A_j. This is not a consideration in the strict domain of pattern recognition but can be incorporated into the theory to some extent in the following way. We introduce the "utility" functions u_{kj} as a measure of advantage of placing an object of class A_j into class A_k. We can assign a positive value if k=j and a negative value if k≠j.

Let us take a two-class case and call R_1 the n-dimensional region or zone which is assigned to class A_1 (i.e., d(x) is to be A_1), and R_2 the region assigned to class A_2, (i.e., d(x) is to be A_2). The utility will then be

$$u = u_{11} \int_{R_1} p(A_1|x)p(x)dx + u_{12} \int_{R_1} p(A_2|x)p(x)dx$$
$$+ u_{22} \int_{R_2} p(A_2|x)p(x)dx + u_{21} \int_{R_2} p(A_1|x)p(x)dx \qquad (8.2.5)$$

where $p(A_j|x)p(x)dx$ is the probability of an item being located in the domain, x and x + dx, <u>and</u> its belonging to class A_j. The border between R_1 and R_2 will be determined by the condition that u becomes maximum. This condition can be formulated as follows: suppose we take a small volume in R_2 and annex it to R_1. The resulting small change in u can be expressed

$$\frac{\delta u}{\delta V_1} = - \frac{\delta u}{\delta V_2} = [u_{11}p(A_1|x) + u_{12}p(A_2|x)$$
$$- u_{22}p(A_2|x) - u_{21}p(A_1|x]p(x) , \qquad (8.2.6)$$

where the right-hand side should be evaluated at the position where the small volume is taken. On the border we shall have $\delta u/\delta V_1 = 0$. In R_2, the differential coefficient $\delta u/\delta V_1 = - \delta u/\delta V_2$ must be negative, because if there is any small volume in which $\delta u/\delta V_1$ is positive then we could add that volume to R_1 and increase u still further. Similarly, in R_1, $\delta u/\delta V_2 = - \delta u/\delta V_1$ must be negative. Thus, we have the following decision procedure: $x \epsilon R_1$ or $x \epsilon R_2$, that is,

$$d(x) = A_1 \quad \text{or} \quad d(x) = A_2 \qquad (8.2.7)$$

according as

$$[(u_{11} - u_{21})p(A_1|x) - (u_{22} - u_{12})p(A_2|x)]p(x) \gtrless 0 , \qquad (8.2.8)$$

or in terms of discriminant functions:

$$g_1 = (u_{11} - u_{21})p(x|A_1)p(A_1)$$
$$g_2 = (u_{22} - u_{12})p(x|A_2)p(A_2) \quad . \tag{8.2.9}$$

Sometimes the negative of utility is called "risk," and the negative of u (8.2.5) the Bayesian risk. In the symmetric case $u_{11} - u_{21} = u_{22} - u_{12} > 0$, we come back to the earlier "disinterested" Bayesian discriminant functions (8.2.4).

The above consideration of the Bayesian risk gives us some insight into the relationship between the error probability and the decision procedure. In the expression (8.2.5) the first and third integrals represent the probability of an item being correctly classified, and the second and fourth integral represent the probability of the item misclassified. The sum of the four probabilities becomes unity, as it should. In a multiple class case also we can write

$$1 = p(\text{correct classification}) + p(\text{misclassification}) \tag{8.2.10}$$

with

$$p(\text{correct classification}) = \sum_{j=1}^{M} \int_{R_j} p(A_j|x)p(x)dx \tag{8.2.11}$$

and

$$p(\text{misclassification}) = \sum_{j=1}^{M} \int_{R_j} \sum_{k \neq j} p(A_k|x)p(x)dx \quad , \tag{8.2.12}$$

where R_j is the zone assigned to A_j (i.e., the region where $d(x) = A_j$). This expression is correct no matter how the assignments R_j are made. The minimum of error probability is equivalent to the maximum of probability of correct classification. The maximum of (8.2.11) is achieved by the condition that each R_j is the domain in which $p(A_j|x)$ is the largest member among other $p(A_k|x)$, because if it were not, $p(A_j|x)$ would not be the largest in some part of R_j. If, for instance, $p(A_k|x)$ is larger than $p(A_j|x)$ in that small region, we could indeed increase the probability of correct classification by cutting away that region from R_j and adding it to R_k. This last prescription is precisely what the disinterested decision procedure tells us to do. The disinterested Bayesian rule is the minimum error algorithm.

It is obviously a tempting enterprise to set an upper bound to the probability of misclassification in a concise mathematical expression. One such upper bound is given in terms of the so-called Bhattacharya coefficient. This coefficient B between two density functions, $p_1(x)$ and $p_2(x)$, is defined by

$$B = \int \sqrt{p_1(x)\; p_2(x)}\, dx \; . \tag{8.2.13}$$

The probability of error is the sum of the second and fourth integral of (8.2.5), which can also be written

$$\begin{aligned} p(\text{misclassification}) &= \int \text{Min}[p(A_1|x),\; p(A_2|x)]\; p(x)\,dx \\ &\leq \int \sqrt{p(A_1|x)\; p(x)\; p(A_2|x)\; p(x)}\,dx \\ &= \sqrt{p(A_1)\; p(A_2)} \int \sqrt{p(x|A_1)\; p(x|A_2)}\,dx \\ &= B\sqrt{p(A_1)\; p(A_2)} \leq \tfrac{1}{2} B \; , \end{aligned} \tag{8.2.14}$$

where $p(A_1)$ and $p(A_2)$ are related to $p(A_1|x)$ and $p(A_2|x)$ by (8.2.1), where B is defined by (8.2.13) with $p(x|A_1)$ and $p(x|A_2)$ as p_1 and p_2. The first inequality in (8.2.14) is due to the simple fact that $\text{Min}(\alpha,\beta) \leq \sqrt{\alpha\beta}$, if $\alpha \geq 0$ and $\beta \geq 0$, and the second inequality is due to the fact that $p(1-p)$ has its maximum value $\frac{1}{4}$ at $p = \frac{1}{2}$. The Bhattacharya coefficient is one of the many quantities that can be used as a measure of the degree of agreement between two density functions. It takes the value unity when the agreement is perfect and becomes zero if there is no overlap. There have been many authors claiming different upper bounds, each asserting how "low" the proposed upper bound is. But, if one wants to have the lowest possible estimate, one needs only to calculate faithfully the integral in the first line of (8.2.14). If one has a certain aversion toward the discontinuous function $\mathrm{Min}[\alpha,\beta]$, I can propose the following. Introducing a step function $\Phi(\xi)$ such that

$$\Phi(\xi) = 1,\ 0,\ -1 \text{ according as } \xi > 0,\ \xi = 0,\ \xi < 0 \tag{8.2.15}$$

we can write

$$\mathrm{Min}[\alpha,\beta] = \tfrac{1}{2}(\alpha+\beta) - \tfrac{1}{2}(\alpha-\beta)\Phi(\alpha-\beta) \ . \tag{8.2.16}$$

Suppose we have an approximation $\Psi(\xi)$ to $\Phi(\xi)$ such that*

$$\Psi(\xi) \leq 1,\ = 0,\ \geq -1 \text{ according as } \xi > 0,\ \xi = 0,\ \xi < 0. \tag{8.2.17}$$

Then obviously

$$\mathrm{Min}[\alpha,\beta] \leq \tfrac{1}{2}(\alpha+\beta) - \tfrac{1}{2}(\alpha-\beta)\Psi(\alpha-\beta) \tag{8.2.18}$$

equality holding if $\Psi = \Phi$. Then we can introduce an upper bound of the probability of error that can be expressed,

$$p(\text{misclassification}) \leq \tfrac{1}{2} - \tfrac{1}{2}\int \xi(x)\Psi[\xi(x)]p(x)\,dx \ , \tag{8.2.19}$$

with

$$\begin{aligned} \xi(x) &= p(A_1|x) - p(A_2|x) \\ &= [p(x|A_1)p(A_1) - p(x|A_2)p(A_2)]/p(x) \ . \end{aligned} \tag{8.2.20}$$

We can suggest as $\Psi(\xi)$, introducing an index $\rho \geq 0$,

---

*Takaasu Ito in his interesting paper [I-2] proposed to use an approximation for Φ, but the function we use is different.

$$\Psi(\xi,\rho) = 2\int_0^{\xi} \Delta(\eta,\rho)d\eta \ , \qquad (8.2.21)$$

where $\Delta(\eta,\rho)$ is a positive even function appreciably different from zero only in the domain of the order of ρ near the origin, such as

$$\Delta(\eta,\rho) = \frac{1}{(2\pi)^{\frac{1}{2}}\rho} \exp[-\eta^2/(2\rho^2)] \ . \qquad (8.2.22)$$

We have thus obtained an upper bound in the form of a continuous function which becomes an exact evaluation of the probability of error in the limit $\rho \to 0$, so that $\Delta(\eta,\rho)$ becomes a delta function and $\Psi(\xi,\rho)$ becomes an exact step function.

All this is fine as a mathematical game, but the practical usefulness of any consideration of the upper bound of error in pattern recognition is highly doubtful. In fact, the estimation of density functions themselves is so unreliable in most of the pattern recognition problems that any discussion of errors based on such dubious density functions is sadly unrealistic, to say the least. This is a typical disease of works in the field of statistical pattern recognition.

We would like to finish this section by giving an example of a statistical decision function for the case in which the density functions are "normal." In general, the normal distribution is applicable when the deviation of individual cases from the mean value is due to the accumulation of many small errors or fluctuations. (This is due to the central limit theorem.) But, in the case of pattern recognition, the statistical distribution of patterns in a class is not of such nature and the normal distribution is usually nothing but an extremely crude approximation used for mathematical convenience.

The density function of a normal distribution in n-dimensional space is given by

$$p(x) = N(x;m,\Sigma) \equiv \frac{1}{(2\pi)^{n/2}(\det\,\Sigma)^{\frac{1}{2}}} e^{-(x-m)^t\Sigma^{-1}(x-m)/2}, \qquad (8.2.23)$$

where x and m are n-dimensional vectors, and Σ is a positive symmetric $n \times n$ matrix and Σ^{-1} its inverse. It is normalized so that

$$\int p(x)\,dx = 1 \tag{8.2.24}$$

and the mean vector and the covariance matrix derived from p(x) are respectively

$$\langle x_i \rangle = \int x_i p(x)\,dx = m_i, \text{ or } \langle x \rangle = m\ , \tag{8.2.25}$$

and

$$\langle (x_i - m_i)(x_j - m_j) \rangle = \int (x_i - m_i)(x_j - m_j) p(x)\,dx = \Sigma_{ij}\ ,$$

or

$$\langle (x-m)(x-m)^t \rangle = \Sigma\ . \tag{8.2.26}$$

By a suitable orthogonal transformation, $T^{-1} = T^t$,

$$x \to x' = Tx, \qquad m' = Tm \tag{8.2.27}$$

$$\Sigma^{-1} \to \Sigma'^{-1} = T\Sigma^{-1}T^{-1} \tag{8.2.28}$$

we can bring the covariance matrix to a diagonal form

$$\Sigma'^{-1}_{ij} = \frac{1}{\sigma_i^2}\,\delta_{ij}\ , \qquad \Sigma'_{ij} = \sigma_i^2 \delta_{ij} \tag{8.2.29}$$

and the probability density p(x) to the form

$$p(x') = \prod_{i=1}^{n} \frac{1}{(2\pi)^{\frac{1}{2}}\sigma_i}\, e^{-(x_i' - m_i')^2/(2\sigma_i^2)} \tag{8.2.30}$$

(i.e., a product of a one-dimensional Gaussian distribution). Note that because $T^{-1} = T^t$ we have the Jacobian $|\partial(x_1', x_2', \ldots, x_n')/\partial(x_1, x_2, \ldots, x_n)| = 1$. The nondiagonal elements of Σ_{ij} represent correlation coefficients. The expressions (8.2.23) and (8.2.30) show that in the normal distribution, the absence of correlation implies a probabilistic independence. By an orthogonal transformation, we can introduce in the case of normal distribution a set of new coordinates that are not only uncorrelated but independent.

Let us assume that all the density functions $p(x|A_j)$ are normal distributions

$$p(x|A_j) = N(x;\, m_j,\, \Sigma_j) \ . \tag{8.2.31}$$

Note that m_i in (8.2.25) is the i-th component of a single mean vector, whereas m_j in (8.2.31) is the j-th mean vector. Since the logarithm is a strictly monotonically increasing function, we can take the logarithm of $p(x|A_j)p(A_j)$ as a discriminant function (8.2.4) and obtain

$$\begin{aligned} g_j(x) &= \log p(x|A_j)p(A_j) \\ &= -\frac{1}{2}(x-m_j)^t\Sigma_j^{-1}(x-m_j) - C_j + \log p(A_j) \ , \end{aligned} \tag{8.2.32}$$

where

$$C_j = \log(2\pi)^{n/2}(\det \Sigma_j)^{\frac{1}{2}} \ . \tag{8.2.33}$$

In the case of two classes the border surface of two zones R_1 and R_2 will be given by

$$g_1(x) - g_2(x) = 0 \ . \tag{8.2.34}$$

It is clear that if the two densities have the same covariant matrix and different mean vectors, the second degree terms in (8.2.34) will vanish and the border surface will become a hyperplane. Remember, however, that a second degree equation could represent two hyperplanes although it represents in general an n-dimensional "conic section."

The decision rule in terms of the discriminant function (8.2.32) can be rephrased by saying that the object at x is classified in the class A_j if the "modified distance" between x and the class mean m_j is the smallest among different classes where the modified distance $D(x, m_j)$ between x and m_j is defined as

$$D(x, m_j) = \sqrt{-g_j(x)}\ , \tag{8.2.35}$$

where $g_j(x)$ is given by (8.2.32). The reason for taking the square root is that the dimension of g is the square of a distance. When the second and third term in (8.2.32) are ignored, the D-function becomes what is usually called the Mahalanobis distance.

8.3 ESTIMATION OF PARAMETERS

In the last section, we assumed that we know already the densities $p(x|A_j)$, $j=1,2,\ldots,M$, and discussed the method of deriving the decision probability $p(A_j|x)$ from them and the procedure of decision making based on the decision probability. In this and the next section, we are going to discuss the methods to determine the probability densities $p(x|A_j)$ from the paradigms of different classes, $j=1,2,\ldots,M$. It is natural to assume that $p(x|A_j)$ depends only on the paradigms of class A_j. Therefore, the determination of $p(x|A_j)$ can be done separately for each class. For this reason, we shall not mention A_j in the density function $p(x|A_j)$ in this and the next section.

There are two approaches to obtain the density function $p(x)$ from paradigms; one parametric, the other nonparametric. We are concerned with the first approach in this section. This method constitutes one of the central topics of mathematical statistics, which have made rapid progress in the last half century, and many excellent expositions are available in textbooks on the market. We shall not try to make a secondhand summary of the technical results. Instead, we shall concentrate on clarifying the meaning of some of the elementary concepts that have been developed in this area. It is often claimed that the newer methods in this field allow us to cope with the case of a small sample* whereas older methods assume that the number of paradigms is infinite, or at least, extremely large. This statement is misleading since the newer methods discuss the statistical behavior of estimates based on a small sample (i.e., an infinite number of cases of a small sample is considered). As a result, we cannot know for certain how good an estimate will be in an individual case of a small sample.

In the parametric approach it is assumed that the functional form of the density function p(x) is known--an assumption in practice seldom justifiable--and that the function contains a parameter or parameters θ whose value(s) are unknown. Hence, it is logical to consider p(x) as a conditional probability $p(x|\theta)$, where the value of p is dependent on θ and the θ themselves have a probability distribution. Suppose that we have paradigms, $x^{(\alpha)}$, $\alpha=1,2,\ldots,\nu$ which we designate collectively by $\mathcal{D}$. The probability of obtaining $\mathcal{D}$ on the assumption H that the probability density is $p(x|\theta)$ is

$$p(\mathcal{D}|H) = p(x^{(1)},x^{(2)},\ldots,x^{(\nu)}|\theta) = \prod_{\alpha=1}^{\nu} p(x^{(\alpha)}|\theta) \;, \tag{8.3.1}$$

where the occurrences of x's are considered probabilistically independent, a requirement usually justifiable. The estimation of θ should then be based on the Bayesian inverse conditional probability density

$$\begin{aligned} p(H|\mathcal{D}) &= p(\theta|x^{(1)},x^{(2)},\ldots,x^{(\nu)}) \\ &= \frac{p(x^{(1)},x^{(2)},\ldots,x^{(\nu)}|\theta)p(\theta)}{\int p(x^{(1)},x^{(2)},\ldots,x^{(\nu)}|\theta)p(\theta)d\theta} \\ &= \frac{\prod_{\alpha=1}^{\nu} p(x^{(\alpha)}|\theta)p(\theta)}{\int \prod_{\alpha=1}^{\nu} (p^{(\alpha)}|\theta)p(\theta)d\theta} \;, \end{aligned} \tag{8.3.2}$$

*In statistics, the word sample is used collectively for a collection of samples.

where $p(\theta)$ is the prior probability density of θ.

The best estimate $\hat{\theta}$ of θ will be given by the condition of maximization of $p(H|\mathcal{D})$

$$p(\hat{\theta}|x^{(1)},x^{(2)},\ldots,x^{(\nu)}) = \operatorname*{Max}_{\theta} p(\theta|x^{(1)},x^{(2)},\ldots,x^{(\nu)}) . \tag{8.3.3}$$

Because the denominator in (8.3.2) does not depend on θ (the θ appearing there being only an integration variable), we can rewrite (8.3.3) also as

$$\prod_{\alpha=1}^{\nu} p(x^{(\alpha)}|\hat{\theta})p(\hat{\theta}) = \operatorname*{Max}_{\theta} \prod_{\alpha=1}^{\nu} p(x^{(\alpha)}|\theta)p(\theta) . \tag{8.3.4}$$

This is the Bayesian estimate which seems to be logically the best estimate of parameters θ. The remarkable merit of this formula is that it makes explicit that the estimate of θ can and should depend in principle on any knowledge or condition about θ other than the fact that the paradigms are found at $x^{(\alpha)}$'s. This flexibility of the Bayesian formula, however, places us in an embarrassing situation. We usually do not know what to do with our privilege of free (i.e., not conditioned by the $x^{(\alpha)}$'s) choice of $p(\theta)$.

A simpler method of estimate of θ is given by the formula known as the maximum likelihood

$$L(x^{(1)},x^{(2)},\ldots,x^{(\nu)};\hat{\theta}) = \operatorname*{Max}_{\theta} L(x^{(1)},x^{(2)},\ldots,x^{(\nu)};\theta), \tag{8.3.5}$$

with

$$L(x^{(1)},x^{(2)},\ldots,x^{(\nu)};\theta) = \prod_{\alpha=1}^{\nu} p(x^{(\alpha)}|\theta) , \tag{8.3.6}$$

whereas the Bayesian estimate can be written as

$$B(x^{(1)},x^{(2)},\ldots,x^{(\nu)};\hat{\theta}) = \operatorname*{Max}_{\theta} B(x^{(1)},x^{(2)},\ldots,x^{(\nu)};\theta), \tag{8.3.7}$$

with

$$B(x^{(1)},x^{(2)},\ldots,x^{(\nu)};\theta) = \prod_{\alpha=1}^{\nu} p(x^{(\alpha)}|\theta)p(\theta) \ . \tag{8.3.8}$$

As we shall see later in more detail, it is often argued as if the maximum likelihood method had a justification **independent** of the Bayesian method, but such an argument does not seem to have much foundation. It would be better to consider the maximum likelihood method as a simplified approximation to the Bayesian method and determine when such a simplification would be permissible.

The poorest argument for dropping $p(\theta)$ from B and using L is to invoke the principle of ignorance: if we don't know the value of probabilities, give the same value to all cases. But the enumeration of cases depends on language or accidental categorization. In the continuous case, why should $p(\theta)$ be uniform in the scale of θ instead of in the scale of θ^2?*

The next possible argument is that if L is a sharp function of θ where $p(\theta)$ is a slowly changing function of θ, then the dependence of $p(\theta)$ on θ does not affect in any way the dependence of B on θ. If this special condition prevails, this argument is tenable, but it is not always easy to show that the conditions are satisfied.

The third argument for dropping $p(\theta)$ is based on the following fact. If ν increases, the effect of $p(\theta)$ on B becomes less and less appreciable. This can be easily seen by taking the logarithm of B

---

*In physics, the volume in the phase-space can be considered as proportional to the a priori probability because it is proportional to the number of quantum states. But, in pattern recognition, there is no such standard of the scale.

$$\log B = \sum_{\alpha=1}^{\nu} \log p(x^{(\alpha)}|\theta) + \log p(\theta) \quad . \quad (8.3.9)$$

We saw in Section 8.1 that as the number of terms ν increases the first summation will overwhelm the effect of the constant (independent of ν) term $\log p(\theta)$. Insofar as ν is finite, the ratio of B's for two values of θ can be made to have any value we want by adjusting the values of $p(\theta)$ for the two values of θ. But, if we fix the $p(\theta)$ for all θ at the beginning and if we increase ν, the effect of $p(\theta)$ will become infinitesimal. This is probably the best argument for the maximum likelihood method, but we should not forget that the argument involves the never-accessible limit of an infinitely large sample: $\nu \to \infty$. One reason why the L-approach is more appealing than the B-approach is that it has no "subjective" and uncertain element represented by $p(\theta)$. But, the inclusion of $p(\theta)$ is definitely more in agreement with the general foundation of probability theory. The reader should remember the discussion and refutation in Chapter 7 of the so-called principle of maximum entropy which also claims the a priori determination of the $p(\theta)$.

If we once abandon the most well-founded Bayesian formula, the estimate by maximum likelihood is not the only conceivable estimate. For instance, if $\hat{\theta}(N)$ is an estimate based on ν paradigms, then $f(\nu)\hat{\theta}(\nu) + g(\nu)$, such that $f(\nu) \to 1$ and $g(\nu) \to 0$ with $\nu \to \infty$, is another estimate which converges to the same limit as $\nu \to \infty$. It is then natural to introduce various criteria for adequacy of an estimate.

The first obvious requirement is that the estimate $\hat{\theta}$ converges to θ in some sense as $\nu \to \infty$. Since $\hat{\theta}(\nu)$ has to be defined as some function of available paradigms, $x^{(\alpha)}$, $\alpha=1,2,\ldots,\nu$, $\hat{\theta}(\nu)$ itself is also a random variable (a statistic in statisticians' jargon). Hence, one of the ways to define such a convergence would be to require that for every $\varepsilon > 0$

$$\lim_{\nu\to\infty} \text{Prob}\,\{|\theta-\hat{\theta}(\nu)| < \varepsilon\} = 1 \ , \qquad (8.3.10)$$

that is, that $\hat{\theta}(\nu)$ converge to θ in probability. If the estimate $\hat{\theta}(\nu)$ satisfies (8.3.10) it is called a "consistent" estimate. [For another condition of convergence for $\nu \to \infty$, see (8.3.13) below.]

Whereas the requirement for convergence for $\nu \to \infty$ is a natural condition for any estimate, it never happens that ν becomes infinite; on the contrary, ν can in practice be rather small. Therefore, it is necessary to require $\hat{\theta}(\nu)$ with a finite ν to satisfy some condition of being a good approximation. Such condition would be that the expected value of $\hat{\theta}(\nu)$ be equal to θ. Thus, it is reasonable to require

$$\langle\hat{\theta}(\nu)\rangle = \theta , \tag{8.3.11}$$

that is,

$$\int \cdots \int \hat{\theta}(\nu) p(x^{(1)}, x^{(2)}, \ldots, x^{(\nu)} | \theta) dx^{(1)} \ldots dx^{(\nu)} = \theta. \tag{8.3.12}$$

If $\hat{\theta}(\nu)$ for any ν satisfies this condition, then the estimate $\hat{\theta}(\nu)$ is said to be an "unbiased" estimate.

An affiliated concept of the unbiased estimate is an "asymptotically unbiased estimate":

$$\lim_{\nu \to \infty} \langle\hat{\theta}(\nu)\rangle = \theta . \tag{8.3.13}$$

This is a very lenient condition and it has no longer the crucial condition that ν be finite. It is another formulation of requirement of convergence for $\nu \to \infty$. We shall discuss in Section 8.4 Akaike's theory [A-3, A-4] on the average value of the discrepancy between θ and its estimate $\hat{\theta}$ based on the maximum likelihood.

Let us take an example of a one-dimensional case, and define the r-th degree moment of a density p(x) by

$$m_r = \langle x^r \rangle = \int x^r \, p(x) dx . \tag{8.3.14}$$

It is not always guaranteed that such moments with arbitrary r exist (since the integral can blow up), but when they exist for some r, we can consider them as characteristic parameters θ of the density $p(x)$. The mean value is m_1. The variance σ^2 defined by

$$\sigma^2 = \langle (x - m_1)^2 \rangle = \langle x^2 \rangle - m_1^2 = m_2 - m_1^2 \qquad (8.3.15)$$

can be considered also as a parameter θ.

When there are ν samples, it may be natural to introduce an estimate of m_r by

$$\hat{m}_r = \frac{1}{\nu} \sum_{\alpha=1}^{\nu} x^{(\alpha)r} . \qquad (8.3.16)$$

Since the ν samples have the same density function and their occurrence is probabilistically independent, we have for any ν

$$\langle \hat{m}_r \rangle = \langle \frac{1}{\nu} \sum_{\alpha=1}^{\nu} \langle x^{(\alpha)r} \rangle = m_r , \qquad (8.3.17)$$

showing that the estimate $\hat{m}_r$ (8.3.16) is an unbiased estimate of m_r (8.3.14). The same is obviously true in the n-dimensional case where the moments are defined by

$$\begin{aligned} m_{r_1 r_2 \ldots r_n} &= \langle x_1^{r_1} x_2^{r_2} \ldots x_n^{r_n} \rangle \\ &= \int \cdots \int x_1^{r_1} x_2^{r_2} \ldots x_n^{r_n} \\ &\quad p(x_1, x_2, \ldots, x_n) dx_1 dx_2 \ldots dx_n , \end{aligned} \qquad (8.3.18)$$

and a simple estimate can be defined

$$\hat{m}_{r_1 r_2 \ldots r_n} = \frac{1}{\nu} \sum_{\alpha=1}^{\nu} x_1^{(\alpha)r_1} x_2^{(\alpha)r_2} \ldots x_n^{(\alpha)r_n} , \qquad (8.3.19)$$

which is an unbiased estimate of $m_{r_1} m_{r_2 \ldots r_n}$.

But, the estimate of variance σ^2 obtained by replacing m_2 and m_1 in (8.3.15) respectively by their respective unbiased estimate $\hat{m}_2$ and $\hat{m}_1$

$$\begin{aligned} \hat{\sigma}^2 &= \frac{1}{\nu} \sum_{\alpha=1}^{\nu} (x^{(\alpha)} - \hat{m}_1)^2 \\ &= \frac{1}{\nu} \sum_{\alpha=1}^{\nu} x^{(\alpha)^2} - (\frac{1}{\nu} \sum_{\alpha=1}^{\nu} x^{(\alpha)})^2 \end{aligned} \tag{8.3.20}$$

is not an unbiased estimate. In fact, the second term can be written

$$< (\frac{1}{\nu} \sum_{\alpha=1}^{\nu} x^{(\alpha)})^2 > = \frac{1}{\nu^2} < \sum_{\alpha=1}^{\nu} x^{(\alpha)^2} + \sum_{\alpha \neq \beta}\sum x^{(\alpha)} x^{(\beta)} > . \tag{8.3.21}$$

In the cross term in (8.3.21) the two stochastic variables $x^{(\alpha)}$ and $x^{(\beta)}$ are independent, therefore the mean value of their product is simply m_1^2. But there are $\nu(\nu-1)$ terms under the summation, hence

$$< (\frac{1}{\nu} \sum_{\alpha=1}^{\nu} x^{(\alpha)})^2 > = \frac{1}{\nu} m_2 + \frac{\nu-1}{\nu} m_1^2 . \tag{8.3.22}$$

Bringing this into (8.3.19) we obtain

$$<\hat{\sigma}^2> = \frac{\nu-1}{\nu} (m_2 - m_1^2) \tag{8.3.23}$$

showing that $\hat{\sigma}^{2*}$ given by

$$\begin{aligned} \hat{\sigma}^{2*} &= \frac{\nu}{\nu-1} \hat{\sigma}^2 = \frac{1}{\nu-1} \sum_{\alpha=1}^{\nu} (x^{(\alpha)} - \hat{m}_1)^2 \\ &= \frac{1}{\nu-1} \sum_{\alpha=1}^{\nu} x^{(\alpha)^2} - \frac{1}{\nu(\nu-1)} \left[\sum_{\alpha=1}^{\nu} x^{(\alpha)} \right]^2 \end{aligned} \tag{8.3.24}$$

but not $\hat{\sigma}^2$ is an unbiased estimate of the variance. In the n-dimensional case, the estimate

$$\hat{\Sigma}^* = \frac{1}{\nu-1} \sum_{\alpha=1}^{\nu} (x^{(\alpha)} - \hat{m}_1)(x^{(\alpha)} - \hat{m}_1)^t$$
$$= \frac{1}{\nu-1} \sum_{\alpha=1}^{\nu} x^{(\alpha)} x^{(\alpha)t} - \frac{\nu}{\nu-1} \hat{m}_1 \hat{m}_1^t \qquad (8.3.25)$$

but not the estimate

$$\hat{\Sigma} = \frac{1}{\nu} \sum_{\alpha=1}^{\nu} (x^{(\alpha)} - \hat{m}_1)(x^{(\alpha)} - \hat{m}_1)^t$$
$$= \frac{1}{\nu} \sum_{\alpha=1}^{\nu} x^{(\alpha)} x^{(\alpha)t} - \hat{m}_1 \hat{m}_1^t \qquad (8.3.26)$$

is an unbiased estimate of the variance

$$\Sigma = \langle (x^{(\alpha)} - m_1)(x^{(\alpha)} - m_1)^t \rangle , \qquad (8.3.27)$$

where m_1 is the mean vector whose k-th component is $m_{r_1 r_2 \ldots r_n}$ with $r_j = 0$ except $r_k = 1$, to use the notation of (8.3.18), and the estimate $\hat{m}_1$ is its estimate in the sense of (8.3.19). The estimates $\hat{\sigma}$ and $\hat{\Sigma}$ are not unbiased, but they are obviously asymptotically unbiased in the sense of (8.3.13), because at the limit they coincide respectively with $\hat{\sigma}^*$ and $\hat{\Sigma}^*$.

The idea of unbiased estimate guarantees only that in the case of a small sample (ν: given) the average of the estimate over an infinity of such cases is the correct value. But in an individual case the actual deviation from the correct value can be very large. The obvious next step is to require that this deviation on the average be small. This leads us to the idea of an efficient estimate. But we should not forget that even if the deviation from the correct value is on the average small, the deviation in each individual case could still be large although the occurrence of a large deviation is relatively rare.

The deviation of an estimate $\hat{\theta}$ of a parameter θ can be measured by

$$D(\hat{\theta}) = \langle|\hat{\theta} - \theta|^2\rangle \ . \tag{8.3.28}$$

For this deviation $D(\hat{\theta})$ there is a famous lower bound (called Cramér-Rao bound) which is a simple function of the density $p(x|\theta)$. We have

$$D \geq R \tag{8.3.29}$$

with

$$R = \frac{1}{\nu \int [\partial \log p(x|\theta)/\partial\theta]^2 \ p(x|\theta)dx} \ , \tag{8.3.30}$$

where ν is as before the size of the sample. Note $R \to 0$ as $\nu \to \infty$, but how small R is for a finite ν depends on $p(x|\theta)$. If the estimate $\hat{\theta}$ is such that the deviation D reaches the lower bound R (i.e., if D = R, and the estimate $\hat{\theta}$ is unbiased), then it is called the "most efficient" estimate. If an estimate $\hat{\theta}_1$ is not the most efficient estimate $\hat{\theta}_{me}$ = R, its relative efficiency is measured by

$$e(\hat{\theta}_1) = \frac{D(\hat{\theta}_{me})}{D(\hat{\theta}_1)} \ . \tag{8.3.31}$$

It can happen that although the relative efficiency $e(\hat{\theta}_1)$ of a certain $\hat{\theta}_1$ at a finite ν is not unity, it tends to unity at the limit $\nu \to \infty$:

$$\lim_{\nu\to\infty} e(\hat{\theta}_1) = 1 \ . \tag{8.3.32}$$

If this is the case, the estimate $\hat{\theta}_1$ is said to be an "asymptotically most efficient estimate."

Referring to (8.3.15), when we know the true value of m_1 but not m_2 we can introduce an estimate of the variance given by:

$$\hat{\sigma}_1^{2**} = \frac{1}{\nu} \sum_{\alpha=1}^{\nu} (x^{(\alpha)} - m_1)^2 \ , \tag{8.3.33}$$

which is unbiased for any distribution since it is essentially an estimate of a moment. It can be shown that this estimate is the most efficient estimate in the case of the normal distribution function. The estimate $\hat{\sigma}^{2*}$ (8.3.24) is an unbiased estimate for any distribution, but not the most efficient estimate. In the case of the normal distribution, the relative efficiency of $\hat{\sigma}^{2*}$ can be shown to be $e = (\nu-1)/\nu$, showing that $\hat{\sigma}^{2*}$ is an asymptotically most efficient estimate.

Now a question arises as to under what condition in general the relative efficiency (for finite ν) reaches unity. The answer to this question is given by the following theorem which will be given here without proof. An unbiased estimate $\hat{\theta}$ of the parameter θ is the most efficient estimate if and only if (a) the estimate $\hat{\theta}$ is "sufficient," and (b) the probability density $p(\hat{\theta}|\theta)$ satisfies

$$\frac{\partial \log p(\hat{\theta}|\theta)}{\partial\theta} = a(\hat{\theta}-\theta) \qquad (8.3.34)$$

(except for the cases whose total probability is zero) where the factor a can depend on θ but not on $\hat{\theta}$. An estimate is a function of $x^{(1)}, x^{(2)}, \ldots, x^{(\nu)}$, hence it is a random variable and has its density function $p(\hat{\theta}|\theta)$ (see below). The meaning of the "sufficiency" of an estimate will be explained presently, but let us notice that it is a necessary condition for the maximum efficiency. An interesting corollary of this theorem is that if there exists the most efficient estimate (which is not always guaranteed to be the case), it is the maximum likelihood estimate. This is an additional merit of the maximum likelihood estimate, but we should not overlook the fact that this theorem does not say that any maximum likelihood estimate is the most efficient estimate.

The idea of sufficient estimate may be the most ingenious one among the many fundamental notions introduced by Fisher in the field of estimation theory [F-1]. Let us explain the meaning of sufficiency in the case of one dimension and one parameter. The probability density for obtaining the experimental data $x^{(1)},x^{(2)},\ldots,x^{(\nu)}$ for a given value θ of the parameter is given by the likelihood function

$$L = p(x^{(1)},x^{(2)},\ldots,x^{(\nu)}|\theta) \qquad (8.3.35)$$

used in (8.3.6). Suppose we introduce a different set of variables to represent the data

$$y^{(j)} = f^{(j)}(x^{(1)},x^{(2)},\ldots,x^{(\nu)}) \qquad j=1,2,\ldots,\nu\ . \qquad (8.3.36)$$

In order that the density function in the x's and the density function in the y's may be related by the condition of conservation of probability:

$$p(x^{(1)},x^{(2)},\ldots x^{(\nu)}|\theta)dx^{(1)}dx^{(2)}\ldots dx^{(\nu)}$$
$$= p(y^{(1)},y^{(2)},\ldots,y^{(\nu)}|\theta)dy^{(1)}dy^{(2)}\ldots dy^{(\nu)} \qquad (8.3.37)$$

we should have

$$p(y^{(1)},y^{(2)},\ldots,y^{(\nu)}|\theta) = p(x^{(1)},x^{(2)},\ldots,x^{(\nu)}|\theta)\cdot|J| \qquad (8.3.38)$$

with

$$J = \frac{\partial(x^{(1)},x^{(2)},\ldots,x^{(\nu)})}{\partial(y^{(1)},y^{(2)},\ldots,y^{(\nu)})}\ . \qquad (8.3.39)$$

We can, of course, write, due to the definition of conditional probability,

$$p(y^{(1)},y^{(2)},\ldots,y^{(\nu)}|\theta)$$
$$= p(y^{(1)}|\theta)p(y^{(2)},y^{(3)},\ldots,y^{(\nu)}|y^{(1)},\theta)\ . \qquad (8.3.40)$$

Now suppose that $y^{(1)}$ is an estimate $\hat{\theta}$ of θ, so that

$$\begin{aligned} &p(\hat{\theta}, y^{(2)}, \ldots, y^{(\nu)} | \theta) \\ &\quad = p(\hat{\theta}|\theta) p(y^{(2)}, y^{(3)}, \ldots, y^{(\nu)} | \hat{\theta}, \theta) \ . \end{aligned} \tag{8.3.41}$$

The second factor on the right side is the probability density of $y^{(2)}, y^{(3)}, \ldots, y^{(\nu)}$, under the condition: "given the parameter value θ and given the value of the estimate $\hat{\theta}$." But, if the estimate $\hat{\theta}$ has all available information about the true value θ then this condition must be equivalent to a simpler condition: "given the value of the estimate $\hat{\theta}$." If this condition is satisfied, that is,

$$\begin{aligned} &p(\hat{\theta}, y^{(2)}, \ldots, y^{(\nu)} | \theta) \\ &\quad = p(\hat{\theta}|\theta) p(y^{(2)}, y^{(3)}, \ldots, y^{(\nu)} | \theta) \ , \end{aligned} \tag{8.3.42}$$

we say that the estimate $\hat{\theta}$ is a sufficient estimate.

Since $|J|$ in (8.3.38) is independent of θ, the value of θ that maximizes $L(x^{(1)}, x^{(2)}, \ldots, x^{(\nu)} | \theta)$ is the same value that maximizes the likelihood function in terms of y,

$$L(y^{(1)}, y^{(2)}, \ldots, y^{(\nu)}; \theta) = p(y^{(1)}, y^{(2)}, \ldots, y^{(\nu)} | \theta) \ . \tag{8.3.43}$$

Let $\hat{\theta}_L$ be the value that maximizes this L or the logarithm of L. If there exists a sufficient estimate $\hat{\theta}_S$, satisfying (8.3.42), we have

$$\begin{aligned} &\frac{\partial}{\partial\theta} \log p(\hat{\theta}_S, y^{(2)}, \ldots, y^{(\nu)} | \theta) \\ &\quad = \frac{\partial}{\partial\theta} \log p(\hat{\theta}_S, \theta) + \frac{\partial}{\partial\theta} \log p(y^{(2)}, y^{(3)}, \ldots, y^{(\nu)} | \hat{\theta}_S) \\ &\quad = \frac{\partial}{\partial\theta} \log p(\hat{\theta}_S, \theta) \ . \end{aligned} \tag{8.3.44}$$

If this sufficient estimate $\hat{\theta}_S$ is also the most efficient estimate, it should, according to (8.3.34) above, satisfy

$$\frac{\partial}{\partial\theta}(\log \hat{\theta}_S, \theta) = a(\hat{\theta}_S - \theta) \ . \qquad (8.3.45)$$

Therefore, if we put $\hat{\theta}_L = \hat{\theta}_S$, then this $\hat{\theta}_L$ will satisfy

$$\frac{\partial}{\partial\theta} p(y^{(1)}, y^{(2)}, \ldots, y^{(\nu)}, \theta)\Big|_{\theta=\theta_L} = 0 \ , \qquad (8.3.46)$$

the condition that $\hat{\theta}_L$ is the maximum likelihood estimate. Thus, if there exists the most efficient estimate, it is bound to be a maximum likelihood estimate.

We have discussed here in a very cursory way various notions with regard to the merits of a "point" estimate. The discussion is based on the probability distribution of the estimate $\hat{\theta}$ derived from the probability distribution $p(x|\theta)$ where θ is not a random variable but a constant of unknown magnitude. The point estimate aims to give the most suitable value of θ in the presence of sample points. There is another kind of discussion, estimating the probability of the true value of θ falling within an interval $(\underline{\theta}, \overline{\theta})$. That is the evaluation of

$$\text{Prob } (\underline{\theta} \leq \theta \leq \overline{\theta}) \qquad (8.3.47)$$

where $\underline{\theta}$ and $\overline{\theta}$ are derived from some observed values of x, hence random variables. The interval $[\underline{\theta}, \overline{\theta}]$ is called the "confidence interval." Suppose, for instance, we have an estimate $\hat{\theta}$ whose distribution density is $p(\hat{\theta}|\theta)$. We can calculate, at least in principle, if $p(x|\theta)$ is known, the probability

$$\text{Prob } (\theta - a \leq \hat{\theta} \leq \theta + b) = \int_{\theta-a}^{\theta+b} p(\hat{\theta}|\theta)d\hat{\theta} \ . \qquad (8.3.48)$$

This probability is the same as

$$\text{Prob } (\hat{\theta} - b \leq \theta \leq \hat{\theta} + a) \ . \qquad (8.3.49)$$

This expression looks as if we consider θ as a random variable, but it is not so. The upper and lower bounds of the interval are random numbers. In this respect, the confidence interval belongs to the same family of consideration as the point estimate. A point estimate whose efficiency is high or a narrow confidence interval with high probability seems to indicate the estimation is quite reliable. But we should not forget that we are assuming a single density function $p(x|\theta)$ and are not comparing different $p(x|\theta)$ with different θ's. For this reason, the conclusion is based only on the self-consistency of an estimate of θ. This method does not utilize our entire resources of information about θ. For instance, apart from the observed values of $x^{(\alpha)}$, $\alpha=1,2,\ldots,\nu$, we may have some reason to believe that θ is an integer. In the theoretical scheme of estimate theory there is no place to accommodate such information. The Bayesian approach is superior to the non-Bayesian approach since it provides, at least in theory, a place to accommodate this kind of extra-evidential information, and, in addition to that in absence of such extra-evidential preference, it reduces to the maximum likelihood estimate which will be the most efficient estimate, provided that such an estimate exists.

Still worse than the estimate theory is the philosophy behind the method called "significance test." According to this method, an assumed probability distribution is rejected, not in competition with other distributions but taken singly, if an observation occurs whose value falls in the region whose probability according to the assumed distribution is less than a certain threshold value. Let our "hypothesis" H_0 be that the probability density of the random variable is $p(x)$. We take a function z of N observed values of x, $z = z(x^{(1)}, x^{(2)}, \ldots, x^{(\nu)})$ whose probability density will be calculated from $p(x)$. Let us assume that the average value of z lies not far from $z = 0$, and assume that the major part of the probability lies in the finite value of z. Then a large value of $|z|$ will happen with small probability. For a given threshold α, let z_0 be defined

$$\text{Prob}\,\{|z| > z_0\} = \alpha \tag{8.3.50}$$

according to H_o. If a set of observations: $x^{(1)}, x^{(2)}, \ldots, x^{(\nu)}$ is such that $|z| > z_o$, we are advised to reject H_o. The value of α is usually fixed at 0.01 or 0.05. If $|z| < z_o$, the hypothesis is retained, but it may be rejected by a later experiment. This method not only commits the same methodological error as the estimate theory of not taking into account the extra-evidential factor, but also depends on an entirely arbitrary number α.

The reasons why these non-Bayesian approaches were popular in earlier years were that determination of prior probability was not required and it can pretend "objectivity" without depending on the personal opinion concerning the hypothesis (the assumed distribution). But, in recent years, it has been established that the personalistic view of probability can be advanced with perfect scientific respectability, and we are no longer afraid of the "subjectivity" of prior probabilities. We should consider that the Bayesian view is the basis and the non-Bayesian methods can be considered as convenient approximations.

As far as pattern recognition is concerned, we can hardly make any assumptions as to the form of the distribution function, or make a null-hypothesis H_o. Already for this reason alone the entire collection of usual tools of evaluation or test theory is almost irrelevant to the practical problem, except in their usefulness of producing publishable papers.

Before passing to the next section we should insert a short description of a method which stands between the parametric and nonparametric approaches. In connection with (8.3.14) and (8.3.18), we treated the moments as parameters of the probability density. But, usually these "parameters" are not explicitly mentioned in the expression of the density. Questions arise then as to whether the moments, if they exist, can characterize a density function and, in the affirmative case, how many of them are necessary. One may ask also if all the moments of any order are equally important. At least in some approximate sense, a small number of them might suffice to determine the general trend of the density. As we have seen, the estimates of the moments by the corresponding sample moments, (8.3.16), (8.3.19), are unbiased, but it can be shown that they are of low asymptotic efficiency. But, leaving these matters to the statisticians, let us briefly review the problem of determination of a probability density from the moments. The estimate of the moments by the sample estimate is after all the oldest and most convenient clue in guessing the density. The only thing we should keep in mind is that the existence of moments is not always guaranteed and that the higher the order of the moments the more probable that the integrals defining them blow up. Thus, this method is applicable when the density becomes very small for larger values of $|x|$.

If the probability is discrete, expressed by p_i, $i=1,2,\ldots,s$, the definition of moments is

$$m_r = \sum_{i=1}^{s} x_i^r \, p_i \qquad (m_o = 1) \ , \qquad (8.3.51)$$

where x_i is the value of a random variable that appears with probability p_i. If we have s equations of this type, $r=0,1,2,\ldots,(s-1)$, we can uniquely determine the s unknown p's from the given m's, provided that all x's are different. Of course, depending on the way the m's are given, the solution p's can become negative. But, if we use the actual estimate the p's obtained by these equations will not become very large in the negative. Similarly, if the density function is defined in a finite domain $[a,b]$ of x, the equation to determine the density $p(x)$ will be

$$m_r = \int_a^b x^r \, p(x)\,dx \quad . \qquad (8.3.52)$$

By a limiting process from the discrete case, we can infer the uniqueness of the solution $p(x)$.

But, if the domain becomes infinite $[-\infty,\infty]$, the solution of

$$m_r = \int_{-\infty}^{\infty} x^r \, p(x)\,dx \qquad (8.3.53)$$

is no longer unique. This can be seen if one notices that there exists a finite $g(x)$ that is not identically zero but has all the moments of zero

$$0 = \int_{-\infty}^{\infty} x^r\, g(x)\,dx\ . \qquad (8.3.54)$$

Examples of such functions can be found in the literature; however, if we impose a condition on $p(x)$--that for large $|x|$, $p(x)$ is bounded by an exponential function: $\exp\ (-\alpha|x|)$, $(\alpha > 0)$--the uniqueness of the solution of (8.3.53) is guaranteed.

Therefore, if we have all the moments, we determine not only the "parameters" of the density, but the density function itself.

But, all this consideration may be called academic since we cannot handle the infinitely many moments. If we can show that the lower order moments are more important than the higher order moments, so that we can approximate the density function using only the lower moments, the situation will be different. As a matter of fact, the Gaussian distribution can be entirely determined by the first two moments, m_1 and m_2, because $m_o = 1$, $m = m_1$ and $\sigma = m_2 - m_1^2$. We know that the actual density function is seldom Gaussian, but we know also that there is good reason to use the Gaussian distribution as the starting approximation. This consideration leads to what is known as Gram's expansion, which is a variant of the well-known expansion by the orthogonal functions consisting of the derivatives of the Gaussian function.

The Hermite polynomials $H_t(x)$, $t=0,1,2,\ldots$, are defined with the help of the derivatives of the Gaussian function by

$$H_t(x) = (-1)^t\, e^{\frac{x^2}{2}}\, \frac{d^2}{dt^2}\, e^{-\frac{x^2}{2}}\ . \qquad (8.3.55)$$

The first few examples are

$$\left.\begin{array}{ll} H_0(x) = 1 & H_1(x) = x \\ H_2(x) = x^2 - 1 & H_3(x) = x^3 - 3x \\ H_4(x) = x^4 - 6x^2 + 3 & \ldots. \end{array}\right\} . \tag{8.3.56}$$

With the aid of the Hermite polynomials, we can define a set of normalized, orthogonal functions $\phi_t(x)$ by

$$\phi_t(x) = \frac{H_t(x)}{\sqrt{t!}} \frac{e^{-\frac{x^2}{4}}}{(2\pi)^{\frac{1}{4}}} . \tag{8.3.57}$$

We can expand any function f(x), provided it vanishes sufficiently fast for large values of $|x|$, in the form:

$$f(x) = \sum_{t=0}^{\infty} \frac{1}{\sqrt{t!}} c_t \phi_t(x) \tag{8.3.58}$$

with

$$c_t = \sqrt{t!} \int f(x) \phi_t(x) dx . \tag{8.3.59}$$

Because all the $\phi_t(x)$ contain the same exponential functions, we can consider (8.3.58) as an expansion in terms of different H's. More explicitly, if we introduce

$$p(x) = \frac{f(x)}{(2\pi)^{\frac{1}{4}}} e^{-\frac{x^2}{4}} \tag{8.3.60}$$

its expansion becomes

$$p(x) = \frac{1}{(2\pi)^{\frac{1}{2}}} e^{-\frac{x^2}{2}} \sum_{t=0}^{\infty} \frac{c_t}{t!} H_t(x) , \tag{8.3.61}$$

where the coefficients c_t are the same as in (8.3.59), but now can be written as

$$c_t = \int_{-\infty}^{\infty} p(x)H(x)dx \ . \tag{8.3.62}$$

Because $p(x)$ in (8.3.60) is proportional to $\exp(-x^2/4)$ times $f(x)$, it must vanish very fast for large $|x|$, but if we take as $p(x)$ the probability density function that appears in pattern recognition, it can be assumed to be zero for large x. Therefore, we can assume that the condition can be easily satisfied in our problems. Equation (8.3.62) shows in view of (8.3.56) that c_t is related to the moment (8.3.14) by simple formula, namely,

$$\begin{aligned} &c_0 = m_0 = 1,\ c_1 = m_1,\ c_2 = m_2 - 1, \\ &c_3 = m_3 - 3\ m_1,\ c_4 = m_4 - 6\ m_2 + 3, \text{ and so on }. \end{aligned} \tag{8.3.63}$$

As a rough approximation, which is all that we need in pattern recognition, we can decide the c's using the sample moments for the m's.

The expansion (8.3.61) with (8.3.62) is called Gram's expansion and insofar as $p(x)$ becomes sufficiently small for large $|x|$, it can be applied to any probability density. Because the first term in expansion is

$$p(x) = \frac{1}{\sqrt{2\pi}} e^{-\frac{x^2}{2}} \tag{8.3.64}$$

it would be wise to adjust the origin of x as the sample average of $x^{(\alpha)}$ and to choose the unit length of x as the square root of the sample average of $x^{(\alpha)2}$, so that the first term becomes the Gaussian approximation of $p(x)$.

As $\phi_t(x)$ forms a complete, orthonormal function system, we can introduce $\phi_{t_1}(x_1), \phi_{t_2}(x_2), \ldots, \phi_{t_n}(x_n)$ which will be a complete orthonormal system for n-dimensional functions, and their coefficients $c_{t_1 t_2 \ldots t_n}$ will be related to $m_{r_1 r_2 r_3 \ldots r_n}$ in some simple way. In this case, it would be desirable to choose the coordinate in such a way that the "observed" covariance matrix becomes diagonal.

8.4 AIC, NUMBER OF PARAMETERS, AND DIMENSIONALITY

We would not be surprised if the last section became tedious to the reader due to the scholastic complexity of the theoretical statistics, which, to the layman's eye, seems to serve nothing but production of an abundance of Ph.D.s and professors. But some scholars think that the essence of pattern recognition resides in a study of these fine points of statistics. In any event, we can show in this section that the method of the theoretical statistics can lead to a conclusion which certainly clarifies a very important problem in the field of pattern recognition. That is the problem of the number of parameters and the dimensionality of representation space. It is obvious that the larger these two numbers, the more faithfully the mathematical model can reproduce the experimental data. But common sense would tell us that this theoretical gain would be paid for by a useless complexity and too much arbitrariness. We have seen already a similar situation when we discussed the problem of curve fitting from the point of view of the heuristic principle of minimum entropy. In this section, we want to explain in our language a theory advanced by Akaike [A-3, A-4], which seems to give theoretical backing to this intuitive feeling.

According to the Bayesian theory, the a posteriori probability of a hypothesis H_j is given by

$$p(H_j|x) = p(x|H_j)p(H_j) \times \text{const} , \qquad (8.4.1)$$

where x is a shorthand for the empirical data and $p(H_j)$ is the a priori probability of the hypothesis. The "likelihood" function L is the degree of confirmation H_j by x

$$L(H_j,x) = p(x|H_j) \qquad (8.4.2)$$

and the maximum likelihood principle recommends to adopt the hypothesis H_k which maximizes the likelihood function

$$L(H_k, x) = \underset{j}{\text{Max}}\ L(H_j, x) \ . \tag{8.4.3}$$

It is important to note that x is a collection of finite samples $x^{(\alpha)}$, $\alpha = 1,2,\ldots,\nu$ which we can assume to take any one of the possible values x_i, $i=1,2,\ldots,R$. Insofar as ν is finite, the choice obeying the maximum likelihood principle is contingent on the accidentally obtained empirical data x. Let β_i be the relative frequency of the number of $x^{(\alpha)}$'s which take the value x_i

$$\beta_i = \frac{\nu_i}{\nu} \ , \tag{8.4.4}$$

where

$$\nu = \sum_{i=1}^{R} \nu_i \ .$$

If the difference between the hypotheses is due to a difference in the value of a parameter or a vector-parameter, θ, we can consider the hypothesis as a function of the values of θ. The logarithm of the probability of the hypothesis $H(\theta)$ can be written in the form of (8.1.9)

$$\log p(\theta|x) = \log L(\theta, x) + \log p(\theta) + \text{const}$$

$$= \nu \sum_{i=1}^{R} \beta_i\ p(x^{(i)}|\theta) + \log p(\theta) + \text{const} \ . \tag{8.4.5}$$

The β_i depends on the sample at hand but we can in many cases assume that it converges to a fixed value γ_i

$$\lim_{\nu\to\infty} \beta_i = \gamma_i \ . \tag{8.4.6}$$

The "const" in (8.4.5) is a term which does not depend on θ.

If $\nu \to \infty$, the first term becomes predominant and we can ignore the second and third terms in the evaluation of the probability of θ. But, the maximum likelihood method insists on ignoring the second and third term even for a finite ν and maximizing

$$\log L^{\nu}(\theta) = \nu \sum_{i=1}^{R} \beta_i \log p(x_i|\theta) \quad . \tag{8.4.7}$$

In reality the maximum likelihood would be legitimately justified only for $\nu \to \infty$, maximizing

$$\lim_{\nu\to\infty} \frac{1}{\nu} L^{(\nu)}(\theta) = \sum_{i=1}^{R} \gamma_i \log p(x_i|\theta) \quad . \tag{8.4.8}$$

In the following, in order to simplify the writing, let us assume the quantization in R steps of the range of x in infinitely fine (which would make each elementary domain i be occupied either by one or zero paradigm) so that we can simply write

$$\frac{1}{\nu} \sum_{i=1}^{R} \text{ for } \sum_{i=1}^{R} \beta_i \quad .$$

Then, we have instead of (8.4.7)

$$\log L^{(\nu)}(\theta) = \sum_{\alpha=1}^{\nu} \log p(x^{(\alpha)}|\theta) \tag{8.4.9}$$

where ν could still be finite. Next, for the limiting case $\nu \to \infty$ we can write

$$\begin{aligned} \lim_{\nu\to\infty} \frac{1}{\nu} \log L^{(\nu)}(\theta) &= E_x[\log p(x|\theta)] \\ &= \int \gamma(x) \log p(x|\theta)\,dx \quad , \end{aligned} \tag{8.4.10}$$

where

$$\int \gamma(x)\,dx = 1 \tag{8.4.11}$$

instead of

$$\sum_{i=1}^{R} \gamma_i = 1 \; . \tag{8.4.12}$$

Let us assume that the density based on θ, $p(x|\theta)$, for a particular value θ_o gives the actual limiting frequency density $\gamma(x)$. Then we can write

$$\lim_{\nu\to\infty} \frac{1}{\nu} L^{(\nu)}(\theta) \to \int \gamma(x) \log p(x|\theta) dx \tag{8.4.13}$$

$$= \int p(x|\theta_o) \log p(x|\theta) dx \; . \tag{8.4.14}$$

The maximum likelihood choice $\hat{\theta}$ at a finite ν can then be considered as a kind of estimate of θ_o, since under fairly general conditions it holds with probability one that

$$\lim_{\nu\to\infty} \hat{\theta} \to \theta_o \; . \tag{8.4.15}$$

According to the Gibbs' theorem, the maximum of (8.4.13) is reached when $p(x|\theta)$ becomes $p(x|\theta_o)$, on the assumption that there is such a hypotehsis that

$$p(x|\theta_o) = \gamma(x) \; . \tag{8.4.16}$$

In other words, θ_o is the maximum likelihood choice of θ on an infinite sample. Under these conditions, if ν is sufficiently large, $\hat{\theta}$ is very close to θ_o; $\hat{\theta}$ depends not only on the number ν but also on the empirical data x which changes from one case to another. Therefore, we can think that $\hat{\theta}$ has a certain probability distribution around θ_o. Since we can assume $\hat{\theta}$ to be close to θ_o, the probability density $p(\hat{\theta})$ can be expanded around θ_o and satisfies a sufficiently good approximation taking only lower powers of $\hat{\theta}-\theta_o$. If we take up only to the second order term, it will be a normal distribution.

It is convenient to introduce the specific likelihood function (i.e., the likelihood function per sample)

$$F^{(\nu)}(\theta) = \frac{1}{\nu} L^{(\nu)}(\theta) = \frac{1}{\nu} \sum_{\alpha=1}^{\nu} \log p(x^{(\alpha)}|\theta) \tag{8.4.17}$$

and

$$\begin{aligned} F^{(\infty)}(\theta) &= \lim_{\nu\to\infty} \frac{1}{\nu} L^{(\nu)}(\theta) \\ &= E_x \log p(x|\theta) = \int \gamma(x) \log p(x|\theta)\,dx \ , \end{aligned} \tag{8.4.18}$$

where $\gamma(x)$ can be replaced by $p(x|\theta_o)$ if (8.4.16) is allowed. As $\hat{\theta}$ is determined by the maximization of the finite likelihood function, we have, if θ is a scalar,

$$\left[\frac{\partial F^{(\nu)}(\theta')}{\partial\theta'}\right]_{\theta'=\hat{\theta}} = 0 \tag{8.4.19}$$

or according to (8.4.17)

$$\left[\frac{1}{\nu} \sum_{\alpha=1}^{\nu} \frac{\partial}{\partial\theta'} \log p(x^{(\alpha)}|\theta')\right]_{\theta'=\hat{\theta}} = 0 \ . \tag{8.4.20}$$

As for θ_o, we have

$$\left[\frac{\partial F^{(\infty)}(\theta')}{\partial\theta'}\right]_{\theta'=\theta_o} = 0 \ , \tag{8.4.21}$$

or

$$\begin{aligned} &\left[\int p(x|\theta_o) \frac{\partial}{\partial\theta'} \log p(x|\theta')\,dx\right]_{\theta'=\theta_o} \\ &= E_x \left[\frac{\partial}{\partial\theta'} \log p(x|\theta')\right]_{\theta'=\theta_o} = 0 \ . \end{aligned} \tag{8.4.22}$$

Since θ_o is not very far from $\hat{\theta}$, we have with the help of (8.4.19) an approximate equality

$$\left[\frac{\partial F^{(\nu)}(\theta')}{\partial\theta'}\right]_{\theta'=\theta_o} = \left[\frac{\partial F^{(\nu)}(\theta')}{\partial\theta'}\right]_{\theta'=\hat{\theta}} \tag{8.4.23}$$

$$+ (\theta_o-\hat{\theta})\left[\frac{\partial^2 F^{(\nu)}}{\partial\theta'^2}\right]_{\theta'=\hat{\theta}} = (\theta_o-\hat{\theta})\left[\frac{\partial^2 F^{(\nu)}(\theta')}{\partial\theta'^2}\right] .$$

From these relationships we can find, after some calculation, that the probability density of $\hat{\theta}$ for large ν_o has the mean value θ_o and the standard deviation $[nC(\theta_o)]^{-1}$ where

$$C(\theta) = -\int p(x|\theta)\left[\frac{\partial^2}{\partial\theta^2}\log p(x|\theta)\right]dx . \tag{8.4.24}$$

In this calculation, we made use of (8.4.22) and the formulae

$$E_x\left[\frac{\partial}{\partial\theta'}\log p(x|\theta')\right]^2_{\theta'=\theta_o} \tag{8.4.25}$$

$$= -\left[E_x\frac{\partial^2}{\partial\theta'^2}\log p(x|\theta')\right]_{\theta'=\theta_o} ,$$

which follows from the definition and the fact

$$\int p(x|\theta')dx = 1 . \tag{8.4.26}$$

When θ is a vector with k components, θ_i, $i=1,2,\ldots,k$, it is convenient to measure the difference between $\hat{\theta}$ and θ_o with the help of the metric $(\nu C_{ij}(\theta))$. Therefore,

$$||\hat{\theta}-\theta_o||^2 = \sum_{i}^{k}\sum_{j}^{k} (\hat{\theta}-\theta_o)_i\ \nu C_{ij}(\theta_o)(\hat{\theta}-\theta_o) \tag{8.4.27}$$

with

$$C_{ij}(\theta) = -\int p(x|\theta) \frac{\partial^2}{\partial\theta_i \partial\theta_j} \left[\log p(x|\theta) \right] dx \ . \quad (8.4.28)$$

We can show that

$$||\hat{\theta}-\theta_o||^2 = \chi_k^2 \ , \quad (8.4.29)$$

where χ_k^2 is the random variable obeying χ^2-distribution with degrees of freedom k (with standard deviation unity). The χ^2-distribution is defined as follows. Suppose we are given independent random variable x_i $(i=1,2,...,k)$ which have the normal distribution with mean value 0 and standard deviation $\sigma=1$: $N(0,\sigma)$. Then distribution of the variable

$$\chi_k^2 = \sum_{i=1} x_i^2 \equiv u \quad (8.4.30)$$

is given by

$$f(u) = \frac{1}{2^{k/2}\ \Gamma(\frac{1}{2}k)} u^{\frac{k}{2}-1} \exp\left(-\frac{u}{2}\right) \ . \quad (8.4.31)$$

The mean value of χ_k^2 is k and the square of the standard deviation is 2k.

Now what we are really interested in is the difference between $F^{(\nu)}(\hat{\theta}_o)$ and $F^{(\nu)}(\theta_o)$, which is by the Taylor expansion,

$$\frac{1}{\nu}\sum_{\alpha=1}^{\nu} \log p(x^{(\alpha)}|\theta) - \frac{1}{\nu}\sum_{\alpha=1}^{\nu} \log p(x^{(\alpha)}|\theta_o)$$

$$= \frac{1}{2}\sum_{i=1}^{k}\sum_{j=1}^{k} (\theta_i-\theta_{oi})(\theta_j-\theta_{oj}) \quad (8.4.32)$$

$$\times \frac{1}{\nu}\left[\frac{\partial^2}{\partial\theta_i'\partial\theta_j'}\sum_{\alpha=1}^{\nu} \log (x^{(\alpha)}|\theta)\right]_{\theta=\theta_o}$$

which we can approximate by

$$\frac{1}{2} \sum_{i=1} \sum_{j=1} (\hat{\theta}_i - \theta_{oi})(\hat{\theta}_j - \theta_{oj}) C_{ij}(\theta_o) \quad ,$$

which we can further approximate by $(1/\nu)$ times

$$\frac{1}{2} \,||\hat{\theta}-\theta_o||^2 = \chi_k^2 \; . \tag{8.4.33}$$

When ν is finite, of course, $F^{(\nu)}(\hat{\theta})$ is larger than $F^{(\nu)}(\theta_o)$. If we take different samples of $\chi^{(\alpha)}$, $\alpha=1,2,\ldots,\nu$, and make the average, we get

$$\mathrm{Av}_x \sum_{\alpha=1}^{\nu} \log p(x^{(\alpha)}|\hat{\theta})$$

$$- \mathrm{Av}_x \sum_{\alpha=1}^{\nu} \log p(x^{(\alpha)}|\theta_o) = \frac{1}{2}\,k \; . \tag{8.4.34}$$

Now if we replace $\frac{1}{\nu} \sum_{\alpha=1}^{\nu}$ by $\int p(x|\theta_o)dx\ldots$, we get, as $F^{(\infty)}(\theta_o)$ is larger than $F^{(\infty)}(\hat{\theta})$,

$$\int p(y|\theta_o) \log p(y|\theta_o) dy - \int p(y|\theta_o) \log p(y|\hat{\theta}) dy$$

$$= \frac{1}{2} \sum_{i=1}^{k} \sum_{j=1}^{k} (\theta_{oi} - \hat{\theta}_i)(\theta_{oj} - \hat{\theta}_j) C_{ij}(\theta_o) \approx \frac{1}{2\nu}\,\chi_k^2 \; , \tag{8.4.35}$$

and

$$\mathrm{Av}_x(\nu Ey \log p(y|\theta_o) - \nu Ey \log p(y|\hat{\theta})) = \frac{1}{2}k \; . \tag{8.4.36}$$

Adding (8.4.34) and (8.4.36), we obtain, noticing that the second term in the first equation and the first term in the second equation cancel each other,

$$\mathrm{Av}_x \sum_{\alpha=1}^{\nu} \log p(x^{(\alpha)}|\hat{\theta}) - \mathrm{Av}_x\, \nu \int p(y|\theta_o) \log p(y|\hat{\theta}) = k \ ,$$

or

$$\log L^{(\infty)}(\hat{\theta}) = \log L^{(\nu)}(\hat{\theta}) - k/\nu \quad (8.4.37)$$

in the sense of average on different finite sets of ν empirical data. This means that if we want to guess $L^{(\infty)}(\hat{\theta})$ from the value of $\hat{\theta}$ in a finite sample, we have to deduct k, the number of parameters.

If we compare this (8.4.37) with (8.4.5), we notice an additional term -k on the right side of the Bayesian equation. The term k, introduced by Akaike [A-3, A-4] may be considered as a correction due to the finiteness of ν. The larger value of k in general tends to increase $L^{(\nu)}$, but we have the penalty for it. This has nothing to do with the evidential data or the logical nature of the problem, hence it may be in a way more natural to include it in the extra-evidential and extra-logical factor $p(\theta)$, that is, we can perhaps think of replacing the a priori probability by

$$P(\theta) \to p(\theta)e^{-k} \ . \quad (8.4.38)$$

For a large value of ν, we get a large value of $L^{(\nu)}$ and the role of the prior probability becomes unimportant; so also does the importance of the Akaike correction.

So far we assumed that k is a given constant. We can enlarge the problem by assuming that in reality there are K parameters, but we restrict our adjustment of contents to only k (<K) parameters. That is, we assume the true θ_o is outside the restricted k-dimensional space. Even then, we can show that the result, (8.4.37), is useful.

The Akaike theory cannot be applied, as it is, to the problem of dimensionality in pattern recognition. However, we can get some hint how to include the problem of dimensionality in the evaluation. As we increase the dimensionality n, the number of parameters involved in any hypothesis about the density function of a class becomes larger. For instance, the number of constants involved in the covariance matrix increases with $n(n+1)/2$. The Akaike theory, as it is, does not allow putting $k \propto k_o n(n+1)/2$. But, it is quite plausible to put $p(\theta) \propto p_o(\theta)_o e^{-g(n)k_o}$ where $g(n)$ is an increasing function of n.

There is a whole literature of speculative ideas to cope with the problem of dimensionality. (See [C-7, D-6, H-13, K-15] among others.) But none is definitive. The approach started by Akaike certainly sheds a new light on the problem. Schwarz proposed $k \log\sqrt{n}$ instead of k, but his n does not correspond exactly to the dimensionality of the representation space [S-17]. See also Akaike's rebuttal to Schwarz [A-5] and Rissanen's new paper [R-8] closely related to the problem started by Akaike. My sincere thanks are due to Dr. Akaike who was kind enough to read the draft of this section to check the correctness of mathematical derivation. He rightly did not approve of (8.4.38) because there is no rigorous justification for shifting a factor from the "confirmation" term to the "a priori" term. Writing this way, however, we can emphasize the extra-evidential nature of the Akaike term. The merit of this section may lie in the fact that we derived the AIC by a straight consideration of the Bayesian formula, without introducing an additional principle or criterion.

8.5 NONPARAMETRIC CURVE MATCHING

The considerations made in this section refer to each class separately, therefore, we shall not mention the class distinction. The points $x^{(\alpha)}$, $\alpha=1,2,\ldots,\nu$ are supposed to be ν random samples from a population which has a probability density function $p(x)$. The task is to reconstruct the function $p(x)$ from the samples $x^{(\alpha)}$, $\alpha=1,2,\ldots,\nu$, without any knowledge about the type of the function $p(x)$. In Section 8.3, we assumed that $p(x)$ is known to have a certain fixed type and only the values of the parameters involved are unknown. In such a case, the task becomes the problem of estimation of parameters from the data $x^{(\alpha)}$. In the present nonparametric case, where even the type of $p(x)$ is not known, the task becomes considerably more complicated. Of course, as we have seen in an example at the end of the last section, we can consider the nonparametric case as a limiting case of the parametric case in which the number of parameters has become infinite. Indeed, we can expand p(x) by a suitable set of base functions and consider the expansion coefficients as the parameters to be determined. But this connection is only a formal one and, in reality, in the nonparametric case we had better adopt an approach from a different point of view.

Before discussing the nonparametric case, we should mention another category of time-honored problems which lie so to speak between the parametric and nonparametric cases. We assume that a nonunimodular density function p(x) is a superposition of many normal distribution densities (or some fixed type distribution density), and we try to determine the parameters of these normal distributions and their relative weights from the observed points. If the observed points are of mixed classes, and if each class, for some reason, is known to have a normal distribution, such a method can be used as a clustering technique. Such an assumption, however, is seldom permissible and this way of posing the problem is not very fruitful.

Concerning the problem of nonparametric estimation of p(x), the most popular and most elementary method is the histogram. Taking the one-dimensional case, let us assume that p(x) is defined in the domain [a,b]. We divide the domain [a,b] into N equal intervals and count the number k of the sample points $x^{(\alpha)}$ that fall into the i-th interval. We divide k/ν by the size of the interval $\Delta x = (b-a)/\mu$, and we consider $k/(\nu\Delta x)$ as the approximate value of p(x)

$$\hat{p}(x) = \frac{k}{\nu\Delta x} \tag{8.5.1}$$

which is constant in the domain Δx. Piecing these p(x) together for different intervals we obtain a stairlike curve. This is the histogram.

The histogram method, however, suffers from a basic difficulty which we may characterize as a conflict: On one hand, we want to have Δx as small as possible in order to determine as accurately as possible the position at which we are evaluating the value of $p(x)$. But on the other hand, if we make Δx smaller and smaller, the number k will become 1 or 0. That is to say that $\hat{p}(x)$ will become unreliable as an indication of the value of $p(x)$ due to the fluctuation.

Let us denote by P the probability of a point falling in one of the domains of size Δx:

$$P = \int_{\Delta x} p(x)\,dx \,, \tag{8.5.2}$$

then the probability of having k points among the total of ν points in the interval Δx will be given by the binomial distribution

$$\text{Prob}\ (k) = \begin{bmatrix} \nu \\ k \end{bmatrix} P^k (1-P)^{\nu-k} \tag{8.5.3}$$

giving the expected value of k by

$$\langle k\rangle = \sum_{k=0}^{\nu} k\ \text{Prob}\ (k) = \nu P \,. \tag{8.5.4}$$

We can consider $\hat{P} = k/\nu = \hat{p}(x)\Delta x$ as an estimate of P; then its expected value will be P and its variance is given by

$$\langle \Delta\hat{P}^2\rangle = P(1-P)/\nu \,. \tag{8.5.5}$$

The relative variance will then be

$$\frac{\langle \Delta P^2\rangle}{\langle \hat{P}\rangle^2} = \frac{\langle \Delta\hat{p}(x)^2\rangle}{\langle p(x)\rangle^2} = \frac{(1-P)}{\nu P} \,. \tag{8.5.6}$$

In order to see the order of magnitude of the right-hand side, we note that 1-P is close to 1 if Δx is relatively small, and P is approximately equal to $p(x)\Delta x$. Hence, we obtain

$$\frac{\langle \Delta\hat{p}(x)^2\rangle}{\langle \hat{p}(x)\rangle^2} \cdot \Delta x \approx \frac{1}{\nu p(x)} \,. \tag{8.5.7}$$

This is a mathematical expression of the conflict mentioned above. If we want to make Δx small, the fluctuation in $\hat{p}(x)^2$ will increase and if we want to make the fluctuation of $\hat{p}(x)^2$ small, we have to increase Δx. The positional inaccuracy Δx would not matter if $p(x)$ were a constant. But, if $p(x)$ changes appreciably in the domain of the order of Δx, the jump at each step of the stairlike function will become intolerably large. This is related to the second difficulty of the histogram method, that of having to add a smoothing prescription to obtain a more realistic function from the histogram.

The statisticians have the usual easy way out of this conflict by letting ν become infinitely large, which according to (8.5.7) allows both $\Delta x \to 0$ and $\langle\Delta\hat{p}(x)^2\rangle/\langle\hat{p}(x)\rangle^2 \to 0$. This, of course, has practically nothing to do with the actual problems of pattern recognition, but for an academic peace of mind it may have some value. In order that $\hat{p}(x)$ in (8.5.1) may converge to a finite value we have to have $k/\nu \to 0$ as $\nu \to \infty$ and $\Delta x \to 0$. And in order that the relative fluctuation of P and of $p(x)$ may vanish with this process, we have to have $k \to \infty$.

Coming back to the histogram with finite N, we can write (8.5.1) in the form

$$\hat{p}(x) = \frac{1}{\nu} \sum_{\alpha=1}^{\nu} \Phi(x^{(\alpha)} - x^i) \qquad (8.5.8)$$

for the value of x is

$$x^i - \frac{\Delta x}{2} < x \leq x^i + \frac{\Delta x}{2} , \qquad (8.5.9)$$

where x^i is the middle point of the i-th region Δx. $\Phi(\xi)$ in (8.5.8) has the value $1/\Delta x$ in the domain $|\xi| \leq \Delta x/2$ and is equal to zero otherwise, so that

$$\int_{-\infty}^{\infty} \Phi(\xi)d\xi = 1 . \qquad (8.5.10)$$

In fact, the sum under (8.5.8) will give $k/\Delta x$ as in (8.5.1) since only those $x^{(\alpha)}$'s that fall in the domain Δx about x^i will have a contribution of $1/\Delta x$ each.

Now, we can improve the expression (8.5.8) in two ways. For one thing, the expression (8.5.8) will be better suited at the center point $x = x^i$ than near the ends of the domain Δx. Therefore, it would be much better to use, for each point x,

$$\hat{p}(x) = \frac{1}{\nu} \sum_{\alpha=1}^{\nu} \Phi(x^{(\alpha)} - x) \tag{8.5.11}$$

in lieu of (8.5.8). If we write this way, we need not bother about the end points of the small domain of size Δx. The expression (8.5.1) or (8.5.8) requires to evaluate $\hat{p}(x)$ at N different values of x, but (8.5.11) requires, at least in thought, to evaluate $\hat{p}(x)$ at continuously many values of x. The function (8.5.11) is smoother than the function (8.5.8) in the following sense. The curve (8.5.8) makes a big jump every time x enters a new fixed region Δx, while (8.5.11) makes a small jump every time a sample point enters or quits the region of Δx about the point x.

To make the curve still smoother it would be desirable if this entrance and exit of a sample point did not cause a sudden jerk on the curve of $\hat{p}(x)$. This could be achieved by making the function $\Phi(\xi)$ gradually taper off at both ends. Thus, we may replace the edgy function $\Phi(\xi)$ by a smoother Δ-function:

$$\hat{p}(x) = \frac{1}{\nu} \sum_{\alpha=1}^{\nu} \Delta(x^{(\alpha)} - x, \rho) , \tag{8.5.12}$$

where $\Delta(x,\rho)$ is a positive even function appreciably different from zero only in the domain of the order of ρ near the origin and satisfying

$$\int_{-\infty}^{\infty} \Delta(x,\rho)\,dx = 1 . \tag{8.5.13}$$

The Δ-function is a finite version of the δ-function so that symbolically

$$\lim_{\rho \to 0} \Delta(x,\rho) = \delta(x) \ . \tag{8.5.14}$$

There are a number of familiar functions of this kind, one of which was given in (8.2.22)

Parzen [P-2] studied the convergence property of the estimate $\hat{p}(x)$ of (8.5.12) for large ν under the assumption (8.5.13) and that the supremum of $\Delta(x,\rho)$ itself as well as the integral of its absolute value over $[-\infty,\infty]$ remain finite and that $\Delta(x,\rho)$ becomes zero faster than $1/x$ for large x. The estimate is found to be asymptotically unbiased and asymptotically consistent provided ρ tends to zero as $\nu \to \infty$ but not as fast as $1/\nu$ when $\nu \to \infty$. But, as we have often stated, we would be happy if we encounter a single case in pattern recognition where ν is so large in reality that these limiting properties acquire some realistic meaning. In the case of finite ν, we have no well-defined condition regarding the size of ρ, but one of the necessary criteria would be that ρ must always be kept large enough to include several sample points so that the shape of the Δ-function will not show so explicitly on the $\hat{p}(x)$ curve. This condition, however, cannot be observed all over the space if the points are concentrated in a limited region of the space. In the case of n-dimension, what we should do with (8.5.12) is obvious. All we need is to interpret (8.5.13) in the n-dimensional sense.

We can consider the function $\Delta(x^{(\alpha)}-x,\rho)$ in (8.5.12) as representing "influence" of the (source) point at $x^{(\alpha)}$ on the (field) point x. This influence function includes as a special case what the Russian researchers call "potential function" [A-1]. In general, since $\Delta(x-x',\rho)$ is a symmetric matrix with a continuous index, it determines a set of base functions by its eigenfunctions, as in (7.5.18),

$$\int \Delta(x-x',\rho)\phi_k(x')dx' = \lambda^{(k)}\phi_k(x) \ , \tag{8.5.15}$$

where the eigenfunctions $\phi_k(x)$ will be assumed to be orthogonal and normalized

$$\int \phi_k(x)\phi_\ell(x)dx = \delta_{k\ell} \ . \tag{8.5.16}$$

The matrix $\Delta(x-x',\rho)$ can then be expressed as

$$\Delta(x-x',\rho) = \sum_{k=1}^{\infty} \lambda^{(k)} \phi_k(x)\phi_k(x') \quad . \tag{8.5.17}$$

We can easily see that (8.5.15) ensues from (8.5.17) with the help of (8.5.16). Since any square-integrable function f(x) can be expanded in terms of the ϕ_k's as

$$f(x) = \sum_{k=1}^{\infty} c_k\phi_k(x) \tag{8.5.18}$$

with

$$c_k = \int f(x)\phi_k(x)\,dx \tag{8.5.19}$$

we can write

$$f(x) = \int f(x')\left[\sum_{k=1}^{\infty} \phi_k(x)\phi_k(x')\right] dx' \quad . \tag{8.5.20}$$

Since this must be true for any function f(x), we can see the quantity in the brackets acts as a delta-function

$$\delta(x-x') = \sum_{k=1}^{\infty} \phi_k(x)\phi_k(x') \quad . \tag{8.5.21}$$

This should be compared to (8.5.17). The λ's in (8.5.17) have the effect of putting more emphasis on some of the ϕ_k's and suppressing some others. Usually, the eigenfunctions of lower orders (smaller k according to a suitable labeling) have less ups and downs and those of higher orders oscillate frequently. Putting more emphasis on the lower order eigenfunctions, we obtain usually the desired properties of $\Delta(x-x',\rho)$ as described under (8.5.12). Compare the case of (8.3.56).

Instead of using a gradually changing $\lambda^{(k)}$ (as dependent of k), we can think of cutting off higher order terms suddenly. Then we obtain

$$\Psi(x-x') = \sum_{k=1}^{\kappa} \phi_k(x)\phi_k(x') \qquad (8.5.22)$$

taking only the first κ terms. The estimate of p(x) in the form

$$\hat{p}(x) = \frac{1}{\nu} \sum_{\alpha=1}^{\nu} \Psi(x^{(\alpha)}-x) \qquad (8.5.23)$$

was introduced by the Russian researchers and the function $\Psi(x-x')$ given in (8.5.22) was called potential function. The function $\Psi(x-x')$ is a special case of what we may call "projection operator" and has the following property in this case: Suppose we have a function f(x) that can be expanded as in (8.5.18), then the convolution of f(x) and $\Psi(x)$ results in picking up only these terms in f(x) that correspond to k=1 to k=κ, for

$$\begin{aligned}\int \Psi(x-x')f(x')dx' &= \sum_{k=1}^{\kappa} \phi_k(x) \int f(x')\phi_k(x')dx' \\ &= \sum_{k=1}^{\kappa} c_k\phi_k(x) \ .\end{aligned} \qquad (8.5.24)$$

If $\kappa \to \infty$, $\Psi(x-x')$ becomes the δ-function as in (8.5.21) and the right-hand side becomes f(x) itself.

But if f(x) from the beginning has only the first κ terms of expansion, then for such a function f(x), the potential function $\Psi(x-x')$ acts as a delta function. If the p-function is such that it has no higher order terms than k=κ, then we shall have

$$p(x) = \int \Psi(x-x')p(x')dx' \ . \qquad (8.5.25)$$

This equation permits an interesting interpretation. Suppose we start from equation (8.5.23) and we increase ν. Then, in each domain dx there will be $\nu p(x)dx$ samples $x^{(\alpha)}$'s. Therefore, (8.5.23) will pass over to (8.5.25). This means that if p(x) is of the form

$$p(x) = \sum_{k=1}^{K} c_k \phi_k(x) \quad , \qquad (8.5.26)$$

then the estimate $\hat{p}(x)$ given in (8.5.23) will converge to p(x) as $\nu \to \infty$. A more rigorous proof shows that this convergence is a convergence in probability. We shall discuss the successive approximation of p(x) in terms of the potential function in Section 9.6.

CHAPTER 9
Pattern Recognition as Discrimination

9.1 FISHER'S DISCRIMINANT

In Chapter 8 we discussed the straightforward statistical theoretical method of deriving the decision probability $p(A_j|x)$ (probability of a point at x belonging to class A_j) from the density function $p(x|A_j)$ (probability of a random sample of class A_j being located at x). The density function was to be determined by the collection of paradigms (class samples). If the number of paradigms were infinite, this determination would be perfect, but in no real cases is the number infinite. When the number is finite, the prior probability intervenes inevitably. The danger of ignoring this factor, as in the case of the likelihood method, is obvious. The methods to be discussed do not assume that the sample-size is infinite. But the justification to these methods often given by the statistically minded researchers runs another kind of risk. It assumes that there is a unique, infinite population, and the researchers show that if the sample size becomes infinite, the decision made by these methods will become the best available. But there is a loop-hole in this argument. There is no such thing as a unique (infinite) population. There can be an infinite number of different (infinite) populations, of which this really existing finite collection of samples can be a partial set. We should appreciate the methods of this chapter as techniques that often work very well with a finite number of paradigms.

We will discuss six different methods in this section: Fisher's discriminant, the least mean square error method, the k-nearest neighbor method, the perceptron method, the weight-and-direction balance method, and the potential function method. Except for the last one which is an unorthodox method to obtain an approximation of the density function from a finite number of paradigms, the methods aim at giving the decision function d(x) directly from the paradigms. The decision function, as explained in Section 2.1, has as possible values, A_1, $A_2, \ldots, A_M$, and its argument x is a point in the n-dimensional representation space. Except the k-nearest neighbor method, the methods apply to the two-class case, M=2, and the border surface between two values of d(x) is assumed to be a single flat hyperplane. Fisher's method is concerned with determination of the normal line to the plane. We speak often of Fisher's "discriminant," but the term is not used strictly in the sense of (8.2.4). What is meant is a plane that would mark the border at which the index k would change in (8.2.3) if the decision probability were known. As we have seen before, we can include as components of x some nonlinear functions of the originally observed quantities. This will produce hyperplanes in the n-dimensional x space including also curved surfaces in the original variables.

We have thus to consider a plane:

$$\sum_{i=1}^{n} c_i x_i + c_o = 0 \ . \tag{9.1.1}$$

The normalized normal of this plane is given by

$$n_i = c_i \Big/ \sqrt{\sum_{i=1}^{n} c_i^2} \ . \tag{9.1.2}$$

The distance p_o of the plane from the origin is given by

$$p_o = -c_o \Big/ \sqrt{\sum_{i=1}^{n} c_i^2} \ . \tag{9.1.3}$$

The signature of p_o as defined by (9.1.3) is such that it will be positive if the vector in the direction given by $\{n_i\}$ (9.1.2) from the origin will encounter the plane, and negative if the vector in the direction $\{-n_i\}$ from the origin encounters the plane.

Fisher's method [F-1] aims to determine the normal of the plane such that it would be appropriate to assign one side of the plane to one class, A_1, and to assign the other side of the plane to the other class, A_2. In determining the direction, Fisher considers two quantities, one of which it is desirable to maximize and the other it is desirable to minimize.

Consider a straight line in the direction $\{n_i\}$ and assume that all the paradigm points of both classes are projected on this straight line. In order to use a plane whose normal is $\{n_j\}$ as the separation of two classes, it would be desirable to have the projection of the mean points of the two classes as far apart as possible. But, if the spread of points within each class becomes large at the same time, we have not gained anything. It is in fact desirable to have the points of each class as compactly condensed as possible on the line. This is a commonsensical requirement, but we have shown that this requirement ensues from our heuristic principle of the minimum entropy.

The projection of a paradigm point $x_i^{(\alpha)}$ on the straight line passing the origin and having the direction $\{n_i\}$ has obviously the coordinate

$$\left(\sum_{k=1}^{n} n_k\, x_k^{(\alpha)}\right) n_i \ . \tag{9.1.4}$$

The distance of this point from the origin on this straight line is

$$\xi^{(\alpha)} = \sum_{i=1}^{n} n_i\, x_i^{(\alpha)} \ . \tag{9.1.5}$$

The position of the sample mean of the points of class A_1 on this straight line is

$$\mu_1 = \frac{1}{N_1} \sum_{\alpha \in A_1} \xi^{(\alpha)} = \frac{1}{N_1} \sum_{\alpha \in A_1} \sum_{i=1}^{n} n_i\, x_i^{(\alpha)} \ , \tag{9.1.6}$$

where N_1 is the number of paradigms of class A_1. Similarly, for class A_2

$$\mu_2 = \frac{1}{N_2} \sum_{\alpha \in A_2} \xi^{(\alpha)} = \frac{1}{N_2} \sum_{\alpha \in A_2}^{n} \sum_{i=1}^{n} n_i \; x_i^{(\alpha)} \tag{9.1.7}$$

As it should be, these expressions show that the mean of the projections is the same as the projection of the mean:

$$\mu_j = \sum_{i=1}^{n} n_i \; m_{j,i} \quad (j = 1,2) \; , \tag{9.1.8}$$

where $\{m_{j,i}\}$ is the mean point (center of mass) of the paradigms of class A_j,

$$m_{j,i} = \frac{1}{N_j} \sum_{\alpha \in A_j} x_i^{(\alpha)} \quad (j = 1,2) \; . \tag{9.1.9}$$

The quantity we should like to make as large as possible would be the distance, or the distance squared, between the projections of the two mean points: $(\mu_1 - \mu_2)^2$. On the other hand, the spread (sample scatter) of points in class A_j on the straight line of direction $\{n_i\}$ is

$$\sigma_j^2 = \sum_{\alpha \in A_j} \left(\xi^{(\alpha)} - \mu_j\right)^2 = \sum_{\alpha \in A_j} \left[\sum_{i=1}^{n} n_i \left(x_i^{(\alpha)} - m_{j,i}\right)\right]^2 . \tag{9.1.10}$$

It would then be desirable to make $\sigma_1^2 + \sigma_2^2$ as small as possible. Then it is understandable that Fisher proposes to determine the direction $\{n_i\}$ so as to maximize a dimensionless quantity:

$$F(\{n_i\}) = \frac{(\mu_1-\mu_2)^2}{\sigma_1^2 + \sigma_2^2} \quad . \tag{9.1.11}$$

This F can be interpreted as the distance between the two mean points in the unit of the average spread of points. It should be noted that both the denominator and numerator are proportional to $|n|^2 = \sum_{i=1}^{n} n_i^2$, hence the maximization condition does not determine the absolute value of $\{n_i\}$ which is supposed to be normalized (see (9.1.2)). We could therefore also use $\{c_i\}$ instead of $\{n_i\}$ in the defining equations of μ_j and σ_j from the beginning. The numerator will converge to a constant value when we increase the numbers of paradigms N_1 and N_2. The denominator will increase indefinitely with $N = N_1 + N_2$. To avoid this, we could divide the entire denominator by N. But this will not change the result of the extremization. It is reasonable that σ_1 and σ_2 as defined in (9.1.10) are respectively proportional to N_1 and N_2. That will give a larger weight to the class whose paradigms are more numerous.

If we define the inter-class scatter H_{ik} by

$$H_{ik}^{inter} = (m_{1,i} - m_{2,i})(m_{1,k} - m_{2,k}) \tag{9.1.12}$$

and the intra-class scatter

$$H_{ik}^{intra} = \sum_{j=1}^{2} H_{j,ik}^{intra} \tag{9.1.13}$$

with

$$H_{j,ik}^{intra} = \sum_{\alpha\varepsilon A_j} \left(x_i^{(\alpha)} - m_{j,i}\right)\left(x_k^{(\alpha)} - m_{j,k}\right) \tag{9.1.14}$$

we can also write $F\{n_i\}$ as

$$F\{n_i\} = \frac{\sum_{i,k} n_i H_{ik}^{inter} n_k}{\sum_{i,k} n_i H_{ik}^{intra} n_k} \tag{9.1.15}$$

The extremum will be obtained by requiring

$$0 = \frac{\partial F}{\partial n_i} = \sum_{j=1}^{2} \frac{\partial F}{\partial \mu_j} \frac{\partial \mu_j}{\partial n_i} + \sum_{j=1}^{2} \frac{\partial F}{\partial \sigma_j^2} \frac{\partial \sigma_j^2}{\partial n_i} , \tag{9.1.16}$$

where

$$\frac{\partial F}{\partial \mu_1} = - \frac{\partial F}{\partial \mu_2} = \frac{2(\mu_1 - \mu_2)}{\sigma_1^2 + \sigma_2^2} , \quad \frac{\partial \mu_j}{\partial n_i} = m_{j,i} \tag{9.1.17}$$

$$\frac{\partial F}{\partial \sigma_1^2} = \frac{\partial F}{\partial \sigma_2^2} = - \frac{(\mu_1 - \mu_2)^2}{(\sigma_1^2 + \sigma_2^2)^2} , \quad \frac{\partial \sigma_j^2}{\partial n_i} = 2 \sum_{k=1}^{n} n_k H_{j,ki}^{intra} .$$

The equation (9.1.16) then becomes

$$m_{1,i} - m_{2,1} = \frac{\mu_1 - \mu_2}{\sigma_1^2 + \sigma_2^2} \cdot \sum_{k=1} n_k H_{ki}^{intra} . \tag{9.1.18}$$

Assuming that H^{intra} is nonsingular, we multiply $(H^{intra})^{-1}_{ik}$ from right on (9.1.18), and we obtain

$$n_k = \frac{\sigma_1^2 + \sigma_2^2}{\mu_1 - \mu_2} \cdot \sum_{i=1}^{n} (m_{1,i} - m_{2,i}) (H^{intra})^{-1}_{ik} . \tag{9.1.19}$$

The factor $(\sigma_1{}^2 + \sigma_2{}^2)$ is proportional to $|n|^2$ and the factor $(\mu_1 - \mu_2)$ is proportional to $|n|$. Hence, (9.1.19) does not interfere with the normalization. In any event, if we are not interested in the magnitude of c_k, then we can write

$$c_k = \sum_{i=1}^{n} (m_{1,i} - m_{2,i})(H^{intra})^{-1}{}_{ik} \tag{9.1.20}$$

and get n_i by (9.1.2).

It is known that Fisher's method gives a fairly reasonable result in many cases with regard to the direction of the normal of the decision plane. There is an attempt to determine the position of the plane by fixing p_o (9.1.3) by requiring minimization of the error probability assuming the normal distribution of paradigms. But, the calculation is complicated, and empirically the result is not so satisfactory. A much simpler but quite satisfactory method to determine p_o seems to be the following. Obviously, the point p_o must lie between μ_1 and μ_2, and it may be reasonable to choose p_o so that $|\mu_1 - p_o|$ and $|\mu_2 - p_o|$ become proportional to the linear spreads $\sqrt{\sigma_1^2/N_1}$ and $\sqrt{\sigma_2^2/N_2}$:

$$-\frac{\mu_1 - p_o}{\mu_2 - p_o} = \sqrt{\frac{\sigma_1{}^2 N_2}{\sigma_2{}^2 N_1}} \tag{9.1.21}$$

or

$$p_o = \left(\sigma_1\sqrt{N_2}\,\mu_2 + \sigma_2\sqrt{N_1}\,\mu_1\right)\Big/\left(\sigma_1\sqrt{N_2} + \sigma_2\sqrt{N_1}\right), \tag{9.1.22}$$

where $\sigma_1 = \sqrt{\sigma_1{}^2}$, $\sigma_2 = \sqrt{\sigma_2{}^2}$. The reason for dividing $\sigma_1{}^1$ and $\sigma_2{}^2$ by N_1 and N_2 to obtain the linear spreads is that the definition of $\sigma_1{}^2$ and $\sigma_2{}^2$ in (9.1.10) gives respectively N_1 times and N_2 times of the sample variances. This method of determining p_o unfortunately does not take the prior probabilities $p(A_1)$ and $p(A_2)$ into consideration. We showed in Section 6.6 another method of determining the position p_0, applying the minimum entropy principle [see the paragraph below formula (6.6.9)].

9.2 LEAST MEAN SQUARED ERROR METHOD

The least mean squared error method has historical roots in the classical problem of the least mean squared curve fitting and has as its aim to determine a linear decision surface of the type (9.1.1) from sets of paradigms of two classes so as to minimize the "errors." This method does not require that the paradigms be linearly separable, and is not an adaptive algorithm. The paradigms of two classes are said to be linearly separable if there exists a hyperplane of the type (9.1.1) such that all paradigms of one class are on one side of the plane, and all paradigms of the other class are on the other side of the plane. A method is called adaptive when the decision surface gradually changes and adapts itself in the measure as new paradigms arrive. The perceptron method which we shall discuss later is an adaptive method which assumes the linearly separable paradigms. The LMSE method we are discussing in this section is a typical method for the nonadaptive case which is applicable also when the paradigms are not linearly separable. Even if the paradigms are linearly separable, the hyperplane obtained by this method is not guaranteed to be a separating one. (See, however, the Ho-Kashyap version of the method explained at the end of this section.) An adaptive version of the LMSE method also will be discussed at the end of this section. The problem of separability and adaptability will be discussed again in connection with the well-balanced perceptron.

Mentally, we can visualize the hyperplane as pulled by the paradigms of two classes from the different sides of the plane, whereby the "potential" of force is positive and proportional to the square of the distance of each point from the plane. The equilibrium position of such a plane is the decision plane obtained by the LMSE method. The force which is pulling the plane from a paradigm is proportional to the distance between the point and the plane. One of the two immediate conclusions we can draw from this picture is that we can change the force law any way we want, and still we shall get a similar separation plane. As a matter of fact, we could even assume a repulsive force instead of the attractive force assumed in the LMSE method. The second point is that in this picture the effect of a point far off the border surface is a strong one, because the potential of the assumed attractive force is proportional to the square of the distance. This is the opposite of the characteristic of the nearest neighbor method in which only the near points have a decisive effect on the determination of the surface. There are several arguments supporting the LMSE method and, as a practical tool, it is a good one because it reflects the global distribution of paradigms. But the "square-law" is just an accidental choice and has very little justification.

Let function F(x) be defined by

$$F(x) = \sum_{i=1}^{n} c_i x_i + c_o \tag{9.2.1}$$

and d(x) by

$$d(x) = \frac{F(x)}{\sqrt{\sum_{i=1}^{n} c_i^2}} \tag{9.2.2}$$

Then $|d(x)|$ is the distance of the point x from the plane $F(x) = 0$. If $c_o < 0$ [hence $p_o > 0$, see (9.1.3)], d(x) will be positive for those points x that lie beyond the plane (i.e., on the other side of the plane than the origin) and negative for those points x that lie on the same side as the origin. If $c_o > 0$ (hence $p_o < 0$), the situation will be just the opposite. Let us note that $d(0) = -p_o$.

Suppose we decide to assign $d(x) > 0$ [i.e., $F(x) > 0$] to class A_1 and $d(x) < 0$ [i.e., $F(x) < 0$] to class A_2. Then, we could think of a possible algorithm that would minimize the mean of the squared distances, $[d(x^{(\alpha)})]^2$. But we would have to incorporate in such an algorithm a mechanism to avoid as much as possible negative values of $d(x^{(\alpha)})$, $\alpha \epsilon A_1$ and $-d(x^{(\alpha)})$, $\alpha \epsilon A_2$. Anything that involves the sign of a function will have to deal with a discontinuous function and will become complicated. (See, however, the Ho-Kashyap procedure at the end of this section.) For this reason, a simple adaptation of the LMSE curve-fitting method would not work for our purpose.

A possible alternative would be to consider two additional planes, $d(x) - \varepsilon_1 = 0$ and $d(x) + \varepsilon_2 = 0$, with $\varepsilon_1 > 0$ and $\varepsilon_2 > 0$. These constants ε_1 and ε_2 will be referred to as "allowances." The former will lie in the domain $d(x) > 0$ (i.e., in the assigned domain of A_1) and is parallel to the decision plane, $d(x) = 0$ at distance ε_1. The latter, will lie in the domain $d(x) < 0$ (i.e., in the assigned domain of A_2) and is parallel to the decision plane at distance ε_2. Let us note that if $d(x) - \varepsilon_1$ for all $x \epsilon A_1$ is larger than $-\varepsilon_1$, and $d(x) + \varepsilon_2$ for all $x \epsilon A_2$ is smaller than ε_2, then all the paradigms are separated. We can then think of an algorithm that would minimize the sum of the (squared) distance of A_1-points from the first auxiliary plane, $d(x) - \varepsilon_1 = 0$, and the distances of A_2-points from the second auxiliary plane, $d(x) + \varepsilon_2 = 0$. What the so-called least-mean squared error method in pattern recognition aims at is not quite the minimization of this sum. What it does aim at, however, is the minimization of this sum multiplied by a factor $(\sum_{i=1}^{n} c_i^2)^{\frac{1}{2}}$, which unfortunately is not a constant but a variable in the process of minimization.

We can write the two auxiliary planes as

$$F(x) = \eta_1 \text{ for } A_1, \quad F(x) = -\eta_2 \text{ for } A_2 \tag{9.2.3}$$

with
$$\eta_j = \varepsilon_j \sum_{i=1}^{n} c_i^2 > 0, \quad j = 1,2 . \tag{9.2.4}$$

We can give a more unified form to the algorithm by introducing a new vector y_i $(i = 0,1,2,\ldots,n)$ by

$$\begin{aligned} y_i &= x_i \text{ and } y_o = +1 \text{ for } x \epsilon A_1 \\ y_j &= -x_i \text{ and } y_o = -1 \text{ for } x \epsilon A_2 . \end{aligned} \tag{9.2.5}$$

Then the two auxiliary planes will become

$$G(y) = \sum_{i=0}^{n} c_i y_i = \eta_j \ , \quad j = 1,2 \ , \tag{9.2.6}$$

The G thus defined is such that $F(x^{(\alpha)}) = G(y^{(\alpha)})$ if $\alpha \epsilon A_1$ and $F(x^{(\alpha)}) = -G(y^{(\alpha)})$ if $\alpha \epsilon A_2$.

Now we can formulate the problem as one of choosing the position of the decision plane by varying its position so as to minimize the sum of the squares of the differences between $G(y^{(\alpha)})$ and η_j, that is,

$$J = \sum_{\alpha=1}^{N} \left[G(y^{(\alpha)}) - \eta^{(\alpha)} \right]^2 , \tag{9.2.7}$$

where $\eta^{(\alpha)} = \eta_1$ or η_2 according as $\alpha \epsilon A_1$ or A_2 . (9.2.8)

It does not make much sense at this stage but we can generalize the formalism so that $\eta^{(\alpha)}$ is not necessarily the same for all the different paradigms of the same class. We assume, however that, $\eta^{(\alpha)} > 0$. In the literature the values $\eta^{(\alpha)}$ are often called the "ideal" or "desired" values of $G(y^{(\alpha)})$, because we minimize the (squared) difference of $G(y^{(\alpha)})$ from $\eta^{(\alpha)}$. We should not, however, forget that the actual distance corresponding to this difference is the difference between $F(x^{(\alpha)})$ and the allowance $\varepsilon^{(\alpha)}$ where

$$\varepsilon^{(\alpha)} = \eta^{(\alpha)} \Big/ \sqrt{\sum_{i=1}^{n} c_i^{\,2}} \tag{9.2.9}$$

At this point, we should already be aware that since we are taking the square of the difference between $G(y^{(\alpha)})$ and $\eta^{(\alpha)}$, we are treating the positive and negative values of the difference on an equal footing. If $G(y^{(\alpha)}) - \eta^{(\alpha)}$ is positive the points $x^{(\alpha)}$ will be farther away from the decision plane than the corresponding auxiliary plane, thus indicating that the point lies in the assigned domain of the class. But if $G(y^{(\alpha)}) - \eta^{(\alpha)}$ is negative this is not guaranteed. Note that if we could cleverly choose the values of positive η's and if the minimum of J could become 0, then the plane $G(y^{(\alpha)}) = 0$ would be the separating hyperplane, when the case is separable.

By introducing a matrix $Y_{\alpha i}$ and a vector η_α, $\alpha = 1,2,\ldots,N$, $i = 0,1,2,\ldots,n$ by

$$Y_{\alpha i} = y^{(\alpha)}{}_i \quad , \quad \eta_\alpha = \eta^{(\alpha)} \tag{9.2.10}$$

We can rewrite (9.2.7) as

$$J = \sum_{\alpha=1}^{N} \left[\sum_{i=0}^{n} Y_{\alpha i}\, c_i - \eta_\alpha \right]^2 . \tag{9.2.11}$$

Since we are looking for a minimum of J varying the decision plane (i.e., varying the c_i's), we should have

$$0 = \frac{\partial J}{\partial c_j} = 2 \sum_{\alpha=1}^{N} Y^t{}_{j\alpha} \left(\sum_{i=0}^{n} Y_{\alpha i}\, c_i - \eta_\alpha \right) \tag{9.2.12}$$

where $Y^t{}_{j\alpha} = y^{(\alpha)}{}_j$.

If we could realize

$$\sum_{i=0}^{n} Y_{\alpha i}\, c_i = \eta_\alpha \tag{9.2.13}$$

we could satisfy (9.2.12). But, the number of equations in (9.2.12) is (n+1), whereas the number of equations in (9.2.13) is N, which could be larger than (n+1). In other words, adjusting (n+1) coefficients c_i's, we cannot in general satisfy N equation (9.2.13). Therefore, we have to retain (9.2.12) which can be rewritten as

$$\sum_{i=0}^{n} (Y^t Y)_{ji}\, c_i = \sum_{i=0}^{n} \left(\sum_{\alpha=1}^{N} Y^t{}_{j\alpha} Y_{\alpha i} \right) c_i = \sum_{\alpha=1}^{N} Y^t{}_{j\alpha} \eta_\alpha . \tag{9.2.14}$$

Here the matrix $(Y^tY)_{ji}$ is an $(n+1) \times (n+1)$ matrix. If we can assume $(Y^tY)_{ji}$ to be nonsingular, we introduce its inverse $(Y^tY)^{-1}{}_{ij}$. Multiplying (9.2.14) by this matrix from the left we obtain the solution of the problem

$$c_i = \sum_{j=0}^{n} \sum_{\alpha=1}^{N} (Y^tY)^{-1}{}_{ij}\, Y^t{}_{j\alpha}\, \eta_\alpha , \qquad (9.2.15)$$

or

$$c_i = \sum_{\alpha=1}^{N} \tilde{Y}_{i\alpha}\, \eta_\alpha \qquad (9.2.16)$$

with

$$\tilde{Y}_{i\alpha} = \sum_{j=0}^{n} (Y^tY)^{-1}{}_{ij}\, Y^t{}_{j\alpha} . \qquad (9.2.17)$$

In case $(Y^tY)_{ji}$ is singular, we cannot write (9.2.17). As in many other similar cases of singular matrices, we add to $(Y^tY)_{ji}$ a small perturbation, say $\varepsilon\delta_{ji}$, so that we can obtain the inverse. Then we take the limit $\varepsilon \to o$. That is to say, $(Y^tY)^{-1}{}_{ii}$ should be understood as $[Y^tY + \varepsilon\delta]^{-1}{}_{ii}$ with $\varepsilon \to o$.

Comparing (9.2.16) with (9.2.13), we see that $\tilde{Y}$ is playing a role similar to the inverse of Y, if such a thing existed. $\tilde{Y}$ is called the pseudoinverse of Y. In fact, if Y^{-1} and $(Y^t)^{-1}$ existed, we could see that $\tilde{Y}$ would reduce to Y^{-1}, because $(Y^tY)^{-1}$ would become $Y^{-1}(Y^t)^{-1}$. Generally, this is not the case. What is always true is

$$\tilde{Y}\, Y = 1 \qquad (9.2.18)$$

but $Y\,\tilde{Y} = 1$ does not hold as a general rule.

We now examine the meaning of the solution (9.2.16) for a given set of values of η_α. We examine the effect of the η_α on the solution in two respects: The effect of the magnitude of the η_α and the effect of the relative values of the η_α for the different α's. If we multiply all the η_α by a positive constant $\lambda > 0$, all the c_i will be according to (9.2.16) multiplied by λ. But, this will not geometrically change the hyperplane (9.1.1).

Further, the allowances $\varepsilon^{(\alpha)}$ will not be changed either, as we can see from (9.2.9) in which both $\eta^{(\alpha)}$ and $\sqrt{\sum_{i=1}^{n} c_i^2}$ will be multiplied by λ. This means that the magnitude of ε_j is not related to the magnitude of η_α. The magnitude of ε_j is determined by the magnitude of $Y_{\alpha i}$. The larger the $Y_{\alpha i}$, the smaller the $\tilde{Y}_{i\alpha}$ due to (9.2.18), and the smaller the $\tilde{Y}_{i\alpha}$ the smaller the ratio of the magnitude of c_i to the magnitude of η_α as can be seen in (9.2.16). This will make the magnitude of the ε_j larger on account of (9.2.9). If we keep the order of magnitudes of y and η and increase the number of paradigms, the order of magnitude of c_i and ε_i will remain unchanged.

When the paradigms, $Y_{\alpha i}$, are given, what we can control is only the relative values of the $\varepsilon^{(\alpha)}$ by changing the relative values of $\eta^{(\alpha)}$. This would result in a change of the hyperplanes. But, on what ground should we use different values of $\eta^{(\alpha)}$ for different α? Unless we know the position of the hyperplane, all the paradigms have to be treated on an equal basis. The only difference we can make is the distinction depending on the class-affiliation. As a result, the actual choice of the relative values of $\varepsilon^{(\alpha)}$, hence of $\eta^{(\alpha)}$, is extremely limited. Since the magnitude of $\varepsilon^{(\alpha)}$ does not depend on the magnitude of $\eta^{(\alpha)}$ and the relative values of $\eta^{(\alpha)}$ leave practically no choice, the $\varepsilon^{(\alpha)}$ are practically determined by the paradigms $Y_{\alpha i}$. The freedom left in our choice of $\eta^{(\alpha)}$ is therefore only apparent and has no practical consequences. It is misleading to call $\eta^{(\alpha)}$ the ideal or desired value of $G(y^{(\alpha)})$.

Consequently we can say that this algorithm is based on a rather weak methodological foundation. But an argument supporting this algorithm [P-12] is provided by the fact that this algorithm in a special case can be considered as a linear approximation to the Bayesian decision function

$$g_B = p(A_1|x) - p(A_2|x) \quad . \tag{9.2.19}$$

The decision function based on the present method is

$$g_{LMS}(x) = F(x) \quad , \tag{9.2.20}$$

where $F(x)$ depends on the c's which are to be determined by (9.2.16) or, equivalently, by minimizing (9.2.7).

If we want to approximate the "true" decision function $g_B(x)$ by a linear function $g_{LMS}(x)$, a possible strategy would be to mimimize the difference

$$\delta = \int \left[g_B(x) - \kappa\, g_{LMS}(x) \right]^2 p(x)\, dx \ , \qquad (9.2.21)$$

where κ is some positive constant.

What we can show is that the condition of minimization of (9.2.21) and the condition of minimization of (9.2.7) coincide, if we assume that $\eta^{(\alpha)}$ for different α's are all equal

$$\eta^{(\alpha)} = \eta \ , \qquad (9.2.22)$$

and if we pass to the limit $N \to \infty$, $N_1 \to \infty$, $N_2 \to \infty$ in such a way that

$$\frac{N_1}{N} = p(A_1) \ , \quad \frac{N_2}{N} = p(A_2) \ . \qquad (9.2.23)$$

Note well that we again resort to the unrealizable case of infinite paradigms, assuming a unique population.

The quantity to be minimized (9.2.7) can be written

$$J = \sum_{\alpha=1}^{n} \left[G(y^{(\alpha)}) - \eta \right]^2$$

$$= \sum_{\alpha \in A_1} \left[F(x^{(\alpha)}) - \eta \right]^2 + \sum_{\alpha \in A_2} \left[F(x^{(\alpha)}) + \eta \right]^2 . \qquad (9.2.24)$$

If there are a very large number N of paradigms, there will be $N_j = N\, p(A_j)$ paradigms of class A_j in total. Of these N_j

$$N_j\, p(x|A_j)\, dx = N\, p(A_j)\, p(x|A_j)\, dx$$

$$= N\, p(A_j|x)\, p(x)\, dx \qquad (9.2.25)$$

will be found in the domain x and x + dx. Hence, we can write

$$J = N\int\{[F(x)-\eta]^2\ p(A_1|x) + [F(x)+\eta]^2\ p(A_2|x)]\}\ p(x)\ dx$$
$$= N\int [F(x)]^2\ p(x)\ dx - 2N\eta\int F(x)\ g_B(x)\ p(x)\ dx + \eta^2 \tag{9.2.26}$$

because $p(A_1|x) + p(A_2|x) = 1$. This can further be rewritten

$$J = N\int [F(x) - \eta\ g_B(x)]^2 p(x)dx$$
$$- N\ \eta\int [g_B(x)]^2 p(x)dx + \eta^2\ . \tag{9.2.27}$$

Because $g_B(x)$ and η have nothing to do with the minimization procedure, the minimization of J is equivalent to the minimization of the first term (i.e., the minimization of δ (9.2.21) with $\kappa = 1/\eta$).

This gives an impression that the LMSE decision rule is a good approximation of the Bayesian decision rule. But this conclusion is too hasty, because the decision function has its meaning in the decision rule based only on three possibilities: $g(x) > 0$, $g(x) = 0$, and $g(x) < 0$. The actual values of $g(x)$ at each point x in the space are irrelevant. Even if the integral (9.2.21) is small, the all-important border surface $g(x) = 0$ may be quite different. Therefore, the smallness of (9.2.21) does not mean much.

Another kind of support for the LMSE method is supplied by a comparison with Fisher's discriminant [K-16]. To return to the description in terms of x's instead of y's, let us write out (9.2.14) separately for index $i = 0$ and index $i = 1,2,...,n$. By straightforward rewriting with the help of (9.2.5) and (9.2.10), we obtain for the coefficients in (9.2.14)

$$\left.\begin{aligned} (Y^tY)_{oo} &= N \\ (Y^tY)_{jo} &= (Y^tY)_{oj} = Nm_j, \quad j=1,2,\ldots,n \\ (Y^tY)_{ij} &= H_{ij}, \qquad i,j=1,2,\ldots,n\ , \end{aligned}\right\} \tag{9.2.28}$$

where $\{m_j\}$ represents the mean vector of all paradigms

$$m_j = \frac{1}{N} \sum_{\alpha=1}^{N} x_j^{(\alpha)} = \frac{N_1}{N} m_{1,j} + \frac{N_2}{N} m_{2,j} \quad j=1,2,\ldots,n , \tag{9.2.29}$$

where $\{m_{1,m}\}$ and $\{m_{2,j}\}$ are given in (9.1.9). H_{ij} is related to $H_{ik}^{intra} \equiv V_{ik}$ of the last section of (9.1.13), (9.1.14) by

$$H_{ij} = \sum_{\alpha}^{all} x_i^{(\alpha)} x_j^{(\alpha)}$$

$$= V_{ij} + \sum_{k=1}^{2} N_k m_{k,i} m_{k,j} . \tag{9.2.30}$$

As a result, the left-hand side of (9.2.14) becomes

$$\sum_{j=0}^{n} (Y^tY)_{oj} c_j = Nc_o + N \sum_{j=1}^{n} m_j c_j$$

$$\sum_{j=0}^{n} (Y^tY)_{ij} c_j = N m_i c_o + \sum_{j=1}^{n} H_{ij} c_j . \tag{9.2.31}$$

Using two values η_1 and η_2 for A_1 and A_2 as in (9.2.8), we can rewrite the right-hand side of (9.2.14) as

$$\left.\begin{aligned} &\sum_{\alpha}^{all} Y^t_{o\alpha} \eta_\alpha = N_1 \eta_1 - N_2 \eta_2 \\ &\sum_{\alpha}^{all} Y^t_{i\alpha} \eta_\alpha = N_1 \eta_1 m_{1,i} - N_2 \eta_2 m_{2,i} . \end{aligned}\right\} \tag{9.2.32}$$

If we put

$$\eta_1 = \frac{1}{N_1}\ , \quad \eta_2 = \frac{1}{N_2} \tag{9.2.33}$$

the first component of the right-hand side becomes zero and we obtain

$$c_o = - \sum_{j=1}^{n} m_j\ c_j \tag{9.2.34}$$

$$N\ m_i\ c_o + \sum_{j=1}^{n} H_{ij}\ c_j = m_{1,i} - m_{2,i}\ . \tag{9.2.35}$$

Substituting the value of c_O from (9.2.34) into (9.2.35), and substituting (9.2.30) for H_{ij}, we obtain

$$\sum_{j=1}^{n} \frac{N_1 N_2}{N}\ (m_{1,i} - m_{2,i})(m_{1,j} - m_{2,j})\ c_j$$

$$+ \sum_{i=1}^{n} V_{ij}\ c_j = (m_{1,i} - m_{2,i}) \tag{9.2.36}$$

or

$$c_j = \sum_{i=1}^{n} V^{-1}{}_{ji}\ (m_{1,i} - m_{2,i})$$

$$\left[1 - \sum_{k=1}^{n} \frac{N_1 N_2}{N}\ (m_{1,k} - m_{2,k})\ c_k\right] . \tag{9.2.37}$$

As far as the relative values of the c_j are concerned, we see from (9.2.37) that

$$c_j \propto \sum_{i=1}^{n} V^{-1}{}_{ji}\ (m_{1,i} - m_{2,i})\ , \tag{9.2.38}$$

which is the same as (9.1.20), because V_{ij} hence $V^{-1}{}_{ji}$ is a symmetric matrix.

This shows that if we take $\eta^{(\alpha)}$ proportional to $1/N_j$ $(j = 1,2)$, the normal of the decision plane according to the LMSE method coincides with the Fisher discriminant. The point where the plane intersects the normal passing the origin, is given, according to (9.2.34), by

$$- \frac{c_o}{\sqrt{\sum c_i^2}} = \frac{\sum m_i c_i}{\sqrt{\sum c_i^2}} = \sum_{i=1}^{n} m_i n_i$$
$$= \frac{N_1}{N} \mu_1 + \frac{N_2}{N} \mu_2 , \tag{9.2.39}$$

where μ_1 and μ_2 are given by (9.1.8). This point is the projection of the center of mass of the paradigms on Fisher's direction.

This is a good argument in support of the LMSE method, but we have to note that the direction of the normal of the decision plane as determined by this method tends to have the following property. The direction as determined by Fisher's method is supposed to maximize the interclass scatter and minimize the intraclass scatter. But, the coincidence of the LMSE and the Fisher methods seem to indicate, at least judged from the intuitive point of view, that the effect of maximization of the interclass scatter is not working as effectively as the effect of minimization of the intraclass scatter. Consider a two-dimensional case where two densities $p(x|A_1)$ and $p(x|A_2)$ are normal and have the same covariance matrix, which is elongated in the x direction and very narrow in the y direction. Assume further that the mean of A_1 and the mean of A_2 are far apart as far as the x direction is concerned and very near as far as the y direction is concerned. According to the meaning of the LMSE method, it can be expected that the border line will lie almost parallel to the x direction and its normal will be in the y direction. But, according to intuition, the border line should, in the present case, rather lie parallel to the y direction. This means the distance between μ_1 and μ_2 is not as large as would be desired.

As far as the position of the plane for the given normal is concerned, the formula (9.2.39) may seem to be better than our previous formula (9.1.22) in the sense that it takes the prior probability (9.2.23) into consideration. But, unfortunately, the effect of the ratio of N_1/N_2 on the position of the plane is just the opposite of what it should be. Suppose that the densities $p(x|A_1)$ and $p(x|A_2)$, hence also the centers of mass μ_1 and μ_2, are kept constant and the ratio of numbers N_1/N_2 increases. Then $p(A_1)/p(A_2)$ increases and the domain of A_1 should increase, but according to (9.2.39), the plane will move closer to μ_1, thus decreasing the domain of A_1. This is definitively an undesirable feature of the method.

We shall explain Widrow-Hoff's successive procedure to obtain the decision plane dictated by the LMSE method mainly because it is historically famous [W-57]. Let us remember some of the elementary facts about the successive methods of finding a maximum or minimum of a function. First, consider the well-known method of finding the "zero" of a function, $y = f(x)$, zero meaning the value of x that makes $y = 0$. It is assumed that it is difficult or impossible to obtain exactly the solution of $f(x) = 0$, but it is possible to obtain the values of $f(x)$ and $f'(x) = df/dx$ for an arbitrary value of x. Suppose we have some hunch about the location of the zero and guess that the zero is near $x = x^{(1)}$. The formula to be obtained is intended to give an improved value $x^{(2)}$ starting from $x^{(1)}$. Using the same formula, we shall be able to obtain a further improved value $x^{(3)}$ starting from $x^{(2)}$, and so forth. Repeating this procedure we shall get a sequence $x^{(1)}, x^{(2)}, x^{(3)}, \ldots$ which we hope will converge to the true zero.

Suppose that $y^{(\nu)}$ is the value of $f(x)$ at $x^{(\nu)}$, and C is the true zero. We replace the curve between the point $(x^{(\nu)}, y^{(\nu)})$ and the guessed position of C by the tangent at $(x^{(\nu)}, y^{(\nu)})$ and call its intersection with the x axis $x^{(\nu+1)}$ which will be closer to C than $x^{(\nu)}$. Then we shall have

$$(x^{(\nu)} - x^{(\nu+1)})\, f'(x^{(\nu)}) = f(x^{(\nu)}) \qquad (9.2.40)$$

or

$$x^{(\nu+1)} = x^{(\nu)} - \frac{f(x^{(\nu)})}{f'(x^{(\nu)})}, \qquad (9.2.41)$$

which is called Newton's formula. We can easily convince ourselves that the same formula works irrespective of whether the slope is positive or negative, irrespective of whether $y^{(\nu)}$ is positive or negative, and irrespective of whether the curvature of the curve near the zero is positive or negative. If we repeat the process (9.2.41), the sequence will ordinarily converge to the zero. But, we can see that this convergence is not always guaranteed, for instance if there is a point of inflection. If there is more than one zero, there is no guarantee as to which one of the zeros the sequence will converge to.

Newton's formula advises us to make a larger correction $(x^{(\nu+1)}-x^{(\nu)})$ if $f(x^{(\nu)})$ is larger and if $f'(x^{(\nu)})$ is smaller. If we obey only the first half of this advice we shall get another formula for successive approach to the zero:

$$x^{(\nu+1)} = x^{(\nu)} - \lambda f(x^{(\nu)}) \tag{9.2.42}$$

with a constant λ. We can see that this amounts to replacing the curve of $f(x)$ between $(x^{(\nu)}, y^{(\nu)})$ and C by a straight line of slope $1/\lambda$. We can see that we have to take λ positive if the curve is cutting the x axis with a positive slope and negative in the opposite case. This procedure will also converge in a favorable situation, but if $|\lambda|$ is too small the convergence will be too slow and if $|\lambda|$ is too large the correction may overshoot and diverge.

Now we can use these formulae to find the maximum or minimum instead of the zero. If we are looking for an extremum of $f(x)$, it is equivalent to looking for the zero of $f'(x)$. Hence, we can immediately obtain from (9.2.41) the formula

$$x^{(\nu+1)} = x^{(\nu)} - \frac{f'(x^{(\nu)})}{f''(x^{(\nu)})} \tag{9.2.43}$$

and from (9.2.42)

$$x^{(\nu+1)} = x^{(\nu)} - \lambda f'(x^{(\nu)}) \, . \tag{9.2.44}$$

It is interesting to note that (5.2.43) applies for both maximum and minimum whereas (9.2.44) applies for a minimum if $\lambda > 0$ and for a maximum if $\lambda < 0$.

There is another way to justify Newton's procedure (9.2.43). Suppose we approximate the curve in the neighborhood of $x^{(\nu)}$ by a second degree curve

$$f(x) = f(x^{(\nu)}) + f'(x^{(\nu)})(x - x^{(\nu)}) + \tfrac{1}{2} f''(x^{(\nu)})(x - x^{(\nu)})^2 . \tag{9.2.45}$$

The extremum of this curve can be obtained by

$$\frac{df(x)}{dx} = f'(x^{(\nu)}) + f''(x^{(\nu)})(x - x^{(\nu)}) = 0 , \tag{9.2.46}$$

which is equivalent to (9.2.43) with $x = x^{(\nu+1)}$. This gives a clue as to how to generalize the result to a multi-dimensional case. Consider c to be a vector whose components are c_i. Then, equations corresponding to (9.2.45) and (9.2.46) will become respectively

$$f(c) = f(c^{(\nu)}) + \sum_i \frac{\partial f(c^{(\nu)})}{\partial c_i} (c_i - c_i^{(\nu)})$$

$$+ \tfrac{1}{2} \sum_i \sum_j \frac{\partial^2 f}{\partial c_i \partial c_j} (c_i - c_i^{(\nu)})(c_j - c_j^{(\nu)}) , \tag{9.2.47}$$

and

$$\frac{\partial f(c)}{\partial c_i} = \frac{\partial f(c^{(\nu)})}{\partial c_i} + \sum_j \frac{\partial^2 f(c^{(\nu)})}{\partial c_i \partial c_j} (c_i - c_j^{(\nu)}) = 0 . \tag{9.2.48}$$

If the matrix

$$K_{ij} = \frac{\partial^2 f(x^{(\nu)})}{\partial c_i \partial c_j} \tag{9.2.49}$$

has its inverse $K^{-1}{}_{ji}$ such that

$$\sum_j K_{ij} K^{-1}{}_{jk} = \sum_j K^{-1}{}_{kj} K_{ji} = \delta_{ki} \tag{9.2.50}$$

we can obtain from (9.2.48), putting $c_i^{(\nu+1)} = c_i$

$$c_i^{(\nu+1)} = c_i^{(\nu)} - \sum_{j=1}^{n} K_{ij}^{-1} \frac{\partial f(c^{(\nu)})}{\partial c_j} . \quad (9.2.51)$$

If we use a constant λ for K_{ij}^{-1}, we obtain

$$c_i^{(\nu+1)} = c_i^{(\nu)} - \lambda \frac{\partial f(c^{(\nu)})}{\partial c_i} , \quad (9.2.52)$$

where $\lambda > 0$ if we look for a minimum and $\lambda < 0$ if we look for a maximum. This formula says in the case $\lambda > 0$, that starting from the ν-th point $x^{(\nu)}$ we should go in the direction of the steepest descent and that the magnitude of the step should be proportional to the steepness of the slope. This last point makes sense becase if $c^{(\nu)}$ is far from the true minimum, the slope will probably be large, and if $c^{(\nu)}$ is near the true minimum the slope will be closer to zero. Note that the gradient vector $(\partial f/\partial c_i)$ gives the steepest direction pointing toward higher values of f, and following that direction we can come quickly to the extremum.

Let us now come back to the LMSE method which aims at obtaining the c_i which minimizes (9.2.11). The equation (9.2.52) will become, with the help of (9.2.12),

$$c_i^{(\nu+1)} = c_i^{(\nu)} - \lambda \sum_{\alpha=1}^{N} y_i^{(\alpha)} \left(\sum_{i=0}^{n} y_i^{(\alpha)} c_i - \eta_\alpha \right) \; i=0,1,2,\ldots,n . \quad (9.2.53)$$

The Widrow-Hoff method is not exactly (9.2.53), in which the correction term is a sum of terms each of which refers to a paradigm. It may be possible to make a correction due to one paradigm at each step. We can change the label of paradigms and call the paradigm that we take for the ν-th correction $y^{(\nu)}$. Then we get the W-H method

$$c_i^{(\nu+1)} = c_i^{(\nu)} - \lambda y_i^{(\nu)}\left(\sum_{i=0}^{n} y_i^{(\nu)} c_i - \eta_\alpha\right). \tag{9.2.54}$$

In practice we have usually a finite number N of paradigms and we have to repeat the same paradigm again and again, for instance by using the label $\nu = 1,2,3,\ldots$, so that $\nu = \alpha \bmod N$. In (9.2.52), if $x^{(\nu)}$ hits the real minimum, the correction term will become zero. But, in (9.2.54), this is not to be expected. Hence, in general, the sequence $\{c^{(\nu)}\}$ will oscillate. To damp the oscillation, we can artificially decrease λ gradually with increasing ν. In practical applications, this successive procedure usually works, but the convergence is notoriously slow. Compared with the exact solution (9.2.16), the successive method has the advantage that it does not assume the nonsingularity of (Y^tY) and is also relatively easier than exact solutions on computer burden.

Another peculiarity of the method, whether in its exact version or in its successive version, is that the position of the plane is too strongly affected by paradigm points far away from the border because the square of the distance of the points from the auxiliary planes comes into calculation. The method such as the perceptron, which takes into consideration only those points that have been misclassified by a trial plane, is strongly affected by points near the border. As far as this problem is concerned the nearest neighbor method we are going to discuss in the next section is at the other extreme and is the most myopic of all the methods.

There could be many attempts to redefine the J-function (9.2.7) to improve the method. For instance, we can set up a J so as to minimize the number of points that fall on the wrong side of the decision plane (i.e, the number of paradigms that make $G(y^{(\alpha)}) < 0$). Such a J can be defined

$$J = \sum_{\alpha=1}^{N}\left[1 - \frac{G(y^{(\alpha)})}{|G(y^{(\alpha)})|}\right]. \tag{9.2.55}$$

This function does not consider the distance of the points to the border. We cannot give a closed-form solution to the minimization of such a J, but, a successive method could be applied.

The LMSE method has a strong point over the perceptron method, which is going to be explained in Section 9.4, namely, the method works whether or not the paradigms are separable. But, it is not guaranteed that in the separable case, the obtained hyperplane actually separates the two groups of paradigms. That it should be called a questionable requirement because the position of the plane should be neither determined only by the global situation of the paradigms, nor influenced too strongly by the local situation. There is a method however, that modifies the LMSE method so that the obtained discriminating hyperplane really separates the two groups in the separable case: the Ho-Kashyap procedure, which we only mention, but do not describe in detail [H-12, H-16].

What the LMSE method does is the following. We choose arbitrarily the vector η_α, $\alpha = 1,2,\ldots,N$, then the method gives us the normal vector c_i, $i = 0,1,2,\ldots,n$ that minimizes (9.2.11) or

$$J = \sum_{\alpha=1}^{N} \left[\sum_{i=0}^{n} y_i^{(\alpha)} c_i - \eta_\alpha \right]^2 . \qquad (9.2.56)$$

The first term, $\sum_{i=0} y_i^{(\alpha)} c_i$, is the distance of the point beyond the plane in the y representation. If the separation is perfect this should be all positive. The separable case means that the data $\{y_i^{(\alpha)}\}$ are such that there exists a vector $\{c_i\}$ which satisfies

$$\sum_{i=0}^{n} y_i^{(\alpha)} c_i = \eta_\alpha^{(\alpha)} > 0, \quad \alpha = 1,2,\ldots,N . \qquad (9.2.57)$$

If we know such $\eta_\alpha^{(\alpha)}$ and use these values in (9.2.56), the LMSE would give the separating plane $\{c_i\}$ which would give $J = 0$. The Ho-Kashyap procedure is the method starting with a set of N positive η_α, it improves, step by step, their values until they reach the optimal values that are conditioned by (9.2.57). The general idea of the method is that whereas the LMSE method considers J as a function of the parameters c_i, the Ho-Kashyap method considers J as a function of both sets of parameters c_i and of η_α, and a successive method of improvement, like the one used in the Widrow-Hoff procedure, is applied.

9.3 NEAREST NEIGHBOR METHOD

Suppose that N paradigms $x^{(\alpha)}$, $\alpha = 1,2,\ldots,N$ are given with their class affiliation $A^{(\alpha)}$, where $A^{(\alpha)}$ could be any one of $A_1, A_2, \ldots, A_M$. Suppose further that the new arrival has a position $x^{(N+1)}$ or simply x, and we are asked to place it in one of the classes A_j, $j = 1,2,\ldots,M$. The simplest possible strategy without referring to the probability density or using any complicated mathematical notions would be to place it in the class to which its nearest neighbor belongs. This is the strategy of the nearest neighbor method.

Such a strategy would be particularly successful if the true border between class domains, if such a thing exists, has an average radius of curvature ρ much larger than the average distance ℓ between the N points.

$$\rho >> \ell \tag{9.3.1}$$

If this is the case the probability will be relatively high that the point and its neighbor are on the same side of the border surface. If, on the other hand, the border surface has gerrymandering with radii of curvature ρ less than ℓ, the chance will be high that the class affiliation of the point in question and the class affiliation of its neighbor will have nothing to do with each other.

A little more sophisticated method than the nearest neighbor method is the k-nearest neighbor method which consists of taking the k-nearest paradigm points of the newcomer x and deciding the class affiliation of x by the plurality of the classes of the k paradigms. Let the radius of a sphere which contains the k-nearest neighbors, but not (k+1), be r. Then, obviously, the assumed border surface has to have an average radius ρ much larger than r:

$$\rho >> r \tag{9.3.2}$$

which makes ρ still larger than the nearest neighbor method.

The rule of decision by the plurality of votes is so familiar in the daily life of men in modern societies that they will be ready to accept it without hesitation. But it may be interesting to see that it agrees with the principle of minimum entropy in the following sense. Let k_j be the number of paradigms of class j in this sphere of k points. The entropy defined by the class representatives is $S = -\sum_{j=1}^{M} p_j \log p_j$, $p_j = k_j/k$. We are now allowed to add one to one of the k_j's. The way to obtain the lowest entropy is obviously to add the one to that class which is already the largest k_j.

This method is well defined and easy to carry out and moreover, as far as the local condition (of the size of radius r) is concerned, it is in some sense a justifiable strategy. But, to adapt this algorithm as a decision rule covering a large domain compared with r is another question. We shall first explain the usual justification given by the statistically minded scholars, and then later we shall return to a more critical attitude. The only warning we should give in advance is that every time they start to talk about the unique infinite population, $N \to \infty$, and a continuous probability distribution, we should already be on guard.

Let N_j be the total number of available paradigms of class A_j, and suppose we take k-nearest neighbors of a point x and let the volume of the sphere containing just these k points be ΔV. Let further k_j be the number of paradigms of class A_j among these k points. Then we may use, as we have seen in (8.5.1),

$$\hat{p}(x|A_j) = \frac{k_j}{N_j}\frac{1}{\Delta V} \tag{9.3.3}$$

as an estimate of the density function $p(x|A_j)$. In fact if we let $k_j \to \infty$ as $N_j \to \infty$, in such a way that $k_j/N_j \to 0$ as we make $\Delta V \to 0$, we can expect (9.3.3) to converge to $p(x|A_j)$. The decision probability $p(A_j|x)$ is proportional to $p(x|A_j)p(A_j)$ and we may use

$$\hat{p}(A_j) = \frac{N_j}{N} , \tag{9.3.4}$$

as an estimate of $p(A_j)$ where $N = \sum_{j=1}^{M} N_j$. Hence, $\hat{p}(x|A_j)p(A_j) = k_j/(N\Delta V)$ and we may consider

$$\hat{p}(A_j|\, x) = \frac{k_j}{N}\frac{1}{\Delta V} \Bigg/ \sum_{\ell=1}^{M} \frac{k_\ell}{N} \cdot \frac{1}{\Delta V} = k_j \Bigg/ \sum_{\ell=1}^{M} k_\ell \tag{9.3.5}$$

as an estimate of the decision probability for a very large N. The decision rule we had in (8.1.1) and (8.1.2) was to choose A_m defined by

$$p(A_m|x) = \operatorname*{Max}_{\ell} p(A_\ell|x) . \tag{9.3.6}$$

If we allow ourselves to use the estimate (9.3.5), this decision rule becomes to choose A_m such that

$$k_m = \operatorname*{Max}_{\ell} k_\ell . \tag{9.3.7}$$

This may be taken as a justification of the k-nearest neighbor method for a very large N. The interesting part is that N_j cancels out and does not appear in the decision rule. But we have to keep in mind that in the k-nearest neighbor method we fix the value of k and do not change it with N as is the case in (9.3.3). Admittedly, however, for relatively large fixed values of k and N, we can justify the k-nearest neighbor method insofar as we are allowed to use the estimate (9.3.5) in lieu of the true decision probability.

Next, let us estimate the "error" committed by the nearest neighbor method in the two-class case k=1, M=2. If the nearest neighbor of x has coordinates x', the error occurs if x happens to belong to class A_1 and x' to A_2 or if x happens to belong to class A_2 and x' to A_1. Hence, the probability of error is

$$e(x,x') = p(A_1|x')\ p(A_2|x) + p(A_2|x')\ p(A_1|x) \ . \tag{9.3.8}$$

If $N \to \infty$, the distance ℓ between x and x' will tend to zero and $p(A_i|x')$ and $p(A_i|x)$ will become equal. In this way, we can satisfy (9.3.1) for any true border surface. Hence,

$$\begin{aligned}\lim_{N \to \infty} e(x,x') = e(x) &= 2\ p(A_1|x)\ p(A_2|x) \\ &= 2\ p(A_1|x)\ [1 - p(A_1|x)] \\ &= 2\ p(A_2|x)\ [1 - p(A_2|x)] \ .\end{aligned} \tag{9.3.9}$$

For comparison, let us remember that if we use the Bayesian decision rule, the error occurs if $p(A_1|x) > p(A_2|x)$ (therefore we decide on A_1) and the point x belongs to A_1 [which happens with probability $p(A_2|x)$] or if $p(A_1|x) < p(A_2|x)$ (therefore we decide on A_2) and the point belongs to A_1 [which happens with probability $p(A_1|x)$]. Hence, the Bayesian error at x, $e_B(x)$ is as we have seen in the first line of (8.2.14)

$$e_B(x) = \mathrm{Min}[p(A_1|x),\ p(A_2|x)] \ . \tag{9.3.10}$$

In the region $p(A_1|x) < p(A_2|x)$, we have $e_B(x) = p(A_2\ x)$ and $e(x) = 2\ e_B(x)[1 - e_B(x)]$ and in the region $p(A_1|x) < p(A_2|x)$ we have $e_B(x) = p(A_1|x)$ and $e(x) = 2\ e_B(x)[1 - e_B(x)]$. Hence, we have in either case

$$e(x) = 2\ e_B(x)\ [1 - e_B(x)] \tag{9.3.11}$$

The average Bayesian error e_B is

$$e_B = \int e_B(x)\ p(x)\ dx \tag{9.3.12}$$

and its variance σ_B^2

$$\sigma_B^2 = \int [e_B(x) - e_B]^2 \, p(x) \, dx = \int e_B^2(x) \, p(x) \, dx - (e_B)^2 \, . \tag{9.3.13}$$

Hence, we can write the average error by the nearest neighbor method for the M=2 as

$$e = \int e(x) \, p(x) \, dx = 2 \, e_B \, (1 - e_B) - 2 \, \sigma_B^2 \, . \tag{9.3.14}$$

On the other hand, the Bayesian error is the minimum error, hence we have

$$e_B \leq e \leq 2 \, e_B \, (1 - e_B) \, . \tag{9.3.15}$$

A similar calculation for the general case where M is not necessarily 2, gives (for k=1)

$$e_B \leq e \leq e_B \, (2 - \frac{M}{M-1} \, e_B) \, . \tag{9.3.16}$$

Hence, for any M, e is always less than 2 e_B. These results of Cover and Hart [C-8] show a very satisfactory feature of the nearest neighbor method, but this method refers to the unattainable case $N \to \infty$. What would be the error bound of the method for a finite N? An answer can be found in Cover's work [C-1]. When N paradigms are given and the (N + 1)-st point is to be classified in either of the two classes (M=2), he considers the set of these (N + 1) points and asks the probability e_N that the nearest neighbor to one of them x_i, i = 1,2,...,N+1 belongs to a different class from x_i. This probability obviously does not depend on i, and $\lim_{N \to \infty} e_N = e_\infty = e$. His result for a finite N is

$$e_N \leq e + \frac{c}{(N+1)^2} = 2 \, e_B(1 - e_B) + \frac{c}{(N+1)^2} \, , \tag{9.3.17}$$

where c is some constant depending on the density function.

A certain peace of mind comes from using the nearest neighbor method for a finite N, but we have to be clear about two points. First, unless we know the value of c, this upper bound does not give any information as to how good the result for a given finite value of N is. This formula is interesting only when we are interested in the manner in which e_N converges to e for $N \to \infty$. Secondly, we have to know the relation between the error in an individual case and the probability of error e_N, which can be obtained by counting in an actual case the number ν_N of indices $i = 1,2,\ldots,N+1$ for which the point x_i and its nearest neighbor belong to different classes and then by taking the expected value of $\nu_N/(N+1)$,

$$e_N = \langle \nu_N/(N+1) \rangle \quad . \tag{9.3.18}$$

The expected value is the ensemble average of (infinitely) many similar cases where the points are random variables belonging to the unknown distributions $p(x|A_1)$ and $p(x|A_2)$ with the ratio of weight, of $p(A_1)$ versus $p(A_2)$. Thus, even if $\langle \nu_N/(N+1) \rangle$ is small, we cannot be sure that the value of $\nu_N/(N+1)$ in the individual case is small. This is the same kind of objection that we raised in connection with the unbiased estimate in the last section. Although we speak of the average in a finite number of samples, its justification as an estimate relies on an infinite number of samples.

In view of this situation, a little more reflection about the validity of the method is in order. We do not know the density functions $f(x|A_i)$ in any way. Therefore, we might as well decide to work with an approximate border surface whose average radius of curvature is of the order of a given value ρ. Then we should take a sufficient number of paradigms so that the average distance ℓ between neighboring points is much smaller than ℓ, so that (9.3.1) is satisfied. Conversely, if a set of paradigms are given, we should be satisfied with a border surface whose average radius of curvature ρ is much larger than the average distance between paradigm points.

If the points are numerous, we can afford to use the k-nearest method with $k > 2$. In fact, for $N \to \infty$, we can show that the larger the k, the smaller the error probability. But, for a finite N, we have to know that the larger the k, the larger the assumed radius of curvature [see (9.3.2)].

Whether or not we want to actually draw a border surface, we can apply, in thought at least, the nearest neighbor method or the k-nearest neighbor method to each point of the space and thus determine a border surface in the space. The surface thus obtained could, however, exhibit gerrymanderings with radia of curvature comparable to ℓ or r. Therefore, the assumed border surface can be only obtained by a smoothing-out process of these small gerrymanderings of the order less than ρ.

So far, we have argued as if the density functions $f(x|A_i)$ existed although unknown. But, in reality, the existence of such functions can be put in doubt. In fact, there does not exist an infinite number of members of each class. If, in principle, only a finite number of members exist, there will be no ground to assume the existence of $f(x|A_i)$, and we should not attribute much meaning to a theoretical justification relying on its existence. If there is no such thing as the maximally defined density function, we should rather think that we are constructing a border surface with a varying measure of precision, every time we are given a certain finite number of paradigms. It is somewhat like drawing the map of a shoreline with a certain given degree of precision. It is from the outset a dubious assumption that there exists a maximally defined shoreline. Should we ignore the zigzags of radius of curvature less than a mile? Should we be satisfied when we go down to the precision of the order of pebbles? Then, the line will be constantly changing. All that depends on the required degree of precision, and that degree is dictated by the use we make of the map. (See [M-8] for a mathematical problem connected with what Mandelbrot calls "fractals.")

One of the reasons that makes the statistical arguments with $N \to \infty$ look plausible is that we are brainwashed to believe that the population with $N \to \infty$ not only exists, at least in the mind, but also is unique. This assumption may be true if there is a single machine which can produce an arbitrarily large number of samples. But, there is no such mechanism. What exists is really a given finite number of samples. Such a finite set can be a subset of an infinite number of different infinite mother sets. It may be true that the mathematical proof works with any one of these infinitely many mother sets. However, this does not give any guarantee that the conclusion based on a finite subset would agree with the conclusion that would be obtained in any one of the imaginary infinite mother sets on the assumption that this one is the unique one. The uniqueness assumption thus has the effect of concealing the fundamental inductive ambiguity and misleading one to believe there exists a unique solution in pattern recognition problems.

In spite of the methodological uncertainty about the ground of justification, the nearest neighbor method and the k-nearest neighbor method remain useful algorithms of pattern recognition. Their only drawback, as compared with, say, the perceptron method, is that we have to keep all the coordinates of the paradigms in the memory. There are certain algorithms to alleviate the computer burden required by these methods, but the essential nature of the difficulty does not change. It is already a costly task to determine the class affiliations of a small number of newcomers. Then in high dimension cases it will easily become almost a prohibitive task to determine actually the border surfaces implied by the nearest neighbor method or the k-nearest neighbor method. Of course, one of the merits of the nearest neighbor and the k-nearest neighbor methods lies in not trying to draw the border surface actually and being nonetheless capable to give an answer in individual cases.

Let us remember the remark we made at the end of the last section. If the LMSE method is "far-sighted," the k-nearest neighbor method is indeed very "near-sighted." It decides the border surface only by the local situation of the paradigm distribution. The perceptron method we are discussing next is, so to speak, moderately near-sighted.

Figure 9.3.1 gives a comparison of the LMSE method (Curve 4) and the nearest neighbor method (Curve 5). Curve 1 is obtained by the Bayesian method assuming the normal distributions for both classes. Curve 2 is obtained by an inadequate method which has not been explained in the text. Curve 3 is obtained by the Fisher discriminant with the point of intersection determined by (9.1.22). The author

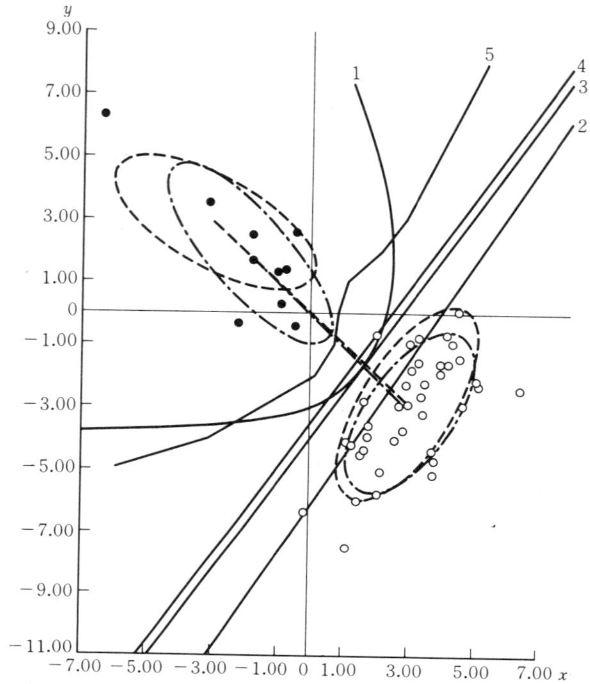

Figure 9.3.1 Comparison of the Bayesian method (1), Fisher's discriminant method (3), the LMSE method (4), and the nearest neighbor method (5).

thanks the student mathematician who contributed the drawing of the figure.

9.4 PERCEPTRON METHOD

The idea of perceptron was first introduced as a model of neural network [R-11], and its success was heralded with great fanfare. What made this success possible was not the brain model as such, but a simple mathematical algorithm that can be programmed easily on any computer. The method, as explained below, provides a decision procedure for the two-class case, M = 2. It assumes the paradigms to be linearly separable and the solution is obtained in a successive, adaptive fashion. Because of its simplicity, the method is still popular and is worth examining.

In Section 9.2, we noted that in the separable case, it is difficult, **unless** we resort to a rather complicated procedure such as Ho-Kashyap's algorithm, to achieve two goals, namely 1. to minimize the average of the squared distance from the plane to the paradigms, that is, to minimize the average of $[d(x^{(\alpha)})]^2$, and 2. to have all the paradigms of one class on one side of the plane and to have all the paradigms of the other class on the other side of the plane. It is then easy to guess that one of two goals will become easy if we abandon the other goal. The perceptron method aims just to separate the two groups by a hyperplane. As a matter of fact the choice of the force law is arbitrary and it serves the purpose of restricting the arbitrariness of induction underlying the problems of pattern recognition. In other words, it is just a heuristic principle which may or may not be the proper one. But, the perceptron in the separable case reveals in fact too much of the arbitrariness, which we have to devise some way to restrict to obtain a usable solution. The method we explain in the next section is one such method of restriction.

The perceptron method will give a prescription of how to improve a plane at hand when a point is encountered that is misclassified by the plane. Instead of taking the distance of the points from the decision plane, it would be still better to take the distance from the two auxiliary planes we considered in (9.2.3). Let us take $\eta_1 = \eta_2 = \eta > 0$ for simplicity. We note that misclassified paradigms of A_i will give nonpositive values to $[F(x^{(\alpha)}) - \eta]$ and misclassified paradigms of A_2 will give nonnegative values to $[F(x^{(\alpha)}) + \eta]$. Hence, the algorithm would be to minimize

$$J = -\sum_{\alpha \in M_1} [F(x^{(\alpha)}) - \eta] + \sum_{\alpha \in M_2} [F(x^{(\alpha)}) + \eta] \tag{9.4.1}$$

where M_1 is the set of misclassified paradigms of A_1 and M_2 is the set of misclassified paradigms of A_2. If we use the y-vectors, (9.2.5), and G-functions (9.2.6), (9.4.1) will become

$$J = -\sum_{\alpha \in M} [G(y^{(\alpha)}) - \eta] , \tag{9.4.2}$$

where M is all the misclassified paradigms, $M = M_1 \cup M_2$, that is, $y^{(\alpha)} \in M$ means

$$G(y^{(\alpha)}) - \eta \leq 0 \ . \qquad (9.4.3)$$

If we apply the gradient method (9.2.52), the "corrected" coefficient $c^{(\nu+1)}$ will be given by

$$c_i^{(\nu+1)} = c_i^{(\nu)} - \lambda^{(\nu)} \frac{\partial J}{\partial c_i}$$

$$= c_i^{(\nu)} + \lambda^{(\nu)} \sum_{\alpha \in M} y^{(\alpha)} \ , \qquad (9.4.4)$$

where M is defined by (9.4.3) where the G-function should be defined with the present values $c_i^{(\nu)}$ of the coefficient:

$$G^{(\nu)}(y) = \sum_{i=0}^{n+1} c_i^{(\nu)} y_i \ . \qquad (9.4.5)$$

For a larger flexibility, we put index ν on the λ in (9.4.4). In fact, we could expect the correction formula (9.2.52) will work with a variable λ insofar as its variability is bounded from above as well as from below. Since we are looking for a minimum of J, the factor $\lambda^{(\nu)}$ should be always positive. In the same way as we passed from (9.2.53) to (9.2.54), we can perform the correction step by step for each misclassified paradigm separately

$$c_i^{(\nu+1)} = c_i^{(\nu)} + \lambda^{(\nu)} y_i^{(\nu)} \qquad (9.4.6)$$

for

$$G^{(\nu)}(y^{(\nu)}) - \eta \leq 0 \qquad (9.4.7)$$

The procedure embodied in (9.4.6) and (9.4.7) constitutes the so-called perceptron algorithm. In practice, we have a given set of paradigms which we try one after another in such a way that each paradigm is taken up again and again. Every time a paradigm is misclassified [i.e., every time (9.4.7) is the case] we perform a correction and update the c's according to (9.4.6). The label ν is only given to the misclassified paradigms, not to those which have passed the test.

A correction induced by $y^{(\nu)}$ will bring to the plane to an "improved" position such that $G^{(\nu+1)}(y^{(\nu)})-\eta$ becomes larger than $G^{(\nu)}(y^{(\nu)})-\eta$ since

$$G^{(\nu+1)}(y^{(\nu)}) = G^{(\nu)}(y^{(\nu)}) + \lambda^{(\nu)} \sum_{i=0}^{n} (y_i^{(\nu)})^2 > G^{(\nu)}(y^{(\nu)}) . \tag{9.4.8}$$

But this does not guarantee that the new plane classifies $y^{(\nu)}$ correctly. In order that this may take place, $\lambda^{(\nu)}$ must be such that

$$\lambda^{(\nu)} > [\eta - G^{(\nu)}(y^{(\nu)})] \Big/ \sum_{i=1}^{n} (y_i^{(\nu)})^2 . \tag{9.4.9}$$

But, we usually do not require this of $\lambda^{(\nu)}$. The most common perceptron procedure assumes $\lambda^{(\nu)}$ is independent of ν. Such a perceptron will be referred to as the constant-λ perceptron. Whether we take a constant procedure or a variable-λ procedure, we have to know that the correction caused by a paradigm could happen in general to change the plane in such a way that another paradigm, which has passed the test previously, may now be misclassified.

The convergence, in a certain sense, of the process (9.4.6) is proven by the famous "perceptron convergence theorem." We want to explain the theorem according to Novikoff's version of the proof [N-1]. For this purpose we assume the following five conditions: 1. The $\lambda^{(\nu)}$ has both an upper and a lower bound

$$0 < \ell \le \lambda^{(\nu)} \le L ; \tag{9.4.10}$$

2. There exists only a finite number N of paradigms;
3. The paradigms are shown to the machine in such a sequence that each paradigm will reappear after any

arbitrary number of terms; 4. The paradigm points are in a finite region of the x-space, hence also of the y-space; and 5. The paradigms are linearly separable, that is, there exists a hyperplane in the y-space such that all the paradigm points satisfy

$$G^{+}(y^{(\alpha)}) > 0 \ , \quad \alpha = 1,2,\ldots,N \ , \qquad (9.4.11)$$

where G^{+} is defined by suitably chosen values of the c's.

A simple lemma that ensues from conditions (2) and (3) is that there exists a positive constant η such that, with the G^{+}-function (9.4.11),

$$G^{+}(y^{(\alpha)}) > \eta \ , \quad \alpha = 1,2,\ldots,N \ , \qquad (9.4.12)$$

because there exists a minimum of $G^{+}(y^{(\alpha)})$, $\alpha = 1, 2,\ldots,N$, N being finite. A further lemma is that, if there is a set of c's that satisfies (9.4.12) with a certain value of η for all paradigms, then there exists a set of c's that satisfies (9.4.12) with any other value of η. This is because if we multiply η by a positive constant, we need only multiply the c's by the same constant in (9.4.12).

The main body of the convergence theorem states that there is a finite integer ν^* such that there will be no revision of the type (9.4.6), (9.4.7) beyond ν^*. This is proven by showing that if the revision were to continue infinitely, we would come to a contradiction.

On the one hand, we have from (9.4.6) and (9.4.7)

$$\begin{aligned}\sum_{i=1}^{n+1} (c_i^{(\nu+1)})^2 &= \sum_{i=1}^{n+1} (c_i^{(\nu)})^2 + (\lambda^{(\nu)})^2 \sum_{i=1}^{n+1} (y_i^{(\nu)})^2 \\ &\quad + 2\,\lambda^{(\nu)} \sum_{i=1}^{n+1} c_i^{(\nu)} y_i^{(\nu)} \le \sum_{i=1}^{n+1} (c_i^{(\nu)})^2 \\ &\quad + (\lambda^{(\nu)})^2 \sum_{i=1}^{n+1} (y_i^{(\nu)})^2 + 2\,\lambda^{(\nu)} \eta \ . \end{aligned} \qquad (9.4.13)$$

Because $\sum_{i=1}^{n+1} (y_i^{(\nu)})^2$ is finite due to condition (4) and $\lambda^{(\nu)}$ is bounded from above by L due to condition (1), there exists a positive number A independent of ν such that

$$\sum_{i=1}^{n+1} (c_i^{(\nu+1)})^2 < \sum_{i=1}^{n+1} (c_i^{(\nu)})^2 + A \; . \qquad (9.4.14)$$

Starting with $\nu = 1$, the value of $\sum_{i=1}^{n+1} (c_i^{(\nu)})^2$ may increase at each step of ν by an increment that is less than A. Hence, taking A larger than $\sum_{i=1}^{n+1} (c_i^{(1)})$, we find

$$\sum_{i=1}^{n+1} (c_i^{(\nu+1)})^2 < (\nu + 1) \; A \; . \qquad (9.4.15)$$

On the other hand, from the condition (5) of separability and the subsequent lemmas we conclude that there exists a set of values c_i^+ such that

$$\sum_{i=1}^{n+1} c_i^+ \; y_i^{(\alpha)} > \eta \qquad (9.4.16)$$

for any given value of η for all paradigms α. From (9.4.6) and (9.4.16)

$$\sum_{i=1}^{n+1} c_i^+ \; c_i^{(\nu+1)} = \sum_{i=1}^{n+1} c_i^+ \; c_i^{(\nu)} + \lambda^{(\nu)} \sum_{i=1}^{n+1} c_i^+ \; y_i^{(\nu)} \qquad (9.4.17)$$

$$> \sum_{i=1}^{n+1} c_i^+ \; c_i^{(\nu)} + \lambda^{(\nu)} \eta \qquad (9.4.18)$$

meaning that the value of $\sum_{i=1}^{n+1} c_i^+ c_i^{(\nu)}$ increases at each step of ν by an increment larger than $\lambda^{(\nu)}\eta$ which is larger than $\ell\eta$ due to condition (1), (5.4.10). Taking a positive constant B smaller than $\ell\eta$ and writing C for $\sum_{i=1}^{n+1} c_i^+ c_i^{(1)}$, we can write

$$\sum_{i=1}^{n+1} c_i^+ c_i^{(\nu+1)} > C + \nu B \qquad (9.4.19)$$

or for sufficiently large ν and a suitable positive constant B'

$$\sum_{i=1}^{n+1} c_i^+ c_i^{(\nu+1)} > \nu B' \qquad (9.4.20)$$

The scalar product of two vectors is never larger than the product of their lengths, therefore, we have

$$\left[\sum_{i=1}^{n+1} (c_i^{(\nu+1)})^2\right]^{\frac{1}{2}} \left[\sum_{i=1}^{n+1} (c_i^+)^2\right]^{\frac{1}{2}} \geq \sum_{i=1}^{n+1} c_i^+ c_i^{(\nu+1)} . \qquad (9.4.21)$$

Noting that the c_i^+ are constant for the given set of paradigms, we conclude, with some positive number B"

$$\sum_{i=1}^{n+1} (c_i^{(\nu+1)})^2 \geq \left[\sum_{i=1}^{n+1} c_i^+ c_i^{(\nu+1)}\right]^2 \Big/ \sum_{i=1}^{n+1} (c_i^+)^2 > \nu^2 B" \qquad (9.4.22)$$

for sufficiently large ν.

If the revision process (9.4.6) continued indefinitely, at some ν, the two inequalities (9.4.15) and (9.4.22) are bound to contradict each other because ν^2 grows faster than ν. Therefore, there must exist the last correction for which the ν will be called ν^*. This completes the proof.

We can consider the coefficients $c_i^{(\nu^*+1)}$ as determined by the ν^*-th correction as the c_i^+. In fact, if they were not c^+, there should exist at least one paradigm $y^{(\alpha)}$ for which

$$G^{(\nu+1)}(y^{(\alpha)}) \leq \eta \ . \tag{9.4.23}$$

But according to condition (3), this particular paradigm will reappear after the ν^*-th correction. This will contradict the condition that the ν^*-th correction is the last correction. Hence, the $c_i^{(\nu^*+1)}$ must be a possible set of c's that qualify as the c_i^+ [i.e., the solution of (9.4.12)]. In practice, we arrange the N paradigms in a row and we repeat this row cyclically, carrying out corrections as required. If correction is no longer needed for one whole cycle of the paradigms, we can consider the current values of the c 's as the solution.

We should be warned against an illusion that we can make the separation of the two auxiliary planes as large as we want by making η large enough. We can satisfy (9.4.12) for a twice as large value of η by simply doubling the magnitude of all the c's, and this will not change the value of ε (9.2.9).

When the paradigms are not linearly separable, the revision process will go on forever and the c-values will oscillate. To dampen the oscillation, we may resort to an ad hoc artifice which consists in making the magnitude of the correction gradually die down, for instance taking

$$\lambda^{(\nu)} \propto e^{-\beta\nu} \tag{9.4.24}$$

with some constant

$$\beta > 0 \ . \tag{9.4.25}$$

Before we discuss disadvantages of the perceptron in the next section, we want to mention some of the merits of the method. Different from most of the other pattern recognition methods, this one deals squarely with the finite number of given paradigms. It gives a separating hyperplane for the two groups of given paradigms whenever such a hyperplane exists. Correspondingly, the "convergence theorem" here does not assume a fictitious infinite number of paradigms. This is a theoretically sound feature of the method.

In addition, the method has a definitive practical advantage. The computation is extremely simple. The convergence is usually much faster than the adaptive version of the LMSE method. If we keep the same set of given paradigms and use them cyclically until the convergence (discontinuation of corrections) takes place, we have of course to keep all the given paradigms in the memory space. But, in practice, we can use the method "on line" as the new paradigms come in, and perform the correction as required, and forget about all these paradigms that were once correctly classified. In this mode of usage, the method does not require the storing of individual paradigms. All the "past experience" is kept in a nutshell in the current values of the coefficients. When the paradigms are plentiful, we can use the method in this mode. The requirements of the memory space are extremely low and the method is truly adaptive.

9.5 WELL-BALANCED PERCEPTRON

An advantage the LMSE method has over the perceptron method is that it gives a decision surface, though perhaps not the best, even when the paradigms are not linearly separable, whereas the perceptron does not give a solution in such a case and is easily disturbed by a single freak paradigm near the border which breaks the separability. We can suppress the oscillation by a method, for example, in (9.4.24) and (9.4.25), but no guarantee can be given that the border surface will finally settle down at a reasonable position. This shortcoming is one of the consequences of the fact that the perceptron does not take the global situation into consideration and tries to decide the border surface by the local situation near the border, namely, only by the misclassified paradigms.

On the other hand, in the separable case, the perceptron method exhibits another kind of inadequacy. If the paradigms are linearly separable, the perceptron will give us any hyperplane that separates the two groups. The plane to which the method converges depends on the original trial solution $\{c_i^{(1)}\}$, the increment coefficient λ, and the order in which the paradigms are shown to the machine. What the convergence theorem guarantees is that in the separable case, the method will land one separating plane and without specifying which plane. In reality, with a constant lambda method, the very "ill-balanced" position of the plane is often given. This effect is particularly marked and causes a nuisance when the two groups of paradigms leave a wide empty space in between. This is theoretically inevitable, because this indetermination is due to the inductive ambiguity inherent in any pattern recognition.

To amend this situation an attempt has been made, and a successful mathematical algorithm was discovered, to draw two parallel hyperplanes between the two groups of points and decide the direction of the planes by maximizing the distance between the hyperplanes [L-1]. This method, though mathematically interesting, is again too sensitive to the local situation near the border surface.

When we state that a perceptron solution has often an "ill-balanced" position, should we not interpret ourselves as meaning that the plane has a wrong location relative to the overall distribution of paradigms? If so, we should consider the positions of all the paradigms in some manner, in particular those paradigms that pass the test and consequently, do not contribute to the decision of the coefficients $\{c_i^{(\nu)}\}$. The perceptron does indeed waste a great deal of useful information carried by those paradigms that do not cause the revision of the coefficients.

In this section, we want to explain a method to improve the perceptron by causing it to settle down on a plane that is "better balanced" relative to the whole assembly of paradigms. This is admittedly a remedy of esthetic nature to eliminate in some cases shortcomings of the perceptron, but not an attempt to revise the entire framework of the approach. Hence, the degree to which we make use of the wasted information is limited and the nature of improvement is rather simple. Yet, the results obtained are rather remarkable and have proved to be quite useful in practice. The idea was originally introduced in

1964, and has since been gradually developed in collaboration with T. Kaminuma [W-9], [W-43], [W-10], [K-18].

As we have also seen relative to the solution of the LMSE method, the position of a decision plane can be evaluated with regard to the direction of the normal and the position of the intersection of the plane and its normal (or the distance of the plane from the origin). We call the former "directional balance" and the latter "weight balance." In the directional balance, the well-balanced method tries to keep the normal direction not too far from the direction connecting the centers of mass of the two classes. In the weight balance, the method tries to keep the distances of the two centers of mass from the plane in good balance. Both corrections are made in such a way that an eventual convergence to a separating position may not be intefered with.

Therefore, the method uses the global situation only to the extent that it is condensed in the position and weight of the centers of mass. Ideally speaking, this is not adequate as the expression of the global situation, but it is a feasible compromise that can be made without stepping entirely out of the framework of the perceptron. There are two modes of using the perceptron: one is to use a limited number of paradigms repeatedly until a convergence is achieved (i.e., until the correction procedure stops), the other, to use only the new paradigms for trial and correction. In the first mode, we keep all the data about the available paradigms in the memory, but in the second we keep the "past experience," in essence , only in the current values of the coefficients. In the second mode, the perceptron is economical on computer burden. In this sense, the demand of the well-balanced method is not very bad either, because all we keep in the memory is the updated values of the coefficients and the updated values of the positions and the weights of the two centers of mass.

The distinction between the adaptive and nonadaptive approaches is largely a relative matter. If an algorithm can be called adaptive on the grounds that it produces an improved solution every time a new paradigm arrives, then any algorithm can act as an adaptive algorithm provided that a large memory space and a sufficiently high-speed computation are available. Indeed, if we keep all the records of the past paradigms in the memory, any algorithm can produce a new solution every time a new paradigm arrives, considering all past and present paradigms. What, therefore, makes an algorithm adaptive is a **relative** smallness of the computer burden, which is a matter of degree. The perceptron in its historical origin was supposed to be a kind of brain model, and its property of being adaptive was highly admired. But, stripped of its glory as a brain model, the property of adaptability has lost its mystical appeal. It is particularly so, since the computer memory and speed have made tremendous progress in recent years.

An amazing bonus one gets by using the well-balanced version of perceptron is that the convergence becomes much faster than the usual version of perceptron. This is a result of the fact that a well-balanced position requires less correction by the later arrivals, because it foresees better what will come later, so to speak. In discussing the function of the perceptron, we usually consider only the training period. The "new" arrival is tested and the correction is made if it is misclassified. This means that all the new arrivals have in reality the known classification. They are not new arrivals in an "application period." Even if the perceptron has reached a stationary position in the training period, we do not know what will happen when true new arrivals with unknown classification start to arrive in the application period. The usual "ill-balanced" solution will tend to fail in the application period. The "well-balanced" solution has a better chance to work correctly in the application period. The fact that the well-balanced method converges much faster in the training period can be taken as evidence supporting the guess that it will fare much better in the application period.

Of the two kinds of balance, let us first discuss the weight balance. Let N_1 and N_2 be, respectively, the number of the paradigms of A_1 and that of A_2 , which have so far been shown to the machine whether or not they have passed the test with the current coefficients. If the paradigms are taken randomly from a given population, we can expect that the ratio N_1/N_2 will fluctuate, but not very violently, about a certain constant value, and the fluctuation will, of course, decrease as the magnitudes of N_1 and N_2 increase. It is understood that if the same point reappears more than once, each appearance will be counted separately in N_1 or N_2. Let D_j (j=1,2) be the distance of the center of mass of class A_j from the plane. In other words, D_j is $(1/N_j)$ times the total sum of the distances of points of class A_j from the plane. The "desirable" position, as far as the weight balance is concerned, is defined by

$$\frac{D_1}{D_2} = \varphi\left(\frac{N_1}{N_2}\right) , \tag{9.5.1}$$

where φ is an arbitrary function of the argument N_1/N_2, which the user can select to suit his sense of balance. Because this relation must be symmetrical with respect to A_1 and A_2, the interchange of N_1 and N_2 should result in the reciprocal value of φ:

$$\varphi(r) = 1/\varphi(1/r) . \tag{9.5.2}$$

This requirement includes, as a special case, also

$$\varphi(1) = 1 , \tag{9.5.3}$$

which is quite natural from the meaning of the φ-function introduced by (9.5.1).

If we want D_1/D_2 not to be affected by N_1 and N_2, we should adopt a constant value (perhaps unity) for the φ-function. But, in general, it seems to be natural to assume that the φ-function is a monotonically increasing function. For, the more points that belong to the class A_j, the larger extension is expected to be occupied by the members of A_j. We have already criticized the LMSE method for the opposite tendency expressed in (9.2.39) which in our present notation would mean

$$\varphi(r) = 1/r . \tag{9.5.4}$$

If paradigm points are distributed with a constant density about their center of mass, the radius ρ_j of the n-dimensional sphere about the center of mass and the number N_j of points inside the sphere will be in a relation of the type

$$N_j \propto \rho_j^{\,n} \quad . \tag{9.5.5}$$

If we assume that D_j is proportional to ρ_j we obtain

$$\left(\frac{D_1}{D_2}\right)^n = \frac{N_1}{N_2} \tag{9.5.6}$$

or

$$\varphi(r) = r^{(1/n)} \quad , \tag{9.5.7}$$

which is a rather slowly increasing function of r if n is large. This is only one of the possible assumptions, but we used it with success for most of our experiments.

What the weight balance algorithm does is to place the "corrected" plane at the desirable position (9.5.1) every time a correction is performed according to (9.4.6), taking advantage of the fact that the $\lambda^{(\nu)}$ need not be a constant. If the $\lambda^{(\nu)}$-value required to satisfy (9.5.1) goes outside the upper or lower bounds (i.e., larger than L or smaller than ℓ), we replace it by L or ℓ, respectively. But, choosing L and ℓ, respectively, sufficiently large and sufficiently small, we can usually satisfy the requirement (9.5.1) easily.

Let us use the index ν for the number of corrections as in (9.4.6), and denote by $A_j^{(\nu)}$ the set of $N_j^{(\nu)}$ paradigms of class A_j as shown up to and inclusive of the ν-th correction. This set will include the same paradigm as different members as many as the number of times it has been shown to the machine. This set will include all the paradigms whether or not they have caused correction according to (9.4.6) and (9.4.7). Then the distance of the center of mass of $A_j^{(\nu)}$ from the corrected plane $G^{(\nu+1)}(y) = 0$ is given by [see (9.2.2) and (9.2.6)]

$$D_j^{(\nu)} = \frac{1}{N_j^{(\nu)}} \sum_{\alpha \in A_j^{(\nu)}} G^{(\nu+1)}(y^{(\alpha)}) \Bigg/ \left(\sum_{i=0}^{n} c_i^{(\nu+1)2} \right)^{\frac{1}{2}} \tag{9.5.8}$$

Even if an individual term $G^{(\nu+1)}(y^{(\alpha)})$ occasionally becomes negative their sum over $A_j^{(\nu)}$ usually becomes positive for a small ν. This, however, should be checked in the program. The condition (9.5.1) at the ν-th stage will become

$$\frac{\sum_{\alpha \in A_1^{(\nu)}} G^{(\nu+1)}(y^{(\alpha)})}{\sum_{\alpha \in A_2^{(\nu)}} G^{(\nu+1)}(y^{(\alpha)})} = \frac{N_1^{(\nu)}}{N_2^{(\nu)}} \varphi \left(\frac{N_1^{(\nu)}}{N_2^{(\nu)}} \right) . \tag{9.5.9}$$

Expressing $G^{(\nu+1)}(y^{(\alpha)})$ in terms of the $c_i^{(\nu+1)}$ of (9.4.6) and writing

$$\kappa^{(\nu)} = \frac{N_1^{(\nu)}}{N_2^{(\nu)}} \varphi \left(\frac{N_1^{(\nu)}}{N_2^{(\nu)}} \right) \tag{9.5.10}$$

we obtain from (9.5.9)

$$\sum_{\alpha \in A_1^{(\nu)}} \sum_{i=0}^{n} (c_i^{(\nu)} + \lambda^{(\nu)} y_i^{(\nu)}) y_i^{(\alpha)}$$

$$= \kappa^{(\nu)} \sum_{\alpha \in A_2^{(\nu)}} \sum_{i=0}^{n} (c_i^{(\nu)} + \lambda^{(\nu)} y_i^{(\nu)}) y_i^{(\alpha)} \tag{9.5.11}$$

or solving for $\lambda^{(\nu)}$

$$\lambda^{(\nu)} = - \frac{\sum_{i=0}^{n} c_i^{(\nu)} \left(N_1^{(\nu)} m_{1,i}^{(\nu)} + \kappa^{(\nu)} N_2^{(\nu)} m_{2,i}^{(\nu)} \right)}{\sum_{i=0}^{n} y_i^{(\nu)} \left(N_1^{(\nu)} m_{1,i}^{(\nu)} + \kappa^{(\nu)} N_2^{(\nu)} m_{2,i}^{(\nu)} \right)} . \tag{9.5.12}$$

In this expression $m_{1,i}^{(\nu)}$ and $m_{2,i}^{(\nu)}$ are the centers of mass (in the x-space) of the paradigms at the ν-th stage:

$$m_{1,i}^{(\nu)} = \frac{1}{N_1^{(\nu)}} \sum_{\alpha \in A_1^{(\nu)}} y_i^{(\alpha)} = \frac{1}{N_1^{(\nu)}} \sum_{\alpha \in A_1^{(\nu)}} x_i^{(\alpha)}$$

$$m_{2,i}^{(\nu)} = - \frac{1}{N_2^{(\nu)}} \sum_{\alpha \in A_2^{(\nu)}} y_i^{(\alpha)} = \frac{1}{N_2^{(\nu)}} \sum_{\alpha \in A_2^{(\nu)}} x_i^{(\alpha)} , \tag{9.5.13}$$

where $x_0^{(\alpha)} = +1$ irrespective of whether $\alpha \in A_1^{(\nu)}$ or $\alpha \in A_2^{(\nu)}$. The value of $\lambda^{(\nu)}$ given by (9.5.12), provided

$$\ell \le \lambda^{(\nu)} \le L \tag{9.5.14}$$

is to be used in (5.4.6) to obtain the revised coefficients $c_i^{(\nu+1)}$ when the revision is caused by the ν-th misclassified paradigm $y_i^{(\nu)}$. The sets $A_1^{(\nu)}$ and $A_2^{(\nu)}$ should include all the paradigms, whether or not misclassified, up to and including the ν-th misclassified paradigms. In the second mode of the usage of perceptron the machine should store, in addition to the updated values of $c_i^{(\nu)}$, the updated values of $m_{1,i}^{(\nu)}$, $m_{2,i}^{(\nu)}$, $(i = 0,1,\ldots,n)$ $N_1^{(\nu)}$, and $N_2^{(\nu)}$. In the first mode, we have to keep all the data about the available paradigms. If $\lambda^{(\nu)}$ is smaller than ℓ, we replace it by ℓ, and if larger than L, we replace it by L. Due to this compromise and to the fact that the weight balancing takes place

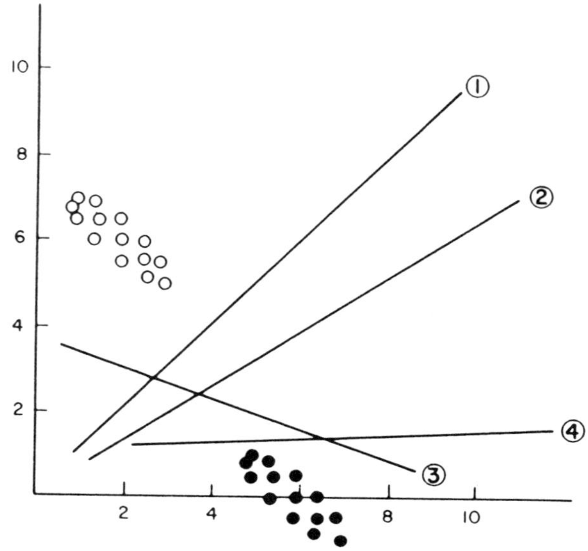

Figure 9.5.1 The ordinary perceptron method leaves the final plane in any odd place as far as it separates the two groups of paradigms.

only when correction is called for by (9.4.7), the final plane occasionally does not rigorously satisfy (9.5.1) for all the paradigms; however, usually the final plane obtained by this method is better-balanced than by the constant lambda method. Particularly, when combined with the directional balancing, it shows an excellent performance. Figure 9.5.1 shows how the final plane in the constant lambda method varies depending on the initial trial function $c_i^{(\nu)}$, the value of the constant λ, and the order in which the paradigms are shown. Figure 9.5.2 shows the corresponding results of the weight balance method.

We tried two alternative algorithms to perform the directional balance, and found that both work well. The directional balance (I) uses the following simple fact. Suppose we perform the revision of the $c_i^{(\nu)}$ with a constant $\lambda^{(\nu)} = \lambda$ every time a new paradigm arrives, whether or not it is misclassified by the current values of the $c_i^{(\nu)}$. Thus, $c_i^{(\nu+1)}$ will be according to (9.4.6)

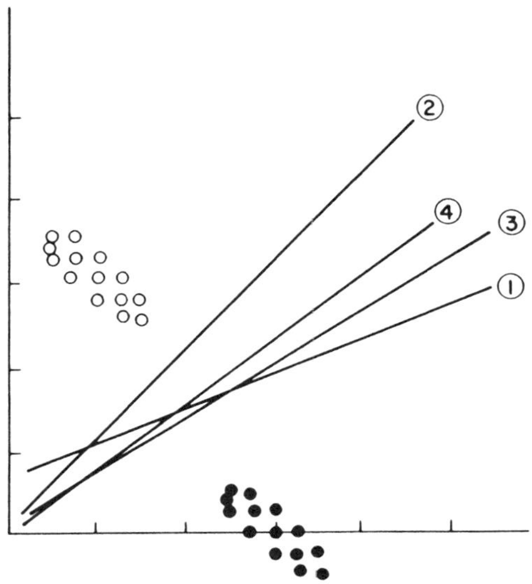

Figure 9.5.2 The weight balance method brings the plane to a more acceptable position such that the centers of mass of the two groups are proportionately distanced from the plane.

$$c_i^{(\nu+1)} = c_i^{(1)} + \lambda \sum_{\nu'=1}^{\nu} Y_i^{(\nu')}$$

$$= c_i^{(1)} + \lambda \left(N_1^{(\nu)} m_{1,i}^{(\nu)} - N_2^{(\nu)} m_{2,i}^{(\nu)}\right). \quad (9.5.15)$$

If the first term $c_i^{(1)}$ is negligible (or put equal to zero) and if $N_1^{(\nu)} = N_2^{(\nu)}$, then

$$c_i^{(\nu+1)} \propto (m_{1,i}^{(\nu)} - m_{2,i}^{(\nu)}) \equiv q_i^{(\nu)} \quad (i = 1,2,\ldots,n) \ , \quad (9.5.16)$$

that is, the normal of the plane defined by $c_i^{(\nu+1)}$ is directed parallel to the line connecting the two centers of mass in the x-plane. We can see from (9.5.16) that all the c_i ($i = 0,1,\ldots,n$) grow roughly proportional to the number of paradigms. In

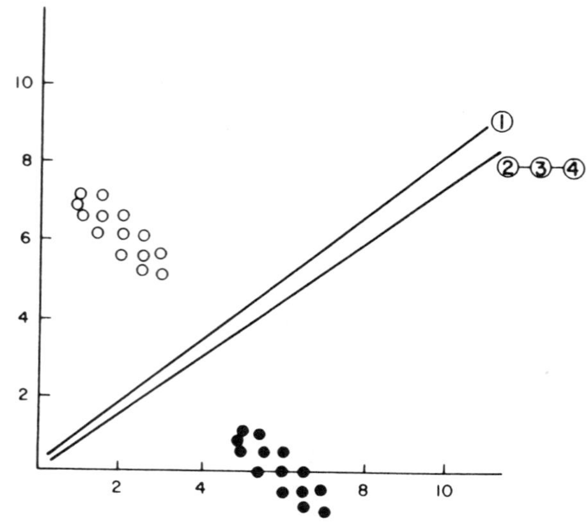

Figure 9.5.3 A result of the combination of weight balance and direction balance (I).

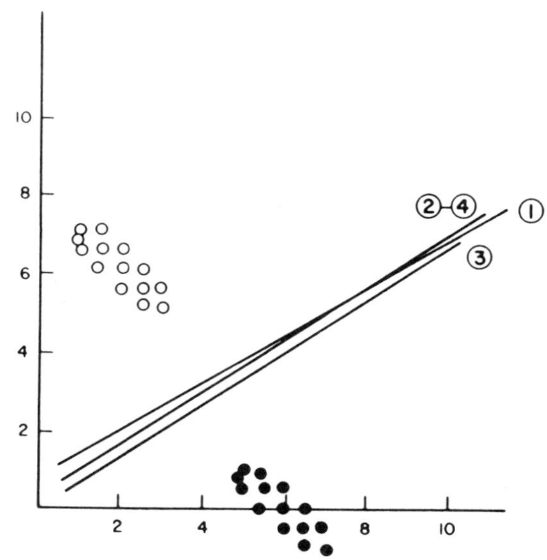

Figure 9.5.4 A result of the combination of weight balance and direction balance (II).

particular, the $c_o^{(\nu+1)}$, apart from $c_o^{(1)}$, gives directly λ-times the difference $N_1^{(\nu)} - N_2^{(\nu)}$ of paradigms so far shown to the machine.

The strategy we adopted was to apply the revision rule (9.4.6) for those paradigms that are not misclassified with the coefficient $\lambda^{(\nu)}$ replaced by

$$\lambda^{(\nu)'} = \lambda^{(\nu)} e^{-\beta\nu} \tag{9.5.17}$$

and apply the revision rule for the misclassified paradigms with $\lambda^{(\nu)}$ without the exponential factor. The $\lambda^{(\nu)}$ here is the value decided by (9.5.12) and (9.5.14). The numbering ν applies to all the paradigms. Because $\lambda^{(\nu)}$ is not a constant and $N_1^{(\nu)}$ and $N_2^{(\nu)}$ are not necessarily equal, the condition (9.5.16) is only approximately realized. But, this procedure at the earlier stages (roughly $\nu < 1/\beta$) brings the plane to a well-balanced position both with respect to direction and weight. After ν becomes large (roughly $\nu > 1/\beta$), only the weight balance remains in force and converges to a final plane according to the convergence theorem. In a way, we can interpret this procedure as preparing a starting plane with a good direction for the converging process for $\nu > 1/\beta$. This procedure not only brings the final plane to a good position, but also accelerates convergence greatly.

The directional balance (II) is based on the following consideration. Let $\xi_i^{(\nu)}$ be the point of intersection between the ν-th plane and the straight line connecting the two centers of mass at the ν-th stage in the x-space. Keeping the point $\xi_i^{(\nu)}$, we turn the plane so that the correctional increment of the normal is in the direction connecting the two centers of mass.

$$\frac{c_i^{(\nu+1)} - c_i^{(\nu)}}{|c_i^{(\nu)}|} = \delta^{(\nu)} \frac{q_i^{(\nu)}}{|q_i^{(\nu)}|} \tag{9.5.18}$$

with

$$q_i^{(\nu)} = m_{1,i}^{(\nu)} - m_{2,i}^{(\nu)} \tag{9.5.19}$$

and

$$|c_i^{(\nu)}| = \sqrt{\sum_{i=1}^{n} c_i^{(\nu)2}} \tag{9.5.20}$$

and

$$|q_i^{(\nu)}| = \sqrt{\sum_{i=1}^{n} q_i^{(\nu)2}} \; . \tag{9.5.21}$$

The scalar factor δ is to be explained later.

Since the the point $\xi_i^{(\nu)}$ should be on the ν-th plane as well as on the $(\nu+1)$st plane, we have

$$\sum_{i=1}^{n} c_i^{(\nu)} \xi_i^{(\nu)} + c_o^{(\nu)} = 0 \tag{9.5.22}$$

and

$$\sum_{i=1}^{n} c_i^{(\nu+1)} \xi_i^{(\nu)} + c_o^{(\nu+1)} = 0 \; . \tag{9.5.23}$$

On the other hand, because the point $\xi_i^{(\nu)}$ is supposed to be on the straight line connecting the two centers of mass, we should have

$$\xi_i^{(\nu)} = a\, m_{1,i}^{(\nu)} + (1-a) m_{2,i}^{(\nu)} \tag{9.5.24}$$

with some real number a. Substituting (9.5.24) into (9.5.22) we obtain

$$a = - \frac{\sum_{i=1}^{n} c_i^{(\nu)} m_{2,i}^{(\nu)} + c_o^{(\nu)}}{\sum_{i=1}^{n} c_i^{(\nu)} q_i^{(\nu)}} \; . \tag{9.5.25}$$

Substituting back this value of a into (9.5.24), we obtain

$$\xi_i^{(\nu)} = m_{2,i}^{(\nu)} - \frac{\left(\sum_{j=1}^{n} c_j^{(\nu)} m_{2,j}^{(\nu)} + c_o^{(\nu)}\right) q_i^{(\nu)}}{\sum_{j=1}^{n} c_j^{(\nu)} q_j^{(\nu)}} \; . \tag{9.5.26}$$

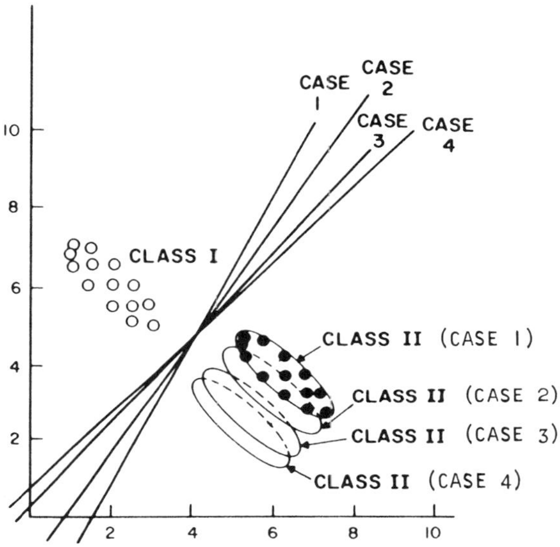

Figure 9.5.5 The paradigms of Class I are fixed, whereas the paradigms of Class II are gradually moved. Our balance method moves the separation plane accordingly.

From (9.5.18)

$$c_i^{(\nu+1)} = c_i^{(\nu)} + \delta^{(\nu)} \frac{|c_i^{(\nu)}|}{|q_i^{(\nu)}|} q_i^{(\nu)}. \qquad (9.5.27)$$

Subtraction of (9.5.22) from (9.5.23) yields

$$c_o^{(\nu+1)} = c_o^{(\nu)} - \sum_{i=1}^{n} \left(c_i^{(\nu+1)} - c_i^{(\nu)}\right) \xi_i^{(\nu)}, \qquad (9.5.28)$$

where $\xi_i^{(\nu)}$ is given by (9.5.26). The multiplier $\delta^{(\nu)}$ consists of three functions

$$\delta^{(\nu)} = \delta_1^{(\nu)} \delta_2^{(\nu)} \delta_3^{(\nu)} \qquad (9.5.29)$$

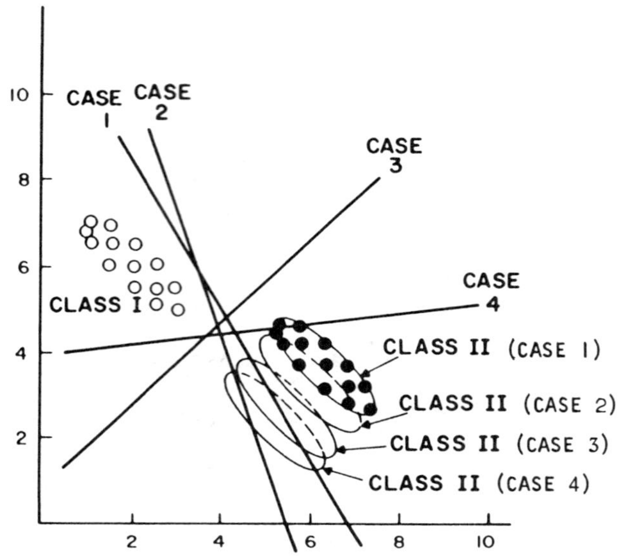

Figure 9.5.6 The exact LMSE method is shown as being too sensitive to the relative positions of the two groups.

with

$$\delta_1^{(\nu)} = e^{-\beta\nu} \tag{9.5.30}$$

and

$$\delta_2^{(\nu)} = \sum_{i=1}^{n} c_i^{(\nu)} q_i^{(\nu)} \Big/ \left|\sum c_i^{(\nu)} q_i^{(\nu)}\right| \tag{9.5.31}$$

and δ_3 is set equal to unity insofar as $|c_i^{(\nu)}|/|q_i^{(\nu)}|$ is less than a certain number K and replaced by $K\,|q_i^{(\nu)}|/|c_i^{(\nu)}|$ beyond that limit. The first factor $\delta_1^{(\nu)}$ means that the directional correction is to be performed at earlier stages and should fade away for larger $\nu(>1/\beta)$. The second factor sees to it that if the cosine between $q_i^{(\nu)}$ and the normal $c_i^{(\nu)}/\,|c_i^{(\nu)}|$ is less than $\pi/2$, the normal will be turned to the direction of $q_i^{(\nu)}$, and if it is more than $\pi/2$, the normal will be turned to the direction of $-q_i^{(\nu)}$. This will not interfere with the rule that A_i should be placed on the positive side of the

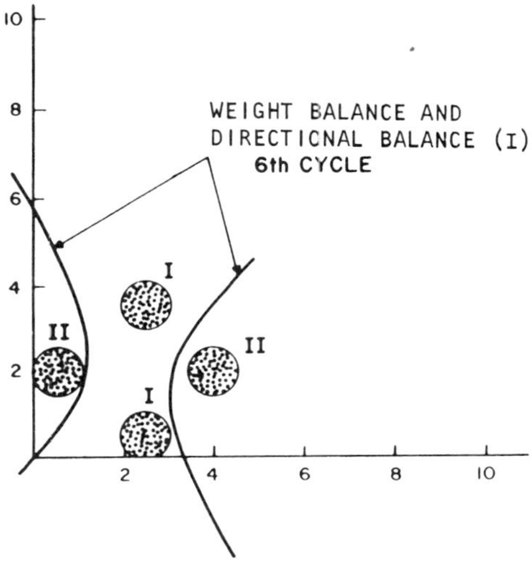

Figure 9.5.7 The result of the combination of weight balance and direction balance (I) using x^2, xy, y^2 as additional independent variables.

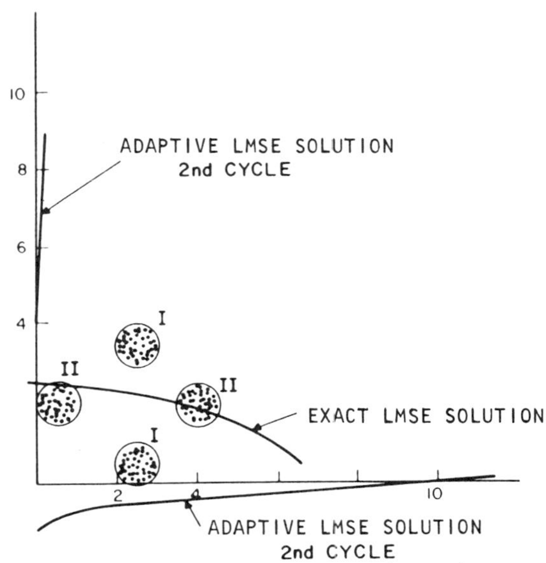

Figure 9.5.8 The same data as in Figure 9.5.7 are used with the help of the second degree variables as additional independent variables, but the method used is the LMSE.

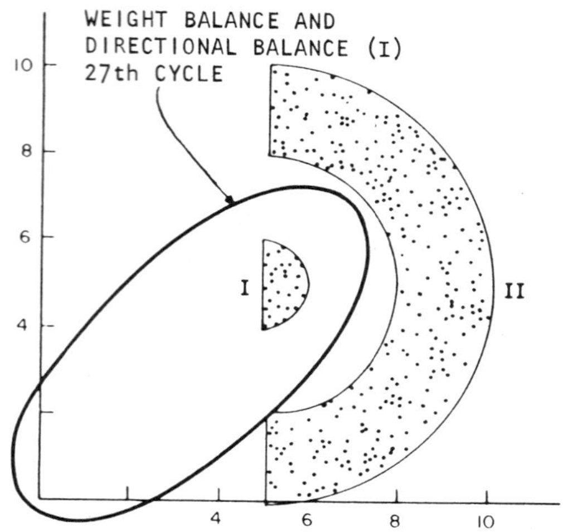

Figure 9.5.9 The method is the same as in Figure 9.5.7, but the data are different.

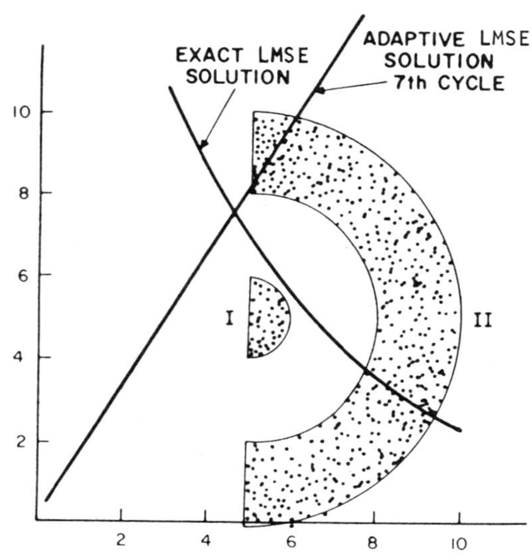

Figure 9.5.10 The method is the same as Figure 9.5.8 and the data are the same as in Figure 9.5.9.

plane, since this last term depends not only on c_i $(i = 1,2,\dots,n)$ but also on c_o.

Figure 9.5.3 shows the result of the combination of the weight balance with the directional balance (I). Figure 9.5.4 shows the result of the combination of the weight balanced with the directional balance (II). Both show that the methods settled on well-balanced positions. Figure 9.5.5 shows how the solution by the weight balance combined with the directional balance (II) gradually changes when the relative position of the two groups of paradigms changes. Figure 9.5.6 shows how the (exact) LMSE method (with $\eta_1 = \eta_2 = 1$) is overly sensitive to the relative position of the two groups.

Figures 9.5.7 and 9.5.9 show the results of the combination of the weight balance and the directional balance (I) using the second degree terms such as x^2, xy, y^2 as independent variables along with x and y (where x and y mean the abscissa and the ordinate). Figures 9.5.8 and 9.5.10 show how the LMSE behaves poorly under the same circumstances.

It should be repeated again that the idea of balancing has no logical necessity, but is a kind of heuristic principle, which gives usually an esthetically agreeable result. It does not necessarily guarantee success in practical problems, but has a good chance of leading to a successful solution or near to it. This is another good example exhibiting that the inductive ambiguity lies in the case of pattern recognition. The illustrations of this section were prepared by T. Kaminuma.

9.6 POTENTIAL FUNCTION METHOD

We learned in Section 8.5 a method to approximate the density function $p(x)$ with the help of an influence function $\Delta(x^{(\alpha)} - x,\rho)$ [see Equation (8.5.12)]. If there are two classes, A_1 and A_2, we can write

$$p(x|A_j) = \frac{1}{N_j} \sum_{\alpha \in A_j} \Delta(x^{(\alpha)} - x,\rho) \ , \tag{9.6.1}$$

where $\alpha \in A_j$ indicates a summation over the N_j available paradigms of A_j. If we approximate the prior probability $p(A_j)$ by N_j/N, $N = N_1 + N_2$, we obtain the decision probability $p(A_j|x)$

$$p(A_j|x) \propto p(x|A_j)p(A_j) \propto \sum_{\alpha \in A_j} \Delta(x^{(\alpha)} - x, \rho). \tag{9.6.2}$$

We can then introduce a discriminant function $g(x)$

$$g(x) \equiv p(x|A_1)p(A_1) - p(x|A_2)p(A_2)$$

$$\propto \sum_{\alpha \in A_1} \Delta(x^{(\alpha)} - x, \rho) - \sum_{\alpha \in A_2} \Delta(x^{(\alpha)} - x, \rho)$$

$$= \sum q^{(\alpha)} \Delta(x^{(\alpha)} - x, \rho) , \tag{9.6.3}$$

where $$q^{(\alpha)} = 1 \text{ or } -1 , \tag{9.6.4}$$

according as $$\alpha \in A_1 \text{ or } A_2 . \tag{9.6.5}$$

We can visualize $g(x)$ as a kind of "potential field" generated by "charges" $q^{(\alpha)}$ such that a positive value of the potential $g(x) > 0$ means that the field point x belongs to class A_1 and a negative value of the potential $g(x) < 0$ means that the field point x belongs to class A_2. Each paradigm acts as the source of this field, and its charge is either positive or negative according to whether the paradigm belong to A_1 or A_2.

It should be noted at this stage that as far as the effect of decision making is concerned, the signature of $g(x)$ is the only thing that matters, and an exact approximation of the value of distribution by (9.6.1) is not important.

The potential function method, in the narrow sense of the word, assumes, as in (8.5.22), that $\Delta(x - x', \rho)$ can be expressed as a sum of a finite number ν of terms in such a way that

$$\Delta(x - x', \rho) = \Psi(x, x') \equiv \sum_{i=1}^{\nu} \phi_i(x)\phi_i(x') , \tag{9.6.6}$$

where $\{\phi_i(x)\}$ is a set of normalized orthogonal base functions

$$\int \phi_i(x)\phi_j(x)dx = \delta_{ij} , \tag{9.6.7}$$

where the integral in general is an n-dimensional one, where n is the number of x's. Equation (9.6.6) implies also that g(x) of Equation (9.6.3) can be expressed as a sum of ν terms

$$g(x) = \sum_{i=1}^{\nu} c_i z_i \equiv F(x) , \tag{9.6.8}$$

where

$$z_i = \phi_i(x) , \quad i = 1,2,\ldots,\nu \tag{9.6.9}$$

$$c_i = \sum_{\alpha} q^{(\alpha)} \phi_i(x^{(\alpha)}) . \tag{9.6.10}$$

The decision procedure for a newcomer x is to be determined by the signature of F(z), where z is to be derived from x by (9.6.9). The decision function becomes a hyperplane in the z-space. This corresponds to one of the methods of linearization explained previously.

Since we have linearized the problem, it suggests that it would apply to the adaptive methods developed in the earlier sections of this chapter to the evaluation of (9.6.8). The formalism, (9.6.8) - (9.6.10), invites us to establish an analogy with the perceptron. It is often the case that a base function system includes a constant as one of the functions. If we call this $\phi_o(x)$, then z_o will correspond to x of the perceptron. The fact that all the paradigms are used to determine the c_i's in (9.6.10) corresponds to our directional balance (I) of Section 9.5. As we have seen, this tends to decide the orientation of the plane so that its normal is parallel to the straight line connecting two centers of mass.

Instead of including all the paradigms in deciding the c_i's, we can adopt the ordinary perceptron method, and introduce the adaptive-corrective procedure similar to (9.4.6). We have then

$$F^{(\mu)}(z) = \sum_{i=1}^{\nu} c_i^{(\mu)} z_i \ , \tag{9.6.11}$$

where $c_i^{(\mu)}$ is corrected according to

$$c_i^{(\mu+1)} = c_i^{(\mu)} + \lambda^{(\mu)} z_i^{(\mu)} \tag{9.6.12}$$

if $$z_i^{(\mu)} \in A_1 \text{ and } F^{(\mu)}(z^{(\mu)}) < 0 \ , \tag{9.6.13}$$

and $$c_i^{(\mu+1)} = c_i^{(\mu)} - \lambda^{(\mu)} z_i^{(\mu)} \tag{9.6.14}$$

if $$z_i^{(\mu)} \in A_2 \text{ and } F^{(\mu)}(z^{(\mu)}) > 0 . \tag{9.6.15}$$

This is identical to the perceptron, and the method will converge in the same way as the perceptron does.

Coming back to the language of the potential function method, the same procedure can be stated as follows. The $g(x)$ is adaptively corrected so that the $(\mu+1)$st stage function is decided by the rule:

$$g^{(\mu+1)}(x) = g^{(\mu)}(x) + \Psi(x^{(\mu)}, x) \ , \tag{9.6.16}$$

if $$x^{(\mu)} \in A_1 \text{ and } g^{(\mu)}(x^{(\mu)}) < 0 \quad \text{and} \tag{9.6.17}$$

$$g^{(\mu+1)}(x) = g^{(\mu)}(x) - \Psi(x^{(\mu)}, x) \ , \tag{9.6.18}$$

if $$x^{(\mu)} \in A_2 \text{ and } g^{(\mu)}(x^{(\mu)}) > 0 \ . \tag{9.6.19}$$

If the paradigm is correctly classified, then there will be no correction to be made. This corrective method was proposed by Aizerman and others [A-1].

The procedure of (9.6.16) to (9.6.19) is in a way more general in the sense that it does not assume the particular form $\Psi(x,x')$ given in (9.6.6). It is enticing to use the same procedure by replacing $\Psi(x,x')$ in (9.6.16) to (9.6.19) by a more general function $\Delta(x - x', \rho)$. This last function is, as seen in (8.5.17), more general than $\Psi(x,x')$ in two senses: It includes an infinite number of terms (i.e., $\nu \to \infty$), and the eigenvalues $\lambda^{(k)}$ can vary from one value of k to another. $\Delta(x - x', \rho)$ is a function only of the difference $x - x'$, whereas $\Psi(x, x', \rho)$ may depend on both x and x'.

The potential function method, whether it uses Ψ or Δ, is a very interesting mathematical idea. But, unfortunately, as a practical algorithm, it is very difficult to choose a good function Δ or a good base function $\{\phi_i\}$. A suitable functional form of Δ or of $\{\phi_i\}$ depends sensitively on problems. In addition to this, if we use a general Δ-function, the computer has to keep in the memory the updated function $g(x)$ for all x with sufficient accuracy, which is a heavy burden for the computer.

CHAPTER 10
Pattern Recognition as Structure Analysis

10.1 CLASSIFICATION BY FEATURES AND DESCRIPTION OF STRUCTURE

In Chapter 6 we introduced the principle of minimum entropy and showed that one way of applying the principle is to consider pattern recognition as a successive information compression, which is a step-by-step decrease of entropy. As an early example of the efforts to achieve such a series of information compressions, we adduced there the case of a ZIP-code reading machine, which performs a chain of information compression, each link of which consists of analysis of a figure into "constituent parts" put together according to some of the fixed "composition rules." This was a technological achievement by engineers in the mid-1960s, but about the same time a group of theoretical studies was done independently, also following the philosophy of "constituent-parts-composition-rules." We want to study anew in this chapter this type of approach in pattern recognition.

Whether we adopt the zone picture or the subspace picture, the methods of pattern recognition studied so far represent objects as vectors, and we aim to classify them according to some salient features they exhibit. The method of structure analysis, which has come to prominence since say, fifteen years ago and which recently started to lose some of its popularity, is claimed to have an entirely different aim from the usual classification by features. In its broadest interpretation, this method regards the objects, which in most cases are limited to two-dimensional images, as composed, according to certain rules, of constituents of known types, and the aim is to describe the structure of this composition. What we here designate by the general term "structure analysis" includes many different yet related methods variously characterized as descriptive, organizational, structural, linguistic, grammatical, syntactical, phrase-structural and so on.

Thus characterized, the approach of structure analysis seems not only to open up an entirely new vista over the problems of pattern recognition but also to bring to the fore one of the basic classical attitudes underlying the scientific tradition, manifest already in the Greek atomism. The idea is to reduce the multifariousness of appearance of objects to different states, arrangements, relations, or organizations occurring among a limited number of atomic entities of fixed types which themselves have a relatively small number of properties. This attitude is basic also to our common mental habits in analytical thinking. In the same way as the atomic description of complex matters, the structure analysis of patterns will have first to identify the constituent atoms and then to describe how these atoms are put together. From this point of view, the method of classification by features might seem to correspond to the simple case where there is no structure, the only task being to determine which kind of atom is there.

But this simplistic comparison obscures from view the more complex relationships between classification by features and structural description. In the first place, a picture is a grayness-function of two independent variables, and any function or functional of this grayness-function that serves as a property characterizing a class or distinguishing classes from one another is a feature. A description in terms of parts and their structure is also a function or a functional of the basic grayness-function, complicated as it may be. The usual classification-by-features method uses only relatively simple functions or functionals as features. By describing the structure, the structural method actually also does a classification, because a given description corresponds usually to more than one individual picture. Instead of giving a name to a group of pictures, it "assigns" a structure. The main difference is to be found in the specially complicated features that are the structure of

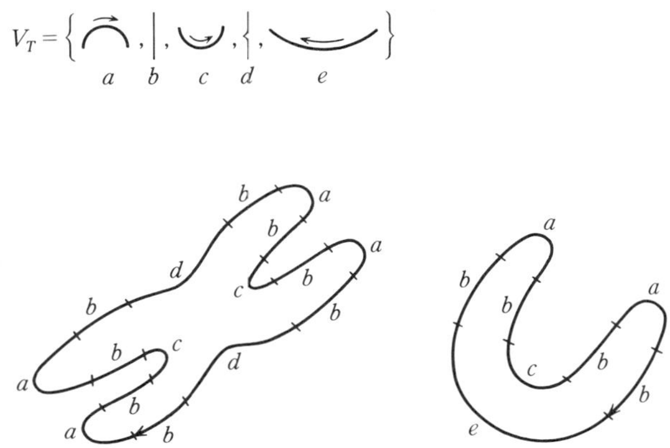

babcbabdbabcbabd *bebabcba*

(a) (b)

Figure 10.1.1 Ledley's analysis of chromosome shapes. A combination of atoms of the terminal vocabulary V_T defines a class of shapes.

components. A further small difference in the structural approach is that the kind of compositions possible (corresponding here to classes) are usually not enumerated at the onset. Possible compositions are defined implicitly by the rules of composition. In spite of these differences, it is perfectly legitimate to consider the aim of structural approach as one of classification using a special kind of feature, which is the structure of components. In the past some proponents of the structural approach used the adjectives, classificatory and nonclassificatory, to characterize the classification-by-feature method and the structure-description method. But, this terminology was rather unfortunately chosen, because both end with a classification.

The above consideration allows us to regard the structural method as a special case of the classification- by-feature method. We can interchange the roles of the two approaches and consider the classification-by-feature method as a special case of the structural approach, in a sense more elaborate than our previous statement to a similar effect. Consider vectors being expanded by a set of base functions and objects being classified by the special

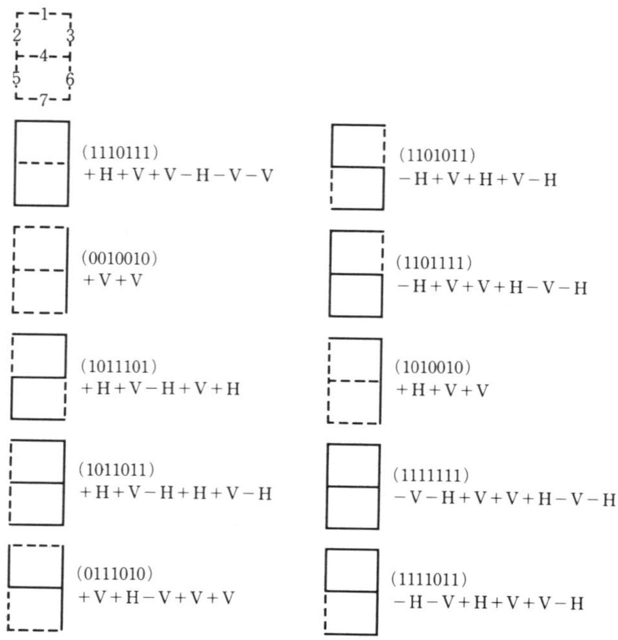

Figure 10.1.2 The familiar digital display of numerals can be analyzed by "grammatical" methods. Two ways of describing are mentioned.

combinations of the expansion coefficients. We can consider the base functions as atoms or components of known kinds and the special relations among the expansion coefficients as the description of structure. Thus, the structural description becomes a description by the special combination of coefficients. Comparing the two methods in this way we notice that what is missing in the structural description method is classification using these descriptions. Ledley's classification of chromosomes illustrates well that such a classification is possible and useful (see Figure 10.1.1). In this illustration V_T is the set of constituent atoms and (a) and (b) are two entirely different types of chromosomes (see [L-5]). But most of the papers on grammatical description neglect this important aspect.

Actually, the structure-description method has to do with classification in two aspects. First, each description corresponds to a class of objects, and second, the classification of descriptions into different categories is a very important task which can be done by this method but which is usually entirely unnoticed.

Before going further to a more detailed discussion of the structure method, let us consider a few simple examples that incorporate the idea of constituent parts or elementary components and structure. First we consider the ten figures used often on digital meters and digital watches, illustrated in Figure 10.1.2. The simplest way to identify them is, of course, to use their customary names: zero, one, two,..., nine. But, if we were Martians we would not use such names and would identify them by a more general analytical way--a way which would allow us to designate any of the $2^7 = 128$ possible configurations. The vectorial approach would be to assign seven coordinates to the seven luminous elements. We can represent any configuration by using seven binary digits such that if the i-th digit is occupied by 1, it means the i-th luminous element is lit and if it is occupied by 0, the corresponding element is not lit. For instance, 2 will be represented by (1011101), meaning that the second and sixth elements are not lit. An advantage of this representation is that the Hamming distance from the correct representation would indicate the number of malfunctioning elements.

It may be noted that this vectorial representation can also be reinterpreted as a case based on the structure description. The elementary components are 1st, 2nd, ..., 7th luminous elements. The 1 on the i-th position is considered as indicating that the i-th component is used. The composition rule is simply that: any of the seven basic elements can be either used or not used.

Another way to apply the point of view of constituent parts and composition is to consider any configuration as composed out of two atoms: V (vertical stroke) and H (horizontal stroke). The rule of composition can be as follows:

1. + V assigns the "head" to the lower end of the stroke and the "tail" to the upper end, and - V assigns the other way around.

2. + H assigns the "head" to the right end of the stroke and the "tail" to the left end, and - H assigns the other way around.
3. The head of an element is connected to the tail of the succeeding (if any) element.

Thus, for instance, 2 can be written, starting from the left upper corner, by one unit to the right, then down, then left, then down and finally right thus engendering a description: + H + V - H + V + H.

There is an interesting relationship between geometrical symmetries and this representation.

1. Changing the signs of all H's, we obtain a mirror image with respect to a vertical axis (e.g., 2 and 5 in Figure 10.1.2).

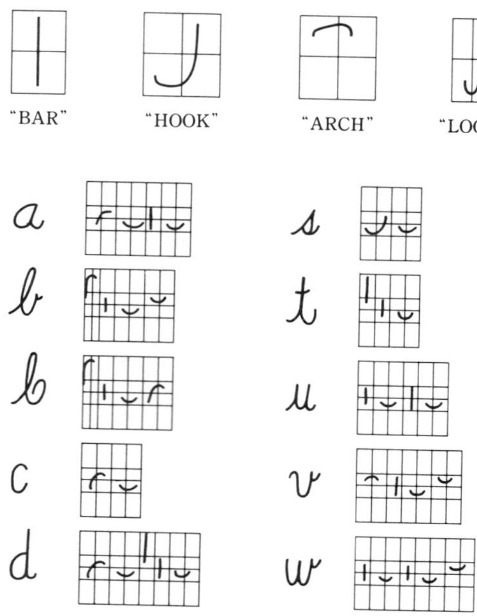

Figure 10.1.3 Probably the earliest work using structure analysis can be attributed to M. Eden. The illustration is taken from Eden's attempt to reconstruct handwritten alphabets using four basic strokes [E-1].

2. Changing the signs of all V's, we obtain a mirror image with respect to a horizontal axis.
3. Therefore, the rotation by 180° is achieved by changing all the signs of the elementary strokes.
4. A rotation by 180° can be obtained also by reversing the order of elements without changing their signs (compare 6 and 9 in Figure 10.1.2).
5. Multiplying the last two transformations, we obtain the identical figure. By reversing the order of the elementary strokes and changing all the signs we obtain an identical transformation.

This last identical transformation amounts to starting from the other end when writing down the description. This is not the only redundancy of this representation. We obtain a different representation every time we start from a different spot in the figure, and every time we take a different branch at first when we come to a branching point. But, we can reduce the redundancy, for instance, by deciding that the shortest representation starting from the uppermost end is the standard representation. Of course, the picture generated according to a representation of this kind has to be required to fit in the 8-shaped quadrilateral frame which is supposed to be given from the beginning. The only ambiguity that remains after this requirement is made is the case of one: + V + V, which could occupy either the 2nd or 5th positions (using the notation of the above vertical representation) or the 3rd and 6th positions. There is no practical usage of these symmetry rules, but we could use the above-mentioned symmetry properties to classify the ten figures and to describe some relationships among them.

Historically, the first papers that proposed the idea of structure analysis in pattern recognition were probably Eden's 1961 papers [E-1, E-4, E-5]. He selected four basic strokes: bar, hook, arch, and loop as the elementary constituents of the handwritten alphabet (see Figure 10.1.3). Eden was also the first to emphasize the "generative" rule to combine these basic strokes to produce, or at least simulate the natural cursive writings. After Eden's work, other authors, such as Kirsch, Narasimhan, and Shaw [K-2, N-2, S-3] emphasized the "grammatical" composition rules, and the interest was shifted toward more and more mathematical elegance instead of practical relevance. We shall discuss the grammatical approach of later developments in Sections 10.3, 10.4, and 10.5 (see [F-2, F-6, F-8, and W-11] for surveys of grammatical algorithm). In Section 10.2 we shall discuss another facet of structural analysis which is not grammatical.

In Section 6.7, we explained the ZIP-code reader that antedated most of the theoretical works in this field [G-6]. It is noteworthy that the philosophy of structure analysis is beautifully and usefully put in practice in this machine, without using the "grammatical" rules. Particularly noteworthy is the fact that three layers of "components" are used instead of one layer as usually considered. Further, it is instructive to see that classification is done according to the structure and that the structure is not identified by a strict compliance with the rules but rather by the nearest approximation to the standard types. All these useful methodological features are usually ignored in theoretical papers on structural analysis.

We stated that the structure analysis has two pillars, namely, "constituent components" and "composition rules." But we can also look at the structure analysis as consisting of two basic elements: "general laws" and "specific instancitation." The general laws are the list of all available constituent components and all valid rules of composition, and the specification is the data about the individual case. The work of analysis is to determine what are the used components and how the rules of composition are used to produce these data. The information we need to produce this final conclusion has two sources, the general laws and the specific data. The situation can be compared, in a rough analogy, to obtaining the particular solution of a differential equation matching a particular set of initial conditions. Or, it can be compared to deciphering of the received concatenation of dots and dashes to obtain the original English sentence using the general law which is the Morse code. We showed elsewhere [W-20] that the information provided by the differential equation is infinitely larger than the information provided by the initial conditions. In the case of Morse code, if we do not have in our memory the list of the code, we have to go through a fantastic job of breaking the code. In general we forget often the importance of the information provided by the general laws. This neglect leads often to a misinterpretation of the true information balance. But, this neglect has some psychological reason. Namely, if it is a realistic problem in physics, we do not need to know the differential equation; nature itself let the phenomena happen automatically. If it is a mechanical simulation by the computer, we need to put the general laws in the Read-Only-Memory, and we can forget even its existence. The elements that change every time are only the specific data. If we eliminate the information supply by the general laws from consideration, the decrease of entropy by the structural method becomes enormous indeed.

In general it is true that the larger the number of components, the smaller the number of composition rules. But, there is an optimum, which is obviously dictated by the total memory capacity we need to store the entire general laws, apart from the requirement that the entire theoretical structure be elegant and simple. The observer, on the other hand, has to start his operation by providing the specific data. The first task in this process is to identify the components, and the next is to find out how these components are put together. This second part is already the beginning of the "parsing" process, which consists of assigning appropriate composition rules to this group of components. Later we shall have a chance to discuss briefly the process of parsing.

The first task of identifying the components is an application of what is called "segmentation" in the discipline of "picture processing." Although we excluded "picture processing" from our book, we shall note a few interesting facts known in this discipline, mainly because it has something to do with the very essence of pattern recognition. In the first chapter, we said that pattern recognition is seeing-one-in-many, and that the first step is to identify a "thing" in the scenery which is at first sight a continuous stretch of gradually changing hues and brightness. Segmentation is essentially recognition of a region that can be considered as one thing--one object--one component. This process should include two operations: Recognition of a set of neighboring parts or subareas which share one property; and recognition of a boundary. As far as the second point is concerned, we have explained in Chapter 2 and in Appendix A-2 how human eyes see a boundary that in itself does not exist. (There are more recent, sophisticated algorithms for boundary detection than those explained in Chapter 2.) The first point has not been mentioned so far, mainly because the idea behind it is straightforward. In reality, both points are not easy operations on the computer. A crude computer method produces a result that contains all kinds of zig-zags, intrusions, and protrusions that from the human point of view are irrelevant to what the human perception would accept as a proper segmentation. Many smoothing and noise-eliminating procedures have been proposed, and we have to expect a lot of work to be done to find a good method of synthesis between the area identification and the boundary.

In order to identify an "area" or a "segment," we can select variables such as brightness, color, texture, and so forth. Brightness and color can be assigned to each of the mesh points, but texture may be determined only by a statistical relation between neighboring points. Anyway, we have to allow a certain range of tolerance ε for the sameness of a property of neighboring points. It is often pointed out that the human perception allows a gradual change of the property within a segment. It is a silly idea to imitate this effect by increasing the allowance ε, because that way we shall include too many points in one segment. We shall define a segment as a disjunctive union of subsegments within each of which ε is not allowed to become too large. The idea of a disjunctive set of similarity was used when we discussed the idea of Wittgenstein of similarity in Chapter 3. The result of segmentation is a partitioning of the whole area into regions, which are disjoint and complete.

When we have obtained the segments we can modify them considering the following conditions:

1. Increase the tolerance ε to reduce the number of too many segments. Decrease

tolerance ε if too few segments are obtained.
2. Merge too many segments to adjacent segments.
3. Eliminate as a meaningless bubble a segment which has only one adjacent segment or a very few adjacent segments. A segment of appreciable size with many adjacent segments may be an important one.
4. Eliminate the contour with parts where the curvature is too high by merging small segments with their adjacent segment.

The number of adjacent segments can be made intuitively easy to visualize when we draw the so-called "region adjacent graph" on the result of a segmentation. In this graph, each region is represented as a node in a graph. The adjacent regions are connected by edges on the graph. The degree of a node is then the number of adjacent regions of the region represented by the node (see Rosenfeld and his collaborators [R-9, S-19]). A concise description of many interesting problems connected with segmentation is given in Pavlidis's books [P-14].

The theory about segmentation has been developed in connection with the problem of identification of constituent components. The identification of grammatical rules that are used in the composition of components is the job of parsing. We shall briefly survey the tests connected with parsing in Section 10.3 .

10.2 GROUP-THEORETICAL DESCRIPTION

This section is included not only because of its intrinsic interest, but also, and more importantly, to dispel the common misconception that the idea of structural analysis is applicable only to the cases where the composition rules are "grammatical" ones. It is naturally difficult to define what grammatical rules in general are or should be. But, it is relatively easy to find some rules which are definitively not grammatical. Suppose there is a rule governing the structure of a compound object, such that if we slightly change a portion of the object the rest of the object has to be automatically

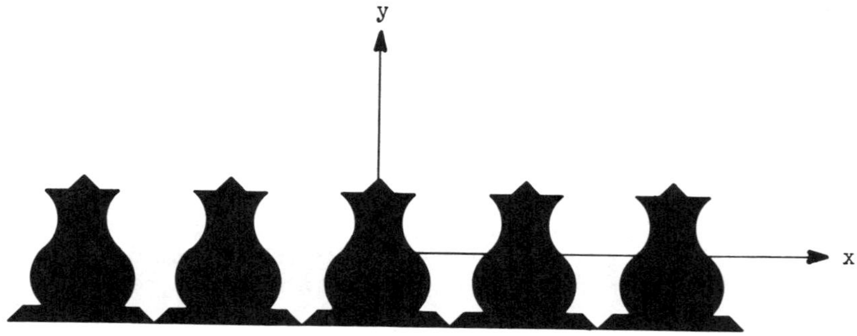

Figure 10.2.1 A typical Islam pattern. Put upside down and shift by 1/2 of the periodicity to the right to get the original pattern with white and black interchanged.

changed. Such a rule cannot be grammatical, because one of the conspicuous facts about any living language is that even after a very long chain of words at the beginning of a sentence has been stated, we still have freedom to choose the remaining part of the sentence. For instance, if there is a noun in any portion of a sentence we can replace it with an adjective plus noun without changing the rest of the sentence in so far as the grammar is concerned. If a grammatical rule becomes so strongly context-dependent that any local modification of a sentence propagates to the entire sentence, it will cease to be a grammatical rule. (The next section contains an example of artificial "grammar" that produces a "sentence" with a certain type of symmetry, exhibiting a global context dependency. Such a case is an exception as a "grammar.")

In the field of pictures, there are many rules which are strongly "Gestalt-forming" in the sense that no isolated local change is allowed. Suppose, for instance, we have a picture of lines of force in an electrostatic field. If we change a small portion of one of the lines of force, provided this is allowed, it has to be accompanied by a major change of lines of force extending over the entire field. This is one of the natures of the rule expressed by a partial differential equation (Poisson's equation) which underlies this picture. Such a rule is nongrammatical in a very fundamental sense.

We want to introduce another example of Gestalt-forming, hence nongrammatical, rules which nonetheless can serve very effectively the purpose of descriptively classifying pictures. The rules in question are not only nongrammatical but also nongenerative although, as we shall show later, they can be transformed into generative rules. They can, however, never be transformed into grammatical rules because no isolated local changes are allowed. Namely, we will discuss geometrical sceneries with different kinds of symmetry.

In Chapter 1, we introduced the idea of "Prägnanz" of the Gestalt psychologists. Prägnanz has never been precisely defined, but the high degree of Prägnanz was associated with simplicity, symmetry, and the like, and it was the contention of the Gestalt theory that the human perception tends to place importance on (and regards as "figure" rather than "ground") that portion or aspect of the scenery which shows a high degree of Prägnanz. We pointed out that this idea agrees well with the conclusion of our heuristic principles that states that pattern recognition seeks a portion or aspect of the scenery that shows small values of entropy. Indeed, a portion of a picture with a high degree of symmetry implies a small value of entropy. Furthermore, it should be noted that a low entropy corresponds to a high degree of redundancy, and a high degree of redundancy entails that a small modification of a small portion results in a large global change. The presence of grammatical rules also restricts the variety of variation, and to that extent, it tends to lower the entropy. But, the redundancy introduced by a grammatical rule is very limited, and the global effect of a small change is very minute.

Let us start by studying an example of a picture with a definite symmetry. Suppose we are given a picture of Figure 10.2.1. Everyone can easily agree that this is a finite portion of a possibly infinitely long picture (admittedly a theoretical construct) which obeys the following rules:

The picture remains invariant for any one of the following two operations and for a successive application of any number of operations of different kinds in any order.

1. Reflections with respect to the vertical line passing through one of the highest points of the black area (the y axis in Figure 10.2.1).
2. Reflections with respect to the horizontal line located halfway between the highest points and the lowest points (the x axis) followed by a one-half unit right-shift with color change. (The horizontal period is called one unit.)

There are many transformations that bring the picture back to an identical picture with the original, and all of them can be engendered by some combinations of these two fundamental ones. Any combination of the two transformations leaves the picture invariant. For instance, the obvious invariance for one-unit shift to the right is obtained by a double application of the transformation (2). If we apply first (2) and then (1), we obtain a 180° rotation about a point of intersection between the bisecting horizontal line and the border curve of the black and white area, followed by color interchange:

(1) $x' = -x, \; y' = y$

(2) $x' = x + \frac{1}{2}, \; y' = -y$; color interchange.

The right-shift by one unit can be expressed by $(2) \times (2) = (2)^2$, and the left-shift by one unit by $(1) \times (2)^2 \times (1)$. The inverse (i.e., the transformation that brings back to the identical transformation) of (1) is (1) itself. The inverse of (2) is $(1) \times (2) \times (1)$. These transformations leave the picture invariant for what mathematicians call "group."

A collection of symbols $G = \{a,b,c,\ldots\}$ is said to form a "group" if we can define an operation $\times$ such that

I. If $a \in G$ and $b \in G$ then $b \times a \in G$.
II. There is an element $\mathbb{1} \in G$ such that $\mathbb{1} \times a = a \times \mathbb{1} = a$ for any $a \in G$.
III. If $a \in G$, then there is an element $a^{-1} \in G$ such that $a^{-1} \times a = a \times a^{-1} = \mathbb{1}$.

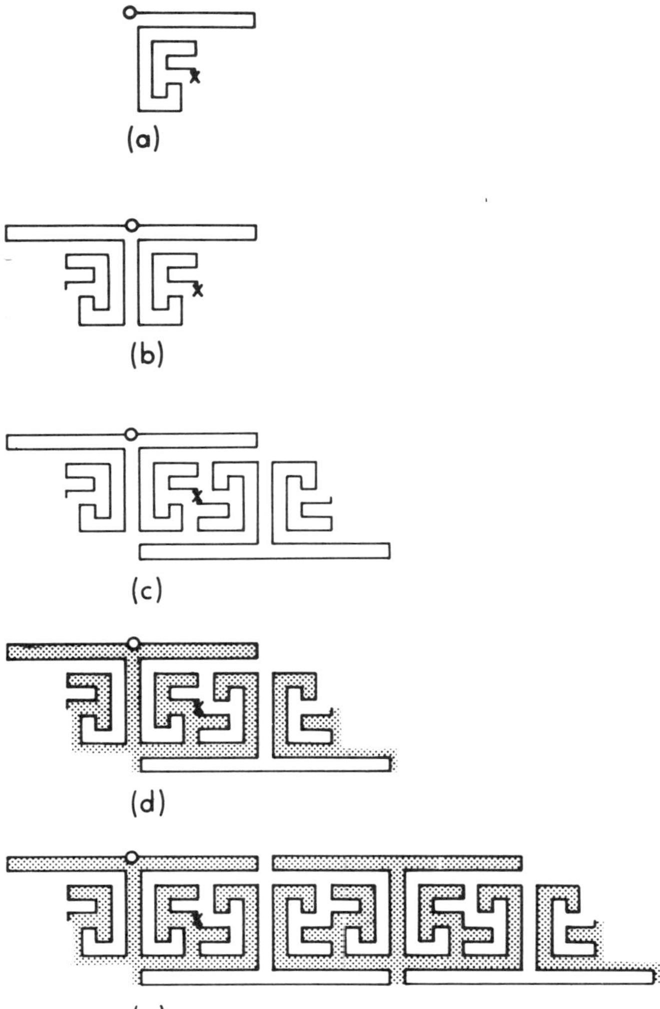

Figure 10.2.2 The pattern is produced by the generative rules (i) through (v), using the curve given in (a) as the atomic component. The completed pattern belongs to the same group theoretical type as Figure 10.2.1.

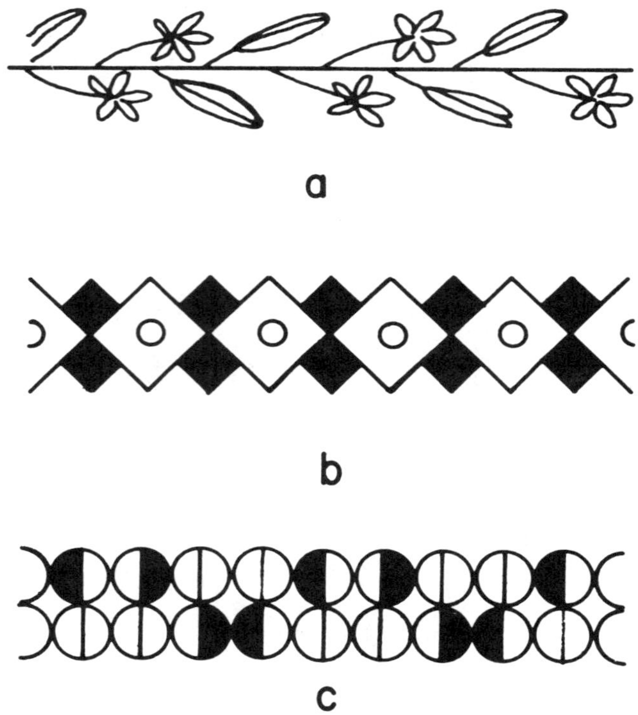

Figure 10.2.3 The reader will be able to write down the group-theoretical rules and the generative rules for each of the three patterns given here.

IV. If $a \in G$, $b \in G$ and $c \in G$, then $c \times (b \times a) = (c \times b) \times a$.

V. If $a \times b = b \times a$ for all $a \in G$ and $b \in G$, then G is an Abelian group. If not, G is a non-Abelian group.

It is clear that all the transformations obtained by products of (1)'s and (2)'s form a group, and that the group is non-Abelian. [Consider for instance (1) × (2) and (2) × (1).] Those readers who are familiar with some elements of the group theory will notice that all the rotations (i.e., the transformations obtained by products of an even number of reflections) (1) or (2) or both mixed, form

Figure 10.2.4 Samples of the so-called "mon," or family crests.

Table 10.2.1

Classification of the 30 mons of Figure 10.2.4 by (n, m). 360 degrees divided by n is the minimum angle of rotation about the center by which the figure returns to itself. m is the number of reflection symmetries.

Classes (n, m)	mon No.
(1, 0)	1, 2
(1, 1)	3, 4
(2, 0)	5, 6, 7
(2, 2)	8, 9, 10
(3, 0)	11, 12, 13
(3, 3)	14, 15, 16
(4, 0)	18
(4, 4)	19, 20
(5, 0)	21, 22
(5, 5)	23, 24
(6, 0)	25
(6, 6)	26
(8, 0)	17
(8, 8)	27, 28
(16, 16)	29
(∞, ∞)	30

an invariant subgroup. Similarly, all those transformations that do not include color interchange (i.e., all those transformations obtained by a product of any number of (1) and an even number of (2)) form another invariant subgroup.

It is well known that the Islams are very fond of this type of group-theoretical pattern, and it is very interesting that we can classify them according to the group-theoretical rules similar to the one mentioned above. See the classical textbook on group theory by Speiser [S-4] and newer books on the subject (see for instance [C-9, T-1]). It is clear that rules (1) and (2) are nongrammatical rules because a slight change at one spot on the upper half will cause another change in the lower half due to (2) and will propagate indefinitely to the left and right infinity by the left and right shifts. Rules (1) and (2) are purely statical rules and not generative, but we can transform them into a set of generative rules as follows:

i. Draw any arbitrary curve connecting two points ($x = 0$, $y = h$) and ($x = \frac{1}{4}$, $y = 0$).
ii. Flip over the picture with respect to the line of symmetry: $x = 0$, i.e., the y axis, and retain both the original curve and the new one obtained by this reflection.
iii. Reflect with respect to the line $y = 0$ (i.e., x axis). Shift the picture to the right by half a unit.
iv. Give two different colors to the corresponding parts in the two pictures before and after the operation.
v. Shift the picture to the left and to the right by integer intervals.

See Figure 10.2.2 for an example of this construction. The two points ($x = 0$, $y = h$) and ($x = \frac{1}{4}$, $y = 0$) are marked by O and x. The generative rule (ii) corresponds to the group-theoretical rule (1) and the generative rules (iii) and (iv) correspond to the group-theoretical rule (2). Instead of (v) we can also simply repeat (ii)-(iv). The arbitrary curve used in (i) corresponds to the "atom" or "component" of the structure. All the rest are the rules of composition. Every time one chooses a different atom, we obtain a different pattern, but remain in the same class insofar as the group-theoretical classification is concerned. To avoid overlapping, the original curve (i) must be not only written within a domain of one-quarter of a unit area, but the boundary of the area must be so chosen that the composition rules do not result in overlapping of the elementary domains.

We stated that the symmetry reduces the entropy. It is easy to calculate the entropy decrease when we bring the symmetry rules (what we called the general laws) to the form of generative rules. Indeed, suppose we take n units of the chain of 10.2.1 or the chain of 9.2.2, we need to know only one unit due to (v), and one unit is determined only one-quarter of the unit due to rules (ii) and (iii). This means the variety of alternatives became 1/(4n). In terms of Hartley's information, this means that the information reduction is - log (4n). The amount of information we save comes naturally from the composition rules. Note here again that this amount of information reduction due to the general rules can become infinite: $\lim_{n\to\infty} \log (4n) \to \infty$.

The reader will be able to find for himself the group-theoretical rules and the corresponding generative rules underlying the three patterns given in Figure 10.2.3. It is not so difficult to discover the underlying group-elements from a given picture because there are only three kinds of geometrical operations: rotation, reflection, and translation. If there are two reflections, they engender a rotation, as was the case with our example of Figures 10.2.1 and 10.2.2. But, there can be cases where there is a rotational invariance but not a reflection invariance.

In Figure 10.2.4 we show some examples of Japanese family crests (mon). Table 10.2.1 classifies these mon according to the rotation symmetry and reflection symmetry. The symbol (n, m) in Table 10.2.1 means the following: The total rotation 360° is divided into n portions, and a rotation by 360°/n degrees brings the picture to the original form. There are m straight lines (passing the center) with respect to which the picture shows reflection invariance. We can note that m is either 0 or equal to n. That means that if there is a line of reflection, there should be n of them. The reason for

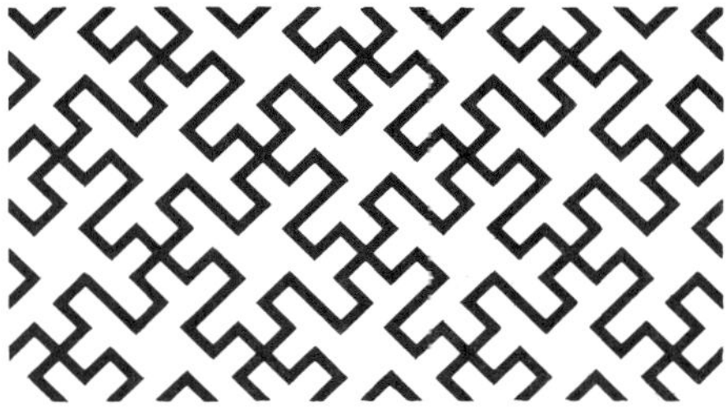

Figure 10.2.5 A pattern with the symmetry type "p4."

this is as follows. If we perform two reflections with respect to two lines intersecting with each other at angle θ between them, the picture rotates by 2θ. If the minimum of 2θ is 360°/n then the minimum of θ has to be 180°/n. This gives 2n lines of reflection symmetries, but the same line is counted twice because two lines intersecting at 180° are the same line.

Apart from the rigorous mathematical rule, we have to note a psychological effect of what may be called approximate symmetry. For instance, mon No. 1 has no line of reflection, but it has a line of approximate symmetry which is a vertical line. The bird's head is easier to draw as a profile than as a front view, as a result, the human observer recognizes a hidden left and right symmetry. Another kind of latent symmetry is generated by a three-dimensional interpretation, e.g., mon No. 11 which has no reflection symmetry. Suppose we rotate the picture as it is by 180° about the vertical line in the three-dimensional space. The result is not the

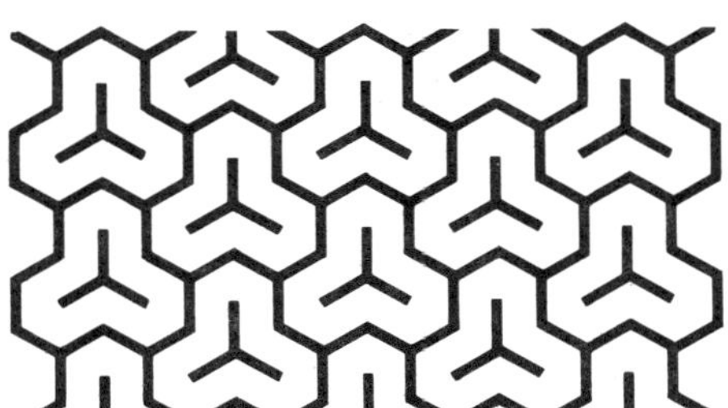

Figure 10.2.6 A pattern with the symmetry type "p3ml."

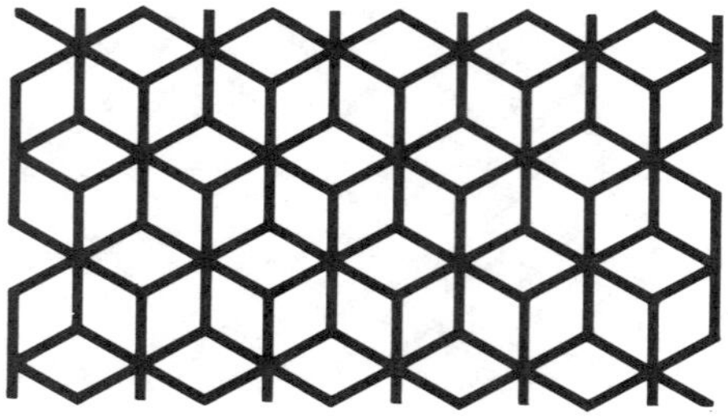

Figure 10.2.7 A pattern with the symmetry type "p6m."

same picture. However, if we consider the picture as a picture of a three-dimensional object, this the object would be invariant by a rotation by 180° about the vertical axis. A similar remark applies to mons No. 17 and No. 25.

We introduced in the physics of elementary particles the notion of chilarity [W-67]. An object is said to have chilarity if it does not return to itself (in a rotated position) by a reflection, and it has no chilarity if it does return to itself. The mons of No. 11, No. 17, and so on have chilarity as two-dimensional objects but have no chilarity as a

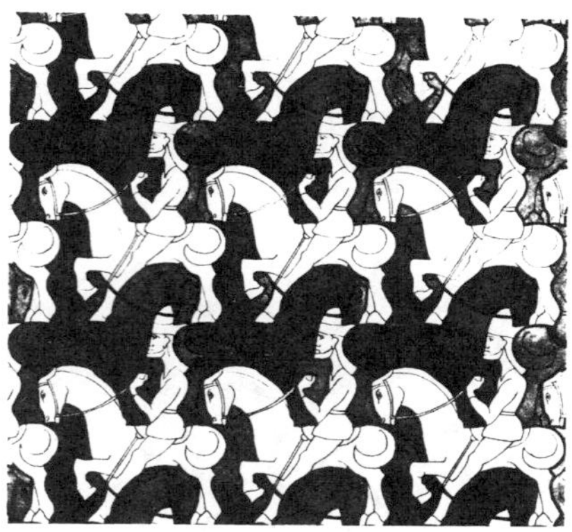

Figure 10.2.8 M.C. Escher's riders. Reprinted from *The Graphic Work of M.C. Escher* by permission of the Collection Haags Gemeenthemuseum - The Hague. Copyright © Beeldrecht, Amsterdam/VAGA, New York.

Figure 10.2.9 "De Imitatione Escheri" by K. Husimi.

three-dimensional object. In the three-dimensional space, a spiral has no chilarity, but a helix has.

The reader can easily convert these group-theoretical rules into a set of generative rules. As the atom of an (n, 0)-type mon we can take a sector of angle 360°/n. The atom of an (n, n)-type mon is an atomic sector of angle 360°/2n.

The kinds of symmetry that came into our consideration were rotations and reflections, because the center of the pattern is a fixed point. In general, a general two-dimensional repeated pattern with symmetry must include translation beside rotation and reflection. An interesting problem would be an appropriate classification of the kinds of symmetry properties and to decide the total number of symmetry properties. The answer is provided by the study of crystallography, and Hermann-Morgan's nomenclature is universally accepted (see [C-9, T-1]). To explain all the details of the theory behind this nomenclature would take too much time, but it may be interesting to know some salient results of this study. There are four groups of symbols which are used in the Hermann-Morgan's classification (p or c), (1,2,3,4, or 6), (m, or mm), (g, or gg). The first group (p or c) refers to translation (see later for explanation). The second group characterizes the rotational symmetry and is the same number as n in our classification of mons. It is noteworthy that 5 is missing and that $n \geq 7$ does not appear. One m means that the pattern has two mutually perpendicular axes of reflection. The symbol g is a glided reflection, as we considered in rule 2 in our analysis of the symmetry of Figure 10.2.1. But the color change is not considered here. It should be noted that not all the symmetries that a pattern allows for are mentioned in the nomenclature. Only the symmetries that are necessary to produce the different kinds of patterns with symmetry are mentioned.

If the translation is only in one direction, the result is somewhat as in Figures 10.2.1 and 10.2.2. We consider only two translations of two directions. We consider the translation group produced by two vectors t_1 and t_2. The lattice consists of a point and all the points that are produced from this point by the translations t_1 and t_2. The same lattice is produced by t_1' and t_2' which are connected to t_1 and t_2:

$$t_1' = \alpha t_1 + \beta t_2, \qquad t_2' = \gamma t_1 + \delta t_2$$

where α, β etc. are positive or negative integers and the determinant made by these coefficients should have an absolute value of 1.

It is easy to see that the lattice points have a rotation symmetry with $n = 2$, but in general they don't show any reflection symmetry. But if there is a reflection symmetry, the mirror image t' of one translation vector t must be also a translation vector. The two vectors

$$t + t' \text{ and } t - t'$$

must be also two translation vectors and the former $t + t'$ must be parallel to the axis of the reflection and the latter $t - t'$ is a vector perpendicular to the axis. Let a and b be the shortest of these two vectors. Then $t' + t = \alpha a$, $t' - t = \beta b$ where α and β are integers. Then the original t and t' will be

$$t = \frac{\alpha}{2} a - \frac{\beta}{2} b, \qquad t' = \frac{\alpha}{2} a + \frac{\beta}{2} b$$

If both α and β are even, then lattice points produced by t and t' will coincide with the rectangle produced by a and b. If both α and β are odd, there will be lattice points produced by t and t' that lie at the centers of the rectangle produced by a and b. The case where one of α and β is even and the other odd does not happen because that would contradict the assumption that a and b are the shortest vectors in their respective directions. In the case where the lattice points produce "centered" rectangles, we write c instead of p. Otherwise, it is p in the first of four characterizations.

Another note necessary to read the Hermann-Morgan's nomenclature concerns the difference between 3ml and 3lm. The existence of the symbol 3 indicates that there is a rotational symmetry with n = 3. Let a be the shortest translation vector and b be the result of 120° rotation of a. The reflection m can have the axis along the direction bisecting the angle between a and b [i.e., it is parallel to (a + b)/2]. Such a reflection is designated ml. If the axis of reflection is perpendicular to this direction [i.e., if it is parallel to (a - b)/2], we write lm.

The result of the group theoretical analysis of all possible symmetric patterns is that there are only 17 categories of symmetry types which are: p1, p2, pm, pg, cm, pmm, pmg, pgg, cmm, p4, p4m, p4g, p3, p3ml, and p3lm, p6, p6m. The examples of Figures 10.2.5, 10.2.6, and 10.2.7 are types: p4, p3ml, and p6m, respectively.

It is a common experience to observe a beautiful symmetrical figure in a tiled floor which is covered by tiles of one kind or two placed in a certain regular fashion. But the tiles have usually simple geometrical shapes. One of Escher's famous pictures is composed of a "tile" (i.e., elementary area), of the shape of a horse-rider and another elementary area of its mirror image. The symmetry it exhibits is Pg. The difficult part is to find an interesting

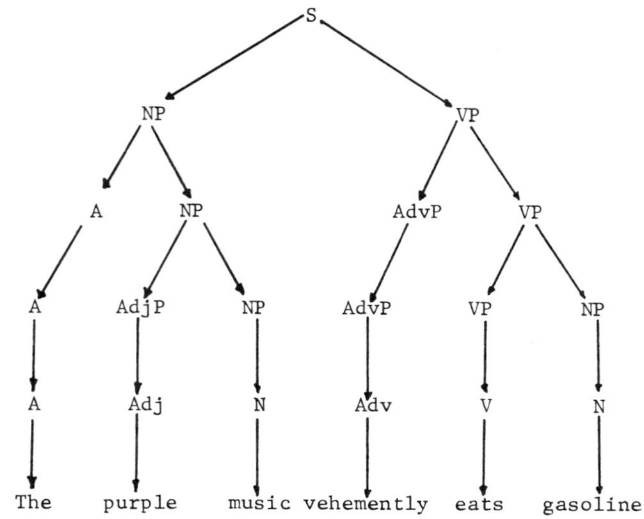

Figure 10.3.1 A grammatical tree produced by Chomsky's substitution rules.

shape such that the tile-laying does not leave any empty gap or make any disturbing overlap [E-2]. Figure 10.2.8 is a reproduction of Escher's famous picture of riders. The next illustration, Figure 10.2.9, is a variation of "De Imitatione Escheri" by Husimi. This has a symmetry pattern of P4. This needs one kind of tile, because it does not involve m or g. The book *Geometry of Beauty* [H-2], written by Husimi and his co-authors, explains how he discovered this pattern by the use of the dragon curve. For the dragon curve, see Scientific American, March 1967. Thanks are due to Professor Husimi for letting me use one of his creations as the motif of the dustcover of this book, and also for many instructive conversations.

10.3 ELEMENTS OF SUBSTITUTION GRAMMAR

Teaching grammar according to Chomsky's [C-3] method has become so popular that it is even adopted for elementary English classes. Therefore, it may be superfluous to explain its basic elements; however we will do so, partly for completeness of our exposition and partly for some useful vocabulary. Chomsky's grammar has two basic methods: substitution and transformation. What is usually relevant to the picture analysis is the part that is called substitution (or rewriting or generative) grammar. We shall limit ourselves only to the substitution grammar, in an elementary way.

Suppose we are given three English sentences:

George walks.
The very tall man is sitting uncomfortably.
They mercilessly hit the boy.

We divide each sentence into two parts so that the first part of each sentence has something in common with each other and the second part has something in common with each other. This is somewhat like a problem of clustering. It would be difficult to answer differently than as follows. The first parts will be: (a) George, (b) The very tall man, (c) They, and the second parts will be: (a) walks, (b) is sitting uncomfortably, (c) mercilessly hit the boy. The first part is a noun or something like a noun (i.e., a group of words or a phrase playing the role of a noun). The second part is a verb or something like a verb (i.e., a group of words or a phrase acting as a verb). So, the sentence (S) can be said to consist of a noun phrase (NP) and a verb phrase (VP).

Next, of what is the noun phrase composed when it is not a noun alone? Sometimes a NP consists of an article A and NP. And, an NP sometimes has a structure like an adjectivelike group + noun (i.e., NP can also become AdjP + NP). Similarly, in the second part, VP can be decomposed as (VP plus an adverb phrase) or (an adverb phrase + VP). And further, a verb, when it is what usually is called a transitive verb, has to be followed by an NP. This NP can be composed in the same way as the NP in the first part. So, the rules of composition are somewhat like this:

$$\begin{aligned}
S &\rightarrow NP + VP \\
NP &\rightarrow A + NP \\
NP &\rightarrow AdjP + NP \\
VP &\rightarrow AdvP + VP \\
VP &\rightarrow VP + AdvP, \\
VP &\rightarrow VP + NP \\
AdjP &\rightarrow AdvP + AdjP,
\end{aligned} \qquad (10.3.1)$$

where → should be understood in the sense "can consist of" or "can be substituted by." It goes without saying that a verb phrase VP can be replaced by a verb V, the adjective phrase AdjP can be replaced by an adjective Adj, and so on.

$$\begin{aligned} NP &\rightarrow N \\ VP &\rightarrow V \\ AdjP &\rightarrow Adj \\ AdvP &\rightarrow Adv \end{aligned} \tag{10.3.2}$$

Finally to obtain a real sentence, we have to replace the symbols N, V, Adj, and so forth, respectively by a real noun, a real verb, a real adjective, and so on.

Conversely, applying these rules successively we can write a grammatically correct sentence:

$$\begin{aligned} &S \rightarrow NP + VP \rightarrow A + NP + AdvP + VP \\ &\rightarrow A + AdjP + NP + AdvP + VP + NP \\ &\rightarrow A + Adj + N + Adv + V + N \\ &\rightarrow \text{The} + \text{purple} + \text{music} + \text{vehemently} \\ &+ \text{eats} + \text{gasoline} \end{aligned} \tag{10.3.3}$$

We can write this generative process in an inverted tree (see Figure 10.3.1).

The important point is that such a set of generative rules will produce grammatical sentences only. The example just mentioned is grammatically correct but semantically nonsense. There have been attempts to include semantic restrictions in the form of production rules, but they are not quite successful. This is not surprising because the semantic restrictions can depend on the global context that extends not only on one sentence, one chapter, or one book but on all the writings of the author. The grammar is a set of rules governing the relatively local relation of words.

When a real sentence is given, we can try to find the generative tree, which would produce the sentence complying with the rules. Such a process is called parsing and it reveals the grammatical structure of the sentence. If we can find a tree according to the rule, we can say that the sentence is grammatically correct. When the sentence is very short, we could try to produce all possible sentences of the given length with the help of the generative grammar from the top down (i.e., starting from S). One of them should coincide with the given sentence. But the number of possible sentences increases with appalling speed with the length of the sentence. In another way, we can think of working backward from the bottom up. But this is not so easy because the grammatical rule is "generative" in nature and is not primarily written for analysis. This can be done for the simple kinds of grammatical rules, but it becomes increasingly difficult with a more complicated type of grammatical rule.

Let us refer to the way we described the regularities governing the English grammatical sentence. As far as the symbols are concerned, we had first the symbol S and then the group of symbols: NP, VP, ... N, V, ... and so on, which are not real words, but stand for words or groups of words. Let us call them nonterminal symbols and, collectively, the nonterminal vocabulary V_N. Then there are real words which form the collection of "atoms" or the vocabulary, or, to make a distinction from V_N, the terminal vocabulary V_T. Also, there are generative rules or production rules such as (10.3.1) and (10.3.2) which directionally (i.e., by an arrow) connect S to a member of V_N^*, or a member of V_N^* to a member of V_N^* or to a member of V_T^*. An asterisk indicates a set of all possible groups or concatenations of some members of the set without an asterisk. Thus, V_T^* for instance, means a set of all possible groups of real words. If we write G for grammar, G and $V_N = \{A,B,C...\}$, $V_T = \{a,b,c...\}$, $P = \{P_1,P_2,...\}$, the G consists of V_N, V_T and P and S. In addition, there are two more symbols $\rightarrow$ and +, but $\rightarrow$ is included in the P's and + can be omitted. P is the set of production rules $\{P_i\}$ and each P_i is of the form in general: $S \rightarrow A^*$, $A^* \rightarrow B^*$ or $A^* \rightarrow a^*$, where A^*, $B^* \in V_N^*$ and $a^* \in V_T^*$. The language is the set of all sentences that can be produced this way. In the examples (10.3.1) and (10.3.2), the term to the left of the arrow consists only of a single symbol. But in general a production rule replaces a <u>group</u> of symbols by another <u>group</u> of symbols.

If the P is of this general type, we have a grammar of the zero-th kind according to the terminology of Chomsky. But we have seen, in the example we adduced at the beginning, that the production rules had only one symbol of V_N or S in the left-hand side of the arrow. P_i is then of the type: $S \to A^*$, $A \to A^*$, $A \to a^*$, $A \epsilon V_N$, $A^* \epsilon V_N$. This means a symbol (S or A) can be replaced by a group of symbols (A^* or a^*) independently of what stands before and after the symbol (S or A). In this sense, this grammar is called context-free grammar or a grammar of the second kind. But in general, the validity of $A \to A^*$ or $A \to a^*$ would be restricted depending on what precedes (α) or succeeds (β) A. In such a case, the production rule will be of the type: $\alpha A \beta \to \alpha A^* \beta$ or $\alpha A \beta \to \alpha a^* \beta$, where $A \epsilon V_N$, $A^* \epsilon V_N^*$, $a^* \epsilon V_N^*$ and α, $\beta \epsilon V_N$ or V_N^*. Such a language is called context-sensitive grammar or a grammar of the first kind. A context-free grammar is sometimes subjected to a further restriction that the production rules are limited to the type: $A \to aB$ and $A \to a$ where A, $B \epsilon V_N$, $a \epsilon V_T$, then we speak of a finite state grammar or a grammar of the third kind.

It is sometimes useful to include S in V_N. It is also sometimes convenient to introduce a symbol $\emptyset$ into V_N which means the absence of any word.

Example 1. The following finite-state grammar, $V_N = \{S\}$, $V_T = \{0, 1\}$

$$\begin{aligned} P_1&: \quad S \to 0S \\ P_2&: \quad S \to 1 \end{aligned} \tag{10.3.4}$$

This grammar produces sentences of the type $0^n 1$, where 0^n means a string of n 0's; n can be any integer. If we want to avoid S in V_N, we can make $V_N = \{A\}$ and use the rules: $S \to 0A$, $A \to 0A$, $A \to 1$.

Example 2. The following context-free grammar, $V_N = \{S\}$, $V_T = \{0, 1, \emptyset\}$

$$\begin{aligned} P_1&: \quad S \to 0S1 \\ P_2&: \quad S \to \emptyset \end{aligned} \tag{10.3.5}$$

produces sentences of the type $0^n 1^n$, where n is an arbitrary integer. It is interesting to see that these sentences exhibit a reflection symmetry with "color-change" (i.e., interchange of 0 and 1).

Example 3. The following context-sensitive grammar, $V_N = \{A\}$, $V_T = \{0, 1, \emptyset\}$

$$\begin{aligned} P_1&: \quad S \rightarrow 0A1 \\ P_2&: \quad 0A1 \rightarrow 01A01 \\ P_3&: \quad 1A0 \rightarrow 10A10 \\ P_4&: \quad A \rightarrow \emptyset \end{aligned} \qquad (10.3.6)$$

produces sentences of the type 010101...010101 which exhibits a translational invariance of period two and a reflection symmetry with color change.

It should be noted that all these examples exhibit some global gestalt and do not allow any local substitution. We have mentioned at the beginning that the local replaceability is vitally important for a living language. Therefore, we should know that the Chomsky grammar can produce artificial languages which lack vital characteristics of living languages. On the other hand, we should emphasize that the Chomskyian grammar is not a systematic or comprehensive tool to cope with the whole area of pictures with different kinds of symmetries and invariants.

It should also be noted that the finite-state grammar as defined above can produce a language which has no regularities at all. For instance, consider a finite state grammar with $V_N = \{S\}$, $V_T = \{0, 1\}$ and P: $S \rightarrow 0S$, $S \rightarrow 1S$, $S \rightarrow \emptyset$. This grammar will produce any arbitrary sequence of 0's and 1's concatenated in any arbitrary order.

Let us next discuss the problem of parsing using as an example a very simple finite state grammar:

$$\begin{aligned} &G_N = \{S, A\}, \qquad V_T = \{0, 1\} \\ &P: \quad \text{(i)} \quad S \rightarrow 0S, \quad \text{(ii)} \ S \rightarrow 0 \\ &\qquad \text{(iii)} \ S \rightarrow 1A, \quad \text{(iv)} \ A \rightarrow 1 \ . \end{aligned} \qquad (10.3.7)$$

From the production rule (i), we can see that a sentence can have any arbitrary number of 0's at the beginning (left end). Then, this chain of 0's can end with another 0 at the end due to (ii). This produces one type of grammatical sentence which consists of any nonzero number of 0's. Another possibility is to have first any number of 0's according to (i), and then go to 1 followed by one A according to the rule (iii). This A then has to be replaced immediately by 1 by rule (iv). Thus, this possibility produces a sentence which has any number (which can be zero) of 0's at the beginning followed by two 1's.

Now let us try the parsing process--the determination of whether a sentence is grammatical or not, and, if grammatical, the determination of which production rules are used in what order. Suppose we are given a sentence 00011. If we use the rule described at the end of the last paragraph, this sentence is found to be grammatical, but we cannot know which rules one used in what order. The fact that the sentence starts with 0 shows that rule (i) or rule (ii) must have been used. But (ii) is excluded because the first 0 is followed by something else. Next, we come to the second 0. We have the same situation, i.e., the rule (i) must have been used again. We have again the same situation with the third zero. That is, so far, (i) is used three times. The next letter is 1. Therefore, rule (iii) must have been used. Then, according to our rules, there is only one possibility to continue, namely to use (iv) to terminate the sentence with the second 1. Thus we have used rules (i), (i), (i), (iii), (iv) to produce the given sentence, which has been simultaneously proved grammatically correct.

This example shows, at least in such a simple case, that parsing is purely "mechanical," and it must be possible to devise a machine which would do the job. To design such a machine it will help to rewrite the rules (ii) and (iv) in the following way:

$$\begin{aligned} &(\text{ii})' \quad S \to 0B \\ &(\text{iv})' \quad A \to 1C, \end{aligned} \tag{10.3.8}$$

where B and C really do not mean any letter but indicate that the sentence ends there, playing the role of "period." Then, all the production rules take the form $X \to aY$. We can now characterize each step in the foregoing analysis as reading a letter a. We passed from nonterminal X to another nonterminal Y according to the production rule of the general type: $X \to aY$, where X, Y could be S, A, B, C.

Suppose we have a machine that can be in any of the four "states"--S, A, B, C--and begins with state S. If when in the state X it reads the sentence from the left end and it encounters a, then it goes to the state Y if there is a rule $X \to aY$ (where X and a may or may not uniquely determine Y). If the result is one of the Y's which represents the "period," then the sentence is proved grammatical.

More generally, we can imagine a "finite state" automaton which can be in any one of the states $\{X_i\}$ $i=1,2,\ldots,n$. The machine is provided with a tape on which a chain of letters out of the alphabet $\{a_i\}$ $i=1,2,\ldots,r$ is written, and the machine reads the tape from the left end. The machine is provided with a program or a set of rules of state transition of the type: $(a_i, X_j) \to X_k$ (i.e., reading the letter a_i), the machine is allowed to pass from state X_j to state X_k. When a letter a_i and the state X_j are given in such a way that there is no state X_k to go, then, the sentence is rejected. If the number of allowed states X_k for a given a_i and X_j is zero or one, we speak of a deterministic automata and otherwise (i.e., the number for at least one pair a_i and X_j is more than one) a nondeterministic automaton. But the difference between the deterministic and nondeterministic automaton is not essential here. There is a particular group of states $\{F_i\}$ $i=1,2,\ldots,s$ which we call final states (or "periods" above). One of the states is called the initial state: I. If the machine starts with I and, after reading the sentence $\{a_{i1}, a_{i2},\ldots\}$, lands one of the F's, then the sentence is accepted.

The correspondence between the grammatical rules and the transition rules of the finite state automaton is obvious: To S corresponds I. To V_N and $\{F_i\}$make up $\{X\}$. To V_T corresponds to $\{a_i\}$. If there is a production rule $X_i \to a_j X_k$ there will be a transition rule $(a_j, X_i) \to X_k$. If there is a production rule $X_i \to a_j$ there will be a transition rule $(a_j, X_i) \to F_k$. To record what rules were used in what order we need an auxiliary machine, but there is no question about its feasibility.

This explanation shows why the finite-state language which has only the production rules of the type $A \to aB$ or $A \to a$ is easy to parse mechanically. The machine needs in fact only to read from the left and can decide at every step the legitimacy of the step. This is no longer the case with the context-free grammar which allows, among other possibilities, both $A \to aB$ and $A \to Ba$. As a matter of fact, the machine which does the parsing job for a context-free language is called "pushdown" automaton. This is a tape-reading machine with an auxiliary memory system called pushdown memory. We can store a string of symbols in this memory but we can read out the symbol at one end. The used symbol is deleted and the next symbol comes to the end to be read out next. There is a correspondence rule between the production rule and the rule of operation of the machine. The acceptance by the machine, which corresponds to a proof of grammaticalness, is signaled by the fact that the pushdown memory has become empty.

The context-sensitive grammar and the general grammar require a Turing machine. A Turing machine has a tape on which it can read and write. The state of the machine-tape configuration is characterized by the state of the machine itself, the contents of the tape, and the position of the tape at which the machine can read and write. The rule of operation is such that the present state of the machine and the input (the symbol on the tape just read) determines the next state of the machine, the symbol to be written in lieu of the symbol read out and also a shift to the left or right by one unit on the tape. The difference between the one corresponding to the context-sensitive grammar and the one corresponding to the general grammar is that the former can use a bounded region of the tape whereas the latter can use the infinite (to the right) region of the tape. In either case the acceptance of the sentence originally written at the left end on the tape is signaled by the stopping of the machine (i.e., the state of the machine becomes one of the final states). But the significant difference from the finite-state case is that the machine goes back and forth, and the acceptance means only that the machine stops in a finite time (i.e., at a certain finite number of steps). At any step when the machine is still moving, we cannot know whether it will eventually stop or not. This is well-nigh tantamount to never knowing whether a sentence is grammatical or not at least in a finite time.

All these mechanical parsing devices assume, of course, that the input is a linear concatenation. In application to the picture analysis, the major difficulty lies in describing a picture in a linear form. Therefore, the existence of parsing machines is a poor consolation. In addition to that, there is a more fundamental problem: what is grammaticalness in the case of pictures? Unless we limit ourselves to pictures produced by certain rules, there is no sense dismissing a picture because it is not "grammatical." In the case of real grammar, what makes the study of grammar interesting and useful is that what is considered to be good construction in ordinary usage of a natural language can be, at least in an approximate sense, produced by a small set of rules.

10.4 CHEMICAL STRUCTURE LANGUAGE

For computer processing of two-dimensional structural formulae in chemistry it is desirable to transform them into one-dimensional linear forms. The so-called Wiswesser system [S-5] of linearization is usually used as a standard linearized notation. But the system is a compromise between a systematic method of transcription and an ad hoc convention introduced for the sole purpose of practical convenience. The chemical structure language (CSL), which will be explained in this section as an example of a grammatical approach to pattern recognition, offers a purely systematic method of linearization. The original version of CSL [W-11] was rather cumbersome, but in this section it is more simple and versatile [W-12]. If we consider atoms in a structure formula as nodes, the formula becomes a simple graph. For this reason, the CSL grammar can be considered also as a generator of a certain family of graphs. It is claimed neither that CSL produces all chemically existing structures and only those chemically existing structures, nor that the CSL is pragmatically more convenient than any other system.

It should be kept in mind that the structure formula in chemistry is meant to exhibit the connectivity of atoms, and the metric aspect (in the geometric sense) of the formula is irrelevant to what is meant to be conveyed by the formula. Therefore, for instance, two formulae in Figure 10.4.1 are equivalent to each other:

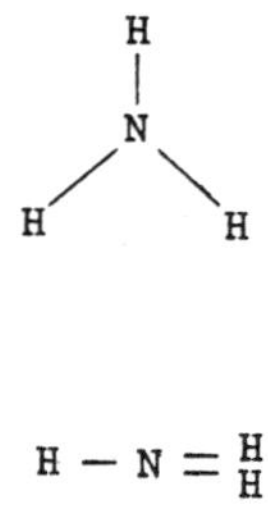

Figure 10.4.1 These two figures are equivalent.

The grammatical theory is par excellence a deductive theory, but it is always helpful to explain, even briefly, the inductive background by which the deductive system was reached. In the case of structure formulae, somewhat as in the case of a language, we have to consider what will happen if we divide a formula into two parts. One important fact is that when we cut a structure formula in half, the number of bonds emerging from the left half and the number of bonds emerging from the right half are the same. If we further cut the left half into two layers, a similar thing will happen at the cutting surface. We can continue the process until the layer becomes one atom thick. In general we may be able to characterize a layer by a symbol like A_{ij}, where i is the number of bonds going to the left and j is the number of bonds going to the right. If we cut A_{ij} into two layers in such a way that the left border of the layer represented by A_{ij} becomes the left border of the left sublayer, and the right border of the layer represented by A_{ij} becomes the right border of the right sublayer, we can write a rule like $A_{ij} \to A_{ik}A_{kj}$ where k can be any nonzero positive integer. If a layer A_{ij} consists of upper and lower parts between which there are no bond connections, we can write

$$A_{ij} \to \begin{matrix} A_{i'j'} \\ A_{i''j''} \end{matrix} ,$$

so that $i = i' + i''$ and $j = j' + j''$. We write for linearity $A_{ij} \to [A_{i'j'}, A_{i''j''}]^T$.

We shall write α_i for an atom of valence i. At the first reading, the reader can understand β_{ii} and γ_i, respectively, something like an atom of valence 2i and something like an atom of valence i. They are actually not atoms, but, the reader will learn their usage through examples.

The grammar for CSL consists of four parts:

$$G = \{S, V_N, V_T, P\}$$

where the vocabularies are

$$V_N = \{A_{ij}, \beta_{ii}\} \qquad i,j = 0,1,2,\ldots$$

$$V_T = \{\alpha_i, \gamma_i, -\} \qquad i = 0,1,2,\ldots$$

and the production rules are

$$P = \{P_1, P_2, \ldots, P_7\}$$

$$P_1: \quad S \rightarrow A_{oo}$$

$$P_2: \quad A_{ij} \rightarrow A_{ik}A_{kj} \qquad i,j = 0,1,2,\ldots; \quad k = 1,2,\ldots,\text{arbitrary}$$

$$P_3: \quad A_{ij} \rightarrow [A_{i(1)j(1)}, A_{i(2)j(2)}, \ldots, A_{i(\nu)j(\nu)}]^T$$

$$i(\sigma), j(\sigma) = 0,1,2,\ldots; \quad \nu = 2,3,\ldots,\text{arbitrary.}$$

$$i = \sum_{\sigma=1}^{\nu} i(\sigma) \quad , \quad j = \sum_{\sigma=1}^{\nu} j(\sigma).$$

$$P_4: \quad A_{ii} \rightarrow \beta_{ii}$$

$$P_5: \quad A_{ij} \rightarrow \overset{=}{\underset{-}{\vdots}}\, \alpha_{i+j}\, \overset{=}{\underset{-}{\vdots}}$$

The number of bonds to the left = i
The number of bonds to the right = j

$$P_6: \quad \beta_{ii} \rightarrow \overset{=}{\underset{-}{\vdots}}$$

The number of bonds = i

$$P_7: \quad A_{io} \rightarrow \overset{=}{\underset{-}{\vdots}}\, \gamma_i$$

The number of bonds to the left = i

$$A_{oi} \rightarrow \gamma_i\, \overset{=}{\underset{-}{\vdots}}$$

The number of bonds to the right = i

We shall add a few explanations:

1. A_{ij} represents an atom or a group of atoms with valence i+j extending i bonds to the left and j bonds to the right.
2. $[A_{i(1)j(1)}, A_{i(2)j(2)}, \ldots, A_{i(\nu)j(\nu)}]^T$ is to be considered to be a column vector with ν components, so that the components are placed one on top of the other. The number of bonds going to the left is $\sum_{\sigma=1}^{\nu} i(\sigma)$, and the number of bonds going to the right is $\sum_{\sigma=1}^{\nu} j(\sigma)$.
3. α_i represents an atom of valence i.
4. β_{ii} is to be considered to be simply 2i bonds, which is introduced for convenience. When we do not use the "loop formula," β_{ii} is needed to describe a molecule that has a closed loop with an odd number of nodes.
5. γ_i serves two purposes: as a free bond of valence i--the neutral molecule should have no γ's; the total sum of i's of the γ's is the valence of the ion or the group of atoms--and as a temporary symbol later to be deleted in the "loop formula" or in the "recursive growth formula."
6. The bonds between two atoms should be connected one by one in a vertical order.
7. If it is necessary to distinguish different atoms or different γ's, we use a superscript, such as $\alpha_i^{(a)}$ or $\gamma_i^{(a)}$, a=1,2,....
8. The graph thus obtained is to be deformed so as to conform with the usually accepted form.
9. To change the order of connection we use symbols $\{i_1, i_2, \ldots, i_n\}$ meaning the k-th bond from the left-hand side atom group should be connected to the i_k-th bond from the right-hand side atom group (see later).
10. A_{io} and A_{oi} which are replaced by γ_i - and $-\gamma_i$ will be sometimes written γ_{io} and γ_{oi}.
11. If a group of atoms often appears in one context, we can treat it as if it were an atom. For instance, the hydroxyl group

(-OH), carbonyl connective (=C=O) and amino group ($-NH_2$) can be treated as "atoms": Q_1, V_2, W_1.

Some examples of how the CSL can describe the chemical structure of some molecules and ions are:

Example 1

$$\begin{aligned} S &\to A_{00} && \text{by } P_1 \\ &\to \alpha_0 && \text{by } P_5 \end{aligned}$$

where α_0 can be any one of the 0-valence atoms, such as He, Ar, and so forth.

Example 2

$$\begin{aligned} S &\to A_{00} && \text{by } P_1 \\ &\to A_{01}\ A_{13}\ A_{33}\ A_{33}\ A_{30} && \text{by } P_2 \\ &\to A_{01}\ A_{13}\ [A_{10}, A_{13}, A_{10}]^T [A_{30}, A_{13}]^T [A_{10}, A_{10}, A_{10}]^T && \text{by } P_3 \\ &\to \alpha_1 - - \alpha_4 \equiv [-\alpha_1, -\alpha_4 \equiv, -\alpha_1]^T [=\alpha_2, -\alpha_4 \equiv]^T \\ &\quad [-\alpha_1, -\alpha_1 - \alpha_1]^T && \text{by } P_5 \end{aligned}$$

If we understand $\alpha_1, \alpha_4, \alpha_2$ to stand for H_1, C_4, O_2, we obtain Figure 10.4.2.

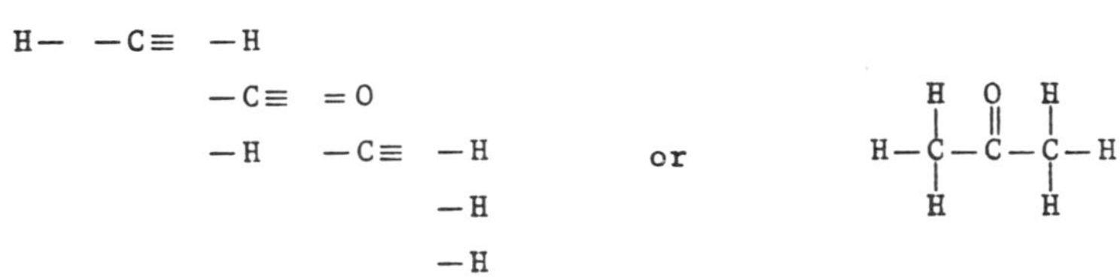

(a) (b)

Figure 10.4.2 Figure (a) is produced by Example 2. It is equivalent to (b).

Example 3

An example of how β is used when there is a closed loop with an odd number of nodes is:

$$S \rightarrow A_{01}\ A_{13}\ [\beta_{11}, A_{22}]^T [A_{12}, A_{12}, A_{10}]^T [A_{10}, A_{31}]^T\ A_{10}$$

$$\rightarrow \alpha_1 - - \alpha_4 \equiv [-, = \alpha_4 =]^T [- \alpha_3 =, - \alpha_3 =, - \alpha_1]^T [- \alpha_1, \equiv \alpha_4]^T - \alpha_1$$

If we understand α_1, α_3, α_4, respectively, as meaning H, N, C, we obtain Figure 10.4.3.

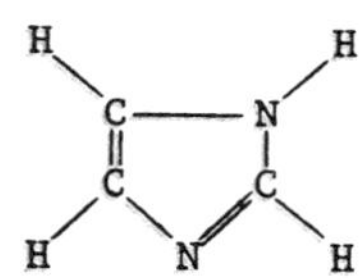

Figure 10.4.3 Example 3 produces this molecule.

Example 4

$$S \rightarrow \alpha_1 - - \alpha_4 \equiv [- \alpha_4 \equiv, = \alpha_4 =]^T [- \alpha_1, = \alpha_4 =, - \alpha_4 \equiv, - \alpha_1]^T$$

$$[- \alpha_4 \equiv, \equiv \alpha_4 -, - \alpha_1]^T [- \alpha_4 \equiv, = \alpha_4 =, - \alpha_4 \equiv]\ [- \alpha_1, = \alpha_4 =,$$

$$- \alpha_4 \equiv, \equiv \alpha_4 -, - \alpha_1]^T [- \alpha_1, \equiv \alpha_4 -, - \alpha_1, - \alpha_1]^T - \alpha_1$$

This linear formula, where α_1 = H, α_4 = C, corresponds to Figure 10.4.4.

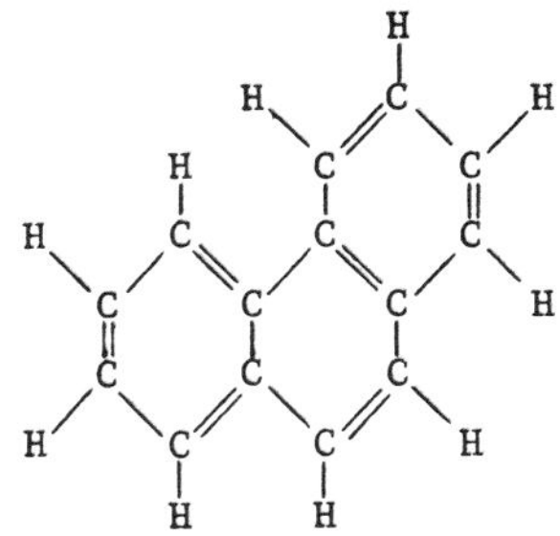

Figure 10.4.4 Example 4 produces this molecule.

Example 5

Kékulé's formula for the benzene nucleus given in Figure 10.4.5

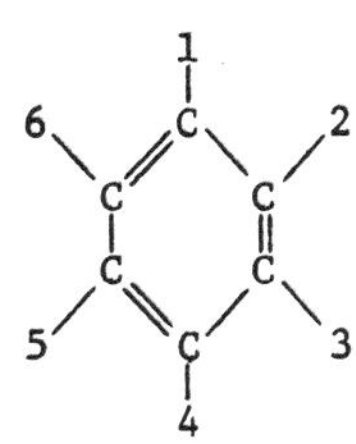

Figure 10.4.5 Example 5.

will be written in our language with the help of γ's:

$$\gamma_1^{(1)} - -C \equiv [-C \equiv,\ =C =]^T [- \gamma_1^{(2)},\ =C =,\ -C \equiv,\ - \gamma_1^{(6)}]^T$$

$$[- \gamma_1^{(3)},\ \equiv C -,\ - \gamma_1^{(5)}]\ \gamma_1^{(4)}$$

We can make our language still more versatile by introducing "loop formulae," "permutators," and "recursive growth" convention. A formula marked by L starting with a γ_i and ending with another γ_i means that the two γ's should be deleted, and the i bonds emanating from the first γ_i and the i bonds received by the second γ_i should be connected one by one in the top-to-bottom order. This can be formally introduced into the grammar by adding

$$P_8:\quad S \rightarrow L:\ \gamma_i\ A_{ii}\ \gamma_i$$

and by adding a symbol L in the V_N and giving an explanation as to how to use it.

Example 6

The molecule considered in Example 3 can now be described without the help of the artificial element β, namely:

$$L:\ \gamma_1\ -N=[-H,\ -C\equiv]^T[-H,\ =N-]^T\ -C\equiv[-H,\ =C=]^T[-H,\ -\gamma_1]$$

Example 7

The formula L: $\gamma_2\ \beta_{22}\ \gamma_2$ is a perfectly legitimate formula according to our grammar which describes a double loop without nodes.

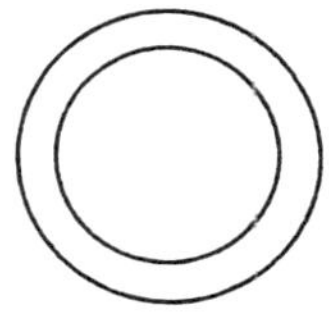

Figure 10.4.6 This can be produced by our rules.

Example 8

Consider a formula

$$L(\gamma_1^{(1)}),\ L(\gamma_1^{(2)}):\ \gamma_1-\alpha_3=[-\alpha_3=,\ -\alpha_3=]^T[-\gamma_1^{(2)}=\alpha_3-,\ -\gamma_1^{(2)}]\ \gamma^{(1)}$$

where the loop operation is done with respect to $\gamma^{(1)}$ and $\gamma^{(2)}$. The molecule would look like Figure 10.4.7.

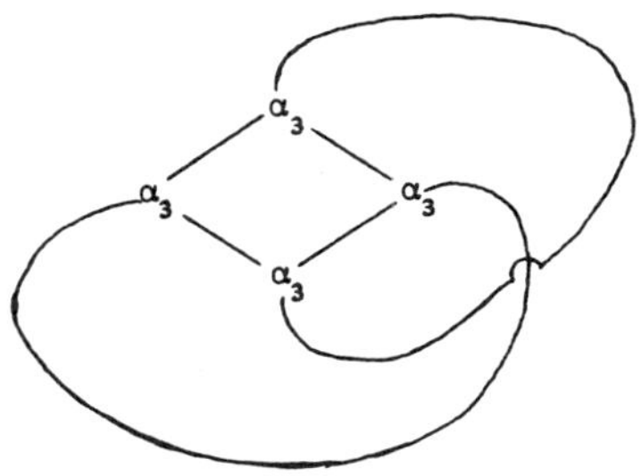

Figure 10.4.7 The use of the loop operation can produce this picture.

Next, let us introduce the permutator U_k. We can change the production rule P_2 to

$$P_2': \quad A_{ij} \rightarrow A_{ik} U_k A_{kj}$$

$$U_k = \{i_1, i_2, \ldots, i_\ell, \ldots, i_k\}$$

adding U's in the U_N. $A_{ik} U_k A_{kj}$ means that the ℓ-th bond coming from the left (i.e., from A_{ik}) should be connected to the i_ℓ-th bond going to the right (i.e., to A_{kj}). If $\{i_1, i_2, \ldots, i_k\}$ is $\{1,2,\ldots,k\}$ then there is no permutation, hence we can omit it, and P_2' becomes P_2.

Example 9

A formula produced by our grammar is

$$\alpha_2 = [-\ \alpha_3 =,\ -\ \alpha_3 =]\{1,3,2,4\}[=\ \alpha_3 -,\ =\ \alpha_3 -] = \alpha_2$$

which represents Figure 10.4.8.

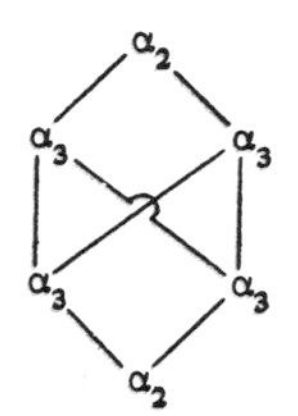

Figure 10.4.8 With the help of a permutator we can produce this picture.

Next let us introduce the "recursive growth" convention. If we have, conforming with P_1 and P_2,

$$S \rightarrow A_{on}\gamma_{no}$$

$$\gamma_{no} \rightarrow A_{nm}\gamma_{mo}, \qquad m \geq n$$

we have a recursively growing graph, depending on how often we use the second formula above. The general form obtained will be $A_{on_1}A_{n_1n_2}A_{n_2n_3}\ldots A_{n_{k-1}n_k}\gamma_{n_k}$. ($\gamma_{no}$ is considered a member of V_N).

Example 10

Let us assume n=m, and let A_{02}, A_{22} (A_{nm} above with n=m) be respectively α_2 =, and $[-\alpha_2-, -\alpha_2-]^T = \alpha_4$ =. Then we have successively formulae (i) $\alpha_2 = \gamma 2$, (ii) $\alpha_2 = [-\alpha_2-, -\alpha_2-]^T = \alpha_4 = \gamma 2$, (iii) $\alpha_2 = [-\alpha_2-, -\alpha_2-]^T = \alpha_4 = [-\alpha_2-, -\alpha_2-]^T = \gamma 2$, etc. The corresponding graphs are given in Figure 10.4.9, which reminds us of a WEB graph [F-9, P-15].

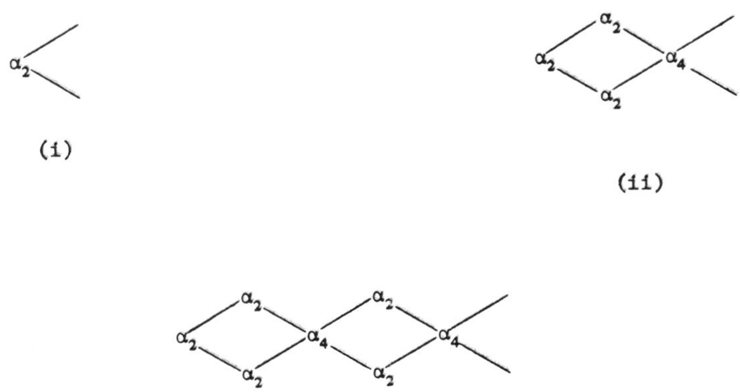

(i) (ii) (iii)

Figure 10.4.9 We can produce also WEB-graph-like pictures.

Example 11

In this example, we have m = n + 2 in the recursive formula, and putting n=2k

$$A_{2k,2k+2} = [-\alpha_3=, =\alpha_4=, \ldots, =\alpha_4=, =\alpha_3-]^T$$

where there are two α_3's and (k-1) α_4's in the brackets. If we put $A_{02} \rightarrow \alpha_2 =$, we shall obtain successively

$$\text{(i)}\quad \alpha_2 = \gamma_2$$

$$\text{(ii)}\quad \alpha_2 = [-\alpha_3=, -\alpha_3=]^T \gamma_4$$

$$\text{(iii)}\quad \alpha_2 = [-\alpha_3=, -\alpha_3=]^T[-\alpha_3=, =\alpha_4=, -\alpha_3=]^T \gamma_6$$

and so on. The corresponding graphs are given in Figure 10.4.10.

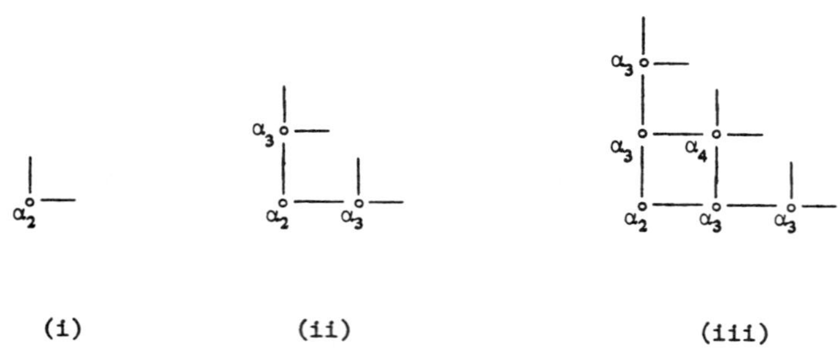

Figure 10.4.10 Example 11 which grows recursively.

Example 12

Putting

$$A_{on} \rightarrow \gamma_{02}\ [-\alpha_2-, -\alpha_2-]^T\{2,1\}$$

$$A_{nm} \rightarrow [-\alpha_2-, -\alpha_2-]^T\{2,1\}$$

in the recursive formula we obtain a result:

$$\gamma_{02}([-\alpha_2-, -\alpha_2-]^T\{2,1\})^n \gamma_{20}$$

where $(\ )^n$ means the n-times multiplication (concatenation) of the content of the parentheses. If we put the loop symbol on the foregoing formula, we obtain

$$L: \gamma_2 = ([-\alpha_2-, -\alpha_2-]^T\{2,1\})^n = \gamma_2$$

which is the linear description of the graph in Figure 10.4.11 (n=8). The difference

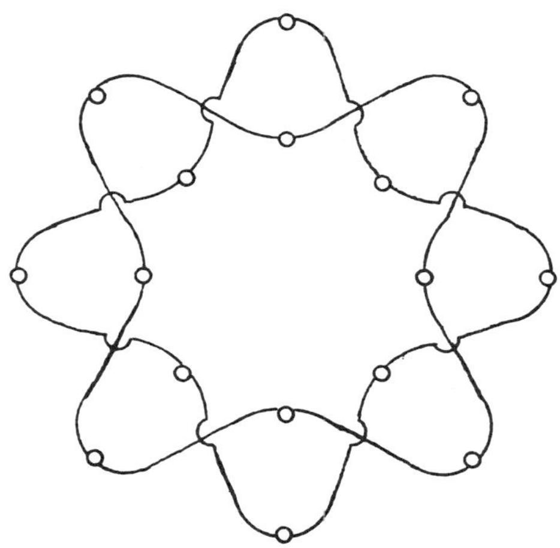

Figure 10.4.11 The reader should try a case with an odd n.

between the presence and absence of the permutator will become more strikingly visible if we take an odd number as n in this example.

The parsing in the sense of an examination as to whether a formula in terms of the members of V_T can be produced by the production rules is very easy in this language. All we need is to check (1) whether the valence of an atom is the same as the number of bonds emanating from the atom and (2) whether the number of bonds going to the right from a term is the same as the number of bonds going to the left from the next term. Note well that there are usually many ways to combine applications of the rule P_2 to obtain the same final formula. Note that not all the structures expressed by our language really exist in nature, although they will obey the rules of valence.

An important problem concerns how we should proceed to transcribe a structural formula into a formula in our language. The rule is to select any one atom and assign it to the first zone. The second zone consists of all atoms to which the first atom is directly connected. Unless there is a triangle of connecting lines, any two atoms belonging to the second zone will not be connected to each other. All the bonds coming from the atoms of the second zone, except those that go to the starting atom, will then cut the border between the second zone and the third zone. We define the third zone as the area covered by the set of atoms which are directly connected with the atoms of the second zone. Unless there is a triangle or a pentagon, all the atoms in the third zone will be disconnected from each other. We continue this process until we can no longer make a further zone. Each zone will correspond to an A_{ij} (in which the atoms are substituted for the α's), where i is the number of bonds cutting the border with the previous zone and j is the number of bonds cutting the border with the next zone.

The top-to-bottom order mentioned in the rules can be interpreted as the left-to-right order when we progress from the starting atom creating new zones. The only ambiguity in the formula stems from the arbitrary choice of the starting atom. We can agree that we take the topmost, leftmost atom in the usual structural formula as the starting atom to avoid this ambiguity.

In case there is a polygon with an odd number of nodes, we can agree to put a fictitious atom (β_{ii}) at a well-defined position. As we proceed from one zone to the next there will be the first atom belonging to the polygon appearing in a certain zone. Then we can agree to place β_{ii} within the next zone on the left branch of the polygon. This will make the transcription unique.

The formula given in Example 3 is obtained by placing β at the position indicated in Figure 10.4.12.

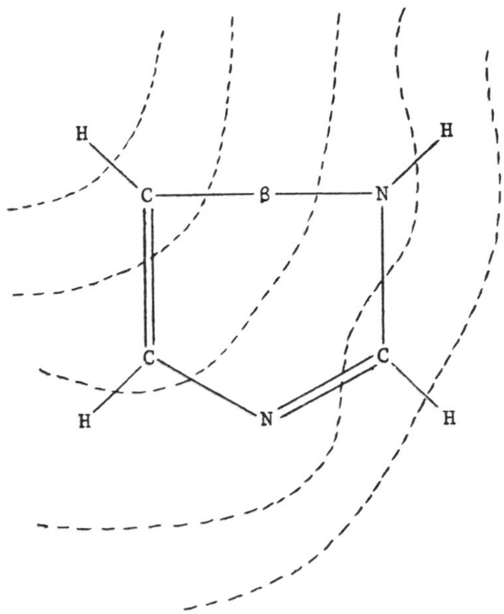

Figure 10.4.12 The use of a β.

10.5 GENERAL REMARKS ON THE GRAMMATICAL METHOD

In the last two sections, we briefly explained what the grammatical method is and showed one example. In this section we want to critically review the basic problems with regard to the way this method functions in relation to actual problems and to comment on the underlying "philosophy."

As we now know, the two major ingredients of the method are "atoms" and "composition rules." But how should we decide the atoms? The basic guidelines about the choice of atoms are that the atoms should be the <u>largest</u> common parts from which the entire set of pictures under consideration can be constructed.

The qualification, "largest," is important because, for instance, two kinds of atoms always come together in a fixed way of combination; it is not necessary to decompose this combination into two atoms. The combined unit can serve as one atom. In addition to this consideration the atoms should be so chosen as to make the composition rules elegant and simple and to make the detection of atoms easy. The detection of atoms by machine in a given picture has to rely on a pattern recognition technique other than the grammatical method, and this task is usually not easy. It is very important to note that even after we have imposed these conditions on the atoms, their choice is not uniquely determined and presents a delicate set of problems. The problems of segmentation, as we discussed briefly in Section 10.1, are not the only difficulties connected with identification of atoms.

In the case of a real language, there is practically no alternative other than choosing the words as atoms. In the applications to pictures, we have to distinguish two entirely different cases. In one case, the set of pictures is defined by some pre-existing (natural) criteria. Such is the case with Ledley's language for the shape of chromosomes and also with our CSL for all the possible structures that can be built according to the law of valence. But, in most of the examples considered in the grammatical approach to picture analysis, the set of pictures is defined by the arbitrarily chosen (artificial) criteria. In the case of "natural" criteria, we have to deal with the difficult problem of making a suitable choice of atoms to cope with the given problem. In the case of "artificial" criteria, the atoms are first decided according to our own arbitrary fancy, and the set of pictures are determined by these atoms and by the composition rules.

In the problem of atom choice, it may be worthwhile to note that the absence rather than the presence of a certain portion of the object can also be a very useful mark of an object. For instance, the holes in Emmenthal cheese (or lotus root) certainly can be considered as an important constituent part of the object. This reinterpretation of absence as presence may be compared with the interpretation of a "bubble" in the sea of negative electrons in negative energy states as a positive electron. It is well known that a method of using "lakes" and "bays" to characterize printed or handwritten alphabetic letters has proved quite successful. The lakes and bays are certainly not components in the strict sense. It seems that for the purpose of real pattern recognition we should be much more flexible in defining components than the mathematical models of grammatical approaches would force us to be.

The next problem is one of deciding the grammatical composition rules. Here again, the "natural" case and "artificial" case are entirely different. In the artificial case, we can set up any rules; the main concern is what kind of "interesting" pictures the chosen set of rules can produce. In the "natural" case, the problem is one of induction. The grammatical rules can produce infinitely many pictures, but we have only a limited number of examples that obey the rules. As is well known [W-10], this type of induction leaves an essential ambiguity as to the inferred general rules. To overcome this ambiguity, we have to resort to an arbitrarily chosen criteria of elegance, simplicity, and so on. The inductive inference of grammatical rules from examples is usually called "grammatical inference" (see [B-2] among others).

In some cases, examples of ungrammatical sentences (pictures) are given together with examples of grammatical sentences (pictures), which makes the task easier. The task becomes still easier if we are allowed to "ask questions" as to legitimacy of freely chosen examples. In the case of a natural language, this tutoring model is not far from reality. To determine grammatical rules, we can make different sentences and ask a native speaker of the language whether they are grammatically correct or not. But in the case of pictures, it is not always easy to realize such a tutorial system.

It is known that the best mathematical model of induction is provided by the Bayesian hypotheses testing [W-10, W-13]. For the application of the Bayesian model to the grammatical method in pattern recognition, see [H-3]. The application of this model implies both that the hypotheses (possible grammatical rules) are assigned credibilities and that the grammatical rules assign probabilities to certain productions. The second probability could be

0 and 1; then the rules become deterministic, which we have assumed in the foregoing explanation of the grammatical approach.

The idea of assigning probabilities (which are not necessarily 0 or 1) to each production rule, and therefore to produced sentences (pictures), goes back to Banerji and Grenander [B-1, G-7]. Fu and his associates have developed this area of stochastic grammar in many papers [F-2].

Suppose we assign p_{0j} to each substitution rule: $S \rightarrow A_j$ and p_{ij} to $A_i \rightarrow A_j$, and so on, so that $\sum_j p_{ij} = 1$, where j covers all possible branching from A_i. Then each string of substitutions ending with a sentence (picture) x will be assigned a probability p(x), which is a product of these probabilities of the type p_{ij}, and if the normalization is correctly done we shall have $\sum_x p(x) = 1$. If there are more than one string of substitutions, producing the identical sentence x, the probability p(x) will be the sum of the probabilities corresponding to these several strings. For the parsing of sentences produced by the probabilistic grammar, we have to consider the so-called stochastic automaton. This stochastic approach to grammar is a good approximation to the realistic situation and for that reason is worth investigation; however, the practical usefulness, in particular in the case of applications to pictures, is somewhat doubtful.

In applications of the grammatical approach (stochastic or nonstochastic) to pictures, we have to keep in mind that a final linear string in terms of the members of the terminal vocabulary is an actual object of study, namely, a sentence. In the case of pictures, however, we need another step to connect the final linear expression in terms of the terminal vocabularity and an actual picture which is the object of study. In the process of production, this step is usually not much of a problem, but in the process of analysis or parsing, we need tremendous pattern recognition work to translate the picture into the linear expression. This effort is usually left out of the discussion of a grammatical approach. But, on the other hand, as can be seen in our example of CSL, this linearization, when its procedure is clearly determined, is of value by itself apart from the grammatical analysis.

In discussing the phrase-structure grammar (Chomskyian grammar), we should not forget the topic of double meaning of sentences. One of the fascinating advantages of the phrase-structure grammar is that if two different parsing trees can be assigned to a given sentence, they correspond to the two different meanings in which the given sentence can be interpreted. This interesting feature is not found in the picture adaptation of this grammar. As a matter of fact, there are often more than one parsing tree for one picture without carrying any different meanings. This meaningless redundancy in pictures in some (but not all) cases stems from the simple fact that a sentence (being a one-dimensional entity) has a well-defined beginning and a well-defined end, while a picture does not.

It is well known that a picture, too, has often a "double meaning." The "figure" and "ground" of a picture come often alternatingly to the foreground of our perception. There are many known geometrical figures whose three-dimensional interpretation oscillates in our mind's eye. We can produce many examples similar to the famous rabbit-duck of Wittgenstein [W-14]. As MacKay [M-1] often points out, one of the most conspicuous facts about the double meaning of a picture is that only one or the other of the alternative interpretations can occupy our mind at one time, and they can never occur simultaneously together. This is very much like the observation of linear polarizations of an elliptically polarized photon in atomic physics, and it perhaps has something to do with the nondistributive logic that governs our psychological experience [W-15, W-35]. Because the phrase-structure grammar is intimately committed to the distributive logic, we cannot expect it to give any satisfactory interpretation to the double-meaning of pictures. We are aware that there are authors who want to explain the double-meaning of a picture by the multiplicity of "grammatical" analyses, but we are not quite persuaded by them (see for instance the fascinating article by Clowes [C-2]).

Before closing this chapter, I should like to invite the reader to reflect upon the historical background of the phrase-structure grammar approach to picture recognition. Phrase-structure grammar [C-3] has become so prestigious within a short period of time that to many people grammar nowadays means exclusively phrase-structure grammar. Correspondingly, many of those who try to make a grammatical theory of pictures take it for granted that they have to emulate the phrase-structure grammar to make a really modern theory of pictures. To understand the strong points and shortcomings of such an attempt, it will be necessary to consider the reason why the phrase-structure grammar has become so popular so quickly.

The intellectual attractiveness of this grammatical theory derives from its kinship with the proof theory developed by logicians and with the automata theory. Certainly the founders of this type of grammar were strongly influenced by the then popular new stream of logical development associated with such fascinating names as Frege, Russel, Gödel, Post, and Turing, among others. The influence of the proof theory on this language theory is so evident that even now there are still people who feel that this theory tries to force a framework which is natural in another entirely different field on the field of language.* But the analogy between grammaticalness and provability (computability) is so beautiful and so enticing that we are tempted to believe that there is something deeper than mere coincidence. But, people tend to forget that this key point of the phrase-structure grammar has no role to play in its adaptation to the picture theory.

The phrase-structure grammar is supposed to produce grammatically correct sentences and only grammatically correct sentences. But, the grammatical, generative rules assumed in a picture theory often produce pictures that can never occur in practice. Furthermore, there are many pictures that occur in practice which cannot be produced by those generative rules. Even limiting ourselves to a certain well-defined family of pictures, we find there is no such thing as "pictureness" corresponding to "grammaticalness" or "provability" or "computability." A grammatical theory is a

*Chomsky himself argued that phrase-structure grammars are inadequate to account for the class of grammatical sentences in a natural language.

descriptive theory, but it derives its utility partly from its normative aspect. In picture applications, however, there are no useful normative concepts. If a single picture appears that violates our grammatical rules, we cannot reject the picture because it is ungrammatical, but we have to modify the rules. The result will probably produce many pictures which we do not want to include in our family of pictures.

About twenty or thirty years ago, a strange myth about human and artificial intelligence was created by a multiple coincidence of events. A myth often has utility, but this myth seems to have played out its resourcefulness, and only superstition lingers. The coincidence of events that occurred was as follows. Nerve cells had been found to have only two states: fired or not fired. The success of the electronic computer was mainly due to the use of binary numbers. Symbolic logic was found tremendously useful in the design of computer circuitries. Gödel [G-12] had proven a mystifying new theorem about the unprovability of certain true theorems in arithmetics. The relationship between provability and computability had just been realized. All these events contributed to the formation of a cluster of half-truths: The Boolean logic is the infallible and all-comprehensive rule of valid thinking. The human brain works on the binary system and is a poor error-prone computer. All the sciences should emulate symbolic logic and should be described as an axiomatic deductive system. The digital computer is intrinsically superior to the analogue computer.

We have shown that the Boolean (i.e., distributive) logic is good only for arithmetics and part of classical physics, and as the set of rules of valid thinking it is not only too narrow but even ill-founded [W-15, W-35]. See also the Appendix of this book. We know by now also that the human brain works in terms of both binary and continuous variables and can do many things that a computer cannot do [W-16]. See the epilogue for the explanation of my idea of "paradigmatic symbols" by which the human brain does its pattern recognition. The functions of paradigmatic symbols is entirely different from a logical process. We are also now becoming aware that in some problems we had better retrieve the once-rejected analogue computers or make a hybrid computer. The phrase structure-grammar was indeed a sparkingly fascinating product of that particular Zeitgeist* of twenty years ago, but now it is the time for a more sober reevaluation, in spite of the undeniable contribution to linguistics made by this new grammar.

Probably, more important than the purely technical achievements of this new grammar was the rationalistic philosophy of learning underlying Chomsky's theory [C-4]. We can learn languages only because we have innate ideas which make it possible to understand and to generate sentences. Our brains are not like a blank paper on which "experience" can be registered as on a photographic plate. This philosophy is basically correct and has a profound significance with reference to pattern recognition. We have shown that there exists no such thing as natural classes in the purely empirical data. It is our internal predilection that makes classification possible. It is surprising that many experts of pattern recognition have adopted so easily all the technicalities of the phrase-structure grammar and did not particularly appreciate the more important underlying philosophy. It is of course to be kept in mind that what seems to be a priori to an individual is the result of a long series of learning processes from experience through the process of evolution [W-18].

The only objection I have to the rationalistic philosophy of learning is that it tends to imply that our innate ideas are logical in nature. We have pointed out [W-10, W-16] that what is needed to make learning possible is not only our innate logical elements but also our internal esthetic elements. Without the latter neither induction nor pattern recognition is possible. This fact is overlooked by the linguists because they are still under the spell of logicalism. Another error of rationalism is that the excessive emphasis on the a priori element in learning makes one forget that learning depends on an

---

*The reader might be tempted to use the Kuhnian term of "paradigm" for the Zeitgeist. But, Kuhn's use of the word paradigm is not in agreement with the proper meaning of the word in English, and, furthermore, we have used the same word in an entirely different meaning in this book. For my objection to Kuhn's theory of theory change, see [W-17].

immense number of empirical data, hence learning has inevitably a statistical aspect. The rationalists usually have a morbid horror of statistical elements in knowledge.

One of the profound weaknesses of the phrase-structure grammar is shared by the theory of deductions in logic. This theory gives a set of rules by which we can derive valid propositions from a set of assumptions. But, there is no universal set of rules by which one can obtain a proof for a given theorem within a fixed number of stages even if this theorem is provable in principle. If we could produce all valid consequences from the assumptions, one of them should be this theorem, but we never know when we encounter this particular one. For this reason, the so-called mechanical theorem proving machine requires various heuristic methods. One of the usual procedures is to start not only from the top (assumptions) but also from the bottom (theorem) and to hope that these two routes will meet somewhere in the middle.

The inverse bottom-up procedure can use, among others, two important tricks. One is to notice that if the assumptions imply the theorem, then the negation of the theorem should imply the negation of the assumptions. Another clue is to find an intermediate theorem that would imply the theorem in question, and, if this intermediate theorem can be proven by the assumptions, then we have proven the theorem in question. The most striking fact here is that in spite of the *deductive* nature of the task of theorem proving, the production of the intermediate theorem from the given theorem is *inductive* in nature (see Chapter 4 of [W-10]). It is well known that there are many interesting works that have been done in this field of theorem proving precisely because there are no foolproof universal algorithms for that task (see, for instance, [G-1]). Here is a vast field of heuristics.

Similarly, the phrase-structure grammar is provided with a set of rules to produce a grammatical sentence, but there is no universal algorithm to produce a parsing tree for a given sentence within a given finite length of time. This fact is already quite disturbing in the case of sentences, but it is even more annoying in the case of pictures, because we are not so much interested in producing a "correct" picture as in analyzing the structure (i.e., in finding the parsing tree for a given picture). This last-named task is indeed the sole purpose, so to speak, of the phrase-structural approach in picture recognition.

Connected with the essentially formal nature of the production rules of grammar is the strange fact that these rules can produce a formally correct sentence, but they cannot produce a particular sentence which should express a desired meaning. The same situation exists in the phrase-structural theory of pictures. You can produce a picture and find out what it represents, but you cannot produce the picture you want.

Epilogue

E1. PARADIGMATIC SYMBOL AND PATTERN RECOGNITION

Content of Perception

What we have studied in this book can be characterized mainly as the "process" of human perception and the methods of mechanical simulation of this process. It may thus be appropriate to complete this book by supplementing the summary with a short survey about the nature of the "content" of human perception, and relatedly that of human memory. This will involve a reflection on the similarity or difference or both of the human and mechanical counterparts.

We have contrasted two epistemological points of view, (1) the Aristotelian viewpoint: what exists is (an enumerable number of) particular objects, with fixed attributes, and (2) the Platonic viewpoint: what exists is the form of which we have an innate idea (see Section 3.1). Briefly, the Platonic view seems to be more strongly favored by the modern neurophysiological experiments. The brain does not seem to have any box, or cell, or cortex region corresponding to a self-identical object, but it has certain definitively identifiable neurons corresponding to the simple Forms (such as circleness, triangleness, clockwiseness, etc.), (see Section 2.4). These neurological forms are, at least as far as some elementary ideas are concerned, innate and permanent.

Now regarding the relation between Form and particular objects (whose ultimate reality is put in doubt by Plato), Plato's viewpoint can be represented by the idea of "paradigms." The paradigm is at once a single example belonging to the Form as well as the Form itself. This is somewhat similar to the situation in ordinary modern languages: the word "pattern" sometimes means a member of a class and sometimes means the class itself (see Section 1.1). The reason for this confused usage is the very fact that perception, or pattern recognition, is a process of "seeing-one-in-many" (Chapter 1).

Recognition of this somewhat perplexing situation resulted in an Aristotelian aberration that the paradigm is the (n + 1)st object that represents a set of n objects, leading to an infinite regression (see Section 3.1). Plato, after Parmemides, became sensitive to that point, and tried to dispel also the caricatured picture of the Platonic world of Forms, cluttered with idealized table, idealized cat, idealized triangle, and so on. But, this does not stop the fact that the paradigm, or Form, or pattern is simultaneously one and many, particularly, it is not one on top of many. The neuron sensitive to triangles is one, but recognizes many triangles. The brain does not care which particular triangle is shown. All that counts is the idea of triangleness that is innate and permanent.

Since the early 60s when the author entered the field of pattern recognition, he has used consistently the term paradigm to mean class-sample. This use of the word turned out to be appropriate according to the modern study of the philosophy of Plato, the man who used the word at the earliest stage of Western civilization. In the 70s, the author used the word paradigmatic symbol to designate what human thought operates with, in contrast to the abstract (empty) symbols with which the computer operates [M-4, W-28, W-29]. This term "paradigmatic symbol" served the purpose of clarifying the difference between human intelligence and artificial intelligence. In this epilogue, we shall continue to use the term "paradigmatic symbol" to designate the nature of content of perception, and consequently also of memory. We shall now enumerate various characteristic properties of paradigmatic symbols.

Elicitory Function of Paradigmatic Symbols

From a logical point of view, a concept can be defined by its intension or extension; it can be represented by an abstract symbol standing for the set of objects corresponding to this concept. However, when a mother wants to teach her child the concept, say, of monkey, she does not give the intension or extension of the class of monkeys. Instead, she shows him just one (or a few) concrete examples of monkey, and the child will seldom make a mistake in recognizing a second monkey he may encounter, although he may never be capable of defining the intension or extension of the class of monkeys. For the child, the first monkey is a paradigmatic symbol. This symbol is a concrete object, or a mental representation thereof, standing for the class of objects of which it is a member; it is a particular standing for a universal. Obviously one object can belong to many, indeed infinitely many, different classes; hence the concept, or "field," for which a paradigmatic symbol stands is not unique and fixed, resulting in what is called inductive ambiguity. But placed in a certain context and applied in each individual case the paradigmatic symbol defines a fairly well-defined field. Fuzziness and flexibility are advantages rather than disadvantages in its usefulness.

The reader may think that paradigmatic symbol is nothing but the so-called "ostensive definition" of a concept. But, the idea of ostensive definition refers only to the manner in which an example of the concept is shown. What is important in the idea of paradigmatic symbol is the capability of a particular example standing for, or more correctly "eliciting," all other examples of the class. The elicitory power is the secret of the mysterious double role of the paradigmatic symbol which is at once one and many.

To avoid misunderstanding, we should not visualize the field as a collection of separate individual particulars, which are connected post hoc by a certain number of bonds of contingent associations. This does not mean that a field does not have internal parts, but it is from the beginning one coherent unit of which one part immediately calls for the other; its vibration of one arouses a resonance on the other. The elicitory capacity is nothing originating from an extraneous agent. It is, so to speak, an intrinsic resonance. The paradigmatic symbol need not be a verbal symbol, but its elicitory power is somewhat like a symbol in the "symbolism" in literature. It evokes, elicits, induces association and repercussion in a field of intrinsically related (if not associated) elements.

There is nothing wrong with using the idea of association among elements, but because even the behaviorists use the word association, we should use coherence or intrinsic relation to express this type of strong "association." But, in the case of the paradigmatic symbol in pattern recognition, a good question to ask is: what is the "cement" that holds the field together? A partial answer is that the "emotional" element plays at least an important role in this cohesion. We shall see later a stronger argument for this point, but we can already say that when we identify a second cat as the "same" thing as a first cat, we definitively evoke the nice feeling of their fur and the cuteness of their behavior. The perception of one paradigm evokes not only other fellow class members, but also it recreates the emotional atmosphere in which both paradigms are found. In this sense, the elicitory power is not only cognitive but also evaluative. In this connection, we should remember also what we learned in Chapter 4 on evaluative ponderation. The gist of that chapter was that the formation of concepts which is the result of pattern recognition is not possible by logical inference except by the help of evaluative ponderation of predicates. This shows also that the paradigmatic symbol requires emotional evaluation for its generation.

Once a paradigmatic symbol elicits a field, there is nothing wrong with giving a name to it. When such a name starts to function, independently of the concrete contents in it, it becomes an abstract symbol. The "concept," divorced from the concrete members, is the empty name. The language deals with such empty abstract symbols. See E.2 for Chirality of the Brain regarding left brain versus right brain.

Computer

Before going further into the nature of human recognition and human memory, let us review how the computer works. It is useless to imagine all sorts of future computers that may have basically different capabilities from the existing computers. It is better to limit ourselves to the present-day computers and those computers that have the same basic functions as these with only improved efficiency. The present-day computer performs three basic functions: storage, sorting, and logical operations.

In mechanical storage, each item of stored information is provided with its address and content. Both address and content are represented in physical states that can be identified by (binary) numbers. We can store and extract numerized symbols under numerized addresses.

We can sort stored items as well as outside data. There are two kinds of sorting: extensional sorting and intensional sorting. Sorting is essentially classification, and according to whether classification is done by virtue of the extension or intension of the class, the sorting becomes, respectively, extensional sorting or intensional sorting.

Consider a case of personal data punched out on IBM cards. Each card has the name of the person and the various data about his properties. If you have a list of names whose data you need, you pull out the desired cards according to the names. This is extensional sorting. If you want to put together those people who have a certain common property, for instance, those who are taller than six feet, then you extract cards according to the data inscribed on them. This is intensional sorting. The search operation is also a special case of sorting where the data are sometimes produced by the program.

Finally, the computer can do logical operations which enable it to carry out arithmetical operations. All higher mathematical operations are reduced to these simple logical operations.

The fundamental fact about these three kinds of "mental" operations of computers is that they are done in terms of pure abstract symbols devoid of any concrete meaning. In order to make the computer effective, we have to introduce from outside the rules of interpretation. Depending on these rules, the computer may be interpreted as meaning entirely different things or meaning nonsense. It is true that we can build these rules of interpretation into a robot so that its concrete behavior can be directly related to the abstract activities of the computer brain; however, we can change these rules and the robot does not cease to be a robot. In other words, the interpretation rules are not organically united with the life or well-being of the robot. It should be noted that paradigmatic symbols need no separate rules of interpretation. We cannot arbitrarily alter the meaning of paradigmatic symbols which are imbedded in the context of life.

Let us now compare these mechanical mental operations to human mental operations. First, human memory does not store abstract symbols. What we remember is backed with emotional impression. It has no address. It is not an isolated item, but it is a general field. The items in the memory can be called out not by the address but by elicitation or association. An item, acting as a paradigmatic symbol, awakens a whole field of memorized items which is flexible and depends on the context and has no similarity to the mechanical memory. In computer technology there is a system called associative memory, but it also has no similarity to the memory system in living organisms. It is working in terms of abstract symbols, and the field of association is limited and fixed. The difference cannot be dismissed as a difference in the degree of complexity. We are going to discuss more in detail the nature of human memory in later sections of the Epilogue in connection with psychological theory and neurological findings.

As far as sorting is concerned, the human brain can do what we call paradigmatic sorting in addition to extensive and intensive sorting. Paradigmatic sorting is the essence of pattern recognition. The human brain can also do basic logical operations and arithmetic operations. These form the basis of deductive inference, but we will show presently that what is considered to be a typical case of deductive inference cannot be carried out solely by means of these purely logical operations. Inductive inference, which is acknowledged by everybody to be outside the domain of logical operations, is obviously outside the capability of the functions of the computer. We will, however, specify more carefully where the difficulties lie for the computer in simulating inductive inference.

Deduction

Deduction is the primary field where the computer has been designed to replace the human mind, functioning on the basic rules of deductive logical operations. Hence, one would imagine that at least in this field the computer can do the job without human aid--but, is this true? The answer is, unfortunately, in the negative.

Take the case of theorem proving, which is one of the most typical deductive operations. We are given a set of axioms, a set of logical rules of deduction, and a theorem to be proved. We are supposed to produce a sequence of theorems such that each one of them is logically derivable from the axioms and/or the preceding theorems and that the last of them coincides with the theorem to be proved.

The machine can produce all possible theorems that ensue from the axioms. If the machine is so programmed as to produce these valid theorems one by one, eventually one of them will turn out to be the theorem to be proved, provided of course it is a "provable" theorem, which we assume; however, this will not serve the purpose of actual theorem proving. The number of valid theorems increases roughly exponentially with the number of steps. As a result, it will take, on the average, a prohibitively long time before the machine will happen to produce the desired theorem, unless this last one requires very few steps from the axioms. That is the reason why any successful theorem-proving program uses some kind of heuristic principles whose main purpose is to limit the fanning process of the number of produced theorems to a reasonable size, and to reach the desired theorem within an acceptable period of computing time (see also Section 10.5).

It is important to note that all these heuristic principles are man-made, and there is at this moment no outlook for a computer program that will produce these heuristic principles by itself. The deep-lying reason seems to be that these heuristics are derived from extralogical inductive reasoning of the human mind. According to one of these heuristic approaches, part of the program starts not from the axioms but from the theorem to be proved. It produces, following various instructions of the program, would-be theorems from which the desired theorem would ensue.

That is, the machine in this mode starts from a more restrictive theorem to a more general statement. If this last is proved, the former will be proved. We have to go upward from the bottom in this fashion until we meet the other process coming down from the axioms.

The process of producing a more general statement from a more particular statement, so that the latter would logically ensue from the former, is the inverse of deductive derivation and constitutes an inductive process. That is also the reason why such a program also has to contain, other than axioms and rules of deduction, all kinds of non-necessary heuristic tricks to produce inductive generalization. The machine, essentially a logical operator, cannot perform the inductive process by itself. If it gives an impression of overcoming the inherent inductive ambiguity, it is only in the appearance.

Theorem proving is not the only case where an ostensively deductive process in reality involves extralogical knowledge or processes or both so that the machine cannot carry it out without human help (see [W-13] for more about the difficulties that the computer encounters in deductive tasks).

Induction

Before discussing induction in detail, let us make a somewhat inexact remark which may give a general perspective of our argument. Induction is a process of producing a general proposition on the ground of a limited number of particular propositions such that these become special instances of the former. It is a process of going from particular to universal, from concrete to abstract. We can then see that the function of a paradigmatic symbol contains in a nutshell the basic task of induction because it is a particular concrete object calling for a general abstract concept. The implication is that the most elementary function of human intelligence executed by paradigmatic symbols is inductive in nature. In a broad sense of the term, induction includes an advancement of argument by analogy. The analogy is considered by some, for instance, Yukawa [Y-1], as the secret of a creative progress of science. By comparison, the logical and deductive processes seem to be secondary acquired behaviors, less germane to the true nature of intelligence.

Induction consists of two major steps. In the first step, new hypotheses are created in the presence of observed facts in a certain domain of experience. In the second step, the hypotheses are evaluated. The first step, which is sometimes called abduction, is an act of creation about which we really do not know much, except that it is a purely extralogical process. Two things, however, may be said about it. First, it is intimately related to the paradigmatic symbolism in the human mind, because it concerns production of a general statement in the presence of concrete incidents. Secondly, it is very much like creation in art because it is the generation of something that did not previously exist and that carries some value. Some people think that computer composition of music is a case of creation, but we do not believe it is. It is not an "expression" of the artist. It is a product of random process obeying certain constraints about harmony and some idiosyncrasy. It is like a program that produces grammatical sentences. The sentences are not an "expression" of a writer who wants to convey something. It would take virtually an infinitely long time before the machine would happen to produce the sentence one wants or needs.

Concerning the evaluation of hypothesis, there is widespread misunderstanding that the plausibility of a hypothesis is determined by the relation between hypothesis and evidence. This error is tragically typified by Carnap's misunderstanding concept of c-function [W-24], [W-10], neglecting to differentiate credibility and the degree of confirmation. The credibility of a hypothesis also depends greatly on extra-evidential factors. Extra-evidential factors affecting the credibility of a hypothesis are, among other things, the credibility of other competing hypotheses, the ease with which the hypothesis can be harmoniously structured into a theoretical system of wider scope, and the esthetic value of the hypothesis, (e.g., its elegance and simplicity). Many of the classical paradoxes with regard to induction can be resolved if we realize that the crucial factor determining the acceptability of a hypothesis is not confirmation but the extra-evidential extralogical consideration (see Section 5.1).

This takes the process of induction out of the reach of purely mechanical data processing. We can produce a semblance of inductive inference with a computer by formulating esthetic criteria in machine-legible sentences, but we have to point out that these rules cannot be produced by a machine and that the criteria of esthetic values cannot be properly formulated in terms of abstract symbols (see also Section E-3). We may, therefore, conclude that all machine imitation of induction has either to omit some important factor of induction or to smuggle in man-made factors under some disguise.

Pattern Recognition

Pattern recognition can mean various things, but a typical task may be defined as being shown a certain limited number of samples (paradigms) of each of the given number of classes, and then shown an object of unknown class and required to place it in one of the classes. It is obviously an inductive process, hence it is not a logical process or mechanical sorting that the computer can perform without human aid; however, it is very instructive to study more closely the nature of the problem (see Chapter 5 and [W-24] for the relationship between pattern recognition and induction).

Pattern recognition is a task of classification, but the classes are defined neither by their intension nor by their extension. They are indicated only by paradigms. If the computer is ever to become capable of doing this job, it has to derive the class-defining properties (i.e., features) from the paradigms so that the task becomes one of intensional sorting, which the computer is capable of doing. But the derivation of class-defining properties from paradigms is not a machine-feasible operation without human aid.

According to the theorem of the Ugly Duckling, any pair of nonidentical objects share an equal number of predicates as any other pair of nonidentical objects, insofar as the number of predicates is finite [W-10]. That is to say, from a logical point of view, there is no such thing as a natural kind. In the case of pattern recognition, the new arrival shares the same number of predicates with any paradigm of any class, which shows that pattern recognition is a logically indeterminate problem. The class-defining properties are generalizations of certain of the properties shared by the paradigms of the class. Which of the properties should be used for generalization is not logically defined. If it were logically determinable, then pattern recognition would have a definite answer in violation of the theorem of the Ugly Duckling.

This conclusion is somewhat disturbing because our empirical knowledge is based on natural kinds of objects. The source of the trouble lies in the fact that we were just counting the number of predicates in the foregoing, treating them as if they were all equally important. The fact is that some predicates are more important than some others. Objects are similar if they share a large number of important predicates.

Important in what scale? We have to conclude that a predicate is important if it leads to a classification that is useful for some purpose. From a logical point of view, a whale can be put together in the same box with a fish or an elephant. For the purpose of building an elegant zoological theory, however, it is better to put the whale together with the elephant; for classifying industries it is better to put it together with the fish. The property characterizing mammals is important for the purpose of theory building in biology, whereas the property of living in water is more important for the purpose of classification of industries.

The conclusion is that classification is a value-dependent task and pattern recognition is mechanically possible only if we smuggle into the machine the scale of importance of predicates. Alternatively, we can introduce into the machine the scale of distance or similarity between objects. This seems to be an innocuous set of auxiliary data, but in reality we are thereby telling the machine our value judgment, which is of an entirely extralogical nature. The human mind has an innate scale of importance of predicates closely related to the sensory organs. This scale seems to have been developed during the process of evolution in such a way as to help maintain and expand life [W-32]. The machine, having no organized life-sustaining inner value structure, cannot form classes of objects or classify objects according to paradigms. In the human mind, on the other hand, paradigmatic symbols, being concrete objects and having their place in the inner value structure, can generate classes as cloud seeds can generate a large cloud around them.

What the paradigmatic symbol does is to form one (class) in a collection of many items. In a manner of speech, pattern recognition is seeing one in many, and this function is performed by the elicitory power of the paradigmatic symbol of the human mind. The inductive faculty cannot be formulated as a necessary, foolproof, unique law. The best we can do is to formulate it as a heuristic principle. The principle of minimum entropy (see Chapter 6) is one such heuristic principle that can be taught to the machine. Because it is a heuristic principle of inductive origin, it cannot be an ever-successful law.

In summary, we may say that artificial intelligence and human intelligence have an unbridgeable gap not only in substance, but also in function. If one wants, however, to narrow the gap, the first thing one could try would be to develop a genuine associative memory--that really deserves the name--to imitate some of the features of paradigmatic symbols. The idea of associating the problem of value to the distinction between human and mechanical intelligence was first announced in 1959 [W-30, W-31].

E2. PARADIGMATIC SYMBOL AND COGNITIVE PSYCHOLOGY

Perception and Memory

It is obvious that the precondition of memory is recognition, because memory registers what is perceived. Recognition requires memory, because perception usually presupposes a certain kind of anticipation originating from memory. The ordinary textbooks of psychology assume that memory is some kind of extension of perception. But in problem-solving of paradigm-oriented pattern recognition the relationship between memory and perception becomes more clearly formulated.

We have the present-stage idea of a class in our memory, and we compare the "newcomer" with this idea and decide whether it belongs or does not belong to the class. The actual judge is not solely the ideas coming from the memory; usually there is an external judge. If this judge decides that the classification according to the present stage of memory is false, then it is the turn of memory that is to be altered. That is, the memory of a class is not a fixed item, it is constantly restructured, which means that the use of memory is a reconstruction of memory. We learned in Chapter 9 of a mathematical model of adaptive memory. It is a primitive model of a complex mechanism of human memory, but it emphasizes the reconstructive aspect of memory.

It is true that very simple fundamental ideas are innate and fixed, or at least very slowly changing. This fact has some neurophysiological backing (see Section 2.4), but the items of memory are usually extremely complex combinations and relationships about simple ideas. These combinations and relationships need not be innate and fixed. As a matter of fact, the most important items of memory are not atomic sensory perceptions; they are "episodes."

Speaking of memory, we have to differentiate rote memory of meaningless concatenations of alphabets and numerals. They usually have a very short retentive life. These are retentions of abstract symbols. What we are interested in is a long-term memory of meaningful episodes. The anecdotic memory has at least three features: (1) It is a combination of many atomic items, (2) it is yet unified as one "story," and (3) it has a meaning. The third feature is the most important characteristic of this type of memory and also of perception. We shall come back to this point later. We should note that the content of a memory item is an integrated whole consisting of many, many atomic items that is not an innate item, but is subjected to modification, improvement, and gradual oblivion (see also Polanyi [P-5]).

We avoid controversy regarding psychological theories about memory, but we have the impression that the so-called reconstruction theory of memory comes the closest to our findings.

Paradigmatic Symbol as a Psychological "Scheme"

According to the reconstructionists, what we remember is not the fixed traces of the components of the past experience, but the "scheme" (i.e., how we construct the past experience out of these components). The term "scheme" in this connection was introduced by Henry Head, but became a favorite technical term of the cognitive psychologists since F.C. Bartlett adopted it in his famous book *Remembering* [B-12], although he "strongly disliked the term schema," (p. 200-201 of [B-12]). He thinks that "active developing pattern," or rather, "organized setting" may be better, but he continues to use the term "schema" in his book. According to him, "schema" is active organization of past reactions, or of past experiences, which must always be supposed to be operating in any well-adapted organic response. The main feature of the theory of schema is that perception and memory are not passive classifications, but the products of an active participation, an active construction by our mind.

The modern followers of Head and Bartlett like to compare the schema to the executive part (or instruction or command part) as distinct from the data part of a computer program [N-4]. This seems to make it easy for the modern mind to understand what schema means. But, this comparison is very misleading, because the real active agent behind the schemata in this case is the programmer who writes them and the operators who put them in the computer. The author of a natural-language-understanding program claimed that, in his program, knowledge is represented as procedures not as fixed verbal structures. This pleased the cognitive psychologists, but their awe will probably disappear as soon as they realize that none of these language-understanding programs understands the language as such. The machine gives one of the many possible answers that the programmer prepared in advance.

A still better explanation is to go back closer to the original idea of Bartlett (who associated the schemata with the memory of bodily posture) and say that the schema is like the content of memory of physical skill. For instance, all elaborate explanations regarding swimming do not help one to swim. The living knowledge of swimming is acquired only by experience, and one can remember it only by actively reconstructing it. It is regrettable that the excellent explanation of the schema in terms of physical skill by Toda is written in Japanese [T-5].

"Remembering" includes so many different types that its theory at this stage is an undifferentiated vague science. The paradigmatic symbol is a certain type of remembering. As we said, the theory of paradigmatic symbol has a close relation to the schema theory of remembering, because the paradigmatic symbol, distinct from the abstract symbol, is par excellence a carrier of the mental activity of elicitation and inductive generalization. The paradigmatic symbol is a schema, but not all the schemata are paradigmatic symbols.

Cognitive Psychology and Neurophysiology

Anderson and Bower [A-6] divided various psychological theories about human memory into two groups: associationism and rationalism. The associationism includes the British empiricism and behaviorism, and the rationalism includes Gestalt theory and reconstruction theory. These authors characterize rationalism by four tendencies: nativism, holism, intuitionism, and vitalism. Except for vitalism, these features may be applicable as a rough characterization to our theory too; nativism in the reconstructionism may require a further elucidation by the proponents of this theory. It is true that most of the cognitive psychologists believe that some basic concepts are innate and permanent. On the other hand, they claim that the schemata are changing and renewed in a modified form every-time the schemata are reconstructed. Their theory requires an elucidation as to how this jump from the static status to a dynamic status takes place. We have already said that a scheme is an integrated whole which includes many elementary ideas, and this integration, not the elementary ideas, can change with time and situations. In terms of paradigmatic symbol, the field of elicitation will change depending on the situation. This explanation, however, is not sufficient. Neurophysiologically, we have seen some evidence showing the innate nature of some of the basic concepts. It is the next urgent assignment to elucidate the mechanism of integration of these basic concepts forming the schema (see discussion in Section E.3).

It is roughly correct to name the cognitive psychology a case of rationalism, in the sense that it lays much emphasis on the introspective data. It has to accept the criticism that it does not place proper emphasis on physical-behavioral data.

Bartlett (p. 200 of [B-12]), objecting to Head's speaking of the cortex as "a storehouse of past impressions," denies the validity of this type of argument: an injury of a certain portion of cortex destroys a certain mental faculty, therefore this portion of cortex is responsible for this mental faculty: Bartlett's argument is logically correct, and his example is so amusing that we want to quote verbatim:

> First, Head gives away far too much to earlier investigators when he speaks of the cortex as 'a storehouse of past impressions.' All that his experiments show is that certain processes cannot be carried out unless the brain is playing its normal part. But equally those very reactions could be cut out by injuries to peripheral nerves or to muscular functions. One might almost as well say that because nobody who is suffering from a raging toothache could calmly recite 'Oh, my love's like a red, red rose,' the teeth are a repository of lyric poetry. In any case, a storehouse is a place where things are put in as they were when first stored away. The schemata are, we are told, living, constantly developing, affected by every bit of incoming sensational experience of a given kind. The storehouse notion is as far removed from this as it well could be.

But Bartlett could no longer object to the modern neurophysiological experiments, which not only negatively use the failure of certain mental faculties caused by destruction of certain portions of the cortex but also positively measure electric potential of different neurons when the brain is actually performing a certain faculty. This positive method has become practically unassailable, because it has become possible to insert microelectrodes in the brain of unanesthetized animals. We, of course, do not mean that every mental event is sharply localizable. Some events may require cooperation of many localities, and a set of mental events and a set of neurophysiological events may have approximate one-to-one correspondence.

What we are maintaining is that we have to take into account, on an equal footing, both the physical-behavioral data and the introspective data to build a sound theory of man. To have an epistemological foundation for such a position, we have to have a solid standpoint with regard to the mind-body problem.

Our standpoint regarding the mind-body problem is given a theoretical expression in [W-33, W-34]. We want to point out that this theory gives us the right to use both the mind-description and the body-description. The theory is conceived in the framework of Niels Bohr's philosophy of complementarity which states that reality can be described according to either of two "incompatible" points of view. Either one of the two "pictures" is consistent, but not "complete," in the sense that both must complement each other to make the full picture of reality. The two pictures are incompatible in the sense that if we want to avoid any inaccuracy, we have to limit ourselves to either one of the pictures, but, if we allow a certain tolerance of joint errors, we can use both pictures.

As is well known, the idea of complementarity was developed to explain the two aspects of an elementary particle, such as electrons, as particle and as wave-motion. The compromise theory which allows both pictures is the one developed by Wigner and von Neumann [W-60]. The joint error is, according to Heisenberg's principle of indeterminacy, of the order of Planck's constant. In our theory of mind-body relation, the mental description and the physical description are the two incompatible pictures. To have a complete picture of the mind-body complex, we can use a "compromise" picture, allowing a joint error of the order of the mind-body "Planck's constant." If the "Planck's constant" were zero, Feigl's famous identity theory would be correct, but the situation is not that simple [F-8]. The philosophy of complementarity is not welcomed by the professional philosophers. This does not mean that we should ignore it.

Integration in the Brain

We have characterized pattern recognition as seeing-one-in-many, and we have called the product of such a faculty "paradigmatic symbol." On the other hand, cognitive psychologists emphasize the "integrative power" of mind. It is obvious that these two do not coincide with each other perfectly, but the overlap between the two notions is overwhelming. For this reason it is meaningful to analyze the notion of "one-in-many-ness" a little more closely than before and to try to see also if there are any neurophysiological facts that may give a backing to this notion.

We can recognize several aspects of "one-in-many-ness" which are, of course, not independent of one another.

1. Spatial Integration, Segment, and Contour. Segmentation is the recognition of an object or part of an object which is to be regarded as a smaller single unit; it requires two processes: (a) recognition of a uniform (or uniformly graduated) domain and (b) recognition of contours or boundaries between such domains. We discussed first the (b) recognition of boundary or contour, which von Békésy's theory attributes to a special combination of positive and inhibitory response of neurons (see Section 2.2). As far as (a) the recognition of a uniform (or uniformly graduated) domain is concerned, we discussed this in connection with the structural approach to pattern recognition (see Section 10.1). Neurophysiologically, it is not surprising that proximate stimuli excite nearby neurons and arouse under certain conditions single sensations or an associated set of sensations.

   Another aspect of spatial integration is the fact that we see "a form" in an entire scene. For this faculty, we made a heuristic mathematical model by introducing the idea of minimum entropy (see Section 6.1). We emphasized that this is not a foolproof law, but a guideline that often succeeds in practice. In the human mind, this corresponds to the feeling that prefers to see simplicity, symmetry, and so on, a mental habit which is not a logically provable law, but is rather an esthetic preference. Hence, if we want to look for a neurophysiological counterpart we should study this phenomenon together with the emotive elements which we are going to discuss in the next section.

2. <u>Temporal Integration</u>. We mention two sets of psychological facts which touch upon temporal integration. One is short-term integration and the other long-term integration. These two kinds of phenomena, however, are not only different in the scale of time measurement, but different in their nature. Tachistoscopic exposure of the order of milliseconds is integrated to form a perception of the temporally continuous existence of an object. This is a constructive effect of temporal integration different from the cinematographic effect. We may call that type of integration short-term integration because the length of exposure is of the order of one thousandth or one hundredth of a second, but the length of temporal retention is comparable to that of long-term memory. A complete collection of short-term temporal integration is reported in Neisser's book [N-4].

   In another experiment a doctor removed an epileptic patient's hippocampus. As a result, the patient was cured, but lost the capacity to put a succession of events as a continuous story into memory. He continued to have some memory of events before the operation and he retained sensory power. Every day and every hour became disparate for the patient who lost his sense of self-identity, apparently because he lost the temporal sequence of sceneries of experience. It is important to remember that the hippocampus is supposedly one of the organs that attach the emotional hues to experience. We shall discuss the mechanism of memory in E.3.

3. Logical and Semantic Integration. The description of the localization of some of the basic perceptual concepts in Chapter 2 might have given the impression that in the brain, "concepts" are standing alone disconnected from one another. In the next section it is stated that one stimulus causes firing of a series of different center cells that seem to be the neurophysiological background of our epistemological structure of concepts. This structure may be called a logical and semantic integration [H-14, K-21, M-7, P-3].

E3. PARADIGMATIC SYMBOL AND NEUROPHYSIOLOGY

Neuron Network

The brain domains where signals from the sensory organs arrive are called primary sensory areas. The primary visual area is located at the end of the occipital lobe, which is the most posterior portion of the cortex. There are four lobes: the frontal lobe located in the forefront of the brain, the parietal lobe located at the top of the brain, the temporal lobe located on the sides, and the occipital lobe at the rear end. The primary auditory area is located on the upper part of the temporal lobe. The olfactory area is located in the central part of the brain behind the temporal lobes and is connected with the amygdala. The body senses arrive at the front end of the parietal lobe next to the frontal lobe. The end part of the frontal lobe next to the parietal lobe is the motor cortex which is directly connected with the motor organs. Apart from the primary sensory area and the primary motor area, the rest of the human brain is not directly committed to any sensory organ or motor organ; it is the association area, where the neurons are connected in a complicated network. The frontal lobe seems to play the role of highest control of a man as a personality. It not only controls body motion but also deals with the planning of future behavior. In addition to control of the motor system, it controls the limbic system which plays a major role in emotion.

The association area is sometimes divided into two portions. One is called the secondary sensory area and is the place where neurons connected to one mode of sensation are associated. They are located in that lobe in which the corresponding primary sensory area is located. The other, called the ternary sensory area, is located at the border of the parietal, temporal, and occipital secondary zones. These are where intermodal association or connection is made and where global association of an object that gives stimuli to different sensory organs is reconstructed.

The arrival of a visual stimulus causes a firing of a succession of neurons in the primary and secondary visual areas. That such a series of fired neurons corresponds to a hierarchical structure of perceptual concepts was first proposed by Hubel and Wiesel [H-14]. For instance, as noted in Chapter 2, each of various simple geometrical forms, such as the cross, circle, and so on, has a definite neuron, innately specific to a particular form. But there is another neuron that is sensitive to any of these different geometrical forms. Such a neuron is sensitive to the "disjunctive" stimuli, because it is sensitive to A <u>or</u> B, where A and B are elementary forms. The term disjunction should, however, not be taken in a strict logical sense.

More generally, the neural connections may roughly correspond to disjunction and conjunction of two (or more) associated neurons. What is done in the ternary association area is essentially conjunctive. By conjunctive connection, the "concept" corresponding to the totality of sensation becomes more specific, whereas by disjunctive connection, it becomes more general. The distinction between secondary and ternary association may perhaps be characterized more abstractly as disjunctive and conjunctive.

The central portion of the brain covered by the four major lobes is called the limbic system, consisting of the thalamus, amygdala, and hippocampus that are related to emotion, desire, instinct, and automatic movement. It is thought that the stimuli that are registered in memory go once to the limbic system, and if "sanctioned" by the limbic system, they go back to major lobes and are stored locally or globally for retention. It is significant that in daily experience the memory is often associated with smell; the olfactory bulb is located very close to the limbic system. It may be claimed that a paradigmatic symbol, if it is to be a full-fledged symbol, has to be the product of the totality of sensation, selected and structured by the perceptual hierarchy and then "colored" by the limbic system. If the limbic system refuses to give permission to the formation of signals as a "symbol," the formation will not be perceived or memorized. This may be a neurophysiological background for what psychoanalysts call "repression." We tend not to remember events that are colored by disagreeable emotions.

Chirality of the Brain

According to Gazzaniga's retrospective survey of 1983 [G-8] of brain chirality (handedness) research, the contemporary series of experimental studies on this subject started 21 years ago [B-13]. The epoch-making discovery of the asymmetry was made public by Sperry in 1968 [S-20] and by Gazzaniga in 1970 [G-9]. It was in the middle of the 1970s that the new knowledge on chirality became one of the sensational conversational topics of intellectual circles. In the 1980s there appeared some skeptical criticism about the clear-cut differentiation of the left-brain and right-brain function.

It was in 1971 that the present author published the idea of paradigmatic symbol [W-28, W-29] as the summarizing notion of his ten-years' study of pattern recognition. It was the 1975 book of Weizenbaum which pointed to the possible implication of split-brain research on artificial intelligence research [W-62]. This book and newer information about split-brain research caused the present author to realize that the action of the paradigmatic symbol roughly corresponds to what was considered to be the right-brain function. This theme was published in 1978 in a short book on pattern recognition in Japanese [W-61]. We intend to summarize the main points here as a synopsis.

In order to avoid the possibility of biasing the report on brain asymmetry in favor of the specific points of the present author's view, let us quote a passage of a recent book on the subject by the scholars of SUNY, Springer and Deutsch [S-21]. They write:

> Since the first split-brain operations, a progression of labels has been used to describe the processes of the left brain and right brain. The most widely cited characteristics may be divided into five main groups, which form a kind of hierarchy. Each designation usually includes and goes beyond the characteristics above it:
>
> Left Hemisphere
>
> Verbal
> Sequential, Temporal, Digital
> Logical, Analytic
> Rational
> Western thought
>
> Right Hemisphere
>
> Nonverbal, Visuo-spatial
> Simultaneous, Spatial, Analogue
> Gestalt, Synthetic
> Intuitive
> Eastern thought

The authors then mention a list of pairs of two contrasting tendencies that many Western thinkers recognized in mental organizations, and say "perhaps, as some have suggested, they correspond to the separate processes of the two cerebral hemispheres." The dichotomic pairs they mention are

Intellect	Intuition
Convergent	Divergent
Intellectual	Sensuous
Deductive	Imaginative
Rational	Metaphoric
Vertical	Horizontal
Discrete	Continuous
Abstract	Concrete
Realistic	Impulsive
Directed	Free

Differential	Existential
Sequential	Multiple
Historic	Timeless
Analytic	Holistic
Explicit	Tacit
Objective	Subjective
Successive	Simultaneous

Reviewing this list, the reader will agree not only that the properties of the paradigmatic symbols, in contrast to those of the abstract symbols, belong to the right side of the list, thus to the right hemisphere, but also that perhaps the paradigmatic symbol as the opposite of the abstract symbol would better characterize the right hemisphere as opposite of the left hemisphere than any single pairs of the opposite notions in the lists, thus avoiding some of the criticisms against sweeping, clear-cut dichotomies used by some writers.

This conviction is enhanced if we know that visual agnosia (failure to recognize objects) arises mostly from damage to the right hemisphere. The only exception is apparently auditory agnosia, which is associated with left-brain damage. This may be explainable if we take into account the fact that auditory capabilities are closely related with verbal faculties.

The greatest difficulty researchers in the field encounter is in selecting the one most basic characterization that distinguishes the left and right hemispheres. The one often used for this purpose is the pair: verbal-nonverbal (or preverbal). But this again has been recently questioned for two reasons. The fact that birds are the only animals besides man that have a predominance of the left-side hemisphere cannot be used as evidence of the necessary relationship between speech and the left hemisphere. In the first place, this coincidence may be accidental. Secondly, the sound that birds make is an inborne "cry," not a "language." What is governed by the human left hemisphere is intellectual faculties associated with linguistic capabilities.

One of the two reasons why we suspect that language is not the prime factor that causes the development of the left brain is the elaborate work by Kimura and Archibald [K-20], which showed that left-side hemisphere specialization for speech is a consequence not so much of an asymmetric evaluation of symbolic functions as it is a consequence of the evolution of certain motor skills "that happen to lead themselves readily to communications," (quoted from [S-21], p. 200).

The second evidence that the linguistic faculty has no inseparable tie with high intellectual capabilities came from the ingenious experiments of Gazzaniga [G-10]. He noted that a small fraction of the left-brain superior split-brain population can have also a linguistic faculty on the right hemisphere. Let us quote him: "A right hemisphere that has a lexicon extensive as the one existing in the left half brain, that also grasps semantic relations, and that can also speak of what it knows, cannot carry out the simplest computations. The startling conclusion is that language qua language confers little to a brain system. Language can be dumb, can be nothing other than a notational system for computational systems that are not only sophisticated but also represent the core system underlying normal human cognition. Talk (language) is cheap; but cognition is not."

To interpret this passage in the context of the present book, we have to understand the term "cognition" in the sense of the opposite of affection or emotion (i.e., in the sense of analytical intelligence). Hence, the term cognition is not used in the sense of "recognitive faculty" in the case of pattern recognition. If we interpret this way, what Gazzaniga states here is in perfect agreement with what we have stated in this book: language is a manipulation of empty symbols and is nothing more than the denotation of what the nonlinguistic faculty crystallized as a paradigmatic symbol.

If this hypothesis is correct, it must be possible to show experimentally that the recognitive power and inductive power of the left brain is impaired by an operational removal of the left-right bridge (corpus callosum, or commissures), which somehow must play the role of translator from the language of the paradigmatic symbol into the language of the abstract symbol. What we usually call, in ordinary language, pattern "recognition" and "induction" is the verbalized version of what the nonlingual right brain has produced.

Before leaving this discussion of brain chirality, we should add a few remarks about characteristic features of the left and right brains. In our effort to find a more synthetic characterization instead of specifically itemized characterizations, we can recall what the mathematicians call geometrical-type and analytical-type mathematicians: strong in spatial visualization and imaginative generalization, strong in logical derivation and axiomatic theory-building, respectively. Poincaré made the surprising statement that traditional mathematical instruction is usually concerned with trivial syllogistic deduction and that the true essence is an invention that is beyond such logical thinking. This is obviously what we would call inductive faculty.

The Western-Eastern dichotomy and the historic-timeless dichotomy are dangerous. For instance, this characterization may apply to the general cultural atmosphere of Japan, but the Japanese educational system is notoriously nonimaginative, formal, conformist, noninductive, vertical (instead of horizontal), deductive, noncreative. Of course, this phenomenon may be the effect of an over-self-correction in the presence of a right-brain civilization. Again, India and China are both typical representatives of the Eastern civilization, but Indian civilization is notoriously ahistoric whereas Chinese civilization is extremely chronologically conscious. Zen Buddhism is emphasizing the importance of the attainment of nonverbal, intuitive truth as exemplified by the motto "We do not erect words," but, on the other hand, is very conscious of temporal inconstance. In an earlier book, the author dichotomized the world civilization into two types: temporal-musical-logical-abstract versus spatial-painting-intuitive-concrete and assigned Western (particularly Germanic) civilization to the first category and the Japanese (and Gallic) civilization to the latter [W-63]. To some extent this dichotomy coincides with the comparison of the left-right brains. But, after World War II, many great musical talents appeared in Japan, invalidating such a simpleminded characterization of civilization. See [T-6] for a controversial analysis of Japanese culture from the point of view of the left-brain concept.

One thing is probably true: the tendency of personality and civilization is strongly influenced by education, although the hereditary element is not entirely negligible. The new consciousness in the Western world that more emphasis should be placed on right-brain type education (i.e., education enhancing the activity of paradigmatic symbols) is certainly a welcome sign. An opposite educational emphasis in the Eastern world has long been started. In some countries this was successful, but for some others not quite so successful. Without losing the special strong points of their traditional civilization, nations should learn at least to understand the opposite kind of civilization.

A serious study of comparison between East and West civilization always shows the existence of a broad unity of human civilization. Similarly, comparison of the left and right brain presupposes a broad similarity of the functions of the two hemispheres. So it is with the human body. The difference between the left half-body and the right half-body is meaningful precisely because of the existence of a broad symmetry between the left and right half-body. The term "chirality" is therefore appropriate to designate the small differences between the faculty of the left- and right-brain hemispheres. The term was a rather old one to designate the slight differences in optical property in two isomers that otherwise behave in the same fashion. The word was revived by Eddington [E-6] and reintroduced into modern physics by Watanabe [W-67], and is now used to designate the slight degree of left and right asymmetry in elementary particle physics which, in a broad sense, is symmetric with regard to spatial reflection.

Finally, it should be pointed out that the validity of the idea of paradigmatic symbol is independent of the validity of the theory and experimental data about brain asymmetry. But the latter can profit from the former by using the idea of paradigmatic symbols to characterize the brain asymmetry, if there is any.

Chemical Neurophysiology

In writing this book, we have had several opportunities to mention that a certain theoretical complex dominated the progress of artificial intelligence with both beneficial and damaging effects. This complex consists of the philosophy of digital computer, logicism, linguistics, deductionism, and axiomatism. There is no doubt that the digital computer is superior to the analogue computer as a calculating machine; there is no doubt that the human brain has a great deal of similarity with the analogue computer. The success of the modern logicalism, and of the ensuing axiomatization is undeniable. But we should not forget that the human brain functions not only with logical elements but also with alogical elements [W-32]. The importance of languages in human cognition cannot be overestimated, but many aspects of human cognitive power can also be found in animals without language. The completed science is usually taught in a deductive style, but, the genesis of a science requires an inductive jump.

One of the most influential products of this "complex" is the McCullough-Pitts model of the human brain [M-9]. Simplifying the excitation mechanism of neurons by the assumption of an all-or-nothing model, it assumes a neuron to be a binary unit (i.e., with 1 bit capacity). And the neuronic connection becomes a simple threshold switch of the algebraic sum of the input impulses. According to the model the cognitive capacity becomes equal, in bit units, to the number of neurons in the human body. That is, the human mental capacity would become somewhere around 10^{10} bits. But, it is known that to learn a single language, we need more than 10^{10} bits. Therefore something is wrong with this model. There have been three proposals to amend this model to allow for a larger capacity. One is to resort to the molecular theory of memory. Another is to emphasize the fact that the interval between two spikes is a continuous variable, hence the all-or-nothing theory (i.e., the characterization of a neuron by a binary variable)is inadequate. The third is to call attention to continuous variables that can be at work at the synapse of two neurons.

From the study of paradigmatic symbols, we learned that the formation of concepts and pseudoconcepts is possible, not on the logical ground, but on the basis of "ponderation" (see Chapter 4). The ponderation depends on the emotional, evaluative faculty of the human brain. This means that continuously variable factors are needed to make cognition possible. In the list of characterizations of the right hemispheres of the brain, we saw adjectives such as analogue, emotional, sensuous, and continuous. Whether or not these features are strictly limited to the right brain, it is important to note that recently scholars have started to notice the importance of such features.

The recent discovery that chemical transmitters--which are the carriers of the signal at synapses--play an important role seems to make possible an introduction of continuous variables in the brain model. In particular, the very fact that these chemicals decide also the emotional atmosphere of the human brain is in surprising agreement with the idea of paradigmatic symbols sustained by the emotional and evaluative factors in the brain.

That a chemical transmission is needed at the synapse is easy to see from the point of view of energy. Each neuron receives signals from many other neurons through synapses that are attached to the dendrite or the cell body of the neuron and emits signals through the synapses at the end of the axon to many other neurons. The signals are not carried by electric current but by the motion of the potential peaks caused by ionic balance. Yet, in analogy, it is like an electric circuit connected to many other circuits through mismatched impedances. In order to effect a postdendric potential comparable to the original potential, it has to interject new energy in addition to the electric energy coming from the other neurons. This is made possible by injections of chemical molecules of high free energy (low entropy). Thus, a signal from one neuron to another is transmitted by way of chemical molecules. The recipient neurons receive the chemicals through their receptacles. A very large number of chemical transmitters have been discovered.

Quite recently, it has been established that there are two kinds of transmitters. One kind is in charge of transmitting the signals themselves; the other kind, called co-transmitters, control the strength of signals. The strength of signals is, in this context, measured not by the magnitude of electric potential, but by the frequency of spikes. The concept of spike frequency, incidentally, is entirely missing in the McCullough-Pitt model and represents a continuous aspect of the neuronic activity.

It would be a tempting assumption--although it is still premature to say anything definitive--to regard the co-transmitter as a carrier of what we called "emotional coloring" of paradigmatic symbols. For instance, the opiates, that form a group of chemicals (both as transmitter and as co-transmitter) which are received by receptacles like morphines, represent "pleasure" elements in the signal transmission.

Another area in which chemical neurophysiology has contributed to cognitive science is the mechanism of memory. Since about 1960, as a side effect of the success of molecular biology in genetics, scholars started to revive the theory of memory trace in the form of a molecular theory of memory, which pretended that the stuff of memory was registered in the molecular structure of an RNA or a peptide. To prove this theory, scientists transplanted the RNA or peptide from an animal who had gone through a learning process to another animal and claimed to have shown that the second animal showed a learned behavior. Another method was to show by chemical analysis that a learning process produced a new RNA or peptide. But, recently, chemical researchers have shown that these two methods do not produce any conclusive evidence in support of a theory that a chemical substance could be a seat of memory.

Another approach is to apply various means to hinder the building up of memory. One kind of memory-obstructing means was an electric shock, and another was the application of various chemical substances. The electric shock destroyed all memory of events that happened about 15 to 30 minutes before the shock but left intact the memory of all events that happened more than about 30 minutes before. It did not alter the memory faculty of an animal after the shock. On the other hand, application of a chemical that hindered synthesis of proteins disturbed the memory of events that had happened about 30 minutes to a few hours before the application, but did not disturb the memory of events that happened much earlier or still closer (than about 30 minutes) to the application. It did not disturb the memory of the events that happened after the application of the chemical.

These results, combined with the fact that the electric impulses sometimes remain a few minutes after the initial instant when the signal enters the brain, and the fact that the synthesis of protein and the allied chemical reactions take time, from 10 minutes to a few hours, seem to support the "neuronic closed circuit theory of memory." This theory was originally proposed by D.O. Hebbs in 1949 [H-15] but has recently acquired a large number of supporters.

According to Hebbs circular connections of neurons often form so that the same impulse comes back again and again until it decays and dies. This should be the memory of a short-term memory. One of the simplest mechanical gadgets of memory is a flip-flop circuit. While memory is in the form of a circular transmission of electric impulses, it can be easily disturbed by an electric shock during the initial ten minutes or so of application.

There are some 10^{10} neurons, and if they are all connected to one another directly or indirectly the "mind" will go "haywire." Fortunately, many of the connections are both positive and inhibitive; as a result the number of possible circular connections is limited, although it is still an immense number. Such circuits may be made possible due to the reinforcing co-transmitters. The reason that a connection can form a closed circuit is yet to be clarified. Perhaps the answer is to be found in the fact we have conjectured previously that in the association domain of cortex both diverging and converging connections must exist.

It is a known fact in neurophysiology that if signals pass the same junction frequently, passage becomes repeatably easier. Probably the chemical environment of synapses gradually changes so that the passage of signals becomes easier and easier. Other than chemical environments, the physical shape of neurons is known to change with the result of learning. Also new synapses are formed. All these effects require more time than several minutes, perhaps up to several hours, corresponding to formation of new proteins. When such a toboggan course of signals is made, it is called a long-term memory. If a new toboggan (a signal) arrives, it tends to slide along the toboggan course with extreme facility and then goes back to the original level due to energy injection.

At each neuron on the circuit (or the toboggan course) there is convergence and divergence of many neurons. If the neuronic circuit gets more and more facility, it is obvious that the neurons of nearby possible circuits will be excited, increasing in number and complication the related networks of associated toboggan courses.

The important question is how this repeated impulse (that is, the signal with small pulse intervals), can cause a long-lasting chemical change that facilitates the passage of the signal. An example of the hypothetical mechanism is described by Y. Kuroda [K-21]. The author thanks Drs. Kuroda and Kumakura for information on chemical neurophysiology.

One of the frequent co-transmitters is ATP (adenosine triphosphate), which is a well-known high-free-energy substance that plays a major role in energy circulation in the living organisms. If the signal frequency is low, the ATP is reabsorbed or dispersed before the next impulse arrives. But, if the frequency is high, the ATP is accumulated near the synapse and is decomposed into adenosine. The adenosine is neither transmitter nor co-transmitter, but is a neuromodulator that controls the emission or action of the transmitter. As a neuromodulator the adenosine rather hinders the signal transmission, but has the effect of producing cyclic AMP (adenylic acid). This substance is known to facilitate the transmission of signals. Probably it acts at the neuron ends to cause phosphorization of proteins, including production of RNA molecules. These RNA will act to produce new proteins which cause long-lasting chemical change of the neuronic circuit.

It is to be noted that the increase of cyclic AMP contributes to the facilitation of not only the original synapse that produced the original ATP but also the facilitation of neighboring synapses, resulting in what the neurophysiologists call "heterosynaptic facilitation." This effect is part of what they call plasticity of the synapses circuit, which means that the synaptic circuit is by no means a fixed route but changes with the accumulation of experience. One other obvious evidence of plasticity of the neuronic circuit is formation of new synapses as a result of learning and memory.

The plasticity of neuronic circuit, incidentally, provides a neurophysiological support for the reconstruction theory of memory maintained by cognitive psychologists, which is irreconcilable with the old fixed cerebral trace theory of memory.

Finally it should be noted that the neuronic circuit is not a single closed loop along which the junctioned neurons are aligned. There must be a great number of closed circuits intertwined and interconnected, making a complicated mass of networks somewhat like an imaginary super-large-scale integrated circuit. Such an inevitably complicated interlocking of neuronic circuits must be a neurophysiological counterpart of the schemata theory of memory.

So far we have sketchily described some of the salient phenomena mainly from the neurophysiological point of view, that is, in the body-side language describing the mind-body complex. If we switch to the mind-side description, to what would all these things correspond? In particular, what, in the mental description, would correspond to the neuronic circuit and the propagation of signals along such a circuit? The only possible answer seems to be "paradigmatic symbol."

It is certainly not an abstract symbol, which would require all verbal and logical appendices. Yet, it carries some information. It is neither a concept of a class, nor a particular instantiation. It is triggered by any one of several particular cases, and thus represents a whole collection of particular cases. In a word it stands for a paradigm. It has a power of inductive generalization and a faculty of eliciting "similar" cases, which corresponds to the so-called plasticity of neuronic circuit. As cognitive psychologists maintain, memory and cognition are the same in essence, as memory is retention of results of cognition (either conscious or unconscious) and anything recognized is a "replay" of old knowledge with a certain degree of overlap. Thus, it is not surprising that the paradigmatic symbol is the essence of cognition and memory.

The most conspicuous agreement between the paradigmatic symbol and the signal flow in the neuronic circuit is that both of them become possible only by graduated emotional valuation. The corollary to this fact is that both are "analogue" or perhaps "hybrid" rather than "digital" as far as the quantitative aspect is concerned.

Finally, it is important to note that the neuronic circuit theory gives a strong support to Hume's theory of general idea [H-6]. Hume is one of the predecessors of the theory of paradigmatic symbol in the sense that he too maintained that the general idea is only the particular idea used "generally." In the neuronic-circuit theory, the same circuit serves as a particular idea as well as the general idea. Particularly interesting is that this theory maintains that the long-lasting circuit is built by the repetitive use of the same circuit; in the same vein, Hume maintained that the formation of a general idea is made by association which repeats itself resulting in a custom in the mind.

As the last remark about the paradigmatic symbol we should emphasize again that this symbol is not a fixed, constant attribute of the mind, but a flexible function which adaptively makes the maintenance and expansion of life possible. In this respect too the neuronic circuit is similar. It is, after all, a plastic tool for survival.

At the writing of this book, the computer experts are talking about the forthcoming fifth generation computer. It is going to be an application of the super-large-scale-integrated circuit. The sixth generation computer, it is hoped, will operate on something similar to the paradigmatic symbol. This will be possible only by a hybrid computer between the digital and analogue computers using nonempty adaptive, flexible symbols (see also [Y-2]). The final and seventh generation computer, on the other hand, has to have an all-unifying purpose to which every function converges making the maintenance and welfare of the life of the computer possible. That computer will no longer be a computer. It will mark the end of the development of computers and perhaps also the end of mankind. We have deliberately avoided in this book any discussion about consciousness. We should perhaps expect the seventh generation computer to have consciousness too. After all, the creation of future according to one's ideal seems to be the act of consciousness [W-63]. Or, will the seventh generation computer never arrive?

APPENDIX A1
Data Taking

The first step in pattern recognition work begins with data taking or measurement, and the second step is the application of preprocessing and processing to raw data to extract pertinent and useful features. The distinction between these two steps is merely conceptual, and in reality the two should be intimately intertwined. The purpose of feature extraction must be already present in mind when we take the "raw" data. In other words, it is desirable that the data be already as close as possible to what may be considered as features.

In this Appendix, we are not going to enumerate all the possible methods of data taking, but, rather, mention a few examples emphasizing the importance of the goal of feature extraction. We have, in Chapter 2, often mentioned what is happening in the perceptive mechanism in living organisms to show how feature extraction is done not only in the brain cortex but also already partially carried out at the peripheral sensory organs. Features are variables directly relevant to ultimate classifications.

It should be kept in mind, however, that a method of data taking that is specialized too much for a particular feature is likely to lack in universality. Thus, an eye specialized to detect a special shape could not see other shapes. An ear that is specially developed to be sensitive to a particular combination of frequencies would not be able to detect another combination. If we want to design a machine that recognizes particular shapes, we should concentrate on the features of these shapes. On the other hand, if we want to design a machine that is sensitive also to different shapes, we should take neutral and nonspecialized data, although there is no such thing as absolute neutrality or absolute universality.

For instance, in the case of character recognition, the method of data taking that is the closest to the "neutral" extreme would be to divide the plane horizontally and vertically into equally wide zones to provide n X n meshes. If the character occupies any portion of a mesh, the mesh will be assigned number 1, and if not, the mesh will be assigned number 0. Reading horizontally from the upper left corner toward the right, and passing to the next line when we come to the right end, we obtain an n^2-digit binary number. We have thus translated the character into an n^2-component vector. If we increase n indefinitely we can achieve as high an accuracy as we want. Such a vectorial representation is neutral in the sense that starting from this vector we could, in principle, extract the features of any nature. Given certain characters, it is meaningless to increase n indefinitely, because this would not add any useful information. This question of the optimum upper limit of n has been discussed in Chapter 7, Section 7.3.

The inconveniences of such a vectorial representation are obvious. For instance, if the same character is shifted a little to the left or right or up or down, the vectorial representation will change considerably. Likewise, a slight change in size of the same character will result in an entirely different distribution of 1's and 0's in the n^2-digit number. This kind of inconvenience can be eliminated to some extent; for instance, by the following method among many other possible ways [W-3]. In the network of n X n meshes, there are n rows, n columns, (2n - 1) "ordinary" diagonals (from upper left to lower right), and (2n - 1) "auxiliary" diagonals (from upper right to lower left). Each of these n + n + (2n - 1) + (2n - 1) lines is a chain of 0's and 1's. We count the number of runs of 1 in each line and attach this number to this line (see Figure A.1.1. and Figure A.1.2.). This number may be called crossing numbers because it represents the number of lines we cross the character where we go along the line in question.

Let α_i be the crossing number of the i-th column, and consider a chain of numbers

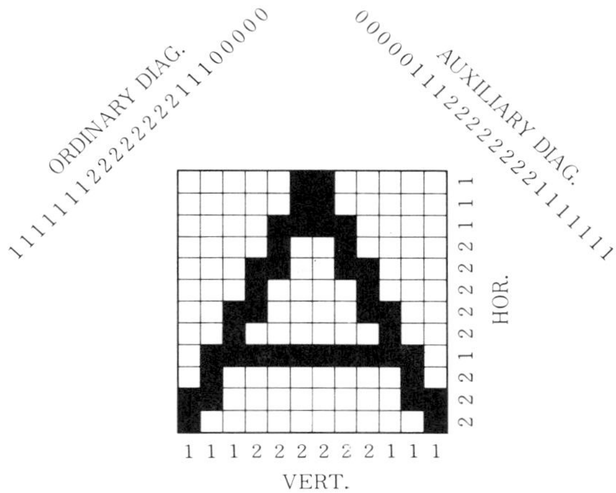

HOR.	02121
VERT.	00121
O.D.	00121
A.D.	00121

Figure A.1.1 On the first vertical column there is one black run. Hence, we have one on the first place in VERT. Similarly, there are two black runs on the fourth vertical column, and so on. Hence, we get 111222222111 as the description of 12 vertical columns. This is abridged to 121. To fill out the five digits we write 00121. We do the same thing for horizontal rows, and two diagonals.

$(\alpha_1, \alpha_2, \ldots, \alpha_n)$. In this chain, if two neighboring α's are equal (except the zeros at the left end), strike one of them out and shift everything standing to the left of the deleted number by one unit to the right, and insert one 0 to the left extremity of the chain. We repeat this process until there are no equal neighbors except the 0's at the left end of the chain which were there from the beginning or which were inserted later. Thus, for instance, if the original chain of crossing numbers is 01122033310, the compressed form will become 000000120310. Because the 0's at the left end and the 0 at the right (if any) are not conveying any information, we can usually decrease the number of digits considerably by agreeing to delete a certain number of 0's at the

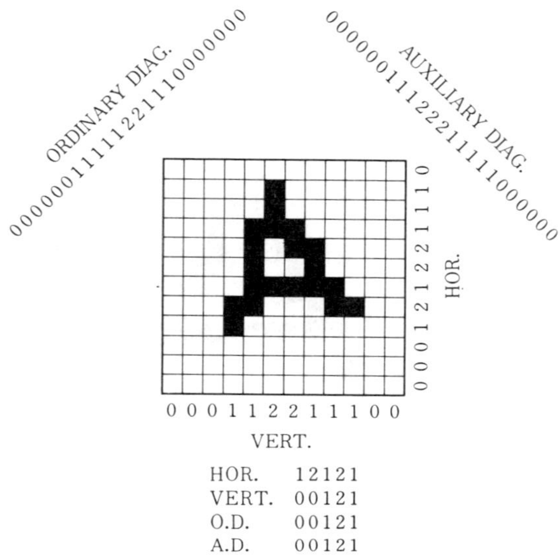

Figure A.1.2 This is a deformed A, but receives almost the same description as that in Figure A.1.1.

left and one 0 (if any) at the right, so that the total length should become, say, m. If we decide m = 6 in the above example where n is 12, we obtain 012031.

We repeat the same thing for the rows, the ordinary diagonals, and the auxiliary diagonals and put these compressed numbers together. If each chain of crossing numbers is compressed to m digits, we shall obtain a 4m-digit number, where each digit could in theory be large, but is in practice never larger than 9, probably even in the case of the most complicated Chinese character. This means that the n^2-digit binary number is compressed to a 4m-digit decimal number. The author has tested this method in a character recognition experiment and found it much better in correct recognition rate than using the n^2-digit binary number directly.

Another method which is simple and often very effective is to take the center of mass of the character, and using this point as the center, draw n rays with equal angular intervals. Each ray is assigned the number (suitably rounded up), which is the largest radius at which the ray intersects the character. Thus, we get a representative of the character in terms of an n-component vector.

If the n X n-mesh representation is tedious but universal, the following method is simple but narrow (i.e., applicable only to a certain class of characters). It consists of representing a character by the numbers of "bays," "lakes," and straight lines. For instance A,B,C,D, and so on, are respectively represented as (1,1,3), (0,2,1), (1,0,0), (0,1,1), and so forth. This is a smart idea, but it must be noticed that it is not so easy to make a machine count the numbers of bays and lakes, either directly or by programming.

In summary, what we should try is to take data as close as possible to pertinent and useful variables. But, when do we say that a variable is pertinent or useful? For instance, in recognizing character A, a variable from one font of A to another font of A would be irrelevant. A pertinent variable keeps a constant value for all types of A. To say the same thing in more mathematical language, we can think of a transformation that allows one to pass from one type of A to another. Then a pertinent variable is an invariant for such a transformation. But, on the other hand, an invariant would be useless if it shows the same value not only for all A's but for all B's. To be pertinent, a variable has to have the power of discrimination.

What kind of transformation can we think of that allows us to pass from one example of a character to another example of the same character? The most obvious one is translation, that is, moving a character from one place to another without rotation or deformation. Also obvious is uniform enlargement or uniform contraction without changing the relative size of all the parts of the character. Rotation, or tilting, is also an allowed transformation. If, however, we allow a rotation of 180°, 6 will become 9. Therefore, rotation has to be limited to small angles. Deformation is risky, but small deformations that do not change topological connectivity are certainly allowed. A change in connectivity and an interchange of straight lines with curved lines are risky.

We can extend the idea of transformation and invariance to the problem of color, greyness, thickness, and so on. A is A whether it is written in red or in yellow, whether it is written in Indian ink or in pencil, whether it is written with a thick pencil or with an extra-thin ballpoint pen.

Data taking should take these invariants into consideration. As far as displacement is concerned, we shall discuss in Appendix 2 the Fourier transformation that serves to extract the invariants for this transformation. Rotation and deformation are usually left out of consideration. Note, however, the lake and bay method allows any rotation and certain deformations. Color, greyness, thickness invariances are taken into consideration in sophisticated character recognizers, such as the ZIP-code reader discussed in Section 6.7.

One way of extracting variables that are invariants is to measure variables that correspond to the average of all cases that can happen within the allowed transformations. One sophisticated suggestion is to "throw" a straight line at random at a character and measure the length of intersection* between the straight line and the character. If we interchange the roles of the character and the random straight line, the "throwing" of the line amounts to changing randomly the position and orientation of the character. If we throw many straight lines we can obtain the average value of the intersection for different positions and orientations. If we could afford to use a great number of observations we could even obtain the probability (frequency) distribution of different lengths of intersection. Otherwise, we could obtain the mean value of intersections for all positions and orientations. The only thing we must be careful about is what is meant by "random" in throwing the straight lines. (Let us remember the paradox of Buffon.) The randomness of the thrown straight lines must reflect the statistical weight of positions and orientation of the character under consideration. For the theoretical backing of the method in terms of integral geometry and the sequential analysis when the number of observations is limited, refer to Eugene Wong's paper [W-45].

---

*When there is more than one point of intersection on the straight line, we take the farthest two points on the straight line, and the distance between these two points will be called the length of intersection.

Another important consideration of data taking concerns the necessity of enhancing or suppressing certain aspects of the incoming signals. For instance, if we ask someone to draw a picture of a face, he will very probably draw the contour of a face. If we compare this with a photograph of a face, we are impressed by the contrast. For us to recognize the shape of an object, we have to see the contour. In the mechanical analysis of aerial photographs of the ground surface, one of the major jobs will be to find the contour of objects. In Section 2.2 we discuss the way the living organism enhances the contour, and we shall explain why this corresponds to the second differentiation of the intensity of light. At the same time we see also that a function corresponding to the first differentiation serves to sharpen the frequency discrimination in the ear. We can simulate these differentiations by computer on a data set which is already taken, but sometimes we can use mechanical methods to do the job before taking the data.

The sharpening of particular temporal frequency bands in sound or the sharpening of particular spatial frequencies in image, whether they are done before or after the data taking, brings forth the different aspects of the incoming signal. The same x-ray picture, filtered through different spatial frequency bands, yields surprisingly diverse information, all vital for different purposes.

Since our book does not emphasize image processing, we go into these problems only to the extent that they serve as good examples as to how the so-called features depend on the purposes for which the job of pattern recognition is subjected, and how the sense of purpose should be present in the recognizer's mind from the very early stages of data taking.

Before discussing the next appendix, let us bring attention to the fact that a simple change of variable sometimes makes the discrimination of classes very easy. Suppose we measure two variables x and y on a collection of samples and obtain the distribution of points like Figure A.1.3a. It is obvious to the human eye that the distribution consists of two groups, I and II. If we rely on the Euclidean distance as a measure of dissimilarity, this discrimination cannot be found. Some of the

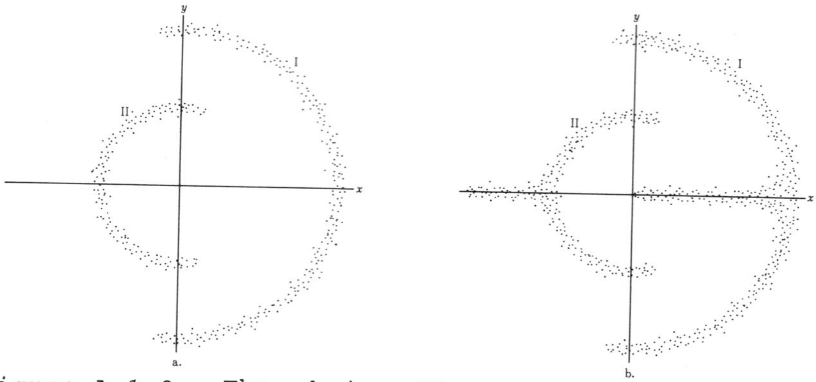

Figure A.1.3 The chain effect. To human eyes, *(a)* and *(b)* are almost the same. But to the machine we have to add a careful instruction so that it recognizes two groups in either *(a)* or *(b)*.

pairs of two points in Group I are indeed farther apart than some points in Group I and Group II. If we, however, measure only the radius $r = \sqrt{x^2 + y^2}$, for instance, the groups will be separated.

If we increase the members of I and II until the distribution becomes like Figure A.1.3b, then the variable r will no longer discriminate Groups I and II. We have to devise a more complicated variable to distinguish them--complicated, of course, in terms of x and y. This is an example of the fact that the distance relation on which the method of pattern recognition usually relies changes drastically when we choose different variables to measure.

It is instructive to reflect on the reasons why the human mind distinguishes Groups I and II. Why, for instance, are two extreme points in Group I considered as belonging to the same group? The reason obviously lies in the fact that there exists a chain of points (for that matter, many chains) connecting these two points such that the distance between the neighboring points in the chain is very small--smaller than the distance between any point in Group I and any point in Group II. This kind of kinship due to the inbetween-lying chain of members is called the "chain effect." The chain effect is one of the cases where the affinity or the "distance" between two items is not solely determined by properties of either of the two groups. It also depends on the existence and absence of the third party.

So far we have discussed data taking in pattern recognition of characters or geometrical forms. For pattern recognition to work in higher level sciences, such as meteorology, geography, medicine, psychology, sociology, we have to use variables that are not directly related to geometrical or physical variables. We shall adduce two examples.

One is an application of pattern recognition to medical diagnosis. The data are medical symptoms or signs and the classes are diseases. The area where the computerized pattern recognition method can become very useful is during medical screening involving a large number of patients where simple data can be taken by paramedical assistants. The sophisticated judgment based on the data obtained by highly specialized instruments and tests should be left to physicians.

The diagnostic task that C.A. Kulikowski of our laboratory succeeded in computerizing was classification into two categories of patients coming to Straub Clinic, Honolulu: (1) hyperthyroidism and (2) nonhyperthyroidism, based on very simple variables. Later the nonhyperthyroidism was again divided into hypothyroidism and euthyroidism (see [K-4]). The principal variables were binary variables that were yes/no answers to the following questions:

1. Has your appetite increased recently?
2. Has your weight decreased over 5% recently?
3. Are there any signs of rapid heartbeat?
4. Are there noticeable heart palpitations?
5. Have you been unusually nervous recently?
6. Have you been unusually irritable recently?
7. Have you been unusually sensitive to heat recently?
8. Have you experienced excessive fatigue recently?
9. Is there history of thyroid disease in your family?
10. Have you been perspiring excessively recently?
11. Is there fine finger tremor?
12. Is the skin warm and moist?
13. Is the thyroid gland enlarged?

The answer to these 13 questions will constitute 13-component binary vectors. To these 13 Kulikowski added three more continuous variables: age, pulse, and Achilles heel reflex time. Applying our CLAFIC method (see Section 7.6) to these variables, he obtained an accuracy of diagnosis (checked later by more detailed tests) better than a physician could using the same data. Some of the variables mentioned above are directly related to physical variables but some of them are far removed from them (see for instance, questions 5 and 6).

Another example we did successfully in our laboratory was a clustering problem in urban geography. The problem and the data were provided by Professor Forrest R. Pitts of the University of Hawaii to whom we owe our thanks. The work was done by T. Kaminuma and T. Takekawa under the author's guidance (see [K-17]). The city of Seoul was divided into 250 subareas, and each subarea was characterized by 180 predicate-variables, such as the numbers of grocery shops, coffee shops, department stores, schools. These data were prepared carefully by the local policemen of Seoul. The purpose of the work was to classify these subareas into several groups, which may or may not agree with the traditional notions such as residential, commercial, or industrial areas. The task was thus a clustering problem with 250 vectors, each with 180 components, whereby the number of classes was not specified. The variables were not simple geometric or physical ones, but were selected on a higher conceptual level. The mathematical methods we used are explained in Section 6.5, but we shall briefly describe the results here.

It should not be expected that the groups obtained by mechanical algorithm should correspond precisely to the ready-made notions of classification. Yet, it is interesting to note that some of the groups can be characterized by our familiar concepts. Group I corresponds mainly to the squatters' area. Group II is semirural areas, which are usually found in suburbs. Sometimes the sections belonging to Group II are found to be in quiet places, such as parks and cemeteries. The third and largest class, which is our Group III, seems to consist mainly of middle-class residential areas which stretch east to west in the form of a belt through the central part of the city. The next largest class, Group VIII, seems to correspond to the commercial areas which are not far from the Central Railroad Station. Some members of this group are scattered in the suburbs, but we could not confirm if they can be characterized as commercial. Seoul has a large number of colleges and schools, so that the presence or absence of some educational institution cannot be used as a good characteristic feature; however, a large number of colleges are found in Groups III or I. We found that those areas which belong to Group X are wards that include buildings which occur seldom, such as women's colleges, the British Embassy, or temples. In short they are not a usual kind of section. The used data were taken during the unstable period after the Korean War, and the clear-cut division of subareas did not exist any way. But for this disadvantage, the results were quite satisfactory. We began with the conceptual variables and yielded categorizations with social scientific meaning.

APPENDIX A2

Fourier Transformation and Fourier Optics

In the early days of the history of pattern recognition, the Fourier transformation was considered a means of feature extraction. This transformation could be done either by a direct optical method or by a computational method. The progress in this field was suddenly accelerated during the last ten years or so by the development of laser technique, on the one hand, for the optical method and the development of fast Fourier transformation programs combined with the growth of computer capability, on the other hand, for the computational method. If the Fourier transformation is done by a computer, it may be considered a kind of preprocessing, whereas if it is done by an optical method, it may be considered part of the data taking. In this appendix, however, we are not so concerned about this distinction. It should, though, be kept in mind that in the optical method the Fourier transformation is done on the amplitude of the electromagnetic waves, whereas in the computational method the transformation is applied usually on the greyness of its image which is proportional to the intensity of the electromagnetic signals.

The underlying reason for the usefulness of Fourier transformations resides obviously in their invariance for spatial translation. Apart from that, however, the Fourier transformation often reveals an unexpected useful common feature of a class of objects. The Fourier transformation is also useful in separating different (spatial) frequency ranges which coexist in the original image, and is extremely valuable, for instance, in the analysis of x-ray pictures for medical purposes. We shall first explain the mathematical properties of the Fourier transformation, and then briefly explain why this can be done also by an optical method.

Suppose we are given a one-valued complex or real function $\psi(x,y)$ of two rectangular coordinate variables, x and y; ψ could represent the amplitude of electromagnetic wave (traveling in the z-direction) or the intensity of black-and-white image. The Fourier transform $\phi(p,q)$ of $\psi(x,y)$ is given by

$$F[\psi(x,y)]\,(p,q) = \phi(p,q)$$
$$= \frac{1}{2\pi}\int_{-\infty}^{+\infty} dx \int_{-\infty}^{+\infty} dy\ \psi(x,y)\exp(ipx + iqy), \tag{A.2.1}$$

and its inverse is

$$F^{-1}[\phi(p,q)](x,y) = F[\phi(-p,-q)](x,y) = \psi(x,y)$$
$$= \frac{1}{2\pi}\int_{-\infty}^{+\infty} dp \int_{-\infty}^{+\infty} dq\ \phi(p,q)\exp(-ipx - ipy)\ . \tag{A.2.2}$$

If we displace the distribution $\psi(x,y)$ in a parallel fashion so that the origin (0,0) of the old coordinate system moves to the point (a,b) of the new coordinate system (i.e., if we perform the transformation of arguments of ψ):

$$\psi(x,y) \to \psi(x-a,y-b) \tag{A.2.3}$$

its Fourier transform will be subjected to the transformation

$$\phi(p,q) \to \exp(ipa + iqb)\phi(p,q)\ , \tag{A.2.4}$$

which indicates that the absolute value of the Fourier transform is invariant for translation (parallel displacement). We often consider $\phi(p,q)$ as a function of the point defined by rectangular coordinates, p and q. This plane is sometimes called frequency domain, but it may be more appropriate to call it wave-number domain in our two-dimensional case.

If we subject the arguments x,y of ψ in (A.2.1) to the transformation

$$\begin{cases} x \to x\cos\theta + y\sin\theta \\ y \to -x\sin\theta + y\cos\theta \end{cases} \tag{A.2.5}$$

the arguments p,q of the resulting transform $\phi(p,q)$ will be subjected to the transformation

$$\begin{cases} p \to p\cos\theta + q\sin\theta \\ q \to -p\sin\theta + q\cos\theta\ , \end{cases} \tag{A.2.6}$$

which illustrates that if we rotate the x-y distribution of ψ by a certain angle, the p-q distribution of ϕ will also rotate by the same angle. The same is, of course, true of the inverse transformation.

Equation (A.2.2) shows that the function $\psi(x,y)$ can be considered as a superposition of waves of the type

$$\exp(-ipx\ -iqy) = \exp\left(-2\pi i\frac{x}{\lambda_x} - 2\pi i\frac{y}{\lambda_y}\right) \tag{A.2.7}$$

with an amplitude proportional to $\phi(p,q)$. The wave (A.2.7) has wave numbers per unit length, $p/2\pi = 1/\lambda_x$, in the x-direction and $q/2\pi = 1/\lambda_y$ in the y-direction. The absolute value of the wave number per length 2π is $\sqrt{p^2+q^2}$ (i.e., the radius on p-q plane) measures the absolute value of the wave number. The larger the radius, the higher the wave number (i.e., the shorter the wave length). The word "frequency" is often used more or less synonymously with wave number, but it should be kept in mind that it means the "spatial frequency" and not the real frequency or "temporal frequency." If we delete the portion of the Fourier transform for radii less than a certain threshold, the effect is the same as passing through a high-pass filter. If we delete the portion for larger radii, it amounts to passing through a low-pass filter.

Before discussing the optical method that realizes the Fourier transformation, let us add, for the convenience of later application, a paragraph or two about the well-known theorem about the Fourier transform of a convolution of two functions. The convolution of two functions $\psi_1(x,y)$ and $\psi_2(x,y)$ is defined as

$$\Psi(x,y) = \int_{-\infty}^{\infty} dx' \int_{-\infty}^{\infty} dy' \psi_1(x',y')\psi_2(x-x',y-y') . \tag{A.2.8}$$

The Fourier transform of $\Psi(x,y)$ is then given by

$$\begin{aligned}\Phi(p,q) &= \frac{1}{2\pi}\int_{-\infty}^{\infty} dx \int_{-\infty}^{\infty} dy \int_{-\infty}^{\infty} dx' \int_{-\infty}^{\infty} dy' \psi_1(x',y')\psi_2(x-x',y-y') \cdot \\ &\qquad \exp[ip(x-x') + iq(y-y')]\exp(ipx' + iqy') \\ &= 2\pi\phi_1(p,q)\phi_2(p,q) ,\end{aligned} \tag{A.2.9}$$

where $\phi_1(p,q)$ and $\phi_2(p,q)$ are respectively the Fourier transforms of $\psi_1(x,y)$ and of $\psi_2(x,y)$. Except for a numerical factor, the convolution in the wave-number domain becomes a simple multiplication.

We shall now briefly explain how we can perform the Fourier transformation by an optical method. The optical phenomenon utilized in this method is a case of what is known as Fraunhoffer diffraction, and a rigorous treatment requires a fairly complicated mathematical calculation based on physical optics. We will offer a very simplified explanation using partly geometrical optics and partly physical (or wave) optics and we mean only to convey the physical meaning of what is going on in this method.

The definition of the focal plane of a converging lens is that a set of parallel rays coming from an object at a great distance converges on one point on the focal plane. In Figure A.2.1, the rays which make angle α with the central rays (z-axis), which is perpendicular to the plane of the lens, will converge at a point P which is u units off the center C of the focal plane, where u is proportional to $\sin\alpha$:

$$u = F\sin\alpha , \tag{A.2.10}$$

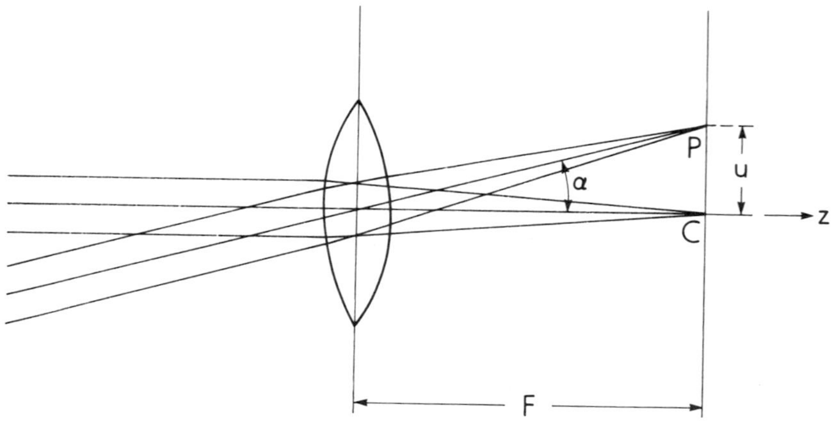

Figure A.2.1 This figure represents the geometric optics of the formation of an image by a convex lens. All parallel rays making an angle α with the axis of the lens converge at point P.

where F is the focal length. The rays that arrive at P are not limited to those lying on the plane of the paper in Figure A.2.1, but also those rays that are parallel to the rays lying on the plane of the paper converge at point P. As far as the angle α is concerned, those rays outside the plane converging on P satisfy the same relation (A.2.10). To avoid complications due to possible optical aberrations, it is assumed that $\alpha \ll 1$. This much can be said in the framework of geometrical optics.

Now suppose we place a picture on a plane perpendicular to the axis of the lens (z-axis) just before the lens, and illuminate it by a parallel coherent light traveling perpendicularly to it. Taking the origin of the x-y coordinate at the axis of the lens, we assume the transparency of the picture is $f(x,y)$ (i.e., the amplitude of the light wave just behind the picture is $f(x,y)$ times the amplitude of the coherent light wave just before the picture). There could be a shift of phase in the light wave crossing the picture, but we assume for simplicity that it does not depend on (x,y) so that we can ignore it in our consideration. We take the x-axis downward in the plane of the paper, so that it is antiparallel to the vector $\vec{CP}$. To avoid optical aberration, we assume that the dimension of the picture is small compared with the focal length F.

According to physical optics, each point of the picture plane becomes a point source of light and emits light waves in all directions. As a result, the light amplitude at P is the superposition of rays coming from all points of the picture traveling in the direction characterized by angle α (i.e., the direction whose direction cosines are $[-\sin\alpha, 0, \cos\alpha]$). To calculate the superposition, we have to know the phase difference of each ray. Indeed, the length of the path from the points on the picture to point P depends on its position (x,y). To see the effect of the difference of path length, it will be easier to visualize conceptually the convergence of rays in two steps. First, we have to consider the formation (in our mind) of a bundle of parallel rays in the direction α, and second their convergence due to the presence of the converging lens onto the point P.

As far as the first step is concerned, we assume that all the points on the picture plane have the same phase. Then, in the bundle in direction α the phase of each ray will be different because of the difference in the path length. Taking the ray that goes through the point x=0, y=0 as the standard, we see, in Figure A.2.2, that the ray going through point x,y, has a path that is longer by $x \sin\alpha$, hence suffers a phase lag in the amount of $(2\pi x \sin\alpha)/\lambda$, which is according to (A.2.10) equal to $2\pi xu/\lambda F$. The coordinate y does not affect the phase. As far as the second step is concerned, the fact that all rays converge on the same point P in the sense of geometrical optics means that all rays have the same optical path length although they have different geometrical path lengths. This means there will occur no further additional phase difference to the different rays in the bundle.

The amplitude of the light wave at point P will then be proportional to

$$\int_{-\infty}^{\infty} dx \int_{-\infty}^{\infty} dy \; f(x,y) \exp\left(\frac{2\pi i u x}{\lambda F}\right) . \quad (A.2.11)$$

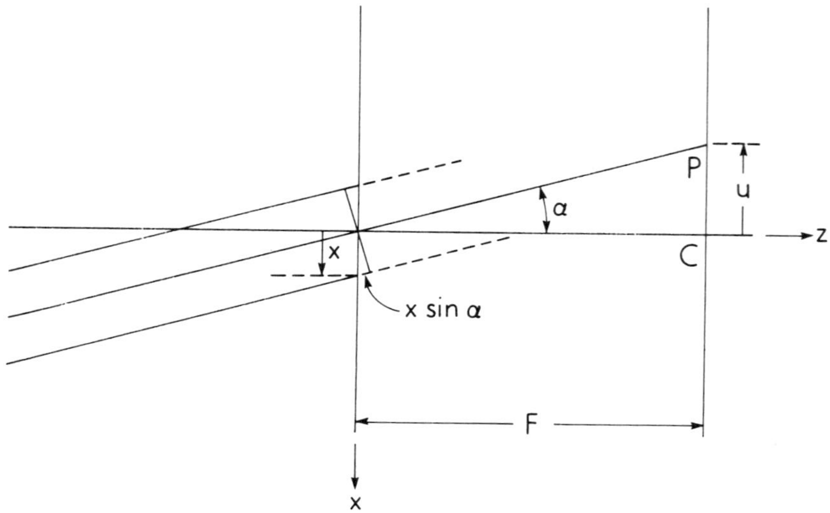

Figure A.2.2 A ray that does not pass through the center of the lens has a geometrical path length longer by $x \sin\alpha$ than the ray that passes through the center of the lens, but after passing the lens the ray does not undergo any additional phase difference.

If we remember that u is the negative of the x-coordinate of point P, we can easily infer that ux + uy would replace ux in (A.2.11) in the general case where point P has the coordinates (-u,-v). The amplitude at (-u,-v) will therefore be proportional to

$$\int_{-\infty}^{\infty} dx \int_{-\infty}^{\infty} dy\ f(x,y)\ \exp \frac{2\pi i}{\lambda F}\ (ux + vy)$$

$$= \int_{-\infty}^{\infty} dx \int_{-\infty}^{\infty} dy\ f(x,y)\ \exp(ipx + iqy) \tag{A.2.12}$$

with

$$p = \frac{2\pi}{\lambda F} u\ , \qquad q = \frac{2\pi}{\lambda F} v\ . \tag{A.2.13}$$

This shows that the amplitude at (-u,-v) is proportional to the Fourier transform $\phi(p,q)$ where p and q are related to u,v, by (A.2.13), that is, if we measure the position of P on the focal plane in the unit of $\lambda F/2\pi$, the amplitude at P is precisely the Fourier transform of the picture f(x,y) placed immediately before the converging lens. The usual methods such as photography and photoamplifier measure the intensity of light. Therefore we can directly measure the squared absolute value of the Fourier transform.

If we place the picture at a finite distance before the lens, instead of immediately before the lens and illuminates it by coherent parallel rays, the only difference will be a constant phase difference at the focal plane. Because what we have on the focal plane is a "real image" representing the Fourier transform, we can further add any optical system to enlarge it, or contract it, or project it, or photograph it in the same way as we can do on any real object or real image.

Suppose we place a second converging lens of the same focal length F at a distance F behind the focal plane of the first converging lens (see Figure A.2.3). Then, the second lens will reverse the whole process and the rays beyond the second lens will be

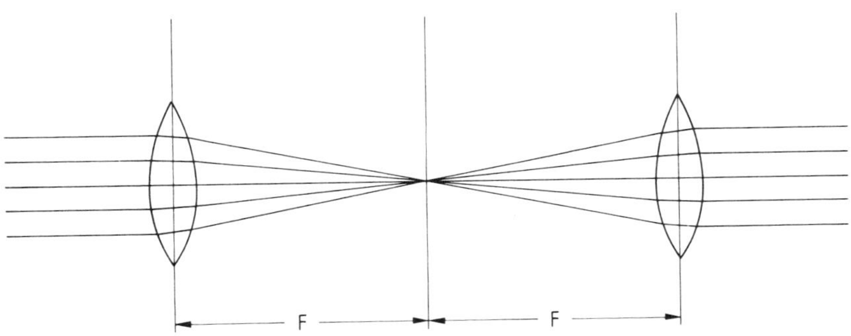

Figure A.2.3 This optical system has a reflection symmetry with respect to the focal plane, due to the reversibility of optical wave propagation, hence the rays after the second lens (on the right) will be exactly the same as the rays before the first lens, only in the reverse direction of propagation.

again a family of parallel rays whose amplitude will be proportional to $f(x,y)$. This arrangement provides a method we are going to use shortly to produce optically the convolution of two functions $f_1(x,y)$ and $f_2(x,y)$. Suppose we can produce a transparency proportional to the Fourier transform of $f_2(x,y)$,

$$\phi_2(p,q) \propto \int_{-\infty}^{\infty} dx \int_{-\infty}^{\infty} dy\; f_2(x,y)\exp(ipx + iqy)\,dx\,dy \;. \tag{A.2.14}$$

Then, placing this transparency at the focal plane where the Fourier transform $\phi_1(p,q)$ of the first function $f_1(x,y)$ is produced, the rays just behind the second transparency will be proportional to the product $\phi_1(p,q)\,\phi_2(p,q)$. Then the light beyond the second lens will be proportional to the convolution of f_1 and f_2 due to the theorem (A.2.9).

The usual measurement technique will, of course, give us the squared absolute value of the convolution. Similarly, we have to be careful in preparing the filter transparency $\phi_2(p,q)$, because if we place $f_2(x,y)$ before the first lens and place the photographic plate at the focal plane, we shall obtain a transparency whose greyness is proportional to the square of $\phi_2(p,q)$. The simplest kind of filter is a low-pass filter, which is an opaque plate with a small transparent circular hole, and a high-pass filter, which is a small circular opaque spot on a transparent plate. The radius determines the threshold frequency.

As an example of the data taking by means of the optical Fourier transformation, we give in Figure A.2.4, a,b,c the Fourier transforms of the three characters A, B, C and also their second reconstruction by the method of Figure A.2.3. We see that straight lines on the original character become stronger angular distributions on the Fourier transforms in the directions perpendicular to the directions of the straight lines. The circular lines become concentric circles.

When the size and the font of the characters are fixed, the optical Fourier transformation can be used to carry out template matching in the following way. Suppose we have two nonnegative functions $\psi_1(x,y)$

A

B

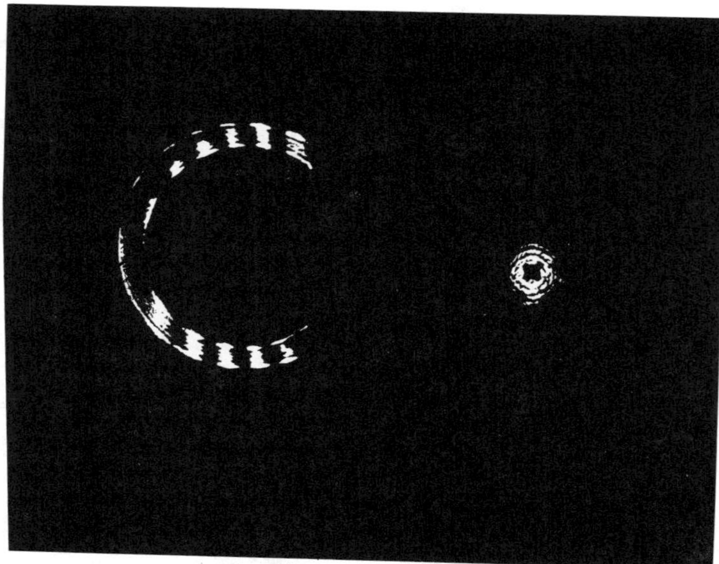

Figure A.2.4a,b,c The figures on the preceeding page are Fourier transforms obtained at the focal plane in an arrangement like Figure A.2.1 and the figures on the left are the images obtained after the second lens in an arrangement like Figure A.2.3.

and $\psi_2(x,y)$ and we want to measure the degree of agreement of the two. There is a simple mathematical theorem which says that

$$\left[\iint \psi_1(x,y)\psi_2(x,y)\,dxdy\right]^2 \leq \int[\psi_1(x,y)]^2 dxdy \int[\psi_2(x,y)]^2 dxdy \, . \tag{A.2.15}$$

This can be understood as a variant of the well-known Schwartz inequality in vector calculus:

$$[\sum a_i b_i]^2 \leq \sum a_i{}^2 \cdot \sum b_i{}^2 \, , \tag{A.2.16}$$

which says that the scalar product is magnitude-wise never larger than the product of the lengths of the two vectors. We need only to replace a_i by $\psi_1(x,y)\sqrt{dxdy}$ and b_i by $\psi_2(x,y)\sqrt{dxdy}$ and consider the index i as corresponding to coordinate (x,y) and replace summation by integration. We shall then obtain (A.2.15) from (A.2.16). Equality in (A.2.16) holds if and only if the absolute value of the direction cosine between the two vectors is unity (i.e., b_i is a constant times a_i). This means that equality in (A.2.15) holds if and only if $\psi_2(x,y)$ is a constant times $\psi_1(x,y)$. We can therefore consider the ratio of the left-hand side of (A.2.15) to the ratio of the right-hand side of (A.2.15) as a good measure of agreement of the two functions $\psi_1(x,y)$ and $\psi_2(x,y)$.

A simple corollary to (A.2.15) is that the degree of agreement between a picture $\psi_1(x,y)$ and the standard picture (template) $\psi_2(x,y)$ is proportional to

$$\max_{a,b}\iint\psi_1(x,y)\psi_2(x-a,y-b)\,dxdy\ , \qquad (A.2.17)$$

that is, the maximum of the convolution of $\psi_1(x,y)$ and $\psi_2(-x,-y)$ if we define the convolution by (A.2.8). The quantity corresponding to the right-hand side of (A.2.15) naturally does not change by a shifting of the origin. Since we can realize the convolution by an optical method, the template matching can be done essentially by such a method, provided care is taken of the necessary details of the process and an appropriate decision rule is adopted for classification.

The progress in Fourier optics has not yet come to an end, and many interesting applications are still being developed. So far, the most spectacular application is, of course, holography which, as is well known, makes three-dimensional image making possible.

It is instructive to consider the problem of the Mach band and lateral inhibition in the wave-number domain. To do that we start out with expressing differentiation as a convolution. This can be done by the use of Dirac's delta function, $\delta(x)$, which is defined by

$$\delta(x) = 0 \qquad \text{except at } x = 0 \qquad (A.2.18)$$

$$\int_{-\infty}^{\infty} \delta(x)dx = 1 \ . \qquad (A.2.19)$$

Then the convolution of a continuous function f(x) with $\delta(a-x)$ is given by

$$\int_{-\infty}^{\infty} f(x)\delta(a-x)dx = f(a) \qquad (A.2.20)$$

which amounts to taking the value of f(x) at x = a. If we consider the "first derivative" of $\delta(x)$ and call it $\delta'(x)$, then we can derive symbolically

$$\int_{-\infty}^{\infty} f(x)\delta'(a-x)dx = \Big| -f(x)\delta(a-x) \Big|_{-\infty}^{\infty} + \int_{-\infty}^{\infty} f'(x)\delta(a-x)dx$$

$$= f'(a) \ , \qquad (A.2.21)$$

although it is difficult to consider the derivative of a discontinuous function. This means that the convolution of f(x) and $\delta'(a-x)$ yields the first derivative of f(x) at x = a. Similarly,

$$\int_{-\infty}^{\infty} f(x)\delta''(a-x)dx = f''(x) \ , \qquad (A.2.22)$$

where $\delta''(x)$ is the second derivative of Dirac's delta function.

It becomes much easier to consider $\delta(x)$ as the limiting case, $\sigma \rightarrow 0$, of some continuous non-negative function $\Delta_\sigma(x)$ that is practically zero outside the domain $(-\sigma, +\sigma)$ such that the integration of $\Delta_\sigma(x)$ from $-\infty$ to $+\infty$ is unity. We may call such a function $\Delta_\sigma(x)$ an extended delta function. We can think of all kinds of functions to express $\Delta_\sigma(x)$, but one of the simplest ones is

$$\Delta_\sigma(x) = \frac{1}{\sqrt{2\pi}\,\sigma} \exp[-x^2/(2\sigma^2)] \ . \qquad (A.2.23)$$

This particular form of $\Delta_\sigma(x)$ has various properties that make its handling easy (see also (8.5.13) and (9.6.6)).

In natural phenomena, we can hardly think that there exists any actual structure whose function can be represented by Dirac's delta-function. It may be in reality something that can be represented by $\Delta_\sigma(x)$ with very small σ. Therefore, the second derivative in Mach's formula (2.2.1) may mean the convolution of intensity with not δ'' but $\Delta''_\sigma = d^2\Delta_\sigma/dx^2$.

The convolution of $f(x)$ with $\Delta_\sigma(x-a)$ is, so to speak, the average of $f(x)$ in a small domain of the order of $(a-\sigma, a+\sigma)$. Let us write therefore

$$\int_{-\infty}^{+\infty} f(x)\Delta_\sigma(a-x)dx = \overline{f(a)}^\sigma . \tag{A.2.24}$$

Then, due to the fact that $\Delta_\sigma(a-x)$ is zero at $-\infty$ and $+\infty$, we can write

$$\int_{-\infty}^{\infty} f(x)\Delta'_\sigma(a-x)dx = \int_{-\infty}^{\infty} f'(x)\Delta_\sigma(a-x)dx = \overline{f'(a)}^\sigma \tag{A.2.25}$$

$$\int_{-\infty}^{\infty} f(x)\Delta''_\sigma(a-x)dx = \int_{-\infty}^{\infty} f''(x)\Delta_\sigma(a=x)dx = \overline{f''(a)}^\sigma . \tag{A.2.26}$$

The convolution of $f(x)$ with $\Delta'_\sigma(a-x)$ and $\Delta''_\sigma(a-x)$ gives respectively the average of $f'(x)$ and $f''(x)$ in the domain $(a-\sigma, a+\sigma)$.

In the case of two dimensions, we have

$$\int_{-\infty}^{\infty} f(x,y)\Delta_\sigma(a-x)\Delta_\sigma(b-y)dxdy = \overline{f(a)f(b)}^\sigma \tag{A.2.27}$$

$$\int_{-\infty}^{\infty} f(x,y)\Delta'_\sigma(a-x)\Delta_\sigma(b-y)dxdy = \overline{\frac{\partial}{\partial x} f(a,b)}^\sigma \tag{A.2.28}$$

and so on. Corresponding to the Laplacian $(\partial^2/\partial x^2) + (\partial^2/\partial y^2)$, we have

$$\int_{-\infty}^{\infty} f(x,y)[\Delta''_\sigma(a-x)\Delta_\sigma(b-y) + \Delta_\sigma(a-x)\Delta''_\sigma(b-y)]dxdy$$

$$= \overline{\left(\frac{\partial^2}{\partial x^2} + \frac{\partial^2}{\partial y^2}\right) f(a,b)}^{\,\sigma} . \tag{A.2.29}$$

If we take the function (A.2.22), the average introduced in (A.2.27) can be interpreted as the average in a disklike domain of radius of the order of σ, because $\Delta_x(x)\Delta_y(y) \propto \exp(-(x^2+y^2)/(2\sigma^2))$. If we adopt (A.2.23) for convenience, we can see that

$$\Delta'_\sigma(x) = \frac{d}{dx}\Delta_\sigma(x) = (-\frac{x}{\sigma^2})\Delta_\sigma(x)$$
$$= -\frac{\sqrt{2}}{\sigma} H_1\left(\frac{x}{\sqrt{2}\,\sigma}\right)\Delta_\sigma(x) \tag{A.2.30}$$

and

$$\Delta''_\sigma(x) = \frac{d^2}{dx^2}\Delta_\sigma(x) = \left(-\frac{1}{\sigma^2} + \frac{x^2}{\sigma^4}\right)\Delta_\sigma(x)$$
$$= -\frac{1}{2\sigma^2} H_2\left(\frac{x}{\sqrt{2}\,\sigma}\right)\Delta_\sigma(x) , \tag{A.2.31}$$

where $H_1(\ )$ and $H_2(\ )$ are Hermite's polynomials of the first and second order:

$$H_1(\xi) = \xi,\ H_2(\xi) = -2 + 4\xi^2 . \tag{A.2.32}$$

The function in the square brackets on the left-hand side of (A.2.29) corresponding to the extended Laplacian will become in this case

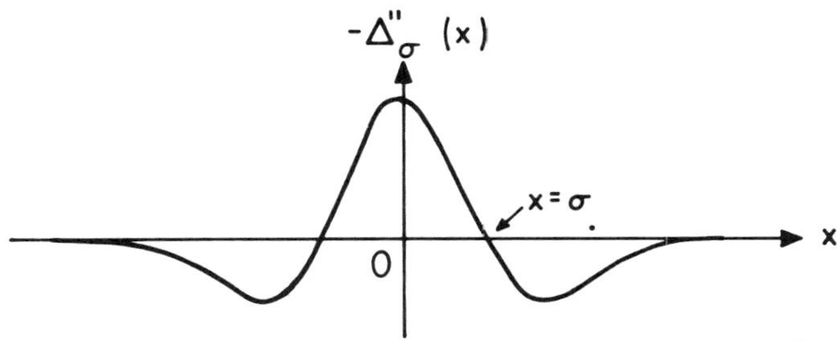

Figure A.2.5 The Békésy filter in the space-domain.

$$\Delta''_\sigma(x)\Delta_\sigma(y) + \Delta_\sigma(x)\Delta''_\sigma(y) = \left(-\frac{2}{\sigma^2} + \frac{x^2+y^2}{\sigma^4}\right)\Delta_\sigma(x)\Delta_\sigma(y) \quad . \tag{A.2.33}$$

We see that this is, again, a function of $r^2 = x^2 + y^2$, because $\Delta_\sigma(x)\Delta_\sigma(y)$ is a function of r^2 due to the functional form of (A.2.22), and the polynomial is also a function of r^2.

Now coming to the wave-number representation, we note that the Fourier transform of a Gaussian function is also a Gaussian function in the wave-number

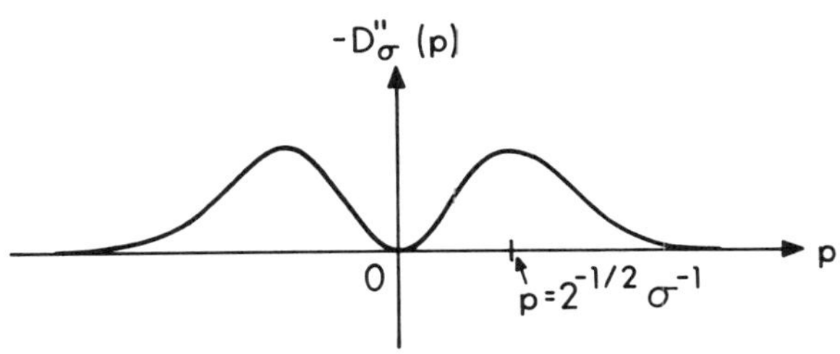

Figure A.2.6 The Békésy filter in the wave-number domain. The application of the two-dimensional version of this filter produced Figure 2.2c of Section 2.2 (Chapter 2).

$$
\begin{aligned}
D_\sigma(p) &= \frac{1}{\sqrt{2\pi}} \int_{-\infty}^{\infty} \Delta_\sigma(x)\exp(ipx)\,dx \\
&= \frac{1}{\sqrt{2\pi}} \exp(-2\sigma^2 p^2)
\end{aligned}
\tag{A.2.34}
$$

$$
\begin{aligned}
D'_\sigma(p) &= \frac{1}{\sqrt{2\pi}} \int_{-\infty}^{\infty} \Delta'_\sigma(x)\exp(ipx)\,dx \\
&= \frac{1}{\sqrt{2\pi}} \left| \Delta_\sigma(x)\exp(ipx) \right|_{-\infty}^{\infty} \\
&= \frac{1}{\sqrt{2\pi}} \int_{-\infty}^{\infty} \Delta_\sigma(x)\,(ip)\exp(ipx)\,dx \\
&= -ip\, D_\sigma(p) \ .
\end{aligned}
\tag{A.2.35}
$$

Similarly,

$$
D''_\sigma(p) = \frac{1}{\sqrt{2\pi}} \int_{-\infty}^{\infty} \Delta''(x)\exp(ipx)\,dx = -p^2 D_\sigma(p) \ . \tag{A.2.36}
$$

In the two-dimensional case, the Fourier transform of $\Delta_\sigma(x) \cdot \Delta_\sigma(y)$ will then be

$$
F[\Delta_\sigma(x)\Delta_\sigma(y)](p,q) = \frac{1}{2\pi} \exp[-2\sigma^2(p^2 + q^2)] \tag{A.2.37}
$$

and the Fourier transform of $\Delta''_\sigma(x)\Delta_\sigma(y) + \Delta_\sigma(x)\Delta''_\sigma(y)$ will be

$$
\begin{aligned}
&F[\Delta''_\sigma(x)\Delta_\sigma(y) + \Delta_\sigma(x)\Delta''(y)](p,q) \\
&= -\frac{1}{2\pi}(p^2 + q^2)\exp[-2\sigma^2(p^2 + q^2)] \ .
\end{aligned}
\tag{A.2.38}
$$

0	-1	0
-1	4	-1
0	-1	0

-1	-1	-1
-1	8	-1
-1	-1	-1

Figure A.2.7 These matrices represent a digitalized version of the Békésy filter (in space domain). These coefficients were invented by computer engineers without knowledge of Békésy's theory (see [K-22]).

As we have seen that convolution of a picture $f_1(x,y)$ and a function $f_2(x,y)$ is simply the product in the wave-number domain, we can learn therefore a very important thing from (A.2.37) and (A.2.38). In general, many noises in pictures can be roughly represented as a Gaussian or near-Gaussian blur of the type (A.2.27) where σ is the spread due to this blur. From (A.2.37), we see that this corresponds in the wave-number domain to a Gaussian or near-Gaussian low-pass filter. That is the effect in cutting off the wave-numbers larger in the order of magnitude than $1/\sigma$.

Second, the formation of Mach band, which corresponds to the negative of the Laplacian, is equivalent to a middle pass-filter roughly representable by (A.2.38). In fact, for small $\rho^2 = p^2 + q^2$, the function goes up roughly as ρ^2 and then decreases rapidly after ρ^2 becomes larger, in the order of magnitude, than $1/\sigma^2$. It should be noted that this σ is different from the σ of blur.

Figure A.2.5 represents the function $-\Delta_\sigma''(x)$ (A.2.31). This is roughly comparable with the Békésy function which is supposed to represent the lateral inhibition. Both functions have the same property as the second derivative which is the limiting value of $[f(x+h) - 2f(x) + f(x-h)]/h^2$, where the values of the function at $(x+h)$ and $(x-h)$ are added and (twice) the value of the function at x is subtracted. Figure A.2.6 represents the Fourier transform $-D_\sigma''(p)$ of $-\Delta_\sigma''(x)$ (see (A.2.31) and (A.2.35)). The curve of Figure A.2.5 crosses the x-axis at $x = \pm\sigma$. The maximum of the curve of Figure A.2.6 happens at $p = \pm 1/(\sqrt{2}\,\sigma)$.

Further, it should be noted that the limiting case of Dirac's delta-function corresponds, in the wave-number domain, to the filter proportional to $\rho^2 = p^2 + q^2$, because the exponential function in (A.2.38) becomes unity at the limit $\sigma \to 0$. We should note that the property that it is proportional to ρ^2 has nothing to do with the particular functional form assumed for the extended delta-function $\Delta_\sigma(x)$, because the factor ρ^2 or p^2 comes from the two-times derivation of the Fourier factor $\exp(ipx + iqy)$ in (A.2.38). This is roughly a high-pass filter and has the opposite effect to the blurring of a low-pass filter, namely the effect of sharpening the edge.

We must be careful, however, because we cannot physically realize a filter with transparency going to infinity. We should rather approximate the situation by assuming that the position of the maximum $[p=1/(\sqrt{2}\sigma)]$ is shifted to a very large value and the value of the function becomes unity for a large value of p (or ρ). In our experiment, we approximated the situation by using a filter where greyness is proportional to a Gaussian distribution. For small values of p, the transparency is then approximately proportional to p^2.

Figures 2.2.2 a,b,c of Section 2.2 are examples of the optical realization of the foregoing method prepared by Seiji Inatsugu in our laboratory. Figure 2.2.2a is the original picture. Figure 2.2.2c is the photographic record obtained by applying a filter of the type Equation A.2.38 at the focal plane in a setup like Figure A.2.3. The greyness in Figure 2.2.2c is proportional to the intensity of light at the plane beyond the second lens in Figure A.2.3. The amplitude of light should show one maximum and one minimum, as in the Mach band. But in terms of intensity, the border line becomes two bright lines. The larger the σ the wider the separation of two border lines.

To obtain a picture like Figure 2.2.2b of Section 2.2 we used a filter, described in the paragraph before last, which can be considered as corresponding to a very small σ instead of $\sigma = 0$. This filter was found to be much better also than a strict high-pass filter with a strict threshold wavelength, which, in terms of a filter, corresponds to a small black dot.

We also used the Fourier optics methods to study the problems of texture of pictures and obtained interesting results, but we do not describe it here. Neither do we describe various technical problems associated with the optical method of Fourier transformations. But, as examples of the problem, which is not immediately obvious in the foregoing explanation, we should mention the size of the Fourier pattern on the focal plane which is determined by the formula similar to (A.2.13):

$$u = \lambda F \frac{p}{2\pi} = \frac{\lambda F}{\lambda'} , \qquad \text{(A.2.39)}$$

where λ' is the "wavelength" of the structure of the original picture we are interested in (i.e., the reciprocal of the wave-numbers in question). As λ is of the order of thousands of Ångstroms, and F is usually of the order of tens of centimeters, the order of u is very small unless an exceptionally small λ' is in question. This makes the centering of the filter with the Fourier image difficult. Also, not so easy is the task of obtaining a flat wave-front of monochromatic light at the plane of the original picture, because the wave-front coming out from a laser tube is necessarily a curved one. We do not go into any details of these and other technical problems.

Before leaving this appendix, we should, however, mention that a rough equivalent of the von Békésy function had been in use by the engineers of pattern recognition before the historical facts about Mach's and von Békésy's works became known. When the greyness is distributed on discrete meshes, we can subtract the total greyness of the neighboring meshes from a certain multiple of the greyness of a mesh we consider, using the coefficients as indicated on Figure A.2.7. This device approximately corresponds to the von Békésy function or the negative Laplacian and has the effect of enhancing the border line. Recently, considerable progress has been made in the field of digital filtering (see for instance [H-5]) and also in the field of scenery analysis, but it is far removed from the purpose of the present appendix. Also, there are many publications on picture processing by Fourier optics now available on the market, but we mention here only some of the classical ones: [A-2, B-3, G-2, T-2]. Our experiments in Fourier optics were started with the collaboration of T. Kaminuma and carried on by Seiji Inatsugu.

APPENDIX A3 Geometrical Representation and Logic

We have N objects on each of which we measure n observable properties. The result is nN quantities: x_i^{α}, $\alpha = 1,2,\ldots,N$; $i = 1,2,\ldots,n$. These quantities can be considered either as N vectors with n components, or as n vectors with N components. The first viewpoint is naturally akin to the Aristotelian world view that the world consists of a finite number of particular objects with fixed attributes, and the second viewpoint may be regarded as a form of rebellion against the Aristotelian philosophy. We discussed the relationship between the two viewpoints in Sections 4.4 and 7.3. In Section 3.1 we explained the Platonic world view which denies the real existence of particular objects. As previously explained, however, most of the theories in pattern recognition are conceived on the Aristotelian assumption, and we have to take the n-dimensional geometrical representation as the starting point of our discussion. The suspicion about the real existence of particular objects is fundamentally healthy, however, and has to be kept in mind throughout our research.

There are two kinds of data $\{x_i^{\alpha}\}$; one kind is such that the absolute magnitude of each component has meaning, whereas the other kind is such that only the relative values of components (with a fixed value of α and different values of i) are important. Usual experimental data belong to the first kind, but, for instance, the amplitudes of vibration in different frequency regions for speech recognition belong to the second kind. The natural representation of vectors of the first kind is an n-dimensional Euclidean space. The metric of the Euclidean space may, or may not, reflect the "distance" in the sense of pattern recognition. The natural representation of vectors of the second kind is an n-dimensional vector space where only the directions of vectors are meaningful. A subclass of the first kind is the case where the components are either 0 or 1. For this subclass, too, an Euclidean space is sometimes used, but such a representation is not consistent because the ordinary addition of two binary vectors is no longer a binary vector.

The most important question is how we should represent predicates in the geometrical representation. The following passage from Charles Peirce is very instructive [P-13].

> "I have maintained since 1867 that there is one primary and fundamental logical relation, that is illation...A proposition, for me, is but an argument divested of the assertiveness of its premise and conclusion. That makes every proposition a conditional proposition at bottom."

A few pages later, we read,

> "This is the very same relation which we express when we say that 'every man is mortal,' or 'men are exclusively mortals.' For this is the same as to say, 'Take anything whatever, M, then if M is a man, it follows necessarily that M is mortal.'"

A proposition P(a) that object a satisfies predicate P means, in the language of pattern recognition, that object a is placed in class P. This is a typical Aristotelian interpretation. Peirce's suggestion is to read this formula as meaning that if an x satisfies A (predicate of being a), then it satisfies P. This is a good way to eliminate the notion of object, liberating us from the Aristotelian framework. This reduces P(a) to $A \rightarrow P$. Another important message of the passage is that the fundamental relation underlying logic is implication. We used this tenet to the fullest extent [W-10], and showed that the logical formalism derivable from implication is a nondistributive logic and that the usual Boolean distributive logic requires an additional condition [W-10, W-35]. In [W-10], we took the standpoint that logic is a set of relations among propositions, but in the present book we take the view that logic is a set of relations among predicates. This is more consistent with the suggestion of the above mentioned passage from Peirce.

Our strategy of deriving logic from the geometrical representation is as follows. We shall first decide the geometrical representation of predicates and then define the geometrical representation of implication, from which the geometrical representations of all logical relations and logical connectives will ensue. If the correspondence between the predicates and their representations is one-to-one, we shall then be able to decide the entire logical system in this picture.

In the representation of the first kind (where the magnitude of each component is meaningful), a predicate A is represented by the set

$$V_A = \{x|A(x)\} \ . \tag{A.3.1}$$

Usually this set becomes a continuous, singly-connected domain. That is why we call this representation the "volume picture."

Following Peirce's advice, we start with implication:

$$A \rightarrow B \ . \tag{A.3.2}$$

The geometrical representation of the implication will be volume-inclusion (set inclusion):

$$V_A \subset V_B \ . \tag{A.3.3}$$

The transitive law:

$$\text{If } A \rightarrow B \text{ and } B \rightarrow C, \text{ then } A \rightarrow C \tag{A.3.4}$$

is obviously true in the geometrical representation, so it will be the basic logical law also.

The predicate $\emptyset$ that represents the constant absurdity has no member, hence

$$V_\emptyset = \{x|\emptyset(x)\} = 0 \ , \tag{A.3.5}$$

which is an empty set or zero volume. The predicate $\square$ that represents the constant truth which is satisfied by any member is

$$V_{\square} = \{x \mid \square(x)\} = \{x\} = \text{all} . \qquad (A.3.6)$$

We have obviously

$$\emptyset \subset A \subset \square \qquad (A.3.7)$$

for any predicate A.

We can now define the conjunction $A \cap B$ and disjunction $A \cup B$ of two predicates A and B with the help of the definition of implication (A.3.3) according to the standard prescription:

1. $A \cap B \rightarrow A$
2. $A \cap B \rightarrow B$
3. If $X \rightarrow A$ and $X \rightarrow B$, then $X \rightarrow A \cap B$. (A.3.8)

This means that the volume corresponding to $A \cap B$ is the largest volume included simultaneously in V_A and V_B. The disjunction $A \cup B$ is defined by (A.3.8) by changing the directions of the arrows of implication. The volume corresponding to the disjunction is the smallest one that includes both A and B. The conjunction and disjunction thus defined obey the four basic laws of lattice:

a) Idempotent law: $A \cap A = A$, $A \cup A = A$ (A.3.9)

b) Commutative law: $A \cap B = B \cap A$, $A \cup B = B \cup A$ (A.3.10)

c) Associative law: $(A \cap B) \cap C = A \cap (B \cap C)$, $(A \cup B) \cup C = A \cup (B \cup C)$ (A.3.11)

d) Absorptive law: $(A \cap B) \cup A = A$, $(A \cup B) \cap A = A$, (A.3.12)

and we have with regard to the constant absurdity and constant truth:

e) $\emptyset \cap A = \emptyset$, $\emptyset \cup A = A$ (A.3.13)

f) $\square \cap A = A$, $\square \cup A = \square$. (A.3.14)

In addition to the four basic laws of lattice, we have in this representation:

g) Distributive law: $(A \cap B) \cup C = (A \cup C) \cap (B \cup C)$ (A.3.15)

$(A \cup B) \cap C = (A \cap C) \cup (B \cap C)$. (A.3.16)

It is not surprising that we have the distributive law in this case, because we have assigned sets to predicates, and the distributive law is the characteristic feature of the set-theory. The first four laws follow directly from the implication and the definition of the conjunction and disjunction. We see that we have the Boolean logic in the case where the geometrization of this type is applicable [W-35].

Let us discuss the "subspace picture," which is useful in the case where the magnitudes of components are not important. To make a consistent theory of the picture, we introduce a basic assumption:

$$\text{If } A(x_1) \text{ and } A(x_2), \text{ then } A(a_1x_1 + a_2x_2) \quad , \qquad \text{(A.3.17)}$$

where a_1 and a_2 are any real numbers, positive or negative or zero. This means that if vector x_1 and vector x_2 satisfy the predicate A, then any linear combination of x_1 and x_2 satisfies the predicate A. This may seem to restrict the admissible predicates, but we can also regard this condition as a prescription for enlargement of the extension of a predicate, which does not satisfy the condition as it is originally given.

The subspace corresponding to A is then defined by the set:

$$M_A = \{x | A(x), A \in Q\} \quad , \qquad \text{(A.3.18)}$$

where Q is the set of predicates that satisfy the condition (A.3.17). For a given subspace M_A, there is an integer m, such that the equation:

$$\sum_{i=1}^{r} a_i x_i = 0, \; x_i \in M_A, \; r < m \qquad \text{(A.3.19)}$$

has no solution for the a_i, except $a_i = 0$ for all $i < (r+1)$. Such m is called the dimension of the subspace M_A.

We define implication (A.3.2) by

$$M_A \subset M_B \ , \tag{A.3.20}$$

which means that if a vector belongs to M_A then it also belongs to M_B. The transitive law of course holds here too.

If we define conjunction and disjunction by the general prescription (A.3.8), we obtain the four basic laws, (A.3.9) through (A.3.12), as well as the two laws, (A.3.13) and (A.3.14), regarding $\emptyset$ and $\square$. But the verbal explication of the disjunction has to be changed. $M_{A \cup B}$ is the set of all vectors that can be expressed as linear combinations of vectors belonging to M_A or M_B or both. The combination of a vector of M_A and a vector of M_B can produce a new vector which belongs neither to M_A nor to M_B. The distributive law, (A.3.15) and (A.3.16), breaks down. For instance, let A be the x-y-plane, B be the y-z-plane, and C be the line in the x-z-plane making 45 degrees with the y-axis. Then the left-hand side of (A.3.15) will be the plane defined by the y-axis and the line represented by C, while the right-hand side will become the entire space. But note that if C becomes the x-axis or the z-axis, the distributive law holds again, conforming with the rule explained next.

Two remarks about the distributive law are:

1. If the dimension of the space is finite, we have the "modular law":

$$(A \cap B) \cup C = A \cap (B \cup C) \ . \tag{A.3.21}$$

This amounts to admitting the distributive law (A.3.15) when $C \rightarrow A$, because $C \rightarrow A$ is equivalent to $A \cup C = A$.

2. If the subspaces corresponding to the predicates under consideration are such that there is n rectangular coordinate axes such that the subspace corresponding to any of the predicates is a subspace subtended by some of the coordinate axes, then the distributive law among the predicates will hold.

The negation in either picture obeys the following rules:

(a) Double Negation: $\neg\neg A = A$ (A.3.22)

(b) Contraposition: if $A \rightarrow B$, then $\neg B \rightarrow \neg A$ (A.3.23)

(c) Selfcontradiction: if $A \rightarrow \neg A$, then $A = \emptyset$ (A.3.24)

(d) de Morgan: $\neg(A \cap B) = \neg A \cup \neg B$ (A.3.25)

(e) Contradiction and Excluded Middle:

$$A \cap \neg A = \emptyset. \quad A \cup \neg A = \square \qquad \text{(A.3.26)}$$

In the volume picture, the negation of A is represented by the set of all the points that are not included in the set representing A. In the subspace picture, the negation of A is represented by the subspace consisting of all the vectors that are perpendicular to all the vectors in the subspace representing A. In the volume picture, the two laws of (e) are sufficient to define $\neg A$ when A is given. But in the subspace picture, they are merely necessary and not sufficient to define $\neg A$.

A more mathematical explanation of the subspace picture is given in Section 7.6 on CLAFIC-MOSS. Usually, this type of nondistributive logic is called quantum logic, but we see that the applicability of this kind of logic is not limited to quantum mechanics. The first paper on quantum logic is due to Birkoff and von Neumann [B-14].

APPENDIX A4

Logic and Probability

In Appendix 3, we stated that Peirce's interpretation of P(a) as "if A(x) (where A is the predicate representing a-ness), then P(x)" is a good way to express the essential function of pattern recognition. By elimination of x, this becomes a relation between two predicates: $A \rightarrow P$. In human pattern recognition, it is seldom that we can affirm yes or no with regard to the implication: $A \rightarrow P$. Rather, what is customary and basic in human thinking is a graduated evaluation of veracity of an implication. Thus, the starting point should be a conditional probability: $p(P|A)$, the probability of P being applicable, when A is known to be applicable. We are going to discuss in Appendix 5 an approach of starting from the conditional probability and reaching the logical structure therefrom, but in this appendix we adopt the standard approach that places logic at the bottom and then build up probability on the basis of logic.

The standard probability theory begins with the unconditional probability, and we are then told how to derive therefrom the concept of conditional probability. We think that this is a wrong way to proceed because there is no such thing as an unconditional probability. The only thing is that the assumed condition is taken for granted during a conversation or an exposition, and we do not mention it as such [W-10]. But with regard to this problem, too, we shall follow the traditional way.

The rigorous way to introduce probability according to Kolmogorov is to define it as a set function of the Borel field, which is different from the Boolean lattice only in that in Borel fields we are allowed to use an enumerably infinite conjunction and disjunction. But we skip the complications due to this difference, because they do not change the essence of the theory.

Each predicate is a set of vectors, and in the volume picture the set of these sets form a Boolean lattice satisfying not only the lattice laws, (A.3.9) through (A.3.14), but also the distributive law, (A.3.15), (A.3.16). Probability is a set function defined on this lattice, that means that a real number is determined every time we select one member of the lattice (i.e., a predicate). But in order for this function to be a probability it has to satisfy certain conditions. The most general law that any probability function has to satisfy is that

$$\text{If } A \rightarrow B, \text{ then } p(A) \leq p(B) \ , \qquad (A.4.1)$$

where p(A) is the probability of predicate A, but, this rule is not sufficient to make the p-function a workable tool. The usually accepted definition is the following four axioms, (A) through (D), which entail also (A.4.1).

(A) $p(A) \geq 0$ (A.4.2)
(B) $p(A) + p(B) = p(A \cap B) + p(A \cup B)$ (A.4.3)
(C) $p(\emptyset) = 0$. (A.4.4)

Another way of expressing (B) is to write

(B') If $A \cap B = \emptyset$, then $p(A \cup B) = p(A) + p(B)$ (A.4.5)

If the lattice is distributive, then (B) follows from (B'). If it is not distributive, (B) does not follow (B'). To prepare ourselves for the nondistributive case which we shall discuss next, it is better to assume (B) instead of (B') as our starting point. If the p-function satisfies (A) through (C), it is called a measure defined on the lattice. If it further satisfies

(D) $p(\square) = 1$ (A.4.6)

it is called probability.

The conditional probability, $p(A|C)$, of A given C is defined by the quotient:

$$p(A|C) = p(A \cap C)/p(C) \ . \qquad (A.4.7)$$

This quantity considered as a set function of A satisfies the axioms. (A) through (D). In particular, it is important to note that the distributive law is necessary to prove that the conditional probability satisfies axiom (B), which in this case becomes

$$p(A|C) + p(B|C) - p(A \cap B|C) = p(A \cup B|C) \ . \qquad (A.4.8)$$

The right-hand side of (A.4.8), multiplied by p(C), is equal to

$$p[(A \cup B) \cap C] \ , \qquad (A.4.9)$$

whereas the left-hand side, multiplied by p(C), becomes

$$p(A \cap C) + p(B \cap C) - p[(A \cap C) \cap (B \cap C)] \ . \qquad (A.4.10)$$

Because the p-function itself is a probability, satisfying the axioms of probability, formula (A.4.10) can be rewritten as

$$p[(A \cap C) \cup (B \cap C)] \qquad (A.4.11)$$

with the help of axiom (B). In order that (A.4.9) and (A.4.11) may be equated as a general rule, we have to have

$$(A \cup B) \cap C = (A \cap C) \cup (B \cap C) \ , \qquad (A.4.12)$$

which is the second form (A.3.16) of the distributive law.

It was Louis de Broglie who was the first to point out the anomaly in the use of probability in quantum mechanics. The reference [W-10] may be the only place where this anomaly is traced down to the breakdown of the distributive law in quantum mechanics. See subsection S-62 [W-10] for a more detailed discussion of the use of probability in quantum mechanics.

In pattern recognition, we can think of two ways to cope with the apparent difficulties in the use of probability in the subspace representation. One way is to apply a nonlinear transformation to the variables of observation so that the predicate subspace in the new variables obey the distributive law. This can be realized if there exists a set of rectangular coordinates in new variables such that each predicate space becomes a subspace subtended by some of the coordinate axes. This corresponds to case (2) under (A.3.21). The mathematical realization of this plan is described in Section 7.6.

Another way to cope with this difficult situation is to relax the definition of probability, in particular, for the application to conditional probability. Suppose we require, instead of axioms (A) through (D), only (A), (C), and (D) and replace (B) or (B') by only

$$\text{(E)} \quad p(A) + p(\neg A) = 1 \, . \tag{A.4.13}$$

This may be considered as a restricted admission of axiom (B) for the case of B being $\neg A$.

What is important for us is the conditional probability $p(A|C)$. In particular, the elementary case we consider is $p(A|x)$ where x stands for C when the subspace corresponding to it is one-dimensional. We assume that

$$p(A|x) = |Ax|^2/|x|^2 \, , \tag{A.4.14}$$

where $|x|$ is the absolute value of the vector x, and Ax is the projection of x on the subspace associated with A. Then we have

$$p(A|x) + p(\neg A|x) = 1 \, , \tag{A.4.15}$$

because the subspace of $\neg A$ is perpendicular to the vectors of subspace of A, and any vector x can be decomposed as a component in A plus a component in $\neg A$.

The quantity $p(A|C)$ can be considered as an average of $p(A|x)$, where x can be any vector in C. Since the average taking is a linear operation, we shall also have

$$p(A|C) + p(\neg A|C) = 1 \tag{A.4.16}$$

satisfying (A.4.13). This gives a useful interpretation to the conditional probability in the subspace picture, without necessitating a complicated transformation of variables.

APPENDIX A5
Propensity Logic

In Appendix 4 we learned how we can introduce the concept of probability on the logical structure that has already been defined. Although this is the standard orthodox way of exposition, it seems to be the opposite to the natural order of development of ideas in human cognition. In fact, in ordinary thinking, a vaguely conceived association between cause and effect with a graduated degree of certainty is generated first in mind, and in rare occasions it is crystallized as an infallible implicational law. The logical axioms can be considered as a formalization of such exceptional cases of singular associations (see [W-16, W-22]).

We have decomposed the recognition of object a as P (i.e., the proposition P(a)) as an implication: $A(x) \rightarrow P(x)$. If we want to introduce a graduated certainty into our formulation, the most natural thing to do is to give a continuous range to the truth value of A(x) or P(x), which is usually supposed to be either 0 or 1. We introduce

$$0 \leq f(A,x) \leq 1 \quad , \qquad \text{(A.5.1)}$$

which should represent the degree of certitude with which x satisfies predicate A. The value 1 means that it is certain that x satisfies A, and the value 0 means that it is certain that x does not satisfy A.

When we limit the possible values of f to 0 and 1, it becomes the usual characteristic function, and the logic we derive from it will become the usual Boolean logic. Our strategy is to define implication with the help of the continuously valued characteristic function, and therefrom the logical axioms. That is the natural way in accordance with the Peirce prescription we quoted in A.4.

The limitation of the values of the f-function to 0 and 1 is a mathematical expression of what has been called the Frege principle, which claims that each predicate has a well-defined, unchanging set of objects that satisfy the predicate. It is the set of all objects for which the f-value is one. In other words, the principle claims that each predicate has a fixed extension. In the technical terms of logic, this is essentially equivalent to the Axiom of Comprehension. It is often the case that somebody who introduces an idea or champions it strongly is at the same time the one who is the most skeptical about the universal validity of the idea. Frege himself became suspicious about the validity of what we call the Frege principle when Russell's paradox became known. He wrote in the appendix of his book that there may be concepts that do not have a definite extension. See [W-10] for the Frege principle, and [W-35] for the self doubt of Frege [Q-3, F-10].

Now to carry out the program suggested by Peirce for the case of continuous values of the f-function. There are actually two ways known to us depending on two different ways of defining the implication with the help of the f-function. In one of them, the f-function will be called "propensity function," and in the other it will be called "fuzzy function" or "membership function." In the propensity theory, we can assume that we have an empirical method of determining whether or not the "object" x satisfies the predicate A. The f-function expresses the degree of expectation of obtaining the positive empirical result in the A-ness test. But once the observation is made, the result will be either definitively affirmative or definitively negative. In the fuzzy theory, there is no empirical method that can affect the values of the f-function. This function expresses a purely subjective evaluation of A-ness of object x. We shall first discuss the propensity function, and then later the fuzzy function.

The propensity theory is based on three assumptions:

1. An observational method can be defined that can decide whether or not object x satisfies predicate A. [This is called A-ness test or A-test on x.]

2. The observer has a "degree of expectation," f(A,x), of obtaining an affirmative result in the A-test on x. (We say that the object has the propensity, in the amount of f(A,x), of giving a positive result on the test. The propensity, however, depends on the object as well as on the observer. We shall explain later how the probability can be derived from the propensity, and how the probability can be related to the empirical fact.)

3. When the observer consecutively carries out two tests, say, A-test and B-test, the result may be different depending on the order of two observations, A-test first and B-test second, or B-test first and A-test second. (If predicate A and predicate B are such that the observational result does not depend on the order of consecutive observations for any object, we say that the predicates are compatible.)

The dependence of results on the order of observations may be attributed (a) to the change of the observed object due to the observation, or (b) to the change of the observer due to the observation, or (c) to both of them. The application of propensity theory to quantum mechanics and to psychology may be justifiable on account of the possibility (a) [W-35]. In the case of medical diagnosis, Sallantin pointed out that when A and B are very close or similar to each other, the ordinary human doctor will tend to classify a patient with a higher probability into A when A is considered before B than when B is considered before A. This may be a case of (b) or (c). (See [S-7] for his interesting argument for the use of non-Boolean logic in many unexpected fields.) It is not certain, however, that all the cases of noncompatibility in pattern recognition can be attributed to case (b) or (c).

We shall now describe briefly, omitting mathematical complexities, how we can derive a general lattice from the propensity function.

We consider dual sets of object $\mathcal{X}$ = {x,y,z,...} and of predicates $\mathcal{A}$ = {A,B,C,...} such that x and y can be identified with each other if f(A,x) = f(A,y) for all A $\in$ $\mathcal{A}$, and A and B can be considered equivalent if f(A,x) = f(B,x) for all x $\in$ $\mathcal{X}$. Note that the term "set" is used here in the metalanguage. The same term will reappear later in our system of object language. $\mathcal{A}$ contains an element ϕ such that

$$f(\phi, x) = 0 \quad \text{for all } x \qquad (A.5.2)$$

and an element $\square$ such that

$$f(\square, x) = 1 \quad \text{for all } x\ . \qquad (A.5.3)$$

If $A \in \mathcal{A}$ and $B \in \mathcal{A}$, then the ordered product $AB \in \mathcal{A}$. An interpretation of this product is that the predicate AB is affirmed if and only if we obtain affirmative results both in the test of A and in the test of B, when the test of A follows immediately the test of B. It is a well-known fact in many branches of science that the results of two observations in general change if we alter the order of the two tests. It is therefore meaningful to distinguish in general AB from BA. In performing the test of AB on x, the object x can be considered to change after the test of B to another object, namely to x', say, if B turns out to be affirmative and to x", say, if B turns out to be negative. If we decide to write x' = Bx, this means that we have the following relations, which may be counted as one of the postulates of the present system:

$$\begin{aligned} f(AB,x) &= f(A,Bx)f(B,x) \quad \text{for all } x \in \mathcal{X} \\ f(BA,x) &= f(B,Ax)f(A,x) \quad \text{for all } x \in \mathcal{X} \end{aligned} \qquad (A.5.4)$$

The formalism we develop in the following corresponds to case (a) of the last page. The formalisms corresponding to cases (b) and (c) are not yet formulated. But we can expect that the final conclusion about the logical scheme will turn out to be the same.

If $A \in \mathcal{A}$ and

$$AA = A\ , \qquad (A.5.5)$$

then we say that A is a simple predicate. If A is simple we have from (A.5.3) and (A.5.4)

$$f(A,Ax) = 1, \quad \text{for all } x \text{ such that } f(A,x) \neq 0. \qquad (A.5.6)$$

We denote the set of simple predicates by $\mathcal{S}$ where $\mathcal{S} \in \mathcal{A}$.

If $A \in \mathcal{A}$, $B \in \mathcal{A}$ and AB = BA, we say that A and B are compatible and we write

$$A \sim B\ . \qquad (A.5.7)$$

If $A \in S$, $B \in S$, $A \sim B$ and $AB = A$, then we say that A implies B and write

$$A \rightarrow B \ . \tag{A.5.8}$$

Implication $\rightarrow$ is nonreflexive, nonsymmetric and transitive within a family of mutually compatible predicates. Compatibility $\sim$ is nontransitive, reflexive, and symmetric. For any $A \in S$, we have

$$\phi \rightarrow A \qquad \text{or}$$
$$A\phi = \phi A = \phi, \quad A\Box = \Box A = A \ . \tag{A.5.9}$$

What we have done is to define implication with the help of the propensity function. Once we have implication, we can easily define conjunction and disjunction. For given $A \in S$ and $B \in S$, $C \in S$ is said to be the conjunction of A and B and is denoted $C = A \cap B$ if and only if $C \rightarrow A$, $C \rightarrow B$ and $Q \rightarrow C$ whenever $Q \in S$ and $Q \rightarrow A$ and $Q \rightarrow B$. By interchanging $\rightarrow$ with $\leftarrow$ and $\cap$ with $\cup$, we obtain the definition of disjunction. We can show that the infinite product of A and B is equivalent to $A \cap B$:

$$A \cap B = \ldots ABAB \ldots \tag{A.5.10}$$

If $A \sim B$, then

$$A \cap B = AB = BA \ . \tag{A.5.11}$$

The negation is defined by

$$f(\neg A,x) = 1 - f(A,x) \qquad \text{for all } x \ . \tag{A.5.12}$$

These definitions are sufficient to prove that S constitutes a complemented lattice, namely, we can prove, for $\cap$, $\cup$ and $\neg$, the idempotent law, commutative law, associative law, absorptive law, law of double negation, law of contraposition, law of self-contradiction, de Morgan's law, and the laws involving ϕ and $\Box$. It is important to note that the distributive law cannot be proven on the present assumption (see Section 7.6).

If $A = \neg B$, we have

$$A \cup B = \Box \qquad \text{and} \qquad A \cap B = \phi \ . \tag{A.5.13}$$

But the converse is not in general true. To prove the converse, we need the distributive law. In the present case, we have that the three relations $A \to B$ and $A \cap B = A$ and $A \cup B = B$ are mutually equivalent. If $A \to B$, we have $A \supset B = \neg A \cup B = \square$, but the converse is true only if the distributive law is available.

For later use, we add two theorems that are valid in the general lattice. Since de Morgan's law is valid here too, we can evaluate the propensity function of disjunction with the help of (A.5.11) and (A.5.9) as follows:

$$\begin{aligned} f(A \cup B,x) &= 1 - f(\neg A \cap \neg B,x) \\ &= 1 - f(\ldots\neg A\neg B\neg A\neg B\ldots,x) \quad \text{for all } x\,. \end{aligned} \tag{A.5.14}$$

Combining (A.5.11) and (A.5.3), we obtain

$$f[(\neg A)B,x] + f(AB,x) = f(B,x) \quad \text{for all } x. \tag{A.5.15}$$

In classical physics and many other sciences which try to imitate classical physics, there is no such thing as incompatibility of two observations. We assume therefore in the following paragraph that the predicates under consideration are all mutually compatible. This assumption is implied by another assumption, usually taken for granted, that the effect of observation on the object can be made as small as desired. We can show that the Frege principle is reestablished in our system if we assume universal compatibility.

If we limit ourselves to those predicates such that any pair of two among them are compatible, we obtain a sublattice within a general lattice. This is intuitively understandable for the following reasons: (1) As $A \cap B \to A \to A \cup B$ we can conclude, due to the premise of (A.5.7), that $(A \cap B) \sim A \sim (A \cup B) \sim (A \cap B)$. Hence, if $A \sim B$, we have that A, B, $A \cap B$, $A \cup B$ are all mutually pairwise compatible. (2) As A and $\neg A$ are decided by the same operation, if $A \sim B$, then A, B, $\neg A$, $\neg B$ are all mutually pairwise compatible. (3) ϕ and $\square$ are compatible with any predicate due to (A.5.8). Hence, starting with mutually compatible predicates we can form a lattice whose elements are all mutually compatible.

The most important fact to note is that among mutually compatible predicates, the distributive laws hold. Under the assumption that $A \sim B \sim C \sim A$, we can prove with the help of (A.5.11), (A.5.13), (A.5.14) that

$$\begin{aligned} A \cup (B \cap C) &= (A \cup B) \cap (A \cup C); \\ A \cap (B \cup C) &= (A \cap B) \cup (A \cap C). \end{aligned} \tag{A.5.16}$$

This completes the task of deriving the Boolean lgoic from the propensity function without resorting to the Frege principle. The formal language of nondistributive logic allows a sublanguage of distributive logic. This is an important feature of our theory. Any attempt to introduce a new logic must see to it that the Boolean logic is allowed in a special case, first because the Boolean logic has definitively a domain in which it is valid and useful and second, the metalanguage in which the formal logic is formulated necessarily uses the Boolean logic.

What has been done has the following significance. The fact that the nondistributive lattice can be derived from the transitive relation of implication is known to those who are familiar with the lattice theory. The introduction of the propensity function, the definition of implication in terms of the propensity function and the proof of distributive laws from the assumption of compatibility are contributions of the present author. A central role in this whole derivation is played by the idea that the most important relation in logic is the implication relation. Refer to [W-35] for the proof of the distributive law for the predicates that are mutually compatible. We use for the proof formulas (A.5.10), (A.5.11), (A.5.13), and (A.5.14). We have stated that it is contrary to the natural structure of our experience to establish first the Boolean logic (or the σ-algebra) before we can introduce the idea of probability. I would rather maintain that probability precedes logic. Our foregoing theory building followed this natural order because we derived the logical structure from a probabilitylike propensity function. It still remains to be shown that propensity function, in the distributive case, reduces to the ordinary probability. At the same time, it would be our theoretical obligation to clarify the relationship between the continuously valued propensity function and the binary valued characteristic function, because we claim that the former is a generalization of the latter.

If all the predicates are mutually compatible, the lattice becomes distributive. For simplicity let us assume that the number of members of the lattice are finite. It is a well-known theorem that among the members of a finite distributive lattice there are a finite number of atoms, $\alpha_1, \alpha_2, \ldots, \alpha_n$ such that $\alpha_i \quad \alpha_j = \phi$ if $i \neq j$ and $\alpha_1 \cup \alpha_2 \cup \ldots \cup \alpha_n = \square$, and $\phi \rightarrow A \rightarrow \alpha_i$ implies that A is ϕ or α_i [W-10]. With the help of some of the atoms, any member A of the lattice can be expressed as their disjunction. $A = \cup_i^{some} \alpha_i$ where i runs over a subset of atoms such that $\alpha_i \rightarrow A$. [Note that the lattice theoretic atom is different from the atom of logical atomism.]

We have defined the negation by (A.5.11), but we can now use it as a law to clarify the property of the propensity function. Since $A \cap \neg A = \phi$, (A.5.12) and $f(\square, x) = 1$ (A.5.2), we can write (A.5.11) as

$$f(A,x) + f(\ A,x) = f(A \cup \neg A,x), \qquad \text{(A.5.17)}$$

where $A \cap \neg A = \phi$. If we apply this to a sublattice consisting of ϕ, α_1, α_2, $\alpha_1 \cup \alpha_2$, we obtain

$$f(\alpha_1,x) + f(\alpha_2,x) = f(\alpha_1 \cup \alpha_2,x) \qquad \text{(A.5.18)}$$

From (A.5.17) we can infer that if

$$A = \bigcup_{\alpha_i \in A} \alpha_i, \quad \text{then}$$
$$f(A,x) = \sum_{\alpha_i \in A} f(\alpha_i,x) \ . \qquad \text{(A.5.19)}$$

We then conclude that if A and B have no common element, that is, if

$$A \cap B = \phi, \quad \text{then}$$
$$f(A \cup B,x) = f(A,x) + f(B,x) \ . \qquad \text{A.5.20)}$$

This, together with (A.5.1) and (A.5.2), constitutes the axioms of probability.

It has been shown that in the presence of the distributive law, we can derive from (A.5.19) for the case where $A \cap B = \phi$ is not necessarily true the famous formula of probability:

$$f(A \cap B,x) + f(A \cup B,x) = f(A,x) + f(B,x). \quad (A.5.21)$$

In short, we have thus derived the probability function from the propensity function in the compatible case.

We have seen that we have in general $f(A, Ax) = 1$ provided $f(A,x) \neq 0$ for any x (see (A.5.5)). In general, an object ξ_A that satisfies $f(A, \xi_A) = 1$ will be called the proper object of predicate A. In particular an object ξ_i such that

$$f(\alpha_i, \xi_i) = 1; \quad f(\alpha_j, \xi_i) = 0 \quad i \neq j \quad (A.5.22)$$

will be called the atomic proper object corresponding to atom α_i. Hence

$$f(A, \xi_i) \begin{array}{ll} = 1 & \text{if } \alpha_i \rightarrow A \\ = 0 & \text{if } \alpha_i \not\rightarrow A . \end{array} \quad (A.5.23)$$

Therefore, according to our assumption of absence of observational disturbance, the relation (A.5.22) is the fixed property of the object. This is precisely the characteristic function in the classical sense. That is to say, the continuously valued propensity function reduces to the binary function, in the mutually compatible case, if the objects are limited to the atomic proper objects of atoms of the lattice.

This does not preclude the existence of nonbinary values of the propensity function even in the case of mutually compatible predicates. Suppose that the specification of the object is not precise and it describes the object only by the propensity of finding x in α_i (i.e., by the probability ρ_i) that it is ξ_i, with $\rho_i \geq 0$, $\sum_{i=1}^{n} \rho_i = 1$. Then the propensity of x affirming predicate A will be

$$f(A,x) = \sum_{i=1}^{n} f(\alpha_i,x) \quad (A.5.24)$$

and

$$f(\alpha_i, x) = \rho_i \ . \qquad \text{(A.5.25)}$$

This corresponds to the case where, owing to our ignorance, we cannot specify the object as an atomic proper object. Since the purpose of the present appendix is to establish the Boolean logic and the concept of probability on a basis other than the Frege principle, we do not go into the details outside the Boolean logic and Kolmogorovian probability, but we can show that our propensity function can express in the general case both kinds of stochasticity: (1) stochasticity due to our ignorance, (2) essential stochasticity which cannot be eliminated by sharpening our knowledge. In the compatible case, the probability is due to our ignorance.

Suppose in the present compatible case, that the objects are all well defined so that $f(\alpha_i, x) = 0$ or 1. This will divide all the x's under consideration into those which have $f(\alpha_i, x) = 1$ for $\alpha_i \to A$ and $f(\alpha_i, x) = 0$ for $\alpha_i \not\to A$. The collection of the first group makes the well-defined extensions of the predicate A. Thus, we land the Frege principle from the propensity function and the compatibility assumption. The idea of extension in combination of Boolean lattice laws can lay the foundation of nonaxiomatic set theory.

We have introduced the propensity as the degree of expectation of the affirmative result in an observation and derived the logical structure from the propensity. Hence, one might argue that the logical structure thus derived depends on the subjective evaluation of future events, and has no empirical anchoring in the world. The propensity in the Boolean case, however, is equivalent to probability, and as we shall explain, probability, in spite of its subjective origin, has definitively an empirical correlation with objective measurement.

As is well known, there are three views about the essential nature of probability: (1) necessary view, (2) subjective view, and (3) frequency view. Necessary view is not tenable, because it cannot justify the prior probability in the Bayesian formula and also because in its combinatorial version it creates a self-contradiction due to its dependence on the accidental linguistic contingency. Frequency view enjoys support of many natural scientists, but it fails to justify the use of probability in nonrepetitive, unique events. The subjective view is often criticized because it is erroneously regarded as divorced from the empirical world. But this criticism can be refuted for two reasons:

(a) Subjective probability can be measured. Toda and Finetti showed that human beings have a fairly accurate feeling of probabilities of possible outcomes in future events, and behave so as to maximize the utility function based on these probabilities. Observing the behavior in a wager situation, we can measure the subjective probabilities [W-10].

(b) Frequency view can be derived from the subjective view but not vice versa. As we have seen in Section 5.3, when there are hypotheses that predict various possible probabilities (i.e., relative frequencies) for a set of alternative outcomes, the subjective a posteriori probability of the hypothesis that predicts the empirical frequencies correctly will receive the maximum value of unity in the process of Bayesian learning.

APPENDIX A6
Fuzzy Logic

The idea of using a continuously valued characteristic function to derive a logical structure was introduced in 1959 in a lecture at the Yale Graduate School, but was published for the first time in 1966 in the special issue of Progress of Theoretical Physics dedicated to Prof. Tomonaga [W-37]. In 1965 Zadeh published his Fuzzy Set Theory which also used a continuously valued characteristic function as a starting point [Z-2].

Although the Fuzzy Set Theory or Fuzzy Logic has a fatal weakness in that it has no anchoring in the empirical world, it has an attractive feature of giving a mathematical appearance to the idea that in human cognition the concepts have only vaguely defined extensions. Although the logical structure is nothing but the rediscovery of the old Lukasiewicz's logic of the kind aleph one, credit has to be given to Zadeh to have pounded energetically into many researchers' minds that human thinking is not a black and white affair. Enthusiastic followers published numerous papers on or around this theme initiating what may be called a movement or subculture. Although the intention lies in the right direction nothing has yet been discovered to connect the subjective "fuzziness" to the empirical measurement. It is quite different from the case of probability [W-64, W-65].

The Fuzzy Set Theory starts with a set of n objects: $X = \{x_1, x_2, \ldots x_n\}$. We assign the "membership function":

$$0 \leq f(A,x) \leq 1 \qquad \text{(A.6.1)}$$

to each "fuzzy set" A and each object x. Every time

we assign a new set of different values of f to the set of n objects x, we define a new fuzzy set A. This produces a set of fuzzy sets: $F = \{A\}$, whose cardinality is continuously infinite and n-dimensional. The value of f is supposed to express the subjective evaluation of the degree to which the object x belongs to the class or concept corresponding to A.

The simplest, but by no means unique, way of introducing half ordering in this set is to define the implication "$\rightarrow$" by

$$A \rightarrow B \quad \text{if } f(A,x) \leq f(B,x), \quad \text{for all } x. \tag{A.6.2}$$

The entire structure of the Zadehian fuzzy-set theory is practically dictated by this simple definition. Simplicity, by itself, is no virtue. Simplicity is often a successful guidance in formulating hypotheses in empirical sciences, but the ultimate criterion of success lies somewhere else, namely in agreement with experience.

Definitions (A.6.1) and (A.6.2) guarantee the existence of the upper bound $\square \in F$ such that

$$A \rightarrow \square, \quad \text{for any } A \in F, \tag{A.6.3}$$

that is,

$$f(\square, x) = 1, \quad \text{for all } x. \tag{A.6.4}$$

Similarly, there exists the lower bound $\phi \in F$ such that

$$\phi \rightarrow A, \quad \text{for any } A \in F, \tag{A.6.5}$$

that is,

$$f(\phi, x) = 0, \quad \text{for all } x. \tag{A.6.6}$$

It is clear that there exists a unique conjunction $C = A \cap B \in F$ if $A \in F$ and $B \in F$, and if we define C by

$$\begin{array}{l} \text{i) } C \rightarrow A,\ C \rightarrow B \\ \text{ii) If } Q \rightarrow A,\ Q \rightarrow B, \text{ then } Q \rightarrow C \end{array} \tag{A.6.7}$$

for we can satisfy (A.6.7) by

$$f(C,x) = \min(f(A,x),\ f(B,x)), \quad \text{for all } x\ . \qquad (A.6.8)$$

Similarly, we can define the disjunction $C = A \cup B \in F$ by changing the direction of arrows in (A.6.7) and changing min in (A.6.8) to max. It is clear also that

$$A \cap \phi = \phi, \quad A \cup \phi = A, \quad \text{for all } A \qquad (A.6.9)$$

$$A \cap \square = A, \quad A \cup \square = \square, \quad \text{for all } A\ . \qquad (A.6.10)$$

This shows that F is a lattice satisfying the 1) idempotent law, 2) associative law, 3) commutative law, and 4) absorptive law (A.3.9) through (A.3.12). In addition to these four lattice laws, the particular definition of implication in this theory allows for the distributive law (A.3.15) through (A.3.16).

It is simple and natural to define, as Zadeh does, the complementation by

$$f(\neg A,x) = 1 - f(A,x), \quad \text{for all } x\ . \qquad (A.6.11)$$

This definition satisfies the law of double negation

$$\neg\neg A = A \qquad (A.6.12)$$

and the law of contraposition

$$\text{If } A \to B, \text{ then } \neg B \to \neg A\ . \qquad (A.6.13)$$

But, it does not satisfy the law of self-contradiction

$$\text{if } A \to \neg A, \text{ then } A = \phi\ , \qquad (A.6.14)$$

the law of excluded middle

$$A \cup \neg A = \square \qquad (A.6.15)$$

or the law of contradiction

$$A \cap \neg A = \phi\ . \qquad (A.6.16)$$

The violation of the three last laws is a serious problem. One possible excuse is to say that the fuzzy-set theory is not a logic. But, this is not acceptable because the members of F are supposed to stand for predicates used in the ordinary language or everyday thinking. In particular, the law of self-contradiction, which requires that a predicate that implies its negation is limited to the constant absurdity, is so fundamental in human thinking that any violation of this law by a proposed logic would deny its qualification as a logic. Another possibility is, of course, to alter the definition of complementation. See [W-25] and [W-65] for the present author's earlier suggestions with regard to these difficulties. In this appendix, however, we shall explain a slightly different view of this problem.

If we acknowledge that the exact values of the membership function have no observable meaning, we can raise a question as to what extent we can change the values of the f-function without altering the logical structure of the fuzzy sets, A's, defined by them. There are three points where the values of the f-function intervene in the definition of the logical relations. One is the definition of implication (A.6.2), the second is the definition of the logical constants (A.6.4), (A.6.6), and the third is the definition of negation (A.6.11). The definitions of conjunction and disjunction will follow automatically from the definition of implication and does not involve any new relation between the f-function and the logic.

In keeping the implication relation invariant, we can take any one-valued, monotone increasing function of f as a new f-function, which we call g.

$$g = F(f),\ dF/df \geq 0, \quad \text{for } 0 \leq f \leq 1 \ . \qquad \text{(A.6.17)}$$

To keep the logical constants, ϕ and $\square$, invariant we have to impose the conditions:

$$F(0) = 0,\ F(1) = 1\ , \qquad \text{(A.6.18)}$$

In order to keep the negation invariant, we still further require

$$F(f) + F(1-f) = 1\ , \qquad \text{(A.6.19)}$$

which includes

$$F(1/2) = 1/2 \; . \qquad \text{(A.6.20)}$$

These conditions still leave us a vast freedom of choice of the F-function, once an f-function is given. For instance, we can take

$$F(f) = \Phi[f - (1/2)] \qquad \text{(A.6.21)}$$

$$\Phi(x) = \int_{-\infty}^{x} \Delta_\sigma(x)\,dx \qquad \text{(A.6.22)}$$

$$\Delta_\sigma(x) = [1/\{(2\pi)^{\frac{1}{2}}\sigma\}]\ \exp\{-x^2/(2\sigma^2)\} \qquad \text{(A.6.23)}$$

with

$$\sigma << (1/2) \; . \qquad \text{(A.6.24)}$$

This function strictly satisfies two conditions (A.6.17) and (A.6.19) and approximately the two other conditions of (A.6.18). In order to satisfy strictly the latter two, we can either make $\sigma \to 0$, or chop off the tails of the normal distribution curve (A.6.23), and renormalize it in the domain $[-(1/2), +(1/2)]$.

No matter how small σ is, we still have the same logical relations as with the original f-function, unless σ is strictly 0. But on the other hand, with a very small σ, one of $g(A,x)$ and $g(\neg A,x)$ practically becomes equal to 0 and the other to 1. As a result, we can realize with any desired accuracy

$$g(A \cup \neg A,x) = \text{Max}[g(A,x), g(\neg A,x)] = 1 \quad \text{for all } x \; , \qquad \text{(A.6.25)}$$

(i.e., the law of excluded middle (A.6.15)). Similarly, with any desired accuracy we can secure the law of contradiction (A.6.16), making σ sufficiently small.

At the limit $\sigma \to 0$, the continuous characteristic function becomes the zero-or-one characteristic function, and the laws of excluded middle and contradiction will become strict laws, re-establishing the old Boolean logic in toto.

Coming back to the ordinary fuzzy set theory, we have to add that if we want to push consistently the idea of fuzzification into the entire theoretical structure, we shall have to attach a fuzzy truth-value even to each judgement that assigns a fuzzified truth-value to a statement. This will inevitably lead to an infinite regression. Zadeh developed a theory along such a line, but we have to say that he has not come up to any reasonable way to cut off the regression.

Prof. M.M. Yanase let us know that he received a private communication from Profs. G. Takeuti and S. Titani which suggested changing the definition of negation in the fuzzy logic and obtaining a logical system which can be considered as a case of Heyting algebra (i.e., an intuitionistic logic reviving the law of contradiction). The present author does not know if the following modification of the rules in the fuzzy logic would be in agreement with the ideas of those logicians, but it is interesting to note that we can reestablish, not approximately but rigorously, either the law of contradiction or the law of excluded middle by the following method. We retain the fundamental law of implication (A.6.2) but change the the definition of negation (A.6.11).

(1) H-Type. We define the negation by the rule:

$$\text{If } 0 \leq f(A,x) \leq 1, \text{ then } f(\neg A,x) = 0 \qquad \text{(A.6.26)}$$

$$\text{If } f(A,x) = 0 \qquad \text{then } f(\neg A,x) = 1 \qquad \text{(A.6.27)}$$

for any x. Then we can easily see that the law of contraposition (A.6.13) remains valid, but the law of self-contradiction (A.6.14) is replaced by

$$\text{If } A \to \neg A, \text{ then } \neg A = \Box \qquad \text{(A.6.28)}$$

and

$$\text{if } \neg A \to A, \text{ then } \neg A = \phi\ . \qquad \text{(A.6.29)}$$

We have here, like in the intuitionistic logic, the law of contradiction (A.6.16), but not the law of excluded middle (A.6.15). We do not have the law of double negation (A.6.12), but as in the intuitionistic logic, the law of triple negation:

$$\neg\neg\neg A = \neg A \qquad (A.6.30)$$

In all this discussion, the definitions of the logical constants (A.6.4), (A.6.6), are supposed to be kept unchanged.

(2) Anti-H-Type. We define the negation by the rule:

$$\text{If } 0 \leq f(A,x) < 1, \text{ then } f(\neg A,x) = 1 \qquad (A.6.31)$$

$$\text{If } f(A,x) = 1, \text{ then } f(\neg A,x) = 0 \qquad (A.6.32)$$

for any x. Then, we have the law of contraposition and, instead of the law of self-contradiction, the laws mentioned in (A.6.28) and (A.6.29). We still have the law of triple negation (A.6.30), but, in contrast to the H-Type case, we have the law of excluded middle (A.6.15) and not the law of contradiction (A.6.16).

In any event, it is an undeniable fact that the class of objects in pattern recognition has, in most cases, a fuzzy extension. It is a worthwhile effort to formulate this situation in a mathematical form, although so far the result has been empirically irrelevant and rationally uncompelling.

References

[A-1] Aizerman, M.A., E.M. Braverman, L.I. Rozonoer, *Theoretical Foundations of the Method of Potential Functions in the Problem of Instructing Automata to Partition Input Situations into Classes*, Moscow, 1963; "*The Probabilistic Problem Concerning the Instruction of Automata to Recognize Classes and the Method of Potential Functions*," Moscow, 1964.

[A-2] Abbe, E., *Archiv. Mikroskopiche Anal.*, v. 9, p. 413, 1873.

[A-3] Akaike, H., "Information Theory and an Extension of the Maximum Likelihood Principle," Petrov and Csaki (eds.), *Proceedings of Second International Symposium on Information Theory*, Akademiai Kiado', Budapest, 1973.

[A-4] Akaike, H., "A New Look at the Statistical Model Identification," *IEEE Transactions on Automatic Control*, v. 19, p. 716-722, 1974.

[A-5] Akaike, H., "A Bayesian Analysis of the Minimum AIC Procedure," *Ann. Inst. Statist. Math.*, v. 30, Part A, p. 9-14, 1978.

[A-6] Anderson, J.R. and Bower, G.H., *Human Associative Memory*, Winston and Sons, Washington , D.C., 1973.

[B-1] Banerji, R.B., "Phase Structure Languages, Finite Machine and Channel Capacity," *Information and Control*, v. 6, p. 153-162, 1963.

[B-2] Biermann, A.W. and J.A. Feldman, "A Survey of Results in Grammatical Inference." In S. Watanabe, (ed.), *Frontiers of Pattern Recognition*, Academic Press, New York, 1972.

[B-3] Born, M. and E. Wolf, *Principles of Optics*, The McMillan Co., New York, 1964.

[B-4] Barnbrough, Renford, "Universals and Family Resemblances," *Proceedings of the Aristotelian Society*, 1960-61.

[B-5] Black, Max, "Induction and Probability." In R. Klibansky, (ed.), *Philosophy in Mid-Century*, Florence, p. 154-163, 1958.

[B-6] Bergson, H., *Evolution Creatrice*, Felix Alcan, Paris, 1907.

[B-7] Boltzmann, L., *Vorlesungen über Gastheorie*, J.A. Barth, Leipzig, 1896.

[B-8] Bohr, N., "Neutron Capture and Nuclear Constitution," *Nature*, v. 137, p. 344, 1936.

[B-9] Bongard, M., *Pattern Recognition*, Spartan Books, Washington, 1970.

[B-10] Bishop, P.O., "Neurophysiology of Binocular Single Vision and Stereopsis." In R. Yung, (ed.), *Handbook of Sensory Physiology*, Vol. 7, *Central Processing of Visual Information*, *A.*, Springer, Berlin: p. 255, 1973.

[B-11] Buchanan, B., G. Sutherland, and Feigenbaum, "Heuristic Dendral: A Program for Generating Explanatory Hypothesis in Organic Chemistry." In *Machine Intelligence*, 4, American Elsevier, New York, 1969.

[B-12] Bartlett, F.C., *Remembering*, University Press, Cambridge, Vol. 4, England, 1932.

[B-13] Bogen, J.E. and M.S. Gazzaniga, "Cerebral Commissurrotomy in Man," *Journal of Neurosurgery*, v. 23, p. 394, 1975.

[B-14] Birkoff, G. and J. von Neumann, Annals of Mathematics, 2nd Ser., 37, p. 823, 1936.

[C-1] Cover, Thomas, "Learning in Pattern Recognition." In S. Watanabe, (ed.), *Methodologies of Pattern Recognition*, Academic Press, New York, p. 111-132, 1969.

[C-2] Clowes, M.B., "Transformational Grammars and the Organization of Pictures." In A. Grasselli, (ed.), *Automatic Interpretation and Classification of Images*, Academic Press, New York, 1969.

[C-3] Chomsky, N., *Syntactical Structures*, Mouton, The Hague, 1957.

[C-4] Chomsky, N., "Recent Contributions of the Theory of Innate Ideas." In R.S. Cohen and M.W. Wartofsky (eds.), *Boston Studies in the Philosophy of Science*, Vol. III, D. Reidel, Dordrecht, 1967.

[C-5] Carnap, R., *Logical Foundations of Probability*, University of Chicago Press, Chicago, 1950.

[C-6] Chavis, D.A. and D.N. Pandya, "Further Observations on Cortico-Frontal Connections in the Rhesus Monkey," *Brain Res.* v. 117, pp. 369-386, 1976.

[C-7] Cover, T.M., "Geometrical and Statistical Properties of Systems of Linear Inequalities with Applications in Pattern Recognition," *IEEE Transactions on Electronic Computers*, EC-14, p. 326-334, 1965.

[C-8] Cover, Thomas M. and Peter Hart, "Nearest Neighbor Pattern Classification," *IEEE Transformations on Information*, IT-13, p. 21-27, 1967.

[C-9] Coxeter, H.S.M. and W.O.J. Moser, *Generators and Relations for Discrete Groups*, Springer-Verlag, New York, 1932.

[C-10] Clausius, R.J., *Die mechanische Wärmetheorie*, Friedrich Vieweg and Sohn, Braunschweig, 1887.

[C-11] Carnot, S., *Réflexion sur la puissance notrice du feu et sur les machines propres à déveloper cette puissance*, Paris, 1824.

[D-1] Dauer, Francis W., *Application of Clustering Technique to Grammatical Substructures*, IBM Internal Publication, 1963.

[D-2] Dallos, P., *The Auditory Periphery, Biophysics and Physiology* , Academic Press, New York, 1973.

[D-3] Duhem, P., *The Aim and Structure of Physical Theory, Part 2*, Princeton University Press, Princeton, N.J., 1954.

[D-4] Dauer, F., "In Defense of the Coherence Theory of Truth," *Journal of Philosophy*, v. 71, p. 791-811, Nov. 21, 1974.

[D-5] Diday, E., G. Govaert and Y. Lemoine, "A New Kind of Representation in Clustering,"

Proceedings of the International Joint Conference on Pattern Recognition, Kyoto, Japan, 1978.

[D-6] Duda, R.O. and P.E. Hart, *Pattern Classification and Scene Analysis*, Wiley-Interscience, New York, 1973.

[D-7] Dias, P.M.C. and A. Shimony, "A Critique of Jaines' Maximum Entropy Principle," *Advances in Applied Mathematics*, v. 2, p. 172-211, 1981.

[E-1] Eden, M., "On the Formalization of Handwriting," *Proceedings of Symposia in Applied Mathematics*, American Mathematical Society, Providence, R.I., Vol. 12, p. 83-88, 1961.

[E-2] Escher, M.C., "The Graphic Work of M.C. Escher," Ballantine Books, New York, 1971.

[E-3] Euler, H., "Uber die Art der Wechsclwirkung in den schweren Atomkernen," *Zertschrift. für Phys.* v. 105, p. 553, 1937.

[E-4] Eden, M. and M. Halle, "The Characterization of Cursive Writing." In C. Cherry, (ed.), *Fourth London Symposium on Information Theory*, Butterworth, London, 1961.

[E-5] Eden, M., "Handwriting and Pattern Recognition," *IRE Transactions on Information Theory*, v. 8, p. 160, 1962.

[E-6] Eddington, A.S., *Fundamental Theory*, University Press, Cambridge, England, 1948.

[F-1] Fisher, R.A., "Theory of Statistical Estimation," *Proceedings of Cambridge Philosophical Society*, Vol. 22, p. 700, 1925.

[F-2] Fu, K.S., *Syntactic Methods in Pattern Recognition*, Academic Press, New York, 1974.

[F-3] Feigl, H., "Validation and Vindication." In Sellars and Hospers, (eds.), *Readings in Ethical Theory*, New York, 1952.

[F-4] Fujisawa, N., "Εχειν, Μετεχιν and Idioms of 'Paradigmatism' in Plato's Theory of Forms," *Phronesis*, v. XIX, no. 1, 1974.

[F-5] Feyerabend, P.K., "Explanation, Reduction and Empiricism." In Feigl and Maxwell, (eds.), *Minnesota Studies in Philosophy of Science*, University Press, Minneapolis, p. 28-97, 1962.

[F-6] Fu, K.S., *Semantical Method in Pattern Recognition and Machine Learning*, Academic Press, New York, 1968.

[F-7] Fukunaga, K. and W.L.G. Koontz, "Application of the Karhunen-Loeve Expansion to Feature Selection and Ordering," in *IEEE Transactions in Computers*, v. C-19, p. 311-318, April, 1970.

[F-8] Feigl, H., *The Mental and the Physical. The Essay and a Postscript.*, University Press, Minneapolis, 1967.

[F-9] Feder, J., "Plex Language," *Information Science*, v. 3, p. 226-241, 1971.

[F-10] Frege, G., *Grundgesetz der Arithmetik*, Georg Olms, Hildesheim, p. 253, 1962.

[G-1] Gelernter, H.L., "Realization of a Geometry Theorem-Proving Machine," *Proceedings of International Conference on Information Processing*, Paris, p. 273, June 1959.

[G-2] Goodman, J.W., *Introduction to Fourier Optics*, McGraw-Hill, New York, 1968.

[G-3] Goodman, N., *Fact, Fiction and Forecast*, Harvard University Press, Cambridge, Massachusetts, 1955.

[G-4] Glansdorf, P. and I. Prigogine, *Thermodynamical Theory of Structure, Stability and Fluctuation*, John Wiley & Sons, Inc., New York, 1971.

[G-5] Gibbs, J.W., *Elementary Principles in Statistical Mechanics*, Yale University Press, New Haven, 1902.

[G-6] Genchi, H., K. Mori, S. Watanabe, and S. Katsuragi, "Recognition of Handwritten Numerical Characters for Automatic Letter Sorting," *IEEE Proceedings*, p. 1292, August 1982.

[G-7] Grenander, U., "Foundation of Pattern Analysis," *Quart. Appl. Math.*, v. 27, p. 1-53, 1969.

[G-8] Gazzaniga, M.S., "Some Contributions of Split-Brain Studies to the Studies of Human Cognition," *Kagaku*, v. 53, no. 4, p. 276-279, 1983.

[G-9] Gazzaniga, M.S., *The Bisected Brains*, Appleton-Century-Croft, New York, 1970.

[G-10] Gazzaniga, M.S. and C.S. Smylie, "Dissociation of Language and Cognition: A Psychological Profile of Two Disconnected Right Hemispheres," in preparation, 1983.

[G-11] Gibbs, J.W., *Elementary Principles of Statistical Mechanics*, Yale University Press, New Haven, 1914.

[G-12] Gödel, Kurt, "Einige mathematische Resultate über Etscheidwrgsdefinitheit und Widerspruchsfreiheit." *Anzeiger der Akademie der Wissenschaften in Wien, mathematische-naturwissenschaftliche Klasse*, Vol. 67, p. 214-215, 1930.

[H-1] Hotelling, Harold, "Analysis of a Complex of Statistical Variables into Principal Components," *Journal of Educational Psychology*, v. 24, p. 417-41, 498-520, 1933.

[H-2] Husimi, K. et al., *Geometry of Beauty*, Tokyo:o Chuokoron-sha, 1979.

[H-3] Horning, J.J., "A Procedure for Grammatical Inference," *Proceedings IFIP Congress*, Yugoslavia, 1971.

[H-4] Hartline, H.K., "Inhibition of Activity of Visual Receptors by Illuminating Nearby Retinal Elements in the Limulus Eye," *Fed Proc.* v. 8, p. 69, 1949.

[H-5] Huang, T.S. (ed.), *Picture Processing and Digital Filtering*, New York, Springer, 1975.

[H-6] Hume, David, *A Treatise of Human Nature*, London, 1739, 1740.

[H-7] Hume, David, *Enquiry Concerning Human Understanding*, London, 1748.

[H-8] Heisenberg, W., "Ueber den Ferromagnetismus," *Zeitschrift für Physik*, v. 49, p. 619, 1928.

[H-9] Haken, H., *Synergetics*, Springer, Berlin, 1978.

[H-10] Hanakata, dissertation, Stuttgart Technical University, 1979.

[H-11] Hartline, H.K. and F. Ratliff, "Spatial Summation of Inhibitory Influence in the Eye of Limulus," *Science*, v. 120, p. 781, 1954.

[H-12] Ho, Y.C. and R.L. Kashyap, "An Algorithm for Linear Inequalities and its Applications," *IEEE Trans. Electronic Computers*, EC-14, p. 683-688, 1965.

[H-13] Highleyman, W.H., "The Design and Analysis of Pattern Recognition Experiments," *Bell Systems Technical Journal*, v. 41, p. 723-744, 1962.

[H-14] Hubel, D.H. and T.N. Wiesel, "Receptive Fields and Functional Architecture in Two Non-striate Visual Areas (18 and 19) of the Cat," *J. Neurophysiol.* v. 28, p. 229-289, 1965.

[H-15] Hebbs, D.C., *The Organization of Behavior*, John Wiley & Sons, Inc., New York, 1949.

[H-16] Ho, Y.C. and R.L. Kashyap, "A Class of Iterative Procedure for Linear Inequalities, *J. SIAM*, Contr. 4, p. 112-115, 1966.

[I-1) Iijima, T., "Fundamental Theory in Observation of Patterns." (in Japanese), *Report of the Research Committee on Automaton and Automatic Control*, Society of Electronic Communication, 1959-12.

[I-2] Ito, T., "Approximate Error Bounds" in Melzer and Mickie, (eds.), *Machine Intelligence*, Vol. 7, University Press, Edinburgh, p. 369-376, 1972.

[K-1] Kelley, Truman L., "Essential Traits of Mental Life," *Harvard Studies in Education*, v. 26, Harvard University Press, Cambridge, Massachusetts, p. 146, 1935.

[K-2] Kirsch, R.A., "Computer Interpretation of English Text and Picture Patterns," *IEEE Trans. Electronic Computers*, v. 13, p. 4, 1964.

[K-3] Kulikowski, Casimir, 1965, unpublished.

[K-4] Kulikowski, Casimir A., "Pattern Recognition Approach to Medical Diagnosis," in *IEEE Transaction on Systems Science and Cybernetics*, Vol. SSC-6, p. 173-178, July 1970.

[K-5] Katsuki, Y. et al., "Neural Mechanism of the Peripheral and Central Auditory System in Monkeys", *J. Acoust. Soc. Amer.*, v. 34, p. 1396-1410, 1962.

[K-6] Keynes, M., *A Treatise on Probability*, Macmillan, London and New York, 1921.

[K-7] Kamentsky, L.A. and C.N. Liu, *IBM Journal of Research and Development*, v. 7, p. 2, 1963.

[K-8] Kuhn, Thomas, *The Structure of Scientific Revolution*, University of Chicago Press, 1970.

[K-9] Kaminuma, T., "Informational Entropy as a Measure of Correlation of Interacting Fermi Particles," Ph.D. Dissertation, University of Hawaii, 1970.

[K-10] Kaminuma, T. and I. Suzuki, "Symmetry of Karhunen-Loeve Systems and Its Applications to Geometric Pattern Analysis," *Proceedings of Fifth International Conference on Pattern Recognition*, Vol. 2, p. 1228, 1980.

[K-11] Kaminuma, T., S. Tomita, and S. Watanabe, "Covariance Matrix Representation and Object-Predicate Symmetry." In Krishnaiah and Kanal, (eds.), *Handbook of Statistics*, Vol. 2, North-Holland, Amsterdam, p. 699-720, 1982.

[K-12] Konorski, J., *Conditional Reflexes and Neuron Organization*, Cambridge University Press, London, 1948; Also reprinted by Hafner Publishing Co., New York, 1968.

[K-13] Koffka, Kurt, *Principle of Gestalt Psychology*, Harcourt, Brace and World, New York, 1935.

[K-14] Kohler, W., *Gestalt Psychology*, H. Liveright, New York and London, 1929.

[K-15] Kanal, L.N. and B. Chandrasekaran, "On Dimensionality and Sample Size in Statistical Pattern Classification, *Pattern Recognition 3*, p. 225-234, 1971.

[K-16] Koford, J.S. and G.F. Groner, "The Use of an Adaptive Threshold Element to Design a Linear Optimal Pattern Classifier," *IEEE Transactions on Information Theory, IT-12*, p. 42-50, 1966.

[K-17] Kaminuma, T., T. Takekawa, and S. Watanabe, "Reduction of Clustering Problem to Pattern Recognition," *Pattern Recognition*, Vol. 1, p. 196-205, 1969.

[K-18] Kaminuma, T. and S. Watanabe, "Fast-Converging Adaptive Algorithms for Well-Balanced Separating Linear Classifier," *Pattern Recognition*, Vol. 4, Pergamon Press, p. 289-305, 1972.

[K-19] Kulikowski, C.A. and S. Watanabe, "Multiclass Subspace Methods in Pattern Recognition," in *Proceeding of the National Electronics Conference*, Vol. XXVI, p. 468-470, 1970.

[K-20] Kimura, D. and Y. Archibald, "Motor Functions of the Left Hemisphere," *Brain*, v. 97, p. 337-350, 1974.

[K-21] Kuroda, Y., "Biochemistry of Memory and Learning," *Kagaku*, v. 32, no. 1, p. 17-23, 1982; *Kagaku*, v. 52, No. 6, p. 399-406, 1982.

[K-22] Kasvand, T., "Experiments on an On-Line Picture Language," in S. Watanabe, (ed.), *Frontiers of Pattern Recognition*, Academic Press, New York, p. 223-265.

[K-23] Kohonen, T. et al., "A Thousand-Word Recognition System Based on the Learning Subspace Method and Redundant Hash Addressing," *Proceedings of the Fifth International Conference on Pattern Recognition*, Miami Beach, p. 158, 1980.

[L-1] Lambert, Peter, "Designing Pattern Categories with Extremal Paradigm Information." In S. Watanabe, (ed.), *Methodologies of Pattern Recognition*, Academic Press, New York, p. 359, 1969.

[L-2] Locke, John, *Essay Concerning Human Understanding*, London, 1960.

[L-3] Lettvin, J.K., H.R. Maturana, W.S. McCulloch, and W.H. Pitts, "What the Frog's Eye Tells the Frog's Brain," *Proc. Inst. Radio Engineers*, v. 47, p. 1940, 1959.

[L-4] Lettvin, J.Y. and R.C. Gesteland, "Speculations on Smell," *Cold Spring Harbor Symposia on Quantitative Biology*, Vol. 30, p. 217, 1965.

[L-5] Ledley, R.S. et al., "FIDAC: Film Input to Digital Automatic Computer." In J. Tippet et al., (eds.), *Optical and Electrical Information Systems*, MIT Press, Cambridge, Massachusetts, 1965.

[L-6] Letov, A.M., *Stability in Non-Linear Control Systems*, Princeton University Press, Princeton, 1961.

[M-1] MacKay, D.M., "Recognition and Action." In S. Watanabe, (ed.), *Methodologies of Pattern Recognition*, Academic Press, New York, 1969.

[M-2] Mach, E., "Über die Wirkung der räumlichen Verteilung des Lichtreizes auf die Netzhaus," *Sitzungberichte der mathematisch-naturuissenschaftlichen Classe der kaiserlichen Akademie der Wissenschaften*, Wien, 52/2, p. 303-322, 1865.

[M-3] Mach, E., "Über den Einfluss räumlich und zeitlich variierender Lichtreizes auf die Gesichtswahrnehmung," *Sitzungsberichte der mathematisch-naturuissenschaftlichen Classe der kaiserlichen Akademie der Wissenschaften*, 115/IIa, p. 633-648, 1906.

[M-4] Morris, Charles, *Signs, Languages and Behavior*, G. Braziller, New York, 1946.

[M-5] Maxwell, J.C., *Philosophical Magazine*, v. 19, p. 1860. Transaction Royal Society, London, 157, p. 49, 1867.

[M-6] Mostofsky, D.I., (ed.), *Stimulus Generalization*, Stanford University Press, 1965.

[M-7] McCulloch, W.S. and W. Pitts, "A Logical Calculus of the Ideas Immanent in Neuron Activity," *Bull. Math. Biophys.*, v. 5, p. 115-133, 1943.

[M-8] Mandelbrot, B., *Fractal*, W.H. Freeman and Co., San Francisco, 1977.

[M-9] McCullough, W.S. and W. Pitts, "How We Know Universals: the Perception of Auditory and Visual Forms," *Bull. Math. Biophysics*, v. 9, p. 127-147, 1947.

[N-1] Novikoff, A.B.J., "On Convergence Proofs for Perceptions," *Proceedings of the Symposium on Mathematics Theory of Automata*, Polytechnic Institute of Brooklyn, New York, p. 615-622, 1962.

[N-2] Narasimhan, R.A., "A Linguistic Approach to Pattern Recognition," *Rep. No. 21, Digital Computer Lab.*, Univ. of Illinois, Urbana, 1962.

[N-3] Newell, A., J.C. Shaw and H. Simon, "A Validity of Intelligent Learning in General Problem-Solver." In M.C. Yovits and S. Cemeron (eds.) *Self-Organizing Systems*, Pergamon Press, New York, p. 153-189, 1960.

[N-4] Neisser, U., *Cognitive Psychology*, Appleton-Century-Croft, New York, 1967.

[P-1] Pearson, Karl, "On Lines and Planes of Closest Fit to Systems of Points in Space," *Phil. Mag.*, v. 6, p. 559-572, 1901.

[P-2] Parzen, E., "An Estimation of a Probability Density Function and Mode," *Ann. Math. Stat.*, v. 33 e, p. 1065-1076, 1962.

[P-3] Price, H.H., *Thinking and Experience*, Hutchinson University Library, London, 1953.

[P-4] Peirce, C.S., *Collected Papers*, Vol. II, Harvard University Press, Cambridge, Mass., 1931-35.

[P-5] Polanyi, M., *Personal Knowledge*. Routledge and Kegan Paul, London, 1958.

[P-6] Popper, Karl, *The Logic of Scientific Discovery*, Hutchinson, London, 1959.

[P-7] Pearl, J., "On the Connection Between the Complexity and Credibility of Inferred Model," *Int. J. Gen. Systems*, v. 4, p. 255, 1978.

[P-8] Pavlov, L.P., *Conditioned Reflexes, An Investigation of Physiological Activity of the Cerebral Cortex* (transl. and ed. by G.V. Anrep) Oxford Univ. Press, Humphrey Milford, 1927.

[P-9] Pavlov, L.P., *Lectures on Conditioned Reflexes*, (transl. and ed. by W. Horsley Ganut, Laurence and Wishant Ltd., London, 1928, 1941.

[P-10] Perrett, D.J. et al., "Visual Neurons Responsive to Faces in the Monkey Temporal Cortex," *Experimental Brain Research*, v. 47, p. 329-342, 1982.

[P-11] Putnam, H., "How Not to Talk about Meaning." In Cohen and Wartofsky (eds.), *Boston Studies in the Philosophy of Science, Humanities*, New York, p. 205-222, 1965.

[P-12] Patterson, J.D. and B.F. Womak, "An Adaptive Pattern Classification System," *IEEE Transactions on Systems Science and Cybernetics*, SSC-2, p. 62-67, 1966.

[P-13] Peirce, C.S., *Collected Papers*, Vol. 3, Harvard University Press, Cambridge, Mass., 1960.

[P-14] Pavlidis, T., *Structural Pattern Recognition*, Springer-Verlag, New York, 1977.

[P-15] Pfalz, J.L. and A. Rosenfeld, "WEB Grammars," *Proceedings of the International Joint Conference on Artificial Intelligence*, Washington, D.C., p. 609-619, May 1969.

[Q-1] Quine, W.V.D., *Ontological Relativity, and Other Essays*, Columbia University Press, New York, 1969.

[Q-2] Quine, W.V.D., *From a Logical Point of View*, 2nd Ed., Harvard University Press, Cambridge, Mass., 1961.

[Q-3] Quine, W.V., On Frege's Way Out, *Mind*, v. N.S. 64, p. 145-159, 1955.

[R-1] Rosenblatt, F., "*The Perceptron--A Perceiving and Recognizing Automaton*," Report-85-460-1, Cornell Aeronautical Laboratory, Ithaca, N.Y., January 1957.

[R-2] Ratliff, F., *Mach Band*, Holden Day, San Francisco, 1965.

[R-3] Rose, J.E., "Discharges of Single Fibers in the Mammalian Auditory Nerve." In R. Plomp and G.F. Smooreuburg, (eds.), *Frequency Analysis and Periodicity Detection in Hearing*, Sijthoff, Leiden, 1970.

[R-4] Russell, Bertrand, *Problems of Philosophy*, H. Holt & Company, New York, 1912.

[R-5] Russell, Bertrand, *An Inquiry Into Meaning and Truth*, W.W. Norton, New York, 1940.

[R-6] Reichenbach, H., *The Theory of Probability*, University of California Press, Berkeley, 1949.

[R-7] Reiter, B. and S. Watanabe, "Orthogonal Subspaces for Multiclass Pattern Recognition." In Art Lew, (ed.), *Proceedings of the Fifth Hawaii International Conference on System Sciences*, Western Periodicals Company, p. 398-400, 1972.

[R-8] Rissanen, J., "A Universal Prior for Integers and Estimation by Minimum Length." *In Annals of Statistics*, July 1983.

[R-9] Rosenfeld, A. and M. Thurston, "Edge and Curve Detection for Visual Scene Analysis," *IEEE Trans. Comp.* C-20, p. 562-569, 1971.

[S-1] Spearman, Charles, "General Intelligence, Objectively Determined and Measured," *American Journal of Psychology*, 15, p. 201-293, 1904.

[S-2] Someya, I., *Propagation of Wave Forms*, Kenkyusha, Tokyo, 1949. (in Japanese).

[S-3] Shaw, A.C., "The Formal Description of Parsing of Pictures," Ph.D. Thesis, Stanford University, 1968.

[S-4] Speiser, A., *Die Theorie der Gruppen von endlicher Ordnung*, Julius Springer, Berlin, 1927.

[S-5] Smith, E.G., *The Wiswesser Line-Formula Chemical Notation*, McGraw-Hill, New York, 1968.

[S-6] Spoendlin, H., "Structural Basis of Peripheral Frequency Analysis." In S. Plomp and G.F. Smoorenburg (eds.), *Frequency Analysis and Periodicity Detection in Hearing*, Sijthoff, Leiden, p. 2-40, 1970.

[S-7] Sallatin, Y., Représentation d'Observations dans le Contexte de la Theorie de l'Information, dissertation for doctorat d'Etat, University Pierre et Marie Curie, Paris, 1979.

[S-8] Strawson, Peter, "Universals," *In Midwest Studies in Philosophy*, Vol. IV, French, Uhling, Wettstein, (eds.), University of Minnesota Press, Minneapolis, p. 3, 1979.

[S-9] Samuel, A., "Some Studies in Machine Learning Using the Game of Checkers." In Feigenbaum and Feldman (eds.), *Computers and Thought*, McGraw - Hill, New York, 1963.

[S-10] Shannon, C.E. and W. Weaver, *The Mathematical Theory of Communication*, University of Illinois Press, Urbana, 1949.

[S-11] Shannon, C.E., *Bell System Tech*. J. v. 30, p. 50, 1951.

[S-12] Schmidt, E., "Zur Theorie der linearen and nicht linearen Integralglesdurgen," *Math. Ann.* v. 63, p. 433-476, 1907.

[S-13] Sakata, H. et al., "Spatial Properties of Visual Fixation Neurons in Posterior Parietal Association Cortex of the Monkey", *J. Neurophysiology*, v. 43, p. 1654-1672, 1980.

[S-14] Sakata, H. et al., "Parietal Neurons with Dual Sensitivity to Real and Induced Movements of Visual Target," *Neurosci. Lett.*, v. 9, p. 165-169, 1978.

[S-15] Sato, T. et al., "Responsiveness of Inferotemporal Single Units to Visual Pattern Stimuli in Monkeys Performing Discrimination," *Exp. Brain Research*, v. 38, p. 313-319, 1980.

[S-16] Stagle, J.R., "A Heuristic Program that Solves Symbolic Integration Problems in Freshman Calculus," *J. ACM.*, v. 10, p. 507-520, 1963.

[S-17] Schwarz, G., "Estimating the Dimension of a Model," *Ann. Statistics*, v. 6-2, p. 461-464, 1978.

[S-18] Schrödinger, E., *"What is Life? The Physical Aspect of the Living Cell, Mind and Matter"*, Cambridge University Press, 1967.

[S-19] Strong III, J.P. and A. Rosenfeld, "A Region Coloring Technique for Scene Analysis," *Communications A.C.M.*, v. 16, p. 237-246, 1973.

[S-20] Sperry, R.W., *The Harvard Lectures*, v. 62, p. 293, 1968.

[S-21] Springer, S.P., and G. Deutsch, *Left Brain and Right Brain*, W.H. Freeman & Co., San Francisco, 1981.

[T-1] Toth, L. Fejes, "Reguläre Figuren," Adakemiai Kiado, Budapest, 1965.

[T-2] Tsujiuchi, J., "Correlation of Optical Images by Compensation of Aberrations and by Spatial Frequency Filtering." In E. Wolf, (ed.), *Progress in Optics*, Vol. II, North-Holland Publishing Company, Amsterdam, 1963.

[T-3] Tomita, S. et al., "Theory of Feature Extraction for Pattern Recognition by Karhunen-Loève Orthogonal System." *Trans. IEEE*. v. 53-C, no. 12, p. 887, 1970.

[T-4] Tomita, S. et al., "On Evaluation of Handwritten Characters by K-L Orthogonal Systems," HICSS-3, Jan. 1973.

[T-5] Toda, M., "What is Memory" In the special issue on *Memory of Suri-Kagaku*, p. 156-163, 1983.

[T-6] Tsunoda, T., *Brain of the Japanese*, Taishukan, Tokyo, 1978.

[V-1] von Neumann, J., *Mathematische Grundluger der Quantenmechanik*, J. Springer, Berlin, 1932.

[V-2] von Weizsäcker, C.F., "Neuere Modellvostellungen über den Bau der Atomkenne," *Naturwissenchaften*, v. 26, Heft 14, p. 209, Heft 15, p. 225, 1938.

[V-3] von Békésy, G., *Sensory Inhibition*, Princeton University Press, Princeton, 1967.

[V-4] von Békésey, G., *Experiments in Hearing*, McGraw-Hill, New York, 1960.

[V-5] von Ehrenfels, Ch., "Über Gestaltqualitäten" *Vierteljahrsschrift für wissenschaftliche Philosophie*, Vol. 4, p. 249, 1890.

[W-1] Watanabe, S., "The Loève-Karhunen Expansion as a Means of Information Compression for Classification of Continuous Signals--Final Report on Research on Advanced Computer Methods for Biological Data Processing", Final Technical Documentary Report to Biomedical Research Lab., Denver, 1964.

[W-2] Watanabe, S., "Karhunen-Loève Expansion and Factor Analysis--Theoretical Remarks and Applications", *Transactions of the Fourth Prague Conference on Information Theory, Statistical Decision Functions, Random Processes*, 1965, Publishing House of the Czechoslovak Academy of Sciences, Prague, p. 635, 1967.

[W-3] Watanabe, S., "Evaluation and Selection of Variables in Pattern Recognition," *Proceedings of the Second Symposium on Computer and Information Sciences* held at Battelle Memorial Institute, August 22-24, 1966, Julius T. Tou, (ed.), Academic Press, p. 91-122, 1967.

[W-4] Whittaker, E.T., "On the Functions which are Represented by the Expansions of the Interpolation-Theory," *Proceedings of Royal Society*, Royal Society of Edinburgh, Edinburgh, v. 35, 181, 1915.

[W-5] Watanabe, Satosi, "Correlation Indices," *Il Nuovo Cimento*, No. 2, Supplemonto, Ser. X, Vol. 13, p. 576, 1959.

[W-6] Watanabe, S., "Information Theoretical Analysis of Multivariate Correlation," *IBM Journal of Research and Development*, v. 4, no. 1, p. 66, January, 1960.

[W-7] Watanabe, S., "A Note on the Formation of Concept and of Association by Information Thoeretical Correlation Analysis," *Information and Control*, v. 4, no. 2-3, p. 291, September, 1961.

[W-8] Watanabe, S., "Object-Predicate Reciprocity and Its Applications to Pattern Recognition," *Information Processing 68*, (IFIP Proceedings), North-Holland Publishing Company, Amsterdam, p. 1608, 1969.

[W-9] Watanabe, S., "A Well-Balanced Adaptive Linear Function Decision Function," presented at the IEEE Workshop on Pattern Recognition, Delft, 1968.

[W-10] Watanabe, S., *Knowing and Guessing*, John Wiley & Sons, Inc., New York, 592 pp., 1969.

[W-11] Watanabe, S., "Ungrammatical Grammar in Pattern Recognition," *Pattern Recognition*, 3, p. 385, 1971.

[W-12] Watanabe, S., "Chemical Structure Language (CSL) and Its Applications," the *Proceedings of the Third International Joint Conference on Pattern Recognition*, San Diego, p. 602-606, November 1976.

[W-13] Watanabe, S., "Information-Theoretical Aspects of Inductive and Deductive Inference," *IBM Journal of Research and Development*, v. 4, p. 208-231, 1960.

[W-14] Wittgenstein, Ludwig, *Philosophical Investigation*, Basil, Blackwell and Mott, Oxford, 1953; Philosophical Investigation (Anscomb, translator) McMillan Co., New York, 1953.

[W-15] Watanabe, S., "Modified Concepts of Logic, Probability, and Information Based on Generalized Continuous Characteristic Function," *Information and Control*, v. 15, p. 1, July, 1969.

[W-16] Watanabe, S., "Can the Cognitive Process be Totally Mechanized?" In C.Y. Cheng, (ed.), *Philosophical Aspects of the Mind-Body Problem*, University of Hawaii Press, Honolulu, 1975.

[W-17] Watanabe, S., "Needed: A Historico-Dynamical View of Theory Change," *Synthese*, v. 32, D. Reidel, Dordrecht, 1975.

[W-18] Watanabe, S., Lecture AAAS Annual Meeting, 1961, unpublished.

[W-19] Watanabe, S., "Une explication mathematique du classement d'objects." In Dockx & Bernays, (eds.), *Information and Prediction in Science*, Academic Press, New York, 1965.

[W-20] Watanabe, S., "Where does the Information Come From." In A. Renyi, (ed.), *Proceedings of the Colloquium on Information Theory, Debrecen*, Kultura, Budapest, p. 511, 1969.

[W-21] Watanabe, S., "MOSS-A Subspace Representation of Classes in Pattern Recognition." In *Transactions of the Seventh Prague Conference in Information Theory, Statistical Decision Functions, and Random Process*, Publication House of the Czechvslovak Academy of Science, Prague, 1974.

[W-22] Watanabe, S., "Logic of the Empirical World, with Reference to the Identity Theory and Reductionism." In C.Y. Cheng, (ed.), *Philosophical Aspects of the Mind-Body Problems*, University of Hawaii Press, Honolulu, p. 162, 1975.

[W-23] Watanabe, S., "Creative Learning and Propensity Automaton," *IEEE Transactions on Systems, Mourand Cybernetics*, Vol. SMC-5, no. 6, p. 603, 1975.

[W-24] Watanabe, S., "Pattern Recognition as Inductive Process." In S. Watanabe, (ed.), *Methodologies of Pattern Recognition*, Academic Press, New York, p. 521-533, 1969.

[W-25] Watanabe, S., "A Generalized Fuzzy Set Theory," *IEEE Transactions*, Vol. SMC-8, no. 10, p. 756, 1978.

[W-26] Watanabe, S., "Pattern Recognition as Information Compression." In S. Watanabe, (ed.), *Frontiers of Pattern Recognition*, Academic Press, New York, 1972.

[W-27] Watanabe, S., "Feature Compression." In J. Tou (ed.), *Advances in Information Systems Sciences*, Vol. 3, Plenum, New York, 1970.

[W-28] Watanabe, S., "Paradigmatic Symbol--A Comparative Study of Human and Artificial Intelligence," *IEEE Transactions on Systems, Man, and Cybernetics*, Vol. SMC-4, no. 1, p. 100, January 1974.

[W-29] Watanabe, S., "Paradigmatic Symbol--Comparative Characterization of Human and Artificial Intelligence," *Abstract Guide of XXth International Congress of Psychology*, August 1972, Science Council of Japan, Tokyo, p. 167, 1974.

[W-30] Watanabe, S., "Civilization and Science--Man and Machine," *Ann. Japan Ass. Philos. Sci.*, Vol. 1. no. 4, p. 216-234, 1959.

[W-31] Watanabe, S., "Comments on Key Issues." In S. Hook, (ed.), *Dimensions of Mind*, New York University Press, New York, p. 143-147, 1960.

[W-32] Watanabe, S., "Les eléménts humains arationnels dans la connaissance scientifique," *Arch. Philos.*, Vol. 34, p. 609-622, 1971.

[W-33] Watanabe, S., "A Model of Mind-Body Relation in Terms of Modular Logic," *Synthese*, v. XIII, no. 4, p. 261, 1961.

[W-34] Watanabe, S., "Entre le monisme et le dualisme," *Epistemologia*, p. 175-194, 1982.

[W-35] Watanabe, S., "Theory of Propensity--A New Foundation of Logic," Cohen and Wartofsky, (eds.), *Language, Logic and Method*, Reidel Publishing Co., 1982.

[W-36] Watanabe, S., "Learning Process and Inverse H-Theorem," *IRE Transactions on Information*, IT-8, p. 246, 1962.

[W-37] Watanabe, S., "Logic of Observation," *Progress of Theoretical Physics*, Supplement Nos. 37 and 38 (dedicated to Prof. Tomonaga), p. 350, 1966.

[W-38] Watanabe, S., "Complexity and Entropy," *Proceedings of the 1975 International Conference on Cybernetics and Society*, IEEE System, Man and Cybernetics Society, p. 407, 1975.

[W-39] Watanabe, S., "Correlation Phenomena in Atomic Nuclei, Parts I, II, III," *Kagaku*, 14, p. 82, 122, 168, 1944.

[W-40] Watanabe, S., "Über die Anwendung Thermodynamischer Begriffe anf den Normalznstand des Atomkerns' *Zeitschrift für Physik*, v. 113, p. 482, 1939.

[W-41] Wiener, Norbert, *Cybernetics*, 2nd Ed. MIT Press and John Wiley & Sons, Inc., New York, 1961.

[W-42] Watanabe, S., "Norbert Wiener and Cybernetical Concept of Time," *IEEE Transactions on S.M.C., 25th Anniversary Symposium of Wiener's Cybernetics*, Vol. SMC-5, no. 3, p. 372, 1975.

[W-43] Watanabe, S., and T. Kaminuma, "A Well-Balanced Adaptive Linear Decision Function," *Proceedings of the N.E.C.*, Chicago, p. 20, 1968.

[W-44] Watanabe, S., and Nikhil Pakvasa, "Subspace Method in Pattern Recognition," *Proceedings of the First International Joint Conference on Pattern Recognition*, Washington, 1973.

[W-45] Wong, E. and J.A. Steppe, "Invariant Recognition of Geometric Shapes." In S. Watanabe, (ed.), *Methodologies of Pattern Recognition*, Academic Press, New York, p. 535, 1969.

[W-46] Watanabe, S., "Le principe de la moindre entropie," *IRIA Seminar*, 1980.

[W-47] Watanabe, S., "Pattern Recognition as a Quest for Minimum Entropy," *Pattern Recognition*, Vol. 13, p. 381-387, 1981.

[W-48] Watanabe, S., lecture notes at summer school on Information Science, Varenna, 1957.

[W-49] Wertheimer, M., *Productive Thinking*, Harper & Bros., New York, 1945 and 1959.

[W-50] Wertheimer, M., "Experimentelle Studien über das Sehen von Bewegung," Z.S. für Psych., v. 61, p. 161, 1912.

[W-51] Watanabe, S., "A Mathematical Explication of Inductive Inference," *Colloquium on the Foundations of Mathematics, Mathematical Machines and Their Applications*, Tihany, September 1962, Budapest: Akademi Kiado, p. 67, 1965.

[W-52] Watanabe, S. et al., "Reduction of Clustering to Pattern Recognition", *Pattern Recognition*, Vol. 1, n. 3, p. 195, 1969.

[W-53] Watanabe, S., "Further Report on Coalescence Model of Clustering," *Proceedings of the Third International Joint Conference on Pattern Recognition*, p. 176-179, 1976.

[W-54] Watanabe, S., "Application of Dynamical Coalescence Model to Paradigm-Oriented Pattern Recognition," *Proceedings to the*

International Joint Conference on Pattern Recognition," Kyoto, p. 320, 1978.

[W-55] Watanabe, S. and E.T. Harada, "Dynamical Model of Clustering," *Proceedings of the Second Joint Conference on Pattern Recognition*," Kyoto, p. 320, 1978.

[W-56] Watanabe, S., "Pattern Recognition as Conceptual Morphogenesis," *IEEE Trans. PAMI*, Vol. 2, p. 161-165, 1980.

[W-57] Widrow, B. and M.E. Hoff, "Adaptive Switching Circuit," *1960 IRE Wescon Convention Record*, Part 4, p. 96-104, 1960.

[W-58] Wang, Hao, "Toward Mechanical Mathematics," *IBM Journal of Research and Development*, v. 4, p. 2, 1960.

[W-59] Watanabe, S., "Creative Time." In Fraser et al., (eds.), *The Study of Time*, Springer-Verlag, Heidelberg, p. 159, 1972.

[W-60] Wigner, E., "On the Quantum Correction for Thermodynamic Equilibrium," *Physical Review*, v. 40, p. 749, 1932.

[W-61] Watanabe, S., *Cognition and Pattern Recognition*, Iwanami, Tokyo, 1978.

[W-62] Weizenbaum, J., *Computer Power and Human Reason*," W.H. Freeman & Co., San Francisco, 1976.

[W-63] Watanabe, S., *Time*, 1st Edition 1949, 2nd Edition 1972, Kawade, Tokyo, 1972.

[W-64] Watanabe, S., "A Generalized Fuzzy-Set Theory," *IEEE Transactions*, Vol. SMC-8, no. 10, p. 756-760, 1978.

[W-65] Watanabe, S., "Fuzzification and Invariance," *Proceedings of International Conference on Cybernetics and Society*, Tokyo, p. 947-951, 1978.

[W-66] Watanabe, S., "A New Entropic Method of Dimension Reduction Specially Designed for Multiclass Discrimination (DIRECLADIS)," *Pattern Recognition Letters*, Vol. 2, p. 1-4, 1983.

[W-67] Watanabe, S., "Chirality of K-Particle," *Physical Review*, v. 106, no. 6, p. 1306, 1957.

[W-68] Watanabe, S., "DIRECLADIS-Dimensionality Reduction for Class Discrimination," *Proceedings of the Seventh International*

Conference on Pattern Recognition, Montreal, p. 1252, 1984.

[Y-1] Yukawa, H., *Creativity and Intuition*, Kodansha International, Tokyo and New York, 1983.

[Y-2] Yamamoto, T., "Analogue Transmission of Signals," *Seibutsu-Kagaku*, v. 32, 1980.

[Z-1] Zwislocki, J.J., "Phase Opposition between Inner and Outer Hair Cells and Auditory Sound Analysis," *Audiology*, 14, p. 443-455, 1975.

[Z-2] Zadeh, L.A., "Fuzzy Sets," *Information and Control*, v. 8, p. 338, 1965.

Index